THE
FOUNDERS
ON THE
FOUNDERS

Word Portraits from the American Revolutionary Era

EDITED BY John P. Kaminski

University of Virginia Press
CHARLOTTESVILLE & LONDON

University of Virginia Press
© 2008 by the Rector and Visitors of the University of Virginia
All rights reserved
Printed in the United States of America on acid-free paper

ISBN 978-0-8139-2757-2

Illustration credits follow the index.

Book Club Edition

For Richard Leffler
Friend and Colleague for Four Decades

Contents

Preface

⇥ THE IDEA FOR THIS BOOK originated about a decade ago when I was commonplacing John Adams, that is, creating a database with entries with interesting quotations from John Adams on a wide array of subjects. Commonplacing was a common practice of the Founding generation, albeit in a notebook rather than a computer file. In 1800 Jefferson wrote that he "had, at an early period of life, read a great deal . . . & commonplaced what I read. This common-place has been my pillar" (quoted in John P. Kaminski, ed., *The Quotable Jefferson* [Princeton, N.J., 2006], 83).

I had already compiled such databases for Thomas Jefferson, Thomas Paine, and John Jay. After poring through about eight volumes of the Adams Papers, I realized that Adams, his wife Abigail, and their son John Quincy Adams regularly commented on their contemporaries. But unlike most of their contemporaries, John and Abigail also loved to write about themselves. That's when I started collecting a database that I called "The Founders on the Founders." My criteria were both broad and restrictive. I collected references to character, mannerisms, physical and intellectual descriptions, and everyday activities but avoided references to political issues. I wanted to put flesh and blood on these people whose personalities we knew little or nothing about. To date, the database is over six thousand pages long and includes descriptions of more than 420 individuals: enough quotations for a single volume each on George Washington and John Adams but sometimes only a single entry or two for others. About fifty entries describing an individual provide enough tiles to make an accurate mosaic of that person, a kind of portrait in words.

⊰ I HAVE CHOSEN thirty individuals for inclusion in this volume: four were U.S. presidents, five were U.S. vice presidents, five were justices on the U.S. Supreme Court (three of whom were chief justice), eleven were state governors. At least twenty served in public office most of their active professional lives. Eleven were lawyers, six were planters, four were what might be called professional soldiers or sailors, two were merchants, one was a physician. Five were born outside the thirteen mainland American colonies. Although many were proficient writers and occasionally wrote important public papers, two earned their living as writers—Benjamin Franklin and Thomas Paine. Two were women. Two—Benjamin Franklin and Thomas Jefferson—might be categorized as Renaissance men.

⊰ SUCH A PROJECT WAS inevitable. It needed one thing—a critical mass of published documentary editions in which reliable, authoritative texts have been painstakingly transcribed by dedicated editors. For the last fifty years, literally thousands of such volumes have been published. Since 1964 the National Historical Publications and Records Commission and the National Endowment for the Humanities have funded a wide variety of documentary editions. Yale University professor Edmund S. Morgan has stated that the publication of documentary editions of the Founding era was the most important contribution to the field of history in the twentieth century. Without these volumes such a database could not have been compiled.

The word portraits compiled in this volume are largely taken from the diaries and correspondence of the Founding generation. Some of the Founders were very cautious in their assessments; others could not resist being brutally frank. Some, like Washington, rarely gossiped; others, like John Adams, couldn't stop communicating the "Tittle Tatle" of the day. Some Founders used their private correspondence to vent off steam. Some avoided introspection, while others, like both John and Abigail Adams, seemed almost obsessed with assessing their own qualities. A few even subconsciously projected their own traits while describing others. For over a hundred years historians have extensively cited

the journal of William Maclay, one of Pennsylvania's two senators in the first federal Congress. Maclay's colorful descriptions
have spiced up the writings of many historians; unfortunately,
readers rarely have been warned that Maclay was neurotic. His
images often were accurate but sometimes were derived from a
less than stable mind. Friends, enemies, colleagues, family members, and occasionally their own introspective feelings provide
over a period of time the individual tiles in these biographical
mosaics. In essence, the Founders themselves become the joint
biographers of each other, or better yet, they become their own
autobiographers.

⊰ OVER THE YEARS, a number of people have helped me by
giving me leads, individual quotations, or copies of manuscripts
from which I could verify a quotation obtained from a printed
source. Such helpful colleagues include Richard B. Bernstein,
Kenneth R. Bowling, Jon Kukla, Richard Leffler, Elizabeth Nux-
oll, Roger Parks, Gaspare J. Saladino, and Michael E. Stevens.

This volume is dedicated to Richard Leffler, my friend and
colleague for forty years. Rich and I have worked together on
*The Documentary History of the Ratification of the Constitu-
tion* for most of this time. For twenty-five years he has served
as deputy director of the Center for the Study of the American
Constitution here in the Department of History at the University of Wisconsin–Madison. We have traveled the country from
Maine to Hawaii, from Oregon to Florida over the last dozen
years giving seminars to federal and state judges in over thirty
states on the early constitutional history of the United States. We
have collaborated on several books and on a number of programs
for WHA-Radio's "University of the Air" here in Madison. We
started and ran two private companies together, a publishing
house and an editing company. Of major significance to me, Rich
has served as a sounding board for all my ideas and writings. He
is my editor. Every manuscript submitted to him is always greatly
improved by his reading. He and his wife Joan have been close
personal friends of my family for all these years; they have been
like an uncle and aunt to my children. It's hard to imagine what
my career would have been without Rich. It's hard to imagine my
life over the last forty years without his friendship.

Introduction

ঌ THE FOUNDERS were extraordinary individuals: they were not cold statues. The fog of fame and time, however, has obscured them as flesh-and-blood human beings. Most of us think of them only as a group—the Founders—not as individuals with their own personalities, strengths, and weaknesses. Those who do warrant individual attention have become caricatures. How many Americans know the real Washington, Franklin, and Jefferson, let alone Madison, Jay, and Hamilton? Occasionally we have been blessed or cursed with a public television documentary on the life of one or another of these Founders. Often they are filled with almost as many errors as facts.

Before the Revolution most of the Founders pictured their ancestors—not themselves—as special individuals who braved the treacherous transatlantic voyage and the subsequent travails of a new hostile, often unforgiving land. Once the Revolutionary movement was well under way, however, the Founders came to appreciate their own unique place in history. It was their "lot to live in perplexing and eventful times." John Adams wrote that "I am but an ordinary Man. The Times alone have destined me to Fame." Thomas Jefferson declared: "Nature intended me for the tranquil pursuits of science, by rendering them my supreme delight. But the enormities of the times in which I have lived, have forced me to take a part in resisting them, and to commit myself on the boisterous ocean of political passions." Speaking for his contemporaries, Adams wrote that "We of this Generation are destined to Act a painful and a dangerous Part, and We must make the best of our Lot."[1]

Adams denigrated the "Idea of the *great Men*. . . . It is a great People that does great Things. They will always find Instruments to employ that will answer their Ends." While attending the First Continental Congress, Adams felt that body's inadequacy for the difficult times ahead. "We have not Men, fit for the Times. We are deficient in Genius, in Education, in Travel, in Fortune—in every Thing. I feel unutterable Anxiety—God grant us Wisdom, and Fortitude!" Three months later Adams significantly elevated his opinion. "There is in the Congress a Collection of the greatest Men upon this Continent, in Point of Abilities, Virtues and Fortunes. The Magnanimity, and public Spirit, which I see here, makes me blush for the sordid venal Herd, which I have seen in my own Province."[2] Increasingly, however, he felt "that every great Character in the World is a Bubble and an Imposture." In outlining what he felt was the ideal form for a state constitution, Adams advocated annual elections for all offices and a mandatory limit of three years in any one office. This would teach "the great political virtue of humility, patience, and moderation, without which every man in power becomes a ravenous beast of prey." Thus the great men, "Like bubbles on the sea of matter borne,/They rise, they break, and to that sea return."[3]

What does seem to separate the Founders from others is a remarkable sense of duty. According to John Jay, "Personal considerations . . . must give way to public ones, and the consciousness of having done our duty to our country and posterity, must recompense us for all the evils we experience in their cause." When about ready to leave his family in New York to travel abroad for at least a year on a diplomatic mission to London, Chief Justice Jay wrote his wife, "I feel the impulse of duty strongly." In accepting the appointment as commander in chief in 1775, George Washington explained to his wife that "it was utterly out of my power to refuse this appointment without exposing my Character to such censures as would have reflected dishonor upon myself and given pain to my friends." To decline the appointment, Washington told Martha, would "have lessen'd me considerably in my own esteem." At the depths of the Revolution, Washington confidently wrote that "there is one reward that nothing can deprive me of, and that is the consciousness of having done my duty with the strictest rectitude and most scrupulous exactness." Toward the end of his presidency, Washington wrote that no amount of lies or censure "shall make me swerve from what I conceive to be the strict line of my duty." Happily retired, Washington could proudly state that "my whole life has been dedicated to the service of my country in one shape or another." Fifteen years after his death, Thomas Jefferson described Washington as having "the singular destiny and merit, of leading the armies of his country successfully through an arduous war, for the establishment of its independence; of conducting its councils through the birth of a government, new in its forms and principles, until it had settled down into a quiet and orderly train; and of scrupulously obeying the laws through the whole of his career, civil and military, of which the history of the world furnishes no other example." Anticipating the presidency, John Adams told his wife that "if the Fates destine one to attempt it, it would be dastardly to shrink if it were in one's Power." Fifteen years later, at age seventy-six, Adams said that he had been "borne along by an irresistible sense of duty."[4]

One of the most remarkable characteristics of the Founding generation was the ferocity with which they defended their traditional rights as Englishmen. The British were taken aback by the American hostility to acts of Parliament, but so too were many Americans like Benjamin Franklin, John Jay, John Dickinson, James Duane, and Thomas Hutchinson, who were fearful of this flagrant disrespect for parliamentary authority. Many of these colonists became reluctant Revolutionaries; others remained loyal to the Crown.

The Founders responded steadfastly to Britain's new imperial policy implemented after the French and Indian War, described by John Adams as "Innovations and illegal Encroachments" and by George Washington as intended "to overthrow our Constitutional Rights & liberties." This new policy provoked a constitutional crisis in defense of common-law rights as defined by a century and a half of colonial experience. Thomas Paine wrote: "When we speak of right we ought always to unite it with the idea of duties: rights become duties by reciprocity. The right which I enjoy becomes my duty to guarantee it to another, and he to me; and those who violate the duty justly incur a forfeiture of the right." Paine believed that every state had three types of men:

"the willing and able, the willing and not able, and the able and *not* willing."[5]

Addressing the freemen of America during the election of the first Congress under the Constitution, "Native American" also suggested:

> Men of talents divide themselves into three classes. The first of which, are those who make a proper use of their talents, when they do so, they exhibit to us examples of the highest virtue and truest piety. The second class, are those who misapply their talents, instead of being the protectors of mankind, they are their worst enemies: then, they commit a most sacrilegious breach of trust, and, as far as in them lies, defeat the designs of providence. This is the greatest of all crimes, and is attended with the worst consequences. The third class, are those who make no use of their talents; these are not so highly culpable as those who misapply their talents—but, as talents are the gift of the Almighty, for the benefit of mankind, he, who makes no use of them is guilty of a crime.
>
> Men of talents were easily discoverable in every community. The good man may be known by his modesty. He courts not praise nor a great name—his desire is to be useful to mankind— he exerts himself for their benefit—his acts are dictated by virtue—they are steady and uniform—the applause of his own conscience, is his best reward—he believes the first duty of men, next to that of worshipping the deity, is ministering to the wants of his fellow-creatures.—Disinterestedness, benevolence, probity, charity, fortitude, and perseverance, are exhibited on all proper occasions—industry and application, carries him to the summit of attainable knowledge—bring him forward into public life—his good qualities do not forsake him—he becomes the guardian angel of his country.—Watchful to avert the most distant evil, and to maintain, or procure good order, due obedience to the laws— peace, plenty—he believes that the true end of government is not to deprive mankind of their natural liberty, but to regulate their conduct, so as to attain the supreme good of the whole— for which purpose, he is ever anxious so to balance the government, that neither tyranny nor licentiousness shall prevail.[6]

These are the kinds of men who should be elected to public office. On the eve of the Revolution, Connecticut congressman

Oliver Wolcott said it was the duty of all members of Congress to protect the constitutions of their colonies. "Experience, Nature's sure hand maid, will guide us right. . . . We shall do our Duty."[7]

In July 1776 representatives from all thirteen mainland colonies assembled in Congress declared their independence from the mightiest nation in the world knowing full well the danger for themselves and their families. Independence, if achievable at all, would come only with great sacrifice. By the end of 1781, these remarkable men and women had torn down an empire and constructed a federal union and thirteen individual state governments. They and European observers quite consciously felt that they constituted a laboratory for a new kind of republican government.

Not all of the Founders agreed on the kind of government to adopt. John Adams and Thomas Paine, for instance, advocated opposite points of view, and each feared the irrevocable damage to be done if the other's plan of government was adopted. Adams explained that Paine's "plan was so democratical, without any restraint or even an Attempt at any Equilibrium or Counterpoise, that it must produce confusion and every Evil Work." After Adams published his own outline for the new state constitutions in a pamphlet entitled *Thoughts on Government,* Paine declared that "it would do hurt, and that it was repugnant to the plan he had proposed in his [pamphlet] Common Sense." Adams responded to Paine that "it was true it was repugnant and for that reason, I had written it and consented to the publication of it: for I was as much afraid of his Work as he was of mine." Never really friends, both men came to despise each other. Paine wrote of Adams: "It has been the political career of this man to begin with hypocrisy, proceed with arrogance, and finish in contempt. May such be the fate of all such characters." Adams in turn described Paine as "a Mongrel between Pigg and Puppy, begotten by a wild Boar on a Bitch Wolf," who had "a Career of Mischief."[8]

When the American experiments in republicanism seemed to have failed, the Founders in 1787–89 drafted, ratified, and implemented a new federal Constitution that would create a powerful, energetic national government. Two years later they tempered that strong Constitution with the Bill of Rights. Over the next generation one state after another revised its own constitution to bring it into alignment with the federal Constitution. Adams pointed to the experience of others who had faced similar crises: "It is much easier to pull down a Government, in such a Conjuncture of affairs as We have seen, than to build up."[9]

Many of the Founders believed they had God's blessing and assistance in their struggle, but even the most religious among them felt that "Providence seldom interposes in human affairs but through the agency of human means."[10] Independence and good government would not be divine gifts miraculously bestowed upon Americans. "Human and natural means" must be used to create governments that would effectively serve mankind.[11] Thus, Americans would have to convince God and the world that they deserved independence. It was a small band of fewer than half a million men sparsely settled along a thin ribbon of unprotected Atlantic coast that would have to stand up against the mightiest navy in the world, against an experienced, well-disciplined army that had a decade before defeated the powerful armies of France and Spain, against thousands of German mercenaries hired by George III, against most of the Indian tribes on their flanks who believed that the colonists could not defeat the British, against at least a third of their own people who remained loyal to the Crown, and against perhaps another third of Americans who were apathetic, pacifistic, or unwilling to take sides.[12]

Within each colony, a small group of men led the anti-British movement. Political factions existed in every colony, with local issues predominating. Often the determining factor in whether one faction was for or against the British was only which faction happened to be in power at the time. Had the Delanceys been out of power in colonial New York when the final crisis loomed, perhaps they would have been the Patriots, while the Livingstons would have remained loyal. Many of these factions continued and new ones formed and subdivided during and after the war.

Within states, factions often developed based on the personalities of their leaders, on religious differences, or on sectional and economic issues. In Virginia the supporters of Thomas Jefferson vied with the supporters of Patrick Henry. In New York, Philip Schuyler and his son-in-law Alexander Hamilton came to loathe their former ally Governor George Clinton, a man they felt was by "family and connections" not entitled to "so distinguished a predominance."[13] The governor returned the antipathy for the aristocratic Schuyler and his shirttail-clinging son-in-law. In Massachusetts various leaders despised the immensely popular John Hancock, whom Abigail Adams described as "the tinkleling cymball."[14] Similarly conservatives hated and feared the uncouth Samuel Chase of Maryland and the democratic Abraham Clark of New Jersey, while in Delaware democrats detested the aristocratic George Read. In Pennsylvania the Constitutionalists and the Republicans battled for a decade and a half over the state's extremely democratic constitution of 1776. Before the adoption of this constitution inspired by Thomas Paine, Pennsylvania politics had fixated on the interminable conflict between the colony's Quakers and Presbyterians. Political conflicts within all the states seemed ever present as opposing forces challenged each other annually in state and local elections.

Local leaders were elected to provincial legislatures, which in turn selected leaders to represent them in Congress meeting in Philadelphia. "Habituated to lead and guide" in their own colonies, many members of Congress vied for leadership roles on the continental stage, while others were content to follow.[15] Posturing occurred in Congress on the most minute matters. Adams styled it "nibbling and quibbling": "There is no greater Mortification than to sit with half a dozen Witts, deliberating upon a Petition, Address, or Memorial. These great Witts, these subtle Criticks, these refined Genius's, these learned Lawyers, these wise Statesmen, are so fond of showing their Parts and Powers, as to make their Consultations very tedious." Jefferson would later agree. "Procrastination is unavoidable. How can expedition be expected from a body which we have saddled with an hundred lawyers, whose trade is talking?"[16]

Coalition building occurred in Congress. New Englanders and southerners often lived apart from each other in different boardinghouses. "The Southern interest, or the Northern; and every man of them ranges himself upon one side or the other, and contends with as much earnestness and warmth as if at an Olympic game." "To people, out of doors, there appears to be the most shameful *party spirit* in that august body—perpetual jarrings—no convictions, nor conciliating temper."[17] Occasionally, however, sectional differences became secondary to personal conflicts. The Lee-Adams Junto connected the democratic cousins John and Samuel Adams of Massachusetts and their supporters with the aristocratic brothers Arthur and Richard Henry Lee of Virginia and their supporters. The Lee-Adams Junto vehemently opposed middle state leaders such as Benjamin Franklin and Robert Morris of Pennsylvania. It was the anomalous Thomas Paine who could attack Morris and his backers in 1778 and yet find himself four years later secretly employed by Superintendent of Finance Morris in writing propaganda for the army and for Congress and in 1785 supporting Morris in Pennsylvania politics.

Foreign affiliations played a key role in coalition building. Those with strong ties toward France bonded together and opposed those wanting to reestablish close political and economic relations with Great Britain. John Jay became a close friend of John Adams as they negotiated the peace treaty with Great Britain in Paris in 1782–83, while they both drifted apart from their fellow peace commissioner Benjamin Franklin. Jay and Adams developed deep suspicions of the French, while Franklin loved and was loved by the French. Adams came to view Franklin as "a Man of Artifice and Duplicity, of Ambition and Vanity, of Jealousy and Envy"; while Franklin believed that Adams "means well for his Country, is always an honest Man, often a wise one, but sometimes, and in some things, absolutely out of his senses." Perhaps, Franklin thought, Adams had a physiological problem that caused "a Disorder in the Brain, which, though not constant, has its Fits too frequent."[18]

Many men elected to the Continental and Confederation congresses had never been outside of their state before, and virtually all of them shared in the animosities that inhabitants of one state felt for people in other states. New Englanders hated New Yorkers and vice versa. Pennsylvanians and Virginians had fought over western lands. Southerners were wary of grasping New England Yankees who always tried to turn an exorbitant profit through shipping southern staples or importing slaves. Even within states, the entrenched coastal establishments withheld legislative representation and costly government services and institutions from the burgeoning backcountry settlements. Separatist movements smoldered in at least half of the states and eventually ignited into civil wars in Vermont, North and South

Carolina, and Pennsylvania. It was the Crown that had previously cemented the colonies together. Increasingly after the war the idea of separate confederacies surfaced, but most Americans sensed the importance of the Union.

With Americans thrust together on the continental scene, forced to address important issues affecting the interests of individual states as well as the country as a whole, it became imperative for politicians to understand each other. John Adams wrote to William Tudor that "We live in Times, when it is necessary to look about Us, and to know the Character of every Man, who is concerned in any material Branch of public affairs." Three months later Adams wrote to his close friend James Warren about the importance of understanding the character of their fellow politicians.

> When it is Said that it is the Prerogative of omniscience to Search Hearts, I Suppose it is meant that no human sagacity can penetrate at all Times into Men's Bosoms and discover with precise Certainty the secrets there: and in this Sense it is certainly true.
>
> But there is a Sense in which Men may be said to be possessed of a Faculty of Searching Hearts too. There is a Discernment competent to Mortals by which they can penetrate into the Minds of Men and discover their Secret Passions, Prejudices, Habits, Hopes, Fears, Wishes and Designs, and by this Means judge what Part they will act in given Circumstances for the future, and see what Principles and Motives have actuated them to the Conduct they have held, in certain Conjunctures of Circumstances which are passed.
>
> A Dexterity and Facility of thus unraveling Men's Thought and a Faculty of governing them by Means of the Knowledge We have of them, constitutes the principal Part of the Art of a Politician.

Adams felt that in a local legislature, "where We know a Man's Pedigree and Biography, his Education, Profession and Connections, as well as his Fortune," it would be relatively "easy to see what it is that governs a Man and determines him to this Party in Preference to that, to this system of Politics rather than another."

But in a continental congress it was different; it was harder. "It requires Time to enquire and learn the Characters and Connections, the Interests and Views of a Multitude of Strangers" to unravel what Adams called the "Mystery of Politics."[19]

Jefferson told James Madison that Adams actually was "a bad calculator of the force and probable effect of the motives which govern men," but he agreed that discerning the character of members of Congress was important. He even offered to send some character sketches of the delegates to Madison, who had just returned to Congress after a three-year absence required by the mandatory rotation-in-office provision of the Articles of Confederation. "It will become of importance that you should form a just estimate of certain public characters; on which therefore I will give you such notes as my knowledge of them has furnished me with. You will compare them with the materials you are otherwise possessed of, and decide on a view of the whole."[20]

Alexander Hamilton always searched for the political affiliations of his colleagues. "I have ever condemned those cold, unfeeling hearts, which no object can animate. I condemn those indifferent mortals, who either never form opinions, or never make them known."[21] To John Adams, "Silence is most commonly design and intrigue."[22] Another leader declared that the intriguer, who used duplicity and machinations on "the road to preferment," was to be despised and guarded against.[23] Perhaps worse was the trimmer, who "in politicks is every way contemptible, and ought never to be trusted. He will certainly *always* be ready to betray you when he conceives that he can serve himself by doing so."[24] But conversations in Congress with trusted friends "constituted feasts of noble sentiments."[25]

The Founders thought it imperative to study the classics of ancient Greece and Rome, the histories of those times, and perhaps of most importance the biographies in Plutarch's *Lives*. Every example of human nature from greed to honor could be found in these works. They believed that "Human nature is the same in all Ages—Habits & Manners vary."[26] If they could identify and compare individuals in their own society with similar types of personalities in ancient Greece and Rome, they could better predict how their contemporaries would act.

John Adams praised his wife's "skill in Physiognomy, and your Talent at drawing Characters," and Abigail instructed her son not to be "a superficial observer, but study Men and Manners that you may be Skillful in both." John Quincy Adams found this hard to do. "To judge Character with impartiality is by no means an easy task. Affection or Resentment will almost always misrepresent things. These passions are the Jaundice of the mind, for they show everything of the same color."[27]

Character sketches were not only useful, they were entertaining. Abigail Adams admonished her close friend Mercy Otis Warren to "fulfill your promise of writing me a long Letter. . . . I love characters drawn by your pen." Abigail's husband also wrote Warren that "the Characters drawn in your last entertained me very agreeably. They were taken off, by a nice & penetrating Eye. I hope you will favor me with more of these Characters. I wish I could draw a Number of Characters for your Inspection. I should perhaps daub on the Paint too thick—but the Features would be very strong." Similarly, John Adams wrote to James Warren, Mercy's husband, saying "I am vastly obliged to you for your Letter. It was like cold Water to a thirsty Soul."[28]

Given the uncertainty of the mail, most correspondents were less than completely candid. John Adams wrote James Warren, "We cannot be too cautious I find what We write, whom We write to, and how it is conveyed." During the war the British on various occasions seized American mail and published letters that embarrassed authors. Adams told Warren, "I wish I could give a Loose to my Pencil and draw Characters for your Inspection, by the Dozen. But Letters don't always go safe." After some letters to her were "kid Napt" by the enemy, Abigail Adams wrote that, "made wise by experience," her husband "is so warry that I dare say, they will get no Booty in politicks from him." Benjamin Rush wasn't so lucky. The British announced that they intended to print an intercepted letter in which Rush "treats the Rebel Senate with great freedom."[29] Each letter was viewed as a child of chance.[30] After the war, opening other people's mail continued "to be a very fashionable Vice."[31]

Diplomats serving abroad understood that their mail was furtively read by foreign government officials. John Jay, serving as American minister-designate to Spain, warned a correspondent that "whenever you write to me, which I hope will be often, recollect that your letters will, in nine instances out of ten, be inspected before they reach me; write nothing, therefore, that you would wish concealed. Jay complained to Secretary of Congress Charles Thomson that "The Want of a regular and safe Communication between Congress and their foreign Ministers, gives occasion to various Inconveniences. Every Letter known or suspected to be for or from me that gets into the post offices, is opened, often kept back for a while and to my certain Knowledge sometimes suppressed entirely. . . . The Expense of private Couriers is intolerable, nor can many in that Character be found who merit Confidence." Thomas Jefferson, U.S. minister to France, described "the infidelities of the post offices both of England and France. . . . The former is the most rascally because they retain one's letters, not choosing to take the trouble of copying them. The latter when they have taken copies, are so civil as to send the originals, re-sealed clumsily with a composition on which they have previously taken the impression of the seal."[32]

The Founders understood the serious consequences of misreading men's characters. John Jay cautioned that one should be well acquainted with a person's character before attempting to describe it. "Much injustice is often done by taking reports as facts, and forming opinions of men from the suggestions which may arise from envy or interested partialities. Though not very old, I have lived too long to credit all I hear; and having been deceived by fair as well as unpromising appearances, they have ceased to decide my judgment of men."[33]

Alternatively, Jay felt that "to see things as being what they are, to estimate them aright, and to act accordingly, are of all attainments the most important." He made "it a Rule to think well of a man as long as I can." Thomas Paine believed that "characters are tender and valuable things; they are more than life to a man of sensibility, and are not to be made the sport of interest, or the sacrifice of incendiary malice." President Thomas Jefferson assured Governor George Clinton not to worry about false accusations by a political opponent. "The uniform tenor of a man's life furnishes better evidence of what he has said or done on any particular occasion than the word of any enemy." It was important, Jefferson believed, to get as many opinions as possible before making a final judgment. "Multiplied testimony, multiplied views will be necessary to give solid establishment to truth. Much is known to one which is not known to another, and no one knows everything. It is the sum of individual knowledge which is to make up the whole truth, and to give its correct current through future time."[34]

Senator William Plumer of New Hampshire realized that he had drawn incorrect conclusions about President Jefferson. "The more critically & impartially I examine the character & conduct of Mr. Jefferson the more favorably I think of his integrity. I am really inclined to think I have done him injustice in not allowing him more credit for the integrity of heart that he possesses." It was important to gather perceptions from different people and at different times. "A city appears very different when viewed from different positions—& so it is with man. Viewed in different situations—different times—places—circumstances—relations & with different dispositions, the man thus examined appears unlike himself." Plumer's object, he said, "is truth—I write for myself—I wish not—I am determined not—to set down ought in malice, or to diminish anything from the fact."[35]

Throughout their public careers many of the Founders employed the same moral compass to plot America's course that they applied in directing their personal lives. Despite the actions of other nations, America would fulfill its destiny only if it was true to the moral imperatives set by God. Success for both men and nations depended upon following a strict code of conduct and a well-balanced system of order. Americans drew upon Alexander Pope, the great English poet who had praised "order and regularity" as "Heaven's first Law."[36] John Jay felt that nations and individuals injure their essential interests in proportion as they deviate from order. "By order I mean that natural regularity which results from attention and obedience to those rules and principles of conduct which reason indicates and which morality and wisdom prescribe. Those rules and principles reach every station and condition in which individuals can be placed, and extend to every possible situation in which nations can find themselves."[37]

For the American Revolution to succeed, America and Americans had to make themselves worthy. Individuals and public officials had to inculcate a whole series of character traits in their personal and official lives. Honesty, morality, integrity, trustworthiness, patriotism, duty, industriousness, dedication, candidness, reserve, prudence, strength, and a resignation to God's will were but a few of the necessary traits. Americans saw the character flaws in the public officials of other countries and how these personal failings adversely affected their countries. Service abroad had shown John Jay the consequences when men and nations failed to live up to proper "rules and principles of conduct." Spain was perhaps the best example of national degeneration. "This Government has little Money, less Wisdom, no Credit, nor any Right to it. They have Pride without Dignity, Cunning without Policy, Nobility without Honor." Great Britain, according to Thomas Jefferson, since the accession of George III to the throne in 1760 had been ruled nine times out of ten by "passion, and not reason." Many Americans felt that the entire British government and economy were totally corrupted and ruled by special interests. Consequently, Jefferson suggested, the way to predict what the British would do during the war was to determine what they should do and then be prepared for the opposite. Thomas Paine agreed. "On our part, in order to know, at any time, what the British government will do, we have only to find out what they ought NOT to do, and this last will be their conduct." Paine acknowledged "that a country has a right to be as foolish as it pleases," as Britain had proved for many years.[38] To avoid a similar fate, American leaders would need strength of character in both their personal and public lives.

Not everyone agreed that the British were all inept. The marquis de Lafayette commanded the American forces in Virginia in 1781. Assessing their chances, Lafayette wrote: "This devil Cornwallis is much wiser than the other generals with whom I have dealt. He inspires me with a sincere fear, and his name has greatly troubled my sleep. This campaign is a good school for me. God grant that the public does not pay for my lessons." To the French minister Luzerne, Lafayette wrote that "I would rather be rid of Lord Cornwallis than of a third of his army. He showers me with courtesies, and we wage war like gentlemen; indeed, he is the only gentleman to have commanded the British in America. But after all this, in the end he will give me a thrashing. . . . Fortune will grow tired of protecting us, and when I am quite alone, I shall be beaten." To his close friend General Henry Knox, Washington's commander of artillery, Lafayette wrote that "Lord Cornwallis's Abilities are to me more Alarming than his Superiority of forces. I ever had a Great opinion of Him. Our Papers Call Him a Mad man but was ever any Advantage taken of Him where

He commanded in Person? To Speak Plain English, I am Devilish Affraid of Him." Lafayette told Knox that during the 1780 campaign "I was Sighing for Opportunities. This Campaign I was trembling for them, as in the Begining there was no difference between a Scarmish and a Battle, a Battle and a total Defeat. We were so lucky as to Escape an Action, and keep ourselves Clear of that Mounted World that was Gallopping Around us."[39]

The Founders did not agree on what was the most important character trait. John Adams felt that morals were more important than all the "arts, sciences, and literature." But Adams and many others believed that "prudence is the first of virtues and the root of all others. Without prudence there may be abstinence but not temperance; there may be rashness but not fortitude; there may be insensibility or obstinacy but not patience." Adams contrasted prudence with levity, which buoys individuals uncontrollably to heights beyond rational limits. Hamilton and Burr and thousands of others possessed this sense of levity. His close friend Dr. Benjamin Rush disagreed on the importance of prudence. He told Adams that General Charles Lee referred to prudence as "a rascally virtue." Rush felt that prudence "certainly has more counterfeits than any other virtue, and when *real* it partakes very much of a selfish nature." It was prudence that made large property holders become Loyalists during the Revolution. Prudence "never achieved anything great in human affairs." Martin Luther lacked prudence, as did William Harvey. So too did the Adamses and John Hancock. "In private life what is commonly called prudence is little else than a system of self-love."[40]

Adams responded immediately. When General Lee characterized prudence as "a rascally virtue," he confused terms. Lee

> meant the spirit which evades when duty requires us to face it. This is cowardice, not prudence; or he meant that subtlety which consults private interest, ease, or safety by the sacrifice or the neglect of our friends or our country. This may be cunning, but is more properly called knavery than prudence. . . . By prudence I mean that deliberation and caution which aims at no ends but good ones, and good ones by none but fair means, and then carefully adjusts and proportions its good means to its good ends. Without this virtue there can be no other. Justice itself cannot exist without

it. A disposition to render to everyone his right is of no use without prudence to judge of what is his right and skill to perform it.[41]

We are truly fortunate that many of the Founders preserved their correspondence and papers for future generations. John Adams hoped that Samuel Adams would make a complete "Collection of his Writings and publish them in Volumes. I know of no greater service that could be rendered to the Rights of Mankind. . . . There Posterity will find a Mass of Principles, and Reasonings, Suitable for them and for all good Men."

John Adams told Jefferson that he hoped "one day your letters will be all published in volumes; they will not always appear Orthodox, or liberal in politics; but they will exhibit a Mass of Taste, Sense, Literature and Science, presented in a sweet simplicity and a neat elegance of Style, which will be read with delight in future ages." Somewhat rationalizing about never writing a history of the Revolutionary era, Jefferson believed that his correspondence afforded, in fact, a more accurate history of his time because it was often "less guarded" and because it was "not meant for the public eye, not restrained by the respect due to that; but poured forth from the overflowings of the heart into the bosom of a friend, as a momentary easement of our feelings." "Written too in the moment, and in the warmth and freshness of fact and feeling," letters carry "internal evidence that what they breathe is genuine." Adams chastised Rush for destroying a collection of anecdotes and documents amassed in order to write his memoirs of the Revolution. Rush said that his history would differ from others and that he would "offend by telling the truth." Adams told Rush that "the burning of your documents was . . . a very rash action, and by no means justifiable upon good principles. Truth, justice, and humanity are of eternal obligation, and we ought to preserve the evidence which can alone support them. I do not intend to let every lie impose upon posterity." It was "from the memoirs [and letters] of individuals the true springs of events and the real motives of actions are to be made known to posterity."[42]

On at least three occasions Abigail Adams pleaded with her husband to destroy her correspondence. He always replied that her letters were more than a mere communication between two people separated by many miles geographically. They were a way for him "to hear you think, or to see your Thoughts." Her letters, he wrote her, make "my Heart throb, more than a Cannonade would. You bid me burn your Letters. But I must forget you first." While riding the circuit in Maine, Adams wrote Abigail every day and sometimes twice a day. He admonished her to "keep these Letters chiefly to yourself, and communicate them with great Caution and Reserve. I should advise you to put them up safe, and preserve them. They may exhibit to our Posterity a kind of Picture of the Manners, Opinions, and Principles of these Times of Perplexity, Danger and Distress."[43]

In a letter labeled "Private and quite confidential," George Washington told Secretary of War James McHenry that he should burn the letter immediately after reading it. Washington told McHenry he would do the same with the response so "that neither the one, nor the other may appear hereafter." Fortunately, the man who (according to Parson Weems) as a child could never tell a lie retained both the file copy of his own letter and the response from McHenry. Washington just could not bring himself to destroy any of his correspondence. Unfortunately, however, after the death of their spouses, both Martha Washington and Thomas Jefferson destroyed their correspondence with their spouses. These were monumental losses because these personal exchanges contained things found nowhere else. Sometimes things were written in letters that never would have been said in person. Abigail Adams wrote John that "my pen is always freer than my tongue. I have wrote many things to you that I suppose I never could have talk'd." Leonard Gansevoort, a New York delegate to Congress, described letter writing as "a Measure which the Almighty has been pleased in his wise providence to dispense to us for the purpose of cultivating the social Virtues and rendering the flames of Friendship, of fraternal Affection and the Ties of Duty flowing from them alive, and not suffer those Ornaments of the Human Mind to be extinguished."[44]

We, individually and as a nation, are enriched because of this literary heritage. It is from this heritage, preserved by a very special generation and brought to light by a myriad of dedicated documentary editors, that the following word portraits have been gleaned.

NOTES

1. John Jay to William Wilberforce, April 14, 1806, *The Correspondence and Public Papers of John Jay,* ed. Henry P. Johnston (4 vols., New York, 1890–93), 4:308; John Adams Diary, April 26, 1779, *Diary and Autobiography of John Adams,* ed. L. H. Butterfield et al. (4 vols., Cambridge, Mass., 1961), 2:362; Jefferson to P. S. du Pont de Nemours, March 2, 1809, *The Quotable Jefferson,* ed. John P. Kaminski (Princeton, N.J., 2006), 75; John Adams to Edmund Jenings, April 13, 1779, *Papers of John Adams,* ed. Robert J. Taylor et al. (Cambridge, Mass., 1977–), 8:35.

2. John Adams to Edmund Jenings, May 22, 1779, *Papers of John Adams* 8:68; John Adams, *Diary,* June 25, 1774, 2:97; John Adams to Abigail Adams, Sept. 8, 1774, *Adams Family Correspondence,* ed. L. H. Butterfield et al. (Cambridge, Mass., 1963–), 1:150.

3. John Adams to Edmund Jenings, May 22, 1779, *Papers of John Adams* 8:68; John Adams, *Thoughts on Government . . .* (Philadelphia, 1776), ibid., 4:90. Adams quoted the couplet from Alexander Pope's *Essay on Man* (London, 1758), Epistle III, lines 19–20.

4. John Jay to Egbert Benson, June 1780, to Sarah Jay, April 15, 1794, in Johnston, *Jay* 1:363, 4:3; George Washington to Martha Washington, June 18, 1775, *The Papers of George Washington,* ed. W. W. Abbot et al. (Charlottesville, Va., 1983–), *Revolutionary Series* 1:3–4; George Washington to Lund Washington, May 19, 1780, to John Eager Howard, Nov. 30, 1795, to James McHenry, July 4, 1798, *The Quotable George Washington: The Wisdom of an American Patriot,* ed. and comp. Stephen E. Lucas (Madison, Wis., 1999), 27, 28, 79; Jefferson to Walter Jones, Jan. 2, 1814, *The Quotable Jefferson,* 438; John Adams to Abigail Adams, Feb. 6, 1796, Adams Papers, Massachusetts Historical Society; John Adams to Benjamin Rush, Aug. 28, 1811, *The Spur of Fame: Dialogues of John Adams and Benjamin Rush, 1805–1813,* ed. John A. Schutz and Douglass Adair (San Marino, Calif., 1966), 207.

5. John Adams to the Comte de Vergennes, Feb. 11, 1779, *Papers of John Adams* 7:402; Washington to Bryan Fairfax, July 20, 1774, *GW Papers, Colonial Series* 10:129–30; Thomas Paine, *Dissertation on First Principles of Government* (1795) and *Serious Address to the People of Pennsylvania* (1778), quoted in *Citizen Paine: Thomas Paine's Thoughts on Man, Government, Society, and Religion,* comp. and ed. John P. Kaminski (Lanham, Md., 2002), 86, 233.

6. New York *Daily Advertiser,* Oct. 6, 1788, in *The Documentary History of the First Federal Elections, 1788–1790,* ed. Merrill Jensen et al. (4 vols., Madison, Wis., 1976–89), 3:204–5.

7. Wolcott to Samuel Lyman, April 17, 1776, *Letters of Delegates to Congress, 1774–1789,* ed. Paul H. Smith et al. (26 vols., Washington, D.C., 1976–2000), 3:553.

8. John Adams, *Autobiography* 3:333; Thomas Paine, "To the Citizens of the United States," *National Intelligencer,* Nov. 22, 1802; section below on Thomas Paine.

9. John Adams to James Warren, Jan. 9, 1787, *Warren-Adams Letters: Being*

Chiefly a Correspondence among John Adams, Samuel Adams, and James Warren (2 vols., Boston, 1917–25), 2:281.

10. John Jay to Richard Peters, March 29, 1811, in Johnston, *Jay* 4:351.

11. John Adams to Benjamin Rush, July 24, 1789, *Documentary History of the First Federal Congress of the United States of America,* ed. Linda Grant De Pauw et al. (Baltimore, 1972–), 16:1125.

12. Of the roughly 3 million people in America in 1776, about 650,000 were African-American slaves, and only about 20 percent of the remaining population was adult white men. Much of the population consisted of children, with ten or more children per family not being unusual. Of the 500,000 adult white men, not more than half favored independence in July 1776.

13. Philip Schuyler to John Jay, July 14, 1777, in Johnston, *Jay* 1:146–47.

14. Abigail Adams to John Adams, July 5, 1780, *Adams Family Correspondence* 3:372.

15. John Adams, *Diary,* Oct. 10, 1774, 2:150.

16. Ibid., Oct. 24, 1774, 2:156; Jefferson to Thomas Leiper, June 12, 1815, *The Quotable Jefferson,* 150–51.

17. Thomas B. Wait to George Thatcher, Aug. 21, 1788, and "Extract of a Letter from New York, 5 September," Litchfield *Weekly Monitor,* Sept. 15, 1788, *First Federal Elections* 1:95, 122–23.

18. John Adams to James Warren, April 13, 1783, *Warren-Adams Letters* 2:210; Franklin to Secretary for Foreign Affairs Robert R. Livingston, July 22, 1783, *Benjamin Franklin: Writings,* ed. J. A. Leo Lemay (New York, 1987), 1065; Franklin to Robert Morris, Dec. 25, 1783, *The Papers of Robert Morris, 1781–1784,* ed. E. James Ferguson et al. (9 vols., Pittsburgh, 1973–99), 8:839.

19. John Adams to William Tudor, July 23, 1775, to James Warren, Oct. 24, 1775, *Papers of John Adams* 3:85, 239.

20. Jefferson to Madison, Jan. 30, 1787, *The Papers of James Madison,* ed. William T. Hutchinson et al. (Chicago and Charlottesville, Va., 1962–), 9:249.

21. Hamilton's speech in the New York Ratifying Convention, June 28, 1788, *The Documentary History of the Ratification of the Constitution,* ed. Merrill Jensen et al. (Madison, Wis., 1976–), 22:1989.

22. John Adams to Benjamin Rush, Sept. 9, 1806, *Spur of Fame,* 69.

23. Elbridge Gerry to James Warren, March 22, 1789, *A Study in Dissent: The Warren-Gerry Correspondence, 1776–1792,* ed. C. Harvey Gardiner (Carbondale, Ill., 1968), 219.

24. "An Inhabitant," *Maryland Journal,* Dec. 26, 1788, *First Federal Elections* 2:163.

25. Benjamin Rush, "Travels through Life," *The Autobiography of Benjamin Rush . . . ,* ed. George W. Corner (Princeton, N.J., 1948), 111.

26. Peter Van Schaack to Henry C. Van Schaack, June 29, 1788, *Documentary History of the Ratification of the Constitution* 21:1239.

27. John Adams to Abigail Adams, Nov. 18, 1775, Abigail Adams to John Quincy Adams, Jan. 21, 1781, *Adams Family Correspondence* 1:327, 4:68; John

Quincy Adams, Diary, Dec. 8, 1785, *Diary of John Quincy Adams,* ed. David Grayson Allen et al. (2 vols., Cambridge, Mass., 1981), 1:368.

28. Abigail Adams to Mercy Otis Warren, April 13, 1776, *Adams Family Correspondence* 1:378; John Adams to Mercy Otis Warren, Nov. 25, 1775, to James Warren, May 21, 1775, *Papers of John Adams* 3:319, 11.

29. John Adams to James Warren, Feb. 11, 1776, Oct. 25, 1775, *Papers of John Adams* 4:21, 3:245; Abigail Adams to Mercy Otis Warren, Jan. 8, 1781, *Adams Family Correspondence* 4:60.

30. Abigail Adams to John Adams, Sept. 15, 1776, *Adams Family Correspondence* 2:125.

31. Leonard Gansevoort to Peter Gansevoort, March 5, 1788, Gansevoort-Lansing Papers, New York Public Library.

32. Jay to William Bingham, Sept. 8, 1781, in Johnston, *Jay* 2:68; Jay to Charles Thomson, April 23, 1781, *John Jay,* ed. Richard B. Morris (2 vols., New York, 1975–80), 2:69; Jefferson to Ralph Izard, Sept. 26, 1785, *The Papers of Thomas Jefferson,* ed. Julian P. Boyd et al. (Princeton, N.J., 1950–), 8:552–53.

33. Jay to William Bingham, Sept. 8, 1781, in Johnston, *Jay* 2:67–68.

34. Jay to Lindley Murray, Aug. 22, 1794, ibid., 4:51; Jay to Alexander Hamilton, Nov. 10, 1798, *The Papers of Alexander Hamilton,* ed. Harold C. Syrett et al. (27 vols., New York, 1961–87), 22:234; Paine, *Pennsylvania Packet,* Dec. 31, 1778; Jefferson to George Clinton, Dec. 31, 1803, to William Johnson, March 4, 1823, Jefferson Papers, Library of Congress.

35. William Plumer, Memorandum, March 16, 1806, *William Plumer's Memorandum of Proceedings in the United States Senate, 1803–1807,* ed. Everett Somerville Brown (New York, 1923), 453.

36. Jeremiah Hill to George Thatcher, March 4, 1789, *Documentary History of the First Federal Congress* 15:10.

37. Jay, Charge to the Grand Jury, Richmond, Va., May 22, 1793, in Johnston, *Jay* 3:478.

38. Jay to Gouverneur Morris, Sept. 28, 1781, *The Emerging Nation: A Documentary History of the Foreign Relations of the United States under the Articles of Confederation, 1780–1789,* ed. Mary A. Giunta et al. (3 vols., Washington, D.C., 1996), 1:238; Jefferson to John Adams, Sept. 28, 1787, to John Jay, Oct. 8, 1787, in Boyd, *Jefferson Papers* 12:190, 216; *Citizen Paine: Thomas Paine's Thoughts on Man, Government, Society, and Religion,* ed. John P. Kaminski (Lanham, Md., 2002), 54.

39. Lafayette to the Vicomte de Noailles, July 9, 1781, to Luzerne, Aug. 14, 1781, to Knox, Aug. 18, 1781, *Lafayette in the Age of the American Revolution: Selected Letters and Papers, 1776–1790,* ed. Stanley J. Idzerda et al. (5 vols., Ithaca, N.Y., 1977–83), 4:241, 322, 332.

40. John Adams to Rush, Nov. 11, 1806, April 12, 1807, Rush to Adams, July 9, 1807, *Spur of Fame,* 73, 84–85, 97–98.

41. John Adams to Rush, Sept. 1, 1807, ibid., 99.

42. John Adams to Abigail Adams, March 28, 1783, *Adams Family Correspondence* 5:111; John Adams to Jefferson, July 12, 1822, Jefferson to John Adams, June 27, 1813, *The Adams-Jefferson Letters . . . ,* ed. Lester J. Cappon (Chapel

Hill, N.C., 1959), 582, 336; Jefferson to William Johnson, March 4, 1823, *The Quotable Jefferson*, 185; Rush to John Adams, Aug. 14, 1805, John Adams to Rush, Aug. 23, Dec. 4, 1805, *Spur of Fame*, 33, 34, 45.

43. John Adams to Abigail Adams, April 28, 1776, *The Book of Abigail and John: Selected Letters of the Adams Family, 1762–1784,* ed. L. H. Butterfield, Marc Friedlaender, and Mary-Jo Kline (Cambridge, Mass., 1975), 125; John Adams to Abigail Adams, July 2, 1774, *Adams Family Correspondence* 1:121.

44. Washington to McHenry, Oct. 1, 1798, *GW Papers, Retirement Series* 3:66, 82; Abigail Adams to John Adams, Oct. 22, 1775, *Adams Family Correspondence* 1:310; Leonard Gansevoort to Peter Gansevoort, March 18, 1788, Gansevoort-Lansing Papers, New York Public Library.

Abigail Adams
1744–1818

⊰ Born in Weymouth, Mass., the second of three daughters and a son, to William Smith, a Congregational minister, and Elizabeth Quincy Smith, daughter of the prominent John Quincy. Because of poor health, she did not attend school but learned from her parents, grandparents, her older brother-in-law Richard Cranch, and her future husband. Surrounded by books, she was an insatiable reader. She met John Adams in 1759 when she was fifteen years old and he twenty-four. They married five years later in October 1764. Over the next ten years, she gave birth to five children: first a daughter, then a son, another daughter, and two more sons. All but the second daughter, Susanna, lived to adulthood. The eldest son was John Quincy Adams. She gave birth to a stillborn daughter in 1777 and then had no more children. Her lawyer husband was often absent, riding the judicial circuit throughout Massachusetts and Maine. As the Revolutionary movement developed, John Adams was increasingly away from home serving in the colonial legislature and the Continental congresses or on diplomatic missions abroad. During his absences Abigail raised the children, supervised the farm, and administered the family finances. She believed in the concept of the republican motherhood. Men and women had separate roles to play. A woman's role was different from a man's but fully as important: no man could achieve his maximum potential without the assistance and cooperation of his wife. She was a sounding board for John's ideas, a defender of his reputation, a soul mate, an inspiration. She advocated the expansion of rights (not necessarily voting rights) for women to protect them from the arbitrary and oppressive rule of their husbands.

She and her daughter left Braintree for London in June 1784 and arrived on July 20. She subsequently lived in Amsterdam, The Hague, Paris, and London. She and John returned to Massachusetts in June 1788. When her husband became vice president of the United States, she lived in New York City and then in Philadelphia. She stayed for a short time in Philadelphia after her husband became president and briefly resided in Washington, D.C., the new federal capital. During most of Adams's presidency, however, Abigail, not in good health, resided in Quincy, a subdivision of Braintree. When separated, they regularly corresponded about all matters, including politics. She was her husband's most trusted adviser. She died of typhoid fever on October 28, 1818.

John Adams, Diary FEBRUARY 1, 1763

Di.* was a constant feast. Tender feeling, sensible, friendly. A friend. Not an imprudent, not an indelicate, not a disagreeable Word or Action. Prudent, modest, delicate, soft, sensible, obliging, action.

John Adams to Abigail Adams PHILADELPHIA, JULY 7, 1775

It gives me more Pleasure than I can express to learn that you sustain with so much Fortitude, the Shocks and Terrors of the Times. You are really brave, my dear, you are an Heroine. And you have Reason to be. For the worst that can happen, can do you no Harm. A soul, as pure, as benevolent, as virtuous and pious as yours has nothing to fear, but every Thing to hope and expect from the last of human Evils.

John Adams, Diary SEPTEMBER 24, 1775

Called upon Stephen Collins who has just returned. . . .

One Thing he told me, for my Wife, who will be peeping here, sometime or other, and come across it. He says when he

---

*John and Abigail Adams often referred to each other with names from Greek and Roman mythology. One of Abigail's mythological names was Diana, the virgin goddess of the moon and the goddess of the wilderness.

called at my House, an English Gentleman was with him, a Man of Penetration, though of few Words. And this silent, penetrating Gentleman was pleased with Mrs. Adams, and thought her, the most accomplished Lady he had seen since he came out of England—Down Vanity, for you don't know who this Englishman is.

John Adams to Abigail Adams PHILADELPHIA, SEPTEMBER 26, 1775

I have seen the Utility of Geometry, Geography, and the Art of drawing so much of late, that I must entreat you, my dear, to teach the Elements of those Sciences to my little Girl and Boys. It is as pretty an Amusement, as Dancing or Skating, or Fencing, after they have once acquired a taste for them. No doubt you are well qualified for a school Mistress in these Studies, for Stephen Collins tells me the English Gentleman, in Company with him, when he visited Braintree, pronounced you the most accomplished Lady, he had seen since he left England, You see a Quaker can flatter, but don't you be proud.

Abigail Adams to John Adams BRAINTREE, MASS., APRIL 7, 1776

I hope in time to have the Reputation of being as good a Farmeress as my partner has of being a good Statesman.

John Adams to Mary Palmer PHILADELPHIA, JULY 5, 1776

In Times as turbulent as these, commend me to the Ladies for Historiographers. The Gentlemen are too much engaged in Action. The Ladies are cooler Spectators.... There is a Lady at the Foot of Penn's Hill, who obliges me, from Time to Time with clearer and fuller Intelligence, than I can get from a whole Committee of Gentlemen.

Abigail Adams to John Adams BRAINTREE, SEPTEMBER 20, 1776

The Best accounts we can collect from New York assure us that our Men fought valiantly. We are no ways dispirited here, we possess a Spirit that will not be conquered. If our Men are all drawn off and we should be attacked, you would find a Race of Amazons in America.

Mercy Otis Warren to Abigail Adams   OCTOBER 15, 1776

When do You Expect to see Mr. Adams. I Really think it a Great trial of patience and philosophy to be so Long separated from the Companion of Your Heart and from the Father of your Little Flock. But the High Enthusiasm of a truly patriotic Lady will Carry Her through Every Difficulty, and Lead Her to Every Exertion. Patience, Fortitude, Public Spirit, Magnanimity and self Denial are the Virtues she Boasts. I wish I Could put in my Claim to those sublime qualities.

James Warren to John Adams   APRIL 27, 1777

After all our Study, I don't know but Mrs. Adams' Native Genius will Excel us all in Husbandry. She was much Engaged when I came along, and the Farm at Braintree Appeared to be Under Excellent Management.

John Adams to Abigail Adams   PHILADELPHIA, MAY 15, 1777

Gen. Warren writes me, that my Farm never looked better, than when he last saw it, and that Mrs. —— was like to outshine all the Farmers.—I wish I could see it.—But I can make Allowances. He knows the Weakness of his Friend's Heart and that nothing flatters it more than praises bestowed upon a certain Lady.

Abigail Adams to John Lowell   BRAINTREE, NOVEMBER 29, 1779

It has been my Lot in Life to be called repeatedly to the painful task of separating from the dearest connection in Life, Honor and Fame of which the world talk, weigh but lightly against the Domestic happiness I resign, and the pain and anxiety I suffer.— One only consideration preponderates the scale, the hope of rendering Essential service to a distressed and Bleeding Country.

Abigail Adams to John Quincy Adams   BRAINTREE, MARCH 2, 1780

You have great reason for thankfulness to your kind perservor, who hath again carried you through many dangers, preserved your Life and given you an opportunity of making further improvements in virtue and knowledge. You must consider that every Moment of your time is precious, if trifled away never to be recalled. Do not spend too much of it in recreation, it will never afford you that permanent satisfaction which the acquisition of one Art or Science will give you, and whatever you undertake aim to make yourself perfect in it, for if it is worth doing at all, it is worth doing well.

Abigail Adams to John Adams APRIL 10, 1782

Adieu my dear Friend. How gladly would I visit you and partake of your Labours and cares, soothe you to rest, and alleviate your anxieties were it given me to visit you even by moon Light, as the fairies are fabled to do.

I cheer my Heart with the distant prospect. All that I can hope for at present, is to hear of your welfare which of all things lies nearest the Heart of your ever affectionate Portia

BRAINTREE, JUNE 30, 1783

But I never shall take a journey which will be truly pleasant to me, unaccompanied by my Friend. And yet how few in the course of 19 years that we have been connected, have we taken together? Though your life has been one continued Scene of journeying, in the early part of my Life, Maternal duties prevented my accompanying you, and in the Later the Stormy Scenes of war. Few persons who so well Love domestick Life as my Friend; have been called, for so long a period, to relinquish the enjoyment of it; yet like the needle to the pole, you invariably turn towards it; as the only point where you have fixed your happiness. It is this belief which has supported me thus far through the voyage, but alas how often have I felt the want of my pilot, obliged "to act my little part alone."

AUGUST 24, 1783

I know not how to realize that I shall see you soon. Hope and Fear have been the two ruling passions of a large portion of my Life, and I have been band[i]ed from one to the other like a tennis Ball.

NOVEMBER 20, 1783

I should have liked very well, to have gone to France, and resided there a year, but to think of going to England in a publick Character, and residing there; engaging at my time of life in Scenes quite New, attended with dissipation, parade and Nonsense; I am sure I should make an awkward figure. The retired Domestick circle "the feast of reason and the flow of soul"* are my Ideas of happiness, and my most ardent wish is, to have you return and become Master of the Feast.

My Health is infirm, I am frequently distressed with a nervous pain in my Head, and a fatigue of any kind will produce it. Neither of us appear to be built for duration. Would to Heaven the few remaining days allotted Us, might be enjoyed together. I have considered it as my misfortune, that I could not attend to your Health, watch for your repose, alleviate your Hours of anxiety, and make you a home where ever you resided. More says a very skillful Dr. depends upon the Nurse than the physician.

My present determination is to tarry at home this winter; lonely as it is without my children; and if I cannot prevail upon you to return to Me in the Spring—you well know that I may be drawn to you.

DECEMBER 15, 1783

I have already written to you in answer to your Letters which were dated September 10th and reached me a month before those by Mr. Thaxter. I related to you all my fears respecting a winter's voyage. My Friends are all against it, and Mr. Gerry as you will see, by the Copy of his Letter enclosed, has given his opinion upon well grounded reasons. If I should leave my affairs in the Hands of my Friends, there would be much to think of, and much to do, to place them in that method and order I would wish to leave them in.

Theory and practice are two very different things; and the object magnifies, as I approach nearer to it. I think if you were abroad in a private Character, and necessitated to continue there; I should not hesitate so much at coming to you. But a mere American as I am, unacquainted with the Etiquette of courts, taught to say the thing I mean, and to wear my Heart in my countenance, I am sure I should make an awkward figure. And then it would mortify my pride if I should be thought to disgrace you. Yet strip Royalty of its pomp, and power, and what are its votaries more than their fellow worms? I have so little of the Ape about me; that I have refused every public invitation to figure in the Gay World, and sequestered myself in this Humble cottage, content

*Alexander Pope, *Satires . . . of Horace* 2.1.128.

with rural Life and my domestick employments in the midst of which; I have sometimes Smiled, upon recollecting that I had the Honor of being allied to an Ambassador. Yet I have for an example the chaste Lucretia who was found spinning in the midst of her maidens, when the Brutal Tarquin plotted her destruction.

JANUARY 3, 1784

Why with a Heart Susceptible of every tender impression, and feelingly alive, have I So often been called to Stand alone and support myself through Scenes which have almost torn it asunder, not I fear, because I have more resolution or fortitude than others, for my resolution often fails me; and my fortitude wavers.

FEBRUARY 11, 1784

You invite me to you, you call me to follow you, the most earnest wish of my soul is to be with you—but you can scarcely form an Idea of the conflict of my mind. It appears to me such an enterprise, the ocean so formidable, the quitting my habitation and my Country, leaving my Children, my Friends, with the Idea that perhaps I may never see them again, without my Husband to console and comfort me under these apprehensions—indeed my dear Friend there are hours when I feel unequal to the trial. But on the other hand, I console myself with the Idea of being joyfully and tenderly received by the best of Husbands and Friends, and of meeting a dear and long absent Son. But the difference is; my fears, and anxieties, are present; my hopes, and expectations, distant.

But avaunt ye Idle Specters, the desires and requests of my Friend are a Law to me. I will sacrifice my present feelings and hope for a blessing in pursuit of my duty.

Abigail Adams to Elizabeth Cranch AUTEUIL, FRANCE, SEPTEMBER 5, 1784

[In a small octagonal room next to Abigail's writing room, all eight walls had floor-to-ceiling mirrors. Abigail abhorred it!] Now that I do not like; for being rather clumsy and by no means an elegant figure, I hate to have it so often repeated to me. This room is about ten or 12 foot large, is 8 cornered and panneld with looking Glasses.

Abigail Adams to Thomas Jefferson LONDON, FEBRUARY 11, 1786

In Europe every being is estimated, and every country valued, in proportion to their show and splendor. In a private station I have not a wish for expensive living, but, whatever my fair countrywomen may think, and I hear they envy my situation, I will most joyfully exchange Europe for America, and my public for a private life. I am really surfeited with Europe, and most heartily long for the rural cottage, the purer and honester manners of my native land, where domestic happiness reigns unrivalled, and virtue and honor go hand in hand. I hope one season more will give us an opportunity of making our escape. At present we are in the situation of Sterne's starling.*

David Humphreys to George Washington LONDON, FEBRUARY 11, 1786

[Rather than describing the birth-night ball for George III,] I will only say in honor of America that Mrs. Adams appeared to very good advantage, being an extremely decent Lady.

Abigail Adams to Elizabeth Smith Shaw LONDON, MARCH 4, 1786

I hope my youngest son has out grown the Rheumatism. This cold weather has stirred up mine, but I am better now than I have been.

Abigail Adams to Mary Cranch LONDON, APRIL 24, 1786

[If I could shed] some pounds I should move nimbler and feel lighter. Tis true I enjoy good Health, but am larger than both my sisters compounded. Mr. Adams too keeps pace with me, and if one Horse had to carry us, I should pity the poor Beast, but your Niece [Nabby Adams] is moulded into a shape as Slender as a *Grey hound,* and is not be sure more than half as large as she was when she first left America. The Spring is advancing and I begin to walk so that I hope exercise will be of service to me.

---

*In Laurence Sterne's *Sentimental Journey through France and Italy,* a starling in a cage cries out to each passerby: "I can't get out." The hero, Yorick, cannot release the bird and reflects on the condition of slavery and the blessings of liberty.

MAY 25, 1786

What a tasteless insipid life do I lead here in comparison with what I used to in Braintree, looking after my children and family—seeing my Friends in a Social way, loving and being beloved by them. Believe me I am not in the least altered, except that I wear my Hair dressed and powdered, and am two years older, and somewhat fatter which you may be sure is no addition to my looks. But the Heart and the mind are the Same.

Abigail Adams to Elizabeth Cranch LONDON, JULY 18, 1786

Could I, you ask, return to my (Rustick) cottage, and view it with the same pleasure and Satisfaction I once enjoy'd in it? I answer I think I could, provided I have the same kind Friends and dear Relatives to enhance its value to me. It is not the superb and magnificent House nor the rich and Costly furniture that can ensure either pleasure or happiness to the possessor. A convenient abode Suitable to the station of the possessor, is no doubt desirable, and to those who can afford them, Parks, Gardens, or what in this Country is called an ornamented Farm, appears to me an Innocent and desirable object. They are Beautiful to the Eye, pleasing to the fancy, and improving to the Imagination, but then as Pope observes,

> 'Tis use alone that sanctifies Expence,
> And Splendor borrows all her rays from Sense.*

Abigail Adams to Thomas Jefferson LONDON, JULY 23, 1786

I suppose you must have heard the report respecting Col. Smith—that he has taken my daughter from me, a contrivance between him and the Bishop of St. Asaph. It is true he tendered me a Son as an equivalent and it was no bad offer, but I had three Sons before, and but one Daughter. Now I have been thinking of an exchange with you sir, suppose you give me Miss Jefferson, and in some future day take a Son in lieu of her. I am for Strengthening the federal Union.

---

*Alexander Pope, *Moral Essays* 4.179–80.

Abigail Adams to Elizabeth Smith Shaw LONDON, OCTOBER 15, 1786

Chastity, Modesty, decency, and conjugal Faith are the pillars of society; Sap these, and the whole fabrick falls sooner or later.

Abigail Adams to Mary Cranch LONDON, JANUARY 20, 1787

I . . . give you some account of my late Tour to Bath, that Seat of fashionable Resort, where like the rest of the World I spent a fortnight in Amusement and dissipation, but returned I assure you, with double pleasure to my own fire side, where only thank heaven, my substantial happiness subsists. Here I find these satisfaction[s] which neither Satiate by enjoyment nor pall upon reflection, for tho I like some times to mix in the Gay World, and view the manners as they rise, I have much reason to be grateful to my Parents that my early Education gave me not an habitual taste for what is termed fashionable Life.

FEBRUARY 25, 1787

I shall quit Europe with more pleasure than I came to it, uncontaminated I hope with its Manners and vices. I have learnt to know the World, and its value. I have seen high Life, I have Witnessed the Luxury and pomp of State, the Power of riches and the influence of titles, and have beheld all Ranks bow before them, as the only shrine worthy of worship. Notwithstanding this, I feel that I can return to my little cottage and be happier than here, and if we have not wealth, we have what is better, Integrity.

Thomas Jefferson to James Madison PARIS, MAY 25, 1788

When he [John Adams] established himself [as a diplomat in Europe], his pecuniary affairs were under the direction of Mrs. Adams, one of the most estimable characters on earth, and the most attentive and honorable economists.

Abigail Adams to John Adams QUINCY, MASS., JANUARY 7, 1789

I have received a Letter every week since you left me, and by this Day's post two, one of the 28th and one of the 29th December for which receive my thanks particularly that part in which you say you are not less anxious to see me than when Separated 20 years ago. Years Subdue the ardour of passion but in lieu thereof a Friendship and affection Deep Rooted Subsists which defies the Ravages of Time, and will Survive whilst the vital Flame exists. Our attachment to Character, Reputation and Fame increase I believe with our Years. . . . My Health . . . is better than the last winter tho very few days pass in which I can say that I feel really well.

Abigail Adams to Mary Cranch RICHMOND HILL, NEW YORK CITY, AUGUST 9, 1789

I have been fully employed in entertaining company, in the first place all the Senators who had Ladies & families, then the remaining Senators, and this week we have begun with the House, and tho we have a room in which we dine 24 persons at a Time, I shall not get through them all, together with the publick Ministers for a month to come. The help I find here is so very indifferent to what I had in England, the weather so warm that we can give only one dinner a week. I cannot find a cook in the whole city but what will get drunk, and as to the Negroes, I am most sincerely sick of them.

Abigail Adams to Cotton Tufts NEW YORK, SEPTEMBER 1, 1789

Our Situation is a very Beautiful one and I feel in that respect quite happy, but I find myself much more exposed to company than in any situation which I have ever before been in. The morning is a time when strangers who come to N. York expect to find Mr. Adams at home. This brings us Breakfast company besides it is a sweet morning retreat for fresh air & a cool Breeze, I should like to visit my friends during the adjournment but our Finances will not admit of much traveling.

Abigail Adams to Mary Cranch RICHMOND HILL, NEW YORK CITY, JANUARY 24, 1790

To many of [my dear Friends] I owe Letters, but I really hate to touch a pen. I am ashamed to say how laizy I am grown in that respect.

NEW YORK, OCTOBER 10, 1790

I do not know of any persons property so unproductive as ours is. I do not believe that it yields us one per cent per Annum. I have the vanity however to think that if Dr. Tufts and my Ladyship had been left to the sole management of our affairs, they would have been upon a more profitable footing. In the first place I never desired so much land. I would have purchased publick securities with. The interest of which, poorly as it is funded, would have been less troublesome to take charge of than Land and much more productive. But in these Ideas I have always been so unfortunate as to differ from my partner, who thinks he never saved any thing but what he vested in Land.

OCTOBER 25, 1790

[Two weeks ago] I retired to my chamber, and was taken with a shaking fit which held me 2 Hours and was succeeded by a fever which lasted till near morning, attended with severe pain in my Head, Back, &c. The next morning I took an Emetic which operated very kindly and proved to me the necessity of it. On Tuesday I felt better and went below stairs, but was again seazd with another shaking fit which was succeeded as the former by the most violent fever I ever felt. It quite made me delirious. No rest for 5 Nights & days. It settled into a Regular intermitting Fever. The Doctor after having repeatedly puked me, gave me James's powders, but with very little effect. I began upon the Bark the 10th day which I have taken in large Quantities and it has appeared to have put an end to my fever, but I am very low and weak. I rode out yesterday and found no inconveniency from it. I shall repeat my ride today. I have great cause to be thankful for so speedy a restoration, but I have a journey before me which appears like a mountain & three Ferries to cross. [The Adamses were moving with the capital from New York City to Philadelphia.]

PHILADELPHIA, APRIL 20, 1792

We proposed setting out on our journey on Monday or Tuesday next. The weather has been so rainy that I have not been able to ride so often as I wished in order to prepare myself for my journey, and how I shall stand it, I know not. This everlasting fever still hangs about me & prevents my entire recovery. A critical period of Life Augments my complaints. I am far from Health, tho much better than when I wrote you last. I see not any company but those who visit me in my chamber.

John Adams to Abigail Adams PHILADELPHIA, FEBRUARY 4, 1794

You Apologize for the length of your Letters and I ought to excuse the shortness and Emptiness of mine. Yours give me more entertainment than all the speeches I hear. There is more good Thoughts, fine strokes and Mother Wit in them than I hear in the Whole Week. An Ounce of Mother Wit is worth a Pound of Clergy and I rejoice that one of my children [John Quincy Adams] at least has an Abundance of not only Mother Wit, but his Mother's Wit. It is one of the most amiable and striking Traits in his Compositions. It appeared in all its Glory and severity in Barneveld.*

Abigail Adams to John Adams QUINCY, FEBRUARY 26, 1794

Some were made for Rule others for Submission, and even amongst my own Sex this doctrine holds good. . . . My ambition will extend no further than Reigning in the Heart of my Husband. That is my throne and there I aspire to be absolute.

John Adams to Abigail Adams PHILADELPHIA, APRIL 3, 1794

I must leave all your Agriculture to your Judgment and the Advice of your Assistants. . . . You are so valorous and noble a farmer that I feel little anxious about Agriculture.

Abigail Adams to John Adams QUINCY, JANUARY 21, 1796

My Ambition leads me not to be first in Rome, and the Event you request me to contemplate is of so serious a Nature that it requires much reflection and deliberation to determine upon it. There is not a beam of Light, nor a shadow of comfort or pleasure in the contemplation of the object. If personal considerations alone were to weigh, I should immediately say retire with the principle. I can only say that circumstances must Govern you. In a matter of such Momentous concern I dare not influence you. I must pray that you may have superior Direction. As to holding the office of v. p. there I will give my opinion. Resign, retire. I won't be second under no Man but Washington.

---

*This pseudonym was used by John Quincy Adams in signing a newspaper article.

FEBRUARY 20, 1796

Whether I have patience, prudence, discretion sufficient to fill a Station so unexceptionably as the Worthy Lady who now holds it, I fear I have not. As Second I have had the happiness of steering clear of censure as far as I know. If the contemplation did not make me feel very serious, I should say that I have been so used to a freedom of sentiment that I know not how to place so many guards about me, as will be indispensable, to look at every word before I utter it, and to impose a silence upon my self, when I long to talk. Here in this retired Village, I live beloved by my Neighbors, and as I assume no State, and practice no pageantry, unenvied I sit calm and easy, missing very little with the World.

John Adams to Abigail Adams PHILADELPHIA, MARCH 1, 1796

I have no concern on your Account but for your health. A Woman can be silent, when she will.

Abigail Adams to John Adams PHILADELPHIA, MARCH 2, 1796

No Man even if he is sixty Years of Age ought to have more than three Months at a Time from his Family, and our Country is a very hard hearted tyrannical niggardly Country. It has committed more Robberies upon me, and obliged me to more sacrifices than any other woman in the Country and this I will maintain against any one who will venture to come forward and dispute it with me. As there never can be a compensation for me, I must sit down with this consolation that it might have been worse.

QUINCY, MARCH 28, 1796

I detest still life, and had rather be jostled than inanimate.

APRIL 10, 1796

What a Jumble are my Letters. Politics, Domestics occurrences, Farming anecdotes. Pray light Your Segars [cigars] with them. Leave them not to the inspection of futurity, for they will never have any other value than that of giving information for the present moment upon those subjects which interest you and Your affectionate A. Adams

John Adams to Abigail Adams PHILADELPHIA, APRIL 21, 1796

You call your Letters a Jumble but they are my Delight and mine are not half as good as Yours.

MARCH 22, 1797

I never wanted your Advice and assistance more in my Life.

APRIL 6, 1797

The Times are critical and dangerous, and I must have you here to assist me.

APRIL 7, 1797

I want Physick and I want Exercise: but I want your Assistance more than either. You must come and leave the Place [their property in Quincy] to the mercy of Winds.

APRIL 11, 1797

You had not received any of my Letters which urge your immediate departure for Philadelphia. I must now repeat this with Zeal and Earnestness. I can do nothing without you. We must resign every Thing but our public Duties, and they will be more than We can discharge, with Satisfaction to ourselves or others I fear. . . . I must entreat you, to lose not a moment's time in preparing to come on that you may take off from me every Care of Life but that of my public Duty, assist me with your Councils, and console me with your Conversation. Every Thing relating to the Farms must be left to our friends.

Abigail Adams to Mary Cranch   PHILADELPHIA, MAY 16, 1797

Mrs Tufts once stiled my situation [as first lady], splendid misery. She was not far from Truth.

MAY 24, 1797

I keep up my old Habit of rising at an early hour. If I did not I should have little command of my Time. At 5 I rise. From that time till 8 I have a few leisure hours. At 8 I breakfast, after which until Eleven I attend to my Family arrangements. At that hour I dress for the day. From 12 until two I receive company, sometimes until 3. We dine at that hour unless on company days which are Tuesdays & Thursdays. After dinner I usually ride out until seven. I begin to feel a little more at Home, and less anxiety about the ceremonious part of my duty, though by not having a drawing Room for the summer I am obliged every day, to devote two Hours for the purpose of seeing company.

Julian Ursyn Niemcewicz, Travels through America
NOVEMBER 8, 1797

I passed then into a room opposite and I found there the true counterpart of Mr. Adams. It was his wife. Small, short and squat, she is accused of a horrible crime. It is said she puts on rouge. What is certain is that if her manner is not the most affable, her mind is well balanced and cultivated.

Abigail Adams to John Adams QUINCY, NOVEMBER 29, 1798

This is our Thanksgiving day. When I look Back upon the Year past, I perceive many, very many causes for thanksgiving, both of a publick and private nature. I hope my Heart is not ungrateful, tho sad; it is usually a day of festivity when the Social Family circle meet together tho separated the rest of the year. No Husband dignifies my Board, no Children add gladness to it, no Smiling Grandchildren Eyes to sparkle for the plumb pudding, or feast upon the mind Eye. Solitary and alone I behold the day after a sleepless night, without a joyous feeling. Am I ungrateful? I hope not.

John Adams to Abigail Adams PHILADELPHIA, JANUARY 1, 1799

You have an Admirable Faculty of employing your Mind. And in the Affairs of the farm materials for it.

Abigail Adams to Mary Cranch PHILADELPHIA, NOVEMBER 26, 1799

Gloom is no part of my Religion.

Benjamin Rush, Sketches C. 1800

The pleasures of these evenings [in conversation with John Adams] was much enhanced by the society of Mrs. Adams, who in point of talent, knowledge, virtue, and female accomplishments was in every respect fitted to be the friend and companion of her husband in all his different and successive stations, of private citizen, member of Congress, foreign minister, Vice President and President of the United States.

Abigail Adams to Mary Cranch PHILADELPHIA, MAY 26, 1800

A strong imagination is said to be a refuge from sorrow, and a kindly solace for a feeling Heart. Upon this principle it was that Pope founded his observation that "hope springs eternal in the human breast."

Fisher Ames to Rufus King DEDHAM, MASS., SEPTEMBER 24, 1800

[Referring to John Adams's praise for Jefferson.] The good Lady his wife has been often talkative in a similar strain, and she is as complete a politician as any Lady in the old French Court.

John Adams to Benjamin Rush QUINCY, APRIL 12, 1809

When I went home to my family in May 1770, from the town meeting in Boston, which was the first I had ever attended, and where I had been chosen in my absence, without any solicitation, one of their representatives, I said to my wife, "I have accepted a seat in the House of Representatives, and thereby have consented to my own ruin, to your ruin, and the ruin of our children. I give you this warning that you may prepare your mind for your fate." She burst into tears, but instantly cried out in a transport of magnanimity, "Well, I am willing in this cause to run all risks with you and to be ruined with you if you are ruined." These were times, my friend, in Boston which tried women's souls as well as men's.

Thomas Jefferson to Benjamin Rush POPLAR FOREST, DECEMBER 5, 1811

Knowing the weight which her opinions had with him [John Adams].

John Adams to Thomas Jefferson QUINCY, OCTOBER 20, 1818

Now Sir, for my Griefs! The dear Partner of my Life for fifty four Years as a Wife and for many Years more as a Lover, now lyes in extremis, forbidden to speak or be spoken to.

John Adams
1735–1826

⇥ BORN IN Braintree, Mass. Graduated from Harvard College, 1755. Taught school and studied law with James Putnam in Worcester. Admitted to Boston bar, 1758; practiced law in that town but lived in Braintree. Married Abigail Smith of Weymouth, 1764. Drafted Braintree resolutions against Stamp Act, 1765. Moved to Boston, 1768. Helped defend British soldiers after Boston Massacre, 1770. Member, colonial House of Representatives, 1770. Election to council rejected by governor, 1774. Returned to Braintree, 1774. Delegate to First Continental Congress, 1774. Represented Braintree in First Provincial Congress, 1774. Author of essays of "Novanglus," 1775. Member, state council, 1775. Chief justice of state Superior Court, 1775–77 (never took seat on bench). Delegate to Continental Congress, 1775–77. Author of *Thoughts on Government,* April 1776. Seconded motion in Congress for independence, June 1776; appointed to committees to prepare a declaration of independence and to plan for foreign alliances, June 1776; a leading advocate for and signer of Declaration of Independence. President, Continental Board of War, 1776–77. Appointed a commissioner to France to replace Silas Deane, 1777. Returned to the United States, 1779. Member, state constitutional convention, 1779; primary author of state constitution of 1780. Appointed minister plenipotentiary to negotiate treaties of peace and commerce with Great Britain, 1779. Appointed commissioner to negotiate treaties of amity and commerce with United Provinces (Holland), 1780. Served as a commissioner to negotiate peace treaty ending war with Great

Britain, 1781–83. Minister plenipotentiary to United Provinces, 1781–88, negotiated loans with Dutch bankers. Along with Benjamin Franklin and Thomas Jefferson empowered to conclude commercial treaties with European and African nations, 1784. Minister plenipotentiary to Great Britain, 1785–88. Author of three-volume *Defence of the Constitutions of the United States,* 1787–88. Returned to America, June 1788. Vice president of the United States, 1789–97. President of the United States, 1797–1801. Wrote his autobiography, 1802–7. Member, state constitutional convention, 1820.

John Adams, Autobiography

Here it may be proper to recollect something which makes an Article of great importance in the Life of every Man. I was of an amorous disposition and very early from ten or eleven Years of Age, was very fond of the Society of females. I had my favorites among the young Women and spent many of my Evenings in their Company and this disposition although controlled for seven Years after my Entrance into College returned and engaged me too much till I was married. I shall draw no Characters nor give any enumeration of my youthful flames. It would be considered as no compliment to the dead or the living. This I will say— they were all modest and virtuous Girls and always maintained this Character through Life. No Virgin or Matron ever had cause to blush at the sight of me, or to regret her Acquaintance with me. No Father, Brother, Son or Friend ever had cause of Grief or Resentment for any Intercourse between me and any Daughter, Sister, Mother, or any other Relation of the female Sex. My Children may be assured that no illegitimate Brother or Sister exists or ever existed. These Reflections, to me consolatory beyond all expression, I am able to make with truth and sincerity and I presume I am indebted for this blessing to my Education. My Parents held every Species of Libertinage in such Contempt and horror, and held up constantly to view such pictures of disgrace, of baseness and of Ruin, that my natural temperament was always overawed by my Principles and Sense of decorum. This Blessing has been rendered the more precious to me, as I have seen enough of the Effects of a different practice. Corroding Reflections through Life are the never failing consequence of illicit amours, in old as well as in new Countries. The Happiness of Life depends more upon Innocence in this respect, than upon all the Philosophy of Epicurus, or of Zeno without it. I could write Romances, or Histories as wonderful as Romances of what I have known or heard in France, Holland and England, and all would serve to confirm what I learned in my Youth in America, that Happiness is lost forever if Innocence is lost, at least until a Repentance is undergone so severe as to be an overbalance to all the gratifications of Licentiousness. Repentance itself cannot restore the Happiness of Innocence, at least in this Life. . . .

I soon perceived a growing Curiosity, a Love of Books and a fondness for Study, which dissipated all my Inclination for Sports, and even for the Society of the Ladies. I read forever, but without much method, and with very little Choice. I got my Lessons regularly and performed my recitations without Censure. Mathematics and Natural Philosophy attracted the most of my Attention, which I have since regretted, because I was destined to a Course of Life, in which these Sciences have been of little Use, and the Classics would have been of great Importance. I owe to this however perhaps some degree of Patience of Investigation, which I might not otherwise have obtained.

John Adams to Robert Treat Paine BRAINTREE, DECEMBER 6, 1759

I cannot think it either Vanity or Virtue to acknowledge, that the Acquisition and Communication of Knowledge, are the sole Entertainment of my Life.

John Adams, Diary FEBRUARY 1, 1763

I employed however, too little of my Time in Reading and in Thinking. I might have spent much more.

John Adams to Cotton Tufts APRIL 9, 1764

I cannot set still without Thinking.

John Adams to Abigail Smith, His Fiancée SEPTEMBER 30, 1764

Candor is my Characteristic.

John Adams, Diary DECEMBER 31, 1772

This Evening at Mr. Cranch's, I found that my constitutional or habitual Infirmities have not entirely forsaken me. Mr. Collins an English Gentleman was there, and in Conversation about the high Commissioned Court, for inquiring after the Burners of the Gaspee at Providence, I found the old Warmth, Heat, Violence, Acrimony, Bitterness, Sharpness of my Temper, and Expression, was not departed. I said there was no more Justice left in Britain than there was in Hell—That I wished for War, and that the whole Bourbon Family was upon the Back of Great Britain—avowed a thorough Dissatisfaction to that Country—wished that any Thing might happen to them, and that as the Clergy prayed of our Enemies in Time of War, that they might be brought to reason or to ruin.

I cannot but reflect upon myself with Severity for these rash, inexperienced, boyish, raw, and awkward Expressions. A Man who has no better Government of his Tongue, no more command of his Temper, is unfit for every Thing, but Children's Play, and the Company of Boys.

A Character can never be supported, if it can be raised, without a good a great Share of Self Government. Such Flights of Passion, such Starts of Imagination, though they may strike a few of the fiery and inconsiderate, yet they lower, they sink a Man, with the Wise. They expose him to danger, as well as familiarity, Contempt, and Ridicule.

John Adams to Abigail Adams PHILADELPHIA, SEPTEMBER 29, 1774

I shall be killed with Kindness in this Place. We go to congress at Nine, and there We stay, most earnestly in Debates upon the most abstruse Mysteries of State until three in the Afternoon, then We adjourn, and go to Dinner with some of the Nobles of Pennsylvania, at four O'Clock and feast upon ten thousand Delicacies, and sit drinking Madeira, Claret and Burgundy. Company, and Care. Yet I hold it out, surprisingly, I drink no Cider, but feast upon Philadelphia Beer, and Porter. A Gentleman, one Mr. Hare, has lately set up in this City a Manufactory of Porter, as good as any that comes from London. I pray We may introduce it into

Massachusetts. It agrees with me, infinitely better than Punch, Wine or Cider, or any other Spirituous Liquor.

OCTOBER 7, 1775

The Situation of Things, is so alarming, that it is our Duty to prepare our Minds and Hearts for every Event, even the Worst. From my earliest Entrance into Life, I have been engaged in the public Cause of America: and from first to last I have had upon my Mind, a strong Impression, that Things would be wrought up to their present Crisis. I saw from the Beginning that the Controversy was of such a Nature that it never would be settled, and every day convinces me more and more. This has been the source of all the Disquietude of my Life. It has lain down and rose up with me these twelve Years. The Thought that we might be driven to the sad Necessity of breaking our Connection with Great Britain exclusive of the Carnage and Destruction which it was easy to see must attend the separation, always gave me a great deal of Grief. And even now, I would cheerfully retire from public life forever, renounce all Chance for Profits or Honors from the public, nay I would cheerfully contribute my little Property to obtain Peace and Liberty. But all these must go and my Life too before I can surrender the Right of my Country to a free Constitution. I dare not consent to it. I should be the most miserable of Mortals ever after, whatever Honors or Emoluments might surround me.

John Adams to Charles Lee PHILADELPHIA, OCTOBER 13, 1775

A Fondness for Dogs, by no means depreciates any Character in my Estimation, because many of the greatest Men have been remarkable for it; and because I think it Evidence of an honest Mind and an Heart capable of Friendship, Fidelity and Strong Attachments being Characteristics of that Animal.

John Adams to Mercy Otis Warren PHILADELPHIA, NOVEMBER 25, 1775

I have no Pleasure or amusements which has any Charms for me. Balls, Assemblies, Concerts, Cards, Horses, Dogs, never engaged any Part of my attention or Concern. Nor am I ever happy in large and promiscuous Companies. Business alone, with the intimate unreserved Conversation of a very few Friends, Books, and familiar Correspondences, have ever engaged all my Time, and I have no Pleasure, no Ease in any other Way. In this Place I have no opportunity to meddle with Books, only in the Way of Business. The Conversation I have here is all in the ceremonious reserved impenetrable Way. Thus I have sketched, a Character for myself of a morose Philosopher and a Surly Politician, neither of which are very amiable or respectable, but yet there is too much truth in it, and from it you will easily believe that I have very little Pleasure here, excepting in the Correspondence of my Friends, and among these I assure you Madam there is none, whose Letters I read with more Pleasure and Instruction than yours. I wish it was in my Power to write to you oftener than I do, but I am really engaged in constant Business of seven to ten in the Morning in Committee, from ten to four in Congress and from Six to Ten again in Committee. Our Assembly is scarcely numerous enough for the Business. Every Body is engaged all Day in Congress and all the Morning and evening in Committees. I mention this Madam as an Apology for not writing you so often as I ought and as a Reason for my Request that you would not wait for my Answers. . . .

The Inactivity of the two Armies, is not very agreeable to me. Fabius's Cunctando was wise and brave. But if I had submitted to it in his situation, it would have been a cruel Mortification to me. Zeal and Fire and Activity and Enterprise Strike my Imagination too much. I am obliged to be constantly on my Guard— yet the Heat within will burst forth at Times.

John Adams to Mercy Otis Warren BRAINTREE, JANUARY 8, 1776

Defeat appears to me preferable to total Inaction.

John Adams to Mercy Otis Warren APRIL 16, 1776

We must move slowly. Patience, Patience, Patience! I am obliged to invoke thee every Morning of my Life, every Noon, and every Evening.

John Adams to Abigail Adams PHILADELPHIA, APRIL 28, 1776

The Conclusion of your Letter makes my Heart throb, more than a Cannonade would. You bid me burn your Letters. But I must forget you first.

John Adams to James Warren   PHILADELPHIA, JULY 27, 1776

My case is worse [than Robert Treat Paine's and Samuel Adams's]. My face is grown pale, my Eyes weak and inflamed, my Nerves tremulous, and my Mind weak as Water. Feverous Heats by Day and Sweats by Night are returned upon me, which is an infallible Symptom with me that it is Time to throw off all Care, for a Time, and take a little Rest. I have several Times with the Blessing of God, saved my Life in this Way, and am now determined to attempt it once more.

John Adams to Abigail Adams   PHILADELPHIA, AUGUST 18, 1776

There are very few People in this World with whom I can bear to converse. I can treat all with Decency and Civility, and converse with them, when it is necessary, on Points of Business. But I am never happy in their Company. This has made me a Recluse, and will one day, make me an Hermit.

Benjamin Rush to Jacques Barbeu-Dubourg   PHILADELPHIA, SEPTEMBER 16, 1776

Lord Howe sent a message to us a few days ago requesting a conference with some members of the Congress. Dr. Franklin, Mr. John Adams, and Mr. [Edward] Rutledge were ordered to wait upon his Lordship. He talked much of his powers to accommodate the dispute between Britain & America, but said he could offer nothing & promise nothing till we returned to our Allegiance. Here the negotiation ended. All America disdains such propositions. I must here mention an anecdote in honor of Mr. Adams. When his Lordship asked in what capacity he was to receive the gentlemen of Congress, Mr. Adams told him "in any capacity his Lordship pleased except in that of BRITISH SUBJECTS." This illustrious patriot has not his superior, scarcely his equal, for Abilities & virtue on the whole continent of America.

Samuel Adams to James Warren   PHILADELPHIA, DECEMBER 12, 1776

Where are your new Members [of Congress]? I greatly applaud your Choice of them. Mr. A. I hope is on the Road [back to Congress]. We never wanted him more.

John Adams to Abigail Adams PHILADELPHIA, SEPTEMBER 2, 1777

I am sick of Fabian Systems in all Quarters. The Officers drink a long and moderate War. My Toast is a short and violent War. They would call me mad and rash &c. but I know better. I am as cool as any of them and cooler too, for my Mind is not inflamed with Fear nor Anger, whereas I believe their's are with both.

John Adams to Benjamin Rush BRAINTREE, FEBRUARY 8, 1778

Patience! Patience! Patience. The first the last and the middle Virtue of a Politician.

John Adams, Autobiography APRIL 9, 1778

Returned and supped with Franklin on Cheese and Beer.

John Adams to Abigail Adams PASSY, FRANCE, APRIL 25, 1778

To tell you the Truth, I admire the Ladies here. Don't be jealous. They are handsome, and very well educated. Their Accomplishments are exceedingly brilliant. And their Knowledge of Letters and Arts, exceeds that of the English Ladies much, I believe.

John Adams to William McCreery PASSY, SEPTEMBER 25, 1778

I have never been used to disguise my sentiments of Men, whom I have been against, in public Life . . . and never was a man of importance enough, to make me deviate from a Rule that I have observed all my Life, vizt. when obliged to be a Man's Enemy to be openly and generously so.

John Adams to James Warren PASSY, DECEMBER 2, 1778

I sincerely grieve for my Country in the News that you are not of either House [of the Massachusetts legislature]. But it is some Comfort to me to think that I shall be soon a private Farmer, as well as you, and both pursuing our Experiments in Husbandry. The longer I live and the more I see of public Men, the more I wish to be a private one. Modesty is a Virtue, that can never thrive, in public. Modest Merit! Is there such a Thing remaining in public Life? It is now become a Maxim with some, who are even Men of Merit, that the World sees a Man in Proportion as he esteems himself, and are generally disposed to allow him, to be what he pretends to be. Accordingly, I am often astonished at the Boldness with which Persons make their Pretensions. A Man must be his own Trumpeter, he must write or dictate Paragraphs of Praise in the News Papers, he must dress, have a Retinue, and Equipage, he must ostentatiously publish to the World his own Writings with his Name, and must write even some Panegyrics upon them, he must get his Picture drawn, his Statue made, and must hire all the Artists in his Turn, to set about Works to spread his Name, make the Mob stare and gape, and perpetuate his Fame. I would undertake, if I could bring my Feelings to bear it, to become one of the most trumpeted, admired, courted, worshipped Idols in the whole World in four or five Years. I have learned the whole Art, I am a perfect Master of it. I learned a great deal of it from [Thomas] Hutchinson and the Tories, and have learned more of it since from Whigs and Tories both, in America and Europe. If you will learn the Art I will teach you.

I have not yet begun to practice this. There is one Practice more which I forget. He must get his Brothers, Cousins, Sons and other Relations into Place about him and must teach them to practice all the same Arts both for themselves and him. He must never do anything for anybody who is not his Friend, or in other Words his tool.

What I am going to say, will be thought by many to be practicing upon some of the above Rules. You and I have had an ugly Modesty about Us, which has destroyed Us of almost all our Importance. We have taken even Pains to conceal our Names, We have delighted in the shade, We have made few Friends, no Tools, and what is worse when the Cause of Truth, Justice, and Liberty have demanded it, We have even Sacrificed Those who called themselves our Friends and have made Enemies.

No Man ever made a great Fortune in the World, by pursuing these Maxims. We therefore do not expect it, and for my own Part, I declare, that the Moment, I can get into Life perfectly private, will be the happiest of my Life.

John Adams to Mercy Otis Warren PASSY, DECEMBER 18, 1778

What shall I say, Madam, to your Question whether I am as much in the good graces of the Ladies as my venerable Colleague [Benjamin Franklin]. Ah No! Alas, Alas No.

The Ladies of this Country [France] Madam have an unaccountable passion for old Age, whereas our Country women you know Madam have rather a Complaisance for youth if I remember right. This is rather unlucky for me for I have nothing to do but wish that I was seventy years old and when I get back I shall be obliged to wish myself back again to 25.

I will take the Liberty to mention an anecdote or two amongst a multitude to show you how unfortunate I am in being so young. A Gentleman introduced me the other day to a Lady. Voila. Madame, says he, Monsieur Adams, notre Ami, Le Colleague de Monsieur Franklin! Je suis enchante de voir Monsieur Adams. Answer'd the Lady. Embrassez le, donc. Reply'd (the Gentleman). Ah No, Monsieur, says the Lady, il est trop jeune.*

So that you see, I must wait patiently, full 30 years longer before I can be so great a favorite.

"I am enchanted to meet you, Mr. Adams," answered the lady.
"Embrace him, then," replied the gentleman.
"Ah, no," says the lady. "He is too young."

John Adams to Abigail Adams PASSY, FEBRUARY 13, 1779

I never had so much trouble in my Life, as here, yet I grow fat. The Climate and soil agree with me—so do the Cookery and even the Manners of the People, of those of them at least that I converse with, Churlish Republican, as some of you, on your side the Water call me. The English have got at me in their News Papers. They make fine Work of me—fanatic—Bigot—perfect Cypher—not one Word of the Language—awkward Figure—uncouth dress—no Address—No Character—cunning hard headed Attorney. But the falsest of it all is, that I am disgusted with the Parisians—Whereas I declare I admire the Parisians prodigiously. They are the happiest People in the World, I believe, and have the best Disposition to make others so.

John Adams, Diary APRIL 26, 1779

There is a Feebleness and a Languor in my Nature. My Mind and Body both partake of this Weakness. By my Physical Constitution, I am but an ordinary Man. The Times alone have destined me to Fame—and even these have not been able to give me,

---

* "Here, Madame," says he, "is Mr. Adams, our friend, the colleague of Mr. Franklin."

much. When I look in the Glass, my Eye, my Forehead, my Brow, my Cheeks, my Lips, all betray this Relaxation. Yet some great Events, some cutting Expressions, some mean Hypocrisies, have at Times, thrown this Assemblage of Sloth, Sleep, and littleness into Rage a little like a Lion. Yet it is not like the Lion—there is Extravagance and Distraction in it, that still betrays the same Weakness.

Benjamin Rush to John Adams PHILADELPHIA, APRIL 28, 1780

I almost envy your Children the happiness of calling that man their father who After contributing his Share towards giving liberty and independence, will finally be honored as the instrument of restoring *peace* to the united States of America.

John Adams to Abigail Adams PARIS, POST MAY 12, 1780

The Science of Government it is my Duty to study, more than all other Sciences: the Art of Legislation and Administration and Negotiation, ought to take Place, indeed to exclude in a manner all other Arts.—I must study Politicks and War that my sons may have liberty to study Mathematics and Philosophy. My sons ought to study Mathematics and Philosophy, Geography, natural History, Naval Architecture, navigation, Commerce and Agriculture, in order to give their children a right to study Painting, Poetry, Music, Architecture, Statuary, Tapestry, and Porcelain.

Benjamin Franklin to the Comte de Vergennes PASSY, AUGUST 3, 1780

I live upon Terms of Civility with him, not of Intimacy.

Comte de Vergennes to the Chevalier de La Luzerne VERSAILLES, AUGUST 7, 1780

I have communicated the whole* to Mr. Franklin, requesting him to report on it to Congress, and I have reason to think that that Minister will make it his duty to comply with my request. I inform you of these details, Sir, so that you may speak of it confidentially to the President and the principal members of Congress and put them in a position to judge whether Mr. Adams is endowed with

---

*Vergennes was referring to the antagonistic attitude of Adams toward France.

a character that renders him appropriate to the important task with which Congress has charged him. As for myself, I anticipate that this plenipotentiary will only incite difficulties and vexations, because he has an inflexibility, a pedantry, an arrogance, and a conceit that renders him incapable of dealing with political subjects, and especially of handling them with the representatives of great powers, who assuredly will not yield either to the tone or to the logic of Mr. Adams.

Benjamin Franklin to Henry Laurens PASSY, AUGUST 9, 1780

Mr. Adams has given Offense to the Court here, by some Sentiments and Expressions contained in several of his Letters written to the Count de Vergennes. I mention this with Reluctance, though perhaps it would have been my Duty to acquaint you with such a Circumstance, even were it not required of me by the Minister himself. He has sent me Copies of the Correspondence, desiring I would communicate them to Congress; and I send them herewith. Mr. Adams did not show me his Letters before he sent them. I have, in a former Letter to Mr. Lovell, mentioned some of the Inconveniencies, that attend the having more than one Minister at the same Court; one of which Inconveniencies is, that they do not always hold the same Language, and that the Impressions made by one, and intended for the Service of his Constituents, may be effaced by the Discourse of the other. It is true, that Mr. Adams's proper Business is elsewhere; but, the Time not being come for that Business, and having nothing else here wherewith to employ himself, he seems to have endeavored to supply what he may suppose my Negotiations defective in. He thinks, as he tells me himself, that America has been too free in Expressions of Gratitude to France; for that she is more obliged to us than we to her; and that we should show Spirit in our Applications. I apprehend, that he mistakes his Ground, and that this Court is to be treated with Decency and Delicacy. The King, a young and virtuous Prince, has, I am persuaded, a Pleasure in reflecting on the generous Benevolence of the Action in assisting an oppressed People, and proposes it as a Part of the Glory of his Reign. I think it right to increase this Pleasure by our thankful Acknowledgments, and that such an Expression of Gratitude is not only our Duty, but our Interest. A different Conduct seems to me what is not only improper and unbecoming, but what may be hurtful to us. Mr. Adams, on the other hand, who, at the same time means our Welfare and Interest as much as I, or any man, can do, seems to think a little apparent Stoutness, and greater air of Independence and Boldness in our Demands, will procure us more ample Assistance. It is for Congress to judge and regulate their Affairs accordingly.

M. Vergennes, who appears much offended, told me, yesterday, that he would enter into no further Discussions with Mr. Adams, nor answer any more of his Letters. He is gone to Holland to try, as he told me, whether something might not be done to render us less dependent on France. He says, the Ideas of this Court and those of the People in America are so totally different, that it is impossible for any Minister to please both. He ought to know America better than I do, having been there lately, and he may choose to do what he thinks will best please the People of America. But, when I consider the Expressions of Congress in many of their public Acts, and particularly in their Letter to the Chev. de la Luzerne, of the 24th of May last, I cannot but imagine, that he mistakes the Sentiments of a few for a general Opinion. It is my Intention, while I stay here, to procure what Advantages I can for our Country, by endeavoring to please this Court; and I wish I could prevent any thing being said by any of our Countrymen here, that may have a contrary Effect, and increase an Opinion lately showing itself in Paris, that we seek a Difference, and with a view of reconciling ourselves to England. Some of them have of late been very indiscreet in their Conversations.

Abigail Adams to John Adams   OCTOBER 8, 1780

I hope you enjoy Health. Dr. Lee says you grow very fat.

John Adams to John Quincy Adams   AMSTERDAM, DECEMBER 28, 1780

Every Thing in Life should be done with Reflection, and Judgment, even the most insignificant Amusements. They should all be arranged in subordination, to the great Plan of Happiness, and Utility.

John Adams to Cotton Tufts   THE HAGUE, AUGUST 1782

I long to be with you, even to share in your Afflictions. The Life I lead is not satisfactory to me. Great Feasts and great Company, the Splendor of Courts and all that is not enough for me. I want my Family, my Friends and my Country. My only Conclusion is, that I have rendered a most important and essential service to my Country, here, which I verily believe no other Man in the World would have done. I don't mean by this, that I have exerted any Abilities here, or any Actions, that are not very common, but I don't believe that any other Man in the World would have had the Patience and Perseverance, to do and to suffer, what was absolutely necessary.—I will never go through such another Scene. Happily, there will never I believe be again Occasion for any body to suffer so much. The Humiliations, the Mortifications, the Provocations, that I have endured here, are beyond all description; yet the Unraveling of the Plot, and the total Change in all these respects make amends for all.

John Thaxter to Abigail Adams THE HAGUE, OCTOBER 9, 1782

Thank God for all things, and especially for that Degree of *Faith, Patience,* and *Perseverance* with which he inspired him, who had the Conduct of this Business. There is no negotiating here without these *Virtues.* Your dearest Friend has gained himself great Honor, and both his Ability and Firmness have been highly complimented and applauded.

John Adams to Abigail Adams THE HAGUE, OCTOBER 16, 1782

Mine has been a hard lot in life, so hard that nothing would have rendered it supportable, especially for the last eight years, but the uninterrupted series of good fortune which has attended my feeble exertions for the public. If I have been unfortunate and unhappy in private life, I thank God I have been uniformly happy and successful as a public man.

John Adams, Journal of Peace Negotiations NOVEMBER 12, 1782

The compliment of "Monsieur, vous êtes le Washington de la négotiation,"* was repeated to me by more than one person. I answered, *Monsieur, vous me faites le plus grand honneur, et le compliment le plus sublime possible.† Eh! Monsieur, en vérité,*

---

*Sir, you are the Washington of negotiation.

†Sir, you pay me the greatest honor and the most sublime compliment possible.

*vous l'avez bien mérité.** (A few of these compliments would kill Franklin if they should come to his ears.)

John Adams to Mercy Otis Warren   PARIS, JANUARY 29, 1783

The Times, Madam have made a Strange Being of me. I shall appear a Domestic Animal, never at home, a bashful Creature, braving the Fronts of the greatest ones of the Earth, a timid Man, venturing on a long Series of the greatest dangers, an irritable fiery Mortal, enduring every Provocation and Disgust, a delicate Valetudinarian bearing the greatest Hardships, an humble Farmer, despising Pomp, Show, Power and Wealth, as profuse as a Prodigal and as proud as Caesar—But an honest Man in all and to the Death.

Alas! who would wish for such a Character! Who would wish to live in Times and Circumstances when to be an honest Man, one must be all the rest? Not I. It can never be the Duty of one Man to be concerned in more than one Revolution, and therefore I will never have anything to do with another.

James Madison to Thomas Jefferson   PHILADELPHIA, FEBRUARY 11, 1783

Congress yesterday received from Mr. Adams several letters dated September not remarkable for any thing unless it be a display of his vanity, his prejudice against the French Court & his venom against Doctor Franklin.

Thomas Jefferson to James Madison   BALTIMORE, FEBRUARY 14, 1783

From what you mention in your letter I suppose the newspapers must be wrong when they say that Mr. Adams had taken up his abode with Dr. Franklin. I am nearly at a loss to judge how he will act in the negotiation [of the peace treaty with Great Britain]. He hates Franklin, he hates Jay, he hates the French, he hates the English. To whom will he adhere? His vanity is a lineament in his character which had entirely escaped me. His want of taste I had observed. Notwithstanding all this he has a sound head on substantial points, and I think he has integrity. I am glad therefore that he is of the commission and expect he will be useful in

---

*Ah! Sir, the truth is you have very much merited it.

it. His dislike of all parties, and all men, by balancing his prejudices, may give the same fair play to his reason as would a general benevolence of temper. At any rate honesty may be extracted
even from poisonous weeds.

John Adams to Abigail Adams PARIS, FEBRUARY 27, 1783

But upon the Rule of Virtue, I hold that Virtue requires We
should serve, where We can do most good. I am soberly of Opinion, that for one or two Years to come I could do more good in
England to the United States of America, than in any other Spot
upon Earth. Much of the immediate Prosperity of the United
States, and much of their future Repose, if not the Peace of the
World, depends upon having just Notions now forthwith instilled
in London. But I think the British Court will be duped by the
French and will entertain that dread of me, which neither ought
to entertain, but which France will inspire because She thinks I
should be impartial—so that I expect some Booby will be sent,
in Complaisance to two silly Courts, upon that most important
of all Services. If Heaven has so decreed, I must submit, and the
Submission will be most pleasant to me as an Individual and as a
Man. I shall be in a Situation where I shall think that I could do
more good in another. But I have been often in such a Situation.
And things must take their Course. We must wait for things to
arrange themselves, when We cannot govern them.

My Mind and Body stand in need of Repose. My Faculties
have been too long upon the Stretch. A Relaxation of a few Years
would be the Life the most charming to me, that I can conceive.

Don't be concerned at anything I have written concerning
Spots, Blemishes, Stains and Disgraces. When all is known, they
will be universally acknowledged to be Laurels, Ornaments and
trophies. They will do neither You nor me nor Ours harm to the
End.

MARCH 28, 1783

I am Sometimes half afraid, that those Persons who procured the
Revocation of my Commission to King George, may be afraid I
shall do them more harm in America, than in England, and therefore of two Evils to choose the least and maneuver to get me sent
to London. By several Coaxing hints of that Kind, which have
been written to me and given me in Conversation, from Persons

who I know are employed to do it, I fancy that Something of that
is in Contemplation. There is another Motive too—they begin
to dread the Appointment of some others whom they like less
than me. I tremble when I think of such a Thing as going to London. If I were to receive orders of that sort, it would be a dull day
to me. No Swiss ever longed for home more than I do. I Shall
forever be a dull Man in Europe. I cannot bear the Thought of
transporting my Family to Europe. It would be the Ruin of my
Children forever. And I cannot bear the Thought of living longer
Separate from them.

APRIL 7, 1783
Supposing a Commission should come to me, I am frightened at
the Thought of it. How will the King and the Courtiers, the City
and the Country, look at me? What Prospect can I have of a tolerable Life there? I shall be Slandered and plagued there, more
than in France. It is a Sad Thing that Simple Integrity should
have so many Enemies in this World, without deserving one. In
the Case Supposed I must go to London and reconnoitre—see
how the Land lies and the faces look, before you think of coming
to me. I will not stay there, to be plagued. One may soon judge.
If I should find a decent Reception and a Prospect of living comfortably a Year or two there I will write for you. All this is you see
upon a supposition which is improbable. It would be infinitely
more agreeable to my own heart to come home and quit Europe
forever. At home I can take Care of my Children, to give them
Education and put them into Business. If I should remain abroad
my Children must suffer for it and be neglected. But in all Events
I will not stay in Holland, the Air of which is totally inconsistent
with my Health. I have tried it, very sufficiently. I can never be
well nor enjoy myself there. In other respects I like that Country
very well.

APRIL 16, 1783
I begin to suspect that French and Franklinian Politics will now
endeavor to get me sent to England, for two Reasons, one that I
may not go to America where I should do them more Mischief
as they think than I could in London. 2. That the Mortifications
which they and their Tools might give me there might disembar-
rass them of me sooner than any where.

    Is it not Strange and Sad that Simple Integrity should have

so many Enemies? that a Man should have to undergo so many Evils merely because he will not betray his Trust? . . .

I have found by Experience, that in this Age of the World that Man has an awful Lot, who "dares to love his Country, and be poor."

Liberty and Virtue! When! Oh When will your Enemies cease to exist or to persecute! . . .

I have Sometimes painted to myself my own Course for these 20 Years, by a Man running a race upon a right line barefooted treading among burning Ploughshares, with the horrid Figures of Jealousy, Envy, Hatred, Revenge, Vanity, Ambition, Avarice, Treachery, Tyranny, Insolence, arranged on each side of his Path and lashing him with scorpions all the Way, and attempting at every Step to trip up his Heels.

I have got through, however to the Goal, but maimed, scarified and out of Breath.

John Adams to James Warren PARIS, APRIL 16, 1783

Our Country is a singular one. It is a Temple of Liberty, set open to all the World. If there is any thing on Earth worthy of being contended for, it is this glorious Object. I never had through my whole Life any other Ambition, than to cherish, promote & protect it, and never will have any other for myself, nor my Children. For this Object, however, I have as much as any Conqueror ever had. For this I have run as great risques & made as great Sacrifices, as any of the pretended Heroes, whose Object was Domination & Power, Wealth & Pleasure. For this I have opened to You Characters with Freedom, which it is to me personally dangerous to touch. But it is necessary, &c, come what will, I will not flinch. These people know me. They know I stand in their Way, & therefore You will hear of Insinuations enough, darkly circulated to lessen me at Home. I care not. Let me come home & tell my own Story.

James Madison to Thomas Jefferson PHILADELPHIA, MAY 6, 1783

Congress have received a long and curious epistle from Mr. Adams dated in February addressed to the president not to the secretary for foreign affairs. He animadverts on the revocation of his commission for a treaty of commerce with Great Britain, presses the appointment of a minister to that court with such a commission, draws a picture of a fit character in which his own likeness is ridiculously and palpably studied, finally praising and recommending Mr. Jay for the appointment *provided* injustice must be done to an older servant.

Benjamin Franklin to Robert R. Livingston PASSY, JULY 22, 1783

I ought not, however, to conceal from you, that one of my Colleagues is of a very different Opinion from me in these Matters. He thinks the French Minister one of the greatest Enemies of our Country, that he would have straitened our Boundaries, to prevent the Growth of our People; contracted our Fishery, to obstruct the Increase of our Seamen; and retained the Royalists among us, to keep us divided; that he privately opposes all our Negotiations with foreign Courts, and afforded us, during the War, the Assistance we received only to keep it alive, that we might be so much the more weakened by it; that to think of Gratitude to France is the greatest of Follies, and that to be influenced by it would ruin us. He makes no Secret of his having these Opinions, expresses them publicly, sometimes in presence of the English Ministers, and speaks of hundreds of Instances when he could produce in Proof of them. None of which however, have yet appeared to me, unless the Conversations and Letter abovementioned are reckoned such.

If I were not convinced of the real Inability of this Court to furnish the further Supplies we asked, I should suspect these Discourses of a Person in his Station might have influenced the Refusal; but I think they have gone no farther than to occasion a Suspicion, that we have a considerable Party of Antigallicans in America, who are not Tories, and consequently to produce some doubts of the Continuance of our Friendship. As such Doubts may hereafter have a bad Effect, I think we cannot take too much care to remove them; and it is, therefore, I write this, to put you on your guard, (believing it my duty, though I know that I hazard by it a mortal Enmity), and to caution you respecting the Insinuations of this Gentleman against this Court, and the Instances he supposes of their ill will to us, which I take to be as imaginary as I know his Fancies to be, that Count de V. and myself are continually plotting against him, and employing the News-Writers of Europe to depreciate his Character, &c. But as Shakespeare says, "Triffles light as Air,"* &c. I am persuaded, however, that he means well for his Country, is always an honest Man, often a wise one, but sometimes, and in some things, absolutely out of his senses.

Elbridge Gerry to Abigail Adams PRINCETON, N.J., SEPTEMBER 18, 1783

Enclosed is an Extract of an official Letter from Doctor F—— to Mr. Livingston, Secretary of foreign affairs dated July 23d. which is calculated to give a private Stab to the Reputation of our Friend; at least it appears so to me.† By the Doctor's Observation that by writing the Letter "he hazarded a mortal Enmity," I think it evident, he did not intend the Letter should be seen by Mr. Adams's particular Friends, but that Mr. Livingston should make a prudent Use of it to multiply Mr. Adams' Enemies. Mr. L. could easily do this, by not communicating to Congress the paragraph: but being now out of Office, the Doctor's Craft is apparent. You will please to keep the Matter a profound Secret, excepting to Mr. Adams, General Warren and Lady; and let the Channel of Communication be likewise a secret.

Benjamin Franklin to Robert Morris PASSY, DECEMBER 25, 1783

My Apprehension, that the Union between France and our States might be diminished by Accounts from hence, was occasioned by the extravagant and violent Language held here by a Public Person, in public Company, which had that Tendency; and it was natural for me to think his Letters might hold the same Language, in which I was right; for I have since had Letters from Boston informing me of it. Luckily here, and I hope there, it is imputed to the true Cause, a Disorder in the Brain, which, though not constant, has its Fits too frequent.

Luigi Castiglioni, Sketches of American Statesmen, 1787

Mr. Adams is 40 to 50 years old, short and corpulent; and his

---

*William Shakespeare, *Othello* 3.3.325.

†For the enclosure sent by Gerry, see Benjamin Franklin to Robert R. Livingston, July 22, 1783, above.

kindly but simple face gives no indication of the range of his
knowledge.

John Adams to James Warren GROSVENOR SQUARE, LONDON, JANUARY 9, 1787

Popularity was never my Mistress, nor was I ever, nor shall I ever
be a popular Man. This Book* will make me unpopular.—But
one Thing I know, a Man must be sensible of the Errors of the
People, & upon his guard against them, & must run the risk of
their displeasure sometimes, or he will never do them any good
in the long run.

Thomas Jefferson to James Madison PARIS, JANUARY 30, 1787

You know the opinion I formerly entertained of my friend Mr.
Adams. Yourself & the governor were the first who shook that
opinion. I afterwards saw proofs which convicted him of a degree of vanity, and of a *blindness* to it, of which no germ had appeared in Congress. A 7 months intimacy with him here and as
many weeks in London have given me opportunities of studying
him closely. He is vain, irritable and a bad calculator of the force
and probable effect of the motives which govern men. This is all
the ill which can possibly be said of him. He is as disinterested
as the being which made him: he is profound in his views: and
accurate in his judgment except where knowledge of the world is
necessary to form a judgment. He is so amiable, that I pronounce
you will love him if ever you become acquainted with him. He
would be, as he was, a great man in Congress.

John Adams to John Jay GROSVENOR SQUARE, LONDON, SEPTEMBER 22, 1787

I shall appear before posterity in a very negligent dress and disor-
dered air. In truth I write too much to write well, and have never
time to correct anything.

Thomas Jefferson to James Madison PARIS, MAY 25, 1788

Of rigorous honesty, and careless of appearances he lived for a
considerable time as an economical private individual. . . . his

*Adams's *Defences of the Constitutions of the United States* (3 vols., London,
1787–88).

pecuniary affairs were under the direction of Mrs. Adams, one of the most estimable characters on earth, and the most attentive and honorable economists. Neither had a wish to lay up a copper, but both wished to make both ends meet. I suspect however, from an expression dropped in conversation, that they were not able to do this, and that a deficit in their accounts appeared in their winding up.

John Adams to Abigail Adams Smith   BRAINTREE, JULY 16, 1788

You may be anxious, too, to know what is to become of me. At my age, this ought not to be a question; but it is. I will tell you, my dear child, in strict confidence, that it appears to me that your father does not stand very high in the esteem, admiration, or respect of his country, or any part of it. In the course of a long absence his character has been lost, and he has got quite out of circulation. The public judgment, the public heart, and the public voice, seem to have decreed to others every public office that he can accept of with consistency, or honor, or reputation; and no other alternative is left for him, but private life at home, or to go again abroad. The latter is the worst of the two; but you may depend upon it, you will hear of him on a trading voyage to the East Indies, or to Surrinam, or Essequibo, before you will hear of his descending as a public man beneath himself.

Benjamin Lincoln to George Washington   HINGHAM, MASS., SEPTEMBER 24, 1788

I am happy in knowing Mr. J. Adams. My acquaintance commenced with him early in life, few men can boast of equal abilities and information and of so many virtues, his foibles are few,—I am happy in knowing his sentiments of your Excellency, there is not virtue in your character which the most intimate of your friends have discovered but it seems to be known and acknowledged by him—I am, from a free conversation with him, as well as from his general character perfectly convinced that there is not a man in this part of the confederacy, if one can be found through the whole of it who would render your Excellency's situation at the head of the government more agreeable or who would make it more his study that your Administration should be honorable to yourself, and permanently interesting to the people.—

Alexander Hamilton to Theodore Sedgwick NEW YORK, OCTOBER 9, 1788

On the subject of Vice President, my ideas have concurred with yours, and I believe Mr. Adams will have the votes of this state. He will certainly, I think, be preferred to the other Gentleman [John Hancock]. Yet, *certainly,* is perhaps too strong a word. I can conceive that the other, who is supposed to be a more pliable man may command Antifoederal influence.

The only hesitation in my mind with regard to Mr. Adams has arisen within a day or two; from a suggestion by a particular Gentleman that he is unfriendly in his sentiments to General Washington. Richard H. Lee who will probably, as rumor now runs, come from Virginia [to the U.S. Senate] is also in this state [of opposing Washington]. The Lees and Adams' have been in the habit of uniting; and hence may spring up a Cabal very embarrassing to the Executive and of course to the administration of the Government. Consider this. Sound the reality of it and let me hear from you.

James Madison to Thomas Jefferson NEW YORK, OCTOBER 17, 1788

J. Adams has made himself obnoxious to many particularly in the Southern states by the political principles avowed in his book. Others recollecting his cabal during the war against General Washington knowing his extravagant self importance and considering his preference of an unprofitable dignity to some place of emolument better adapted to private fortune as a proof of his having an eye to the presidency conclude that he would not be a very cordial second to the general and that an impatient ambition might even intrigue for a premature advancement.

Alexander Hamilton to James Madison NEW YORK, NOVEMBER 23, 1788

On the whole I have concluded to support Adams [for vice president]; though I am not without apprehensions on the score we have conversed about. My principal reasons are these—First He is a declared partisan of referring to future experience the expediency of amendments in the system (and though I do not *altogether* adopt this sentiment) it is much nearer my own than certain other doctrines. Secondly a character of importance in the Eastern states, if he is not Vice President, one of two worse things will be likely to happen—Either he must be nominated to some important office for which he is less proper, or will become a malcontent and possibly espouse and give additional weight to the opposition to the Government.

Comte de Moustier to the Comte de Montmorin NEW YORK, APRIL 7, 1789

Mr. Adams, having failed in the negotiation of a treaty of commerce with England, which was the cherished object of his desires and no longer being able to remain decorously in a country where, in spite of the praise lavished on England in his writings, he suffered only unpleasantness, arrives just a little before the task of forming a new government is at hand. This man, lauded in advance, before his success has been determined, captures the attention of his compatriots who on his word believe him as great in politics as General Washington is in war and who, thinking that a profound politician is needed more today than an able general, see him as the leading figure in the United States and accordingly, in the world. Thus it is that small talents mustered and employed with perseverance often elevate an ordinary man, who possesses the art of self-promotion and sometimes the imprudence to make use of it for himself above men who are superior to him in talent; in virtue; in merit of all kinds. I do not at all mean to apply this observation specifically to Mr. Adams, but it arises from circumstance because it proves that should Mr. Adams not turn out to be as distinguished a man as we are assured he is, he will have succeeded nonetheless in this manner.

Governor John Pickering to John Langdon PORTSMOUTH, N.H., APRIL 17, 1789

I rejoice that the American FABIUS & SOLON are chosen President and Vice-President of the United States—their known & tried integrity and talents bode well to the Union.

Henry Wynkoop to Reading Beatty NEW YORK, APRIL 23, 1789

Enclosed a paper containing an Account of the Reception & Address of his Excellency the Vice President, on whom I waited yesterday morning, found him in perfect Health & Spirits with no small Addition of corpulence since I saw him in Philadelphia in 1775.

John Adams to Abigail Adams   NEW YORK, MAY 14, 1789

I have as many difficulties here, as you can have; public and private, but my Life from my Cradle has been a series of difficulties and that series will continue to the Grave.

Thomas FitzSimons to Benjamin Rush   NEW YORK, MAY 15, 1789

I said nothing to you in my last upon a Subject, which has Very much Agitated the Senate, and in which the V.P. has given recent proofs of his Superlative Vanity.

Victor Marie du Pont to His Brother Éleuthère Irenée du Pont NEW YORK, MAY 15, 1789

Mr. Adams arrived the twentieth. They gave him a very nice reception and he received it with much dignity. This is a small man, quite vain and ambitious, but, we are assured, of great talent. It is incredible with what enthusiasm the inhabitants of New England extol him. The best politician, the best negotiator, the best legislator of the century, are the epithets which accompany his name in our newspapers. These trite and exaggerated flatteries must be quite disagreeable to a man who is portrayed as the most austere, humble, and simple republican; but it seems that he does not dislike it as much as it is said he does; and under the philosophical cloak, a tiny bit of ear is showing. As for the rest, he is an economist.

John Adams to Benjamin Rush   NEW YORK, MAY 17, 1789

[On being elected vice president with so few electoral votes.] You Say I had not a firmer Friend in the late Election. I must protest against this mode of reasoning. I am not obliged to vote for a Man because he voted for me, had my Office been ever so lucrative or ever so important. But ask your own heart, is not my Election to this Office, in the Scurvy manner in which it was done, a curse rather than a Blessing? Is there Gratitude? Is there Justice? Is there common Sense or decency in this Business? Is it not an indelible Stain on our Country, Countrymen and Constitution? I assure You I think it so, and nothing but an Apprehension of great Mischief, and the final failure of the Government, from my Refusal and assigning my reasons for it, prevented me from Spurning it.

Now my Friend We start fair—Never must I again hear a Selfish motive urged to me, to induce my Vote or Influence in publick affairs.

I never served the Public one moment in my Life, but to the loss and injury of myself and my Children, and I suffer as much by it, at this moment as ever.

Comte de Moustier to the Comte de Montmorin NEW YORK, MAY 17, 1789

I should inform You, Sir, that, in spite of Mr. Adams's tenacious opinions and the haughty republicanism that he shares with his countrymen I find him much more open and disposed to good sense than Mr. Jay.

John Adams to Nathaniel P. Sargeant NEW YORK, MAY 22, 1789

Despondency is not one of my Characteristics: on the contrary the world in general suppose me too much inclined to be sanguine. However this may be I have seen the dangers which surround me, and I hope have never been afraid to meet them. If I had been I should have perished long ago. I had more reasons to say that I should wear a Crown of Thorns than you can be aware of. Indeed I have been astonished to see how little informed Massachusetts Gentlemen who have never been before in Congress are of the real state of American Politics—fifteen years cruel experience has made an indelible impression on my heart—New England is reproached with local Attachments. But the Truth is she is the least influenced by State Prejudices of any in the Union. She sacrifices her interests to the good of the Union. She sacrifices one after another all her ablest & meritorious Characters, She mortifies herself, and all her Friends in complaisance to southern Pride. Insolence and scorn—on the contrary She cries up to the Stars Southern Characters, to enable them to make her humiliation and Abasement the more Remarkable—a greater Insult was never offered to a People than the Maneuveres by which she was horse jockeyed in the late election of Vice President; yet she does not feel it nor see it—you may depend upon it, every honest man in whatever Station in the new Govt. will wear a Crown of

Thorns until New England shall be more attentive, generous and Consistent—till then her honor & Interest will be sacrificed by one Adventurer after Another.

William Maclay, Diary MAY 28, 1789

I began now to think of what Mr. Morris had told me. That it was necessary to make Mr. Adams Vice President to keep him quiet. He is antifederal, but one of a very different turn from the general Cast, a mark may be missed as well above as below, and he is an high flyer.

St. George Tucker to Thomas Tudor Tucker NEW YORK, JUNE 3, 1789

Stimulated by my Indignation I have actually begun a political farce, the object of which is to ridicule the frivolity of the proceedings of the Senate [in debating titles], & to expose in its proper Colors the Character of *their* President, whom I consider as the high priest of Monarchy; ready to immolate a Hecatomb of his most virtuous Countrymen at that shrine.

John Adams to Benjamin Rush NEW YORK, JUNE 9, 1789

I also, am as much a Republican as I was in 1775. I do not "consider hereditary Monarchy or Aristocracy as Rebellion against Nature." On the contrary I esteem them both Institutions of admirable Wisdom and exemplary Virtue, in a certain Stage of Society in a great Nation. The only Institutions that can possibly preserve the Laws and Liberties of the People. And I am clear that America must resort to them as an Asylum against Discord, Seditions and Civil War and that at no very distant Period of time. I shall not live to see it—but you may: I think it therefore impolitick to cherish Prejudices against Institutions which must be kept in View as the Hope of our Posterity. I am by no means for Attempting any Such thing at present. Our Country is not ripe for it, in many respects and it is not yet necessary but our Ship must ultimately land on that shore or be cast away.

I do not "abhor Titles, nor the Pageantry of Government"— if I did I should abhor Government itself—for there never was, and never will be, because there never can be, any Government without Titles and Pageantry. There is not a Quaker Family in

Penn, governed without Titles and Pageantry, not a School, nor a College, nor a Club can be governed without them.

"I love the People," with you—too well to cheat them, lie to them or deceive them. I wish those who have flattered them so much had loved them half as well. If I had not loved them I never would have Served them—if I did not love them now, I would not Serve them another hour—for I very well know that Vexation and Chagrine, must be my Portion, every moment I shall continue in public Life.

John Adams to John Quincy Adams   NEW YORK, JULY 9, 1789

This is entre nous. Independence, my Boy and freedom from humiliating Obligations, are greater Sources of happiness, than Riches.

My office requires, rather Severe duty, and it is a kind of Duty, which if I do not flatter my self too much, is not quite adapted to my Character. I mean it is too inactive, and mechanical. The Chancellor sometimes wishes to leave the Woolsack, and engage in debate. But as it cannot be done, I am content, tho it sometimes happens that I am much inclined to think I could throw a little light upon a subject—if my health and Patience should hold out my four years, I can retire and make Way for some of you younger folks, for one Vacancy makes many Promotions.

David Stuart to George Washington   ABINGTON, FAIRFAX COUNTY, VA., JULY 14, 1789

Nothing could equal the ferment and disquietude, occasioned by the proposition respecting titles—As it is believed to have originated from Mr. Adams & [R. H.] Lee, they are not only unpopular to an extreme, but highly odious—Neither I am convinced, will ever get a vote from this State again. As I consider it very unfortunate for the Government, that a person in the second office should be so unpopular, I have been much concerned at the clamor and abuse against him—Perhaps I feel it more sensibly, from being reminded of my insignificant exertions for him, as an Elector— . . . It has given me much pleasure to hear every part of your conduct spoke of, with high approbation, and particularly your dispensing with ceremony occasionally, and walking the streets; while Adams is never seen but in his carriage & six—As trivial as this may appear, it appears to be more captivating to the generality, than matters of more importance—Indeed, I believe the great herd of mankind, form their judgments of characters, more from such light occurrences, than those of greater magnitude, and perhaps they are right, as the heart is more immediately consulted with respect to the former, than the latter, and an error of judgment, is more easily pardoned, than one of the heart.

George Washington to David Stuart NEW YORK, JULY 26, 1789

One of the Gentlemen whose name is mentioned in your letter, though [high ton]ed has never, I believe, appeared with more than *two* horses in his Carriage—but it is to be lamented that *he,* and *some others,* have stirred a question which has given rise to so much animadversion; and which I confess, has given me much uneasiness.

Thomas Jefferson to James Madison PARIS, JULY 29, 1789

[In response to Adams's advocacy of aristocratical titles for the president.] It is a proof the more of the justice of the character given by Doctr. Franklin of my friend: always an honest man, often a great one, but sometimes absolutely mad.

Abigail Adams to Mary Cranch RICHMOND HILL, NEW YORK CITY, AUGUST 9, 1789

His Rule through life has been to vote and act, independent of Party agreeable to the dictates of his conscience.

Abigail Adams to Cotton Tufts NEW YORK, SEPTEMBER 1, 1789

Mr. Adams is well and will write to you soon. The Senate are so close to Business & he frequently has so much reading to do & such constant attention to the debates, that he comes home quite exhausted & unable to take his pen.

John Adams to James Lovell NEW YORK, SEPTEMBER 1, 1789

I have not yet answered your letter of the 26 of July. You guess well—I find that I shall have all the unpopular questions to determine: and shall soon be pronounced Hostis Republicam generis*—What they will do with me I know not, but must trust to providence. You insinuate that I am accused "of deciding in favor of the power of the prince because I look up to that goal."

*An enemy of the Republic.

That I look up to that goal sometimes is very probable because it is not far above me, only one step, and it is directly before my eyes: so that I must be blind not to see it—I am forced to look up to it and bound by duty to do so, because there is only the breath of one mortal between me and it. There was lately cause enough to look up to it, as I did with horror, when that breath was in some danger of expiring. But deciding for the supreme, was not certainly the way to render that goal more desirable or less terrible nor was it the way to obtain votes for continuing in it, or an advancement to it. The way to have ensured votes would have been to have given up that power—There is not however to be serious, the smallest prospect that I shall ever reach that goal. Our beloved Chief is very little older than his second, has recovered his health and is a much stronger man than I am—a new Vice president must be chosen before a new President—This reflection give[s] me no pain but on the contrary great pleasure: for I know very well that I am not possessed of the confidence and affection of my fellow Citizens, to the degree that he is. I am not of Caesar's mind. The second place in Rome is high enough for me. Although I have a spirit that will not give up its right or relinquish its place whatever the world or even my friends, or even you who knew me so well may think of me, I am not an ambitious man. Submission to insult and disgrace is one thing: but aspiring to higher situations is another. I am quite contented in my present condition and should not be discontented to leave it.

John Adams to Henry Marchant NEW YORK, SEPTEMBER 17, 1789

There is more confinement, in my present situation than in any I have ever been in these thirty years, and another evil is come upon me, under which I suffered formerly, but from which I have been wholly relieved during my absence from America. Public speaking ever gave me a pain in my breast, which was not only troublesome for the time, but dangerous for the future. My present office not only obliges me to a constant and close attention of mind, but to continual reading and speaking, which has again affected la poitrine* as it used to do, and raises many doubts how long I shall be able to go on.

*The chest or breast.

John Adams to John Trumbull NEW YORK, APRIL 25, 1790

They may depend upon it, they will find in me a Man who has Patience but will not be a Sport nor a Dupe.

Alexander Hamilton to Charles Cotesworth Pinckney
PHILADELPHIA, OCTOBER 10, 1792

Mr. Adams, whatever objections may be against some of his theoretic opinions, is a firm honest independent politician.

Alexander Hamilton to John Steele PHILADELPHIA, OCTOBER 15, 1792

Mr. Adams like other men has his faults and his foibles. Some of the opinions he is supposed to entertain, we do not approve—but we believe him to be honest firm faithful and independent—a sincere lover of his country—a real friend to genuine liberty; but combining his attachment to that with the love of order and stable government. No man's private character can be fairer than his. No man has given stronger proofs than him of disinterested & intrepid patriotism.

John Adams to Abigail Adams PHILADELPHIA, DECEMBER 7, 1792

How the Election is gone I know not. It cannot go amiss for me, because I am prepared for every Event. Indeed I am of the Cat kind and fall upon my feet, throw me as they will. I hear some very good Stories to this purpose sometimes.

JANUARY 24, 1793

I cannot say that my desire of Fame increases. It has been Strong in some Parts of my Life but never so strong as my Love of honesty. I never in my Life that I know of sacrificed my Principles or Duty to Popularity, or Reputation. I hope I am now too old ever to do it. But one knows not how tryals may be borne, till they are made.

FEBRUARY 17, 1793

The Personal hatreds and Party Animosities which prevail here, have left me more in tranquility than any other Person. The Altercations between the humble Friends of the two or three Ministers have done no service to the Reputation of either. The S[ecretary] of the Treasury has suffered as much as the Secretary of State. Ambition is imputed to both, and the Moral Character of both has Suffered in the Sensing. . . . Hamilton has been intemperately puffed and this has excited green Eyed Jealousy and haggard Envy. Jay's Friends have let Escape feelings of Jealousy as well as Jefferson's. And it is very natural. Poor me who have no Friends to be jealous, I am left out of the question and pray I ever may.

DECEMBER 22, 1793

My office renders me so compleatly insignificant that all Parties can afford to treat me with a decent respect which accordingly they do, as far as I observe, or hear or suspect. They all know that I can do them neither much good nor much harm.

FEBRUARY 10, 1794

I am weary of this eternal Indecision. I wish for the Time when Old Sam And Old John conducted with more wisdom and more success. This is Egotism enough to deserve the Guillotine to be sure but I cannot but recollect old scenes, and old Results.

JANUARY 20, 1795

Cold as it is, my heart is as warm as ever towards her whom I commit.

JANUARY 31, 1796

I read forever, and am determined to sacrifice my Eyes like John Milton rather than give up the Amusement without which I should despair. . . .

Search We the Spot which mental power contains? Go where Man gets his living by his Brains. If I had my Living by my Brains for seven Years past I should have had more mental Power. But Brains have not only been Useless but even hurtful and pernicious in my Course. Mine have been idle a long time—till they are rusty.

FEBRUARY 10, 1796

I am weary of the Game. Yet I don't know how I could live out of it. I don't love Slight, neglect, Contempt, disgrace nor Insult more than others. Yet I believe I have firmness of Mind enough to bear it like a Man, a Hero and a Philosopher.

MARCH 1, 1796

As to the Subject of yours of the 20th [about the presidency]. I am quite at my Ease. I never felt less Anxiety when any considerable

Change lay before me. Aut transit aut fin.* I transmigrate or come
to an End. The Question is between living at Phila. or at Quincy,
between great Cares and Small Cares. I have looked into myself and see no meanness nor dishonesty there. I see weakness
enough. But no timidity.

MARCH 11, 1796

Oh that I had a Bosom to lean my Head upon: But how dare you
hint or Lisp a Word about Sixty Years of Age. If I were near, I
would soon convince you that I am not above forty.

DECEMBER 16, 1796

Elevated Expectations of Grandeur and Glory as well as Prosperity have accompanied me through Life and been a great source of
my Enjoyment. They are not diminished by the present Prospect.

DECEMBER 30, 1796

I think a Man had better wear than rust.

Oliver Wolcott Sr. to Oliver Wolcott Jr. MARCH 20, 1797

We have done the best we could in our election. We have chosen
a very honest man, a friend to order and to our national independence and honor; but that you may know that I am not mistaken,
I will for once, under a strong seal, venture to tell you that I always considered Mr. Adams a man of great vanity, pretty capricious, of a very moderate share of prudence, and of far less real
abilities than he believes he possesses. I therefore sincerely wish
he may have able counsellors, in whom he will confide; though,
as he will not be influenced but by an apparent compliment to
his own understanding, it will require a deal of address to render
him the service which it will be essential for him to receive.

John Adams to Abigail Adams PHILADELPHIA, APRIL 18, 1797

My Eyes will totally fail me in six months. I shall be obliged to
resign for Want of sight, if I go on as I began. The Number of
Papers to read is prodigious. My Eyes complain most bitterly.

John Marshall to Mary W. Marshall PHILADELPHIA, JULY 3, 1797

I dined on Saturday in private with the President whom I found

*Either it is a transformation, or it is the end.

a sensible plain candid good tempered man & was consequently much pleased with him.

Julian Ursyn Niemcewicz, Travels through America
NOVEMBER 8, 1797

At one o'clock I was presented to Mr. Adams. He was sitting, reading a newspaper, facing the fireplace with Mr. [Samuel B.] Malcolm, a young man 20 years old, his private secretary. I saw a dumpy little man dressed wholly in gray, well-powdered hair and a long pigtail. His face appeared to me that of a good and honest man, touched nevertheless with a grain of malice.

James Monroe to Thomas Jefferson ALBEMARLE, VA., APRIL 8, 1798

Mr. A: will never surprise me by any act of the wild & extravagant kind. If he was in a sober and discreet manner to repair the breach between this country & France, & heal the wounds which his predecessor has given to the reputation & interest of his country, I should be surprised. His passion is to out-do his predecessor, & thus I expect to find no difference, between the knight of the present day and the former one, than what the superior violence of his passion may lead to.

John Adams to Abigail Adams PHILADELPHIA, DECEMBER 4, 1798

If you come on, you must expect to find me cross. Sam. Adams Says Old Men are fractious and appealed to his Wife, if she did not find it so. I shall be more fractious than he, I fear for I shall be plagued.

Rufus King to Alexander Hamilton LONDON, DECEMBER 19, 1798

The President has no talent for war.

John Dawson to James Monroe PHILADELPHIA, APRIL 20, 1800

[In predicting Jefferson's victory over Adams in the presidential election of 1800,] I think "Old Codfish" may prepare for Braintree & "red breeches" to quit the mountain.

Alexander Hamilton to James McHenry NEW YORK, JUNE 6, 1800

The man is more mad than I ever thought him and I shall soon be led to say as wicked as he is mad.

Oliver Wolcott Jr. to George Cabot PHILADELPHIA, JUNE 16, 1800

It is with grief and humiliation, but at the same time with perfect confidence, that I declare that no administration of the government by President Adams can be successful. His prejudices are too violent, and the resentments of men of influence are too keen, to render it possible that he should please either party, and we all know that he does not possess, and cannot command the talents, fortitude, and constancy necessary to the formation of a new party. . . . I am no advocate for rash measures, and know that public opinion cannot be suddenly changed; but it is clear to my mind that we shall never find ourselves in the straight road of federalism while Mr. Adams is President.

Timothy Pickering to Rufus King PHILADELPHIA, JUNE 26, 1800

I am informed that the President denies that there has been any coalition between him & Mr. Jefferson. He has also denied that he ever said there was a British faction in the Senate and among those American citizens who may be called *public men.* On this I will only say that the President is not always consistent or accurate in his remembrance. To me, he said, that Mr. Jefferson had very little of that knowledge which was necessary for a statesman; and shortly after to McHenry, that Mr. Jefferson was a very proper person to be President of the U. States; "and that he would sooner serve as Vice-President under him, or even as Minister resident at the Hague, than be indebted for his election to *such a being* as Hamilton;" whom in the same sentence he called a *bastard* and as much an alien as Gallatin. No one could have imagined Mr. Adams capable of such billingsgate language. But a man so entirely under the dominion of violent passion, is capable of anything.

Alexander Hamilton to Charles Carroll of Carrollton
NEW YORK, JULY 1, 1800

That this gentleman ought not to be the object of the federal wish, is, with me, reduced to demonstration. His administration has already very materially disgraced and sunk the government. There are defects in his character which must inevitably continue to do this more and more. And if he is supported by the federal party, his party must in the issue fall with him. Every other calculation will, in my judgment, prove illusory.

Doctor *Franklin,* a sagacious observer of human nature, drew this portrait of Mr. Adams:—"He is always honest, *sometimes* great, but *often mad.*" I subscribe to the justness of this picture, adding as to the first trait of it this qualification—"as far as a man excessively *vain* and *jealous,* and *ignobly* attached to *place* can be."

AUGUST 7, 1800

As between Pinckney & Adams I give a decided preference to the first. If you have not heard enough to induce you to agree in this opinion I will upon your request enter into my reasons. Mr. Adams has governed & must govern from *impulse* and *caprice,* under the influence of the two most mischievous of Passions for a Politician, to an extreme that to be portrayed would present a caricature—*Vanity* and *Jealousy.* He has already disorganized & in a great measure prostrated the Federal Party.

Oliver Wolcott Jr. to Fisher Ames WASHINGTON, D.C., AUGUST 10, 1800

But however dangerous the election of Mr. Jefferson may prove to the community, I do not perceive that any portion of the mischief would be avoided by the election of Mr. Adams. We know the temper of his mind to be revolutionary, violent, and vindictive; he would be sensible that another official term would bring him to the close of life. His passions and selfishness would continually gain strength; his pride and interest would concur in rendering his administration favorable to the views of the democrats and jacobins; public offices would be frequently bestowed on men capable of servile compliances; the example of a selfish attention to personal and family interests would spread like a leprosy in our political system, and by corrupting the fountains of virtue and honor would destroy the principles by which alone a mild government under any form can be sustained.

James A. Bayard to Alexander Hamilton WILMINGTON, DEL., AUGUST 18, 1800

What is the charm which attaches the East so much to Mr. A.? It can be nothing personal. . . . He is liable to gusts of passion little short of phrenzy which drive him beyond the control of any rational reflection.

I speak of what I have seen. At such moments the interest of those who support him or the interest of the nation, would be outweighed by a single impulse of rage.

This is enough but not all. He wants Magnanimity. The President is not exempt from the little interests—the little jealousies and little animosities of Mr. Adams.

We may thank the guardian Genius of the country which has watched over its destinies for the last 4 years.

Fisher Ames to Rufus King SEPTEMBER 24, 1800

This man I allude to is too much the creature of *impulse* or freakish humor—he is a revolutionist from temperament, habit and lately what he thinks policy—he is too much irritated against many if not most of the principal sound men of the country ever to bestow on them *his* confidence or to retrieve *theirs*. In particular he is implacable against a certain great little man whom we mutually respect [Alexander Hamilton]. With so much less than the old & requisite harmony with the best friends of the country, he has certain antipathies and prejudices connected with them that are equally strange, stubborn & pernicious. He really thinks it a light matter to have a war with G. B. as he hates that government in every thing but its theory, believes it corrupt and affects to believe it possesses *influence* here; he can scarcely refrain and he seldom tries to refrain from inveighing against British influence, and to conciliate to himself the mob honors that cant will obtain. He does not hesitate to say that public debt would go down and paper money come up in that case. But he loves to bluster and vapor about the courage he once displayed when *he* was not afraid of that great power when we had not half our present force. He has the *os magne soniturum** and with all the ignorance of men & business that must belong to the possessor of the before mentioned tenets, he indulges the vanity, so much his favorite & his master.

Alexander Hamilton, Letter concerning the Public Conduct and Character of John Adams NEW YORK, OCTOBER 24, 1800

Few go as far in their objections [to the reelection of Adams as president] as I do. Not denying to Mr. Adams patriotism and integrity, and even talents of a certain kind, I should be deficient in candor, were I to conceal the conviction, that he does not possess the talents adapted to the *Administration* of Government, and that there are great and intrinsic defects in his character, which unfit him for the office of Chief Magistrate. . . .

I was one of that numerous class who had conceived a high veneration for Mr. Adams, on account of the part he acted in the first stages of our revolution. My imagination had exalted him to a high eminence, as a man of patriotic, bold, profound, and comprehensive mind. But in the progress of the war, opinions were ascribed to him, which brought into question, with me, the solidity of his understanding. . . . I remember also, that they had the effect of inducing me to qualify the admiration which I had once entertained for him, and to reserve for opportunities of future scrutiny, a definitive opinion of the true standard of his character. . . .

But this did not hinder me from making careful observations upon his several communications, and endeavoring to derive from them an accurate idea of his talents and character. This scrutiny enhanced my esteem in the main for his moral qualifications, but lessened my respect for his intellectual endowments. I then adopted an opinion, which all my subsequent experience has confirmed, that he is a man of an imagination sublimated and eccentric; propitious neither to the regular display of sound judgment, nor to steady perseverance in a systematic plan of conduct; and I began to perceive what has been since too manifest, that to this defect are added the unfortunate foibles of a vanity without bounds, and a jealousy capable of discoloring every object. . . .

**Os magna sonaturum.* "Mouth formed for great utterances." Horace, *Satires* 1.4.42.

The particulars of this Journal [Adams's diary entries while a peace commissioner] cannot be expected to have remained in my memory—but I recollect one which may serve as a sample. Being among the guests invited to dine with the Count de Vergennes, Minister for Foreign Affairs, Mr. Adams thought fit to give a specimen of American politeness, by conducting Madame de Vergennes to dinner; in the way, she was pleased to make retribution in the current coin of French politeness—by saying to him, "Monsieur Adams, vous etes le Washington de negotiation." Stating the incident, he makes this comment upon it: "These people have a very pretty knack of paying compliments." He might have added, they have also a very dexterous knack of disguising a sarcasm. . . .

A primary cause of the state of things which led to this event, is to be traced to the ungovernable temper of Mr. Adams. It is a fact that he is often liable to paroxysms of anger, which deprive him of self command, and produce very outrageous behavior to those who approach him. Most, if not all his Ministers, and several distinguished Members of the two Houses of Congress, have been humiliated by the effects of these gusts of passion.

John Adams, Autobiography 1802

Here I will interrupt the narration for a moment to observe that from all I have read of the History of Greece and Rome, England and France, and all I have observed at home, and abroad, that Eloquence in public Assemblies is not the surest road, to Fame and Preferment, at least unless it be used with great caution, very rarely, and with great Reserve. The Examples of Washington, Franklin and Jefferson are enough to show that Silence and reserve in public are more Efficacious than Argument or Oratory. A public Speaker who inserts himself, or is urged by others into the Conduct of Affairs, by daily Exertions to justify his measures, and answer the Objections of Opponents, makes himself too familiar with the public, and unavoidably makes himself Enemies. Few Persons can bare to be outdone in Reasoning or declamation or Wit, or Sarcasm or Repartee, or Satire, and all these things are very apt to grow out of public debate. In this Way in a Course of Years, a Nation becomes full of a Man's Enemies, or at least of such as have been galled in some Controversy, and take a secret pleasure in assisting to humble and mortify him.

Thomas Paine, "To the Citizens of the United States," National Intelligencer NOVEMBER 22, 1802

It has been the political career of this man to begin with hypocrisy, proceed with arrogance, and finish in contempt. May such be the fate of all such characters.

Thomas Jefferson to Benjamin Rush WASHINGTON, D.C., OCTOBER 4, 1803

General Washington had his eye on him, whom he certainly did not love.

Mercy Otis Warren, History of the American Revolution 1805

In his diplomatic character, Mr. Adams had never enjoyed himself so well, as while residing in the Dutch republic. Regular in his morals, and reserved in his temper, he appeared rather gloomy in a circle; but he was sensible, shrewd, and sarcastic, among private friends. His genius was not altogether calculated for a court life, amidst the conviviality and gaiety of Parisian taste. In France he was never happy: not beloved by his venerable colleague, Doctor Franklin; thwarted by the minister, the Count de Vergennes, and ridiculed by the fashionable and polite, as deficient in the *je ne sais quoi,* so necessary in highly polished society; viewed with jealousy by the court, and hated by courtiers, for the perseverance, frigidity, and warmth, blended in his deportment; he there did little of consequence, until the important period when, in conjunction with Dr. Franklin and Mr. Jay, a treaty of peace was negotiated between Great Britain and the United States of America....

Mr. Adams was undoubtedly a statesman of penetration and ability; but his prejudices and his passions were sometimes too strong for his sagacity and judgment....

On Mr. Adams's return from England, he undoubtedly discovered a partiality in favor of monarchic government, and few scrupled to assert for a time, that he exerted his abilities to encourage the operation of those principles in America....

Mr. Adams, in private life, supported an unimpeachable character; his habits of morality, decency and religion, rendered him amiable in his family, and beloved by his neighbors. The opinions of a man of such sobriety of manners, political experience, and general knowledge of morals, law and government, will ever have a powerful effect on society, and must naturally influence the people, more especially the rising generation, the young men, who have not had the opportunity of acquainting themselves with the character, police, and jurisprudence of nations, or with the history of their own country, much less with the principles on which the American revolution was grounded.

Thomas Jefferson to William Short WASHINGTON, D.C., JUNE 12, 1807

He has a better heart than head.

John Adams to Skelton Jones QUINCY, MARCH 11, 1809

My temper in general has been tranquil, except when any instance of extraordinary madness, deceit, hypocrisy, ingratitude, treachery or perfidy, has suddenly struck me. Then I have always been irascible enough, and in three or four instances, very extraordinary ones, too much so. The storm, however, never lasted for half an hour, and anger never rested in the bosom.

Thomas Jefferson to Benjamin Rush MONTICELLO, JANUARY 16, 1811

I think it part of his character to suspect foul play in those of whom he is jealous, and not easily to relinquish his suspicions.

John Adams to Benjamin Rush JUNE 21, 1811

I am well, my appetite is as good as ever. I sleep well o'nights; no burdens, whether grasshoppers or mammoths of body or mind, affect me. I still enjoy a chair in this study, but avoid close thinking from principle. My natural vision is not bad, but I use glasses for ease to my eyes, which you have known to be weak and subject to inflammations for almost forty years. My hearing, for anything that I perceive or my friends have remarked to me, is as good as ever. So much for the bright side.

On the other I have a "quiveration." What in the name of the medical dictionary, you will say, is a "quiveration"? A wild Irish boy, who lives with my son T.B.A. [Thomas Boylston Adams], let a horse run away with a chaise. One of the family ran out and cried out, "Nat! Why did you not scream and call for help?" "Sir!

Sir!" said Nat, "I was seized with such a *quiveration* that I could not speak." Nat's quiveration is the best word I know to express my palsy. It does not as yet much incommode me in writing, although my hands are chiefly affected. Another circumstance on the dark side is, my organs of speech are gone. It would divert you to witness a conversation between my ancient friend and colleague, Robert T. Paine, and me. He is above eighty. I cannot speak, and he cannot hear. Yet we converse.

Benjamin Rush to John Adams SEPTEMBER 4, 1811

No hand but your own must compose your voice from the tomb. Your style is bold, original, occasionally brilliant, and at all times full of nerve. There is not a redundant word in it. . . . It is the artillery of language.

PHILADELPHIA, FEBRUARY 17, 1812

I rejoice in the correspondence which has taken place between you and your old friend Mr. Jefferson. I consider you and him as the North and South Poles of the American Revolution. Some talked, some wrote, and some fought to promote and establish it, but you and Mr. Jefferson *thought* for us all. I never take a retrospect of the years 1775 and 1776 without associating your opinions and speeches and conversations with all the great political, moral, and intellectual achievements of the Congresses of those memorable years.

Benjamin Rush to Thomas Jefferson PHILADELPHIA, MARCH 3, 1812

[On the resumption of correspondence between Adams and Thomas Jefferson.] If Mr. Adams' letters to you are written in the same elevated and nervous [i.e., vigorous] style, both as to matter and language, that his letters are which he now and then addresses to me, I am sure you will be delighted with his correspondence. Some of his thoughts electrify me. I view him as a mountain with its head clear and reflecting the beams of the sun, while all below it is frost and snow.

John Adams to Thomas Jefferson QUINCY, SEPTEMBER 14, 1813

It has been long, very long a settled opinion in my Mind that there is now, never will be, and never was but one being who can

Understand the Universe. And that it is not only vain but wicked for insects to pretend to comprehend it.

Thomas Jefferson, Conversation with Daniel Webster 1824

John Adams was our Colossus on the floor. He was not graceful, nor elegant, nor remarkably fluent; but he came out occasionally with a power of thought & expression, that moved us from our seats.

John Adams to Thomas Jefferson QUINCY, JANUARY 14, 1826

I am certainly very near the end of my life. I am far from trifling with the idea of Death which is a great and solemn event. But I contemplate it without terror or dismay, "aut transit, aut finit,"* if finit, which I cannot believe, and do not believe, there is then an end of all but I shall never know it, and why should I dread it, which I do not; if transit I shall ever be under the same constitution and administration of Government in the Universe, and I am not afraid to trust and confide in it.

Timothy Pickering to Daniel Webster BOSTON, JULY 19, 1826

All unpleasant feelings towards Mr. Adams, had ceased long before the occurrence of the above mentioned correspondence. A subsequent event obliged me, in my own vindication, to expose publicly his faults. Still I view, as I have always viewed him, as a man of eminent talents, zealously, courageously & faithfully exerted in effecting the Independence of the Thirteen United Colonies: and I believe that he, more than any other individual, roused and prepared the minds of his fellow citizens to decide positively and timely that greatest revolutionary question.

---

*Either it is a transformation, or it is the end.

Samuel Adams

1722–1803

⊰ BORN IN Boston. Graduated from Harvard College, 1740 (M.A., 1743). Tax collector of Boston, 1756–65. Drafted Massachusetts Resolves against Stamp Act, 1765. Member, colonial House of Representatives, 1766–74. Revolutionary publicist and agitator. Member, three provincial congresses, 1774–75, and Committee of Safety of the Provincial Congress, 1775. Delegate to Continental Congress, 1774–81; signed Declaration of Independence and Articles of Confederation. Member, state council, 1775–76, 1779–80; state constitutional convention, 1779–80; and state senate, 1781–85, 1786–88 (president, 1781–85, 1787–88). Member, Massachusetts Convention, voted to ratify, despite earlier opposition to Constitution, 1788. Defeated by Fisher Ames for U.S. representative, 1788. Lieutenant governor, 1789–93. Assumed governorship upon Governor John Hancock's death, 1793. Governor, 1793–97; did not seek reelection, 1797.

John Adams, Diary DECEMBER 22, 1765

Adams is zealous, ardent and keen in the Cause, is always for Softness, and Delicacy, and Prudence where they will do, but is staunch and stiff and strict and rigid and inflexible, in the Cause.

DECEMBER 30, 1772

Spent this Evening with Mr. Samuel Adams at his House.... Adams was more cool, genteel and agreeable than common—concealed, and restrained his Passions—&c. He affects to despise Riches, and not to dread Poverty. But no Man is more ambitious of entertaining his Friends handsomely, or of making a decent, an elegant Appearance than he. He has lately new covered and glazed his House and painted it, very neatly, and has new papered, painted and furnished his Rooms. So that you visit at a very genteel House and are very politely received and entertained.

John Adams to Abigail Adams PHILADELPHIA, SEPTEMBER 16, 1774

When the Congress first met, Mr. Cushing made a Motion, that it should be opened with Prayer. It was opposed by Mr. Jay of N. York and Mr. Rutledge of South Carolina, because we were so divided in religious Sentiments, some Episcopalians, some Quakers, some anabaptists, some Presbyterian and some Congregationalists, so that We could not join in the same Act of Worship. Mr. S. Adams arose and said he was no Bigot, and could hear a Prayer from a Gentleman of Piety and Virtue, who was at the same Time a Friend to his Country. He was a Stranger in Philadelphia, but had heard that Mr. Duche (Dushay they pronounce it) deserved that Character, therefore he moved that Mr. Duchè, an episcopal Clergyman, might be desired to read Prayers to the Congress.

John Adams to James Warren PHILADELPHIA, SEPTEMBER 17, 1775

Be it known to you then that two of the most unlikely Things, within the whole Congress of Possibility, have really, and actually happened. The first is the Sudden Marriage of our President [John Hancock], whose agreeable Lady honors us with her Presence and contributes much to our good Humor, as well as to the Happiness of the President. So much for that.

The next Thing is more wonderful Still.

You know the aversion which your Secretary* has ever entertained to riding Horseback. He never would be persuaded to mount a Horse. The last time we were here, I often labored to persuade him, for the Sake of his Health, but in vain. Soon after We Set out, on the last Journey, I reflected that Some Degree of

---

*Samuel Adams was the Massachusetts secretary of state.

Skill and Dexterity in Horsemanship, was necessary to the Character of a Statesman. It would take more Time and Paper than I have to Spare, to show the Utility of Horsemanship to a Politician; So I shall take this for granted. But I pointed out the particulars to him, and likewise showed him that Sociability would be greatly promoted, by his mounting one of my Horses.

On Saturday the second day of September 1775, in the Town of Grafton He was prevailed on to put my Servant with his, into Harrison's Chaise and to mount upon my Horse, a very genteel, and easy little Creature. We were all disappointed and Surprised. Instead of the Taylor riding to Brentford We beheld, an easy, genteel Figure, upon the Horse, and a good deal of Spirit and facility, in the Management of the Horse, insomuch that We soon found our Servants were making Some disagreeable Comparisons, and Since our arrival here I am told that Fessenden (impudent Scoundrel) reports that the Secretary rides fifty per Cent better than your Correspondent.

In this manner, We rode to Woodstock, where we put up for the Sabbath. It was Soon observed that the Secretary, could not Sit so erect in his Chair as he had Sat upon his Horse, but Seemed to be neither sensible of the Disease or the Remedy. I Soon perceived and apprised him of both. On Sunday Evening, at Mr. Dexter's, where we drank Coffee & Spent an agreeable Evening I persuaded him to purchase two yards of flannel which we carried to our Landlady, who with the assistance of a Taylor Woman in the house, made up a Pair of Drawers, which the next Morning were put on, and not only defended the Secretary from any further Injury, but entirely healed the little Breach which had been begun.

Still an Imperfection remained. Our Secretary had not yet learned to mount and dismount. Two Servants were necessary to attend upon these Occasions, one to hold the Bridle and Stirrup, the other to boost the Secretary. This was rather a ridiculous Circumstance Still. At last, I undertook to instruct him the necessary Art of mounting. I had my Education to this Art, under Bates, the celebrated Equerry, and therefore might be Supposed to be a Master of it. I taught him to grasp the Bridle, with his Right Hand over the Pummell of his Saddle, to place his left Foot firm in the Stirrup; top twist his left Hand into the Horse's Mane, about half Way between his Ears and his Shoulders, and then a vigorous Exertion of his Strength would carry him very gracefully into the Seat, without the least Danger of falling over on the other Side. The Experiment was tried and Succeeded to Admiration.

Thus equipped and instructed, our Horseman rode all the Way from Woodstock to Philadelphia, Sometimes upon one of my Horses, Sometimes on the other—and acquired fresh Strength, Courage, Activity and Spirit every day. His Health is much improved by it, and I value myself, very much upon the Merit of having probably added Several Years to a Life So important to his Country, by the little Pains I took to persuade him to mount and teach him to ride.

James Warren to Samuel Adams WATERTOWN, MASS., SEPTEMBER 28, 1775

[Commenting on Adams learning how to ride a horse while traveling to Congress in Philadelphia.] I had the pleasure Yesterday of hearing for the first Time of your safe Arrival at Philadelphia, and of your performing the Journey in a manner that Contributed much to your Health, it is said that Horsemanship and dexterity in riding on the Saddle are necessary to Complete that Character, I really give you Joy on this Occasion and that this Important Acquisition was made by the help of flannel without Injury. I am obliged to my Friend, Mr. Adams, for this Intelligence, whose Letter I received yesterday by Mr. Cabot wholly on that Subject, which shows the Importance of it in his mind and his fondness for fame and Glory, for he assumes the whole merit of first Advising and then giving the Necessary Instructions. I never feel disposed to lessen his Glory and Fame and shall readily in this Instance allow him the Honor of Completing the Character of a great Statesman and prolonging the Life of a distinguished Patriot.

Joseph Galloway, Historical and Political Reflections on the Rise and Progress of the American Rebellion 1790

Samuel Adams—a man, who though by no means remarkable for brilliant abilities, yet is equal to most men in popular intrigue, and the management of a faction. He eats little, drinks little, sleeps little, thinks much, and is most decisive and indefatigable in the pursuit of his objects. It was this man, who by his superior application managed at once the factions in Congress at Philadelphia, and the factions in New England. Whatever these patriots in Congress wished to have done by their colleagues without . . . Mr. Adams advised and directed to be done, and when done, it was dispatched by express to Congress.

John Adams, Autobiography MARCH 1776

Mr. Samuel Adams had become very bitter against Mr. Hancock and spoke of him with great Asperity, in private Circles, and this Alienation between them continued from this time till the Year 1789, thirteen Years, when they were again reconciled.

John Adams to James Warren PHILADELPHIA, JULY 27, 1776

The Secretary, between you and me, is completely worn out. I wish he had gone home Six months ago, and rested himself. Then, he might have done it, without any Disadvantage. But in plain English he has been so long here, and his Strength, Spirit and Abilities so exhausted, that an hundred such delegates here would not be worth a Shilling.

Ambrose Searle, American Journal JANUARY 2, 1777

Saml. Adams has often publicly boasted in Philadelphia of late, that for 20 Years past he has been inculcating his republican Opinions among all the young Gentlemen in & about Boston, and that he now saw the happy Fruit of it. Mr. Andrew Allen says, that of all the men he ever knew, this Adams is the most capable of leading or inflaming a Mob. He has vast Insinuation, & infinite Art, by which he has been able to impose upon most Men.

Elbridge Gerry to James Warren YORK, PA., NOVEMBER 13, 1777

Our Friends the Mr. Adams left this place two Days since. . . . The Absence of these Gentlemen occasions a Chasm in Congress, who employed the microscopic Eye of the One to penetrate the obscure Designs of intriguing Adversaries and the deep Erudition of the other to raise Barriers against them.

Samuel Adams to Samuel P. Savage PHILADELPHIA, JULY 3, 1778

I now begin to promise myself the Pleasure of seeing the Liberties of our Country established on a solid Foundation. It will then be my most earnest Wish to be released from all public Cares, and sit down with my Family and a little Circle of *faithful* Friends in the Cottage of Obscurity. There we will give Thanks to the God of Heaven for the great Things he has done for America, and fervently pray that she may be virtuous, without which she cannot long enjoy the Blessings of Freedom.

OCTOBER 6, 1778

You tell me that Boston is become a new City, and explain yourself by mentioning the exceeding Gaiety of Appearance there. I would fain hope this is confined to Strangers. Luxury & Extravagance are in my opinion totally destructive of those Virtues which are necessary for the Preservation of the Liberty and Happiness of the People. . . . Shall we not again see that Sobriety of Manners, that Temperance, Frugality, Fortitude, and other manly Virtues which were once the Glory and Strength of my much loved native Town. Heaven grant it speedily!

Samuel Adams to Elizabeth Adams   PHILADELPHIA, OCTOBER 20, 1778

My Boston Friends tell me with great Solicitude that I have Enemies there. I thank them for their Concern for me, and tell them I knew it before. The Man who acts an honest Part in public Life, must often counteract the Passions, Inclinations or Humors of weak and wicked Men and this must create him Enemies. I am therefore not disappointed or mortified. I flatter myself that no virtuous Man who knows me will or can be my Enemy; because I think he can have no Suspicion of my Integrity. But they say my Enemies "are plotting against me." Neither does this discompose me, for what else can I expect from such kind of Men. If they mean to make me uneasy they miss their Aim; for I am happy and it is not in *their* Power to disturb my Peace. They add, the design is to get me recalled from this Service. I am in no Pain about such an Event; for I know there are many who can serve our Country here with greater Capacity (though none more honestly). The sooner therefore another is elected in my Room the better. I shall the sooner retire to the sweet Enjoyment of domestic Life. This, you can witness, I have often wished for; and I trust that all gracious Providence has spared *your* precious Life through a dangerous Illness, to heighten the Pleasures of my Retirement. If my

Enemies are governed by Malice or Envy, I could not wish them a severer Punishment than their own Feelings. But, my Dear, I thank God, I have many Friends.

Samuel Adams to Samuel P. Savage PHILADELPHIA, NOVEMBER 1, 1778

You was mistaken in supposing that I ascribed the Independence of America to New England *only*. I never was so assuming as to think so. My words are that America is obliged to Massachusetts, and this is an acknowledged Truth. It is the opinion of others as well as myself, that the Principles and Manners of New England from time to time led to that great Event. I pray God she may ever maintain those Principles, which in my Opinion, are essentially necessary to support & perpetuate her Liberty. You may see my Sentiments of the Patriotism of other States in the Union, in a Letter I lately wrote to Mrs. A (if it is in Being), in which I relate a Conversation which passed between Monsieur —— and myself. But enough of this, I love my Country. My Fears concerning her are that she will ruin herself by *Idolatry*.

A part of your Letter you tell me is confidential. I will always keep the Secrets of my Friends when I can do it honestly, though I confess I do not like to be encumbered with them.

Samuel Adams to Elizabeth Adams PHILADELPHIA, DECEMBER 13, 1778

It is diverting enough to hear the different Language held forth concerning me, by a kind of Men whom I despise beyond Expression. In New England they say I am averse to an Accommodation with Great Britain, and make that an Exception against me. In Philadelphia I am charged, indirectly at least, with a frequent Exchange of Visits with the Companion of Berhenhout, Lord Lindsay, Governor Johnston & the Son of Lord Bute, with a View of secretly bringing about an Accommodation with that King and Nation which I have solemnly abjured. What is there which Malice joined with a small Share of Wit will not suggest! I am not apt to conceal my Sentiments. They are far from being problematical. They are well known here & at Boston; and I can trust my Consistency in the Judgment of every honest and sensible Man that is acquainted with me. The Censure of Fools or Knaves is Applause.

Samuel Adams to Samuel Cooper PHILADELPHIA, DECEMBER 25, 1778

A Politician must take men as he finds them and while he carefully endeavors to make their Humors & Prejudices, their Passions & Feelings, as well as their Reason & Understandings subservient to his Views of public Liberty & Happiness, he must frequently observe among the many if he has any Sagacity, some who having gained the Confidence of their Country, are sacrilegiously employing their Talents to the Ruin of its Affairs, for their own private Emolument. Upon such Men he stamps the Stigma *Hic niger est,** and if he thinks them capable of doing great Mischief to prevent it, he ventures to hold them up to the public Eye. This he does at the Risk of his own Reputation; for it is a thousand to one but those whose Craft he puts at Hazard will give him the odious Epithets of suspicious, dissatisfiable, peevish, quarrelsome, &c, and honest, undiscerning Men may be induced for a time to believe them pertinent; but he solaces himself in a conscious Rectitude of Heart, trusting that it will sooner or later be made manifest; perhaps in this World, but most assuredly in that Day when the secret Thoughts of all Men shall be unfolded.

James Lovell to Abigail Adams PHILADELPHIA, AUGUST 9, 1779

And has not that very philosophic Politician been yet to see you?

John Adams to Thomas Diggers MARCH 14, 1780

The Committee of Correspondence is purely an American Invention. It is an Invention of Mr. Samuel Adams, who first conceived the Thought, made the first Motion in a Boston Town Meeting, and was himself chosen the first Chairman of a Committee of Correspondence, that ever existed among men.

Samuel Adams to James Warren PHILADELPHIA, NOVEMBER 20, 1780

In your Letter of the 17th of September which is still before me you say, that "the Tongue of Malice has always been employed

---

*"That man's heart is black." Horace, *Satires* 1.4.81.

against me," and in mentioning it, you discover the Feelings of a Friend. It may perhaps in some Measure relieve those Feelings, if I tell you that it serves to make me the more watchful over my self, lest by any Misconduct, I should afford Occasion to malicious Men, to say that of me which would give me just Cause to be ashamed. It is said to be a Misfortune to a Man, when all speak well of him. Is it then an Advantage to a Man, that he has Enemies? It may be so, if he has Wisdom to make a good Use of them. We are apt to be partial, in our own Judgment of ourselves. Our friends are either blind to our Faults, or not faithful enough to tell us of them. The malicious Man will utter all Manner of Evil of us, and contrive Means to send it post haste to our Ears; and if among much Slander, they say some Truths, what have we to do, but to correct past Errors, & guard against future ones. The Report you mention as propagated of me, is groundless. Would any Man in his Senses, who wishes that the War may be carried on with Vigor, prefer the temporary and expensive Drafts of Militia, to a permanent and well appointed Army! But Envy knows no other Business than to calumniate.

Samuel Adams to Elizabeth Adams PHILADELPHIA, NOVEMBER 24, 1780

You seem, my Dear, to express more Concern than I think you ought, at certain Events that have of late taken Place in the Common Wealth of Massachusetts. Do you not consider that in a free Republic, the People have an uncontrollable right of choosing whom they please, to take their Parts in the Administration of public Affairs? No Man has a Claim on his Country, upon the Score of his having rendered public Service. It is the Duty of every one to use his utmost Exertions in promoting the Cause of Liberty & Virtue; and having so done, if his Country thinks proper to call others to the arduous Task, he ought cheerfully to acquiesce, and he may Console himself with the Contemplation of an Honest Man in private Life. You know how ardently I have wished for the Sweets of Retirement. I am like to have my Wish. You are witness that I have not raised a fortune in the Service of my Country. I glory in being what the World calls a poor Man. If my Mind has ever been tinctured with Envy, the Rich & the Great have not been its objects. If I have been vain, Popularity, though I had as much of it as any Man ought to have, is not the

Phantom I have pursued. He who gains the Approbation of the Virtuous Citizens, I will own may feel himself happy; but he is in Reality much more so, *who knows he deserves it.* Such a Man, if he cannot retreat with Splendor, he may with Dignity. I will trust in that all gracious Being, who in his own good Way, has provided us with Food and Raiment; and having spent the greatest Part of my Life in public Cares, like the weary Traveller, fatigued with the Journey of the Day, I can rest with you in a Cottage. If I live till the Spring, I will take my final Leave of Congress and return to Boston. I have Reasons to be fixed in this Determination which I will then explain to you. I grow more domestic as I increase in years.

Peter Oliver, *"The Origin and Progress of the American Rebellion"* 1781

I shall next give you a Sketch of some of Mr. *Samuel Adams's* Features; & I do not know how to delineate them stronger, than by the Observation made by a celebrated Painter in *America,* vizt. "That if he wished to draw the Picture of the devil, that he would get *Sam Adams* to sit for him": & indeed, a very ordinary Physiognomist would, at a transient View of his Countenance, develop the Malignity of his Heart. He was a Person of Understanding, but it was discoverable rather by a Shrewdness than Solidity of Judgment; & he understood human Nature, in low life, so well, that he could turn the Minds of the great Vulgar as well as the small into any Course that he might choose; perhaps he was a singular Instance in this Kind; & he never failed of employing his Abilities to the vilest Purposes. He was educated at *Harvard College;* and when he quitted that Scene of Life, he entered upon the Business of a Malster, the Profits of which afforded him but a moderate Maintenance; & his Circumstances were too well known for him to gain a pecuniary Credit with Mankind.

He was so thorough a *Machiavilian,* that he divested himself of every worthy Principle, & would stick at no Crime to accomplish his Ends. He was chosen a Collector of Taxes for the Town of *Boston;* but when the Day of Account came, it was found that there was a Defalcation of about £1700 Sterling. He was apprised of it long before, & formed his plans accordingly—he knew the Temper of the Town of *Boston,* that the most Part of them were inclined to Opposition of Government, and he secured an Interest with them. This he did, by ingratiating himself with *John Hancock Esqr.,* a considerable Merchant of that Town, in the same Manner that the Devil is represented seducing *Eve,* by a constant whispering at his Ear. . . .

I here . . . return to Mr. *Adams,* when he had embezzled the public Monies of *Boston*—in order to extricate himself, he duped Mr. *Hancock,* by persuading him to build Houses & Wharves which would not bring him 2 percent Interest for his Money. This Work necessarily engaged a Variety of Artificers, whom *Adams* could prefer. This secured these Orders of Men in his Interest; & such Men chiefly composed the Voters of a *Boston* Town Meeting. At one of their Meetings the Town voted him a Discharge of ds of his Debt, & Mr. *Hancock* & some others, into whose Graces he had insinuated his baleful Poison, subscribed to a Discharge of the other Third—thus was he set at large to commit his Ravages on Government, until he undermined the Foundations of it, & not one Stone had been left upon another. He soon outrivalled Mr. *Otis* in popularity. His was all serpentine Cunning, Mr. *Otis* was rash, unguarded, foulmouthed, & openly spiteful; all which was disgustful to those who piqued themselves upon their Sanctity. The other [i.e., Adams] had always a religious Mask ready for his Occasions; he could transform his self into an Angel of Light with the weak Religionist; & with the abandoned he would disrobe his self & appear with his cloven Foot & in his native Blackness of Darkness—he had a good Voice, & was a Master in vocal Music. This Genius he improved, by instituting singing Societies of Mechanics, where he presided; & embraced such Opportunities to the inculcating Sedition, 'till it had ripened into Rebellion. His Power over weak Minds was truly surprising.

Thomas Rodney, *"Caractors of Some of the Members of Congress"* POST MARCH 8, 1781

Samuel Adams of Massachusetts has been in Congress from their first Meeting has a pretty general knowledge of their affairs and is particularly attentive to every thing that affects his own State or friends; he is neither eloquent nor Talkative; but having the full command of his passions, and possessing a great deal of caution and Court cunning he is fitted for a politician in every Case Where great and good abilities are not requisite.

Marquis de Chastellux, Travels in North-America, in the Years 1780, 1781, and 1782

Mr. Samuel Adams, Deputy for Massachusetts Bay, was not at this dinner, but on rising from the table I went to see him. When I entered his room, I found him *tête-à-tête* with a young girl of fifteen who was preparing his tea; but we shall not be scandalized at this, on considering that he is at least sixty. Every body in Europe knows that he was one of the prime movers of the present revolution. I experienced in his company the satisfaction one rarely has in the world, nay even in the theater, of finding the person of the actor corresponding with the character he performs. In him, I saw a man wrapt up in his object, who never spoke but to give a good opinion of his cause, and a high idea of his country. His simple and frugal exterior, seemed intended as a contrast with the energy and extent of his ideas, which were wholly turned towards the republic, and lost nothing of their warmth by being expressed with method and precision; as an army, marching towards the enemy, has not a less determined air for observing the laws of tactics.

John Adams to Abigail Adams PARIS, MARCH 28, 1783

I have one favor for you to ask of Mr. Adams the President of the [Massachusetts] Senate. It is that he would make a complete Collection of his Writings and publish them in Volumes. I know of no greater Service that could be rendered to the Rights of Mankind. At least that he would give you a List of them. They comprise a Period of forty Years, and although they would not find so many Rakes for Purchasers, as the Writings of Voltaire, they would do infinitely more good to mankind especially in our rising Empire. There Posterity will find a Mass of Principles, and Reasonings, suitable for them and for all good Men. The Copy, I fancy would sell to Advantage in Europe.

John Adams to John Quincy Adams THE HAGUE, JUNE 11, 1784

In a Letter I wrote a Year ago to Mr. Adams, I urged upon him to make and publish a Collection of his Writings and I have mentioned it many Times in Conversation with Americans. It is a Work which ought to be given to the public; But Mr. Adams will never do it. It will be done, imperfectly by some other, hereafter.

My Advice to you is to Search for every Scratch of his Pen, and lay it up with Care.

Luigi Castiglioni, Sketches of American Statesmen 1787

Lean, small, a great talker, and crudely dressed, he reveals at first sight both by his words and behavior the turbulent and intolerant character of those individuals who, like death-dealing instruments of war, if they are necessary in disturbed times, should be removed from the sight of men in times of peace.

James Warren to John Adams MILTON, MASS., MAY 18, 1787

Our old Friend Mr. A., however, is re-chosen [president of the Massachusetts senate], though he seems to have forsaken all his old principles and professions and to have become the most arbitrary and despotic Man in the Commonwealth.

New York Journal JANUARY 7, 1788

That father of patriots SAMUEL ADAMS.

James Madison to Edmund Randolph NEW YORK, JANUARY 10, 1788

The accounts [on the newly proposed Constitution] from Massachusetts vary extremely according to the channels through which they come. It is said that S. Adams who has hitherto been reserved, begins to make open declaration of his hostile views. His influence is not great, but this step argues an opinion that he can calculate on a considerable party.

"Common Sense," Boston Independent Chronicle DECEMBER 18, 1788

The friends to good government have long since determined to give their votes [for U.S. representative] to Mr. Adams; and it is not in the power of any writer, by descanting on the abilities of any other man in the country, to change their purpose. . . . They have long thought on Mr. Adams and determined him to be the man. They have experienced his abilities and his integrity; they have invariably found him attached to good government; and they know that the dignity of his character will have an influence in Congress upon some younger politicians, who upon first taking the reins, may be disposed to ride the people too hard. In this old and steady patriot, they are sure of sending an upright man, above temptation, and who scorns a bribe. *He is the poor man's friend,* and *if he has a prejudice in his politics, it leans to the rights and privileges of the common people.*

It has been said he is old and Antifederal. My fellow citizens, be not deceived; his age and experience are the very qualifications you want. *His influence caused the Constitution to be adopted in this state,* and if he fails to give it his support for a fair trial, remember it will be the first time he ever failed you. In forty years he has never deceived you; in times of more consequence than the present, he has proved true; and for his own sake as well as yours, he will not now forfeit your good opinion.

James Iredell to Hannah Iredell BOSTON, NOVEMBER 1, 1792

I had the honor of dining with the Committee and Corporation of the College, and of being seated next to the Lieutenant Governor, the famous Sam. Adams who though an old Man has a great deal of fire yet. He is polite and agreeable. I think he is the very image of the Pictures I have seen of Oliver Cromwell.

John Quincy Adams to John Adams BOSTON, MARCH 24, 1794

The old gentleman has hurt himself by this improper compliance with an insolent request [calling and then canceling a feast honoring French military victories]. The general opinion seems to be that there will be no choice of a governor by the people at our ensuing election. It is my opinion however that Mr. Adams will be chosen.* He may do less harm than some others, but he will certainly never do any good. *Stat magni nominis umbra.*† His present impotence leans for support on his former services, and the office will be given him as a reward, not as an employment.

John Adams to Abigail Adams PHILADELPHIA, APRIL 7, 1794

At nine o Clock at night I suppose your Election is over, and another fortnight will enable Us to guess whether An Adams or a Cushing is to be the great Man. Although the Old Gentleman's Conduct is not such as I can approve in many Things of late

---

*If no candidate for governor received a majority of the popular vote, the election was decided by the state legislature.

†He stands, the shadow of a great name.

Years, Yet I find it difficult to believe that the People of Massachusetts will forsake him in his last moments. Alas! His Grandeur must be of short duration if it ever commences. I shall be happier at home, if Cushing succeeds and the State I believe will be more prudently conducted.

Abigail Adams to John Adams   QUINCY, APRIL 11, 1794

You will see by the return of votes that Mr. Adams is undoubtedly chosen Governor by a large Majority of the people, and it is probable Mr. Gill will be Lieut. Governor. Judge Cushing stands high upon the list, but the cry of Gratitude towards an old Servant of the publick, whose Years could not be long, was powerful, nor would they fix a Stigma upon him by placing an other over his Head. Their Principal was good, and I wish they may always act as wisely. Yet at this very critical Time, a more National and unprejudiced Man as well as a more active one, might have proved a greater Blessing to the State.

John Quincy Adams to John Adams   BOSTON, APRIL 12, 1794

Our election of Governor took place last Monday. The numerous candidates of whom everybody talked, and for whom nobody intended to vote, had silently sunk into oblivion, and Judge Cushing alone remained to be opposed to the claimant *by succession.** In this town uncommon pains were taken by both parties. There were 500 votes more than have ever been given upon any former election. Mr. Adams had 1400, and Judge Cushing 900. Our federalists droop the head and think all is lost. They know not so much of the human heart, or of the American character as you do. You told me what the event of the elections would be last October, and I then thought your "oracle *plus sure que celui de Chalcas.*"† A friend of mine who lives in the country, by the name of [Horatio] Townsend, a sensible man and a warm Federalist, has repeatedly told me previous to the election, that he did not think the prophet would even have votes enough to make him a candidate for the election. Why? Because he is superannuated

*Samuel Adams was serving as lieutenant governor when Governor John Hancock died.

†More certain than Chalcas, a Trojan priest or soothsayer who predicted that Troy would not be taken.

and antifederal. I have so often told him that I believed the choice of the people would be for this doting antifederalist. Since the election he writes me "I give you joy of the prospect of your old friend's being elected Governor. The votes went very different from what I expected. *I was not sufficiently acquainted with the moral habits of the people.* The main argument of his being a scapegoat of seventy-five had more weight than I had expected."

John Adams to Abigail Adams PHILADELPHIA, FEBRUARY 2, 1796

It is devoutly to be wished that the Massachusetts had a Governor capable of diffusing his Thoughts over fifteen states and seeing their Dependences on each other as well as their Relations with foreign Nations. Mr. Adams cannot. His Pride and Vanity are vastly more extensive than his Abilities. He always had a contracted Mind—tho a subtle and a bold one. He never was over honest nor over candid. He will lie a little for his own Vanity and more for his Party, and as much as a Spartan for his notions of the public good.

Abigail Adams to John Adams PHILADELPHIA, APRIL 4, 1796

Tomorrow is our Election Day, and after scolding and abusing the Old Man some, their Hearts relent towards him, and I am very certain from what I have read and what I have heard, all of which will serve rather than injure his cause, he will again be Re-elected and I believe by a large proportion of the State. In the first place he lives in the Town of Boston. That has its Weight with their Pride and Ambition. In the next place, they recollect his former Services, his Age, and his Virtues. Those take hold of their gratitude, and they know not how to bring his grey Hairs with sorrow to the Grave. There they have some merit. They know there is not any other Man held up sufficiently popular to unite the people. These are the considerations of the Patriots. The Antis support him, because they think him a spoke in their Wheel. I own for myself, whilst I pity his infirmities I should have been sorry to have had him dropped.

QUINCY, APRIL 10, 1796

Mr. Adams as I expected is undoubtedly Elected, tho he lost many votes by his, I will not say conduct, but want of Conduct.

Thomas Jefferson to James Sullivan MONTICELLO, FEBRUARY 9, 1797

I am always glad of an opportunity of inquiring after my most ancient & respected friend Mr. Samuel Adams. His principles, founded on the immovable basis of equal right & reason, have continued pure & unchanged. Permit me to place here my sincere veneration for him.

Benjamin Rush, "Travels through Life" c. 1800

Upon the motion for leaving Philadelphia Samuel Adams (who seldom spoke in Congress) delivered a short, but very animating speech. His feelings raised him frequently upon his toes at the close of his sentences. There was nothing very oratorical in his manner, but what he said infused a sudden vigor into the minds of every member of the House.

Benjamin Rush, Sketches c. 1800

He was near sixty years of age when he took his seat in Congress, but possessed all the vigor of mind of a young man of five and twenty. He was a republican in principle and manners. He once acknowledged to me "that the independence of the United States upon Great Britain had been the first wish of his heart seven years before the war." About the same time he said to me "if it were revealed to him that 999 Americans out of 1000 would perish in a war for liberty, he would vote for that war, rather than see his country enslaved. The survivors in such a war, though few (he said), would propagate a nation of freemen." He abhorred a standing army, and used to say that they were the "shoeblacks of Society." He dreaded the undue influence of an individual in a Republic, and once said to me "Let us beware of continental and State great men." He loved simplicity and economy in the administration of government, and despised the appeals which are made to the eyes and ears of the common people in order to govern them. He considered national happiness and the public patronage of religion as inseparably connected; and so great was his regard for public worship, as the means of promoting religion, that he constantly attended divine service in the German church in York town [Pa.] while the Congress sat there, when there was no service in their chapel, although he was ignorant of the German language. His morals were irreproachable, and even ambition and avarice, the usual vices of politicians, seemed to have no place in his breast. He seldom spoke in Congress, but was active in preparing and doing business out of doors. In some parts of his conduct I have thought he discovered more of the prejudices of a Massachusetts man than the liberal sentiments of a citizen of the United States. His abilities were considerable, and his knowledge extensive and correct upon Revolutionary subjects, and both friends and enemies agree in viewing him as one of the most active instruments of the American Revolution.

Thomas Jefferson to Samuel Adams PHILADELPHIA, FEBRUARY 26, 1800

Your principles have been tested in the crucible of time, and have come out pure. You have proved that it was monarchy, and not merely British monarchy, you opposed.

Mercy Otis Warren, History of the American Revolution 1805

Mr. Adams was a gentleman of a good education, a decent family, but no fortune. Early nurtured in the principles of civil and religious liberty, he possessed a quick understanding, a cool head, stern manners, a smooth address, and a Roman-like firmness, united with that sagacity and penetration that would have made a figure in a conclave. He was at the same time liberal in opinion, and uniformly devout; social with men of all denominations, grave in deportment; placid, yet severe; sober and indefatigable; calm in seasons of difficulty, tranquil and unruffled in the vortex of political altercation; too firm to be intimidated, too haughty for condescension, his mind was replete with resources that dissipated fear, and extricated in the greatest emergencies. Thus qualified, he stood forth early, and continued firm, through the great struggle, and may justly claim a large share of honor, due to that spirit of energy which opposed the measures of administration, and produced the independence of America. Through a long life he exhibited on all occasions, an example of patriotism, religion, and virtue honorary to the human character.

John Quincy Adams to Skelton Jones BOSTON, APRIL 17, 1809

Samuel Adams was many years older than my father. He received his degree of Master of Arts at Harvard College in 1743. It was then the custom of that college, that the candidates for this degree should each of them propose a question having relation to any of the sciences, in which they had been instructed, and assuming the affirmative or negative side of the proposition, profess to be prepared to defend the principle contained in it at the public Commencement against all opponents.

The question proposed by Samuel Adams was, "whether the people have a just right of resistance, when oppressed by their rulers," and the side that he asserted was the affirmative.

John Adams to Thomas Jefferson   QUINCY, JULY 16, 1814

I am sometimes afraid that my "Machine" will not "surcease motion" soon enough; for I dread nothing so much as "dying at top" and expiring like Dean Swift "a driveller and a Show" or like Sam. Adams, a Grief and distress to his Family, a weeping helpless Object of Compassion for Years.

John Adams to Dr. J. Morse   QUINCY, JANUARY 1, 1816

[Immediately after the Boston Massacre on March 5, 1770,] Samuel Adams appeared in his true character. His caution, his discretion, his ingenuity, his sagacity, his self-command, his presence of mind, and his intrepidity, commanded the admiration and loud applauses of both parties. The troops were ordered to the Castle, and Lord North called them from this time, "Sam Adams's two regiments."

Thomas Jefferson to Benjamin Waterhouse   MONTICELLO, JANUARY 31, 1819

I was the youngest man but one in the old Congress, and he the oldest but one; as I believe. His only senior, I suppose, was Stephen Hopkins. . . . Although my high reverence for Samuel Adams was returned by habitual notices from him which highly flattered me, yet the disparity of age prevented intimate and confidential Communications. I always considered him as more than any other member the fountain of our important measures. And although he was neither an eloquent nor easy speaker, whatever he said was sound, and commanded the profound attention of the House. In the discussions on the floor of Congress, he reposed himself on our main pillar in debate, Mr. John Adams. These two gentlemen were verily a host in our councils.

John Adams to William Tudor QUINCY, FEBRUARY 9, 1819

Samuel Adams, to my certain knowledge, from 1758 to 1775, that is, for seventeen years, made it his constant rule to watch the rise of every brilliant genius, to seek his acquaintance, to court his friendship, to cultivate his natural feelings in favor of his native country, to warn him against the hostile designs of Great Britain, and to fix his affections and reflections on the side of his native country. I could enumerate a list, but I will confine myself to a few. [Adams listed John Hancock, Joseph Warren, Benjamin Church, and Josiah Quincy] . . . If Samuel Adams was not a Demosthenes in oratory, nor had the learning of a Mansfield in law, or the universal history of a Burke, he had the art of commanding the learning, the oratory, the talents, the diamonds of the first order that his country afforded, without anybody's knowing or suspecting he had it, but himself, and a very few friends.

John Adams to Thomas Jefferson QUINCY, MAY 27, 1819

His . . . character however will never be accurately known to posterity, as it never was sufficiently known to its own age: his merit in the Revolution, if there was any merit in it, was and is beyond all calculation. I know but one superior to it, and that was James Otis.

Thomas Jefferson, Conversation with Daniel Webster 1824

For depth of purpose, zeal, & sagacity, no man in Congress *exceeded,* if any equalled Sam Adams; & none did more than he, to originate & sustain revolutionary measures in Congress. But he could not speak, he had a hesitating grunting manner.

Aaron Burr
1756–1836

⚜ BORN IN Newark, N.J. Father was Aaron Burr, second president of the College of New Jersey (Princeton). Maternal grandfather was Jonathan Edwards. Graduated from Princeton, 1772. Continental army, 1775–79 (served in Canada and at Valley Forge and Monmouth). Studies law with William Paterson, 1780. Admitted to New Jersey bar, 1782. Moves to New York City, fall 1783. New York state attorney general, 1789–91. U.S. senator, 1791–97. Unsuccessful candidate for governor and U.S. vice president, 1792. Defeated for reelection as senator, receives thirty electoral votes for U.S. president, and elected New York Assembly, 1797. Defeated for reelection to assembly, 1798. Ties Jefferson in presidential election of 1800. Loses balloting in House of Representatives. U.S. vice president, 1801–5. Defeated in election for New York governor, 1804. Kills Alexander Hamilton in duel, July 1804. Leads western conspiracy. Tried and acquitted of treason, 1807. Travels to Europe, 1808. Returns to the United States, 1812.

Eliphalet Dyer to Joseph Trumbull PHILADELPHIA, JULY 18, 1775

This Letter is by Mr. Burr only son of the late President Burr, his Sister Married Mr. Reeves of Litchfield. He is Accompanied by one Mr. [Matthias] Ogden of the Jerseys. They are both young Gentlemen of fortune & regulation. They have so great ardor for Military that they are determined to join our Army as Volunteers and go into the Ranks if they can get Nothing better.

Oliver Wolcott to Samuel Lyman PHILADELPHIA, FEBRUARY 3, 1776

Young Mr. Burr is amongst the News Paper Heroes. He behaved Very bravely and I hope will not get killed—he has an Appointment in the Army.

Alexander Hamilton to Hugh Seton NEW YORK, JANUARY 1, 1785

Mr. Burr . . . is a member of the Assembly, of influence and abilities.

James Kent to Theodorus Bailey JANUARY 16, 1791

The insinuation of his manners is equal to the refinement of his taste and the activity of his mind.

Morgan Lewis to Robert R. Livingston PHILADELPHIA, JANUARY 24, 1791

If you have the same Opinion of Mr. Burr that many have, you will not rely much on his friendship. . . . 'tis pretty prevalent, that he is a Man who makes every Thing subservient to his private Views.

James Watson to Alexander Hamilton NEW YORK, FEBRUARY 2, 1792

The cautious distance observed by this gentleman towards all parties, however exceptionable in a politician may be a real merit in a Governor.

Aaron Burr to Jacob Delamater NEW YORK, JUNE 15, 1792

It would, indeed, be the extreme of weakness in me to expect friendship from Mr. [George] Clinton. I have too many reasons to believe that he regards me with jealousy and malevolence.

From Alexander Hamilton PHILADELPHIA, SEPTEMBER 21, 1792

Mr. Clinton's success [in winning the vice presidency] I should think very unfortunate. I am not for trusting the Government too much in the hands of its enemies. But still Mr. C—— is a man of property, and, in private life, as far as I know of probity. I fear the other Gentleman is unprincipled both as a public and private man. When the constitution was in deliberation, his conduct was equivocal; but its enemies, who I believe best understood him considered him as with them. In fact, I take it, he is for or against nothing, but as it suits his interest or ambition. He is determined, as I conceive, to make his way to be the head of the popular party and to climb per *fas et nefas** to the highest honors of the state; and as much higher as circumstances may permit. Embarrassed, as I understand, in his circumstances, with an extravagant family—bold enterprising and intriguing, I am mistaken, if it be not his object to play the game of confusion, and I feel it a religious duty to oppose his career.

SEPTEMBER 26, 1792

Mr. Burr's integrity as an Individual is not unimpeached. As a public man he is one of the worst sort—a friend to nothing but as it suits his interest and ambition. Determined to climb to the highest honors of State, and as much higher as circumstances may permit—he cares nothing about the means of effecting his purpose. Tis evident that he aims at putting himself at the head of what he calls the "popular party" as affording the best tools for an ambitious man to work with. Secretly turning Liberty into ridicule he knows as well as most men how to make use of the name. In a word, if we have an embryo-Caesar in the United States 'tis Burr.

John Nicholson to James Madison   PHILADELPHIA, OCTOBER 3, 1792

I take the liberty of addressing you by the Bearer on a subject which concerns the republican interests of the United States. Those in that interest I believe pretty generally desire a change in the vice presidency of the United States at [the] ensuing election, and at the first Governor Clinton was thought of to succeed him; however the circumstances of the State In which he presides combined with his own wishes induced us here to agree to the Honorable Mr. Burr whose talents, abilities and firmness of character are I believe fully equal, with a prospect of some accessional Strength from Middle and Eastern States which would not be given to Clinton. The people here however only desire a

*Legally or illegally.

communication with their southern brethren on the subject and although they would I believe generally prefer *Burr* to *Clinton* will unite in either that will be thought most likely to succeed, for although Clinton wishes to decline in favor of Burr he does not absolutely refuse to serve if elected.

James Monroe to James Madison OCTOBER 9, 1792

[In response to a letter from Melancton Smith and Marinus Willett of New York recommending the substitution of Aaron Burr for Governor George Clinton as the Republican candidate to oppose the reelection of Vice President John Adams.] My opinion is briefly this: that if Mr. Burr was in every respect inexceptionable it would be impossible to have him elected [vice president]. He is too young, if not in point of age, yet upon the public theatre, to admit the possibility of an union in his favor. If formed at all, it must be upon the recommendation & responsibility of particular characters in the several States; & if this could succeed it would be an unpleasant thing to those who would stand as sponsors. But for an office of this kind it could not, nor should it succeed. Some person of more advanced life and longer standing in publick trust should be selected for it, and particularly one who in consequence of such service had given unequivocal proofs of what his principles really were. A person who had marked a line of conduct so decisively that you might tell what he would be hereafter by what he had been heretofore. To place this gentleman, or any other of his standing in the chair of the present incumbent, would not be well thought of in America; nor would it produce the desired effect; for some compunction always attends the rejection of an old servant, especially when accompanied with any kind of reproach. To lessen this if the ground of exception is well founded, the person preferred should in that respect, at least, be universally known to be sound, and to balance in other respects against him as nearly as possible an equal weight of character. Having this impression I consider the effort in New York in his favor as highly injurious & improper, & which if persisted in will certainly defeat the object. The particular arrangement of things there it might perhaps suit well enough; but they should not endeavor to make the more important interests of the union subservient to their accommodation—The path, however, to be pursued is difficult to be marked.

Alexander Hamilton to Charles Cotesworth Pinckney
PHILADELPHIA, OCTOBER 10, 1792

[Burr] has no other principle than to *mount at all events* to the first honors of the State & to as much more as circumstances will permit—a man in private life not unblemished.

Alexander Hamilton to John Steele PHILADELPHIA, OCTOBER 15, 1792

My opinion of Mr. Burr is yet to form—but according to the present state of it, he is a man whose only political principle is, to *mount at all events* to the highest legal honors of the Nation and as much further as circumstances will carry him. Imputations not favorable to his integrity as a man rest upon him; but I do not vouch for their authenticity.

John Adams to Abigail Adams PHILADELPHIA, NOVEMBER 18, 1794

A Senate was made to Day, by the Arrival of Col. Burr, as fat as a Duck and as ruddy as a roost Cock. An hundred Thousand Pounds is a very wholesome Thing I believe, and I suppose my manifold Infirmities are owing to my Poverty. I know not whether fame lies, on this occasion, but she begins to whisper that Burr has been very fortunate and successful as well as several others of Govr. Clinton's friends, by means that I will not explain till fame explains them more in detail.

MARCH 12, 1796

I dined Yesterday with Mr. Burr, who lives here in Style.

Robert Troup to Rufus King NEW YORK, JUNE 24, 1800

It is impossible to say who will be the man set up as Governor by the Democrats, Burr has undoubtedly a view to the office, if he should fail in being President or Vice-President. He certainly means to avail himself of all chances to become a great man; and if he should be finally disappointed, it will not be owing to his want of industry—or to his modesty or virtue.

Fisher Ames to Rufus King BOSTON, JULY 15, 1800

Col. B. of New York . . . may give his influence to the highest bidder.

Alexander Hamilton to James A. Bayard NEW YORK, AUGUST 6, 1800

There seems to be too much probability that Jefferson or Burr will be President. The latter is intriguing with all his might in New Jersey, Rhode-Island & Vermont. And there is a possibility of some success to his intrigues. He counts positively on the universal support of the Antis: & that by some adventitious aid from other quarters, he will overtop his friend Jefferson. Admitting the first point the conclusion may be realized. And if it is Burr will certainly attempt to reform the Government *a la Buonaparte*. He is as unprincipled & dangerous a man as any country can boast; as true a *Cataline* as ever met in midnight conclave.

Aaron Burr to Samuel Smith NEW YORK, DECEMBER 16, 1800

It is highly improbable that I shall have an equal number of Votes with Mr. Jefferson; but if such should be the result every Man who knows me ought to know that I should utterly disclaim all competition—Be assured that the federal party can entertain no wish for such an exchange. As to my friends—they would dishonor my Views and insult my feelings by harboring a suspicion that I could submit to be instrumental in Counteracting the Wishes & expectations of the U.S.

Alexander Hamilton to Oliver Wolcott Jr. NEW YORK, DECEMBER 16, 1800

It is now, my Dear Sir, ascertained that Jefferson or Burr will be President and it seems probable that they will come with equal votes to the House of Representatives. It is also circulated here that in this event the Federalists in Congress or some of them talk of preferring Burr. I trust New England at least will not so far lose its head as to fall into this snare. There is no doubt but that upon every virtuous and prudent calculation Jefferson is to be preferred. He is by far not so dangerous a man and he has pretensions to character.

As to *Burr* there is nothing in his favour. His private character is not defended by his most partial friends. He is bankrupt beyond redemption except by the plunder of his country. His public principles have no other spring or aim than his own aggrandizement per *fas* et *nefas*.* If he can, he will certainly disturb our institutions to secure to himself *permanent power* and with it *wealth*. He is truly the *Cataline* of America—& if I may credit Major Wilcocks, he has held very vindictive language respecting his opponents.

But early measures must be taken to fix on this point the opinions of the Federalists. Among them, from different motives—Burr will find partisans. If the thing be neglected he may possibly go far.

Yet it may be well enough to throw out a lure for him, in order to tempt him to start for the plate & thus lay the foundation of dissention between the two chiefs.

Alexander Hamilton to Theodore Sedgwick NEW YORK, DECEMBER 22, 1800

The appointment of Burr, as President would disgrace our Country abroad. No agreement with him could be relied upon. His private circumstances render disorder a necessary resource. His public principles offer no obstacle. His ambition aims at nothing short of permanent power and wealth in his own person. For heaven's sake let not the Federal party be responsible for the elevation of this Man.

Alexander Hamilton to Harrison Gray Otis NEW YORK, DECEMBER 23, 1800

Burr loves nothing but himself; thinks of nothing but his own aggrandizement, and will be content with nothing, short of permanent power in his own hands. No compact that he should make with any passion in his breast, except ambition, could be relied upon by himself. How then should we be able to rely upon any agreement with him. Jefferson, I suspect, will not dare much. Burr will dare every thing, in the sanguine hope of effecting every thing.

Alexander Hamilton to Gouverneur Morris NEW YORK, DECEMBER 24, 1800

Another subject—*Jefferson* or *Burr?*—the former without all doubt. The latter in my judgment has no principle public or

*Legally or illegally.

private—could be bound by no agreement—will listen to no monitor but his ambition; & for this purpose will use the *worst* part of the community as a ladder to climb to permanent power & an instrument to crush the better part. He is bankrupt beyond redemption except by the resources that grow out of war and disorder or by a sale to a foreign power or by great peculation. War with Great Britain would be the immediate instrument. He is sanguine enough to hope every thing—daring enough to attempt every thing—wicked enough to scruple nothing. From the elevation of such a man heaven preserve the Country!

DECEMBER 26, 1800
That the Convention with France ought to be ratified as the least of two evils. That on the same ground Jefferson ought to be preferred to Burr.

I trust the Federalists will not finally be so mad as to vote for the latter. I speak with an intimate & accurate knowledge of character. His elevation can only promote the purposes of the desperate and profligate. If there be a man in the world I ought to hate it is Jefferson. With Burr I have always been personally well. But the public good must be paramount to every private consideration. My opinion may be freely used with such reserves as you shall think discreet.

Gouverneur Morris, Diary   DECEMBER 27, 1800
Today Mr. Harper calls, and Mr. Latimer. The former is, he says, an intimate friend of Burr, and thinks it advisable for the House of Representatives to give him their voice, without asking or expecting any assurances or explanation respecting his future administration. He thinks Burr's temper and disposition give an ample security for a conduct hostile to the democratic spirit which Mr. Harper considers as dangerous to our country, while Mr. Jefferson, he thinks, is so deeply imbued with false principles of government, and has so far committed himself in support of them, that nothing good can be expected from him. I give him some reasons why it would be better for gentlemen in his House to suspend their determinations until they can have more light as to the merit and probable conduct of the candidates.

Alexander Hamilton to James Ross NEW YORK, DECEMBER 29, 1800

Letters which myself and others have received from Washington give me much alarm at the prospect that Mr. Burr may be supported by the Federalists in preference to Mr. Jefferson. Be assured, my Dear Sir, that this would be a fatal mistake. From a thorough knowledge of the character I can pronounce with confidence that Mr. Burr is the last man in the United States to be supported by the Federalists.

1. It is an opinion firmly entertained by his enemies and not disputed by his friends that as a man he is deficient in *honesty*. Some vary sad stories are related of him. That he is bankrupt for a large *deficit* is certain.

2. As a politician discerning men of both parties admit that he has but one principle—to *get power* by *any* means and to *keep* it by *all* means.

3. Of an ambition too irregular and inordinate to be content with institutions that leave his power precarious, he is of too bold and sanguine a temper to think anything too hazardous to be attempted or too difficult to be accomplished.

4. As to talents they are great for management and intrigue—but he is yet to give the first proofs that they are equal to the art of governing well.

5. As to his theory, no mortal can tell what it is. Institutions that would serve his own purpose (such as the Government of France of the present day) not such as would promote lasting prosperity and glory to the Country would be his preference because he cares only for himself and nothing for his Country or glory.

6. Certain that his irregular ambition cannot be supported by *good* men, he will *court* and *employ* the worst men of all parties as the most eligible instruments. Jacobinism in its most pernicious form will scourge the country.

7. As to foreign policies, War will be a necessary mean of power and wealth. The animosity to the British will be the handle by which he will attempt to wield the nation to that point: Within a fortnight he has advocated positions which if acted upon would in six months place us in a state of War with that power.

From the Elevation of such a man may heaven preserve the Country. Should it be by the means of the Federalists I should at once despair. I should see no longer anything upon which to rest the hope of public or private prosperity.

John Adams to Elbridge Gerry WASHINGTON, D.C., DECEMBER 30, 1800

Your anxiety for the issue of the election is, by this time, allayed. How mighty a power is the spirit of party! How decisive and unanimous it is! Seventy-three for Mr. Jefferson and seventy-three for Mr. Burr. May the peace and welfare of the country be promoted by this result! But I see not the way as yet. In the case of Mr. Jefferson, there is nothing wonderful; but Mr. Burr's good fortune surpasses all ordinary rules, and exceeds that of Bonaparte. All the old patriots, all the splendid talents, the long experience, both of Federalists and Antifederalists, must be subjected to the humiliation of seeing this dexterous gentleman rise, like a balloon, filled with inflammable air, over their heads. And this is not the worst. What a discouragement to all virtuous exertion, and what an encouragement to party intrigue, and corruption! What course is it we steer, and to what harbor are we bound? Say, man of wisdom and experience, for I am wholly at a loss.

Theodore Sedgwick to Alexander Hamilton WASHINGTON, D.C., JANUARY 10, 1801

As to the other candidate there is no disagreement as to his character. He is ambitious—selfish—profligate. His ambition is of the worst kind—it is a mere love of power, regardless of fame but as its instrument—his selfishness excludes all social affections & his profligacy unrestrained by any moral sentiment, and defying all decency. This is agreed, but then it is known that his manners are plausible, that he is dexterous in the acquisition & use of the means necessary to effect his wishes. Nothing can be a stronger evidence of this than the situation in which he stands at this moment—without any pretension from connections, fame or services, elevated, by his own independent means, to the highest point to which all those can carry the most meritorious man in the nation. He holds to no pernicious theories, but is a mere matter-of-fact man. His very selfishness prevents his entertaining any mischievous predilections for foreign nations. The situation

in which he lives has enabled him to discern and justly appreciate the benefits resulting from our commercial & other national
systems; and this same selfishness will afford some security that he
will not only patronize their support but their invigoration. . . .

It must be confessed that there is a part of the character of
Burr more dangerous than that of Jefferson. Give to the former a
probable chance & he would become an usurper; the latter might
not incline, he certainly would not dare, to make the attempt. I
do not believe that either would succeed, & I am even confident
that such a project would be rejected by Burr as visionary.

Alexander Hamilton to James A. Bayard NEW YORK, JANUARY
16, 1801

As to Burr these things are admitted and indeed cannot be denied, that he is a man of *extreme & irregular* ambition—that he
is *selfish* to a degree which excludes all social affections & that
he is decidedly *profligate.* But it is said, 1st. that he is *artful &
dexterous* to accomplish his ends—2nd. that he holds no pernicious theories, but is a mere *matter of fact* man—3rd. that his
very selfishness is a guard against mischievous foreign predilections. 4th That his *local situation* has enabled him to appreciate the utility of our Commercial & fiscal systems, and the same
quality of selfishness will lead him to support & invigorate them.
5th. that he is now disliked by the Jacobins, that his elevation will
be a mortal stab to them, breed an invincible hatred to him, &
compel him to lean on the Federalists. 6th. That Burr's ambition
will be checked by his good sense, by the manifest impossibility
of succeeding in any scheme of usurpation, & that if attempted,
there is nothing to fear from the attempt. These topics are in
my judgment more plausible than solid. As to the 1st point the
fact must be admitted, but those qualities are objections rather
than recommendations when they are under the direction of bad
principles. As to the 2nd point too much is taken for granted. If
Burr's conversation is to be credited he is not very far from being
a visionary. It is ascertained in some instances that he has talked
perfect *Godwinism.* I have myself heard him speak with applause
of the French system as unshackling the mind & leaving it to its
natural energies, and I have been present when he has contended
against Banking Systems with earnestness & with the same arguments that Jefferson would use. The truth is that *Burr* is a man of

a very subtle imagination, and a mind of this make is rarely free from ingenious whimsies. Yet I admit that he has no fixed theory & that his peculiar notions will easily give way to his interest. But is it a recommendation to have *no theory*? Can that man be a systematic or able statesman who has none? I believe not. *No general principles* will hardly work much better than erroneous ones. As to the 3rd. point—it is certain that Burr generally speaking has been as warm a partisan of France as Jefferson—that he has in some instances shown himself to be so with passion. But if it was from calculation who will say that his calculations will not continue him so? His selfishness so far from being an obstacle may be a prompter. If corrupt as well as selfish he may be a partisan for gain—if ambitious as well as selfish, he may be a partisan for the sake of aid to his views. No man has trafficked more than he in the floating passions of the multitude. Hatred to G. Britain & attachment to France in the public mind will naturally lead a man of his selfishness, attached to place and power, to favor France & oppose G. Britain. The Gallicism of many of our patriots is to be thus resolved, & in my opinion it is morally certain that Burr will continue to be influenced by this calculation. As to the 4th point the instance I have cited with respect to Banks proves that the argument is not to be relied on. If there was much in it, why does Chancellor Livingston maintain that we ought not to cultivate navigation but ought to let foreigners be our carriers? France is of this opinion too & Burr for some reason or other, will be very apt to be of the opinion of *France.* As to the 5th point—nothing can be more fallacious. It is demonstrated by recent facts that Burr is *solicitous* to *keep* upon *Antifederal ground,* to avoid compromising himself by any engagements with the Federalists. With or without such engagements he will easily persuade his former friends that he does stand on that ground, & after their first resentment they will be glad to rally under him. In the mean time he will take care not to disoblige them & he will always court those among them who are best fitted for tools. He will never choose to lean on good men because he knows that they will never support his bad projects; but instead of this he will endeavor to disorganize both parties & to form out of them a third composed of men fitted by their characters to be conspirators, & instruments of such projects. That this will be his future conduct may be inferred from his past plan, &

from the admitted quality of irregular ambition. Let it be remembered that Mr. Burr has never appeared solicitous for fame, & that great Ambition unchecked by principle, or the love of Glory, is an unruly Tyrant which never can keep long in a course which good men will approve. As to the last point—The proposition is against the experience of all times. Ambition without principle never was long under the guidance of good sense. Besides that, really the force of Mr. Burr's understanding is much overrated. He is far more *cunning* than *wise,* far more *dexterous* than *able.* In my opinion he is inferior in real ability to Jefferson. There are also facts against the supposition. It is past all doubt that he has blamed me for not having improved the situation I once was in to change the Government. That when answered that this could not been done without guilt—he replied—"Les grands ames se soucient peu des petits morceaux"*—that when told the thing was never practicable from the genius and situation of the country, he answered, "that depends on the estimate we form of the human passions and of the means of influencing them." Does this prove that Mr. Burr would consider a scheme of usurpation as visionary. The truth is with great apparent coldness he is the most sanguine man in the world. He thinks every thing possible to adventure and perseverance. And though I believe he will fail, I think it almost certain he will attempt usurpation. And the attempt will involve great mischief.

Gouverneur Morris to Alexander Hamilton WASHINGTON, D.C., JANUARY 26, 1801

[The members of the House of Representatives] consider the Candidates as equal in Worth or (if you like the other Mode of Expression best) as equally void of it with this Difference that Mr. Burr's Defects do not arise from Want of Energy and Vigor. They believe that to Courage he joins Generosity and cannot be branded with the Charge of Ingratitude.

Gouverneur Morris to Robert R. Livingston MARCH 18, 1802

Burr is trying to place himself well with us, and his measures are not without some success. His friends the democrats fear and hate him, and he knows it.

*Great souls worry little about small morsels.

William Dickson to Andrew Jackson WASHINGTON, D.C.,
DECEMBER 10, 1802

The popularity of the President [Jefferson] continues to increase.
But the Vice President has lost irretrievably the confidence of the
American People.

Manasseh Cutler to Joseph Torrey WASHINGTON, D.C., MARCH
13, 1804

The [impeachment] trial of Judge Pickering was closed yesterday, and sentence of condemnation passed—ayes, 20, nays, 10.
This trial, so far as respects mere forms, has been conducted with
much dignity and solemnity. This is wholly owing to Mr. Burr.
He presides in the Senate in a manner which reflects much honor
and respectability upon him as a man of taste and judgment.

William Plumer, Memorandum NOVEMBER 7, 1804

This day the Senate made a quorum for the first time this session. Mr. Burr, the Vice President, appeared and took his seat in
the Senate the very first day of the session. It has been unusual
for the Vice President to take his seat the first day of the session.
But this man, though indicted in New York & New Jersey for the
murder of the illustrious Hamilton, is determined to brave public
opinion. What a humiliating circumstance that a man Who for
months has fled from justice—& who by the legal authorities is
now accused of murder, should preside over the first branch of
the National Legislature!

I have avoided him—his presence to me is odious—I have
merely bowed & spoken to him—Federalists appear to despise,
neglect & abhor him. The democrats, at least many of them, appear attentive to him—& he is very familiar with them—What line
of conduct they will generally observe to him is yet uncertain.

Thomas C. Cushing to Manasseh Cutler SALEM, MASS.,
NOVEMBER 15, 1804

It is a matter of curiosity and inquiry, whether that —— Burr will
have the audacity to take his seat in the Senate, and, if he does,
how will he be received and treated by that body. Can they submit to the degradation of the presidency of a man lying under
the legal imputation of murder? Will not N. jersey claim him as a

fugitive from justice? Will not an impeachment be moved against him in your House? But, doubtless, impeachment against ten judges would be voted, before one would be against a murderer.

Thomas Jefferson, "Anas" 1804

I had never seen Colo. Burr till he came as a member of the Senate. His conduct very soon inspired me with distrust. I habitually cautioned Mr. Madison against trusting him too much. I saw afterwards that under Genl. W[ashington]'s and Mr. A[dams]'s administrations, whenever a great military appointment or a diplomatic one was to be made, he came post to Philadelphia to show himself & in fact that he was always at market, if they had wanted him. He was indeed told by Dayton in 1800 he might be Secretary at War; but this bid was too late. His election as V.P. was then foreseen. With these impressions of Colo. Burr there never had been any intimacy between us, and but little association. When I destined him for a high appointment, it was out of respect for the favor he had obtained with the republican party by his extraordinary exertions and successes in the N.Y. election in 1800.

John Quincy Adams to Louisa Catherine Adams QUINCY, JULY 19, 1804

The conduct of Mr. Burr through the whole affair [the challenge and duel with Alexander Hamilton] appears to me strongly to corroborate that opinion of his character which his enemies have long ascribed to him.

William Plumer, Memoranda DECEMBER 5, 1804

'Tis now more than a month since we have been in session, & day by day, when in the Senate Chamber, have I attentively watched the conduct of Aaron Burr. After the minutes of the preceding day have been read—the little business before us dispatched— he would leave the chair—come to one Senator, & intimate in strong terms that it was best to adjourn—& sometimes request a senator to move an adjournment—& in a few moments he was gone—He appears to have lost those easy graceful manners that beguiled the hours away the last session—He is now uneasy, discontented, & hurried.—So true it is, "Great guilt never knew great joy at heart." What course he will take after the 3d of march is very uncertain—He can never I think rise again. But surely he is a very extraordinary man, & is an exception to all rules.—No man is better fitted to brow beat or cajole public opinion. And considering of what material the mass of men are formed—how easily they are gulled—& considering how little restraint laws human or divine have on his mind is impossible to say what he will attempt—or what he may obtain.

FEBRUARY 28, 1805

The Vice President is an ambitious man—he aspired to the Presidency—disappointed ambition will be restless. You put arms into his hands to attack your government—He may disseminate seditious pamphlets, newspapers & letters at the expense of the very government he is destroying.

MARCH 2, 1805

At two O'clock Mr. Burr informed the Senate that he should now take leave of the Senate. His address was very correct & elegant & the sentiments very just.

He said he hoped that the Constitution of the U.S. would never be destroyed but he would venture to predict that if such an unfortunate event should ever take place, on this floor it would meet with its 1st & most noble defense—Here it would draw its last gasp.—This house is the last portion of the people, the last branch in the government that will abandon it.

As to his conduct in office—he said he had with great care endeavored to know no party—no friend or political enemy—He had acted with promptitude & decision—that he thought this more correct although he might thereby sometimes err—than a wavering undecisive conduct—which would stamp ignorance on him & produce confusion & insubordination in the Senate. He had in that promptitude no doubt sometimes wounded the feelings of an individual senator—on these occasions, which he trusted were few, he never had suffered any explanation at the time because the animation of the moment always rendered it improper. He was proud to say that during the four years he had presided he had never seen a single senator but what appeared anxious to support the authority of the Chair. That it was with great consolation he could review his official conduct & with conscious pride could say he had not degraded the dignity of that Chair which he now resigned to his successor. For each individual senator he entertained & felt a spirit of friendship, & he trusted that the regret on parting was mutual.

He bowed & retired—several shed tears very plentifully.

MARCH 2, 1806

For a long time it has been bandied about from New Hampshire to Georgia in the newspapers &c that Aaron Burr was to be appointed Envoy Extraordinary & Minister plenipotentiary to Great Britain. I have Myself given no credit to the relation. Mr. Jefferson has no confidence in him. He knows him to be capable of the darkest measures—a designing dangerous man.

APRIL 4, 1806

[Vermont senator Stephen Roe Bradley said] That Mr. Jefferson was a visionary man—never qualified for the presidency—That we must now turn our attention to an eastern man—That Rufus King would make a good president—that Burr a better. That Mr. Jefferson had explicitly told him he would not be a candidate at the next election.

NOVEMBER 30, 1806

In after visits I became more particularly attentive to the language of Mr. Burr—& I found he possessed the talent of making an impression of an opinion upon the subject, on the person with whom he conversed, without explicitly stating or necessarily giving his sentiments thereon. In every thing he said or did, he had a design—& perhaps no man's language was ever so apparently explicit, & at the same time so covert & indefinite.

DECEMBER 24, 1806

I am still at a loss to know what Burr is doing—& to what object he is driving.

As a conspirator—or as a politician—he has a fault—he is too cunning—too secret—even in business where frankness & openness would not injure him. The reputation of being a *cunning* man, is enough to blast any man's popularity—It at once renders him an object of suspicion. Burr's lawful business always appears enveloped in mystery. This trait in his character is strong, & marks all his conduct.

Thomas Jefferson to Charles Clay WASHINGTON, D.C., JANUARY 11, 1807

Burr's enterprise is the most extraordinary since the days of Don Quixote. It is so extravagant that those who know his understanding, would not believe it if the proofs admitted doubt. He has meant to place himself on the throne of Montezuma, and extend his empire to the Allegheny, seizing on New Orleans as the instrument of compulsion for our western States.

William Plumer, Memorandum JANUARY 15, 1807

This evening my colleague, Nicholas Gilman, told me, That Mr. Jefferson a few days since informed him, That the last winter Aaron Burr made several visits to him—& requested that as he was out of employ that the President would give him an appointment as minister to some foreign court. That at the last visit, Mr. Burr pressed the subject—The President then replied to him— You once had my confidence—the people & myself have now lost that confidence they had in you—I cannot therefore gratify you with an appointment. Burr then intimated to the President, that he would find he had it in his power to do Mr. Jefferson much injury.

John Adams to Benjamin Rush FEBRUARY 2, 1807

What shall I say of the Democratical Vice-President and the Federal would-be President, Burr? Although I never thought so highly of his natural talents or his acquired attainments as many of both parties have represented them, I never believed him to be a fool. But he must be an idiot or a lunatic if he has really planned and attempted to execute such a project as is imputed to him.

Thomas Jefferson to Robert R. Livingston WASHINGTON, D.C., MARCH 24, 1807

Burr has indeed made a most inglorious exhibition of his much over-rated talents. He is now on his way to Richmond for trial.

Thomas Jefferson to Unknown WASHINGTON, D.C., MARCH 25, 1807

Burr is on his way to Richmond for trial. No man's history proves better the value of honesty.

Benjamin Rush to John Adams PHILADELPHIA, APRIL 3, 1807

I concur with you in your reflections upon the western insurrection, but not altogether in your opinion of Colonel Burr's objects. "Prudence in enterprises and even common business and a guilty conscience," Sully long ago remarked in his character of Count Byron, "are generally incompatible." Burr's plans have been directed like doctors' prescriptions by *pro re nata* circumstances.* I will give you a specimen of them. He applied indirectly to Governor McKean for the chief-justiceship of Pennsylvania just before he set off for Kentucky last year. Success here was as improbable as revolutionizing the western states. "To be unfortunate," says Richelieu, "is to be imprudent." The history of Colonel Burr's pursuits verifies this remark. He failed 1st. in obtaining a foreign embassy the first year he took his seat in the Senate; 2. in supplanting Mr. Jefferson; 3. in obtaining the government of New York [as governor]; 4. in his western enterprises, and 5. in being chief justice of Pennsylvania. There is often something said or done by men in their youth that marks their destiny in life. I attended the commencement at Princeton at which Mr. Burr took his degree. He was then between 16 and 17 years of age. He spoke an elegant oration and with great spirit upon "Building Castles in the Air," in which he exposed its folly in literary, political, and military pursuits.

Thomas Jefferson to William Branch Giles MONTICELLO, APRIL 20, 1807

Against Burr, personally, I never had one hostile sentiment. I never indeed thought him an honest, frank-dealing man, but considered him as a crooked gun, or other perverted machine, whose aim or stroke you could never be sure of. Still while he possessed the confidence of the nation, I thought it my duty to respect in him their confidence, & to treat him as if he deserved it.

William Plumer, Memorandum JUNE 22, 1807

Alexander Hamilton, who fell by his shot, once said to an acquaintance of mine (*Jona. Mason, Esq.*) "The talents of Mr. Burr are over-rated—the world will ere long know it—His arguments at the bar were concise—his address was pleasing, his manners

*According to the present appearances.

were more, they were fascinating. When I analyzed his arguments I could not discover in what his greatness consisted. But
his ambition is unlimited." Mr. Mason stated these observations
of Hamilton to me this day.

Benjamin Rush to John Adams PHILADELPHIA, JULY 9, 1807

Colonel Burr retains in his confinement his usual good spirits.
He is nondescript in the history of human nature. Should he be
acquitted [of treason], you say he may yet be President of the
United States. It is possible. Some worse men hold high appointments in every part of our country.

John Adams to Samuel B. Malcolm QUINCY, AUGUST 6, 1812

Colonel Burr, Attorney-General Burr, Senator Burr, Vice-
President Burr, almost President Burr, has returned to New York
[from abroad]. What is to be his destiny?

James Wilkinson, **Memoirs of My Own Times** 1816

At taking leave, I observed to him [Alexander Hamilton], "well,
Sir, having fatigued you with my prattle, I now propose to visit
an old friend whom I have not seen for several years. I know you
are twain in politics, but I hope there is no disagreement between
you, which might render the renewal of my acquaintance with
him indecorous to my superior officer"; he asked me if it was
"Lamb," meaning Colonel [John] Lamb, I replied in the negative, and named Colonel Burr. "Little Burr," said he, "Oh no, we
have always been opposed in politics but always on good terms,
we set out in the practice of the law at the same time, and took
opposite political directions. Burr beckoned me to follow him,
and I advised him to come with me; we could not agree, but I
fancy he now begins to think he was wrong and I was right."

James Kent, Memoirs

Colonel Burr was acute, quick, terse, polished, sententious, and
sometimes sarcastic in his forensic discussions. He seemed to
disdain illustration and expansion, and confined himself with
stringency to the point in debate.

Samuel Chase

1741–1811

⫸ BORN IN Somerset County, Md. Lawyer. Maryland Assembly, 1765–66, 1768–71, 1773–77, 1777–88. Radical leader. Member Maryland committee of correspondence, 1773–75. Delegate to Continental Congress, 1774–78; signed Declaration of Independence. Member of committee sent to Canada, 1776. Charged with using privileged information to try to corner flour market, 1778. Opposed U.S. Constitution; voted against ratification in Maryland Convention, 1788. Judge, Maryland General Court, 1791–96. Associate justice, U.S. Supreme Court, 1796–1811. Impeached, 1804, but acquitted.

John Adams, Diary PHILADELPHIA, OCTOBER 10, 1774.
Chase speaks warmly.

John Adams, Diary SEPTEMBER 15, 1775
Upon recollecting the Debates of this Day in Congress, there appears to me a remarkable Want of Judgment in some of our Members. Chase is violent and boisterous, asking his Pardon. He is tedious upon frivolous Points.

SEPTEMBER 18, 1775
In the afternoon Mr. S.A. [Samuel Adams] and I made visit at Mrs. Bedford's to the Maryland Gentlemen. We found Paca and Chase and a polite Reception from them. Chase is ever social and talkative. He seems in better Humor, than he was before the

Adjournment. His Colony have acted with Spirit in Support of the Cause. They have formed themselves into a System and enjoined an Association, if that is not an Absurdity.

John Adams to James Warren PHILADELPHIA, FEBRUARY 11, 1776

Chace is a Man of common sense.

John Adams to James Warren FEBRUARY 18, 1776

Dr. Franklin, and Mr. Chase of Maryland, and Mr. Charles Carroll of Carrollton, are chosen a Committee to go to Canada. I must confess I have very great Confidence, in the Abilities and Integrity, the Political Principles and good Disposition of this Committee. . . .

Chase is in younger Life, under forty; But deeply impressed with a sense of the Importance of securing Canada, very active, eloquent, spirited, and capable.

Charles Carroll of Carrollton to Charles Carroll Sr. PHILADELPHIA, JULY 29, 1776

I hope Mr. [Thomas] Johnson is secure of a seat [in Congress]. Chase I know is—& I know these two men have the will & power to be useful.

John Adams to Horatio Gates PHILADELPHIA, AUGUST 13, 1776

I showed your last Letter to Mr. Chase, who begged it to write you an answer. I have exactly the same Idea of him, which you express. He had the good of the Service at Heart, but was too Sanguine, and had too little Experience in such Scenes, and too little Penetration into the Characters of Men.

Mayor and Aldermen of Annapolis, Md. DURING REVOLUTION

[Chase was a] busy, restless incendiary, a Ringleader of Mobs—a foul-mouth'd and inflaming son of Discord and Faction—a common Disturber of the public Tranquility, and a Promoter of the lawless excesses of the multitude.

William Williams to Ezekiel Williams PHILADELPHIA, AUGUST 23, 1776

[Chase is] a most bold, voluble & overbearing man.

Samuel Chase to John Sullivan DECEMBER 24, 1776

I hope America will never submit to the Tyrant of Britain. I declare as an Individual I would rather become a Subject of France, but I am afraid all my Countrymen are not of my stubborn Temper. The sullen unrelenting Monarch of Britain should never lord it over me.—I despise, I hate, and wish to destroy him, and all such Tyrants.

Charles Carroll of Annapolis to Charles Carroll of Carrollton
NOVEMBER 7, 1777

I wrote to Chase with reflection and Cool deliberation. I do & must continue to look upon Him as a Rogue unworthy the Society of Honest Men unless He acknowledges His fault & endeavors Sincerely to Atone for it.

Charles Carroll of Carrollton to Charles Carroll of Annapolis
NOVEMBER 25, 1777

Chase is too impetuous & gives his adversaries by this a great advantage over him.

Louis Guillaume Otto, Biographies FALL, 1788

Elder member of Congress. Man of superior talents, as much for jurisprudence as for legislation, but whose moral character has often been attacked, without his excuses ever fully justifying himself.

Matthew Ridley to John Jay, Susquehanna, Md. SEPTEMBER 7, 1789

I forgot when with you to mention Mr. Samuel Chase—I wish if it should lay in your Power to save him that you would—He has a large Family—has met with many hard Rubs, and I believe at this Time feels heavily the weight of his Family from the difficulty of making such a provision for them as he might heretofore have reasonably expected—He has on many Occasions been a useful Man in our public Affairs—I have never had any Conversation with him but am led to believe he would willingly accept the appointment of one of the Supreme Judges—He gets rather too much advanced in Life for the drudgery of the Law—If a Judge should be taken out of this State I know no Man more proper—His Abilities as a Lawyer, or Integrity in the profession I have never heard questioned—His uprightness as a Judge in this state (of the Criminal Court) has been much approved—Added to this I am informed that Mr. Harrison, who would in all probability be the Person preferred to any other in this state, is satisfied with his present Office of Judge of our General Court—

Alexander Contee Hanson, Description of Chase

I am constrained by candour to declare, that vile as Chase has been held by most of the better kind of his fellow Citizens, he has been the mover of almost every thing, this State has to boast of. Strange inconsistent man! Without him, how very seldom would any thing good have passed the Legislature, and yet could he *always* have prevailed, how soon would he have defeated every thing good which has been done! . . . I have viewed him with admiration and with horror, with kindness and with detestation. In the main I always liked tho' never would I trust him for more than a single turn.

George Washington to Alexander Hamilton PHILADELPHIA, OCTOBER 29, 1795

Mr. Chase of Maryland is, unquestionably, a man of abilities; and it is supposed by some, that he would accept the appointment of Attorney General. Though opposed to the adoption of the Constitution, it is said he has been a steady friend to the general government since it has been in operation. But he is violently opposed in his own State by a party, and is besides, or to speak more correctly has been; accused of some impurity in his conduct.

John Adams to Abigail Adams FEBRUARY 6, 1796

Mr. Chase is a new Judge, but although a good 1774 Man his Character has a Mist about it of suspicion and Impurity which gives occasion to the Enemy to censure. He has been a warm Party Man, and has made many Enemies. His Corpulency . . . is against his riding Circuit very long.

Oliver Wolcott Sr. to Oliver Wolcott Jr. LITCHFIELD, CONN., FEBRUARY 15, 1796

I knew Samuel Chase, and to you I will say, that I have but an unworthy opinion of him.

Abigail Adams to John Adams QUINCY, FEBRUARY 21, 1796

I am very sorry that Judge Cushing has refused his appointment [as chief justice]. Chase is not a Man from all I have heard, who will make Mr. Jay's place good. "How can a judge enforce that Law against some poor elf Which conscience tells him, he hath broke himself?" The fountain of Justice should be as Virgin innocence. The Laws can neither be administered or respected, if the minister of them is not unspotted.

Bushrod Washington to James Iredell ALEXANDRIA, VA.,
AUGUST 20, 1799

I went from and returned to Baltimore with our Brother Chace, whose excellent flow of spirits & good sense rendered pleasant a Journey which would otherwise have been fatiguing & disagreeable.

Benjamin Rush, Sketches 1800

This man's life and character were a good deal checkered. He rendered great services to his country by awakening and directing the public spirit of his native State in the first years of the Revolution. He possessed more learning than knowledge, and more of both than judgment. His person and attitude in speaking were graceful, and his elocution commanding, but his speeches were more oratorical than logical. He always voted with the friends to Independence. In the year 1778 he made his public station subservient to his private views, and exhibited marks of a mind tainted with that spirit of speculation which at that time pervaded nearly all ranks of citizens of the United States.

Stevens Thomson Mason to James Madison PHILADELPHIA,
APRIL 23, 1800

Thos. Cooper of Northumberland was tried and convicted on Saturday last for a libel on the President. A more oppressive and disgusting proceeding I never saw. Chase in his charge to the Jury (in a speech of an hour) showed all the zeal of a well fee'd Lawyer and the rancor of a vindictive and implacable enemy.

Philadelphia Aurora JUNE 20, 1800

Judge Chase [is] An Unprincipled tyrant, totally unfit to be intrusted with any power over the lives or liberties of the free citizens of America.

John Adams to John Marshall QUINCY, AUGUST 7, 1800

The Merit of Judge Chase, of which I have been a Witness at times for Six and twenty years are very great in my estimation: and if his son's [Thomas Chase] are as well qualified as others, it is quite consistent with my Principles to consider the sacrifices and services of a Father, in weighing the Pretensions of a Son. The Old Gentleman will not probably last very long, and it can hardly be called accumulating offices in a Family, to appoint the son of a Judge of the United States, Marshall of a particular state.

John G. Jackson to James Madison CLARKSBURG, VA., SEPTEMBER 25, 1800

But stop! I must not forget that a Sedition Law and a modern Jeffreys* (alias Chase) are in existence.

Wilmington, Del., Mirror of the Times NOVEMBER 15, 1800

Naturally proud, imperious, & overbearing—positive in his dogmas—supercilious in his manners—prejudiced in his decisions—and headstrong in his opinions.

William Charles Cole Claiborne to Andrew Jackson NEAR NATCHEZ, MISSISSIPPI TERRITORY, MARCH 20, 1802

The impeachment and conviction of the American Jeffries (Samuel Chase) will I flatter myself, all be announced, in a few weeks.

Manasseh Cutler to F. Poole WASHINGTON, D.C., FEBRUARY 13, 1804

Judge Chase (one of the largest men I ever saw) is as remarkable for the largeness as Johnny [John Randolph of Roanoke] for the smallness of his size.

William Plumer, Memorandum MARCH 2, 1805

The removal of Judge Chase was deemed an imprudent measure—public opinion so far as it could be collected was decidedly

---

*George Jeffreys was a seventeenth-century English judge who despotically ruled from the bench and disregarded constitutional forms.

opposed to the measure. In this case a great point is gained in favor of the Constitution. A prosecution commenced with the rage of party has been arrested—& to the honor of the Accused his political foes his enemies have acquitted him.

Joseph Story to Matthew Bramble PHILADELPHIA, JUNE 10, 1807

Accompanied by Mr. Harper, I paid a visit to Judge Chase, who is a rough, but very sensible man. He has counted nearly seventy winters, and yet possesses considerable vigor and vivacity; but the flashes are irregular and sometimes ill-directed. In his person, he is tall, and not unlike [Theophilus] Parsons [i.e., corpulent]. I suspect he is the American Thurlow,—bold, impetuous, overbearing, and decisive.* He received us very kindly and with all his plainness of manners, I confess that he impressed me with respect.

Joseph Story to Samuel P. P. Fay WASHINGTON, D.C., FEBRUARY 25, 1808

Of Chase I have formerly written. On a nearer view, I am satisfied that the elements of his mind are of the very first excellence; age and infirmity have in some degree impaired them. His manners are coarse, and in appearance harsh; but in reality he abounds with good humor. He loves to croak and grumble, and in the very same breath he amuses you extremely by his anecdotes and pleasantry. His first approach is formidable, but all difficulty vanishes when you once understand him. In person, in manners, in unwieldy strength, in severity of reproof, in real tenderness of heart; and above all in intellect, he is the living, I had almost said the exact image of Samuel Johnson. To use a provincial expression, I like him hugely.

---

*Edward Thurlow, first Baron Thurlow, British jurist and statesman, was known as the dictator of the House of Lords.

George Clinton
1739–1812

⚘ BORN IN Little Britain, Ulster County, N.Y. Served on privateer and in militia during French and Indian War. Studied law in New York City with William Smith Jr. (who had defended John Peter Zenger); admitted to bar, 1764; and began practice in Ulster County. Clerk, Ulster County Court of Common Pleas, 1759–1812. Member, colonial Assembly, 1768–75; Continental Congress, 1775–76 (left for military duty before Declaration of Independence was signed); Provincial Convention, 1775; and Third and Fourth Provincial congresses, 1776–77. Brigadier general in militia, 1775–77, and Continental army, 1777–83; brevet major general, Continental army, 1783. Governor, 1777–95, 1801–4. Vice president, New York Society for the Manumission of Slaves, 1785. Member for Ulster County, New York Convention, 1788, and as president did not vote. Unsuccessful candidate for U.S. vice president, 1788, 1792. Member, state Assembly, 1800–1801. U.S. vice president from 1805 until his death. Candidate for U.S. president, 1808. Alleged to have written "Cato" essays during ratification debate.

Edward Rutledge to John Jay PHILADELPHIA, JUNE 29, 1776
[In the Second Continental Congress] Clinton has Abilities but is silent in general and wants (when he does speak) that Influence to which he is entitled.

Philip Schuyler to John Jay ALBANY, JUNE 30, 1777

General Clinton I am informed has a majority of votes for the Chair [i.e., governor of New York]. If so he has played his cards better than was expected.

FORT EDWARD, JULY 14, 1777

I hope Gen. Clinton's having the chair of Government will not cause any divisions amongst the friends of America. Altho' his family and connections do not entitle him to so distinguished a predominance; yet he is virtuous and loves his country, has abilities and is brave, and hope he will experience from every patriot what I am resolved he shall have from me, support, countenance and comfort.

Alexander Hamilton to Israel Putnam CORYELL'S FERRY, N.J., JULY 30, 1777

General Clinton informs His Excellency [George Washington], that he is called to attend at Kingston and take the oath of office conformable to his appointment as Governor of the State of New York. It is to be regretted that so useful an officer is obliged to leave the posts under his superintendency at a time like this.

George Washington to the New York Council of Safety PHILADELPHIA, AUGUST 4, 1777

The appointment of General Clinton to the government of your state is an event that in itself gives me great pleasure, and very much abates the regret I should otherwise feel for the loss of his services in the Military line. That Gentleman's character is such as will make him peculiarly useful at the head of your state in a situation so alarming and interesting as it at present experiences.

Alexander Hamilton to Robert R. Livingston HEADQUARTERS NEAR GERMANTOWN, PA., AUGUST 7, 1777

In a Conversation I lately had with Mr. Jay he mentioned sending Governor Clinton with all the New York Militia of the upper part of your State to assist in opposing Mr. Burgoyne. I wish you may do this of all things. General Clinton is an excellent officer, the people have Confidence in him, will once act with zeal and Serve with Spirit & perseverance under him; his being wanted in the

Civil line should be no Objection. It imports you more to take measures for preserving your State than for Governing what you may not long have to Govern. Governor Clinton I am persuaded can render you the most Essential Services in the way proposed.

George Washington to Israel Putnam BUCKS COUNTY, AUGUST 11, 1777

I am glad to hear that Govr Clinton has determined to resume the command of Fort Montgomery, for there cannot be a properer Man upon every Account.

Henry Laurens to the Marquis de Lafayette YORK, PA., OCTOBER 12, 1777

He is a brave Officer in the field, cautious & timid only upon paper, therefore I am not diffident of his success.

Alexander Hamilton to Susanna Livingston MIDDLEBROOK, N.J., MARCH 18, 1779

I shall therefore only tell you, that whether the governor & the general are more honest, or more perverse, than other people, they have a very odd knack of thinking alike; and it happens in the present case, that they both equally disapprove the intercourse [of people back and forth into British-held territory].

Nathanael Greene to Udny Hay FISH KILL, N.Y., NOVEMBER 9, 1779

I have wrote the Governor on the subject [of the workers' demand for higher pay], who I know has great influence over the minds of every Class of people in this State, and whose good will towards the [Quartermaster's] Department I have had many proofs of.

Udny Hay to Nathanael Greene MORRISTOWN, N.J., DECEMBER 14, 1779

I agree with you, in opinion, respecting the influence of the Governor that it is great; but the people are not so patriotic or so warmly attached to the Governor as to sacrifice their property, to comply with an unreasonable request from him. I am sensible the Inhabitants (that is) certain classes of them, will do everything that is reasonable for you to ask, or them to comply with; but it cannot be expected that they will beggar themselves, for the National benefit upon a principle of private obligation.

Marquis de Lafayette, Memoir of 1779

He found George Clinton, the governor of the state of New York, resolute, enlightened, and cooperative.

John Morin Scott to Ezra L'Hommedieu PHILADELPHIA, JUNE 6, 1780

I think the Governor's presence in the upper part of the Country is highly necessary; and flatter myself that his good Sense & military active Spirit will have salutary Effects.

Alexander Hamilton to Robert Morris ALBANY, AUGUST 13, 1782

There is no man in the government [of the state of New York] who has a decided influence in it. The present governor has declined in popularity, partly from a defect of qualifications for his station and partly from causes that do him honor—the vigorous execution of some necessary laws that bore hard upon the people, and severity of discipline among the militia. He is, I believe, a man of integrity and passes with his particular friends for a statesman; it is certain that without being destitute of understanding, his passions are much warmer, than his judgment is enlightened. The preservation of his place is an object to his private fortune as well as to his ambition; and we are not to be surprised, if instead of taking a lead in measures that contradict a prevailing prejudice, however he may be convinced of their utility, he either flatters it or temporizes; especially when a new election approaches.

Marquis de Chastellux, Travels in North-America, in the Years 1780, 1781, and 1782

I only regretted not having seen Governor Clinton, for whom I had letters of recommendation. He is a man who governs with the utmost vigor and firmness, and is inexorable to the tories, whom he makes tremble, though they are very numerous: he has had the address to maintain in its duty this province, one extremity of which borders on Canada, the other on the city of New York.

George Washington to George Clinton MOUNT VERNON,
NOVEMBER 25, 1784

A few days ago I had the pleasure to receive your favor of the
12th Instant. Altho' I felt pain from your Silence, I should have
imputed it to any cause rather than a diminution of friendship.
The warmth of which I feel too sensibly *for* you, to harbor a suspicion of the want of it *in* you, without being conscious of having
given cause for the change—having ever flattered myself that our
regards were reciprocal.

Philip Schuyler to John Jay ALBANY, MAY 30, 1785

It is conceived now that the business of a reform in a government
cannot be accomplished unless Mr. Clinton is ousted, and it is
therefore determined to attempt a change and almost every character of respectability and indeed a great majority of all ranks will
support the attempt. But who is to be the person? It is agreed
that none have a chance of succeeding but you, the Chancellor
or myself. The second on account of the prejudices against his
family name, it is believed would fail. With respect to me, altho'
I should carry a majority of at least fifteen hundred voices in this
and Montgomery County and some in Washington, yet I am so
little known in the Southern part of this state that I should fail
there. Besides this reason, which suffices with my friends here as
well as myself, there is another arising from my great and many
bodily infirmities which render me incapable of that attention
which the office requires. I therefore could not accept of it even if
unanimously offered. Hence the wishes of me and my friends are
directed to you, and we have not only sanguine but well founded
hopes, that you will obtain a great majority.*

David Humphreys to Thomas Jefferson HARTFORD, JUNE 5,
1786

Governor Clinton is said to have become an Antifederalist. He
was not in N. York when I was there. Certain it is the issue of a
paper currency in that State depended upon him.

---

*Clinton ran unopposed for a fourth consecutive three-year term as governor
in 1786.

Luigi Castiglioni, Sketches of American Soldiers 1787

Some charge him with being very unsociable, with not spending in vain pomp, with failure to pay court to strangers. But if he occupies the time that he might give to conversation in attending to business, if he gives in charity to the poor the money that he would otherwise throw away in costly dinners and luxury, the nation must venerate this supposed defect as a virtue, and enlightened foreigners will be glad to see him sacrifice his time for the benefit of the state. In fact, the people do render him justice and speak of this man with great esteem. I did not have the fortune to meet him since he flees presentation to strangers, because they would distract him from his methodical manner of living; but persons who know him intimately assure me that he really deserves the praise given him, and that beyond the already mentioned fields of knowledge he possesses an extensive background in the sciences, which he cultivates in his hours of leisure.

Governor Clinton is about 50 years of age—or more. Both he and his wife are always simply dressed, and his office inspires in him no haughtiness or sense of superiority.

Alexander Hamilton, New York Daily Advertiser SEPTEMBER 15, 1787

There is no danger that the rights of a man, at the head of the Government (possessing all the influence to be derived from long continuance in office, the disposition of lucrative places, and *consummate talents* for popularity) can be injured by the voice of a private individual.

"Examiner," No. 2, New York Journal DECEMBER 14, 1787

Cato [George Clinton] has cast a net, which I believe will catch very few fish. He affects the appearance of a true son of liberty, but he is an hypocrite, and may be compared to a carved image with a double-head one within the other; the inner head cohering with the trunk or body, and the outer being moveable about the inner, and painted in front the color of an human face, not unlike the wooden heads exposed to view in a barber's shop.

Samuel Blachley Webb to Joseph Barrell NEW YORK, JANUARY 13, 1788

This City are very unanimous [in favor of the new Constitution]— but we have as you have before heard four or five characters violently opposed, none however whose influence is to be feared but Govr. Clinton's. His has been astonishingly great in the back country's, but is undoubtedly daily lessening.

St. John de Crèvecoeur to William Short NEW YORK, FEBRUARY 20, 1788

I flatter myself that the State at large is more strongly Federalist than the Members of both Houses [of the legislature]; if the Tide turns here in favor of the new Constitution down goes the Idol of the People, that tool of Popularity of which you have often heard me speak, our Governor I mean.

New York **Daily Advertiser** APRIL 26, 1788

The Antifederal Party in this city, despairing of success by open and fair exertions, at the ensuing Election, are industriously employed in procuring the suffrages of some of the citizens, by insidious personal applications. They pretend that they will not oppose the Federal Ticket, in order to lull into security the friends of order and good government. They hope by such unmanly conduct, to foist into the Convention, as the representation of New-York, the following list, or at least the *pendulum* of Antifederalism, the great Goliath of their party, his Ex——y G——r C——n.

Alexander Hamilton to James Madison NEW YORK, MAY 19, 1788

As Clinton is truly the leader of his party, and is inflexibly obstinate I count little on overcoming opposition [to the Constitution] by reason.

Alexander Hamilton to Gouverneur Morris NEW YORK, MAY 19, 1788

In this state, as far as we can judge, the elections [for the state ratifying convention] have gone wrong. The event however will not certainly be known till the end of the month. Violence rather than moderation is to be looked for from the opposite party. Obstinacy seems the prevailing trait in the character of its leader. The language is, that if all the other states adopt, this is to persist in refusing the Constitution. It is reduced to a certainty that Clinton has in several conversations declared the UNION unnecessary; though I have the information through channels which do not permit a public use to be made of it.

Abigail Adams Smith to Abigail Adams NEW YORK, JUNE 15, 1788

We are treated, here, with great politeness, civility, and friendship. We were invited to dine with the Governor, which was a *very particular* favour. He nor his family either visit, or are visited by, any families, either in public or private life, of this place. . . . That he is a man of no decided character, no one who sees him will say. To me he appears one whose conduct and motives of action are not to be seen through upon a slight examination. The part he has taken upon the subject of the new Constitution is much condemned. What are his motives, I do not pretend to judge; but I do believe that he acts or thinks without some *important* motives.

Alexander Hamilton to James Madison POUGHKEEPSIE, JULY 2, 1788

[On the debates in the New York ratifying convention.] Our arguments confound, but do not convince. Some of the leaders however appear to me to be convinced by circumstances and to be desirous of a retreat. This does not apply to the Chief, who wishes to establish Clintonism on the basis of Antifederalism.

Samuel Blachley Webb to Catherine Hogeboom NEW YORK, JULY 13, 1788

The Southern District are determined on a Separation to join the union, and I do not believe the life of the Governor & his party would be safe in this place.

Nicholas Gilman to John Langdon NEW YORK, JULY 17, 1788

This is merely to accompany the paper of the day, by which you will discover the temper of the Poughkeepsie Convention. They are still in session and the heart of their Pharaoh is still unrelenting.

Samuel Blachley Webb to Catherine Hogeboom NEW YORK, JULY 20, 1788

The Governor has rendered himself extremely obnoxious to the Inhabitants of this City, so much so, that they have lost all respect for him. However I shall be cautious not to render myself the personal enemy of him or any other Character;—God mend his ways.

Brissot de Warville, **New Travels in the United States of America** AUGUST, 1788

Governor Clinton . . . is anything but a man of learning.

Louis Guillaume Otto, Biographies FALL 1788

All the wealthy in the state of New York and all those who favor the new Constitution, cry loudly against Governor Clinton, a man of the people, who was governor during the war and who distinguished himself militarily. It is possible that to support his family [i.e., his party], Mr. Clinton flatters the people a little too much, that he speculates in public money, and that he works secretly against the establishment of the new Constitution. It is not less true that, of all his enemies, none is more truly attached to France and none has rendered us more essential services. I will even add that, with the exception of [Robert R.] Livingston, most of the *Federalists* of this state are attached to England or at least are very cool toward France. Mr. Clinton having been elected President of the New York Convention, he has fervently combated the efforts of the Federalists, and the amendments proposed by this state are much more prejudiced against the system of consolidation than those of the other states. Mr. Clinton's opinion is that Americans should be satisfied with tilling their fields without wanting to play a role in the world.

Robert R. Livingston to St. John de Crèvecoeur CLERMONT, DECEMBER 1788

The Governor has as you observe been long soured—He finds himself lessened in the esteem of the publick & tho' (which I think very probable) the strength of the antifederal party & the want of concert in the opposition may serve to continue him in office with all its emoluments loses many of its charms when it is not attended with the respect & favor of the people—

St. John de Crèvecoeur to Thomas Jefferson   NEW YORK, JANUARY 5, 1789

Our Governor who Sees That nothing can Stop the Federal Tide is very much Chagrined—He Loses daily Some degree of popularity among his Warmest Partisans who perceiving that, [in]spite of the Idea, they had of his abilities as well as of the righteousness of their Cause every thing goes against them begin to think him less Infallible & the New System less obnoxious.... our Governor is not a man of sufficient abilities to become the head of a Party.

John Lamb to John Smith   NEW YORK, JANUARY 7, 1789

The Federalists in Philadelphia, have got the horrors from an apprehension that Governor Clinton, will be elected Vice-President—This alarm (on their part) I believe must arise from some intelligence which it is probable they have received of the intentions of the Electors in the Southern States.—God grant, that their fears may be well grounded.

Joshua Atherton to John Lamb   AMHERST, N.H., FEBRUARY 23, 1789

To have rendered any service to so distinguished a patriot and ornament of his country as Governor Clinton, to have put it more in the power of his great abilities to secure to the United States freedom and happiness, to have placed him as one of the principal directors of the scene in so interesting a period would indeed have been rendering a service highly honorable to myself, and of the utmost importance to our tottering country.

To the Independent Electors of the State of New-York   MARCH 1788

But it is alleged, that he is parsimonious, and lives beneath the dignity of his station. Passion and prejudice are apt to put a false coloring on things. By these, frugality will be represented as parsimony, and temperance and regularity of living as meanness. It becomes the chief magistrate, in a republican government, to set an example of temperance, frugality, and simplicity of manners; such examples are eminently proper at this time in our country, and are really essential to its prosperity. Would it be agreeable to the citizens of this state to see the principal magistrate constantly engaged in a scene of dissipation and luxury? To see him employed in making feasts, or attending them; seldom, if ever, at leisure to pursue the important concerns of the state, and so difficult of access, as never to be seen, but in the company of those, whose rioting and intemperance in the excesses of the table are their only recommendation? This, we presume, can never be the wish of those citizens who feel themselves interested in preserving the morals of the people, and the welfare of the state. If the Governor errs, it is on the side of prudence and propriety, and we ought to think ourselves happy in this respect, that instead of having the first officer in the state, taking the lead in extravagance and dissipation, he is an example of decent frugality and orderly living.

"Cassius," Poughkeepsie Country Journal MARCH 3, 1789

Every scheme and artifice which can be devised are now using, and will be used to oust our present Governor at the next election, for no other reason but because he is a whig, a republican, a friend to the liberties of the common people, and a professed enemy to aristocracy; which he and all writers and thinkers upon the subject, justly esteem to be the most oppressive kind of government on earth. They can justly find no fault with his character, none with his public administration; and I believe that no one who is acquainted with the history of his life, will dare to accuse me of partiality, when I say I believe him to be one of the best public characters on the continent. From his (legal) infancy he has been in our assembly an able and steady asserter of the rights of the people, until the commencement of the late war, through which, amidst innumerable difficulties, he has defended them with equal activity, abilities and firmness in the field. Nor was his merit less conspicuous, in the peace and good order which immediately took place upon our taking possession of the southern district of this State, between the jarring elements which came together upon that occasion. When resentments ran so high as to threaten the destruction of part of the community, the peace was preserved, the dignity of government kept up, and the authority of the laws prevailed.—And what is now peculiar to his character, and distinguishes it from most of the shining ones of the time, is, that he does not ask, he does not wish, as a reward for his services, a surrender of those rights into his own hands, but still remains the same steady and sincere friend to the liberties of his country, and the same determined opposer of tyranny, whether it comes in the shape of a royal Prerogative, an act of Parliament, or in one less alarming, and consequently more dangerous.

Killian K. Van Renssalaer to Samuel Blachley Webb
CLAVERACK, N.Y., MARCH 14, 1789

I believe old Clinton the *sinner* will get *ousted* [as governor].

Samuel Blachley Webb to Catherine Hogeboom NEW YORK, MARCH 22, 1789

I am fully persuaded that we can have no Peace nor political happiness, until Mr. Clinton retires from the Administration.—If he ever had any Claims on his Country he is amply paid.

Samuel Blachley Webb to Killian K. Van Renssalaer NEW YORK, MARCH 22, 1789

I am favored with your letter of the 14th Instant, it gives me great pleasure to find the great people of Columbia [County] are in opinion with us, respecting a change in the Administration, and I haven't a doubt if the Northern Counties exert themselves we shall have the pleasure of hearing Judge [Robert] Yates announced our Governor.—It adds much to my satisfaction to hear that our friend Col. Hogeboom has thrown his influence into the scale, but wishes alone will not answer, you well know the art and cunning of Clinton and his party, and that they are using every possible exertion for his reelection. We must work double tides to defeat them. In this quarter we have nothing to fear. He is most heartily despised except by a few Sycophants whom he has put in office and their dependents "whose price of office has been obedience to their chief."

Federalist Committee of New York City (Alexander Hamilton), To the Independent and Patriotic Electors of the State of New York NEW YORK, APRIL 7, 1789

But when the Governor is objected to, as the head of a party, we presume, it is not on account of the side he took in the question concerning the new constitution. It is true, indeed, that the friends of that constitution are of opinion, that circumstances have attended the Governor's conduct in relation to it, before it appeared, after it appeared, and before its adoption, and even since its adoption, which savor of prejudice and intemperance, and subject him to suspicions derogatory to his prudence and patriotism. But the objection to him as the head of a party, reaches much further back than the new constitution. Discerning men, soon after the peace, perceived, that he had formed a close connection with a particular set of characters, in whose public and private views he was continually embarked.

It is asked, what could have been his object in thus devoting himself to a party? The answer is plain—to keep himself in place—to perpetuate himself in the enjoyment of the power and profit of the office he holds.

But it is asked again, why, if that was his wish, did he not connect himself with the wealthy and the great? These, it is pretended, would have been better instruments of a scheme of personal aggrandizement.

Such a suggestion has scarcely the merit of plausibility. It is well known, that large property is an object of jealousy in republics, and that those who possess it, seldom enjoy extensive popularity. The Governor was aware that he would have risked the loss, rather than have promoted the continuance of that which he possessed, by connecting himself with men of that class; and that his purpose could be better answered by an opposite course. Besides, from men who would suppose their pretensions not inferior to his, he would be more likely to experience competition and contradiction. The history of republics affords more examples of individuals arriving at dangerous pre-eminence, by a policy similar to that which seems to have been pursued by the Governor, than in any other mode.

William Grayson to Patrick Henry NEW YORK, JUNE 12, 1789

There has been a most severe attack upon Governor Clinton. He has been slandered and abused in all the public newspapers for these five months by men of the first weight and abilities in the state. Almost all the gentlemen, as well as all the merchants & mechanics, combined together to turn him out of his office: he has had nothing to depend on but his own integrity & the integrity of an honest yeomanry, who supported him against all his enemies. . . . As this gentleman is the great palladium of republicanism in this state, you may guess at the situation of anti-ism here, as he did not carry the election by more than 5 or 600.

George Lux to George Read BALTIMORE, JULY 28, 1789

I am also happy to learn, that Governor Clinton has abandoned his virulent opposition to the New Government & become moderate & dispassionate.

Thomas Jefferson to James Madison JUNE 21, 1792

[Speaking of Clinton's narrowly won contested victory over John Jay for governor in spring 1792.] It does not seem possible to defend Clinton as a just or disinterested man if he does not decline the Office [of governor] of which there is no symptom; and I really apprehend that the cause of republicanism will suffer and its votaries be thrown into schism by embarking it in support of this man [for vice president], and for what? To draw over the antifederalists who are not numerous enough to be worth drawing over.

Alexander Hamilton to Rufus King PHILADELPHIA, JUNE 28, 1792

I have not, as you will imagine, been inattentive to your political squabble. I believe you are right (though I have not accurately examined) but I am not without apprehension that a ferment may be raised which may not be allayed when you wish it. Tis not to be forgotten that the opposers of Clinton are the real friends to order & good Government; and that it will ill become them to give an example of the contrary.

Rufus King to Alexander Hamilton NEW YORK, JULY 10, 1792

But Mr. Clinton is in fact Governor, and though he may not be free from anxieties & Doubts [over the disputed gubernatorial election of 1792], he will not willingly relinquish the Office—the majority, and a very great one are against him—should he persist, and the sword be drawn, he must go to the wall—but this my dear Sir, is a dreadful alternative, and what & whom it may affect is altogether uncertain. If this case will justify a recurrence to first Principles, what are we not to expect from the disputes, which must & will arise in the Succession of the Presidency? And how are we able to place confidence in the security of our Government?

James Monroe to Thomas Jefferson WILLIAMSBURG, JULY 17, 1792

I was favored at Richmond with yours giving a statement of the votes & eventual decision upon the New York election. The declaration in favor of Clinton on the part of the convention was perhaps right, tho' it requires more accurate information of their election & sheriff laws to determine it than I possess. How far he might with propriety have declined the appointment, without an imputation upon the rectitude of the canvassers, seems doubtful—or what would have been the intermediate condition of the government, who have discharged the Executive functions, whether the legislature must have been convened to relieve them from the dilemma, are circumstances which merited attention & no doubt had weight in the decision. The terms however upon which he has accepted his re-election, are not flattering to him and cast an air upon the whole proceeding, which how fair soever it may have been, will give the adversary party an advantage they will not fail to avail themselves of. Certain it is with respect to this gentleman, that altho' as a center of union to the republican party in that State it may be necessary to support him, yet there are traits in his character and particularly that of extreme parsimony, which are highly exceptionable. No one would point to him as a model for imitation; but comparatively with others in that quarter, & especially his late competitor & confreres [Aaron Burr], I have no hesitation which to prefer. If an unequivocal fact is known & principles understood, altho' in some respects vicious, yet in any given situation you can determine his course and as the effect of the alloy may be ascertained, it may be guarded against.

Alexander Hamilton to John Adams PHILADELPHIA, AUGUST 16, 1792

[In speaking about Clinton's parsimoniousness.] You forgot that Mr. Clinton could feast upon what would starve another.

From Alexander Hamilton PHILADELPHIA, SEPTEMBER 21, 1792

Mr. Clinton's success [in winning the vice presidency] I should think very unfortunate. I am not for trusting the Government too much in the hands of its enemies. But still Mr. C—— is a man of property, and, in private life, as far as I know of probity.

Alexander Hamilton to John Steele PHILADELPHIA, OCTOBER 15, 1792

As to Mr. Clinton he is a man of narrow and perverse politics, and as well under the former as under the present Government, he has been steadily since the termination of the war with Great Britain opposed to national principles.

Oliver Wolcott Sr. to Oliver Wolcott Jr. MIDDLETOWN, CONN., DECEMBER 5, 1792

I am here, and have attended, with all the other electors of the state, the election of President and Vice President of the United States, and am happy to be able to inform you that upon counting their votes, they were united in their choice of President Washington and Vice President Adams. In this election, they were very cordial, and impressed with the deepest conviction of the propriety of continuing those officers in their present stations. The efforts which have been made to affect the election of the Vice President, I sincerely wish and trust, may be found effectual. I am certain that no choice could be more improper than that of George Clinton. I have a vile opinion of the man, and believe nothing but the grossest ignorance, or the most nefarious designs, could have proposed such a candidate. The enemies of Mr. Adams are mistaken if they conceive that George Clinton can ever engage a vote in this state. His friends in New York wish to give him an honorable retreat from the resentment of the majority of the people of the state; those who think unworthily of him, wish to remove him from the state government. It is melancholy to think that a government which has been found so beneficial in its operations, should be so soon attacked by a set of ambitious, partial and selfish men.

Abigail Adams to John Adams QUINCY, JANUARY 2, 1793

Amidst all that has been written upon the occasion [the vice presidential election], no one has ventured to State the comparative merits, and Services of the Candidates, but have contented themselves with saying that they would not bear a comparison that Clinton's were lighter than a feather when weighed against Yours.

John Adams to Abigail Adams PHILADELPHIA, DECEMBER 2, 1794

If Fame says true Clinton cares little for Popularity: for The Miser has made himself immensely rich, and all his Friends and Tools besides.

William Plumer, Memoranda JULY 16, 1805

For the first time George Clinton the Vice President took his seat in the Senate. He is an old feeble man—he appears altogether unacquainted with our rules—his voice is very weak & feeble—I cannot hear the one-half of what he says—he has a clumsy awkward way of putting a question—Preserves little or no order— What a vast difference between him & Aaron Burr! One would think that the office was made for Clinton, & not he for the office. This however being his first day it is to be hoped he will in time do better—though he is too old to make improvements.

DECEMBER 12, 1805

I am very confident the old gentleman will make a sorry figure as president of the Senate. Tho' he complained to me that the office was too inactive for him, yet, I fear, he will find it too laborious for his advanced age.

MARCH 15, 1806

Early this morning I called upon Mr. Clinton the Vice President & conversed with him in private for the space of two hours. I owe it to him—I owe it to myself—to say that the more I see & know of this man the more highly he rises in my estimation. He is an old man—time has impaired his mental faculties as much as it has the powers of his body. He is too old for the office he now holds; little as are its duties—he is from age rendered incapable of discharging them. He cannot preserve order—He frequently forgets the state of business before the Senate—he reads deliberately but his voice is too feeble to be distinctly heard. And he assured me that the sitting three hours in the Chair at a time was extremely fatiguing to him. But there is something venerable in his appearance—There is that pleasing cheerfulness—that easy access—that flow of good humor—& docile manners, that are so seldom found in men of his age—& which renders him, to me, a very interesting companion. He appears honest.

MARCH 1, 1807

Mr. Clinton, always comes to the city in his own carriage, accompanied by one of his daughters, & a servant. He is immensely rich—but lives out at board like a common member—keeps no table—or invites anybody to dine. A style of living unworthy of the 2d officer in our government.

He is old, feeble & altogether uncapable of the duty of presiding in the Senate. He has no mind—no intellect—no memory—He forgets the question—mistakes it—& not infrequently declares a vote before it's taken—& often forgets to do it after it is taken—Takes up new business while a question is depending.

Thomas Jefferson to Benjamin Rush POPLAR FOREST, AUGUST 17, 1811

It is wonderful to me that old men should not be sensible that their minds keep pace with their bodies in the progress of decay. Our old revolutionary friend Clinton, for example, who was a hero, but never a man of mind, is wonderfully jealous on this head. He tells eternally the stories of his younger days to prove his memory, as if memory and reason were the same faculty. Nothing betrays imbecility so much as the being insensible of it.

John Adams to the Printers of the **Boston Patriot** JUNE 1812

George Clinton has been one of the most important Characters, in the Nation. With a Strong Mind, a brave intrepid heart, with understanding and information enough to satisfy his Party, he has been supported by it with more Uniformity, Constancy and Perseverance than any Man in America. Hancock, Bowdoin, Sam Adams, Jay, Livingstons, Lees, Henry, Rutledges, Gadsdens, Pinckneys, Washington himself; no Man has ever been supported in North America like George Clinton. Washington himself with all his real Merit, all his Advantages of Person, Manners and Fortune, and all his millions of Puffers, all his Statues, Mausoleums and Benevolent Societies, nay with his ten thousand officers of his Army all sworn to trumpet him to the Skies; nay with all his funding systems and banking systems by which he chained all the avarice of the Nation to his Carr; Washington, himself has never been supported with the Steadiness that George Clinton, has uniformly held up.

James Kent to Mrs. Elizabeth Hamilton NEW YORK, DECEMBER 10, 1832

Though I felt strong political prejudices against Governor Clinton, as the leader of the Anti-Federal party, yet during the course of that Convention [that ratified the Constitution in 1788], I became very favorably struck with the dignity with which he presided, and with his unassuming and modest pretensions as a speaker. It was impossible not to feel respect for such a man, and for a young person not to be somewhat over-awed in his presence, when it was apparent in all his actions and deportment that he possessed great decision of character and a stern inflexibility of purpose.

John Dickinson
1732–1808

⊰ BORN IN Talbot County, Md. Family moved to Kent County, Del., 1740. Studied law in Philadelphia and at Middle Temple, London. Admitted to Philadelphia bar, 1757. Kent delegate to house and speaker, 1760–61. Philadelphia County delegate to assembly, 1762–65, 1774–77. Author of *The Late Regulations respecting the British Colonies* (1765). Pennsylvania delegate to Stamp Act Congress, 1765 (drafted declaration of rights). Author of "Letters from a Farmer in Pennsylvania," 1767–68. Philadelphia City delegate to assembly, 1770–71 (author of petition to the king, 1771). Pennsylvania delegate to Congress, 1774–76 (author of first and second petitions to the king, 1774, 1775; revised Thomas Jefferson's draft of Declaration of Taking up Arms, 1775; chairman of committee to draft Articles of Confederation, 1776; voted against resolution declaring independence and absent when Declaration of Independence was adopted, 1776). Chairman Philadelphia committee of correspondence, 1774. Chairman Pennsylvania committee of safety, 1775–76. Pennsylvania militia colonel, 1775–76. Philadelphia County delegate to Assembly, 1776–78 (resigned in dispute over new state constitution). Delaware delegate to Congress, 1779 (signed Articles of Confederation). New Castle member of council, 1781. President of Delaware, 1782–83. President Supreme Executive Council of Pennsylvania, 1783–85. Delaware delegate to and chairman of Annapolis Convention, 1786. Delaware delegate to Constitutional Convention, 1787. (George Read signed Constitution for him.) Author of "Fabius" letters supporting Constitution, 1788. President Delaware constitutional convention, 1792. Author of "Fabius" letters supporting continued alliance with France, 1797.

John Adams, Diary PHILADELPHIA, AUGUST 31, 1774

Made a Visit to Governor Ward of Rhode Island at his Lodgings. There We were introduced to several gentlemen.

Mr. Dickinson the Farmer of Pennsylvania, came to Mr. Ward's Lodgings to see us, in his Coach and four beautiful Horses. He was introduced to Us, and very politely said he was exceedingly glad to have the Pleasure of seeing these Gentlemen, made some Enquiry after the Health of his Brother and Sister, who are now in Boston. Gave us some Account of his late ill Health and his present Gout. This was the first Time of his getting out.

Mr. Dickinson has been Subject to Hectic Complaints. He is a Shadow—tall, but slender as a Reed—pale as ashes. One would think at first Sight that he could not live a Month. Yet upon a more attentive Inspection, he looks as if the Springs of Life were strong enough to last many Years.

Robert Treat Paine, Diary PHILADELPHIA, SEPTEMBER 12, 1774

We returned & dined at Mr. John Dickinson's, the Celebrated Farmer, whose Seat is 2½ miles from the City, & is a convenient, decent, elegant, Philosopher's Rural Retreat.

John Adams, Diary OCTOBER 24, 1774

Mr. Dickinson is very modest, delicate, and timid.

John Adams to James Warren PHILADELPHIA, JULY 24, 1775

A certain great Fortune and piddling Genius whose Fame has been trumpeted so loudly, has given a silly Cast to our whole Doings. We are between Hawk and Buzzard.

Robert Whitehill to Various Friends PHILADELPHIA, JUNE 10, 1776

Dickinson, Wilson, and the others, have Rendered themselves obnoxious to Every Whig in town, and Every Day of their Existence are losing the Confidence of the people.

Edward Rutledge to John Jay PHILADELPHIA, JUNE 29, 1776

I have been much engaged lately upon a plan of a Confederation which Dickenson has drawn. It has the Vice of all his Productions to a considerable Degree; I mean the Vice of Refining too much. Unless it is greatly curtailed it never can pass, as it is to be submitted to Men in the respective Provinces who will not be led or rather driven into Measures which may lay the Foundation of their Ruin.

John Adams to Jonathan Dickinson Sergeant PHILADELPHIA, JULY 21, 1776

What is the Cause, that Mr. Dickinson never can maintain his Popularity for more than two or three years together, as they tell me has ever been the Case! He may have a good Heart, and certainly is very ready with his Pen, and has a great deal of Learning, but his Head is not very long, nor clear.

Samuel Adams to James Warren PHILADELPHIA, DECEMBER 12, 1776

Non Resistance is the professed Principle of Quakers, but the Religion of many of them is to get money & sleep as the vulgar Phrase is, in a whole Skin. The Interest of the Proprietor is at Antipodes with that of America, at least I suppose he thinks so— and though he is apparently inactive, there are many Engines which he can secretly set to work. These are no doubt partly the Causes of the Evil. Besides there are many Tories here who have been for months past exciting a violent Contest among the well affected about their new form of Government on purpose to embitter their Spirits & divert their Attention from the great Cause. But the foundation of all was laid Months ago through the Folly, I will not say a harsher word of that excellent, superlatively wise and great Patriot D., who from the 10th of September 1774 to the 4th of July 1776 has been urging every Individual & Body of Men over whom he had any influence, the Necessity of making Terms of Accommodation with Great Britain. With this he has poisoned the Minds of the People, the Effect of which is a total Stagnation of the Power of Resentment, the utter Loss of every manly Sentiment of Liberty & Virtue. I give up this City & State for lost until recovered by other Americans.

Robert Morris to John Jay PHILADELPHIA, JANUARY 12, 1777

Dickinson & A. Allen have given mortal stabs to their own Characters & pity it is the wounds should penetrate any further, but they were men of property, Men of fair private Characters & what they have done, seems to pierce through their sides into the Vitals of those who have similar pretensions to Fortune & good Character. The defection of these men is supposed to originate in a desire to preserve their Estates & consequently glances a suspicion on all that have Estates to lose. I pity them both exceedingly. Dickinson's Nerves gave way & his fears dictated a letter to his Brother advising him not to receive Continental money. His Judgment & his virtue should have prevented this act of Folly, I call it such because I believe his Heart to be good & regret much that his exalted Character should be degraded, by what could hardly be called a crime at the time he did it, but he thought the Game was up.

William Hooper to Robert Morris BALTIMORE, FEBRUARY 1, 1777

I am much pleased with our Success against the foraging party, & the more so from General [Philemon] Dickinson having had the Command. He has laid up a kind of Reputation as a patriot & an officer which will be sufficient not only for himself for life but upon which his Brother the Farmer may make drafts to repair that loss of Credit into which a constitutional weakness of nerves has betrayed him & in which I sincerely believe his heart had no share.

John Adams to Abigail Adams APRIL 8, 1777

The F [i.e., the Farmer of Pennsylvania] turns out to be the Man, that I have seen him to be, these two Years. He is in total Neglect and Disgrace here. I am sorry for it, because of the forward Part he took, in the Beginning of the Controversy. But there is certainly such a Thing as falling away, in Politicks, if there is none in Grace.

John Adams, Diary JUNE 20, 1779

[The chevalier de La Luzerne] enquired after Mr. Dickinson, and the Reason why he disappeared. I explained, as well as I could in French, the Inconsistency of the Farmers Letters and his Perseverance in that Inconsistency in Congress. Mr. Dickinson's Opposition to the declaration of Independency, I ventured as modestly as I could to let him know that I had the Honour to be the Principal Disputant in Congress against Mr. Dickinson upon that great Question. That Mr. Dickinson had the Eloquence, the Learning and the Ingenuity on his Side of the Question, but that I had the Hearts of the Americans on mine, and therefore my Side of the Question prevailed. That Mr. Dickinson had a good Heart, and an amiable Character. But that his Opposition to Independency, had lost him the Confidence of the People, who suspected him of Timidity and Avarice, and that his Opposition sprung from those Passions: But that he had since turned out with the Militia, against the B[ritish] troops and I doubted not might in Time regain the Confidence of the People.

Benjamin Rush to John Montgomery PHILADELPHIA, NOVEMBER 5, 1782

There can be little doubt of Mr. Dickinson being president [of Pennsylvania]. Shame will compel some to vote for him whom inclination would not. He is everything that his friends would wish him to be. His enemies (who are enemies of virtue and public justice) sicken and tremble at his name.

Edmund Pendleton to James Madison VIRGINIA, JULY 14, 1783

[Speaking of President of the Supreme Executive Council John Dickinson's failure to call out the state militia to suppress a mutiny of Pennsylvania troops that surrounded the State House where both Congress and the Pennsylvania Assembly were meeting.] The Supine neglect of the Executive to interpose the force of the State on this Occasion, probably had its source in the t[imi]d Spirit of the C[hie]f M[a]g[istrat]e, whose nerves are too weak for any exertions, but those of Oratory or the pen.

Charles Thomson to Hannah Thomson PRINCETON, N.J., JULY 26, 1783

You know how open a certain person [John Dickinson] is to flattery & who, though he has shining parts, is not remarkable for solidity of judgment. His passions are too ungovernable and he is apt to suffer himself when under their influence to be the dupe of those who will flatter his vanity. And yet he has many good qualities. I am much afraid that a young, sly & crafty politician, of whose principles & conduct I have not the best Opinion, has found out his foible, and has had too much influence in the late transactions.

Benjamin Rush to John Montgomery PHILADELPHIA, DECEMBER 10, 1784

The professorship of divinity [at Dickinson College] which Mr. D. promised to endow must for a while fall to the ground. . . . Our poor friend Mr. D. is alas! steady in nothing but in his *instability*. This is the only fixed trait in his character.

Thomas Jefferson, Answers to François Soulés' Queries SEPTEMBER 13–18, 1786

Mr. Dickinson, a lawyer of more ingenuity than sound judgment, and still more timid than ingenious.

William Pierce, "Character Sketches of Delegates to the Federal Convention" 1787

Mr. Dickinson has been famed through all America, for his farmers Letters; he is a Scholar, and said to be a Man of very extensive information. When I saw him in the Convention I was induced to pay the greatest attention to him whenever he spoke. I had often heard that he was a great Orator, but I found him an indifferent Speaker. With an affected air of wisdom he labors to produce a trifle,—his language is irregular and incorrect,—his flourishes (for he sometimes attempts them), are like expiring flames, they just show themselves and go out;—no traces of them are left on the mind to clear or animate it. He is, however, a good writer and will ever be considered one of the most important characters in the United States. He is about 55 years old, and was bred a Quaker.

Benjamin Rush to John Dickinson PHILADELPHIA, JULY 15, 1788

The Success of the new government in restoring Order to our country, will depend very much upon the talents & principles of the Gentlemen who are to compose the federal legislature.— Your friends in Philadelphia have destined you to be one of the

members of the Senate from the Delaware state. I know how perfectly your present tranquil mode of life, accords with the present
happy frame of your Mind. But remember my Dear friend—that
"none liveth to himself." Even our Old Age is not our own property. All its fruits of Wisdom, & experience belong to the public.
"To do good" is the business of *life.* "To enjoy *rest*" is the happiness of heaven. We pluck premature, of forbidden fruit when
we grasp at *rest* on this Side the grave. I know too, your present
infirm state of body, but an active interest in the great Objects &
business of the new legislature for a few years, by giving tone to
your mind, will invigorate your body.—Should you only assist
with your advice for one or two years 'till all the wheels of the
great machine are set in motion, your Country will forgive your
resignation of your Seat in the Senate afterwards.—

Louis Guillaume Otto, Biographies FALL 1788

Author of the *Letters of a Pennsylvania Farmer.* Very rich man,
was of the anti-English party at the beginning of the Revolution,
without however favoring independence, which he actually voted
against publicly. He is old, feeble, and without influence.

Benjamin Rush to John Adams PHILADELPHIA, APRIL 13, 1790

[Recalling a conversation with John Adams in October 1776.]
Upon my asking Mr. J. Adams what he thought of sending Mr.
Dickinson to Europe as a minister, he said, "Mr. D. is the most
unfit man in the world to be sent abroad. He is such a friend
to monarchy that he would prostrate himself at the feet of every
throne he saw. I would prefer Dr. Witherspoon to him."

Benjamin Rush, Sketches C. 1800

Few men wrote, spoke and acted more for their country from the
years 1764 to the establishment of the federal government than
Mr. Dickinson. He was alike eloquent at the bar, in a popular assembly, and in convention. Count [Thomas Cajetan] Wengier-
ski, a Polish nobleman who travelled thro' the United States soon
after the peace, said he was the most learned man he had met
with in America. He possessed the air of a camp and the ease of
the court in his manners. He was opposed to the Declaration of
Independence at the time it took place, but concurred in supporting it. During the war and for some years after it, he admired

and preferred the British constitution. Towards the close of his life he became a decided and zealous Republican.

Thomas Jefferson to Joseph Bringhurst WASHINGTON, D.C., FEBRUARY 24, 1808

I have to acknowledge the receipt of your letter of the 16th. It gave me the first information of the death of our distinguished fellow citizen, John Dickinson. A more estimable man, or truer patriot, could not have left us. Among the first of the advocates for the rights of his country when assailed by Great Britain, he continued to the last the orthodox advocate of the true principles of our new government, and his name will be consecrated in history as one of the great worthies of the Revolution. We ought to be grateful for having been permitted to retain the benefit of his counsel to so good an old age; still the moment of losing it, whenever it arises, must be a moment of deep-felt regret. For himself, perhaps, a longer period of life was less important, alloyed as the feeble enjoyments of that age are with so much pain. But to his country every addition to his moments was interesting. A junior companion of his labors in the early part of our Revolution, it has been a great comfort to me to have retained his friendship to the last moment of his life.

John Adams to Thomas Jefferson QUINCY, NOVEMBER 12, 1813

There was a little Aristocracy, among Us, of Talents and Letters. Mr. Dickinson was primus inter pares;* the Bell Weather; the leader of the Aristocratical flock. Billy, alias Governor Livingston, and his Son in law Mr. Jay were of this privileged order.

*First among equals.

Oliver Ellsworth

1745–1807

≼ BORN IN Windsor, Conn. College of New Jersey (Princeton), B.A., 1766. Admitted to bar, 1771. Windsor delegate to house, 1773–75. Hartford County justice of the peace, 1774–80. State's attorney for Hartford County, 1777–85. Delegate to Congress, 1778–83. Member, Council of Safety, 1779. Hartford delegate to house, 1779. Delegate to Hartford Convention, 1779. Member of council, 1780–85. Judge of Connecticut Superior Court, 1785–88. Delegate to Constitutional Convention, 1787 (member Committee of Detail). Author of "Landholder" essays, 1787–88. Delegate to Connecticut Convention, voted to ratify the Constitution, 1788. U.S. senator, 1789–96. Chief justice of the United States, 1796–1800. Peace commissioner to France, 1799–1800. Member of council, 1802–7.

William Pierce, "Character Sketches of Delegates to the Federal Convention," 1787

Mr. Ellsworth is a Judge of the Supreme Court in Connecticut;— he is a Gentleman of a clear, deep, and copious understanding; eloquent, and connected in public debate; and always attentive to his duty. He is very happy in a reply, and choice in selecting such parts of his adversary's arguments as he finds make the strongest impressions,—in order to take off the force of them, so as to admit the power of his own. Mr. Ellsworth is about 37 years of age, a Man much respected for his integrity, and venerated for his abilities.

Connecticut Courant JANUARY 9, 1788

[On speeches in the Connecticut ratifying convention.] Suffice it
to say that all the objections to the Constitution vanished before
the learning and eloquence of a [William Samuel] Johnson, the
genuine good sense and discernment of a [Roger] Sherman, and
the Demosthenian energy of an Ellsworth.

Louis Guillaume Otto, Biographies FALL 1788

Former member of Congress, is a man of absolutely the same
cast of mind and disposition [as Samuel Huntington]. The same
can be said of Mr. Sherman. In general the men of this state
[Connecticut] have a national character that is rarely found in
the other parts of this continent. They are nearing republican
simplicity; they are completely at ease without opulence. Rural
economy and domestic industry have grown for a long time in
Connecticut; the people are happy there.

Abigail Adams to John Adams HARTFORD, NOVEMBER 16, 1788

Our Landlord who is an intelligent man fell into politicks today,
inquired who were talked of for Senators in our state, &c. but
finding no politicians in company few observations were made.
He was high in praise of Dr. Johnson and Judge Ellsworth, hop'd
the rest of the States would send as good Men and then he did
not believe that the House of Lords in England could equal them.
. . . he wanted those Men in office whose Fame had resounded
throughout all the States.

John Adams to William Tudor NEW YORK, MAY 9, 1789

The Sentiments that I have read and heard in America these fifteen Years, and that I still continue to hear every day, even from
Men of Education, Reading, Age, and travel, upon the subject
of Government appear to me as extravagant, as the drivelings of
Idiotism, or the ravings of delirium, a total inattention to every
Thing in human nature by which Mankind ever were or ever will
be governed is obvious in numbers who have the Reputation,
and who really are Men of Sense and Experience as well as of
letters. Our Chief has some just notions, and here and there one
is to be found, who is quite right. Mr. Ellsworth of Connecticut,
appears to me to be more exactly and completely right, than any

Man I ever met in Congress, and what crowns all, is, he is not afraid to think or Speak.

William Maclay, Diary APRIL 9, 1790

I can with Truth pronounce him the most uncandid man I ever knew possessing such Abilities. I am often led to doubt Whether he has a particle of Integrity, perhaps such a Quality is Useless in Connecticut.

JUNE 12, 1790
Ellsworth a Man of great Faculties, and eloquent in debate, but he has taken too much on himself. He wishes to reconcile the Secretary's [Alexander Hamilton's] System to the public Opinion, and Welfare but it is too much. He cannot retain the Confidence of the People & remain in the Good graces of the Secretary. He may lose both.

FEBRUARY 10, 1791
This man has abilities, but Abilities without candor and integrity, are the characteristics of the Devil.

Jonathan Trumbull to John Trumbull PHILADELPHIA, MARCH 4, 1796

Our Mr. Ellsworth has been taken from *our Corps* to fill the Seat of Chief Justice on the federal Bench—in room of Mr. Rutledge dementated—a great Loss this to the Senate!—but a valuable acquisition to the Court—an acquisition which has been much needed.

John Adams to Abigail Adams PHILADELPHIA, MARCH 5, 1796

Yesterday Mr. Ellsworth's Nomination was consented to as Chief Justice, by which We loose the clearest head and most diligent hand We had. It will give a Nobility to the Government however, to place a Man of his Courage, Constancy, fortitude and Capacity in that situation. The Nomination of Mr. Chase had given Occasion to uncharitable Reflections and Mr. Wilson's ardent Speculations had given offence to some, and his too frequent affectation of Popularity to others. Though Ellsworth has the Stiffness of Connecticut: though His Air and Gilt are not elegant: though He cannot enter a Room nor retire from it with the Ease and Grace of a Courtier: Yet his Understanding is as sound, his Information as good and his heart as steady as any Man can boast.

Jeremiah Smith to William Plumer PHILADELPHIA, MARCH 5, 1796

I write merely to inform you that yesterday Mr. Ellsworth was appointed Chief Justice of the United States—The vote was unanimous in Senate except *Mason* of Virginia who is a very ill natured & sour *man* as well as *politician.*—I presume no appointment in the U.S. has been more wise or judicious than this: He is a very able lawyer, a very learned man, a very great Politician & a very honest man. In short he is every thing one would desire.—I know this will give you much pleasure as you are a sincere well wisher to good Government & especially to a good judiciary; a thing which *we* know the Value of by the want of it. I hope he will accept.—

Connecticut can not send his equal into the Senate—He was the life & soul of that body & they will severely feel his loss— He was a man of investigation & uncommon Industry—Nothing passed without his examination.—I believe his enemies placed as much Confidence in him as his friends, if this is not an improper expression—

Oliver Wolcott Sr. to Jonathan Trumbull LITCHFIELD, CONN., MARCH 14, 1796

Mr. Ellsworth's appointment [as chief justice of the United States] will be very satisfactory to all who are willing to be pleased. If our country shall be preserved from anarchy and confusion, it must be by men of his character.

Abigail Adams to John Adams QUINCY, MARCH 20, 1796

I both rejoiced and mourned at the Appointment of Mr. Ellsworth as Chief Justice, but what the Senate lose, the Bench will acquire. I rejoice that they have obtained a Man of a fair Fame, distinguished abilities and integrity. Caesar's Wife ought not to be suspected. This will apply to that office.

Oliver Wolcott Sr. to Oliver Wolcott Jr. LITCHFIELD, CONN., MARCH 21, 1796

The established principles and abilities of Mr. Ellsworth render his appointment [as chief justice] proper.

Abigail Adams to John Adams QUINCY, APRIL 17, 1797

I have just been reading Chief Justice Ellsworth's Charge to the Grand jury at New York! Did the good gentleman never write before? Can it be genuine. The language is stiffer than his person. I find it difficult to pick out his meaning in many sentences. I am sorry it was ever published.

John Adams to Abigail Adams PHILADELPHIA, APRIL 24, 1797

You and Such petit Maitres and Maitresses* as you, are forever criticizing the Periods and Diction of Such great Men as Presidents and Chief Justices. Do you think their Minds are taken up with such Trifles? There is solid, keen, deep sense in that Morsel of Ellsworth's. You ought to be punished for wishing it not published.

Frederick Wolcott to Oliver Wolcott Jr. HARTFORD, JANUARY 23, 1798

Mr. Ellsworth will not go to Philadelphia till some time the next week.—He is considerably unwell, I understand quite hypochondriac.

Oliver Ellsworth to Oliver Wolcott Jr., LE HAVRE, OCTOBER 16, 1800

Sufferings at sea and by a winter's journey through Spain, gave me an obstinate gravel, which, by wounding the kidneys, has drawn and fixed my wandering gout to those parts. My pains are constant, and at times excruciating; they do not permit me to embark for America at this late season of the year, nor, if there, would they permit me to discharge my official duties. I have, therefore, sent my resignation of the office of chief justice, and shall, after spending a few weeks in England, retire for winter-quarters to the south of France.

Theodore Sedgwick to Alexander Hamilton WASHINGTON, D.C., DECEMBER 17, 1800

The mind as well as body of Mr. Ellsworth are rendered feeble by disease. He has resigned as Chief Justice.

---

*Dandies, fops.

Benjamin Franklin
1706–1790

⊰ BORN IN Boston. Arrives in Philadelphia, 1723. Becomes successful printer and publisher. Retires from private business, 1748, to pursue public affairs. Gains prominence and wins awards for scientific studies concerning electricity, 1753. Proposes Albany Plan of Union, 1754. Delegate Pennsylvania Assembly, 1751–57. Colonial agent for Pennsylvania and other colonies (New Jersey, Georgia, and lower house of Massachusetts), 1757–74. Returns to the United States, 1775. Delegate to Continental Congress, 1775–76. Commissioner to France, 1776–78; minister plenipotentiary to France, 1778–85. Peace negotiator, 1782–83. Returns to Philadelphia, September 1785. Claimed as leader by Constitutionalists; nominated for councillor from Philadelphia; elected unanimously Oct. 1785; president, Supreme Executive Council, 1785–88. Delegate to Constitutional Convention, 1787; delivered conciliatory address at close of convention that was widely published by Federalists in late 1787 and early 1788. Nominated for state convention by Constitutionalists but defeated, 1787. Last public act was to sign a petition to Congress encouraging abolition of slavery, 1790.

James Madison to William Bradford JUNE 19, 1775

Little did I ever expect to hear that Jeremiah's Doctrine that "the heart of man is deceitful above all things & desperately wicked" was exemplified in the celebrated Dr. Franklin, & if the suspicions against him be well founded it certainly is remarkably exemplified. Indeed it appears to me that the bare suspicion of his guilt amounts very nearly to a proof of its reality. If he were the man he formerly was, & has even of late pretended to be, his conduct in Philadelphia on this critical occasion could have left no room for surmise or distrust. He certainly would have been both a faithful informer & an active member of the Congress. His behavior would have been explicit & his Zeal warm and conspicuous.

John Adams to Abigail Adams JULY 23, 1775

Dr. Franklin has been very constant in his Attendance on Congress from the Beginning. His Conduct has been composed and grave and in the Opinion of many Gentlemen very reserved. He has not assumed any Thing, nor affected to take the lead; but has seemed to choose that the Congress should pursue their own Principles and sentiments and adopt their own Plans: Yet he has not been backward: has been very useful, on many occasions, and discovered a Disposition entirely American. He does not hesitate at our boldest Measures, but rather seems to think us, too irresolute, and backward. He thinks us at present in an odd State, neither in Peace nor War, neither dependent nor independent. But he thinks that We shall soon assume a Character more decisive.

He thinks that We have the Power of preserving ourselves, and that even if We should be driven to the disagreeable Necessity of assuming a total independency, and set up a separate state, We could maintain it. The People of England, have thought that the Opposition in America, was wholly owing to Dr. Franklin: and I suppose their scribblers will attribute the Temper, and Proceedings of this Congress to him: but there cannot be a greater Mistake. He has had but little share farther than to cooperate and assist. He is however a great and good Man.

John Adams to James Warren PHILADELPHIA, SEPTEMBER 30, 1775

Dr. Franklin needs nothing to be said. There is no abler or better American, that I know of.

Abigail Adams to John Adams BRAINTREE, NOVEMBER 5, 1775

I hope you have received several Letters from me in this fortnight past. I wrote by Mr. Lynch, and by Dr. Franklin the latter of whom I had the pleasure of dining with, and of admiring him whose character from my Infancy I had been taught to venerate. I found him social, but not talkative, and when he spoke something useful dropped from his Tongue; he was grave, yet pleasant, and affable.—You know I make some pretensions to physiognomy and I thought I could read in his countenance the Virtues of his Heart, among which patriotism shined in its full Lustre—and with that is blended every virtue of a Christian, for a true patriot must be a religious Man.

John Adams to James Warren FEBRUARY 18, 1776

Dr. Franklin, and Mr. Chase of Maryland, and Mr. Charles Carroll of Carrollton, are chosen a Committee to go to Canada. I must confess I have very great Confidence, in the Abilities and Integrity, the Political Principles and good Disposition of this Committee.

Franklin's Character you know. His masterly Acquaintance with the French Language, his extensive Correspondence in France, his great Experience in Life, his Wisdom, Prudence, Caution, his engaging Address, united to his unshaken Firmness in the present American System of Politics and War, point him out as the fittest Character for this momentous Undertaking.

William Carmichael to C. W. F. Dumas LE HAVRE, JANUARY 21, 1777

You will no doubt have our Paris news from the prophet who draws down fire from heaven.

Jonathan Williams Jr. to Benjamin Franklin NANTES, JANUARY 25, 1777

I am treated here with as much Respect as if I were the Nephew of a prince. So much is your name respected that I hear the Ladies of Nantes are about making an addition to their heads in imitation of your Hair Cap, which they intend to call a la Franklin.

Benjamin Franklin to Emma Thompson PARIS, FEBRUARY 8, 1777

Figure me in your mind as jolly as formerly, and as strong and hearty, only a few Years older, very plainly dressed, wearing my thin grey straight Hair, that peeps out under my only Coiffure, a fine Fur Cap, which comes down my Forehead almost to my Spectacles. Think how this must appear among the Powdered Heads of Paris. I wish every Gentleman and Lady in France would only be so obliging as to follow my Fashion, comb their own Heads as I do mine.

Silas Deane to President of Congress John Hancock PARIS, C. MARCH 16, 1777

[Franklin] is universally esteemed and respected here, as well as in America, and, I may say, through the learned world.

William Carmichael to William Bingham PARIS, JUNE 25, 1777

The age of Dr. Franklin in some measure hinders him from taking so active a part in the drudgery of business as his great zeal and abilities would otherwise enable him to execute. He is the master to whom we children in politics all look up for counsel, and whose name is everywhere a passport to be well received.

John Adams, Diary APRIL 16, 1778

Dr. F. is reported to speak French very well, but I find upon attending to him that he does not speak it Grammatically, and indeed upon inquiring, he confesses that he is wholly inattentive to the Grammar. His Pronunciation too, upon which the French Gentlemen and Ladies compliment him, and which he seems to think is pretty well, I am sure is very far from being exact.

Indeed Dr. Franklin's Knowledge of French, at least his Faculty of speaking it, may be said to have begun with his Embassy to this Court. He told me that when he was in France before, Sir John Pringle was with him, and did all his Conversation for him as Interpreter, and that he understood and spoke French with great Difficulty, until he came here last, although he read it.

John Adams to Abigail Adams PASSY, APRIL 25, 1778

My venerable Colleague enjoys a Privilege here, that is much to be envied. Being seventy Years of Age, the Ladies not only allow him to embrace them as often as he pleases, but they are perpetually embracing him.—I told him Yesterday, I would write this to America.

John Adams, Autobiography MAY 27, 1778

I found that the Business of our Commission would never be done, unless I did it. My two Colleagues would agree in nothing. The Life of Dr. Franklin was a Scene of continual dissipation. I could never obtain the favour of his Company in a Morning before Breakfast which would have been the most convenient time to read over the Letters and papers, deliberate on their contents, and decide upon the Substance of the Answers. It was late when he breakfasted, and as soon as Breakfast was over, a crowd of Carriages came to his Levee or if you like the term better to his Lodgings, with all Sorts of People; some Philosophers, Academicians and Economists; some of his small tribe of humble friends in the literary Way whom he employed to translate some of his ancient Compositions, such as his Bonhomme Richard and for what I know his Polly Baker &c.; but by far the greater part were Women and Children, come to have the honor to see the great Franklin, and to have the pleasure of telling Stories about his Simplicity, his bald head and scattering strait hairs, among their Acquaintances. These Visitors occupied all the time, commonly, till it was time to dress to go to Dinner. He was invited to dine abroad every day and never declined unless when We had invited Company to dine with Us. I was always invited with him, till I found it necessary to send Apologies, that I might have some time to study the French Language and do the Business of the mission. Mr. Franklin kept a horn book always in his Pocket in which he minuted all his invitations to dinner, and Mr. [Arthur] Lee said it was the only thing in which he was punctual. It was the Custom in France to dine between one and two O'clock: so that when the time came to dress, it was time for the Voiture to be ready to carry him to dinner. Mr. Lee came daily to my Apartment to attend to Business, but we could rarely obtain the Company of Dr. Franklin for a few minutes, and often when I had drawn the Papers and had them fairly copied for Signature, and Mr. Lee and I had signed them, I was frequently obliged to wait several days, before I could procure the Signature of Dr. Franklin to them. He went according to his Invitation to his Dinner and after that went sometimes to the Play, sometimes to the Philosophers but most commonly to visit those Ladies who were complaisant enough to depart from the custom of France so far as to procure Sets of Tea

Gear as it is called and make Tea for him. Some of these Ladies I knew as Madam Hellvetius, Madam Brillon, Madam Chaumont, Madam Le Roy &c. and others whom I never knew and never inquired for. After Tea the Evening was spent, in hearing the Ladies sing and play upon their Piano Fortes and other instruments of Music, and in various Games as Cards, Chess, Backgammon, &c. &c. Mr. Franklin I believe however never played at any Thing but Chess or Checkers. In these Agreeable and important Occupations and Amusements, the Afternoon and Evening was spent, and he came home at all hours from Nine to twelve O'clock at night. This Course of Life contributed to his Pleasure and I believe to his health and Longevity. He was now between Seventy and Eighty and I had so much respect and compassion for his Age, that I should have been happy to have done all the Business or rather all the Drudgery, if I could have been favoured with a few moments in a day to receive his Advice concerning the manner in which it ought to be done. But this condescension was not attainable. All that could be had was his Signature, after it was done, and this it is true he very rarely refused though he sometimes delayed.

Ralph Izard to Henry Laurens PARIS, JUNE 28, 1778

His abilities are great and his reputation high. Removed as he is at so considerable a distance from the observation of his constituents, if he is not guided by principles of virtue and honor those abilities and that reputation may produce the most mischievous effects. (In my conscience I declare to you, that I believe him to be under no such internal restraint; and God knows that I speak the real unprejudiced sentiments of my heart. If at any time I have been under the influence of prejudice, it has been in his favor, and nothing but my own observation could have convinced me so thoroughly how undeservedly it is possible for public approbation to be bestowed.)

Silas Deane to Henry Laurens PHILADELPHIA, OCTOBER 12, 1778

[In criticizing the letters of Arthur Lee and Ralph Izard that censured Benjamin Franklin.] Gratitude as well as justice to that truly great man, to whose friendship and counsel I owe much, oblige me to say on this occasion that I not only believe, but know, that this is, to say no more of it, directly the reverse of the character which Dr. Franklin has ever sustained, and which he now most eminently supports. It gives me pleasure to reflect on the honors and respect universally paid him by all orders of people in France, and never did I enjoy greater satisfaction than in being the spectator of the public honors often paid him. A celebrated cause being to be heard before the parliament of Paris, and the house and streets leading to it crowded with people, on the appearance of Dr. Franklin way was made for him in the most respectful manner, and he passed through the crowd to the seat reserved for him amid the acclamations of the people; an honor seldom paid to their first princes of the blood. When he attended the operas and plays similar honors were paid him, and I confess I felt a joy and pride which were pure and honest, though not disinterested, for I considered it an honor to be known to be an American and his friend. What were the sensations of the writers of these letters on such occasions, I leave their letters and conduct towards him to speak, and I can not now express the indignation and grief I feel at finding such a character represented as the worst that human depravity is capable of exhibiting, and that such a representation should be made by an American in a public character.

John Adams to Samuel Adams PASSY, DECEMBER 7, 1778

The other [i.e., Franklin] you know personally, and that he loves his Ease, hates to offend, and seldom gives any Opinion until obliged to do it. I know also and it is necessary you should be informed, that he is overwhelmed with a Correspondence from all Quarters, most of them upon trifling subjects, and in a more trifling Style; with unmeaning Visits from Multitudes of People, chiefly from the Vanity of Having it to say that they have Seen him. There is another Thing which I am obliged to mention, there are So many private Families, Ladies and Gentlemen that he visits So often, and they are So fond of him that he cannot well avoid it, and So much Intercourse with Academicians, that all these Things together keep his Mind in Such a constant State of Dissipation, that if he is left alone here, the public Business, will Suffer in a degree beyond Description, provided our Affairs are continued upon the present footing.

John Adams to James Lovell PASSY, FEBRUARY 20, 1779

On the other Hand, there was a Monopoly of Reputation here, and an Indecency in displaying it, which did great Injustice to the real Merit of others, that I do not wonder was resented. There was an Indolence—there was a Dissipation—which gave just Occasion of Complaint—there was a Complaisance to interested Adventurers. There was an Intimacy, with stock jobbers, there was an Acquaintance with Persons from England, which gave just Occasion of Jealousy, however innocent the intentions were. I have learned that total silence is enough to procure a Character for Prudence, whatever Indiscretions a Man may commit.

John Adams, Autobiography MAY 10, 1779

[Rev. Hezekiah Ford told me]: I came to France with the highest opinion of Dr. F.—as a Philosopher, a Statesman and as even the Pater Patriae.* But I assure you Tempora mutantur.†

He has very moderate Abilities, He knows nothing of Philosophy, but his few Experiments in Electricity; He is an Atheist, he don't believe any future State: Yet he is terribly afraid of dying.

This is Ford's Opinion. This is his Character of the great Man.

I believe it is too much to say that he is an Atheist, and that he don't believe a future State: though I am not certain his Hints, and Squibs sometimes go so far as to raise Suspicions:—and he never tells any Body, I fancy that he believes a G[od], a P[urgatory] or f[uture] s[tate]. It is too rank to say that he understands nothing of Philosophy, but his own electrical Experiments, although I don't think him so deeply read in Philosophy, as his Names imputes.

He has a Passion for Reputation and Fame, as strong as you can imagine, and his Time and Thoughts are chiefly employed to obtain it, and to set Tongues and Pens male and female, to celebrating him. Painters, Statuaries, Sculptors, China Potters, and all are set to work for this End. He has the most affectionate and insinuating Way of charming the Women or the Man that he fixes on. It is the most silly and ridiculous Way imaginable, in the Sight of an American, but it succeeds, to admiration, fulsome and sickish as it is, in Europe.

*Father of his country.
†The times are changed.

John Adams, Diary JUNE 18, 1779

[Reporting a conversation with François, marquis de Barbé-Marbois.] That it was often affirmed that Mr. Franklin spoke French as fluently and elegantly, as a Courtier at Versailles, but every Man that knew and spoke sincerely, agreed that he spoke it very ill. Persons spoke of these Things, according to their Affections.

He said it was Flattery. That he would not flatter, it was very true that both Mr. F. and I spoke French, badly.

JUNE 23, 1779

I said that Mr. Franklin had great Merit as a Philosopher. His Discoveries in Electricity were very grand, and he certainly was a Great Genius, and had great Merit in our American Affairs. But he had no Title to the Legislator of America.

Mr. M[arbois] said he had Wit and Irony, but these were not the Faculties of Statesmen. His Essay upon the true Means of bringing a great Empire to be a small one was very pretty.—I said he had wrote many Things, which had great Merit and infinite Wit and Ingenuity. His bonhomme Richard was a very ingenious Thing, which had been recommended by Curates and Bishops to so many Parishes and Dioceses.

State Papers Read by Conrad Alexandre Gérard before Congress JULY 14, 1779

The king and ministry were extremely pleased with the resolution which Congress has taken to maintain only one minister plenipotentiary at this court, as well as with the exclusive appointment of so steady and honest a man and so firm and solid a patriot as Dr. Franklin. . . .

There is every reason to believe that Congress will very soon receive proofs of the confidence which this court was always willing to show to the servants of these States. The personal character of Dr. Franklin will enable the court to act with a frankness becoming the alliance, and they will have no occasion to withhold any more the secrets which may interest the United States and the alliance.

John Adams to Thomas McKean BRAINTREE, SEPTEMBER 20, 1779

I presume Congress intend to appoint a secretary to the Commission, and Consuls for the Management of Commercial and maritime matters. It is highly necessary. Franklin is a Wit and a Humorist, I know. He may be a Philosopher, for what I know, but he is not a sufficient Statesman, he knows too little of American Affairs or the Politicks of Europe, and takes too little Pains to inform himself of Either. He is too old, too infirm, too indolent and dissipated, to be sufficient for the Discharge of all the important Duties of Ambassador, Secretary, Admiral, Commercial Agent, Board of War, Board of Treasury, Commissary of Prisoners, &c. &c. &c. as he is at present in that Department, besides an immense Correspondence, and Acquaintance, each of which would be enough for the whole Time of the most active Man in the Vigor of Youth.

Yet such is his Name on both Sides the Water, that it is best, perhaps that he should be left there. But a secretary and Consuls should be appointed to do the Business, or it will not be done, or if done it will not be done by him, but by busy People who insinuate themselves into his Confidence without either such Heads or Hearts as Congress should trust.

John Paul Jones to Robert Morris L'ORIENT, JUNE 27, 1780

I thank God that I am of no party and have no brothers or relations to serve, but I am convinced that Mr. [Arthur] Lee has acted in this matter merely because I would not become the enemy of the venerable, the wise, and good Franklin, whose heart as well as head does and will always do honor to human nature. I know the great and good in this kingdom better, perhaps, than any other American who has appeared in Europe since the treaty of alliance, and if my testimony could add anything to Franklin's reputation I would witness the universal veneration and esteem with which his name inspires all ranks, not only at Versailles and all over this kingdom, but also in Spain and Holland. And I can add from the testimony of the first characters of other nations that with them envy is dumb when the name of Franklin is but mentioned.

John Jay to Benjamin Franklin MADRID, OCTOBER 30, 1780

I have often congratulated my country and myself on your being at present in France. I once expected to have seen you there, and to have profited by the lessons which time and much experience have taught you. Miracles have ceased, and my constitution does not promise length of days, or I should probably desire you, when you ascend, to drop me your mantle.

Benjamin Franklin to President of Congress Samuel Huntington PASSY, MARCH 12, 1781

I must now beg leave to say something relating to myself; a Subject with which I have not often troubled the Congress. I have passed my 75th. Year, and I find that the long & severe Fit of the Gout which I had the last Winter, has shaken me exceedingly, and I am yet far from having recovered the bodily Strength I before enjoyed. I do not know that my mental Faculties are impaired; perhaps I shall be the last to discover that; but I am sensible of great Diminution in my Activity; a Quality I think particularly necessary in your Minister for this Court. I am afraid therefore that your Affairs may some time or other suffer by my Deficiency. I find also that the Business is too heavy for me and too confining. The constant Attendance at home which is necessary for receiving and accepting your Bills of Exchange, (a Matter foreign to my ministerial Functions) to answer Letters and perform other Parts of my Employment, prevents my taking the Air and Exercise which my annual Journeys formerly used to afford me, and which contributed much to the Preservation of my Health. There are many other little personal Attentions, which the Infirmities of Age render necessary to an old Man's Comfort, even perhaps in some Degree to the Continuance of his Existence, and with which Business often interferes. I have been engaged in public Affairs, and enjoyed public Confidence in some Shape or other, during the long Term of fifty Years, an Honor sufficient to satisfy any reasonable Ambition, and I have no other left, but that of Repose, which I hope the Congress will grant me, by sending some Person to supply my Place. At the same time, I beg they may be assured, that it is not any Disgust received in their Service, that induces me to decline it, but purely and simply the Reasons above-mentioned.

John Jay to President of Congress Samuel Huntington MADRID, APRIL 21, 1781

By the letter from Doctor Franklin, herewith enclosed, and which he was so obliging as to leave open for my perusal, I find he has requested permission to retire on account of his age and infirmities. How far his health may be improved I know not, since the letters I have received from him bear no marks of age. There is an acuteness and sententious brevity in them which do not bespeak an understanding injured by years. I have many reasons to think our country is much indebted to him, and I confess it would mortify my pride as an American if his constituents should be the only people to whom his character is known that should deny his merit and services. Justice demands of me to assure you that his reputation and respectability are acknowledged and have weight here, and that I have received from him all that uniform attention and aid which was due to the importance of the affairs committed to me.

APRIL 25, 1781

I perceive that Dr. Franklin desires to retire. This circumstance calls upon me to assure Congress that I have reason to be perfectly satisfied with his conduct towards me, and that I have received from him all the aid and attention I could wish or expect. His character is very high here, and I really believe that the respectability, which he enjoys throughout Europe, has been of general use to our cause and country.

Arthur Lee to James Warren PHILADELPHIA, JUNE 15, 1781

What I always knew must now be clear to everyone—that it was not Dr. Lee but his principles that were offensive to the French Court: since in conjunction with Dr. Franklin, they have commenced the very same intrigues against our friend Mr. J. Adams. They know that his intentions are too honest, and his mind too firm, for their purposes; and therefore they are endeavoring to disgrace him, or shackle him with the wiles of that old, corrupt Serpent, who has constantly sold this Country to them.

Abigail Adams to James Lovell BRAINTREE, JUNE 30, 1781

[On Franklin's influence over French foreign secretary Vergennes or former French minister to the United States Luzerne.] If the [influence is over the] Latter I am very Sorry that he should become a dupe to the wiles of the Sorcerer. . . .

   [On Benjamin Franklin's attacks on John Adams and others.] Was the Man a Gallant I should think he had been monopolizing the Women from the enchanter. Was he a Modern Courtier

I should think he had outwitted him in court intrigue. Was He a selfish avaricious designing deceitful Villain I should think he had encroached upon the old Gentleman's prerogatives but as he is neither, what can raise his malice against an honest republican? Tis fear, fear, that fear which made the first grand deceiver start up his own shape when touched by Ithuriel's Spear.* The honest Zeal of a Man who has no Sinister views to serve, no Friends to advance to places of profit and Emolument, no ambition to make a fortune with the Spoil of his country, or to eat the Bread of Idleness and dissipation—this man must be crushed, he must be calumniated and abused. It needs great courage Sir to engage in the cause of America, we have not only an open but secret foes to contend with. It comes not unexpected upon me I assure you, he who had unjustly traduced the character of one Man, would not hesitate to attack every one who should obstruct his views and no Man however honest his views and intentions will be safe whilst this Gentleman holds his office. I hope you will be very particular not only in transmitting the accusation but what Effect it has had in your Body [Congress], what measures have been taken in consequence, and whether you have acquainted my Friend with it. If not I beg it may be done that he may take proper measures in his defense.

Abigail Adams to Alice Lee Shippen BRAINTREE, JUNE 30, 1781

Your favor of June 17 . . . explained to me the machinations of a Man, Grown old in the practice of deception and calumny. . . .

If upright and good intentions with a fair full and diligent discharge of the duties of his office will merit the approbation of his employers I dare say my absent Friend will be able to justify his conduct and to exculpate himself from the Slander of his accuser whose sly secret Malice is of a more dangerous kind than the open attacks of an avowed Enemy. It is some consolation however to have an associate even in misfortune, and my Friends character is not the first which has been immolated by this unprincipled Gentleman to the Altars of envy, Calumny and disappointed ambition. It has been the Misfortune of America in the unhappy tragedy in which She has been engaged, that some of

---

*In John Milton's *Paradise Lost,* Ithuriel, the guardian angel of the Garden of Eden, used his sword to touch the devil disguised as a toad and made him reveal his true form as a grisly king.

her principal characters have disgraced the Scenes. Her Franklin, Dean, and Arnold may be ranked with her Hutchinson and Galloway. If the Aspersions you mention are such as to obtain the Notice of Congress, I hope they will do my Friend the justice to acquaint him with them before they give credit to a Gentleman whom they have long had reason to execrate and who if continued in office will still embarrass their affairs and discourage the faithfulest servants of the public from engaging in its service.

Abigail Adams to James Lovell BRAINTREE, JULY 14, 1781

Join with him [John Adams] an upright honest Man of real abilities and he will thank you for an assistant should a negotiation [for peace] commence, but do not Saddle him with a Man who looks no further than the present state of existence for a retribution of his virtues or his vices, but who considering this world as the summum bonum* of Man might I think have a little more regard to the happiness of his fellow Mortals in the present state, and not quite so willing to relinquish their Natural Rights. One will speak a bold and firm language becoming a free sovereign and Independent Nation, the other will be indecisive yielding fawning flattery.

Abigail Adams to Elbridge Gerry BRAINTREE, JULY 20, 1781

The plan which appears to be adopted both at Home and abroad, is a servile adulation and complaisance to the Court of our Allies, even to the giving up some of our most valuable privileges. The Independent Spirit of your Friend, abroad, does not coincide with the selfish views and inordinate ambition of your Minister, who in consequence of it, is determined upon his destruction. Stung with envy at a merit he cannot emulate, he is alarmed with the apprehension of losing the Honor of some Brilliant action; and is using his endeavors that every enterprise shall miscarry, in which he has not the command. To Effect this purpose he has insinuated into the minds of those in power the falsest prejudices against your Friend, and they have so far influenced the united Counsels of these States, as to induce them to join this unprincipled Man, in Commission with him for future Negotiations. If Congress had thought proper to have joined any Gentleman

*Supreme good.

of real abilities and integrity with our Friend, who could have acted in concert with him; he would have gratefully received his assistance—but to clog him with a Man, who has shown himself so Inimical to him, who has discovered the marks of a little and narrow Spirit by his malicious aspersions, and ungenerous in-sinuations, and whose measures for a long time they have had no reason to be gratified with, is such a proof to me of what my ab-sent Friend has reason to expect, and what you know, Sir, I very early feared; that I can see nothing but dishonor, and disgrace attending his most faithful, and zealous exertions for the welfare of his Country.

Arthur Lee to James Warren   PHILADELPHIA, JULY 27, 1781

Congress have very injudiciously I fear, and contrary to their resolutions when there was a plot to remove me, joined Dr. F. in commission with Mr. Adams when they know that unprin-cipled old man has created differences with Mr. Adams and is endeavoring to ruin his reputation. Mr. Jay, Laurens the elder and Governor Jefferson are added. But their Instructions are such as throw them at the feet of Count Vergennes in everything but Independency. Mr. Adams can no more escape the Snares of old Franklin with the Count to assist him, than I could. I do not say that such treatment of Mr. Adams is unwise and unworthy; only, it is as cruel as if they had stretched him upon an iron bed of torture and left the old man at full liberty to glut himself with tormenting him.

Alice Lee Shippen to Abigail Adams   PHILADELPHIA, AUGUST 1781

Money and power are now in the hands of bad men, and there is no popular Ear. You are acquainted by this time with particulars. It is a little surprising is it not that Congress should have joined Dr. Franklin in commission with your Friend after what has pass'd; Can harmony be expected by joining a man's calumnia-tor with him? It is certainly putting your friend in a disagreeable situation, 'tis most probable if an advantageous peace should be negotiated, Dr. Franklin will take the credit: if otherwise, he will throw the blame on him he has already marked out; but my dear Madam, the slander of corrupt men in a corrupt age, is better than their praise. The Dr. appears to be no respecter of persons, he breaks through every tie of gratitude, and of Country, all his affections center in one character. He loves a knave wherever he finds him.

Elkanah Watson, Memoirs NOVEMBER 19, 1781

On November 19. I dined and spent the evening with Franklin, at Passy; arriving at an early hour, I observed him in a distant room reading, in the exact position he is represented in an excellent engraving, his left arm resting on a table, and his chin in his right hand thumb. I was soon conducted to him, and was cordially received, as usual. From a long habit of mixing with courtiers and men of eminence, as well in America as in Europe, he possesses an urbanity of manners, in connection with his venerable locks suspended over his shoulders, and his personal dignity, which commands reverence and respect; and yet so natural and fascinating in his deportment, that I always find myself perfectly at ease in his presence. Although he loves adulation, he woos it and hugs it to his heart in a manner unperceived, and therefore diminishes naught from his sterling merit. Not so with the vain boaster, trumpeting his own fame above all the fraudulent men who float upon borrowed plumes. Such men are always detected; soon sink into contempt, and hold a short run with posterity. But the name of Franklin will freshen with posterity, and increase in fame, through a long line of generations, while America shall bear a name. . . . He asked me if I knew he was a musician, and then conducted me across the room to an instrument of his own invention, fixed as a harpsichord. On my intimating a wish to see him perform, he immediately placed himself before it with his habitual condescension, touching the ends of his fingers on a moistened piece of sponge, and commenced playing with his right foot, bearing upon a treadle fixed in the manner of a spinning wheel, which turned a set of musical glasses, presenting their edges in perpendicular positions, in the shape of saucers graduated of different sizes, so as to produce all the requisite tones. He touched the edges with the ends of his fingers, playing a Scottish pastoral tune, in sweet delicate melody, which thrilled me to my very soul.—Besides, the novel spectacle was highly gratifying to my high toned American pride, to contemplate a native son of my native state, a distinguished philosopher in his 76th year, exhibiting on an instrument of his own invention, which he has named

Harmonica. . . . At times his Philosophy seemed to abandon him in gloomy despondency—& then viewing the issue in an opposite light, his hopes would flash into a concertion of complete success. Although in his 76th year, yet his whole machinery appeared in a state of elasticity, and in active play—So much was he exhilarated when hope predominated.

John Paul Jones to Benjamin Franklin PORTSMOUTH, N.H., DECEMBER 13, 1781

Enjoy, dear Sir, your present happiness! You are beloved; and will ever, while Virtue is honorable, be revered as a Father and Savior of your Country.

John Jay to Benjamin Franklin MADRID, JANUARY 30, 1782

France has done, and is still doing so much for us that Gratitude as well as Policy demands from us the utmost Moderation & Delicacy in our Applications for Aids. And considering the very singular plan of drawing Bills at a Venture I think we have no less Reason to admire the Patience, than to be satisfied with the Liberality of our good & generous Allies—

Mr. De Neufville had given me a Hint of the Embarrassments occasioned by "the Affair of our Goods in Holland." It seems as if Trouble finds its Way to you from every Quarter.—Our Credit in Holland leans upon you on one hand &, in Spain, on the other,—thus you continue like the Key Stone of an Arch, pressed by both sides & yet sustaining each. How grateful ought we to be to France for enabling you to do it!—

Peter Oliver, "The Origin and Progress of the American Rebellion" 1782

There was one Person more who might, now, be termed, the *instar omnium** of Rebellion. The Features of whose Soul were so minutely expressed in the Lines of his Countenance, that a Gentleman, whose Acumen was so great as to strike out a Character from a very slight View of a Face, was introduced to his Company many Years since; and upon his being asked his Opinion of the Man, he replied, "that he was calculated to set a whole Kingdom in a Flame." This was his Opinion of Dr. Benjamin Franklin. . . .

*The one who is the likeness of all.

Dr. Franklin (pardon the Expression) was cursed with a full Share of Understanding, he was a Man of Genius, but of so unprincipled an Heart, that the Merit of all his political & philosophical Disquisitions can never atone for the Mischiefs which he plunged Society into, by the Perversion of his Genius. He had such an Insight into human Nature, that he insinuated himself into various public Departments in the Province of Pennsylvania, & at last arrived to the Office of one of the Post Masters in America, a Place worth 4 or £500 Sterling p[er] Year. He was now released from the necessary Cares for a moderate Support; & was at Leisure to indulge in what might first strike his Fancy. . . .

Pride is Dr. Franklin's ruling Passion, & from this Source may be traced all the Actions of his life. He had a Contempt of Religion, of Mankind, & even of those whom he had duped; & had he viewed the Subject in a moral Light, he would have contemned hisself.

John Jay to Robert R. Livingston PARIS, JUNE 25, 1782

I shall endeavor to get lodgings as near to Dr. Franklin as I can. He is in perfect good health, and his mind appears more vigorous than that of any man of his age I have known. He certainly is a valuable Minister, and an agreeable companion.

Arthur Lee to James Warren AUGUST 1782

Congress had the fullest evidence and conviction that Dr. Franklin was both a dishonest & incapable man.

John Adams to Abigail Adams THE HAGUE, OCTOBER 12, 1782

Dr. Franklin has been a long time much indisposed as I lately learn with the Gout and Strangury.*

John Jay to Robert R. Livingston PARIS, DECEMBER 12, 1782

Dr. Franklin's firmness and exertions on the subject of the Tories did us much service. I enclose herewith a copy of a letter he wrote [on November 26] about that matter to Mr. [Richard] Oswald. It had much weight, and is written with a degree of acuteness and spirit seldom to be met with in persons of his age.

---

*Slow and painful urination, drip by drip.

Arthur Lee to John Adams PHILADELPHIA, JANUARY 26, 1783

The servility, envy, & avarice of the old man you mention have been the more pernicious to our cause, as he is most unaccountably rooted in the opinion of many, and nothing but success will in their eyes justify a conduct founded upon opposite principles.

Arthur Lee to James Warren PHILADELPHIA, MARCH 12, 1783

Mr. J. Adams is so persuaded, that Peace is settled that he has desired leave to resign & return home. I am not of opinion that we can spare him yet. He & Mr. Jay have acted a spirited, independent, & therefore, in my judgment, a most laudable part; & will be necessary in Europe to counteract the treachery of old Franklin. I had drawn up a vote of thanks to Mr. Adams for the extraordinary Services he has rendered us in Holland; but upon sounding I found the jealousy which Dr. F's friends, after his example, entertain of any approbation bestowed upon another, being a censure upon him, would render the passage of it doubtful. It was therefore thought more prudent not to move it. There never I think existed a man more meanly envious & selfish than Dr. Franklin. The reason probably why it is not seen so as to make men despise him is, that men in general listen much to professions, & look little to actions.

James Madison to Edmund Randolph PHILADELPHIA, MARCH 12, 1783

Franklin's correspondence on this occasion denotes a vigor of intellect, which is astonishing at his age, a letter to the British Minister on the case of the Tories in particular is remarkable for strength of reasoning, of sentiment & of expression. He concludes his letter to Congress with observing that he is now entering on his 78th year, 50 of which have been spent in the public Service; and that having lived to see like Simeon of old the salvation of his Country, his prayer is that he may be permitted to retire from public life.

John Adams to James Warren PARIS, APRIL 13, 1783

I have in some late Letters opened to You in Confidence the Dangers, which our most important Interests have been in, as well as the Opposition and Jealousy and Slanders, which your Ministers have met with, from the vain, ambitious and despotic Character of one Minister, I mean the C. de Vergennes. But You will form but an imperfect Idea after all of the Difficulties We have had to encounter, without taking into Consideration another Character equally selfish and interested, equally vain and ambitious, more jealous and envious, and more false and deceitful, I mean Dr. Franklin.

It is a saying of Algernon Sidney concerning Sir Walter Raleigh, that "his Morals were not sufficiently exact for a great Man." And the Observation can never be applied with more propriety than to Dr. Franklin. His whole Life has been one continued Insult to good Manners and to Decency. . . .

A sacred regard to Truth is among the first and most essential Virtues of a public Man. How many Kings have involved themselves and their Kingdoms in Misfortunes, by a Laxness in this particular? How much Mischief has been done in all Ages by Ministers of State, who have indulged themselves in a Duplicity and Finesse, or in other Words, in an Hypocrisy and falsehood, which some are even abandoned enough to recommend and prescribe to Politicians, but which never yet did anything but Harm and Mischief. I am sorry to say, but strict and impartial Justice obliges me to say, that from five complete Years of Experience of Dr. Franklin, which I have now had in Europe, I can have no Dependence on his Word. I never know when he speaks the Truth, and when not. If he talked as much as other Men, and deviated from the Truth as often in proportion as he does now, he would have been the Scorn of the Universe long ago. But his perpetual Taciturnity has saved him.

It would be Folly to deny that he has had a great Genius, and that he had written several things in Philosophy and in Politics, profoundly. But his Philosophy and his Politics have been infinitely exaggerated, by the studied Arts of Empiricism, until his Reputation has become one of the grossest Impostures, that has ever been practiced upon Mankind since the Days of Mahomet.

A Reputation so imposing in a Man of Artifice and Duplicity, of Ambition and Vanity, of Jealousy and Envy, is as real a Tyranny as that of the Grand Seignor. It is in vain to talk of Laws and Justice, of Right, of Truth, of Liberty, against the Authority of such a Reputation. It produces all the Servility of Adulation, all the

Fear, all the Expectation and Dependence in Court and of Imperial Splendor. He had been very sensible of this, and has taken Advantage of it.

As if he had been conscious of the Laziness, Inactivity and real Insignificance of his advanced Age, he has considered every American Minister, who has come to Europe, as his natural Enemy. He has been afraid that some one would serve his Country, acquire a reputation, and begin to be thought of by Congress to replace him.

Sensible that his Character has not been so much respected in America as in Europe, he has sought an Alliance to support him with Mr. de Sartine and the Comte de Vergennes and their "Autours"—Satellites. It is impossible to prove, but from what I know of him, I have no doubt, that he is the Man, who, by means of the Emissaries or Satellites just alluded to, made to those Ministers all the malicious Insinuations against Mr. Lee and Mr. Izard, which, although absolutely false and groundless, have made as much Noise in the World, and had almost the same Effects, as if they had been true. From the same detestable Source came the Insinuations and Prejudices against me, and the shameless abandoned Attack upon me, the History of which You know better than I. Hence too the Prejudices against Mr. [Francis] Dana, Mr. Jay and every other. These are my Opinions, though I cannot prove them, otherwise than by what I have seen and heard myself, what results from a long Series of Letters and Transactions, and what I know of the Characters of Men. The C[omte] has had his Head filled with so many Prejudices against others, and in favor of him, and has found him so convenient a Minister, ready always to comply with every Desire, never asking anything but when ordered and obliged to ask for Money, never proposing anything, never advising anything, that he has adopted all his Passions, Prejudices and Jealousies, and has supported him, as if his own Office depended upon him. He and his Office of Interpreters have filled all the gazettes of Europe with the most senseless Flattery of him, and by means of the Police set every Spectacle, Society, and even private Club and Circle to clapping him with such Applause, as they give to Opera Girls. This being the unfortunate Situation of foreign Affairs, what is to be done?

Franklin has, as he gives out, asked Leave to resign. He does not mean to obtain it, but to save the Shame of being recalled. I wish with all my Soul he was out of public Service, and in Retirement, repenting of his past Life, and preparing, as he ought to be, for another World. But as the Peace is made, and he is old, and it will make a horrid Wonder in the World to remove him, and it would be impossible to publish the whole Truth in Justification of it to the People of America as well as of Europe, perhaps it may be as well to let him alone. But at least Congress should firmly and steadily support their other Ministers against his insidious Maneuvers. They should add no more Feathers to his Cap. French Influence will forever aid him, and both will be eternally attacking openly and secretly every other Minister. So that I am persuaded he will remain as long as he lives, the Demon of Discord among our Ministers, and the Curse and Scourge of our foreign Affairs.

John Adams, Diary MAY 2, 1783

In Truth Congress and their Ministers have been played upon like Children, trifled with, imposed upon, deceived. Franklin's Servility and insidious faithless Selfishness is the true and only Cause why this Game has succeeded. He has aided Vergennes with all his Weight, and his great Reputation, in both Worlds, has supported this ignominious System and blasted every Man and every Effort to shake it off. I only have had a little Success against him.

James Warren to John Adams MILTON, MASS, OCTOBER 27, 1783

I don't know that I detest any Character more than that of the Old Man, who is, as you might expect your determined Enemy. You will before this reaches you get a paragraph of one of his Letters, which if you should by an Interval be in possession of your right Mind will put the Matter out of Doubt; How long will he live? and if he lives how long can he be able to preserve the good Opinion and Confidence of his Country? The Bubble must burst soon, or Mankind are more lost to Sentiment and Virtue, than I can suppose.

Comte de Vergennes to the Chevalier de La Luzerne
VERSAILLES, FEBRUARY 15, 1784

We think that Congress has acted wisely in recalling most of its agents in Europe; their character is too little conciliatory, and their head too much excited, to admit of their being useful to their country. The calmness and the prudence of Mr. Franklin are certainly grave faults in their eyes; but it is by those qualities that this minister has inspired us with confidence. I do not believe that the superior services which this minister has rendered to his country will be requited; I can say that it will be very difficult for Congress to replace him.

John Quincy Adams, Diary FEBRUARY 26, 1785

Mr. Franklin has been so long in France, that he is more a Frenchman than an American: I doubt whether he will enjoy himself perfectly if he returns to America.

Benjamin Rush to Richard Price PHILADELPHIA, OCTOBER 15, 1785

Dr. Franklin . . . has succeeded Mr. Dickinson as our governor. . . . The Doctor enjoys in his eightieth year the full exercise of all faculties of his mind. While Spain boasts of her Ximenes, France of her Fleury, and Britain of her Mansfield, all of whom sustained the burden of government after they passed the eightieth year of their lives, America claims a Franklin, inferior to none of them in activity of mind and clearness of perception on the great affairs of government. We expect, in consequence of his arrival, a revolution in favor of reason, justice, and humanity in our country. He has already begun to point out abuses and to propose schemes that are full of wisdom and benevolence.

Elkanah Watson, Memoirs 1786

On my first entering the room, he observed that all his old friends were dead, and he found himself alone, in the midst of a new generation, and added the remark, alike characteristic of the man and the philosopher, "he was in their way, and it was time he was off the stage." Yet he delighted a circle of young people (for he was a most instructive companion to youth in his old age) the whole evening with pleasant anecdote and interesting stories. His voice was very sonorous and clear, but at the same time hollow and peculiar.

Franklin was the first and greatest of American philosophers—a brilliant star in the galaxy of America's best benefactors—a child of nature, destitute of early literary acquirements, yet occupying a lofty position among the most distinguished literary men of his age. His own history will most adequately illustrate his useful career in a long life devoted to the promotion of the happiness of his fellow-men, and by his last will dispensing his beneficence centuries after his decease. Franklin was not averse to popular applause; he loved fame—not the blast of surreptitious honors; but that renown which was based on his own great deeds.

Benjamin Rush to Richard Price PHILADELPHIA, MAY 25, 1786

Our venerable friend Dr. Franklin continues to enjoy as much health and spirits as are compatible with his time of life. I dined with him a few days ago in a most agreeable circle, where he appeared as cheerful and gay as a young man of five-and-twenty. But his conversation was full of the wisdom and experience of mellow old age. He has destroyed party rage in our state, or to borrow an allusion from one of his discoveries, his presence and advice, like oil upon troubled waters, have composed the contending waves of faction which for so many years agitated the State of Pennsylvania.

William Pierce, "Character Sketches of Delegates to the Federal Convention" 1787

Dr. Franklin is well known to be the greatest philosopher of the present age;—all the operations of nature he seems to understand,—the very heavens obey him, and the Clouds yield up their Lightning to be imprisoned in his rod. But what claim he has to the politician, posterity must determine. It is certain that he does not shine much in public Council,—he is no Speaker, nor does he seem to let politics engage his attention. He is, however, a most extraordinary Man, and tells a story in a style more engaging than anything I ever heard. Let his Biographer finish his character. He is 82 years old, and possesses an activity of mind equal to a youth of 25 years of age.

John Adams to Benjamin Rush NEW YORK, APRIL 4, 1790

The History of our Revolution will be one continued Lie from one end to the other. the essence of the whole will be that Dr. Franklin's electrical Rod, smote the Earth and out sprung General Washington. That Franklin electrified him with his rod—and thence forward these two conducted all the Policy, Negotiations, Legislatures and War.

Benjamin Rush, Commonplace Book APRIL 18, 1790

Last evening at 11 o'clock died the venerable Dr. Franklin. He had been reduced by the stone in his bladder, but died finally of a pleurisy which terminated in an abscess in his lungs from which he discharged matter a few days before his death. This pleurisy was caught by lying with his windows open. He possessed his reason to the last day of his life, but spoke nothing of his future existence or expectation beyond the grave.

Thomas Jefferson to Ferdinand Grand NEW YORK, APRIL 23, 1790

The good old Doctor Franklin, so long the ornament of our country and I may say of the world, has at length closed his eminent career: he died on the 17th instant, of an imposthume of his lungs, which having suppurated and burst, he had not the strength to throw off the matter, and was suffocated by it: his illness from this imposthume was of sixteen days. Congress wear mourning for him by a resolve of their body.

James Madison, Motion in House of Representatives, New York Daily Advertiser APRIL 23, 1790

Mr. Madison rose and made the following motion: Mr. Speaker said he, Though we have been informed not only through the channel of the newspapers but by a more direct communication, of the decease of an illustrious character whose native genius has rendered distinguished services to the cause of science and of mankind in general, and whose patriotic exertions have contributed in a high degree to the independence and prosperity of this country in particular—the occasion seems to call upon us to pay some tribute to his memory expressive of the tender veneration his country feels for such distinguished merit. I therefore move the following resolution:

The house being informed of the decease of Benjamin Franklin, a citizen whose native genius was not more an ornament to human nature, than his various exertions of it have been precious to science, to freedom, and to his country, do resolve, as a mark of the veneration due to his memory, that the members wear the customary badge of mourning for one month.

John Adams to John Trumbull NEW YORK, APRIL 25, 1790

Franklin is gone, Peace to his Shade—Personal Resentments and Hatreds are not to be found in my nature in public affairs. I feel no ill will to his Memory—but I owe more to Truth than to his Fame; and I owe the Truth to my Country and Posterity. The last Letter of abuse to Congress in which he mentioned me he said I "was always an honest Man."—I wish my Conscience would allow me to say as much of him.—But from the first to the last of my acquaintance with him, I can reconcile his Conduct in public affairs neither to the Character of an honest Man, nor to that of a Man of Sense.

Thomas Jefferson to William Smith PHILADELPHIA, FEBRUARY 19, 1791

I can only therefore testify in general that there appeared to me more respect & veneration attached to the character of Doctor Franklin in France, than to that of any other person in the same country, foreign or native. I had opportunities of knowing particularly how far these sentiments were felt by the foreign ambassadors & ministers at the court of Versailles. The fable of his capture by the Algerines, propagated by the English newspapers, excited no uneasiness; as it was seen at once to be a dish cooked up to the palate of their readers. But nothing could exceed the anxiety of his diplomatic brethren, on a subsequent report of his death, which, though premature, bore some marks of authenticity.

I found the ministers of France equally impressed with the talents & integrity of Doctor Franklin. The Comte de Vergennes particularly gave me repeated and unequivocal demonstrations of his entire confidence in him. . . .

His death was an affliction which was to happen to us at some time or other. We have reason to be thankful he was so long spared; that the most useful life should be the longest also; that it was protracted so far beyond the ordinary span allotted to man, as to avail us of his wisdom in the establishment of our own freedom, & to bless him with a view of its dawn in the east, where they seemed, till now, to have learned everything, but how to be free.

The succession to Doctor Franklin, at the court of France, was an excellent school of humility. On being presented to any one as the minister of America, the commonplace question used in such cases was "C'est vous, Monsieur, qui remplace le Docteur Franklin?" "It is you, Sir, who replaces Doctor Franklin?" I generally answered, "No one can replace him, Sir; I am only his successor."

Thomas Paine, Rights of Man, *Part 1* 1791

The situation of Dr. Franklin as Minister from America to France, should be taken into the chain of circumstances. The diplomatic character is of itself the narrowest sphere of society that man can act in. It forbids intercourse by a reciprocity of suspicion; and a Diplomatic is a sort of unconnected atom, continually repelling and repelled. But this was not the case with Dr. Franklin. He was not the diplomatic of a Court, but of MAN. His character as a philosopher had been long established, and his circle of society in France was universal.

Thomas Paine, Age of Reason, *Part 2* 1795

To be happy in old age, it is necessary that we accustom ourselves to objects that can accompany the mind all the way through life, and that we take the rest as good in their day. The man of pleasure is miserable in old age, and the mere drudge in business is but little better: whereas natural philosophy, mathematical, and mechanical science, are a continual source of tranquil pleasure. . . . Those who knew Benjamin Franklin will recollect that his mind was ever young; his temper ever serene. Science, that never grows grey, was always his mistress. He was never without an object; for when we cease to have an object, we become like an invalid in an hospital waiting for death.

Thomas Jefferson to Samuel Smith MONTICELLO, AUGUST 22, 1798

Dr. Franklin, the greatest man and ornament of the age and country in which he lived.

Benjamin Rush, "Travels through Life" c. 1800

I never visited him without learning something.

John Adams to John Marshall WASHINGTON, D.C., FEBRUARY 10, 1801

Dr. Franklin, the most concise, sprightly, and entertaining writer of his time.

Mercy Otis Warren, History of the American Revolution 1805

The celebrity of Doctor Franklin has been so just and so extensive, that it is painful even for the impartial historian, who contemplates the superiority of his genius, to record the foibles of the man; but intoxicated by the warm caresses and unbounded applauses of all ranks, among a people where the art of pleasing is systematized, he appeared, notwithstanding his age and experience, in a short time after his residence in France, little less a Gallican than an American. This might be from policy. It was said, however, that he attached himself to the interest of the Count de Vergennes, who, though he countenanced the American revolution, and co-operated in measures that completed it, yet it was afterwards discovered, that he secretly wished to embarrass their councils, and dreaded the rising glory of the United States. Whatever suggestions there might have been, it was never supposed that Doctor Franklin was led off from his attachment to the interest of America; yet this distinguished sage became susceptible of a court influence, that startled his jealous and more frigid colleague, Mr. Lee.

John Adams to Benjamin Rush SEPTEMBER 19, 1806

My experience is perfectly conformable to yours respecting silent men. Silence is most commonly design and intrigue. In Franklin it was very remarkable, because he was naturally a great talker. I have conversed with him frequently in his garrulous humors, and his grandson, or son, Billy, has told me that he never knew a greater talker than his grandfather. But at other times he was as silent as midnight, and often upon occasions and in relation to subjects on which it was his duty to speak. Arthur Lee told me he had known him to sit whole evenings in London, without uttering a word, in company with the first men for science and literature, when the conversation had turned upon subjects on which he was supposed to be well informed.

Benjamin Rush to John Adams OCTOBER 31, 1807

Dr. Franklin thought a great deal, wrote occasionally, but read during the middle and latter years of his life very little, and hence the errors of several of his opinions upon government.

Thomas Jefferson to Thomas Jefferson Randolph WASHING-TON, D.C., NOVEMBER 24, 1808

It was one of the rules which, above all others, made Doctor Franklin the amiable of men in society, "never to contradict anybody." If he was urged to announce an opinion, he did it rather by asking questions, as if for information, or by suggesting doubts.

John Adams to Benjamin Rush QUINCY, APRIL 12, 1809

Dr. Franklin's behavior had been so excessively complaisant to the French ministry, and in my opinion had so endangered the essential interests of our country, that I had been frequently obliged to differ from him, and sometimes to withstand him to his face; so that I knew he had conceived an irreconcilable hatred of me, and that he had propagated and would continue to propagate prejudices, if nothing worse, against me in America from one end of it to the other.

Benjamin Rush to John Adams PHILADELPHIA, AUGUST 19, 1811

The Doctor was a rigid economist, but he was in every stage of his life charitable, hospitable, and generous. In his private intercourse with his fellow citizens he was honest even above suspicion, and from all I have ever seen and know of him I believe he was strictly upright and correct as a servant of the public.

Thomas Jefferson to Robert Walsh MONTICELLO, DECEMBER 4, 1818

As to the charge of subservience to France, besides the evidence of his friendly colleagues before named [Arthur Lee and John Adams], two years of my own service with him at Paris, daily visits, and the most friendly and confidential conversation, convince me it had not a shadow of foundation. He possessed the confidence of that government in the highest degree, insomuch, that it may truly be said, that they were more under his influence, than he under theirs. The fact is, that his temper was so amiable and conciliatory, his conduct so rational, never urging impossibilities, or even things unreasonably inconvenient to them, in short, so moderate and attentive to their difficulties, as well as our own, that what his enemies called subserviency, I saw was only that reasonable disposition, which, sensible that advantages are not all to be on one side, yielding what is just and liberal, is the more certain of obtaining liberality and justice. Mutual confidence produces, of course, mutual influence, and this was all which subsisted between Dr. Franklin and the government of France.

Reminiscence of Manasseh Cutler (as related by Ira Cheever)
POST 1821

As I walked up the avenue to his house, I reflected, I am going into the presence of a *great man*—one who had stood before kings and mighty ones of the earth. I hesitated; my knees smote together; but I could not retreat. I was greatly surprised to see in Dr. Franklin a small, lively, old man in his morning-gown, perfectly simple and unaffected in his appearance and manners. He immediately recognized me as the author of a botanical work— invited me to walk in his spacious and elegant garden; and in five minutes I felt as free and as much at home with him as with my own family or my most intimate friend.

James Madison, Conversation with Jared Sparks APRIL 25, 1830

In the Convention Dr. Franklin seldom spoke. As he was too feeble to stand long at a time, his speeches were generally written. He would arise and ask the favor of one of his colleagues to read what he had written. Occasionally, however, he would make short extemporaneous speeches with great pertinency and effect.

James Madison, Detached Memorandum BEFORE 1832

I did not become acquainted with Dr. Franklin till after his return from France and election to the Chief Magistracy of Pennsylvania. During the Session of the Grand Convention, of which he was a member and as long after as he lived, I had opportunities of enjoying much of his conversation, which was always a feast to me. I never passed half an hour in his company without hearing some observation or anecdote worth remembering. . . .

On entering his chamber in his extreme age when he had been much exhausted by pain and was particularly sensible of his weakness, Mr. M. said he, these machines of ours however admirably formed will not last always. Mine I find is just worn out. It must have been an uncommonly good one I observed to last so long, especially under the painful malady which had co-operated with age in preying on it; adding that I could not but hope that he was yet to remain some time with us, and that the cause of his suffering might wear out faster than his Constitution. The only alleviation he said to his pain was opium, and that he found as yet to be a pretty sure one. I told him I took for granted he used it as sparingly as possible as frequent doses must otherwise impair his constitutional strength. He was well aware he said that every Dose he took had that effect; but he had no other remedy; and thought the best terms he could make with his complaint was to give up a part of his remaining life, for the greater ease of the rest.

Elbridge Gerry

1744–1814

⚔ BORN IN Marblehead, Mass. Graduated from Harvard College, 1762. Entered family's mercantile business. Member, colonial House of Representatives, 1772–74, three provincial congresses, 1774–75, and Committee of Supplies of Provincial Congress, 1775. Delegate to Congress, 1776–80, 1783–85 (elected 1780–81 but refused to serve); signed Declaration of Independence and Articles of Confederation; member and often president of congressional Treasury Board, 1776–79. Member, state House of Representatives, 1776–77, 1780–81, 1786–87. Moved to Cambridge, Mass., 1786. Elected commissioner to Annapolis Convention but resigned, 1786. Delegate to Constitutional Convention, 1787. Refused to sign Constitution. U.S. representative, 1789–93, and Federalist presidential elector, 1796. Along with Charles Cotesworth Pinckney and John Marshall appointed by President John Adams envoy to treat with France, 1797 (XYZ Affair). Unsuccessful Republican candidate for governor, 1800–1803. Republican presidential elector, 1804. Governor, 1810–12 (defeated for reelection). Vice president of the United States, 1813 until death.

John Adams, Autobiography FEBRUARY 1776

Mr. Gerry was chosen [as a delegate to Congress], who went with me to Philadelphia, and We took our Seats in Congress on Friday 9 February 1776. In this Gentleman I found a faithful Friend, and an ardent persevering Lover of his Country, who never hesitated to promote with all his abilities and Industry the boldest measures reconcilable with prudence.

John Adams to James Warren JULY 15, 1776

The News, you will learn from my very worthy Friend Gerry. He is obliged to take a Ride for his Health, as I shall be very soon or have none. God grant he may recover it for he is a Man of immense Worth. If every Man here was a Gerry, the Liberties of America would be safe against the Gates of Earth and Hell.

John Adams to Abigail Adams PHILADELPHIA, JULY 15, 1776

My very deserving Friend, Mr. Gerry, sets off, tomorrow, for Boston, worn out of Health, by the Fatigues of this station. He is an excellent Man, and an active able statesman. I hope he will soon return hither.

JULY 29, 1776

Gerry carried with him a Cannister for you. But he is an old Bachelor, and what is worse a Politician, and what is worse still a kind of Soldier, so that I suppose he will have so much Curiosity to see Armies and Fortifications and Assemblies, that you will lose many a fine Breakfast at a Time when you want them most.

Nathaniel Peabody to Meshech Weare MORRISTOWN, N.J., JUNE 11, 1780

I have only at this time to recommend to your particular Notice the Honorable Elbridge Gerry Esq—Gentleman of distinguished Honor, integrity & Abilities—whose long and unremitted exertion in the Cause of America—Zeal & attachment to her Interest, has Justly entitled him to the most entire Esteem & Confidence of those Citizens who have had the Honor of an acquaintance with him.

Abigail Adams to Elbridge Gerry BRAINTREE, JULY 20, 1781

When I looked for your Name among those who form the Representative Body of the people this year I could not find it. I sought for it with the Senate, but was still more disappointed. I however had the pleasure of finding it amongst the delegates of this Commonwealth to Congress, where I flatter myself you will still do us Honor which posterity will gratefully acknowledge; and the virtuous few now confess. But as you are no worshiper of the rising Sun, or Adulator at the shrine of power, you must expect with others, who possess an Independent Spirit, to be viewed in the shade, to be eyed askance, to be malign'ed and to have your Good evil spoken of. But let not this Sir discourage you in the arduous Business. I hope America has not yet arrived at so great a pitch of degeneracy as to be given up by those alone who can save her; I mean the disinterested patriot—who possessing an unconfined Benevolence will persevere in the path of his duty. Tho the Ingratitude of his constituents and the Malevolence of his Enemies should conspire against him, he will feel within himself the best Intimation of his duty and he will look for no external Motive.

History informs us that the single virtue of Cato, upheld the Roman Empire for a time, and a Righteous few might have saved from the impending Wrath of an Offended deity the Ancient cities of Sodom and Gomorah. Why then my dear Sir, may I ask you, do you wish to withdraw yourself from publick Life?

You have supported the cause of America with zeal, with ardour and fidelity, but you have not met even with the gratitude of your fellow citizens—in that you do not stand alone.

You have a mind too Liberal to consider yourself only as an Individual, and not to regard both your Country and posterity—and in that view I know you must be anxiously concerned when you consider the undue Influence exercised in her Supreme Counsels. You can be no stranger I dare say Sir, to matters of the Highest importance to the future Welfare of America as a Nation; being now before her Representatives—and that she stands in need of the collected wisdom of the United States, and the Integrity of her most virtuous Members.

Charles Thomson to Hannah Thomson PRINCETON, N.J.,
OCTOBER 20, 1783

Though he is far from being distinguished for his talents in Oratory, and cannot boast of the thunder of his voice, the harmony of his periods or any of those high strokes of eloquence which transport and captivate the hearers, nor of a just arrangement of arguments or soft insinuating address which commands the attention of an Audience and leads them insensibly and almost involuntarily to the point he means to carry, yet with his feeble voice and uncouth delivery broken and interrupted with many a heck & hem & repetition of ofs & ands he assumed such a superiority over [his opponents].

OCTOBER 21, 1783

Mr. Gerry . . . seems to be used as the instrument for setting this continent in a flame.

Elbridge Gerry to John Adams PHILADELPHIA, JUNE 16, 1784

Here I am after a six Month Session at Annapolis, on my Way to Massachusetts, & altho my Opposition to the same System in America, which You have opposed in Europe, has perhaps rendered me equally obnoxious here to the aristocratic Party, yet I assure You the Pleasure resulting from a Reflection on the Measures adopted by Congress, overbalances every trifling Consideration of the Loss of Friendships, which being for the most part ostensible, are generally applied as Incentives to our Rewards of Servility, Baseness & Treachery, but rarely if ever of Fidelity, Honor or Patriotism.

Francis Dana to Elbridge Gerry ANNAPOLIS, JUNE 17, 1784

I am glad you had so agreeable a journey from hence, and so good an opportunity of entertaining yourself on the way with reflecting upon the congressional scenes: You have acted one of the principal parts in them, & cannot but derive much solid satisfaction from this reflection, "that what has been done, is pro bono publico,* *well done*." The interested views, absurd projects, prejudices, & partialities, of which you speak, are so many irresistible arguments against your conclusion, viz. that your own happiness can never be promoted by partaking in the politics of such an extensive republican government &c. Reflect, my dear Sir, again upon these things, and you will be convinced, that altho a Man shou'd not be able to effect much positive good, in such a heterogeneous a body, yet if he can prevent mischief, 'tis his duty to struggle hard to do it: And what it is our duty to do, that upon due reflection we shall find productive of our happiness. But you are out of your element when you are out of politicks: to talk of making pleasure *your* business, is to attempt a violence upon your disposition. You have not that levity of mind which is alone fitted for the pursuits of pleasure. Be yourself Man, and

*For the public good.

you will be happy. When I seem to interdict to you pleasurable pursuits, remember I do not mean to oppose an *inkling,* or as the French say the *penchant,* you seem to have to Matrimony. No, quite the contrary, I wou'd encourage it by every means in my power. This is a duty you still owe to God & your Country. "Take unto thyself a wife, & obey the ordinance of God." But look well to your choice, in that indeed is involv'd much happiness or much misery.

JULY 20, 1784

I agree you have attacked my position "that out of politicks you are out of your element" with your wonted ingenuity, and shall be thoroughly satisfied if you keep out of them for a short time with a view of entering *bona fide** into the holy state of matrimony. There are many duties incumbent upon us in this life, perfectly consistent with each other; but unless you can settle it in your own mind, that a proper attention to the woman of your choice, will not require of you a renunciation of your political career: I must urge it upon you to remain as you are. For without flattery, my friend, I know of no one in our State, whose experience and abilities have better fitted him to assist in the deliberation & guidance of our great national concerns. And it appears there never was a moment which called louder for the attention of such characters to them. . . . Remember the important matters which have been affected of late, by your personal exertions and perseverance, and which, I verily believe, wou'd not otherwise have been obtained. I know your feelings must have been frequently very sensibly touched by that sort of barbarous opposition you have met with; but have you not almost constantly borne it down, & carried your points? And what grateful sensations and reflections hath success brought along with it! I renew my charge to you then, *persevere.*

John Adams to Mercy Otis Warren AUTEUIL, FRANCE, MAY 6, 1785

I promise myself from Mr. Gerry's Attendance in Congress all those changes for the better in the Management of the general Affairs of the Union, which I have often seen proceed from the Clearness of his Head and the goodness of his heart. I know of

*In good faith.

scarcely any Man of more Address, more Industry or Perseverance. He never appeared in Congress without a great Influence.
He deserves to stand higher in the Estimation of Massachusetts
than he has appeared to me at this distance to stand. He has merited more of that State than I am afraid they know of.

Mercy Otis Warren to John Adams   MILTON, MASS., SEPTEMBER 1785

Mr. Gerry will not be eligible by the Confederation as a Delegate
after November. I wish his Countrymen may never forget his
Merits. But if his Happiness depended on their Favor, probably
he might long pursue without ever overtaking the Phantom. But
I have Reason to believe he means in future to build on the more
solid Base of Domestic Felicity.

John Jay to John Adams   NEW YORK, MAY 4, 1786

Our friend Gerry has retired from Congress with a charming,
amiable lady, whom he married here. I regret his absence, for he
discharged the trust reposed in him with great fidelity, and with
more industry and persevering attention than many are distinguished by.

William Pierce, "Character Sketches of Delegates to the Federal Convention" 1787

Mr. Gerry's character is marked for integrity and perseverance.
He is a hesitating and laborious speaker; possesses a great degree of confidence and goes extensively into all subjects that he
speaks on, without respect to elegance or flower of diction. He is
connected and sometimes clear in his arguments, conceives well,
and cherishes as his first virtue, a love for his Country. Mr. Gerry
is very much of a Gentleman in his principles and manners;—he
has been engaged in the mercantile line and is a Man of property.
He is about 37 years of age.*

Unknown to Jefferson   PHILADELPHIA, OCTOBER 11, 1787

After four months session the house [i.e., the Constitutional
Convention] broke up. The represented states, eleven & a half,
having unanimously agreed to the act handed to you, there were

---

*Gerry was actually forty-three years old.

only three dissenting voices; one from New England, a man of sense, but a Grumbletonian. He was of service by objecting to every thing he did not propose.

Portland, Maine, **Cumberland Gazette** JANUARY 24, 1788

Why gentlemen should be opposed to the introduction of Mr. Gerry [as a guest] to the [Massachusetts ratifying] Convention, we are unable to determine.—His greatest enemies allow him to be a man of ability, integrity, and to use their own expressions, "a politician of mathematical nicety."

Louis Guillaume Otto, Biographies FALL 1788

Mr. Elb. Gerry is a small man, very intriguing and without much finesse, who until recently has been rather successful. He has been the most active member of Congress for the longest time. He has acquired a great knowledge of public affairs, which he makes the best use of to appear worthy in the opinion of his fellow-citizens. In 1782 he delivered a speech in the state legislature at Boston to persuade it not to ratify the consular convention. He pretended to like M. Luzerne very much, but one must mistrust all his noble protestations. In general we have very few friends among the powerful men of Massachusetts. Our commerce does not interest them and our fisheries impede them. Mr. [James] Bowdoin, Mr. [Rufus] King, Mr. Samuel Adams, etc., get all of their political ideas from writing or talking with Mr. [John] Jay and John Adams. The people in general like the French, since they have often seen our ships and they remember the services we have rendered them.

James Warren to Elbridge Gerry PLYMOUTH, MASS., MARCH 3, 1789

I suppose you are now just launching into the ocean of politics, an ocean always turbulent, perhaps now more tempestuous than usual. I wish your habits and Experience may preserve you from Seasickness, while the uniformity of your Conduct, and the rectitude of your Mind may lead you to stem the rolling Billows. Your situation may be singular, but you may as well oppose the Billows as run with an easy Sail before them. Your antifederal Sins will never be forgiven by a Party who while they wish you to support their System, are malignant enough to represent you as puerile and unsteady in your own, that is they report that you was greatly elated with your Election [to the U.S. House of Representatives], and had become the highest federal in the Country. All this & much more would be too Contemptible to be mentioned for any other purpose than to show the Temper of the Party. I often reflect on your situation & think where you will fix your Confidence. A man that has been used to Act with the old Patriots will feel a defect in modern Sentiments & modern views which even Considerable abilities will not supply the place of.

Elbridge Gerry to James Warren NEW YORK, MARCH 22, 1789

I foresaw it was impossible for me to feel easy in a branch of the federal legislature, where I had few or no connections & friends, whilst these were in the same body but politically sequestered. Whatever the State of my case upon republican principles may be, I cannot Separate from my mind the idea of a degradation, when I reflect that the flower of my life has been spent in the arduous business and see a preference to those who have endured very few of the toils of the revolution. But we both know that republican governments never were remarkable & probably never will be for gratitude, & therefore private life is the System which we ought to pursue for happiness whilst the road to preferment is thro the maizes of intrigue, Servility and corruption, & there is no great prospect of attaining it if we mean to preserve a "reverence for ourselves."

New York Daily Advertiser APRIL 30, 1789

[Gerry] has become the avowed friend of the Constitution.

Samuel Henshaw to Theodore Sedgwick BOSTON, JUNE 14, 1789

Consult Mr. Gerry—I advise you to take pains to be on good terms with Mr. Gerry—I am sure you wont find a better Man—a better friend.

Elbridge Gerry to James Warren NEW YORK, JULY 10, 1789

I am on good terms with the person you allude to [Vice President John Adams], but have kept a distance in consequence of the pompous ideas with which our new Government commenced, for a person sinks in my esteem in proportion as he rises in his

Own on account of federal station. I ask no favor of Government & expect none, & therefore hold myself very independent in sentiment & conduct: this I suppose is criminal in the eyes of sycophants, but the society of such is painful to us both & to displease them is the best mode of a separation.

Abigail Adams to Mary Cranch RICHMOND HILL, NEW YORK CITY, JULY 12, 1789

The Senate is composed of many men of great abilities, who appear to be liberal in their sentiments and candid towards each other. The House is composed of some men of equal talents. Others, the debates will give you the best Idea of them, but there is not a member whose sentiments clash more with my Ideas of things than Mr. G——y. He certainly does not comprehend the Great National System which must Render us respectable abroad & energetic at Home and will assuredly find himself lost amidst Rocks & sands. . . . I really believe Mr. G——y to be an honest Man.

Benjamin Goodhue to Samuel Phillips NEW YORK, AUGUST 11, 1789

Gerry . . . has as high notions of profusive grants as any person I ever knew, and has manifested such an illiberal and ugly a disposition since he has been in Congress that I believe no man has fewer friends then Mr. Gerry.

Benjamin Goodhue to Stephen Goodhue NEW YORK, AUGUST 20, 1789

We have done all in our power to prevent it [large pay for Congress], I mean our Massachusetts members, (Gerry excepted). . . . Perhaps it may not be well to have it publickly Known that Gerry was on that side, but he is a high blade, and a troublesome member.

James Sullivan to Elbridge Gerry NEW YORK, AUGUST 30, 1789

Your Enemies wish to find you in an unpopular Singularity that they may the more completely foil you. They represent you as Speaking often and in opposition to all measures but the people have Confidence in you.

Abigail Adams to Cotton Tufts NEW YORK, SEPTEMBER 1, 1789

Mr. G—— What can I say. You see him always in the minority, you see him very frequently wrong and the poor man looks ghastly. I believe he is worried, mortified and quite in the horrors. A constant correspondent of W[arre]n and his Wife, all of whom see nothing but ruin & destruction before them, & who will again Set our State by the ears if possible. Watch them closely.

Elbridge Gerry to John Wendell MAY 16, 1790

The indisposition of myself & family, & a constant attention to business when in health have induced me of late to suspend answers to all the letters of my friends; indeed the measure has been indispensable, for the influenza has disqualified me a great part of the time from attending to any business.

John Page, Speech in U.S. House of Representatives JULY 8, 1790

[Gerry] is remarkable for his coolness and his particular attention to every sentiment offered in debate.

James Iredell to Hannah Iredell BOSTON, OCTOBER 7, 1792

He is certainly a very agreeable Man, and I am persuaded from every thing I have heard & observed a very worthy one.

John Adams to Abigail Adams PHILADELPHIA, JUNE 21, 1795

One of the Company expressed such Inveteracy against my old Friend Gerry that I could not help taking up his Vindication. The future Election of a Governor, in Case of an empty Chair, excites Jealousy which I have long perceived. These Things will always be so. Gerry's Merit is inferior to that of no Man in Massachusetts, except the present Governor [Samuel Adams], according to My Ideas and Judgment of Merit. I wish he was more enlarged however and more correct in his Views. He never was one of the threads tyed into the knot, and was never popular with that Sett.

Abigail Adams to Mary Cranch PHILADELPHIA, JUNE 23, 1797

The President has now nominated Mr. Gerry [as an envoy to France]. This I know will be cavilled at by some, and he will be blamed for it, but the responsibility rests with him, and he must bear it. He would not have nominated him if he had not thought him an honest Man and a Friend to his Country, who will neither be deceived nor warped. I hope he will not refuse.

Charles Cotesworth Pinckney to Rufus King PARIS, APRIL 4, 1798

I never met with a man of less candor and so much duplicity as Mr. Gerry.

William Vans Murray to John Quincy Adams THE HAGUE, APRIL 13, 1798

Though I know that he is a very well informed one upon Congress business, and of a most friendly turn of heart, good husband, father and neighbor, yet I know him so well as to say that of all men I know in America he is perhaps the least qualified to play a part in Paris, either among the men or the women. He is too virtuous for the last, too little acquainted with the world and with himself for the first, and could do no possible good but in a relative character as one of three envoys.

Robert Troup to Rufus King NEW YORK, OCTOBER 2, 1798

As to Mr. Gerry, I can say nothing honorable to him, or pleasing to you. *De mortuis nil nisi bonum** is a maxim as applicable to him as if he was in his grave.

Timothy Pickering to John Marshall TRENTON, OCTOBER 19, 1798

The President ought to be acquainted with Mr. Gerry's whole conduct. Your journal shows it to have been characterized, not only with timidity, indecision and meanness, but with treachery.

George Cabot to Timothy Pickering BROOKLINE, MASS., NOVEMBER 17, 1798

Mr. Wolcott can tell you that in a dispute with the President at his (Mr. Wolcott's) table, concerning the character of Mr. Gerry, I was provoked to be rude; and that I pronounced him "totally unfit to conduct any great affair of himself, and from his captious

*Of the dead say nothing but good.

and jealous temper altogether unqualified to act with others." Such he has always been; such his late colleagues have found him; and such, I am persuaded, even the French now think him.

FEBRUARY 14, 1799

I think it impossible for any man of common sense to avoid seeing that Gerry is too great a fool to have been employed by a wise government in a business of so much consequence.

Robert Troup to Rufus King NEW YORK, NOVEMBER 6, 1799

Little Gerry is crawling out of his obscurity and giving entertainments as a candidate for the office of Governor of Massachusetts. I understand he expects to be supported by the independent of both parties.

Benjamin Rush, Sketches c. 1800

He was a respectable young merchant, of a liberal education, and considerable knowledge. He was slow in his perceptions and in his manner of doing business, and stammering in his speech, but he knew and embraced truth when he saw it. He had no local or state prejudices. Every part of his conduct in 1775, 1776, and 1777 indicated him to be a sensible, upright man, and a genuine friend to republican forms of government.

Fisher Ames to Oliver Wolcott Jr. DEDHAM, MASS., JANUARY 2, 1800

Massachusetts is threatened with Gerry, who, though a weak creature, would unite the confidence of the anarchists and would gain and abuse a portion of that of his adversaries.

Mercy Otis Warren, History of the American Revolution 1805

This gentleman entered from principle, early in the opposition to British encroachments, and continued one of the most uniform republicans to the end of the contest. He was the next year chosen a delegate to the continental Congress. Firm, exact, perspicuous, and tenacious of public and private honor, he rendered essential service to the union for many years that he continued a member of that honorable body.

John Adams to Thomas Jefferson   QUINCY, MAY 21, 1812

Though Mr. Gerry is not too old for the most arduous Service, he is one of the earliest and oldest Legislators in the Revolution and has devoted himself, his fortune and his family in the Service of his Country.

Rufus King to John Adams   NOVEMBER 23, 1814

Another of the patriots of the revolution is gone; the Vice President was dressed as usual to attend the Senate this morning, went in his carriage to call upon Mr. Nourse of the Treasury department, complained while there of feeling unwell, was helped by Mr. Nourse into the carriage to return to his quarters, distant not more than a quarter of a mile, was senseless when he arrived there & being taken out & laid upon a bed immediately expired without a groan or a struggle. Knowing your long & constant friendship for Mr. Gerry, I have thought it to be my duty to impart to you the melancholy information.

Alexander Hamilton
1757–1804

⫫ BORN ON Nevis, Leeward Islands, British West Indies. Came to America in 1772. Entered King's College (Columbia), 1773. Wrote pamphlets and newspaper essays favoring independence, 1774–75. Commissioned by Second Provincial Congress to command artillery company, 1776. George Washington's aide-de-camp with rank of lieutenant colonel, 1777–81. Married Elizabeth Schuyler, daughter of the wealthy Albany manor lord Philip Schuyler, 1780. Led attack on redoubt at Yorktown, 1781. Settled in Albany, studied law, and admitted to bar, 1782. Member, Confederation Congress, 1782–83, 1788. Opened law office in New York City, 1783. Argued case of *Rutgers v. Waddington,* 1784. A founder of Bank of New York, 1784. Delegate to Annapolis Convention, 1786; drafted report of convention. Member, state Assembly, 1787. Delegate to Constitutional Convention, 1787; signed Constitution as only New York delegate. Published attack on Gov. George Clinton, July 21, 1787. Possible author of "Cæsar" essays, 1787. Coauthor of "Publius": *The Federalist,* 1787–88. Member, New York Convention, 1788; voted to ratify Constitution. U.S. secretary of the treasury, 1789–95. Leader of Federalist Party. After retirement from Treasury, returned to New York City to practice law; remained active in politics. Major general (second in command) of Provisional Army raised to meet potential threat from France, 1798. Opposed Aaron Burr's election as U.S. senator, 1797, as president, 1800–1801, and as governor of New York, 1804. Killed in duel with Burr.

Alexander Hamilton to Edward Stevens ST. CROIX, NOVEMBER 11, 1769

To confess my weakness, Ned, my Ambition is prevalent that I contemn the groveling and condition of a Clerk or the like, to which my Fortune &c. condemns me and would willingly risk my life though not my Character to exalt my Station. I'm confident, Ned, that my Youth excludes me from any hopes of immediate Preferment nor do I desire it, but I mean to prepare the way for futurity. I'm no Philosopher you see and may be justly said to Build Castles in the Air. My Folly makes me ashamed and beg you'll Conceal it, yet Neddy we have seen such Schemes successful when the Projector is Constant. I shall Conclude saying I wish there was a War.

Alexander Hamilton to John Laurens MIDDLEBROOK, N.J., MAY 22, 1779

I hate money making men.

RAMAPO, N.J., JUNE 30, 1780

Have you not heard that I am on the point of becoming a benedict? I confess I am guilty. Next fall completes my doom. I give up my liberty to Miss Schuyler. She is a good hearted girl who I am sure will never play the termagant; though not a genius she has good sense enough to be agreeable, and though not a beauty, she has fine black eyes—is rather handsome and has every other requisite of the exterior to make a lover happy. And believe me, I am lover in earnest, though I do not speak of the perfections of my Mistress in the enthusiasm of Chivalry.

Marquis de Lafayette to George Washington PARAMUS, N.J., NOVEMBER 28, 1780

[On the appointment of an adjutant general for Washington's army.] Unless, however you was to cast your Eye on a man who, I think, would suit better than any other in the world. Hamilton is, I confess, the officer whom I would like to see in that station. At equal advantages his services deserve from you the preference on any other. But his knowledge of Your opinions and intentions on Military arrangements, his love of discipline the advantages he would have on all the others principally when both armies will operate together, and his Uncommon Abilities would render him perfectly agreeable to you. The use of him would be increased by this preferment, and on other points he would render the same services. An Adjutant General ought always to be with the Commander in chief. Hamilton should therefore remain in your family, and his Great Industry for Business would render him perfectly serviceable in all circumstances. On every public or private account, My dear General, I would advise you to take him.

Alexander Hamilton to John Laurens NEW WINDSOR, N.Y., FEBRUARY 4, 1781

A politician My Dear friend must be at all times supple—he must often dissemble.

George Washington to John Sullivan NEW WINDSOR, N.Y., FEBRUARY 4, 1781

How far Colo. Hamilton, of whom you ask my opinion as a financier, has turned his thoughts to that particular study I am unable to answer because I never entered upon a discussion on this point with him; but this I can venture to advance from a thorough knowledge of him, that there are few men to be found, of his age, who has a more general knowledge than he possesses, and none whose Soul is more firmly engaged in the cause, or who exceeds him in probity and Sterling virtue.

Philip Schuyler to Alexander Hamilton ALBANY, FEBRUARY 25, 1781

Long before I had the least Intimation that you intended that connection with my family, which is so very pleasing to me, and which affords me such entire satisfaction I had studied Your Character, and that of the other Gentlemen who composed the General's family. I thought I discovered in all an attention to the duties of their station, in some a considerable degree of ability, but (without a compliment for I trust there is no necessity of that between us), in you only I found those qualifications so essentially necessary to the man who is to aid and council a commanding General, environed with difficulties of every kind, and these perhaps more, and of greater magnitude, than any other ever has had to encounter, whose correspondence must of necessity be extensive always interesting, and frequently so delicate as to require much Judgment and address to be properly managed. The public voice has confirmed the Idea I had formed of You, but what is more consoling to me and more honorable to you, men of genius, Observation and Judgment think as I do on the occasion. Your quitting your station must therefore be productive of very material Injuries to the public, and this consideration, exclusive of others, impels me to wish that the unhappy breach should be closed, and a mutual Confidence restored. You may both of you Imagine when you separate, that the cause will remain a secret, but I will venture to speak decidedly, and say It is impossible, and I fear the Effect, especially with the French Officers, with the French Minister, and even with the French Court; these already Observe so many divisions between us; they know and acknowledge your Abilities and how necessary you are to the General. Indeed how will the loss be replaced? He will if you leave him, have not one Gentleman left sufficiently versed in the French to convey his Ideas. And if he obtains one, it is more than probable that he will be a mere interpreter, without being able to afford his General an Idea, and Incapable of conducting business with any competent degree of address, propriety or delicacy.

It is evident my Dear Sir that the General conceived himself the Aggressor, and that he quickly repented of the Insult; "he wished to heal a difference which could not have happened but in a moment of passion." It falls to the lot of few men to pass through life without one of those unguarded moments which wound the feelings of a friend; let us then impute them to the frailty of human nature, and with [Laurence] Sterne's recording angel, drop a tear, and blot It out of the page of life. I do not mean to reprehend the maxims you have formed for your conduct; they are laudable, and though generally approved, yet times and circumstances sometimes render a deviation necessary and Justifiable. This necessity now exists in the distresses of Your country. Make the sacrifice, the greater it is, the more glorious to you, your services are wanted, they are wanted in that particular station which You have already filled so beneficially to the public, and with such extensive reputation. I am as incapable of wishing as you are of doing, any thing injurious to those principles of honor, which If I may use the expression, are the test of virtue; my wishes, which are very earnest for a reconciliation I am convinced you will impute to their true motives, public good and the best affections of the human heart.

Alexander Hamilton to Elizabeth Hamilton HEAD OF ELK, MD., SEPTEMBER 6, 1781

Every day confirms me in the intention of renouncing public life, and devoting myself wholly to you. Let others waste their time and their tranquillity in a vain pursuit of power and glory; be it my object to be happy in a quiet retreat with my better angel.

Alexander Hamilton to the Marquis de Lafayette ALBANY, NOVEMBER 3, 1782

I have been employed for the last ten months in rocking the cradle and studying the art of fleecing my neighbors. I am now a Grave Counselor at law, and shall soon be a grand member of Congress. The Legislature at their last session took it into their heads to name me pretty unanimously one of their delegates. I am going to throw away a few months more in public life and then I retire a simple citizen and good paterfamilias. I set out for Philadelphia in a few days. You see the disposition I am in. You are condemned to run the race of ambition all your life. I am already tired of the career and dare to leave it.

James McHenry to Alexander Hamilton PRINCETON, N.J., OCTOBER 22, 1783

The homilies you delivered in Congress are still recollected with pleasure. The impressions they made are in favor of your integrity and no one but believes you a man of honor and republican principles. Were you ten years older and twenty thousand pounds richer, there is no doubt but that you might obtain the suffrages of Congress for the highest office in their gift. You are supposed to possess various knowledge, useful—substantial—and ornamental. Your very grave and your cautious—your men who measure others by the standard of their own creeping politics think you sometimes intemperate, but seldom visionary, and that were you to pursue your object with as much cold perseverance as you do with ardor and argument you would become irresistible. In a word, if you could submit to spend a whole life in dissecting a fly you would be in their opinion one of the greatest men in the world.

Hugh Knox to Alexander Hamilton ST. CROIX, JULY 28, 1784

I have always had a just & secret pride in having Advised you to go to America, & in having recommended you to Some of my old friends there; Since you have not only Answered, but even far Exceeded, our most Sanguine hopes & Expectations. I am glad to find that your popularity increases, & that your fine talents are coming into play, in a way that Contributes so much to your own honor & Emolument, & to the Good of the public. Perhaps Camps & marches & the hardy deeds of War, may have a little fortified & Steeled your Constitution (which used to be rather delicate & frail). But beware you do not enfeeble & impair it again, by plunging into intense Studies, & the anxieties of the Bar: For I know your laudable Ambition to Excel, & that you will Strain Every Nerve to be among the first of your profession. And, great as your talent[s] are, I should imagine that the accurate Study of So Complex & Voluminous a Science as the law, & Acquiring all the habits of a pleader, would cost you a deal of Labor.

Your Matrimonial Connection, I should think, might Enable you to live at your ease (I do not mean the Otium inglorisum,* but the otium honestum†) As a Gentleman of Independent fortune, & to pursue Studies more pleasing to yourself & perhaps more profitable to the Commonwealth, & to posterity. You guess at the meaning of this hint. But you are certainly a better Judge of the propriety & Expediency of your present pursuits, than I can possibly be.

William Pierce, "Character Sketches of Delegates to the Federal Convention" 1787

Colo. Hamilton is deservedly celebrated for his talents. He is a practitioner of the Law, and reputed to be a finished Scholar. To a clear and strong judgment he unites the ornaments of fancy, and whilst he is able, convincing, and engaging in his eloquence the Heart and Head sympathize in approving him. Yet there is something too feeble in his voice to be equal to the strains of oratory,—it is my opinion that he is rather a convincing Speaker, than a blazing Orator. Colo. Hamilton requires time to think— he enquires into every part of his subject with the searchings

*Inglorious leisure.
†Honorable leisure.

of philosophy, and when he comes forward he comes highly charged with interesting matter, there is no skimming over the surface of a subject with him, he must sink to the bottom to see what foundation it rests on.—His language is not always equal, sometimes didactic like Bolingbroke's at others light and tripping like Stern's. His eloquence is not so defusive as to trifle with the senses, but he rambles just enough to strike and keep up the attention. He is about 33 years old, of small stature, and lean. His manners are tinctured with stiffness, and sometimes with a degree of vanity that is highly disagreeable.

New York Journal SEPTEMBER 20, 1787

I have also known an upstart attorney, palm himself upon a great and good man, for a youth of extraordinary genius, and under the shadow of such a patronage make himself at once known and respected; but being sifted and bolted to the brain, he was, at length, found to be a superficial, self-concerted coxcomb, and was of course turned off, and disregarded by his patron.

DECEMBER 5, 1787

What in nature, observes a correspondent, is more despicable than a FOP, ——The Fop, says a modern poet, most resembles the gay mushroom;—as,

> From his own dunghill lately sprung,
> So buxom, debonair, and young;
> Yet on his brow sits empty scorn,—
> "He hates mechanics, meanly born."
> Stranger to merit—genius—sense—
> He owes his rise to impudence,
> With strutting self-importance fraught,
> Free—from each particle of thought;
> He'll not debase himself to think,—
> " 'Tis too damn'd low,"—but he will drink.
> From his own lips his praises flow,
> With—"Damme! I did so and so!—
> I've e'en in paths of honor trod;
> I'd soon, go to hell!—by God!—
> Than lose my honor!"—yet his genius
> Consists in blasphemy and meanness;
> In what true honor interdicts,

And in diverting little tricks.
He'll, all at once, start from his chair,
Twirl his whip and sing an air,
Dance, to show his grace and shape,
Brisk and sprightly as an—Ape.
To the glass he often goes,
There adjusts his stock and clothes,
Meets his image with a glance,
Of the sweetest complaisance.
He's first,—and oft the only one,—
To laugh at his own jest or pun.
Suppose it is wond'rous witty,
But men of sense will—smile and pity.
Such is the hero of my poem,
Readers—you must surely know him.

James Kent to Nathaniel Lawrence POUGHKEEPSIE, DECEMBER 21, 1787

You may praise who you please & I will presume to say that I think Publius is a most admirable writer & wields the sword of Party dispute with justness, energy, & inconceivable dexterity. The Author *must be* Hamilton who I think in Genius & political Research is not inferior to Gibbon, Hume or Montesquieu.

Hugh Hughes, "'Interrogator' to Publius or the Pseudo-Federalist" DECEMBER 1787

You appear to be much bloated by a vain Opinion of a little Learning and Knowledge, and not infrequently to have written like a Person, who considered himself as the sole Proprietor of all common Sense, permit me to remind you of the Fable of the Ox and the Frog, who, ambitious to make as great an Appearance as the Former, kept straining its lanky Sides till it burst, which, must be the Fate of every Individual whatever, that attempts to put his scanty Knowledge or Acquirements in Competition with the Aggregate Knowledge of a Nation—Only reflect on how little you know of your own mental and corporal Composition, as well as of what daily and momently contributes to your Support and Existence or, that many of the most simple Plebeians, or Mechanics, can teach you some of the first Principles of Philosophy. Or how very little you know of any Thing, when compared with what is

unknown to you and Thousands who are much wiser, & you will
not find much Cause to value yourself an Omniscience.*

Samuel Blachley Webb to Joseph Barrell NEW YORK, JANUARY 13, 1788

We have in the Press a Pamphlet written by Colonel Hamilton
under the Signature of Publius on the subject of a Federal Government, which I will send you by the first conveyance. He is
undoubtedly one of the most sensible men in America, though
yet not much more than Thirty years old.

"A Citizen, and Real Friend to Order and Good Government" New York Daily Advertiser MARCH 21, 1788

The publications of Col. Hamilton, in defense of the liberties of
America previous to the late war, when a youth in the college of
New York; his great military services, and the confidential line
in which he stood with that good and great man General Washington, during that war, are indubitable proofs of his virtue. As a
lawyer, a politician, and a statesman, Col. Hamilton is certainly
great; as a public speaker he is clear, pointed and sententious;
he excels most men in reply, being possessed of the powers of
reasoning in an eminent degree, and he is endowed with a most
benevolent and good heart.

David S. Bogart to Samuel Blachley Webb POUGHKEEPSIE, JUNE 14, 1788

Mr. Hamilton, the American Cicero.

Charles Tillinghast to John Lamb POUGHKEEPSIE, JUNE 21, 1788

You would be surprised, did you not know the Man, what an
amazing Republican Hamilton wishes to make himself to be considered—But he is known—

Philip Schuyler to John Bradstreet Schuyler POUGHKEEPSIE, JUNE 26, 1788

Though all [the Federalist speakers in the New York Convention
are eloquent, Hamilton's] sentiments are so true, his judgment

*In the Hugh Hughes Papers, Library of Congress.

so correct, his elocution so pleasing, so smooth, and yet so [forcible] that he reaches the heart and carries conviction, where every avenue to conviction is shut up. I fear there are too many, who labor under this prejudice.

Samuel Blachley Webb to Catherine Hogeboom POUGHKEEPSIE, JUNE 27, 1788

We have been entertained for upwards of two hours this morning by Colonel Hamilton in one of the most elegant speeches I ever heard. He is indeed one of the most remarkable genius's of the Age, his Political knowledge exceeds, I believe, any Man in our Country, and his Oratorial abilities has pleased his friends and surprised his Enemies.

Robert C. Johnson to William Samuel Johnson POUGHKEEPSIE, JUNE 28, 1788

I am this moment returned from hearing Hamilton [at the state ratifying convention]—warm, animated, clear, logical & convincing; attracting, nay, forcing universal admiration & applause. And he is at present an Enthusiast—

. . . I have heard Hamilton with rapture & admiration.

Melancton Smith to Nathan Dane POUGHKEEPSIE, JUNE 28, 1788

Hamilton is the champion, he speaks frequently, very long and very vehemently—has, like Publius, much to say not very applicable to the subject—

New York **Daily Advertiser** JULY 21, 1788

Mr. Hamilton made another display of those great abilities for which he is justly distinguished; he was powerful in his reasoning, and so persuasively eloquent and pathetic [i.e., emotional], that he drew tears from most of the audience.

Richard Platt to Winthrop Sargent NEW YORK, AUGUST 8, 1788

Little Hamilton shines like a Star of the first magnitude. Think how great his Victory in our Convention when with only 19

Federalists opposed to 46 most violent Anti's with Clinton, Yates, Lansing, Smith & Jones at their head, after six or seven weeks, he triumphed & gave us the Constitution.

Louis Guillaume Otto, Biographies FALL 1788

Great orator, intrepid in public debates. Zealous partisan, to an extreme over the new Constitution, and declared enemy of Governor Clinton, whom he had the courage to attack publicly in a newspaper without any provocation. He is one of those rare men who have distinguished themselves equally on the field of battle and at the bar. He owes everything to his talents. An indiscretion got him into trouble with General Washington for whom he served as confidential secretary; other indiscretions obliged him to leave Congress in 1783. He has a little too much pretension and too little prudence.

Here is what M. Luzerne said about him in 1780: "Mr. Hamilton, one of the aides de camp of General Washington who has the most influence with him, man of spirit, of a mediocre integrity; he left the English territory where he was born of low extraction. . . . Also a favorite of M. de Lafayette. Mr. Conway thinks that Hamilton hates the French, that he is absolutely corrupted and that the connections that he will appear to have with us will never be anything but deceptive."

Mr. Hamilton has done nothing that could justify this last opinion; he is only too impetuous and because he wants to control everything, he fails in his intentions. His eloquence is often out of place in public debates, where precision and clarity are preferred to a brilliant imagination. It is believed that Mr. Hamilton is the author of the pamphlet entitled *The Federalist*. He has again missed his mark. This work is of no use to educated men and it is too learned and too long for the ignorant. It has, however, made him a great celebrity and a small frigate has been named *Hamilton* which was pulled through the streets of New York during the great federal procession. But these parades only make a momentary impression here and as the Antifederalist party is the largest in the state, Mr. Hamilton has lost more than he has gained by his zeal on this occasion.

A stranger in this state, where he rose by benevolence, Mr. Hamilton has found the means to run off with the daughter of

General Schuyler,* a great proprietor and very influential. After being reconciled with the family, he now possesses the esteem of his father-in-law.

Thomas Lee Shippen to Thomas Jefferson LONDON, FEBRUARY 3, 1789

Mr. S. Morris son of General Morris of New York is just arrived from America. He gives me a very interesting account of the proceedings of the New York Convention in which Hamilton makes a godlike figure indeed.

Alexander Hamilton to Isaac Ledyard JAMAICA, N.Y., FEBRUARY 18, 1789

In Politics as in war the first blow is half the battle.

Abraham Clark to Jonathan Dayton MARCH 1789

I feel myself out of all patience with Col. Hamilton. He really appears to be, what I have some times thought him, a shim sham politician. He must needs soon run himself aground. His politics are such as will not stand the test. He will soon refine them to nothing.

Tristram Lowther to James Iredell NEW YORK, MAY 9, 1789

The popularity of Col. Hamilton has been hurt by his declining to represent this district in Congress; it is supposed he looks up to be Financier-General, for which he has been preparing himself, or to be appointed a foreign ambassador, for either of which he is extremely well qualified. He is said and believed to be a man of such extraordinary powers as to be able to render himself master of any subject in a week.

Fisher Ames to John Lowell NEW YORK, SEPTEMBER 13, 1789

I think so highly of Col. Hamilton's moral & intellectual qualities that I consider his appointment to the head of the Treasury as an auspicious event.

---

*Otto: Elopement is more common in America than in France; the parents are offended at first, they wait and are reconciled after a few months. Everyone is interested in these passionate marriages, since they seem to conform to the primitive natural impulses.

John Fenno to Joseph Ward OCTOBER 10, 1789

Great things are anticipated from Hamilton. I think that he considers his fame as much at stake as ever a General of an Army did—and I think further, that he is one of those sort of men that consider wealth as less than nothing and vanity contrasted with Honor & reputation—These things being so—it appears to me that now is the time for a stroke—but your penetrating eye may see dangers in Ambush which escape me.

Oliver Wolcott Sr. to Oliver Wolcott Jr. LITCHFIELD, CONN., FEBRUARY 8, 1790

The gentleman at the head of the department, with whom I am most acquainted, I have always known to be a man of strict integrity and honor.

Samuel Johnston to James Iredell FEBRUARY 25, 1790

The great difficulty seems to rest on the ways and means; but your favorite, the Secretary of the Treasury, whose application is as indefatigable as his genius is extensive, encourages us to hope that they may be found.

John Trumbull to John Adams MARCH 30, 1790

Is our Hamilton a great politician or only a theoretical genius. He has great abilities but I doubt his knowledge of mankind. I have never spoken my sentiments on his report but I really fear some parts of his plan are too complicated and perhaps at this period too impolitic as well as impracticable.

John Adams to John Trumbull NEW YORK, APRIL 25, 1790

Our Secretary [of the Treasury] has however I think good Abilities and certainly great Industry. He has high minded Ambition and great Penetration.—He may have too much disposition to intrigue.—If this is not indulged I know not where a better Minister for his Department could be found. But nothing is more dangerous, nothing will be more certainly destructive in our Situation than the Spirit of Intrigue.

William Maclay, Diary JUNE 28, 1790

Hamilton has a very boyish giddy Manner. Our Scotch Irish People would call him a Skite.

Rhode Island Senators Joseph Stanton Jr. and Theodore Foster to Governor Arthur Fenner PHILADELPHIA, FEBRUARY 17, 1791

The Confidence of the Nation at large in the Secretary of the Treasury is deservedly great. Possessed of a contemplative, comprehensive, energetic, independent Mind, he Knotes the strictest Integrity to the most Indefatigable Industry, which on all occasions he incessantly applies to the Service of the Public. Prudent, active yet deliberate, Studious, firm and candid he may be said to investigate the whole fiscal System of our Country. Ability, Foresight, Direction and a comprehensive View of the remotest Consequences, are so conspicuous in all his Reports respecting the Finances and National Arrangements which he recommends that they seem generally to carry conviction as they go. With a Fertile Invention, added to real Science and Patriotic Views, he has the Talent of bringing his Information into Action, with that Propensity, Method & Forcibleness of Reasoning that his Country Generally acquiesces in the Propriety of the Measure he recommends.

Thomas Jefferson to James Madison SEPTEMBER 8, 1793

Hamilton is ill of the [yellow] fever as is said. He had two physicians out at his house the night before last. His family think him in danger, & he puts himself so by his excessive alarm. He had been miserable several days before from a firm persuasion he should catch it. A man as timid as he is on the water, as timid on horseback, as timid in sickness, would be a ph'nomenon if the courage of which he has the reputation in military occasions were genuine.

DeWitt Clinton to Miss Cornelia Clinton ALBANY, JANUARY 23, 1794

The two great financiers, i.e., the two great pests of the World— Hamilton and Pitt must now fall like Lucifer never to rise again.

Abigail Adams to John Adams QUINCY, MAY 10, 1794

I have ever thought with respect to that Man, "beware of that Spair Cassius." This might be done consistant with prudence, and without the illibral abuse in many respects so plentifully cast upon him.

George Washington to Alexander Hamilton PHILADELPHIA, FEBRUARY 2, 1795

After so long an experience of your public services, I am naturally led, at this moment of your departure from office—which it has always been my wish to prevent—to review them.

In every relation, which you have borne to me, I have found that my confidence in your talents, exertions and integrity, has been well placed. I the more freely render this testimony of my approbation, because I speak from opportunities of information which cannot deceive me, and which furnish satisfactory proof of your title to public regard.

James McHenry to Alexander Hamilton NEAR BALTIMORE, FEBRUARY 17, 1795

The tempest weathered and landed on the same shore I may now congratulate you upon having established a system of credit and having conducted the affairs of our country upon principles and reasoning which ought to insure its immortality as it undoubtedly will your fame. Few public men have been so eminently fortunate as voluntarily to leave so high a station with so unsullied a character and so well-assured a reputation, and still fewer have so well deserved the gratitude of their country and the elogiums of history. Let this console you for past toils and pains, and reconcile you to humble pleasures and a private life. What remains for you having ensured fame but to ensure felicity. Seek for it in the moderate pursuit of your profession, or if public life still flatters in that office most congenial to it, and which will not withdraw you from those literary objects that require no violent waste of spirits, and those little plans that involve gentle exercise and which you can drop or indulge in without injury to your family.

I have built houses, I have cultivated fields, I have planned gardens, I have planted trees, I have written little essays, I have made poetry once a year to please my wife, at times got children and at all times thought myself happy. Why cannot you do the same, for after all if a man is only to acquire fame or distinctions by continued privations and abuse I would incline to prefer a life of privacy and little pleasures.

William Bradford to Alexander Hamilton PHILADELPHIA, JULY 2, 1795

It will always give me pleasure to hear from you: & I will endeavor to repay you with what you may consider "as a smack of the Whip." Yet I hear that you have renounced every thing but your profession—that you will not even pick up money when it lies at your feet, unless it comes in the form of a fee! But it is in vain to kick against the pricks. You were made for a Statesman, & politics will never be out of your head.

Thomas Jefferson to James Madison MONTICELLO, SEPTEMBER 21, 1795

Hamilton is really a colossus to the antirepublican party. Without numbers, he is an host within himself. They have got themselves into a defile, where they might be finished; but too much security on the Republican part, will give time to his talents & indefatigableness to extricate them. We have had only middling performances to oppose him. In truth, when he comes forward, there is nobody but yourself who can meet him. His adversaries having begun the attack, he has the advantage of answering them, & remains unanswered himself. . . . For god's sake take up your pen, and give a fundamental reply to Curtius & Camillus.

John Adams to Abigail Adams PHILADELPHIA, FEBRUARY 27, 1796

[On the constitutionality of the carriage tax.] Hamilton argued this last for three hours with his usual Splendor of Talents and Eloquence as they say. In the Course of his argument he said no Man was obliged to pay the Tax. This he knew by Experiment: for after having enjoyed the Pleasure of riding in his Carriage for six Years he had been obliged to lay it down and was happy.

Alexander Hamilton to George Washington NEW YORK, SEPTEMBER 5, 1796

Had I had *health* enough, it was my intention to have written it [i.e., Washington's Farewell Address] over, in which case I could both have improved & abridged. But this is not the case. I seem now to have regularly a period of ill health every summer.

John Adams to Abigail Adams PHILADELPHIA, DECEMBER 31, 1796

You may recollect, that I have often said to you H is a Man ambitious as Julius Caesar. A subtle intriguer, his abilities would make him dangerous if he was to espouse a wrong side. His thirst for Fame is insatiable. I have ever kept my Eye upon him. He has obtained a great influence over some of the most worthy and amiable of our acquaintance whom I could name. He has always busied himself in the Election of v. p. as you well know.

JANUARY 9, 1797

Hamilton I know to be a proud Spirited, conceited, aspiring Mortal always pretending to Morality, with as debauched Morals as old Franklin who is more his Model than any one I know. As great an Hypocrite as any in the U.S. His intrigue in the Election I despise. That he has Talents I admit but I dread none of them. I shall take no notice of his Puppy head but retain the same Opinion of him I always had and maintain the same Conduct towards him I always did, that is keep him at a distance.

Abigail Adams to John Adams QUINCY, JANUARY 28, 1797

Beware of that spair Cassius, has always occured to me when I have seen that cock Sparrow. O I have read his Heart in his wicked Eyes many a time. The very devil is in them. They are laciviousness itself, or I have no skill in Physiognomy.

Timothy Pickering to George Washington PHILADELPHIA, JULY 6, 1798

[Considering the appointment of officers to lead the U.S. Provisional Army.] There is one man who will gladly be *Your Second;* but who will not, I presume, because I think he ought not to be, the Second to any other military commander in the U. States. You too well know Colo. Hamilton's distinguished ability, energy and fidelity, to apply my remark to any other man. But to ensure his appointment, I apprehend the weight of your opinion may be necessary. From the conversation that I and others have had with the President, there appears to us to be a disinclination to place Colo. Hamilton in what we think is his proper station, and that alone in which we suppose he will serve—the *Second* to You—and the *Chief in your absence.* In any war, and especially in such a war as now impends, a Commander in Chief ought to know and have a confidence in the officers most essential to ensure success to his measures. In a late conversation with the president, I took the liberty to observe that the army in question not being yet raised, the only material object to be contemplated in the early appointment of the Commander in Chief, would be, that he might be consulted, because he ought to be satisfied, in the choice of the principal officers who serve under him.

If any considerations should prevent your taking the command of the army, I deceive myself extremely, if you will not think it should be conferred on Colo. Hamilton, and in this case, it might be equally important as in the former that you should intimate your opinion to the President. Even Colo. Hamilton's political enemies, I believe, would repose more confidence in him than in any military character that can be placed in competition with him.

George Washington to President John Adams MOUNT VERNON, SEPTEMBER 25, 1798

It is an invidious task, at all times, to draw comparisons, and I shall avoid it as much as possible; but I have no hesitation in declaring, that if the Public is to be deprived of the Services of Colonel Hamilton in the Military line, that the Post he was destined to fill will not be easily supplied; and that this is the sentiment of the Public, I think I can venture to pronounce. Although Colonel Hamilton has never acted in the character of a General Officer, yet his opportunities, as the principal & most confidential aid of the Commander in chief, afforded him the means of viewing every thing on a larger scale than those whose attentions were confined to Divisions or Brigades; who knew nothing of the correspondences of the Commander in Chief, or of the various orders to, or transactions with, the General Staff of the Army. These advantages, and his having served with usefulness in the Old Congress; in the General Convention; and having filled one of the most important departments of Government with acknowledged abilities and integrity, has placed him on high ground; and made him a conspicuous character in the United States, and even in Europe. To these, as a matter of no small consideration may be added, that as a lucrative practice in the line of his Profession is his *most certain* dependence, the inducement to relinquish it, must, in some degree, be commensurate. By some he is considered as an ambitious man, and therefore a dangerous one. That he is ambitious I shall readily grant, but it is of that laudable kind which prompts a man to excel in whatever he takes in hand. He is enterprising, quick in his perceptions, and his judgment intuitively great: qualities essential to a great military character, and therefore I repeat, that his loss will be irrepairable.

George Cabot to Timothy Pickering BROOKLINE, MASS., NOVEMBER 17, 1798

I lament with you the misfortune of Knox on his own account, and, I am sorry to add, on that of the public; for already he begins to intimate, though obscurely, that Hamilton is a man of insatiable ambition and not to be trusted.

Abigail Adams to John Adams QUINCY, JANUARY 12, 1799

The Idea which prevails here, is that Hamilton will be first in command, as there is very little Idea that Washington will be any thing more than, Name as to actual Service, and I am told that it ill suits the N. England Stomach. They say He is not a Native, and besides He has so damned himself to everlasting Infamy, that He ought not to be Head of any thing. The Jacobins Hate him and the Federalists do not Love him. Serious people are mortified, and every Uriah must tremble for his Bathsheba.*

JANUARY 13, 1799

I would however as soon trust Col. S—h [William Stephens Smith] as Genll. Hamilton. I have not any Confidence in the honour, integrity or patriotism of any Man, who does not believe that Thou shalt not commit Adultery is a possitive prohibition of God. Thou shalt not covet thy Neighbour's wife, is an other, and yet I have been credibly informd that the Audacious publication of that Man† has only renderd him more bold, and hardened in iniquity. It only requires a temptation sufficiently powerfull

---

*King David had an affair and a child with Bathsheba. Her husband, Uriah, was killed when David ordered him to be sent to the most dangerous part of the battle.

†This is a reference to Hamilton's public acknowledgment that he had an affair with Maria Reynolds and his assertion that he was totally honest in his public duties.

to Ambition to lead from the path of political Rectitude; it is a strange way of Reasoning. I would not upon any consideration do a publick wrong or injury, but I can be guilty of breaking the most solemn private engagement and that to one whom I am bound by affection, and by Honor to protect, to Love and Respect. I can disgrace and stigmatize my Lawful o[ff]spring, and feel neither Shame or compunction, but I would not betray a public trust. I cannot see that I commit any breach of Charity in this comment.

Alexander Hamilton to Henry Knox NEW YORK, MARCH 14, 1799

My heart advises otherwise and my heart has always been the Master of my Judgment.

John Beckley to Ephraim Kirby OCTOBER 25, 1799

The turbulent and intriguing spirit of Alexander Hamilton, has again manifested itself, in an insidious publication to defeat Mr. Adams's election, and in a labored effort to belittle the character of the president, he has in no small degree belittled his own. Vainly does he essay to seize the mantle of Washington, and cloak the moral atrocities of a life spent in wickedness and which must terminate in shame and dishonor. His career of ambition is passed, and neither honor or empire will ever be his. As a political nullity, he has inflicted upon himself the sentence of "*Aut Caesar, aut Nullus.*"*

Philadelphia Aurora MARCH 1, 1800

After he became governor Mr. [Henry] Lee in his free suavity mode soon forgot his political enmity—Hamilton *never* forgets.

James McHenry to Alexander Hamilton, War Department WASHINGTON, D.C., MAY 31, 1800

[Recollections of a conversation between Secretary of War McHenry and President John Adams on May 5, 1800.] President Adams: Hamilton is an intriguant—the greatest intriguant in the World—a man devoid of every moral principle—a Bastard, and as much a foreigner as Gallatin. Mr. Jefferson is an infinitely better

*Either Caesar or nothing; either first or nothing.

man, a wiser one, I am sure, and, if President, will act wisely. I know it, and would rather be Vice President under him, or even Minister Resident at the Hague, than indebted to such a being as Hamilton for the Presidency.

William North to Alexander Hamilton NEW YORK, JUNE 15, 1800

To you, my dear General, all eyes, look, & on you, everything will depend in a great measure, & as you are amongst the saints, it will not be improper to cite a text of scripture, "Be wise as serpents harmless as doves."* Your head is always right, I would, your heart was a little less susceptible. I pray you, when it is about to carry you out of the direct path, you will, like the deacons & Select men, throw a cloak over your shoulders.

You will consider this as a letter, not from an adjutant General to his Commander in chief, but from a citizen, a plain, private Citizen, who is anxious for the welfare of his country, & for the personal happiness of the man who under heaven, he hopes will one day, save that country from ruin.

James McHenry to Alexander Hamilton BALTIMORE, SEPTEMBER 4, 1800

I sincerely believe that there is not one of your friends who have paid the least attention to the insinuations attempted to be cast on the legitimacy of your birth, or who would care or respect you less were all that your enemies say or impune on this head true. I think it will be most prudent and magnanimous to leave any explanation on the subject to your biographer, and the discretion of those friends to whom you have communicated the facts.

Abigail Adams to Mary Cranch PHILADELPHIA, NOVEMBER 10, 1800

I shall not say any thing to you upon political subjects, no not upon the little Gen'l's Letter but reserve it for a future Letter when I arrive at Washington and you have more health to laugh at the folly, and pity the weakness, vanity and ambitious views of, as very a sparrow as Sterne commented upon, in his Sentimental Journey, or More describes in his fables.

*Matthew 10:16.

John Adams to Dr. Ogden WASHINGTON, D.C., DECEMBER 3, 1800

This last pamphlet [Hamilton's attack on Adams] I regret more on account of its author than on my own, because I am confident it will do him more harm than me. I am not his enemy, and never was. I have not adored him, like his idolaters, and have had great cause to disapprove of some of his politics. He has talents, if he would correct himself, which might be useful. There is more burnish, however, on the outside, than sterling silver in the substance.

Robert Troup to Rufus King NEW YORK, DECEMBER 31, 1800

The current of public opinion still sets strongly against the discretion of Hamilton's late letter respecting the character and conduct of Mr. Adams. I do not believe it has altered a single vote in the late election. . . . The influence however of this letter upon Hamilton's character is extremely unfortunate. An opinion has grown out of it, which at present obtains almost universally, that his character *is radically deficient in discretion,* and therefore the Federalists ask, what avail the most preeminent talents—the most distinguished patriotism—without the all important quality of discretion? Hence he is considered as an unfit head of the party—and we are in fact without a rallying point.

APRIL 9, 1802

Hamilton is closely pursuing the law, and I have at length succeeded in making him somewhat mercenary. I have known him latterly to dun his clients for money, and in settling an account with me the other day, he reminded me that I had received a fee for him in settling a question referred to him and me jointly. These indications of regard to property give me hopes that we shall not be obliged to raise a subscription to pay for his funeral expenses.

JUNE 6, 1802

The fatigue occasioned by the constant sitting of our courts exhausted us all very much. I find that Hamilton's health, notwithstanding the quickness and enormous strength of his mind, is impairing, as well as mine. This man's mind, by the by, seems to be progressing to greater and greater maturity; such is the common opinion of our bar; and I may say with truth that his powers are now enormous! And the only chance we have of success is now and then when he happens to be on the weaker side: and yet he is always complaining that he does not get his share of judgments and decrees!

AUGUST 24, 1802

No mortal can yet calculate the present state of public opinion. Federalism is looking up. At the last 4th of July the toasts everywhere given prove that Hamilton is regaining that general esteem and confidence, which he seems to have lost, and his standing is very much our political thermometer.

Rufus King to Christopher Gore NEW YORK, NOVEMBER 20, 1803

Hamilton is at the head of his profession, and in the annual receipt of a handsome income. He lives wholly at his house 9 miles from town so that on an average he must spend three hours a day on the road going and returning between his house and town, which he performs four or five days each week. I don't perceive that he meddles or feels much concerning Politics. He has formed very decided opinions of our System as well as of our administration, and as the one and the other has the voice of the country, he has nothing to do but to prophecy!

George Cabot to John Lowell BOSTON, JULY 18, 1804

Newspapers of the day . . . will announce and explain to you the public misfortune experienced here by the untimely death of Hamilton. You know how well his friends loved him, and all esteemed him. You can therefore judge of the general sensibility at his death. I have always thought his virtues surpassed those of other men almost as his talents. His errors, unfortunately for the country, were conspicuous, and diminished his influence, which otherwise would have been irresistible, and was always directed to the noblest purposes. All reflecting men seem now to be sensible that he was our *hope* in the crisis to which our affairs necessarily drive us.

John Adams, Autobiography

Of Hamilton, when he came into the General's Family I need say nothing. For my Part I never heard of him till after the Peace, and the Evacuation of the City of New York. The World has heard enough of him since. His Petulance, Impertinence and Impudence, will make too great a figure in these memories hereafter. . . .

Here again the Honesty of Hamilton appears. The Articles of War and the Institution of the Army during the War, were all my Work, and yet he represents me as an Enemy to a regular Army. Although I have long since forgiven this Arch Enemy, yet Vice, Folly and Villainy are not to be forgotten, because the guilty Wretch repented, in his dying Moments. Although David repented, We are no where commanded to forget the Affair of Uriah: though the Magdalene reformed, We are not obliged to forget her former *Vocation:* though the Thief on the cross was converted, his Felony is still upon Record. The Prodigal Son repented and was forgiven, yet his Harlots and riotous living, and even the Swine and the husks that brought him to consideration, cannot be forgotten. Nor am I obliged by any Principles of Morality or Religion to suffer my Character to lie under infamous Calumnies, because the Author of them, with a Pistol Bullet through his Spinal Marrow, died a Penitent. Charity requires that We should hope and believe that his humiliation was sincere, and I hope he was forgiven: but I will not conceal his former Character at the Expense of so much Injustice to my own, as this Scottish Creolian Bolingbroke in the days of his disappointed Ambition and unbridled Malice and revenge, was pleased falsely to attempt against it. Born on a Speck more obscure than Corsica, from an Original not only contemptible but infamous, with infinitely less courage and Capacity than Bonaparte, he would in my Opinion, if I had not controlled the fury of his Vanity, instead of relieving this Country from Confusion as Bonaparte did France, he would have involved it in all the Bloodshed and distractions of foreign and civil War at once.

John Adams to Benjamin Rush AUGUST 23, 1805

You say that Washington and Hamilton are idolized by the tories. Hamilton is; Washington is not. To speak the truth, they puffed Washington like an air balloon to raise Hamilton into the air. Their preachers, their orators, their pamphlets and newspapers have spoken out and avowed publicly since Hamilton's death what I very well knew to be in their hearts for many years before, viz: that Hamilton was everything and Washington but a name. . . .

Hamilton's talents have been greatly exaggerated. His knowledge of the great subjects of coin and commerce and their intimate connections with all departments of every government, especially such as are so elective as ours, was very superficial and imperfect. He had derived most of his information from [William] Duer, who was a brother-in-law of Mr. Rose, the deputy secretary of the treasury under Mr. Pitt. Duer had long been secretary to the board of treasury. [Arthur] Lee, [Samuel] Osgood, and [Walter] Livingston were all men of abilities and kept the books of the treasury in good order.... [Oliver] Wolcott's indefatigable industry with a seven year's experience at the Connecticut pay table came in aid of Hamilton and Duer, so that I see no extraordinary reason for so much exclusive glory to Hamilton.

Gouverneur Morris to Aaron Ogden DECEMBER 28, 1805

Our poor friend Hamilton bestrode his hobby [i.e., a monarchical government], to the great annoyance of his friends and not without injury to himself. More a theoretic than a practical man, he was not sufficiently convinced that a system may be good in itself and bad in relation to particular circumstances. He well knew that his favorite form was inadmissible, unless as the result of civil war, and I suspect that his belief in that which he called an approaching crisis arose from a conviction that the kind of government most suitable, in his opinion, to this extensive country, could be established in no other way.

John Adams to Benjamin Rush JANUARY 25, 1806

Although I read with tranquility and suffered to pass without animadversion in silent contempt the base insinuations of vanity and a hundred lies besides published in a pamphlet against me by an insolent coxcomb who rarely dined in good company, where there was good wine, without getting silly and vaporing about his administration like a young girl about her brilliants and trinkets, yet I lose all patience when I think of a bastard brat of a Scottish pedlar daring to threaten to undeceive the world in their judgment of Washington by writing an history of his battles and campaigns. This creature was in a delirium of ambition; he had been blown up with vanity by the tories, had fixed his eyes on the highest station in America, and he hated every man, young or old, who stood in his way or could in any manner eclipse his laurels or rival his pretensions.

William Plumer, Memorandum MARCH 15, 1806

That Hamilton was a great man—a great lawyer—a man of integrity—very ambitious—& was very anxious to effect, that ruinous measure, a consolidation of the States.

John Adams to Benjamin Rush SEPTEMBER 1807

Hamilton had great disadvantages. His origin was infamous; his place of birth and education were foreign countries; his fortune was poverty itself; the profligacy of his life—his fornications, adulteries, and his incests—were propagated far and wide. Nevertheless, he "affich'd"* disinterestedness as boldly as Washington. His myrmidons asserted it with as little shame, though not a man of them believed it. All the rest of the world ridiculed and despised the pretext. He had not, therefore, the same success. Yet he found means to fascinate some and intimidate others. You and I know him also to have been an intriguer.

FEBRUARY 25, 1808

At the time of Hamilton's death, the Federal papers avowed that Hamilton was the soul and Washington the body, or in other words that Washington was the painted wooden head of the ship and Hamilton the pilot and steersman.

John Adams, Draft of a Letter to the Printer of the Boston Patriot [1809?]

[Hamilton's] exuberant Vanity and insatiable Egotism prompt him to be ever restless, and busy and meddling, with Things far above his Capacity and inflame him with an absolute rage to arrogate to himself the Honor of Suggesting every measure of Government. He is no more fit for a Prompter than Phaeton to drive the Chariot of the Sun. If his Projects had been followed they would absolutely have burnt up the World.

Thomas Jefferson to Joel Barlow MONTICELLO, JANUARY 24, 1810

The dissensions between two members of the Cabinet are to be lamented. But why should these force Mr. Gallatin to withdraw? They cannot be greater than between Hamilton and myself, and

*Flaunted.

yet we served together four years in that way. We had indeed no personal dissensions. Each of us, perhaps, thought well of the other as a man, but as politicians it was impossible for two men to be of more opposite principles.

Robert Troup, Narrative ALBANY, MARCH 22, 1810

Whilst at [King's] College, the General was attentive to public worship; and in the habit of praying upon his knees both night and morning. I lived in the same Room with him for sometime; and I have often been powerfully affected, by the fervor and eloquence of his prayers. The General had read most of the polemical writers on Religious subjects; and he was a zealous believer in the fundamental doctrines of Christianity; and I confess, that the arguments with which he was accustomed to justify his belief, have tended, in no small degree, to confirm my own faith in revealed Religion. When he commanded a company of Artillery in the summer of 1776, I paid him a visit; and at night, and in the morning, he went to prayer in his usual mode.

Thomas Jefferson to Benjamin Rush MONTICELLO, JANUARY 16, 1811

I received a letter from President Washington, then at Mount Vernon, desiring me to call together the Heads of departments, and to invite Mr. Adams to join us in order to determine on some measure which required despatch; and he desired me to act on it, as decided, without again recurring to him. I invited them to dine with me, and after dinner, sitting at our wine, having settled our question, other conversation came on, in which a collision of opinion arose between Mr. Adams and Colonel Hamilton, on the merits of the British constitution, Mr. Adams giving it as his opinion, that, if some of its defects and abuses were corrected, it would be the most perfect constitution of government ever devised by man. Hamilton, on the contrary, asserted, that with its existing vices, it was the most perfect model of government that could be formed; and that the correction of its vices would render it an impracticable government. And this you may be assured was the real line of difference between the political principles of these two gentlemen. Another incident took place on the same occasion, which will further delineate Mr. Hamilton's political principles. The room being hung around with a collection of the portraits of remarkable men, among them were those of Bacon, Newton and Locke, Hamilton asked me who they were. I told him they were my trinity of the three greatest men the world had ever produced, naming them. He paused for some time: "the greatest man," said he, "that ever lived, was Julius Caesar." Mr. Adams was honest as a politician, as well as a man; Hamilton honest as a man, but, as a politician, believing in the necessity of either force or corruption to govern man.

Gouverneur Morris to Robert Walsh FEBRUARY 5, 1811

Speaking of General Hamilton, he had little share in forming the Constitution. He disliked it, believing all republican government to be radically defective. He admired, nevertheless, the British constitution, which I consider as an aristocracy in fact, though a monarchy in name. General Hamilton hated republican government; and he detested the latter, because he believed it must end in despotism, and, be in the mean time, destructive to public morality. He believed that our administration would be enfeebled progressively at every new election, and become at last contemptible. He apprehended that the minions of faction would sell themselves and their country as soon as foreign powers should think it worth while to make the purchase. In short, his study of ancient history impressed on his mind a conviction that democracy, ending in tyranny, is, while it lasts, a cruel and oppressing domination. One marked trait of the General's character was the pertinacious adherence to opinions he had once formed. From his situation in early life, it was not to be expected that he should have a fellow-feeling with those who idly supposed themselves to be the natural aristocracy of this country. In maturer age, his observation and good sense demonstrated that the materials for an aristocracy do not exist in America; wherefore, taking the people as a mass in which there was nothing of family, wealth, prejudice, or habit to raise a permanent mound of distinction. . . .

General Hamilton was of that kind of man which may most safely be trusted; for he was more covetous of glory than of wealth or power. But he was of all men the most indiscreet.

James McHenry to Timothy Pickering NEAR BALTIMORE, FEBRUARY 23, 1811

Mr. Adams, for reasons best known to himself, endeavors to represent General Hamilton as a man without fair pretensions to sound judgments or useful talents, a visionary politician consumed by indelicate pleasures and a censurable ambition. . . . As to their minds abstractly considered, Hamilton's was profound, penetrating, and invariably sound, and his genius of that rare kind which enlightens the judgment without misleading it; the mind of Mr. Adams, like the last glimmering of a lamp, feeble, wavering, and unsteady, with occasionally a strong flash of light, his genius little, and that little insufficient to irradiate his judgment.

John Adams to Benjamin Rush AUGUST 28, 1811

If I should inculcate fidelity to the marriage bed, it would be said, that it proceeded from resentment to General Hamilton and a malicious desire to hold up to posterity his libertinism.

John Adams to the Printers of the Boston Patriot JUNE 1812

The Truth is, that Hamilton's soul was corroded by that mordant sublimated Spirit of Ambition, that subjugates every Thing to its own Interest; and considers every Man of superior Age and merit, or who had the reputation of superior merit, as its Enemy. . . .

But it seems my "Personal Friends" "disparaged" his "motives" from another Topic, namely by calling him a "Factious Spirit," a "versatile Spirit," who could not be long satisfied with any Chief however meritorious.

Really, if I should believe this to be true, I must take Mr. Hamilton's Word for it. I never knew that I had such "personal Friends." I never knew that I had any Friends who had so much sagacity as to penetrate this Truth, or so much fortitude as to declare it. I will say nothing of the "factious Spirit." Let Posterity judge. Let the World judge. But "a versatile Spirit" he cannot be called, unless in an hypocritical sense. His invariable object was the head of this Nation, whether as President, as Monarch, or as Despot with an Army of Conscripts at his heels. "Empire! Empire! Empire! Let that Word make sacred all I do or can attempt." This was his whole creed, theological, philosophical, moral, political and civil. From this Principle, which in my opinion was his only Principle, he scorned and defamed Washington, whenever Washington would not be his Tool, from this Principle he calumniated Burr, with a cool deliberate, insidious, persevering malice, the parallel of which I never knew, and which finally cost him his life. From this Principle, he libeled Adams. From this Principle he calumniated every Man who stood before him, every Man who stood on equal ground with him, and every Man who was after him near enough, to have a probability or possibility of coming up with him. From this Principle he gave the go by to Mr. Jay, by propagating the Idea that he was a "degraded Character" and became a religious "Fanatick." He could not surely be called "a versatile Spirit." My personal Friends were in an error; quite mistaken, if they called him a "versatile Spirit." His object was invariable, not versatile, viz. Supreme Power; his means were invariably the same, viz. Libels, lies and slanders, therefore certainly not versatile. . . .

Hamilton had no more gratitude than a Cat. If you give a hungry famished Cat a slice of meat, she will not accept it as a Gift; she will snatch at it by Force, and express in her countenance and air, that she is under no obligation to you; that she got it by her own cunning and activity, and that you are a fool for giving it to her.

John Adams to Thomas Jefferson   QUINCY, JULY 12, 1813

A bastard Bratt of a Scotch Pedlar.

OCTOBER 15, 1822

Hamilton's hobby was the Army.

James Kent, Memoirs

Colonel Hamilton was indisputably pre-eminent [at the bar]. This was universally conceded. He rose at once to the loftiest heights of professional eminence by his profound penetration, his power of analysis, the comprehensive grasp and strength of his understanding, and the firmness, frankness, and integrity of his character.

He generally spoke with much animation and energy and with considerable gesture. His language was clear, nervous [i.e., strong, powerful], and classical. His investigations penetrated to the foundation and reason of every doctrine and principle which he examined, and he brought to the debate a mind filled with all the learning and precedents applicable to the subject. He never omitted to meet, examine, and discover the strength or weakness, the truth or falsehood of every proposition with which he had to contend. His candor was magnanimous and rose to a level with his abilities. His temper was spirited but courteous, amiable and generous, and he frequently made pathetic [i.e., emotional] and powerful appeals to the moral sense and patriotism, the fears and hopes of the assembly, in order to give them a deep sense of the difficulties of the crisis and prepare their minds for the reception of the Constitution.

John Hancock
1737–1793

⊰ BORN IN Braintree, Mass. Graduated from Harvard College, 1754. Wealthy Boston merchant, learned mercantile trade from his uncle Thomas Hancock in Boston and London. His ship *Liberty* was seized by British in 1768 for smuggling, resulting in mob action and Hancock's prosecution, which was dropped in 1769. Member, colonial House of Representatives, 1766–72, 1774, and colonial council, 1772–74. Member, three provincial congresses, 1774–75 (president, first and second congresses); chairman, Committee of Safety of the Provincial Congress, 1774–75. Member, state council, 1775–76. Delegate to Continental Congress, 1775–78 (president, 1775–77); signed Declaration of Independence and Articles of Confederation. Major general, Massachusetts militia; commanded state forces in unsuccessful expedition in Rhode Island, 1778. Member, state House of Representatives, 1777–80 (speaker in 1779–80), and state constitutional convention, 1779–80. Governor, 1780–85, 1787–93 (died in office). Elected to Congress, 1785; elected president but never attended, and resigned as president, 1786. Member, state ratifying convention; elected president but did not attend until late in session when he introduced amendments and voted to ratify the Constitution, 1788.

John Adams, Autobiography JUNE 1775

Mr. Hancock himself had an Ambition to be appointed Commander in Chief. Whether he thought, an election, a Compliment due to him and intended to have the honor of declining it or whether he would have accepted I know not. To the Compliment he had some Pretensions, for at that time his Exertions, Sacrifices and general Merit in the Cause of his Country, had been incomparably greater than those of Colonel Washington. But the Delicacy of his health, and his entire Want of Experience in actual Service, though an excellent Militia Officer, were decisive Objections to him in my Mind. In canvassing this Subject out of Doors, I found too that even among the Delegates of Virginia there were difficulties. The Apostolical Reasonings among themselves which should be greatest were not less energetic Among the Saints of the Ancient dominion, than they were among Us of New England. In several Conversations I found more than one very cool about the Appointment of Washington, and particularly Mr. Pendleton was very clear and full against. Full of Anxieties concerning these Confusions, and apprehending daily that We should hear very distressing News from Boston, I walked with Mr. Samuel Adams in the State house Yard, for a little Exercise and fresh Air, before the hour of Congress, and there represented to him the various dangers that surrounded Us. He agreed to them all, but said what shall We do? I answered him, that he knew I had taken great pains to get our Colleagues to agree upon some plan that We might be unanimous: but he knew that they would pledge themselves to nothing: but I was determined to take a Step, which should compel them and all the other Members of Congress, to declare themselves for or against something. I am determined this Morning to make a direct Motion that Congress should adopt the Army before Boston and appoint Colonel Washington Commander of it. Mr. Adams seemed to think very seriously of it, but said Nothing.—Accordingly When Congress had assembled I rose in my place and in as short a Speech as the Subject would admit, represented the State of the Colonies, the Uncertainty in the Minds of the People, their great Expectations and Anxiety, the distresses of the Army, the danger of its dissolution, the difficulty of collecting another, and the probability that the British Army would take Advantage of our delays, march out of Boston and spread desolation as far as they could go. I concluded with a Motion in form that Congress would Adopt the Army at Cambridge and appoint a General, that though this was not the proper time to nominate a General, yet as I had reason to believe this was a point of the greatest difficulty, I had no hesitation to declare that I had but one Gentleman in my Mind for that important command, and that was a Gentleman from Virginia who was among Us and very well known to all of Us, a Gentleman whose Skill and Experience as an Officer, whose independent fortune, great Talents and excellent universal Character, would command the Approbation of all America, and unite the cordial Exertions of all the Colonies better than any other Person in the Union. Mr. Washington, who happened to sit near the Door, as soon as he heard me allude to him, from his Usual Modesty darted into the Library Room. Mr. Hancock, who was our President, which gave me an Opportunity to observe his Countenance, while I was speaking on the State of the Colonies, the Army at Cambridge and the Enemy, heard me with visible pleasure, but when I came to describe Washington for the Commander, I never remarked a more sudden and sinking Change of Countenance. Mortification and resentment were expressed as his Face could exhibit them. Mr. Samuel Adams Seconded the Motion, and that did not soften the President's Physiognomy at all.

Benjamin Harrison to George Washington PHILADELPHIA, JULY 21, 1775

I do not know what to think of some of these Men, they seem exceeding hearty in the Cause, but still wish to keep every thing among themselves. Our President is quite of a different Cast, Noble, Disinterested & Generous to a very great Degree.

Charles Carroll of Carrollton to Charles Carroll of Annapolis MARCH 15, 1776

I dine this day with the Massachusetts Deputies—Mrs. Hancock will be of the party: she is not very handsome, yet handsome enough, and appears to be a most affectionate wife, of an easy & amiable temper. Hancock is well behaved, and generally liked, a proof of a good disposition.

John Adams, Diary FEBRUARY 17, 1777

Mr. H. told C.W. [Colonel Whipple] Yesterday, that he had determined to go to Boston in April. Mrs. H. was not willing to go till May, but Mr. H. was determined upon April. Perhaps the Choice of a Governor, may come on in May. What aspiring little

Creatures we are! How subtle, sagacious and judicious this Passion is! How clearly it sees its Object, how constantly it pursues it, and what wise Plans it devises for obtaining it!

Jacob Duché to George Washington PHILADELPHIA, OCTOBER 8, 1777

[In denigrating the character of members of Congress.] From the New-England provinces, can you find one, that as a gentleman, you could wish to associate with? Unless the soft & mild address of Mr. Hancock, can atone for his want of every other qualification necessary for the Station he fills.

Henry Laurens to John Lewis Gervais YORK, PA., OCTOBER 16, 1777

Our President gave notice yesterday of his purpose to quit the Chair & Congress next week. I moved the House to entreat & solicit his continuance, to my surprise I was seconded & no more.

Henry Laurens to John Laurens YORK, PA., JANUARY 8, 1778

We are tottering, & without the immediate exertions of wisdom & fortitude we must fall flat down. Among the Causes of this melancholy state are to be found some Men in whom your friend [George Washington] reposed an implicit confidence. I do not mean in the Army—did not I intimate to you some distress I was under in answering a Letter soon after I was called to the Presidency, because I could not flatter? The Man I alluded to [Hancock], against whom I can have no prejudice, for we always in our short acquaintance sat & drank together in great cordiality has contributed largely to the promotion of *party*. His fawning mild address & obsequiousness procured him toleration from great Men on both sides, a sort of favoritism from some. His Idleness, duplicity & criminal partialities in a certain Circle laid the foundation of our present deplorable state. If your friend knew these things as well as I do, he would see as clearly as I do, how his honest heart has been deceived but enough of this till we meet.

Abigail Adams to John Thaxter BRAINTREE, MAY 21, 1778

Our Great Man designs soon for Congress it has been said for more than a month, tomorrow and tomorrow and tomorrow. Was there ever any thing decisive in him?

JULY 23, 1778

Tis reported here that Mr. H——k is returning out of Health. Is it really or politically so? Did he expect an offer, which he never made himself. I fancy he did, and his Disease is mortification. A little of it will do no injury.

James Warren to Samuel Adams BOSTON, AUGUST 18, 1778

You can hardly Conceive with how much pleasure this, and indeed every other Story to your disadvantage is received and propagated here by a Party who are determined at all Events to ruin your Interest. I stopped their Career in this by reading and telling a paragraph in your Letter relating to that matter. I shall always oppose the measures of this Party, for if I have no partiality for you, I have a prejudice against many of them. I can't bare the Influence of Men who were so hid in Holes and Corners a few Years ago that it was difficult to find them; and when found dared not tell you which side they belonged to. Especially when that Influence is directed against the Capital and most Staunch Friends this Country ever had. Those men must have an Idol. They most of them worshipped Hutchinson; they all now worship another [Hancock] who, if he has not H[utchinson]'s Abilities, certainly equals him in Ambition and Exceeds him in Vanity. I wish I could give you a few Anecdotes. They would Excite your Indignation and perhaps ridicule. The servility and flattery I am daily a Witness of is disgusting enough.

Marquis de Lafayette to the Comte d'Estaing, Rhode Island, Letter of Introduction AUGUST 24, 1778

It is so much the greater a pleasure for me, Monsieur le Comte, to present Mr. Hancock to you through this letter, as I know how eager you are to make his acquaintance. We in the eighteenth century are very glad to see a Brutus in the flesh, and this one's role in the revolution should make him as interesting to persons in the present age as he will be to posterity.

(Private) AUGUST 24, 1778

Mr. Hancock is leaving for Boston. Here is a Jesuitical twist: the man has only the wit necessary to get him out of difficulty wherever he goes, and his vanity equals the reputation that has so readily been given him in Europe; yet he is all-powerful in

Boston. His zeal for France, combined with the lack of eagerness he displays for English bullets, compelled him to go and offer you his services. I am giving him a letter of recommendation that flatters his self-esteem and may persuade him to give us some proof of that popularity which he has obtained and which he delights in showing off. Fear of English vengeance will make him a loyal ally of our country; he is a man to be treated entirely with respect in the town whose assistance is unfortunately essential to you.

Henry Laurens to Rawlins Lowndes PHILADELPHIA, SEPTEMBER 6, 1778

The Major's [Lewis Morris] words in a whisper to me were "I do assure you Sir, we are indebted to that good Man General Washington for our escape [from the Rhode Island campaign], he gave us notice and pressed again our Retreat." The day following 5000 [British] Men landed from New York at Newport—Sir Henry Clinton said to be at the head of them—when General Sullivan had determined to retreat he covered his design by a stratagem which completely deceived the Enemy and happily effected his purpose. The Enemy were then at least equal in number Man for Man with himself—the retreat of Major General Hancock and his Volunteers and of the Militia &c who had followed his example had nearly ruined our cause, or to say the least reduced America to extreme distress—we have cause to be thankful for an almost unparalled escape.

James Warren to John Adams BOSTON, OCTOBER 7, 1778

Genl. Hancock went [to Congress] last June, after he had taken Care of the public here at Election. He returned very soon finding the Climate did not agree with him. He was not gone but about six weeks. It used to agree with him better than with any of you. Perhaps the Air in the President's Seat is purer than it is in more humble Stations. After his return he went on the Rhode Island Expedition and there stayed Just long enough to gain among the Multitude the popular Eclat, and then left it so soon as to make the more discerning laugh. He is making great Entertainments and figuring away in a most Magnificent Manner. The Eyes of many People are open and see his views and Motives, and some of the Judicious think Nothing Necessary but to veer away rope.*

*To let out ripe.

Samuel Adams to Samuel P. Savage PHILADELPHIA, NOVEMBER 1, 1778

Can a difference between Mr. —— [Hancock] & me, either real or imaginary, be of any consequence to the World? I think not. Tories you say triumph. They may make Sport of it; but indeed my Friend, it is too unimportant a Matter for a sensible Whig to weep and break his Heart about. I am desirous of making you easy. And I do assure you, that so far from brooding in my Heart an unfriendly Disposition towards that Man, I seldom think of him unless I happen to take up a Boston Newspaper, or hear his Name mentioned in Chit Chat Conversation. You call upon me by all that is sacred to forgive him. Do you then think *he* has injured *me*? If he has, Should not *he* ask for forgiveness? No man ever found me inexorable. I do not wish him to ask me to forgive him. This would be too humiliating. If he is conscious of having done or designed me Injury, let him do so no more, and I will promise to forgive & forget him too. Or, I would add, to do him all the Service in my Power; but this is needless. It is not in my Power to serve him. *He* is above it.

If you wish to know the Foundation of this wonderful Collision, ask my friend J.W. [James Warren], or another whom you properly call my "closest" Friend [John Adams]. To them I have related the trifling Tale, & they can repeat it to you.

John Jay to John Hancock PHILADELPHIA, DECEMBER 26, 1778

The Respect & Esteem I have long had for your private as well as public Character renders the commencement of a Correspondence with You very agreeable, and will always lead me to every mark of Attention due to a Patriot, and a Gentleman.

James Warren to John Adams BOSTON, JUNE 13, 1779

H. has been [to Congress] once but was gone but about six weeks. He tarried at Congress but about 2 weeks. The air of Philadelphia did not suit him on a Common Seat, he returned for better Health. He is now Speaker of our House, and a sinecure delegate to Congress. The last serves as a feather among others in his cap, to decorate an Illustrious Speaker.

Abigail Adams to John Adams JULY 5, 1780

The Man [James Bowdoin] who from Merit, fortune and abilities ought to be our *Chief* is not *popular,* and tho he will have the votes of the sensible judicious part of the State, he will be more than out Numbered by the Lovers of the tinkleling cymbal.

James Warren to John Adams BOSTON, JULY 11, 1780

The Election of Governor, Lt. Governor and Senate to be made on the beginning of September. Mr. B[owdoin] has again come into public Life that he may with greater Advantage stand as a candidate, in competition with H. for the highest honor and rank in this State. Who will carry the Election is very uncertain. I don't envy either of them their feelings. The Vanity of one of them will Sting like an Adder if it is disappointed, and the Advancements made by the other if they don't succeed will hurt his *Modest* pride. The upper counties will be for H., the Interest of the other will lay in the lower ones.

William Gordon to John Adams JAMAICA PLAINS, N.Y., JULY 22, 1780

We begin to think of the ensuing elections. It is thought that Mr. Bowdoin or Mr. Hancock will be chosen governor. Heavens grant that it may be the former and not the latter, who is one of the most egregious triflers I know! He hath not yet settled his accounts as treasurer of the college—and probably never will by *fair* means. The corporation and overseers have the comfort to infer, that he means not any particular affront to them, from his serving every one else in the like manner. A hint has been given me, that he would serve as Lieut. Govr. under Mr. Bowdoin, but no one else; and this is not a little stoop for his ambition. I would have him kept out of the chair. He can't as Lt. Govr. do much hurt. I mean therefore to propagate the hint that has been given me; and probably some may by that be taken off from voting for him as Govr. The most knowing and sensible I apprehend will not be for him, unless any of them should be induced by sinister views; but the common people who are ignorant of his character—his *true* character—and have had his name so often ding'd in their ears will be likely to pitch upon him.

Abigail Adams to John Adams BRAINTREE, SEPTEMBER 3, 1780

This is a Great and important day in the political System of this State. Mr. B[owdoi]n has merrit and integrity, all the judicious people will vote for him, but popular Clamour will elect another, who ought to forfeit every vote, by the low mean Arts he has taken to procure them. I could tell you many, if prudence did not restrain me, yet nothing that would surprise you, for you know every Avenue of his vain Heart. Give an extensive cord, and you know the adage.

Samuel Adams to Elizabeth Adams PHILADELPHIA, OCTOBER 3, 1780

I expect soon to see it announced in the Papers that Mr. Hancock is elected Governor of the Common Wealth of Massachusetts. I confess I did not foresee that Boston would have been so united as I find they were, when two such Candidates as he and Mr. Bowdoin were set up. Their respective Characters, Abilities and Merit were well-known to the Electors, who therefore acted with their Eyes open. It is to be presumed they have been influenced to this Choice by the pure Motives of publick Affection. A due Attention to the Administration of Government I fancy, will soon determine whether they have acted with Wisdom or not.

Samuel Adams to James Warren PHILADELPHIA, OCTOBER 3, 1780

Why will you upbraid me, my Friend, with the Votes of "my *beloved* Town," in Favor of a Man, whom neither you nor I would set up for the Governor of the Common Wealth? It is true, I love the People of Boston. I have spent much of my Time in their Service, and have labored to promote their Reputation and true Interest. I confess, I feel chagrined and disappointed at the Preference they have given. But is an honest & virtuous People incapable of Error? They acted, you will say, with their Eyes open. They knew the different Characters, Abilities and Merit of the Candidates. But may they not have been deceived with false Appearances for the Moment? A due Attention to the Administration of Government, will enable them to measure the Capacity of him whom they have made the Object of Their present Choice. That Watchfulness and Jealousy which I still hold to be the best

Securities of the publick Liberty will guard them against future Mistakes.

James Warren to John Adams BOSTON, OCTOBER 12, 1780

The New Government is the Principal Topic of Conversation. The General Court [the state legislature] meets under the New Constitution the Week after next. Hancock is undoubtedly chosen Governor by a very great Majority. His Popularity is greater than ever. No Body was set in Competition with him but Mr. Bowdoin and he stood no Chance. Frequent and brilliant Entertainments strengthen his popularity, and whether it will End in Absolute Adoration, or in the Exhaustion of the Sources of profusion I can't say. He this day feasts the French Minister (who came to Town last Evening) and the Council at the Castle.

Samuel Adams to Elizabeth Adams PHILADELPHIA, OCTOBER 17, 1780

You was mistaken when you supposed that I had heard who were chosen into the highest Places under our new Constitution. We are not so well informed. I had Reason to believe that Mr. Hancock would be the Governor. I am disposed to think, that my Fellow Citizens had upright Views in giving him their Suffrages. Many Circumstances have combined to make this Election appear to be politically necessary; and if the People, who are now blessed with so great a Privilege, will exercise that Watchfulness over Men whom they exalt to Places of Power, which their Duty & Interest should lead them to, I flatter myself that his will prove a happy Choice. You may wonder at my saying so; but I think I am not misguided in my Judgment in this Instance. If they have now chosen a wise & virtuous governor, a few only will be disappointed; if otherwise, Many will see their Error, and will be induced to greater Vigilance for the future. I am far from being an Enemy to that Gentleman, tho' he has been prevailed upon to mark me as such. I have so much Friendship for him, as to wish with all my Heart, that in the most critical Circumstances, he may distinguish between his real Friends & his flattering Enemies. Or, rather between the real Friends of the Country & those who will be ready to offer the Incense of Flattery to him who is the first Man in it. This will require an accurate Knowledge of Men. I therefore again wish that he may have the most able faithful Councellors to assist him in the Administration of Affairs. Can I say more? If, with the best Advice he is able to hold the Reins of Government with Dignity, I wish him a Continuance of the Honor. If he renders our Country secure in a flourishing Condition, I will never be so partial & unjust as to withhold my Tribute of Applause.

Samuel Adams to James Warren PHILADELPHIA, OCTOBER 24, 1780

It ill becomes you, my Friend, to think of retiring into private Life, who can lay your hand on your heart and say, that in your publick Conduct you have in no Instance deviated from virtuous Principles. If ever the Time shall come, when vain and aspiring Men shall possess the highest Seats of Government, our Country will stand in Need of its experienced Patriots, to prevent its Ruin. There may be more Danger of this, than some, even of our well disposed Citizens may imagine. If the People should grant their Suffrages to Men, only because they conceive them to have been Friends to the Country, without Regard to the necessary Qualifications for the Places they are to fill, the Administration of Government will become a mere Farce, and our publick Affairs will never be put on a Footing of solid Security. We should mark the Tempers as well as the Abilities of Men, if we would form a Judgment in what Manner the Trusts to be reposed in them will probably be executed. You know the character of Pisistratus.* He was a Citizen of Athens, supposed to have many excellent Qualities; but he had an insatiable Lust of Preeminence. Solon would discover his Vanity, but the People were blinded by a false Glare of Virtues, and he was their Idol. Under Pretense of his having escaped imminent Danger from a violent Faction, and the further Insecurity of his Person, he artfully obtained a Guard of Soldiers, by which Means he possessed himself of the Citadel and usurped the Government. But though he made himself Sovereign, and thus far overthrew the popular Election, the Historian tells us, that he made no Change in the Magistracy or the Laws. He was content that others should hold their Places according

---

*Twice a tyrant of Athens (561–556 and 546–527 BC), Peisistratus was noted for his long, moderate, benevolent rule while keeping to the letter of the constitution.

to the Rules of the Constitution, so that he might continue himself *Archon*,* independent of the Suffrages of the People. This he effected; for though several Attempts were made to deprive him of the Sovereignty which he had with equal Art & Violence obtained, he held it till his Death and left it to his Children. Such was the Ambition of a Man, who indeed assumed Authority, and such were the Effects of it. Power is intoxicating, and Men who have been legally vested with it, have too often discovered the same dangerous Disposition. How different a Man was Pisistratus from the Roman Hero and Patriot Lucius Quinctius Cincinatus, who, though vested with the Authority of Dictator, was so moderate in his Desires of a Continuance of Power, that having in six Weeks fulfilled the Purpose of his Appointment, he resigned the dangerous office which he might have held till the Expiration of Six Months. When we formerly had weak & corrupt Governors, it was our Misfortune; but for the future, while we enjoy and exercise the inestimable Right of choosing them ourselves, it will be our *Disgrace*. I hope our Countrymen will always keep a watchful Eye over the publick Conduct of those whom they exalt to Power, making at the same Time, every just Allowance for the Imperfections of human Nature. And I pray God, we may never see Men, filling the sacred Seats of Government, who are wanting in adequate Abilities, or influenced by any Motives or Feelings separate from the publick Welfare.

Samuel Adams to Elizabeth Adams PHILADELPHIA, NOVEMBER 13, 1780

By the next we expect to receive Accounts of the Organization of our government under the new Constitution, in all its Splendor— to see the Speech from the Chair, the Answers from the several Branches of the Legislature—Congratulatory Addresses &c, &c. I have been anxious lest our Countrymen should misjudge in the Choice of their first Governor. They are grateful; and I was afraid that from the goodness of their Hearts they might be induced to give their Suffrages for a Man, who, they might conceive, had done them eminent Services, in other Stations, without a due Consideration whether he possesses those excellent Qualities

---

*The highest office in most Greek city states, the archon had executive, judicial, and religious duties.

which should characterize and dignify their chief Magistrate. Our present Governors may probably stamp the moral as well as political Character of the People. I shall most heartily rejoice, if the *"Abilities and disinterested Zeal"* of the Gentleman called to fill the Chair prove adequate to the strong Expectations of my fellow Citizens in Boston expressed in their late Vote of Thanks. But why do I trouble you with a Subject of this Nature?

Mercy Otis Warren to John Adams BOSTON, NOVEMBER 15, 1780

The Arrangement of officers under the New Constitution you will have from other hands, and a Detail of the administration, as well as operation, of a system, so complete in all its parts, that the Wishes of all parties are concentered in one Great Object, and Whigs and Tories, Infidel and Religionists all agree that some portion of Idolatry is Necessary for the support of the political Machine. Of course the Daily Incense is offered in the Capital, and the Guilded puppet placed on the public Theater a few years ago (for certain purposes) is Become the Idol to whom the supple Homage of Adulation is paid, by a people once Disinterested, Firm, Discerning, and Tenacious of their Rights.

That tincture of Enthusiasm which is perhaps characteristic of the North American is now heated with the Emulation of Exhibiting the Highest Instances of Worship. Yet the Image whose Feet are of Clay, may in a short time become as the Chaff of the summer Threshing Floor, unless like another *Pisastratus,* for the sake of prolonging his power, he should Govern according to the Minutest Forms of the Constitution.

John Sullivan to John Hancock PHILADELPHIA, NOVEMBER 18, 1780

Permit me my Dear Sir with the most unfeigned Sincerity to Congratulate Your Excellency on Your Advancement to the Chair of Government in the State of the Massachusetts Bay. It affords me inexpressible Pleasure to find that the Freemen of Your State have been guided by their Judgment, Their Gratitude and regard for Publick Virtue to give their Suffrages to a Gentleman who not only Possesses sufficient Skill to regulate the Political Wheels of Government but has the Abilities and Disposition to Draw forth all the resources of that Important State in time of Publick

Danger and lead its Forces against the Common Enemy with that Judgment and Bravery which must insure Success.

Samuel Adams to James Warren PHILADELPHIA, NOVEMBER 20, 1780

Your Friend [i.e., the letter writer] makes no Claim on his Country, nor does he set himself in Competition with Mr. —— whose Connections have made him a necessary Man. He is, I confess, one whom I have esteemed for his Honesty and easy good Humor. We have been entertained with the Speeches both before and after putting on the Regalias, and we expect to see Congratulatory Addresses from various Orders, civil and ecclesiastic. I shall pity the Governor if he is apt to be discomposed with the high Complimentary Stile. I could wish, if we must have abundant Addresses to see the manly Simplicity of Barckly the Quaker in his Dedication to Charles the 2d of England. Excepting that Instance, I do not recollect ever to have seen an Address to a Great Man, that was not more or less, and very often deeply, tinctured with Flattery.

James Warren to John Adams BOSTON, NOVEMBER 22, 1780

Our New Government has taken place. The Papers will tell you, who are the Governing Powers, that Compose the Administration, it is only necessary for me to tell you that it is now perfectly Systematic. The Influence here is as Uniform and Extensive as in England, and the Criterion to determine the Qualifications for Office much the same as in the most Arbitrary Governments, or in the most servile Nations. How long this will last I don't know. Whether Pisistratus will be able to Establish himself Perpetual Archon, or whether he will be able to Convey that Honor and rank to his Family by hereditary right Time must determine. He has no Guards, yet Established, but he has unbounded Adulation, and Submission and that may Effect here all the purposes for which Guards were necessary at Athens. It is certain there is a greater Influence and a more unlimited Confidence here than is Consistent with a Republican Government. That Influence has already Effected here what [Governor Thomas] Hutchinson was never Able to do, it has not only removed S.A. [Samuel Adams] from all Share on the Govt. but taken from him his Bread and given all Secretaryship to Mr. [John] Avery Son in Law to the

Lieut. Govr. [Thomas Cushing]. Your Friend Gerry is the next Object and who among you that at Congress Committed the unpardonable Sin, of opposing or not submitting to his Measure, is uncertain. Perhaps the Extent of the Atlantic may secure you and Mr. [Francis] Dana for a while.

John Adams to Arthur Lee AMSTERDAM, DECEMBER 6, 1780

Yours from Lebanon [Conn.] 28 Sept. is just come to hand. I wish Massachusetts happy in their Governor. It would not have been otherwise, as you Suggest, had an Absent Citizen been at home.* Popularity is a Witch. The Gentleman chosen has long been So, to a great degree. The Absent one could Scarcely ever be Said to be so.

So it has ever been. Objects must be set up for popular Admiration, Confidence, and Affection, and when the Habit is formed, it is impossible to wean it, tho it may become dangerous, or even pernicious. It is So in the freest Governments, and even in the most virtuous. I hope however, in this Instance, We shall do well—and have no Reason to think otherwise. More Penetration, Knowledge, and Steadiness might have been found, perhaps. But the Meaning is good, as I believe.

Mercy Otis Warren to John Adams PLYMOUTH, MASS., DECEMBER 28, 1780

The political situation, the state of Commerce, and the Military operations, of Your Country is a Field I dare not Enter. They are subjects too much above the Delineation of my pen. The state of parties, the Rapid Growth of Idolatry, the Worship of the pageant, the Mimic Greatness of Monarchy in Embrio, are too much below Its Exertions to describe.

Peter Oliver, "The Origin and Progress of the American Rebellion" 1781

Here I am almost necessarily led into a Digression upon Mr. *Hancock's* Character, who was as closely attached to the hindermost Part of Mr. *Adams* as the Rattles are affixed to the Tail of the

---

*In his September 28 letter, Lee had written that "Mr. Hancock is chosen Governor, much owing to your absence and the in-attention of those who wish well to their Country and will probably repent of their inactivity."

Rattle Snake. Mr. *Hancock* was the Son of a dissenting Clergy-man, whose Circumstances in Life were not above Mediocrity, but he had a rich uncle. He was educated at *Harvard College,* was introduced into his uncle's Warehouses as a Merchant, & upon his Death was the residuary Legatee of £60,000 Sterling. His Understanding was of the Dwarf Size; but his Ambition, upon the Accession to so great an Estate, was upon the Gigantic. He was free from Immoralities, & Objects of Charity often felt the Effects of his Riches. His Mind was a mere *Tabula Rosa* & had he met with a good Artist he would have enstamped upon it such Character as would have made him a most useful Member of Society. But Mr. *Adams* who was restless in endeavors to disturb the Peace of Society, & who was ever going about seeking whom he might devour, seized upon him as his prey, & stamped such Lessons upon his Mind, as have not as yet been erased. Sometimes, indeed, by certain Efforts of Nature, which he was insensible of the Causes of his self, he would almost disengage himself from his assailant; but *Adams,* like the Cuddlefish, would discharge his muddy Liquid, & darken the Water to such an Hue, that the other was lost to his Way, & by his Tergiversation in the Cloudy Vortex would again be seized, & at last secured. Mr. *Hancock,* in Order to figure away as a Merchant, entered deeply into Trade; but having no Genius for it, (by monopolizing & other Misfortunes, together with his Ambition for being a Politician for which he was as little qualified as for a Merchant) he very soon reduced his Finances to a very low Ebb, & rendered it difficult for a Creditor to procure from him a small Balance of Debt; & some Things he did, by reason of his distressed Circumstances, which were not compatible with the Rules of strict Justice. Mr. *Adams,* after bringing him into such a Situation, could do no less than shove him up to the last Round of the Ladder, & he was president of the *American Congress.* Here he was at the Summit of his Ambition; but he has descended so far as to be the Governor of *Massachusetts* Province; & if the British Government should succeed in subduing the Rebellion, it requires no second Sight to foresee, that whereas he was once vain, that he would then be less than nothing & Vanity itself.

Abigail Adams to John Adams BRAINTREE, JANUARY 28, 1781

The G[overno]r as has been heretofore predicted, when any

thing not quite popular is in agitation, has the Gout and is confined to his Bed.

Samuel Cooper to Benjamin Franklin BOSTON, FEBRUARY 1, 1781

The popular Interest of Governor Hancock in this Common Wealth is great. He is a warm Friend to you and your Friends in the civil Line and in the Army: Some are opposed to him but the Body of the People are staunch to the Men and Measures that began the Revolution.

Artemas Ward to Samuel Osgood MARCH 13, 1781

Measures ought to be taken by the States to inform Congress of everything they have done in consequence of their requisitions for men & money. Since Novr. last the Governor gives no more information than if he was at the East Indies, notwithstanding it is his duty. If he don't know his duty I wish his Council would advise him; if they don't know it to be his duty, do let some body be appointed to teach them.

Mercy Otis Warren to Elbridge Gerry TREMONT, MASS., JUNE 6, 1783

Caesar had talents,—he had valor, intrepidity, activity, and magnanimity as well as ambition,—he had the capacity and inclination for the dispatch of business—thus qualified, it was easy to deceive by intrigue, while he captivated by generosity. But modern times exhibit more wonderful phenomenons;—we have seen a man without abilities idolized by the multitude, and fame on the wing to crown the head of imbecility;—we have seen a people trifling with the privilege of *election,* and throwing away the glorious opportunity of establishing liberty and independence on the everlasting basis of virtue, we have heard them trumpet the praises of their idol of straw, and sing of sacrifices he never had the courage to make. You very well know, Sir, he was first brought into political existence, and supported, on the shoulders of men of less fortune, but infinitely more merit than himself. We have seen this state *baby* of Massachusetts repeatedly chosen the first magistrate of this Commonwealth;—we see him triumph in the zenith of popularity, though so debilitated, as literally to be borne about on the shoulders of his sycophants. Much artifice has been necessary for this general deception, but nothing has had a more powerful effect, than squandering gratuities among the weak and the worthless.

Stephen Higginson to Elbridge Gerry BOSTON, OCTOBER 6, 1783

His Excellency [Governor Hancock] has treated me very coolly & indeed rather Cavalierly, he told me when I first met him, as I was going to the Council Chamber to pay him my respects, that he was happy he had by meeting me saved me the trouble of going there. This I considered as an intimation that he wished for no Conversation with me. I have therefore kept clear of him since & shall not put myself out of the way to show *him* any respect.

James Warren to Elbridge Gerry MILTON, MASS., DECEMBER 17, 1783

We have Nothing new here, tho' we have been threatened with a very Extraordinary Event, the Resignation of our Governor. He declared before very large and respectable Companies, among which were at one time the Supreme Court, and at another the Governors of the College that the Last thing he Intended to do as Governor was to Nominate a Person to fill the Supreme Bench, and that he would absolutely resign on the 26th of November. That Time is past without a resignation, and there are those who do not despise him secretly, nor ridicule him openly. However singular his good Luck is, if you ask what determined him to make such a declaration, I can only say that opinions are various. Some say it arose from disappointment and Chagrin that his Speech was not Echoed Back in the usual style of fulsome address, and the late publications of some of his small Fools Justify this Opinion, while others say that it happened at a Certain time, that an Idea of the dignity of General Washington in retiring to private Life happened to float across his Pericranium, and to make such an Impression as Induced him to think he should be a great Man too, if he followed the Example. But alas, his Fortitude did not support his resolution, and enable him to do this wise and prudent thing. But it is a matter of very trifling Consequence and so I dismiss it.

From Elbridge Gerry ANNAPOLIS, DECEMBER 20, 1783

Your Information respecting the Governor is curious, & there is not the least probability in my Mind, that he is sincere in his Declaration. I cannot account for the Maneuver on any other principles, than that his Excellency has experienced less Flattery of late, than was formerly paid him, & the Love of this, being his master passion, he is determined to recover the Loss by intimating an Intention to give up the Reins, & leave an ungrateful people to their own Destruction. Such a proposition must naturally produce in the Minds of his Constituents, a Conviction of their Error; & an increased Exertion to do Justice to his Merits, & to regain his Favour, without which, what will become of the unfortunate Commonwealth of Massachusetts?

Abigail Adams to John Adams BRAINTREE, DECEMBER 27, 1783

The present Gentleman's Health is much upon the decline. He has been confined more than half of the last year and unable to do any business on account of the Gout.

James Warren to Elbridge Gerry MILTON, MASS., FEBRUARY 25, 1784

My last was principally on the subject of an Intended resignation or at least a pretended one, but for your Comfort and Consolation I have the pleasure to Inform you, that we hear no more of it. We may still be happy in the possession of a Chief Magistrate, whose Merits are of such an Extraordinary kind that no Conduct on his own can sully them with ridicule or Contempt.

JANUARY 31, 1785

Every thing here has gone on in the Usual way till last Saturday, when a great political Phenomenon made its Unexpected Appearance. Our first Magistrate made his resignation in form. This I am well Informed is the Fact. I am not Philosopher enough to Account for this strange Event, whether the *Gas* that has so long supported this political Balloon is Expended, or whatever other Cause has produced this singular Event, must be left to the Sagas of the airy regions of Caprice and Vanity to determine. For my part, I am satisfied with a Conviction that no Change can be for the worse.

Mercy Otis Warren to John Adams MILTON HILL, MASS., APRIL 27, 1785

A late Resignation you have doubtless heard of. And had you been with us when the period of annual Election Revolved, it is probable your Country would have manifested some tokens of Gratitude by giving you their Suffrages for the first office of State. Yet there is no dependence on the popular Voice. There would have been a maneuvering against it, lest you should have held it too long for the convenience of another [Hancock] who means to come in again the next year.

There is such a blind Attachment to this man of *straw* that I have little doubt he will have the opportunity of establishing himself for life—perhaps the power of entailing an Hereditary succession. If that should be the Case many would cry *"Come over into Macedonia and help us,"* for I cannot suppose you think we are *yet* ripe for Monarchic Government.

James Warren to Elbridge Gerry MILTON, MASS, OCTOBER 4, 1785

H—— has got the Gout; whether it is a political, or natural fit, I don't know. If the former, he may have some reason to despair of the Presidency, and may wrap up in Baize, as a preparatory when the [General] Court meets. If every Body loved him as I do, they would save him that trouble, and excuse without the Expense of a single piece of Baize.

Luigi Castiglioni, Sketches of American Statesmen 1787

There is perhaps no name more celebrated, and perhaps with less reason, than that of Hancock. He was a moderately wealthy Boston businessman, of a fiery temperament, one of the first to take a firm stand against the English, and one of the three proscribed when proposals of peace were made to the Americans. He was repaid for this proscription with the lofty office of President of Congress, which he held for a number of years in a row. A lover of festivity and amusements, in which he spent the greater part of his fortune, he made himself greatly beloved by the people, who are satisfied with appearances, and although he is of limited talents, he was for many consecutive years elected and confirmed as governor of the State of Massachusetts.

James Madison to Edmund Pendleton NEW YORK, APRIL 22, 1787

Governor Bowdoin is already displaced in favor of Mr. Hancock, whose acknowledged merits are not a little tainted by a dishonorable obsequiousness to popular follies.

James Madison to Thomas Jefferson NEW YORK, APRIL 23, 1787

Mr. Hancock takes the place of Mr. Bowdoin. His general character forbids a suspicion of his patriotic principles; but as he is an idolater of popularity, it is to be feared that he may be seduced by this foible into dishonorable compliances.

John Quincy Adams to John Adams BRAINTREE, JUNE 30, 1787

Mr. Hancock was again elected governor this year, and out of 18,000 votes he had more than 13,000. This plainly shows that the people in general are displeased with some part of Mr. Bowdoin's conduct; but it is the caprice of an ungrateful populace, for which it must ever be impossible to account. Mr. Hancock is very much involved in debt, if common report be true. It is even confidently asserted that his present estate would not by any means do justice to his creditors. It is therefore concluded that he would favor tender acts, paper currencies, and all those measures which would give the sanction of the law to private fraud and villainy.

Rufus King to James Madison BOSTON, JANUARY 30, 1788

This day for the first our President Mr. Hancock took his Seat in [the Massachusetts ratifying] convention, and we shall probably terminate our business on Saturday or Tuesday next. I cannot predict the issue, but our Hopes are increasing—if Mr. Hancock does not disappoint our present Expectations our wishes will be gratified. But his character is not entirely free from a portion of caprice—this however is confidential.

William Gordon to George Washington LONDON, APRIL 3, 1788

Expect the pleasure of having to congratulate your Excellency before the year is out upon being chosen President to the American parliament. I know of no one whom I could wish so heartily to fill that place as yourself. But I do not wish you to have Mr. Hancock for your vice-president; there are many I think much better qualified, on one of whom I hope the choice will fall.

William Cranch to His Sister Lucy Cranch BOSTON, JUNE 2, 1788

High *'Tillery* today.—All the town is running into the Common to see his Gouty *Excellency set in his Chair*. A Wonderful sight! That a man with his legs wrapt in Baize should be able to set in Chair!—

I hate to see that antirepublican spirit which is shown whenever his Excellency appears in public. I do not believe any Monarch in Europe or Asia is more idolized than this same Governor—or is more fond of it—

Brissot de Warville, New Travels in the United States of America JULY 30, 1788

Samuel Adams is one of the strongest supporters of Governor Hancock's party in this state. You are familiar with the prodigious sacrifices Hancock made during the Revolution and you know how courageously he declared his position in the early days of the insurrection. The same patriotic spirit still inspires him. His character is a mixture of great generosity and lofty ambition. He possesses the virtues and the talents of the population; that is to say, without any effort he makes himself every man's friend and equal. I supped at his home in the company of a hatter who seemed to be an intimate friend. Mr. Hancock is amiable and polite when he wishes to be, but he is accused of not always having this wish. At such times, he develops a miraculous case of gout which protects him against all visitors and bars the door of his house. Mr. Hancock is not as highly educated as his rival, Mr. Bowdoin, and seems even to scorn learning. Bowdoin is more esteemed by men of education; Hancock is more loved by the people.

Christopher Gore to Rufus King BOSTON, AUGUST 30, 1788

It is said the Governor aims at the Presidency, and disdains a second seat. How far this is true you can determine as well as myself.

Christopher Gore to Theodore Sedgwick BOSTON, AUGUST 31, 1788

The other character acts with such increasing capriciousness that every man of reason and virtue is afraid of him—He is intending a journey in the ensuing week to Providence—probably from thence will go to Connecticut—and I think there can be little doubt but his flatterers have persuaded him of his election as president being more probable than Washington's—

James Madison to Thomas Jefferson NEW YORK, OCTOBER 17, 1788

Hancock is weak, ambitious, a courtier of popularity given to low intrigue and lately reunited by a factious friendship with S. Adams.

James Madison to Edmund Randolph NEW YORK, OCTOBER 28, 1788

The public mind seems not to be yet settled on the Vice President. The question has been supposed to lie between Hancock & Adams. The former is far the more popular man in N. England but he has declared to his lady, *it is said,* that she had once been the first in America, & he would never make her the second.

Tobias Lear to Benjamin Lincoln MOUNT VERNON, FEBRUARY 5, 1789

An idea has been held up here, & I believe has been pretty current through the States, that Mr. H—— would not accept of the *second* post in the Government if he should be chosen to it;—he has gained no credit by this—and indeed he seems not to be in that high estimation at present that he was a few years ago—several circumstances have tended to lessen his popularity—

William Tudor to John Adams BOSTON, JUNE 21, 1789

This Silliness [the Senate debate over titles] pleases Mr. Han., Mr. S.A. & Dr. J. [Hancock, Samuel Adams, and Charles Jarvis]. I most heartily wish all the Fools of the same Stamp throughout the Union would unite & colonize. There is Land enough upon the Banks of the Ohio for all the democratic Simpletons in the united States. There let them found a Utopia & crack Acorns with the *equal* Commoners of the Woods. It is owing to Envy & a contemptible Pride, that our chief Magistrates are to be denied those Titles which would be expressive of their Posts, because two only can possess them, and because thirteen Excellencies would be then out titled.

Samuel A. Otis to Theodore Sedgwick NEW YORK, OCTOBER 13, 1789

After all a glare of popularity dazzles all eyes & Mr. H will probably as usual prevail.

John Adams to Abigail Adams HARTFORD, NOVEMBER 24, 1789

Governor H. has been here and made a Dinner for the Gentlemen of this Town. One asked after the V.P. "The Governor has not Spoken to the V.P. this year. He was not one of the Well born." A Gentleman remarked upon it afterwards What would Mr. H. have been if he had not been well born the Nephew of the rich Uncle Thomas? In short his Silly Envy of the V.P. is perceived and ridiculed by all the World out of Massachusetts. He is considered as a mere rich Man prodigal of his Wealth to obtain an empty Bubble of Popularity.

PHILADELPHIA, DECEMBER 28, 1789

I am Surprised to find how little Popularity Mr. Hancock has in any of the States out of Mass[achusetts].

John Quincy Adams to John Adams NEWBURYPORT, MASS., MARCH 19, 1790

The internal politics of the State are in a state of tranquility, very unusual at this season. The opposers of the Governor [John Hancock], discouraged I presume by the ill success which they have always experienced, seem determined to leave him in quiet possession. He has been confined as usual all winter with the gout, and his judicial appointments have been the only public circumstances which have for some time past been the subject of animadversion. The appointment of [Robert Treat] Paine was rather popular. That of Mr. Cushing was far otherwise. The friends of the Governor only insist upon the disinterested magnanimity of nominating a man who it is said has been invariably opposed to his measures, while his enemies are so far from acknowledging his disinterestedness, that they censure him very highly for nominating to one of the most important offices in the State, a man totally unqualified to sustain it, merely to be freed from his troublesome opposition as a councillor.

John Trumbull to John Adams HARTFORD, MARCH 30, 1790

I agree that the strongest *Envy* against you lies in the Breasts of the two Men you mentioned, who could not bear your elevation above them—Each of them probably flattered his own vanity with an expectation of the Rank of V.P.—Hancock particularly, after his grand maneuver of limping forth, "With all his imperfections on his heels," to propose nonsensical amendments to the Convention of Massachusetts, supposed himself almost sure of the appointment—not knowing that the whole affair was planned & conducted as a political measure by men of more discernment than himself.

Jeremy Belknap, Remarks Written in 1796 on the Cover of Peter Thacher's Sermon, On the Death of Governor Hancock 1793

This sermon contains the best part of Gov. H's Character honestly drawn by a friend who knew his failings but kept them out of sight—there was no need of reciting them at his funeral.*

George Cabot to Christopher Gore JUNE 9, 1799

It has been a part of the cant of Democratic writers to ascribe to kings exclusively an undue love of praise, and to *subjects* the disgrace of giving it, however unmerited. Few kings I believe could be named, who swallowed grosser flattery than our Governor Hancock daily required and received from servile citizens. You recollect how entirely men of dignity and worth were excluded from his confidence, because they could not yield the adulation he desired. It must be unhappy for our country if ever a man of such character should be raised to the head of the Union.

Benjamin Rush, Sketches C. 1800

He was a man of plain understanding, and good education. He was fond of the ceremonies of public life, but wanted industry

*In the personal collection of the editor.

and punctuality in business. His conversation was desultory, and his manners much influenced by frequent attacks of the gout, which gave a hypochondriacal peevishness to his temper. With all these infirmities he was a disinterested patriot, and made large sacrifices of an ample estate to the liberties and independence of his country.

Mercy Otis Warren, History of the American Revolution 1805

Mr. Hancock was a young gentleman of fortune, of more external accomplishments than real abilities. He was polite in manners, easy in address, affable, civil, and liberal. With these accomplishments, he was capricious, sanguine, and implacable: naturally generous, he was profuse in expense; he scattered largesses without discretion, and purchased favors by the waste of wealth, until he reached the ultimatum of his wishes, which centered in the focus of popular applause. He enlisted early in the cause of his country, at the instigation of some gentlemen of penetration, who thought his ample fortune might give consideration, while his fickleness could not injure, so long as he was under the influence of men of superior judgment. They complimented him by nominations to committees of importance, till he plunged too far to recede; and flattered by ideas of his own consequence, he had taken a decided part before the battle of Lexington, and was president of the provincial congress, when that event took place.

By the appearance of zeal, added to a certain alacrity of engaging in any public department, Mr. Hancock was influential in keeping up the tide of opposition; and by a concurrence of fortuitous circumstances, among which this proscription was the most capital, he reached the summit of popularity, which raised him afterwards to the most elevated stations, and very fortunately he had the honor of affixing his signature as president, to many of the subsequent proceedings of the continental congress, which will ever hold an illustrious rank in the page of history. . . .

Mr. Hancock retained his popularity to the end of his life. His death did not take place until 1793. He was chosen governor of Massachusetts in 1780, and though a remarkable debilitation of body rendered him to appearance little able to discharge the duties of the first magistrate, yet the suffrages of the people kept him long in the chair, after he was reduced to such a state of weakness as to be lifted by his servants into his carriage, and thence into the state house, to deliver his public speeches. In this he acquitted himself with a degree of elocution, pleasing and popular, though his health did not admit of his writing them previously, seldom had he strength to add his signature to the acts of the legislature. But his mental faculties were not much impaired by the infirmities of his bodily constitution; they were not indeed composed of those elementary sparks of genius that soon burn themselves out; nor were the energies of his mind blunted by industry and application. . . .

An ample measure of gratitude was repaid to Mr. Hancock, both for public services and private benefits; a mantle of love was thrown over his foibles by his countrymen, and his memory was embalmed in the affections of his townsmen.

Fisher Ames to Timothy Pickering DEDHAM, MASS., MARCH 10, 1806

It is a mark of a little mind in a great man, to get such people about him for favorites as our chief [President Jefferson] is said to prefer. Hancock thought himself a Jupiter, and filled his Olympus with buffoons, sots, and blockheads.

John Adams to Richard Rush QUINCY, JULY 31, 1812

The Anecdotes of Hancock and Gadsden excited more sensibility than you can conceive. Names that I never hear or read but with Tenderness and Reverence. When will the Character of Hancock be understood? Never. I could melt into Tears when I hear his Name. The Property he possessed when his Country called him, would purchase Washington and Franklin both. If Benevolence, Charity Generosity were ever personified in North America, they were in John Hancock. What shall I say of his Education? His literary Acquisitions, his Travels, his military civil and political services? His sufferings and sacrifices? I dare not say even to you, at this time what I think and what I know.

John Adams to Elkanah Watson QUINCY, AUGUST 10, 1812

Hancock [could be compared] with nobody—he never had his equal in generosity.

John Adams to William Tudor QUINCY, JUNE 1, 1817

You "never profoundly admired Mr. Hancock. He had vanity

and caprice." I can say, with truth, that I profoundly admired him, and more profoundly loved him. If he had vanity and caprice, so had I. And if his vanity and caprice made me sometimes sputter, as you know they often did, mine, I well know, had often a similar effect upon him. But these little flickerings of little passions determine nothing concerning essential characters. I knew Mr. Hancock from his cradle to his grave. He was radically generous and benevolent. He was born in this town, half way between this house and our congregational temple, son of a clergyman of this parish, and grandson of a clergyman of Lexington, both of excellent characters. We were at the same school together, as soon as we were out of petticoats. His father died when he was very young. His uncle, the most opulent merchant in Boston, who had no children, adopted him, placed him in Mr. Lovell's school, educated him at Harvard college, and then took him into his store. And what a school was this! Four large ships constantly plying between Boston and London, and other business in proportion. This was in 1755. He became an example to all the young men in the town. Wholly devoted to business, he was as regular and punctual at his store as the sun in his course. His uncle sent him to London, from whence, after a residence of about a year, he returned to his store, with the same habits of business, unaltered in manners or deportment, and pursued his employments with the same punctuality and assiduity, till the death of his uncle, who left him his business, his credit, his capital, and his fortune; who did more—he left him the protector of his widow. This lady, though her husband left her a handsome independence, would have sunk into oblivion, like so many other most excellent widows, had not the public attention been fastened upon her by the fame of her nephew. Never was a nephew to an aunt more affectionate, dutiful, or respectful. No alteration appeared in Mr. Hancock, either from his travels in England, or from his accession to the fortune of his uncle. The same steady, regular, punctual, industrious, indefatigable man of business; and, to complete the character with the ladies, always genteelly dressed, according to the fashions of those days.

What shall I say of his fortune, his ships? His commerce was a great one. Your honored father told me, at that time, that not less than a thousand families were, every day in the year, dependent on Mr. Hancock for their daily bread. Consider his real estate in

Boston, in the country, in Connecticut, and the rest of New England. Had Mr. Hancock fallen asleep to this day, he would now awake one of the richest men. Had he persevered in business as a private merchant, he might have erected a house of Medicis. Providence, however, did not intend or permit, in this instance, such a calamity to mankind. Mr. Hancock was the delight of the eyes of the whole town. There can be no doubt that he might have had his choice, and he had his choice of a companion; and that choice was very natural, a granddaughter of the great patron and most revered friend of his father. Beauty, politeness, and every domestic virtue justified his predilection.

At the time of this prosperity, I was one day walking in the mall, and, accidentally, met Samuel Adams. In taking a few turns together, we came in full view of Mr. Hancock's house. Mr. Adams, pointing to the stone building, said, "This town has done a wise thing today." "What?" "They have made that young man's fortune their own." His prophecy was literally fulfilled; for no man's property, was ever more entirely devoted to the public. The town had, that day, chosen Mr. Hancock into the legislature of the province. The quivering anxiety of the public, under the fearful looking for of the vengeance of king, ministry, and parliament, compelled him to a constant attendance in the House; his mind was soon engrossed by public cares, alarms, and terrors; his business was left to subalterns; his private affairs neglected, and continued to be so to the end of his life. If his fortune had not been very large, he must have died as poor as Mr. S. Adams or Mr. Gerry.

I am not writing the life of Mr. Hancock; his biography would fill as many volumes as Marshall's *Washington,* and be quite as instructive and entertaining. Though I never injured or justly offended him, and though I spent much of my time, and suffered unknown anxiety, in defending his property, reputation, and liberty from persecution, I cannot but reflect upon myself for not paying him more respect than I did in his lifetime. His life will, however, not ever be written. But if statues, obelisks, pyramids, or divine honors were ever merited by men, of cities or nations, James Otis, Samuel Adams, and John Hancock, deserved these from the town of Boston and the United States. Such adulations, however, are monopolized by profligate libelers, by cringing flatterers, by unprincipled ambition, by sordid avarice, by griping usurers, by scheming speculators, by plundering bankers, by blind enthusiasts, by superstitious bigots, by puppies and butterflies, and by every thing but honor and virtue. Hence the universal slavery of the human species. Hence a commentary on the well known and most expressive figure of rhetoric, "It grieved the Almighty, at his heart, that he had made man." Nevertheless, this is a good world, and I thank the Almighty that he has made man.

Mr. Hancock had a delicate constitution. He was very infirm; a great part of his life was passed in acute pain. He inherited from his father, though one of the most amiable and beloved of men, a certain sensibility, a keenness of feeling, or, in more familiar language, a peevishness of temper, that sometimes disgusted and afflicted his friends. Yet it was astonishing with what patience, perseverance, and punctuality he attended to business to the last. Nor were his talents or attainments inconsiderable. They were far superior to many who have been much more celebrated. He had a great deal of political sagacity and penetration into men. He was by no means a contemptible scholar or orator. Compared with Washington, Lincoln, or Knox, he was learned.

Patrick Henry
1736–1799

⚜ BORN AT Studley, Hanover County, Va. Farmer and storekeeper until 1760, when admitted to Virginia bar. Represented Louisa County, 1765–68, and Hanover County, 1769–76, in House of Burgesses; Hanover County in Revolutionary conventions, 1774–76; Henry County, 1780–84, and Prince Edward County, 1787–91, in House of Delegates. Delegate to Congress, 1774–75. Commander, Virginia forces, 1775–76. Governor, 1776–79, 1784–86 (did not seek reelection in 1786). Declined appointment to the Constitutional Convention, 1787. Led opposition to the Constitution in Virginia. Represented Prince Edward County in state convention, voted against ratification of the Constitution, 1788. Retired from public life, 1791. Moved to Red Hill, Charlotte County, in 1796. Declined appointments as U.S. senator, 1794, U.S. secretary of state, 1795, and chief justice of the United States, 1796. Elected Charlotte County delegate to the House of Delegates in 1799 but died before taking seat.

William Wirt, *Account of the Parson's Cause Trial* NOVEMBER 1763

The courthouse was crowded with an overwhelming multitude, and surrounded with an immense and anxious throng, who, not finding room to enter were endeavoring to listen without, in the deepest attention. But there was something still more awfully disconcerting than all this; for in the chair of the presiding magistrate sat no other than his own father.... And now came on the first trial of Patrick Henry's strength. No one had ever heard him speak, and curiosity was on tiptoe. He rose very awkwardly, and faltered much in his exordium. The people hung their heads at so unpromising a commencement; the clergy were observed to exchange sly looks with each other; and his father is described as having almost sunk with confusion from his seat. But these feelings were of short duration, and soon gave place to others, of a very different character. For now were those wonderful faculties which he possessed, for the first time, developed; and now was first witnessed that mysterious and almost supernatural transformation of appearance, which the fire of his own eloquence never failed to work in him. For as his mind rolled along, and began to glow from its own action, all the *exuviae* of the clown seemed to shed themselves spontaneously. His attitude, by degrees, became erect and lofty. The spirit of his genius awakened all his features. His countenance shone with a nobleness and grandeur which it had never before exhibited. There was a lightning in his eyes which seemed to rive the spectator. His action became graceful, bold, and commanding; and in this tone of his voice, but more especially in his emphasis, there was a peculiar charm, a magic, of which anyone who ever heard him will speak as soon as he is named, but of which no one can give any adequate description. They can only say that it struck upon the ear and upon the heart, *in a manner which language cannot tell.* Add to all these, his wonder-working fancy, and the peculiar phraseology in which he clothed its images; for he painted to the heart with a force that almost petrified it. In the language of those who heard him on this occasion, "he made their blood run cold, and their hair to rise on end. . . ."

I have tried much to procure a sketch of this celebrated speech. But those of Mr. Henry's hearers who survive, seem to have been bereft of their senses. They can only tell you, in general, that they were taken captive; and so delighted with their captivity, that they followed implicitly, whithersoever he led them: that, at his bidding, their tears flowed from pity, and their cheeks flushed with indignation: that when it was over, they felt as if they had just awakened from some ecstatic dream, of which they were unable to recall or connect the particulars. It was such a speech as they believe had never before fallen from the lips of man; and to this day, the old people of that county cannot conceive that a higher compliment can be paid to a speaker, than to say of him, in their own homey phrase:—"*He is almost equal to Patrick, when he plead against the parsons.*"

George Mason to Martin Cockburn WILLIAMSBURG, MAY 26, 1774

At the request of the gentlemen concerned, I have spent an evening with them upon the subject, where I had an opportunity of conversing with Mr. Henry, and knowing his sentiments; as well as hearing him speak in the house since, on different occasions. He is by far the most powerful speaker I ever heard. Every word he says not only engages but commands the attention; and your passions are no longer your own when he addresses them. But his eloquence is the smallest part of his merit. He is in my opinion the first man upon this continent, as well in abilities as public virtues, and had he lived in Rome about the time of the first Punic war, when the Roman people had arrived at their meridian glory, and their virtue not tarnished, Mr. Henry's talents must have put him at the head of that glorious Commonwealth.

John Adams, Diary AUGUST 28, 1774

He [Jonathan Dickinson Sergeant] says the Virginians speak in raptures about Richard Henry Lee and Patrick Henry—one the Cicero and the other the Demosthenes of the Age.

Silas Deane to Elizabeth Deane PHILADELPHIA, SEPTEMBER 10, 1774

Mr. Henry is also a Lawyer, and the completest Speaker I ever heard. If his future Speeches, are equal to the small Samples he had hitherto given Us, they will be worth preserving, but in a Letter I can give You no Idea of the Music of his Voice, or the highwrought, yet Natural elegance of his Style, & Manner.

John Adams, Diary PHILADELPHIA, OCTOBER 10, 1774

[Richard Henry] Lee, Henry, and [William] Hooper are the orators [in Congress].

OCTOBER 11, 1774

Spent the Evening with Mr. Henry at his Lodgings consulting about a Petition to the King.

Henry said he had no public Education. At fifteen he read Virgil and Livy, and has not looked into a Latin Book since. His father left him at that Age, and he has been struggling thro Life ever since. He has high Notions. Talks about exalted Minds, &c. He has a horrid Opinion of Galloway, Jay, and the Rutledges. Their System he says would ruin the Cause of America. He is very impatient to see such Fellows, and not be at Liberty to describe them in their true Colors.

John Adams to Abigail Adams PHILADELPHIA, FEBRUARY 13, 1776

In the Beginning of a War, in Colonies like this and Virginia, where the martial Spirit is but just awakened and the People are unaccustomed to Arms, it may be proper and necessary for such popular Orators as Henry and Dickinson to assume a military Character. But I really think them both, better Statesmen than Soldiers, though I cannot say they are not very good in the Latter Character. Henry's Principles, and Systems, are much more conformable to mine than the other's however.

George Lux to John Sullivan AUGUST 22, 1776

Our Friend Pat: Henry Esqr. is now Governor of Virginia. . . . I have the Pleasure to inform you, that he discharges his Office with the Integrity & Ability natural to him—

Benjamin Rush, Autobiography

Patrick Henry from Virginia was my patient under the inoculation for the small pox. He was amiable in his manners, and a zealous advocate of the claims of his country. I never heard him speak in public, but his private opinions upon men and things, showed a deep and correct knowledge of human nature.

Thomas Jefferson to Isaac Zane RICHMOND, DECEMBER 24, 1781

The trifling body [George Nicholas] who moved this matter* was below contempt; he was more an object of pity. His natural ill-temper was the tool worked with by another hand [Patrick

*The motion was to have the Virginia House of Delegates censure Jefferson for his role as governor when the British invaded Virginia. Jefferson was exonerated by the house.

Henry]. He was like the minners [minnows] which go in and out of the fundament of the whale. But the whale himself was discoverable enough by the turbulence of the water under which he moved.

Thomas Jefferson to George Rogers Clark NOVEMBER 26, 1782

I was not a little surprised however to find one person hostile to you as far as he has personal courage to show hostility to any man. Who he is you will probably have heard, or may know him by this description as being all tongue without either head or heart. In the variety of his crooked [i.e., devious or tortured] schemes however, his interests may probably veer about so as to put it in your power to be useful to him; in which case he certainly will be your friend again if you want him.

George Mason to Patrick Henry GUNSTON HALL, MAY 6, 1783

It is in your Power, my dear Sir, to do more Good, and prevent more Mischief than any Man in this State; and I doubt not that you will exert the great Talents with which God has blessed you, in promoting the public Happiness & Prosperity.

Thomas Jefferson to James Madison TUCKAHOE, MAY 7, 1783

Henry as usual is involved in mystery. Should the popular tide run strongly in either direction, he will fall in with it. Should it not he will have a struggle between his enmity to the Lees & his enmity to every thing which may give influence to Congress.

Edmund Randolph to James Madison PETTUS'S, JUNE 21, 1783

Mr. Henry left the assembly last Saturday, and at the same time the field open to his adversary [Richard Henry Lee]. He can always recover himself in interest by an exertion, but his sighs for home expose him to a daily loss of his popularity.

John Marshall to James Monroe RICHMOND, DECEMBER 12, 1783

Henry retorted with a good deal of tartness but with much temper; 'tis his peculiar excellence when he altercates to appear to be drawn unwillingly into the contest & to throw in the eyes of others the whole blame on his adversary. His influence is immense.

Edward Bancroft to William Frazer PHILADELPHIA, MAY 28, 1784

Mr. Jefferson is just now informed, as he tells me, that the great leader of the Virginians, Mr. Patrick Henry, who has been violently opposed to every idea of increasing the powers of Congress, is convinced of his error, and has within these few days pledged himself to Mr. Madison, Mr. Jones, and others, to support a plan which they are to prepare and propose to the legislature of Virginia, for amending the confederation by a further concession of powers to Congress.

Thomas Jefferson to James Madison PARIS, DECEMBER 8, 1784

The proposition for a Convention has had the result I expected. If one could be obtained I do not know whether it would not do more harm than good. While Mr. Henry lives another bad [Virginia] constitution would be formed, & saddled forever on us. What we have to do I think is devoutly to pray for his death, in the mean time to keep alive the idea that the present is but an ordinance & to prepare the minds of the young men.

Luigi Castiglioni, Sketches of American Statesmen 1787

His knowledge extends not only to politics and government but also to literature and the sciences, the study of which he still pursues in hours free of affairs.

He is a man of about 50 years of age, and his features, fine but not too noble, show the liveliness of his talent.

James Madison to George Washington NEW YORK, MARCH 18, 1787

I hear from Richmond with much concern that Mr. Henry has positively declined his mission to Philadelphia [to the Constitutional Convention]. Besides the loss of his services on that theatre, there is danger I fear that this step has proceeded from a wish to leave his conduct unfettered on another theatre where the result of the Convention will receive its destiny from his omnipotence.

Henry Lee to James Madison STRATFORD, DECEMBER 7, 1787

[On a vote in the House of Delegates on an issue collateral to the Constitution.] Henry whose art is equal to his talents for declamation, conducted this business & gained a majority on the vote of sixteen.

Edward Carrington to James Madison MANCHESTER, VA., FEBRUARY 10, 1788

My Route has been pretty much within the Neighborhood of Mr. Henry, and I find his politics to have been so industriously propagated, that the people are much disposed to be his blind followers. As an evidence of it the demagogues in the opposition [to the Constitution] suppose that their popularity is increased in proportion to the loudness of their clamors, whilst the Friends to the Constitution think it prudent to suppress their opinions, or at least to advance them with Caution

Cyrus Griffin to James Madison NEW YORK, APRIL 14, 1788

Henry is weighty and powerful but too interested [in the Virginia ratifying convention].

Edward Carrington to Thomas Jefferson NEW YORK, APRIL 24, 1788

Mr. H—— does not openly declare for a dismemberment of the union, but his Arguments in support of his opposition to the Constitution, go directly to that issue. He says that three confederacies would be practicable & better suited to the good of America, than one.

George Washington to John Jay MOUNT VERNON, JUNE 8, 1788

Upon the whole, the following inferences seem to have been drawn. . . . That Mr. Henry & Colonel Mason took different & awkward ground—& by no means equalled the public expectation in their Speeches [in the Virginia ratifying convention]— That the former has, probably, receded somewhat from his violent measures to coalesce with the latter—and that the leaders of the opposition appear rather chagreened& hardly to be decided as to their mode of opposition.

Gouverneur Morris to Alexander Hamilton RICHMOND, JUNE 13, 1788

Matters are not going so well in this State as the Friends of America could wish. If indeed the Debates in Convention were alone attended to a contrary Inference would be drawn for although Mr. Henry is most warm and powerful in Declamation being perfectly Master of Action, Utterance and the Power of Speech to stir Men's Blood yet the Weight of Argument is so strong on the Side of Truth as wholly to destroy even on weak Minds the Effects of his Eloquence but there are as you well know certain dark Modes of operating on the Minds of Members which like contagious Diseases are only known by their Effects on the Frame and unfortunately our moral like our physical Doctors are often mistaken in their Judgment from Diagnostics.

Henry Knox to Rufus King NEW YORK, JUNE 19, 1788

I fear that overwhelming torrent, Patrick Henry. I would it were well over and the parchment [documenting Virginia's ratification of the Constitution] lodged in the Secretary's office.

Louis Guillaume Otto, Biographies FALL 1788

Man of the people, whom nature has given an amazing facility in a spirited manner. His eloquence astonishes and condemns even the most skillful adversaries to silence. He is the head of the plebeian party.

Edmund Randolph to James Madison RICHMOND, OCTOBER 23, 1788

Mr. Henry, I learn, has been urged to take a seat in the [U.S.] Senate. But he refuses, being unwilling to submit to the oath.

Richard Bland Lee to James Madison OCTOBER 29, 1788

Our Assembly is *weak*. Mr. Henry is the only orator we have amongst us—and the friends to the new government, being all young & inexperienced—form but a feeble band against him.

Edmund Randolph to James Madison RICHMOND, NOVEMBER 5, 1788

H——y is . . . all powerful.

George Washington to James Madison MOUNT VERNON, NOVEMBER 17, 1788

The Accounts from Richmond are indeed, very unpropitious to fœderal measures. The whole proceedings of the Assembly, *it is said* may be summed up in one word—to wit—that the Edicts of Mr. H—— are enregistered with less opposition by the Majority of that body, than those of the Grand Monarch are in the Parliaments of France. He has only to say let this be Law—and it is Law.

Henry Lee to James Madison ALEXANDRIA, VA., NOVEMBER 19, 1788

Mr. H is absolute, & every measure succeeds, which menaces the existence of the government.

James Madison to Thomas Jefferson PHILADELPHIA, DECEMBER 8, 1788

Mr. Henry . . . is omnipotent in the present legislature.

Henry Lee to James Madison ALEXANDRIA, VA., DECEMBER 8, 1788

[Reference to] Henry's influence & venom.

George Lee Turberville to James Madison RICHMOND, DECEMBER 14, 1788

The violence of the Antifederals has begun to arouse suspicion—& so soon as the people become acquainted with the Conduct of their *great high priest* I have no doubt, but that they will take that direction which reason & moderation point out to them.

William Grayson to Patrick Henry NEW YORK, JUNE 12, 1789

Your agreable favor was handed to me about a week ago. With respect to the unmerited attacks [in the "Decius" newspaper series] on your character I think they deserve nothing but contempt on your part: you have certainly adopted the dignified line of conduct, and I trust & hope you will persevere in it: nothing would please the author so well as to enter into a literary altercation with you: he would expect to aggrandize himself from the character of his competition: In my opinion such ill founded bad digested calumny ought to give you no manner of uneasiness: such kind of attacks on characters that are high in the public estimation have been so frequent & are so well understood as not to deserve a moment's attention—Envy & detraction says Mr. [Joseph] Addison is a tax which every man of merit pays for being eminent & conspicuous.

David Stuart to George Washington ABINGTON, FAIRFAX
COUNTY, VA., JULY 14, 1789

[On the debate in the U.S. Senate on titles.] The Opponents to
the government affect to smile at it, and consider it as a verifica-
tion of their prophecies about the tendency of the government.
Mr. Henry's description of it, that it squinted towards monarchy,
is in every mouth, and has established him in the general opinion, as a true Prophet—

Thomas Jefferson to William Short EPPINGTON, DECEMBER 14,
1789

Antifederalism is not yet dead in this country. The gentlemen who
opposed it retain a good deal of malevolence towards the new government. Henry is its avowed foe. He stands higher in public estimation than he ever did. Yet he was so often in the minority in
the present assembly that he has quitted it, never more to return,
unless an opportunity offers to overturn the new constitution.

William Madison to James Madison RICHMOND, DECEMBER 3,
1791

I wish to suggest to you the renewal of a correspondence with
Col. Henry. I am authorized, by a particular and intimate acquaintance of his, to say that such an intercourse will not only be
extremely acceptable but its decline is a subject of regret to Col.
Henry and his Lady. For my part I do not see any impropriety
but on the other hand great advantage probably resulting from
the communication as it is in his power to give you more information of the disposition of the different parts of the State than
perhaps any other Man in it. I wish to know your sentiments on
the subject and if you do not see any greater obstacle than I do I
hope you will gratify the old gentleman.

John Beckley to James Madison PHILADELPHIA, OCTOBER 17,
1792

A jealous eye is cast toward Virginia in her impending choice of a
Senator and the most marked anxiety for the reelection of R:H.L.
[Richard Henry Lee]—*perhaps* an attentive observer on the spot,
might mark the secret workings of Mr. H. *even in the Virginia
Legislature,* through the agency of one or more of those closeted

friends of his, of whom I wrote you during the summer—it would be wise to be watchful; there is no inferior degree of sagacity in the combinations of this *extraordinary* Man, with a comprehensive Eye, a subtle and contriving mind, and a Soul devoted to his object, all his measures are promptly and aptly designed, and like the links of a chain, dependent on each other, acquire additional strength by their union & concert.

James Iredell to Hannah Iredell   RICHMOND, MAY 27, 1793

We began on the great British Causes the second day of the Court, and are now in the midst of them. The great P. Henry is to speak today. I never was more agreeably disappointed than in my acquaintance with him. I have been much in his company, and his manners are very pleasing and his mind I am persuaded highly liberal.

Rufus King to Alexander Hamilton   NEW YORK, MAY 4, 1796

I am entirely of opinion that P. H. declining [to be the Federalist candidate for president], Mr. P[inckney] ought to be our man. It is even an idea of which I am fond in various lights. Indeed on latter reflection, I rather wish to be rid of P.H., that we may be at full liberty to take up Pinckney.

John Taylor to James Madison   CAROLINE, VA., MARCH 4, 1799

Yesterday I received a letter from the southward of this state, written by a gentleman [Creed Taylor] upon whom I can rely, containing the following sentence. "Mr. Henry has certainly declared for the next [Virginia] Assembly, in obedience to the call from General Washington, who has called on him to step forward and save his country—this is laughable; after the abuse formerly lavished upon that character, they now look up to as the savior of his country—I hope to see you in the next assembly, and pray exert your influence to prevail on Mr. Madison, to come forward—now is the time when all the friends to our free government should exert themselves."

Shall I write to my correspondent, that all your friends are in a state of grief and dejection, from a despair of prevailing with you to come forward, and save them and yourself; or will any considerations overset a resolution, so baleful to your country?

Fathom Mr. Henry's motives, and consider your personal situation. When I recollect his conduct respecting Mr. Jefferson . . . his apostasy is capable of a solution, only by considering it as the issue of a personal enmity to Mr. Jefferson and yourself, to gratify which he has sacrificed his principles to a party, determined on your destruction.

Ralph Wormeley Jr. to George Washington ROSEGILL, MAY 12, 1799

Report (too well founded I fear) announces the death of Mr. Patrick Henry; he died 'tis said the day after he was elected a delegate to the Assembly: alarmed and indignant at the measures of the majority of the late assembly he offered himself and was elected, and intended to exert all the force of his eloquence to endeavor to change the Temper of the Delegates should that of the present members be similar to that of their predecessors. He is surely a great loss; at *this crisis* and with *this* disposition, what mighty good, would not such a man, with his great powers of Oratory and his known character of integrity, have wrought! But alas! He is gone, leaving behind him few who excel him as an Orator, or, as a Patriot.

George Washington to John Marshall MOUNT VERNON, JUNE 16, 1799

In the Death of Mr. Henry (of which I fear there is little doubt) not only Virginia, but our Country at large has sustained a very serious loss. I sincerely lament his death as a friend; and the loss of his eminent talents as a Patriot I consider as peculiarly unfortunate at this critical juncture of our affairs.

Archibald Blair to George Washington RICHMOND, JUNE 19, 1799

It is much to be lamented that a Man of Mr. Henry's merits should be so little personally known in the world—I remember at the commencement of the revolution he was dreaded as the Cromwell of America, and since, he has been counted upon by the opposition Party as a rival to you, and the Destroyer of our happy & most valuable Constitution. I had the honor of qualifying to my present office* when Mr. Henry commenced the Administration

*Blair had been clerk of the Virginia Council of State since its inception in July 1776.

of our revolutionary Government, from which period to the day of his death, I have been upon the most intimate, and I believe, friendly terms with him; And I can with truth say that I never saw any thing tyrannical in his Disposition, nor otherwise ambitious than to be serviceable to Mankind. With regard to you sir, I may say as he said of Marshall—that he *loved you*—and for the same reason—*because you felt & acted as a republican—as an American.*

William Heth to Alexander Hamilton PETERSBURG, VA., JUNE 20, 1799

You must have heard ere this, of the death of our great HENRY. In the loss of this wonderful man, AMERICA itself, hath received a deep wound. But, Virginia, unfortunate, distracted Virginia! hath received a blow, which she will long feel. The good, the virtuous, and the liberal minded of all classes, seem truly sensible of the severe stroke & show much, & deep affliction; while some few of the Jacobin tribe, are found so lost to every sense of decency & humanity, as openly to express their pleasure at an event, melancholy in the extreme, & which at this crisis of American affairs, may truly be called a *national misfortune.* But, what are not such degenerate, & contemptible wretches capable of? You have our last paper, to show how this misfortune has been mentioned here & in Richmond. . . . I should like to see this published in one of your papers, *embellished* by you—in order to get into ours. If you approve of this, send me your paper.

Edmund Randolph, History of Virginia

He was respectable in his parentage, but the patrimony of his ancestors and of himself was too scanty to feed ostentation or luxury. From education he derived those manners which belonged to the real Virginia planter and which were his ornament, in no less disdaining an abridgment of personal independence than in observing every decorum interwoven with the comfort of society. With his years the unbought means of popularity increased. Identified with the people, they clothed him with the confidence of a favorite son. Until his resolutions on the Stamp Act, he had been unknown, except to those with whom he had associated in the hardy sports of the field and the avowed neglect of literature.

Still he did not escape notice, as occasionally retiring within himself in silent reflection, and sometimes descanting with peculiar emphasis on the martyrs in the cause of liberty. This enthusiasm was nourished by his partiality for the dissenters from the Established Church. He often listened to them while they were waging their steady and finally effectual war against the burdens of that church, and from a repetition of his sympathy with the history of their sufferings, he unlocked the human heart and transferred into civil discussions many of the bold licenses which prevailed in the religions. If he was not a constant hearer and admirer of that stupendous master of the human passions, George Whitefield, he was a follower, a devotee of some of his most powerful disciples at least.

All these advantages he employed by a demeanor inoffensive, conciliating, and abounding in good humor. For a short time he practiced the law in an humble sphere, too humble for the real height of his powers. He then took a seat at the bar of the General Court, the supreme tribunal of Virginia, among a constellation of eminent lawyers and scholars and was in great request even on questions for which he had not been prepared by much previous erudition. Upon the theater of legislation, he entered regardless of that criticism which was profusely bestowed on his language, pronunciation, and gesture. Nor was he absolutely exempt from an irregularity in his language, a certain homespun pronunciation, and a degree of awkwardness in the cold commencement of his gesture. But the corresponding looks and emotions of those whom he addressed speedily announced that language may be sometimes peculiar and even quaint, while it is at the same time expressive and appropriate; that a pronunciation which might disgust in a drawing room may yet find access to the hearts of a popular assembly; and that a gesture at first too much the effect of indolence may expand itself in the progress of delivery into forms which would be above the rule and compass but strictly within the prompting of nature. Compared with any of his more refined contemporaries and rivals, he by his imagination, which painted to the soul, eclipsed the sparklings of art, and knowing what chord of the heart would sound in unison with his immediate purpose, and with what strength or peculiarity it ought to be touched, he had scarcely ever languished in a minority at the time up to which his character is now brought. Contrasted with the most renowned of British orators, the older William Pitt, he was not inferior to him in the intrepidity of metaphor. Like him, he possessed a vein of sportive ridicule, but without arrogance or dictatorial malignity. In Henry's exordium there was a simplicity and even carelessness, which to a stranger, who had never before heard him, promised little. A formal division of his intended discourse he never made; but even the first distance, which he took from his main ground, was not so remote as to obscure it, or to require any distortion of his course to reach it. With an eye which possessed neither positive beauty nor acuteness, and which he fixed upon the moderator of the assembly addressed without straying in quest of applause, he contrived to be the focus to which every person present was directed, even at the moment of the apparent languor of his opening. He transfused into the breast of others the earnestness depicted in his own features, which ever forbade a doubt of sincerity. In others rhetorical artifice and unmeaning expletives have been often employed as scouts to seize the wandering attention of the audience; in him the absence of trick constituted the triumph of nature. His was the only monotony which I ever heard reconcilable with true eloquence; its chief note was melodious, but the sameness was diversified by a mixture of sensations which a dramatic versatility of action and of countenance produced. His pauses, which for their length might sometimes be feared to dispel the attention, riveted it the more by raising the expectation of renewed brilliancy. In pure reasoning, he encountered many successful competitors; in the wisdom of looks, many superiors; but although he might be inconclusive, he was never frivolous; and arguments which at first seemed strange were afterwards discovered to be select in their kind, because adapted to some peculiarity in his audience. His style of oratory was vehement, without transporting him beyond the power of self-command or wounding his opponents by deliberate offense: after a debate had ceased, he was surrounded by them on the first occasion with pleasantry on some of its incidents. His figures of speech, when borrowed, were often borrowed from the Scriptures. The prototypes of others were the sublime scenes and objects of nature; and an occurrence at the same instant he never failed to employ with all the energy of which it was capable. His lightning consisted in quick successive flashes, which rested only to alarm the more.

His ability as a writer cannot be insisted on, nor was he fond of a length of details; but for grand impressions in the defense of liberty, the Western world has not yet been able to exhibit a rival. His nature had probably denied to him, under any circumstances, the capacity of becoming Pitt, while Pitt himself would have been but a defective instrument in a revolution the essence of which was deep and pervading popular sentiment.

In this embryo state of the Revolution, deep research into the ancient treasures of political learning might well be dispensed with. It was enough to feel, to remember some general maxims coeval with the colony and inculcated frequently afterwards. With principles like these, Mr. Henry need not dread to encounter the usurpation threatened by Parliament, for although even his powerful eloquence could not create public sentiment, he could apply the torch of opposition so as fortunately to perceive that in every vicissitude of event, he concurred with his country.

Thomas Jefferson to William Wirt MONTICELLO, APRIL 12, 1812

Mr. Henry's ravenous avarice [was] the only passion paramount to his love of popularity. . . .

In ordinary business [in the House of Burgesses] he was a very inefficient member. He could not draw a bill on the most simple subject which would bear legal criticism, or even the ordinary criticism which looks to correctness of style & ideas, for indeed there was no accuracy of idea in his head. His imagination was copious, poetical, sublime, but vague also. He said the strongest things in the finest language, but without logic, without arrangement, desultorily.

John Adams to Thomas Jefferson QUINCY, NOVEMBER 12, 1813

In the Congress of 1774 there was not one member, except Patrick Henry, who appeared to me sensible of the Precipice or rather the Pinnacle on which he stood, and had candor and courage enough to acknowledge it.

Thomas Jefferson to William Wirt MONTICELLO, AUGUST 5, 1815

You ask some account of Mr. Henry's mind, information and manners in 1759–60, when I first became acquainted with him.

We met at Nathan Dandridge's, in Hanover, about the Christmas of that winter, and passed perhaps a fortnight together at the revelries of the neighborhood and season. His manners had something of the coarseness of the society he had frequented; his passion was fiddling, dancing and pleasantry. He excelled in the last, and it attached every one to him. The occasion perhaps, as much as his idle disposition, prevented his engaging in any conversation which might give the measure either of his mind or information. Opportunity was not wanting, because Mr. John Campbell was there, who had married Mrs. Spotswood, the sister of Colonel Dandridge. He was a man of science, and often introduced conversations on scientific subjects. Mr. Henry had a little before broke up his store, or rather it had broken him up, and within three months after he came to Williamsburg for his license, and told me, I think, he had read law not more than six weeks.

Archibald Stuart to William Wirt STAUNTON, VA., AUGUST 25, 1816

I was with Mr. H. in the [Virginia ratifying] Convention, when a storm rose in the midst of his speech, I sat too far from him to hear distinctly, but it was said he seemed to rise on the wings of the Tempest to seize upon the Artillery of Heaven & direct it against his adversaries.

Spencer Roane, Memorandum POST 1817

It is to be also observed that although his language was plain, and free from unusual or high-flown words, his ideas were remarkably bold, strong, and striking. By the joint effect of these two faculties, I mean of the power of his tone of voice and the grandness of his conceptions, he had a wonderful effect upon the feelings of his audience.

William Wirt, Sketches of the Life and Character of Patrick Henry 1817

In criminal cases Mr. Henry was perfectly irresistible. He adapted himself, without effort, to the character of the cause; seized, with the quickness of intuition, its defensible point, and never permitted the jury to lose sight of it. Sir Joshua Reynolds has said of

Titian, that, by a few strokes of his pencil, he knew how to mark the image and character of whatever object he attempted; and produced by this means a truer representation than any of his predecessors, *who finished every hair.* In like manner, Mr. Henry, by a few master-strokes upon the evidence, could in general stamp upon the cause whatever image or character he pleased; and convert it into tragedy or comedy, at his sovereign will, and with a power which no efforts of his adversary could counteract. He never wearied the jury by a dry and minute analysis of the evidence; he did not expend his strength in *finishing the hairs;* he produced all his high effect by those rare master-touches, and by the resistless skill with which, in a very few words, he could mold and color the prominent facts of a cause to his purpose. He had wonderful address, too, in leading off the minds of his hearers from the contemplation of unfavorable points, if at any time they were too stubborn to yield to his power of transformation. He beguiled the hearer so far from them, as to diminish them by distance, and soften, if not entirely cast into shade, their too strong natural colors. At this distance, too, he had a better opportunity of throwing upon them a false light, by an apparently casual ray of refraction from other points in the evidence, whose powers no man better knew how to array and concentrate, in order to disguise or eclipse an obnoxious fact. It required a mind of uncommon vigilance, and most intractable temper, to resist this charm with which he decoyed away his hearers; it demanded a rapidity of penetration which is rarely, if ever, to be found in a jury-box, to detect the intellectual juggle by which he spread his nets around them; it called for a stubbornness and obduracy of soul which does not exist, to sit unmoved under the pictures of horror or of pity which started from his canvass. They might resolve, if they pleased, to decide the cause against him, and to disregard every thing which he could urge in the defense of his client. But it was all in vain. Some feint, in an unexpected direction, threw them off their guard, and they were gone; some happy phrase, burning from the soul, beautiful and genuine impress, struck them with delightful surprise, and melted them into conciliation; and conciliation toward Mr. Henry, was victory inevitable. In short, he understood the human character so perfectly; knew so well all its strength and all its weaknesses, together with every path and by-way which winds around to the citadel of the best fortified heart

and mind, that he never failed to take them, either by stratagem or storm. Hence he was, beyond doubt, the ablest defender of criminals in Virginia, and will probably never be equalled again.
. . .

The lax habits of his early life had implanted in him an insuperable aversion to the drudgery of details. He could not endure confinement of any sort, nor the labor of close and solitary thinking. His habits were all social, and his mind delighted in unlimited range. His conclusions were never reached by an elaborate deduction of thought; he gained them as it were *per saltum;** yet with a certainty not less infallible than that of the driest and severest logician.

John Adams to William Wirt QUINCY, JANUARY 23, 1818

From a personal acquaintance, perhaps I might say a friendship, with Mr. Henry of more than forty years, and from all that I have heard or read of him, I have always considered him as a gentleman of deep reflection, keen sagacity, clear foresight, daring enterprise, inflexible intrepidity, and untainted integrity; with an ardent zeal for the liberties, the honor, and felicity of his country, and his species. All this you justly, as I believe, represent him to have been.

Thomas Jefferson, Autobiography 1821

Mr. Pendleton, . . . taken all in all, was the ablest man in debate I have ever met with. He had not indeed the poetical fancy of Mr. Henry, his sublime imagination, his lofty and overwhelming diction. . . .

When the famous Resolutions of 1765, against the Stamp-act, were proposed, I was yet a student of law in Williamsburg. I attended the debate, however, at the door of the lobby of the House of Burgesses, and heard the splendid display of Mr. Henry's talents as a popular orator. They were great indeed; such as I have never heard from any other man. He appeared to me to speak as Homer wrote. . . .

. . . he was the laziest man in reading I ever knew.

*By a single bound.

Thomas Jefferson, Conversation with Daniel Webster 1824

Patrick Henry was originally a bar-keeper. He was married very young, & going into some business on his own account, was a bankrupt before the year was out. . . .

He was as well suited to the times as any man ever was, & it is not now easy to say, what we should have done without Patrick Henry. He was far before all, in maintaining the spirit of the Revolution. His influence was most extensive, with the Members from the Upper Counties, & *his* boldness & their votes overawed & controlled the more cool, or the more timid Aristocratic gentlemen of the lower part of the State. His eloquence was peculiar; if indeed it should be called eloquence, for it was impressive & sublime beyond what can be imagined. Although it was difficult when he had spoken, to tell what he had said, yet while he was speaking, it always seemed directly to the point. When he had spoken in opposition to *my* opinion, had produced a great effect, & I myself been highly delighted & moved, I have asked myself when he ceased, "What the devil has he said," & could never answer the enquiry.

His person was of full size, & his manner & voice free & manly. His utterance neither very fast nor very slow. His speeches generally short from a quarter to an half hour. His pronunciation, was vulgar & vicious, but it was forgotten while he was speaking.

He was a man of very little knowledge of any sort, he read nothing & had no books. Returning one November from Albemarle Court, he borrowed of me Hume's Essays, in two vols. saying he should have leisure in the winter for reading. In the Spring he returned them, & declared he had not been able to go farther than twenty or thirty pages, in the first volume. He wrote almost nothing, he *could not* write. The resolutions of '75 which have been ascribed to him, have by many, been supposed to have been written by Mr. [Thomas] Johnson, who acted as his second, on that occasion. But if they were written by Henry himself, they are not such as to prove any power of composition. Neither in politicks nor in his profession was he a man of business, he was a man for debate only. His biographer [William Wirt] says, that he read Plutarch every year,—I doubt whether he ever read a volume of it in his life. His temper was excellent, & he generally observed decorum in debate.

On one or two occasions I have seen him *angry*—and his anger was terrible. Those who witnessed it, were not disposed to rouse it again. In his opinions he was yielding & practicable, & not disposed to differ from his friends. In private conversation he was agreeable, & facetious & while in genteel society appeared to understand all the decencies & proprieties of it; but in his *heart,* he preferred low society, & sought it as often as possible. He would hunt in the pine woods of Fluvannah, with overseers, & people of that description, living in a camp for a fortnight at a time without a change of raiment. I have often been astonished at his command of proper language; how he obtained the knowledge of it, I never could find out, as he read so little & conversed little with educated men.

After all, it must be allowed that he was our leader, in the measures of the Revolution, in Virginia. In that respect more is due to HIM than to any other person. If we had not had *him,* we probably have got on pretty well, as you did by a number of men of nearly equal talents, but he left us all far behind.

John Jay
1745–1829

⊰ BORN IN New York City of French Huguenot descent. Graduated King's College (Columbia), 1764. Studied law with Benjamin Kissam in New York City; admitted to bar, 1768. Secretary of royal commission to fix boundary between New York and New Jersey, 1773. Married Sarah Livingston, daughter of William Livingston, 1774. Member, New York committee of correspondence, 1774. Delegate to Continental and Confederation congresses, 1774–76 (but absent and did not sign Declaration of Independence), 1778–79 (president), 1784. Member, Provincial Convention, 1775; Third and Fourth Provincial congresses, 1776–77, where he favored agreeing to Declaration of Independence and played major role in drafting and adoption of state constitution of 1777. Member, First Council of Safety, 1777. First chief justice, New York Supreme Court, 1777–79. Appointed minister plenipotentiary to Spain, 1779. Joint commissioner for negotiating peace with Great Britain, 1782–83. Returned to the United States, July 1784. Confederation secretary for foreign affairs, 1784–90. President, New York Society for the Manumission of Slaves, 1785–90. Coauthor, "Publius": *The Federalist*, 1787–88; author, as "A Citizen of New-York," *An Address to the People of the State of New-York*, 1788. Injured in "Doctor's Riot" in New York City, April 1788. Member, New York Convention, 1788; voted to ratify Constitution. Chief justice, U.S. Supreme Court, 1789–95. Unsuccessful Federalist candidate for governor, 1792. As special envoy to Great Britain, negotiated Jay Treaty, 1794. Returned to the United States, 1795. Governor, 1795–1801. Declined appointment as chief justice of the United States, December 1800. Retired from public life to his estate near Bedford, Westchester County, 1801.

John Adams, Diary AUGUST 22, 1774

Mr. Jay is a young Gentleman of the Law of about 26, Mr. Scott says an hard Student and a good Speaker.

John Jay to Sarah Jay SALISBURY, JULY 29, 1776

I always endeavor to anticipate good instead of ill Fortune, and find it turns to good Account. Were this Practice more general, I fancy Mankind would experience more Happiness than they usually do.

John Vardill to William Eden APRIL 11, 1778

Jay . . . is possessed of a strong Understanding though much perverted by the Study of the Law joined to a Temper naturally controversial. You can sooner gain him to your opinion by submitting to be confuted by him, than by a direct attempt to convince him. . . . He is obstinate, indefatigable, & dogmatical, but by his Courage, Zeal & abilities as a Writer & Speaker has much Popularity.

Gouverneur Morris to Robert R. Livingston PHILADELPHIA, SEPTEMBER 22, 1778

I repose myself entirely with you and Jay. You shall act for me. Let me tell you that your Tempers are so very different that you will make the best Friends in the World. You are too lazy, he is too proud. He is too hasty, you too inattentive to the public Affairs. Shall I go on. No. With all the Faults both of you have I have as many as both of you together. You both pardon me therefore you must pardon each other. And do you hear. None of your Stomaching.

Gouverneur Morris to George Clinton PHILADELPHIA, DECEMBER 10, 1778

I have the Pleasure to inform your Excellency that the honorable John Jay Esqr. is elevated to the Chair of Congress, which as well from your Friendship for him, as for Reasons of public Importance will, I am confident, be agreeable to you. The weight of his personal Character contributed as much to his Election as the Respect for the State which hath done and suffered so much or the Regard for its Delegates which is not inconsiderable. The Public will I am confident experience many good consequences from the Exchange.

Edward Langworthy to William Duer PHILADELPHIA, DECEMBER 18, 1778

I'm sorry we shall in a great measure lose the Oratory of Mr. Jay by placing him in the Chair—he appears to me to be a man of Ability & to have that Ornament of the understanding a lively imagination.

William Carmichael to Charles Carroll of Carrollton PHILADELPHIA, JANUARY 16, 1779

Mr. Jay is more judicious than his predecessor in the chair, and less prolix.

John Jay to Catherine W. Livingston PHILADELPHIA, FEBRUARY 27, 1779

Perseverance in doing what we think Right, and Resignation to the Dispensations of the great Governor of the World, offer a Shield against the Darts of these Afflictions, to every body that will use it.

John Adams, Diary JUNE 20, 1779

I said that Mr. Jay was a Man of Wit, well informed, a good Speaker and an elegant Writer.

John Jay to Governor George Clinton PHILADELPHIA, AUGUST 27, 1779

Popularity is not, among the number of my objects. A seat in Congress I do not desire, and as ambition has in no instance drawn me into public life, I am sure it will never influence me to continue in it.

John Jay, Instructions to William Carmichael CADIZ, JANUARY 27, 1780

Although I have confidence in your prudence, yet permit me to recommend to you the greatest circumspection. Command yourself under every circumstance; on the one hand, avoid being suspected of servility, and on the other, let your temper be always even and your attention unremitted.

John Jay to Robert R. Livingston   MADRID, MAY 23, 1780

I am approaching the Age of Ambition without being influenced by its Allurements. Public Considerations induced me to leave the private Walk of Life; when they cease, I shall return to it. Believe me I shall not remain here a Moment longer than the Duties of a Citizen may detain me; and that I look forward with Pleasure to the Day when I shall again follow peaceably the Business of my Profession, and make some little Provision for my Family, whose Interests I have so long neglected for public Concerns. My Conduct moves on fixed Principles, from which I shall never deviate; and they will not permit me to leave the unfortunate part of my Family destitute of my Care and Attention longer than higher Duties call me from them.

Don Diego de Gardoqui, Memoirs 1786

The American, Jay, who is generally considered to possess talent and capacity enough to cover in great part a weakness natural to him, appears (by a consistent behavior) to be a very self-centered man [*es hombre muy interesado*], which passion his wife augments, because, in addition to considering herself worthy of merit and being rather vain, she likes to be catered to [*gusta que la obsequien*], and even more to receive presents. This woman, whom he loves blindly, dominates him and nothing is done without her consent, so that her opinion prevails, though her husband at first may disagree: from which I infer that a little management in dealing with her and a few timely gifts will secure the friendship of both, because I have reason to believe that they proceed resolved to make a fortune. He is not the only one in his country who has the same weakness [*flanco*], for there are many poor persons [*muchos necesitados*] among the governing body, and I believe a skillful hand which knows how to take advantage of favorable opportunities, and how to give dinners and above all to entertain with good wine, may profit without appearing to pursue them.

John Jay to Robert R. Livingston MADRID, OCTOBER 6, 1780

My Heart is in America, and I am impatient for the Time when the Rest of my Body will be there also.

John Jay to Benjamin Franklin MADRID, OCTOBER 30, 1780

To be active, prudent, and patient is in my power; but whether I shall reap as well as sow and water, God only knows.

John Jay to Silas Deane MADRID, NOVEMBER 1, 1780

I believe that a wise and good Being governs this World, that he has ordered us to travel through it to a better, and that We have nothing but our Duty to do on the Journey which will not be a long one. Let us therefore travel on with Spirits and Cheerfulness without grumbling much at the Bad Roads, bad Inns or bad Company we may be obliged to put up with on the Way. Let us enjoy Prosperity when We have it, and in adversity endeavor to be patient and resigned without being lazy or insensible. . . .

I believe firmly the old adage nil utile nisi quod honestum,* and therefore before Politicians or others deviate from Integrity they should well consider the Consequences.

John Jay to President of Congress Thomas McKean ST. ILDEFONSO, SPAIN, SEPTEMBER 20, 1781

[On Jay being appointed peace commissioner with Adams, Franklin, and Laurens and instructed by Congress to keep the French informed of their actions.] So far as personal pride and reluctance to humiliation may render this appointment disagreeable, I view it as a very unimportant circumstance; and should Congress, on any occasion, think it for the public good to place me in a station inferior and subordinate to the one I now hold, they will find me ready to descend from the one, and cheerfully undertake the duties of the other. My ambition will always be more gratified in being useful than conspicuous; for, in my opinion, the solid dignity of a man depends less on the height or extent of the sphere allotted to him, than on the manner in which he may fulfill the duties of it.

But, sir, as an American, I feel an interest in the dignity of my country, which renders it difficult for me to reconcile myself to

*Nothing is useful except what is honorable.

the idea of the sovereign independent States of America, submitting, in the persons of their ministers, to be absolutely governed by the *advice* and *opinion* of the servants of another sovereign, especially in a case of such national importance.

John Jay to Peter Van Schaack PARIS, SEPTEMBER 17, 1782

In the Course of the present Troubles I have adhered to certain fixed Principles, and faithfully obeyed their Dictates, without regarding the Consequences of such Conduct to my Friends, my Family or myself; all of whom, however dreadful the Thought, I have ever been ready to sacrifice, if necessary, to the public Objects in Contest.

James Warren to John Adams MILTON, MASS., NOVEMBER 1, 1782

I have a great Opinion of Mr. Jay. He has conducted, if I am well informed, with great dignity.

John Adams, Diary NOVEMBER 5, 1782

Mr. Jay likes Frenchmen as little as Mr. Lee and Mr. Izard did. He says they are not a Moral people. They know not what it is. He don't like any Frenchmen.—The Marquis de la Fayette is clever, but he is a Frenchman.

Alexander Hamilton, Speech in Congress (from James Madison's Notes) PHILADELPHIA, MARCH 19, 1783

[In speaking of the peace commissioners' failure to fully consult France as instructed by Congress.] He observed particularly with respect to Mr. Jay that although he was a man of profound sagacity & pure integrity, yet he was of a suspicious temper, & that this trait might explain the extraordinary jealousies which he professed [of the French].

John Adams to Abigail Adams PARIS, APRIL 16, 1783

Mr. Jay has been my only Consolation. In him I have found a Friend to his Country, without Alloy. I shall never forget him, nor cease to love him, while I live. He has been happier than I, having his Family with him, no Anxiety for his Children, and his Lady with him, to keep Up his Spirits. His Happiness in this

particular, has made me more unhappy for what I know under
the Separation from mine.

Comte de Vergennes to the Chevalier de La Luzerne PARIS, JULY 21, 1783

I understand that Mr. Franklin has asked for his recall, but that
Congress has not yet acted on his request. I desire that it reject it,
at least for the present, because it will be impossible to give Mr.
Franklin a Successor as wise and also conciliating as he; moreover, I fear that we will be left with Mr. Jay, and he is the man with
whom I would least like to treat of affairs: he is egotistical, and
too accessible to prejudices and ill-humor.

John Adams to Abigail Adams PARIS, SEPTEMBER 4, 1783

Mr. Jay has been my Comforter. We have compared Notes, and
they agree. I love him so well that I know not what I should do
in Europe without him. Yet how many times have I disputed
Sharply with him in Congress! I always thought him however an
honest Man. He is a virtuous and religious Man. He has a Conscience, and has been persecuted, accordingly, as all conscien-
tious Men are. Don't suspect me of Cant. I am not addicted to it.
He and I have Tales to tell, dismal Tales: But it will be most for
his Happiness and mine to forget them. So let them be forgotten. If the public Good should not absolutely require them to be
told.

John Jay to Catherine W. Livingston BATH, ENGLAND, DECEMBER 24, 1783

Experience has taught me reserve.

John Jay to Gouverneur Morris PARIS, FEBRUARY 10, 1784

Pecuniary considerations ever held a secondary place in my estimation. I know how to live within the bounds of any income,
however narrow.

John Jay to Silas Deane CHAILLOT, NEAR PARIS, FEBRUARY 23, 1784

I love my country and my honor better than my friends, and even
my family, and am ready to part with them all whenever it would
be improper to retain them.

Charles Thomson to John Jay   PHILADELPHIA, JUNE 18, 1784

I have the pleasure to inform you that on the 7th of May Congress elected you Secretary for Foreign Affairs. I do not know how you will be pleased with the appointment, but this I am sure of—that your country stands in need of your abilities in that office.

John Adams to James Warren   THE HAGUE, JUNE 30, 1784

Jay is minister of foreign Affairs. This is a great Point gained in favor of our Country. Wisdom and Virtue have triumphed, for once. And I hope and believe, he will give an entire new Cast, to the Complexion of our foreign Affairs, and you may depend upon it, that for some time to come as for a long time past, the Character and the System of our Country has been entirely decided by our foreign affairs.

John Jay to Richard Price   NEW YORK, SEPTEMBER 27, 1785

All that the best men can do is, to persevere in doing their duty to their country, and leave the consequences to Him who made it their duty; being neither elated by success, however great, nor discouraged by disappointments however frequent and mortifying.

Louis Guillaume Otto to the Comte de Vergennes   NEW YORK, DECEMBER 25, 1785

The inconsistency of Congress, My Lord, is gradually giving the Ministers of the various departments a power incompatible with the spirit of liberty and jealousy that reigns in this land. They do not want Members of Congress to hold office for more than three years, but the Secretaries of State are removable only for bad conduct. It follows that these Ministers, perfectly informed about current affairs, enjoy a great superiority over the delegates that chance has assembled from all parts of the Continent, and who are for the most part strangers to their task. Mr. Jay especially has already acquired a particular ascendancy over the members of Congress. All the important business passes through his hands; he makes his report on it, and it is rare that Congress is of an opinion different from his own. Instead of appointing Committees, they will gradually become accustomed to see only through the eyes of Mr. Jay, and although this Minister may be as capable as anyone to direct the conduct of the United States well, his influence must necessarily strike a blow to the liberty and the impartiality that should reign in the national Senate.

James Monroe to James Madison NEW YORK, DECEMBER 26, 1785

His character is too well established to be called in question upon any unimportant or trivial occasion.

Louis Guillaume Otto to the Comte de Vergennes NEW YORK, JANUARY 10, 1786

Mr. Jay's political importance increases every day. Congress appears to govern itself only by his impulses, and it is as difficult to obtain anything without the concurrence of this minister as to have a measure that he has proposed rejected. The indolence of most of the members of Congress and the ignorance of some others occasion this Superiority. It is much more convenient to ask the opinion of the minister of foreign affairs regarding all current business than to resolve themselves into a Committee, so that Mr. Jay's prejudices and passions insensibly become those of Congress, and that without being aware of it this Assembly is no more than the instrument of its first Minister. Happily Mr. Jay is a patriot and generally well disposed, but his grievances against France render him highly inflexible regarding our most just requests. I have already had the honor to inform you that neither M. de Marbois nor I have received any response to the various memoranda that we have delivered for nearly a year. This minister always tells me that Congress is too busy to take them into consideration, but I know that this Assembly has not had anything very important to decide for a long time, and that these delays are due only to the ill will of Mr. Jay. I would not complain, My Lord, if I did not have reason to fear that the long silence of Congress may be attributed to my inactivity, but I am pained to see that for the simplest things, and what requires only two hours of discussion, this minister has put off responding for several months. Such is among others the Treaty proposed by M. le Baron d'Ogny [over postal matters between France and the United States] I have not yet obtained any response on this Subject, and I cannot importune Mr. Jay since his response is always ready; it is to say that he will seize the first occasion to bring this affair to the attention of Congress.

Besides, this Minister has the character, for which the Quakers are reproached, of never responding directly to any question that is put to him. As he never makes his opinion known, it is impossible to rectify it, and although it may be he who inspires most of the resolutions of Congress, he always has the air of referring to this assembly for all clarifications that are asked of him. It is very troublesome for us, My Lord, that for so important a position, the choice of Congress has justly fallen on a man who does not like us. The article of the fisheries is always on his mind, and it is impossible to make him see reason regarding a subject on which we have not really been prejudicial to the United States. Besides, whatever this minister's prejudices may be in our regard, I cannot deny that there are few men in America more able to fill the position that he occupies. The veneration that he has inspired in almost all members of Congress proves more than anything else that even the jealousy so inseparable from the American character has not found a hold on him, and that he is as circumspect in his conduct as he is firm and unshakeable in his political principles and in his coldness for France.

MAY 20, 1786
Mr. Jay . . . is only the echo of the delegates of Massachusetts Bay.

William Livingston to John Jay ELIZABETH TOWN, N.J., AUGUST 28, 1786

Are you totally discouraged from coming to Elizabeth Town by our bad luck at fishing on our last jaunt? Pray let us try again, and I can almost assure you of better success.

John Jay to Matthew Ridley NEW YORK, JANUARY 4, 1788

We have not yet tried the Beer you were so kind as to send us, thinking it best to let it rest a while before we tap it—However it may turn out you have our Thanks for your friendly attention. There is at present a Scarcity of Segars [cigars], & one of the best kind to be had—a sample of some of the highest Price is sent [to you] by Capt. White; but I doubt your being much pleased with them—my Stock is consumed, & I will endeavor to supply you & myself out of the first Parcel of good ones that may arrive from the Havannah.

New York Daily Advertiser FEBRUARY 20, 1788

[Nominated for state ratifying convention.] From his long services abroad and at home, and the nature of his present office as minister of foreign affairs, must be supposed to possess the best information of any man in the United States, on our relative situation with foreign nations.

"A Citizen, and Real Friend to Order and Good Government,"
New York Daily Advertiser MARCH 21, 1788

The distinguished abilities, and unshaken integrity of Mr. Jay, recommended him at an early period in life, to all his acquaintance, as well as to the notice of the British Government, in the late Province of New York, antecedent to the war; insomuch, that he would have been appointed to one of the first offices in that Province, upon the first vacancy that should happen: Nevertheless when the rights of his country became invaded by the British, he took a decided and active part in her favor; his uniform services since, both at home and abroad, particularly in the formation of the Treaty of Peace, so peculiarly advantageous and beneficial to the interest of the United States; in the management and prosecution of which, he had a principal share. Mr. Jay's legal knowledge is incontrovertible; his arguments are methodically arranged and drawn forth with judgment; he reasons logically and well, and excels most men in dissecting the arguments of his opponents, and rendering them futile and nugatory; he is able and pointed in reply, and possesses the powers of persuasion in an eminent degree; in short, Mr. Jay is endowed with the necessary qualifications to constitute a Statesman.

Charles Tillinghast to John Lamb POUGHKEEPSIE, JUNE 21,
1788

I am happy to inform you that our Friends here continue firm in the opposition, and that all the Arts of a Hamilton &c will have no effect, although he, the Chancellor, & Mr. Jay are continually singling out the Members in Opposition (when out of Convention) and conversing with them on the subject. The latter's manners and mode of address would probably do much mischief, were the members not as firm as they are—

Extract of a letter from a Gentleman at Poughkeepsie, New York Daily Advertiser JUNE 28, 1788

Mr. Jay arose [in the New York ratifying convention], commanding great respect and remarkable attention, he was heard with great pleasure and satisfaction; and, no doubt, he spoke convincingly on the points raised. He has the most peculiar knack of expressing himself I ever heard. Fancy, passion, and in short every thing that marks an orator, he is a stranger to; and yet none who hear but are pleased with him, and captivated beyond expression. He appears to me not to speak as a scribe, but as a man having a right to speak, and at the same time having authority to command them to obey:—he was up about fifteen minutes.

Peter Van Schaack to Henry C. Van Schaack JUNE 29, 1788

I am told Mr. Jay's Arguments like the Rock of Ajax knocked down all opposition, and like the Pillar of Fire which conducted the Israelites through the Wilderness, showed Us the Way out of our many Embarrassments.

John Jay to Robert R. Livingston UNDATED

When our friendship first commenced, or rather when it was particularly professed to each other (the 29 March 1765) and for sometime after, I took it into my head that our dispositions were in many respects similar. Afterwards I conceived a different opinion. It appeared to me that you had more vivacity. Bashfulness and pride rendered me more staid. Both equally ambitious but pursuing it in different roads. You flexible, I pertinacious. Both equally sensible of indignities, you less prone to sudden resentments. Both possessed of warm passions, but you of more self-possession. You formed for a citizen of the world, I for a College or a Village. You fond of large acquaintance, I careless of all but a few. You could forbid your countenance to tell tales, mine was a babbler. You understood men and *women* early, I knew them not. You had talents and inclination for intrigue, I had neither. Your mind (and body) received pleasure from a variety of objects, mine from few. You was naturally easy of access, and in advances, I in neither. Unbounded confidence kept us together—may it ever exist!

Robert Barnwell to John Kean NEW YORK, JANUARY 10, 1789

I have had the satisfaction of being introduced to a number of valuable characters, and amongst them though at the head in my opinion is Mr. Jay, from some cause unknown to my self I had ever entertained the highest estimation of the Ability and Principle of this gentleman. Neither his Official writings nor his conversation gave me room to think this predilection misplaced. The most happy talent in the distribution of his Subjects, the closest reasonings and the most impartial Reports combine to render him the most proper person for the Office which he holds, and on seeing him and hearing him speak (the purity of his language excepted) could I believe the transmigration of souls. I could readily distinguish the same Spirit and appearance which belonged to and inspired a Ham[p]den and a Pym.

Abigail Adams to John Adams NEW YORK, JANUARY 12, 1789

Mr. and Mrs. Jay desire their affectionate Regards to you. He is as plain as a Quaker, and as mild as New Milk. Out under all this, an abundance of Rogury in his Eye's. I need to say to you who so well know him, that he possesses an excellent Heart.

Tench Coxe to James Madison NEW YORK, JANUARY 27, 1789

Mr. Jay who is the only candidate besides [John Adams] that is talked of [for U.S. vice president] will have but little support in this Matter left. He appears to have no Views himself. Tho well qualified for more important station than the proper Duties of the VP. render that yet I think it would be wrong to draw him for the Office of foreign affairs. Our treaties are all unformed—he alone knows the whole Negotiations—he is among the very few who have been in the way of qualifying themselves for foreign negotiations. He is much esteemed in Pennsylvania but her votes & influence would be exerted against him in the present state of the question on the seat of Government.

Tench Coxe to Benjamin Rush NEW YORK, FEBRUARY 12, 1789

Mr. Adams will undoubtedly be V. President. Mr. Jay (entre nous) would not have objected I think—and is not without views of a higher situation at a future day. A good use may be made of this in the Business of the Government.

Comte de Moustier to the Comte de Montmorin NEW YORK,
JUNE 29, 1789

It is not unlikely that this Minister Plenipotentiary [Thomas
Jefferson] would become, upon his return, Minister of Foreign
Affairs, if Mr. Jay obtains the post of Chief Justice as expected.
Although Mr. Jefferson has been delayed, there will be nothing
lost for him because the slowness of the Congress in all its operations will give him time to arrive, perhaps even well before all the
departments, and especially the judiciary department are formed
and organized. However, Mr. Jefferson's views on the post of
Secretary of Foreign Affairs are unknown. It is generally believed
only that if he is disposed to accept it, it will be offered to him,
just as it is believed that Mr. Jay would like a permanent position better than one that could be revoked without process. This
change suits us in every regard. Mr. Jefferson being better informed about the customs and conventions between Sovereigns
and Nations, having more elevated sensibilities, more conciliatory manners, and inclinations that are more suitable to the good
of his country (which demand the approbation of the King) than
the man he would replace.

SEPTEMBER 8, 1789

Mr. Jay is fulfilling the functions [of the secretary of state] while
awaiting the nomination that will be made by the President. This
Secretary has not suppressed anything of his repulsive manners,
his unpleasant character or his extreme bias against France. Born
into a refugee family, he retained the feelings of a religious per-
secutee and he is the only man from the State of New York, who
is opposed to tolerance of the Catholic religion, saying that the
lands cleared by his ancestors would never be used to nourish
those who chased them from their homeland. Although Mr. Jay
never ceases to demand generosity from those who negotiate
with him, he gives none in return. Attached to the New England
party, he is easily tempted by the smallest gains and he neither
can nor will see the big picture. His reserve, taciturnity, and grave
demeanor give him greater regard than he seems to merit; he is
neither an Orator, nor a good writer, nor assiduous in his office
and the Department of State will not make him more approach-
able or more hard-working. I believe that, in spite of the arrogance of this Secretary, it would be possible to win him over if

as much account is taken of his personal interest, as he seems to take himself.

Samuel A. Otis to John Langdon NEW YORK, SEPTEMBER 20, 1789

The *Keeper of the Tower* is waiting to see which Salary is best, that of Lord Chief Justice or Secretary of State.

Comte de Moustier to the Comte de Montmorin NEW YORK, OCTOBER 3, 1789

Mr. Jay whose spite is more active and whose conduct is more cautious, would have been more dangerous if he had held on to the department of Foreign Affairs. Fortunately, he was just replaced by the man whom we could most hope to see at the head of this department. Mr. Jefferson whose return we expect at any moment is named Secretary of State and it is presumed that he will accept this post to which Interior Affairs other than Finance and War are attached as well as foreign affairs. Mr. Jay is named Chief Justice, a permanent position and third in dignity. He is well known for his Jurisprudence and well suited to the important position he is going to fill. His personal qualities, the dryness of his manner, his irascible character and his tendency to put himself first render him inappropriate for the position that he formerly occupied, rather than filled well. He has shown me greater regard recently than he was accustomed to, and I think Gen. Washington must have insinuated to him not to give the King's Minister reason to believe that Mr. Jay harbored prejudices against France, because my personal conduct toward him, which never varied, could not induce him to treat me either better or worse. It will always be of interest to maintain a good outward relationship with Mr. Jay, while waiting for an inner change, because of the great influence his position gives him on the decision of many questions that must be decided by the federal courts of which he is the first Judge and where he will try to raise himself up as an Oracle.

George Washington to John Jay NEW YORK, OCTOBER 5, 1789

It is with singular pleasure that I address you as Chief Justice of the supreme Court of the United States, for which office your Commission is here enclosed.

In nominating you for the important station which you now fill, I not only acted in conformity to my best judgement; but, I trust, I did a grateful thing to the good citizens of these united States: and I have a full confidence that the love which you bear our Country, and a desire to promote general happiness, will not suffer you to hesitate a moment to bring into action the talents, knowledge and integrity which are so necessary to be exercised at the head of that department which must be considered as the Key-Stone of our political fabric.

William Samuel Johnson, Conversation with George Beckwith, NEW YORK, 1789

I regret Mr. Jay's removal from the Department of Foreign Affairs, as he is a man of a just and firm character; his successor Mr. Jefferson I do not so much approve of.

Joshua Loring to Jonathan Palfrey BOSTON, MAY 13, 1790

We have had the first Circuit Court opened here lately; Jay of New York Chief Justice; who appears quite in Court Style with respect to attendance, having Mr. Jackson the Marshal, Col. Samuel Bradford Deputy Marshal always attending him upon his excursions or visits; otherwise he is a plain dressing Man & makes but a poor figure, being rather of a small size, remarkably thin & in my opinion looks more like an high Lad alias a worn out Buck* than a Judge of the first Court in America. This proves the falsity of judging by appearances as it is allowed he is a man of superior abilities & understanding.

Christopher Gore to Rufus King BOSTON, MAY 15, 1790

The Chief Justice hath delighted the people of Massachusetts— they regret that Boston was not the place of his nativity—and his manners, they consider, so perfect as to believe that New York stole him from New England.

John Jay to Catharine Ridley PHILADELPHIA, FEBRUARY 1, 1791

My Life has for many Years past been in several Respects various—It is the Fortune of few to choose their Situations—it

---

*A dandy or a fop.

is the Duty & Interest of all to accommodate themselves to the one which Providence chooses for them—on my Return from Europe I was placed in an office which confined me to my Desk & Papers—I am now in one which takes me from my Family half the Year, and obliges me to pass too considerable a part of my Time on the Road, in Lodging Houses & Inns.

Thomas Jefferson to James Monroe PHILADELPHIA, 1791

Jay covering the same [monarchical] principles under the veil of silence, is rising steadily on the ruins of his friends.

John Jay to Sarah Jay EAST HARTFORD, CONN., JUNE 18, 1792

[On his loss to George Clinton in the disputed New York gubernatorial election of 1792.] The reflection that the majority of the Electors were for me is a pleasing one; that injustice has taken place does not surprise me, and I hope will not affect you very sensibly. The intelligence found me perfectly prepared for it. Having nothing to reproach myself with in relation to this event, it shall neither discompose my temper, nor postpone my sleep. A few years more will put us all in the dust; and it will then be of more importance to me to have governed myself than to have governed the State.

Edmund Randolph to James Madison GERMANTOWN, PA., AUGUST 12, 1792

An opinion, which has been long entertained by others, is riveted in my breast, concerning the C.J. [chief justice]. He has a nervous [i.e., strong] and imposing elocution; and striking lineaments of face, well-adapted to his real character. He is clear too in the expression of his ideas. But that they do not abound on legal subjects has been proved to my conviction. In two judgments, which he gave last week; one of which was written, there was no method, no legal principle, no system of reasoning.

John Adams to Abigail Adams NEW YORK, DECEMBER 2, 1792

The C.J. [chief justice] has been very Sick but is recovered. He looks very thin and pale however.

To Lord Grenville

He argues closely but is long-winded and self-opinioned. He can bear any opposition to what he advances provided that regard is shown to his abilities. He may be attached by good treatment, but will be unforgiving if he thinks himself neglected. . . . almost every man has a weak and assailable quarter and Mr. Jay's weak side is *Mr. Jay.**

John Alsop to Rufus King NEW YORK, APRIL 17, 1794

[On the appointment of an envoy to negotiate with Britain.] I wish Mr. Jay was appointed and would accept; we all know his abilities and firmness.

John Jay to Colonel Read LONDON, AUGUST 14, 1794

To see things as being what they are, to estimate them aright, and to act accordingly, are of all attainments the most important.

John Jay to Lindley Murray, Royal Hotel, Pall Mall LONDON, AUGUST 22, 1794

I perceive that we concur in thinking that we must go home to be happy, and that our home is not in this world. Here we have nothing to do but our duty, and by it to regulate our business and our pleasures, and travelers through the world (as we all are) may, without scruple, gratefully enjoy the good roads, pleasant scenes, and agreeable accommodations with which Providence may be pleased to render our journey more cheerful and comfortable; but in search of these we are not to deviate from the main road, nor, when they occur, should we permit them to detain or retard us. The theory of prudence is sublime and in many respects simple. The practice is difficult; and it necessarily must be so, or this would cease to be a state of probation.

Jeremiah Smith to William Plumer PHILADELPHIA, FEBRUARY 7, 1795

The Supreme Court commenced their session on Monday.— Much of the dignity of the Court is lost by the absence of the Chief Justice—

FEBRUARY 24, 1795
I shall attend the Supreme Court today—I am told that the

---

*Quoted in Samuel Flagg Bemis, *Jay's Treaty: A Study in Commerce and Diplomacy* (New Haven, Conn., 1923), 282.

Judges will this day deliver their opinions *seriatim* in the Mc-
Clary Cause—This indicates that a difference in opinion exists
on the Bench—They miss the chief-Justice—He was the ornament of the Bench—

Gouverneur Morris, Diary LONDON, JUNE 14, 1795

[Referring to the Jay Treaty.] I presume that it will be confirmed
by a feeble Majority but it will I imagine hang about Mr. Jay's
Neck like a Mill Stone in his political Voyages.

Alexander J. Dallas, Features of Mr. Jay's Treaty 1795

We heard of Mr. Jay's diplomatic honors; of the royal and ministerial courtesy which was shown to him; and of the convivial
boards to which he was invited; but, no more! Mr. Jay enveloped
by a dangerous confidence in the intuitive faculties of his own
mind, or the inexhaustible fund of his diplomatic information,
neither possessed nor wished for external aid.

Committee of Federal Freeholders of the City of New York to Governor John Jay NEW YORK, JANUARY 13, 1801

We have been long accustomed to contemplate, sentiments of
exalted satisfaction, the virtues, public and private, which adorn
your character, and the distinguished talents and services which
place you in the first rank of citizens eminently useful to their
Country. To attempt to retrace the variety of arduous and honorable exertions which have marked your public career, would be
an office to which we do not feel ourselves equal. Neither does it
require our testimony to record, what will ever find an indelible
memorial in the minds and hearts of the enlightened and just,
that in the great events which accomplished the American Revolution, you were among the most conspicuous, and that your
abilities, patriotism and energy, then and since, have been repeatedly displayed with luster, as well in the councils of this State and
of the United States, as in the different diplomatic trusts confided
to your charge. The part you acted in forming the constitution of
the State, and in promoting the adoption of the National Government, the important treaty which terminated the controversy for
independence, and the Convention which lately preserved your
Country from being involved in a pernicious war (defeating the
predictions of evil, and confirming the anticipations of good), are

a few of the many Acts that bear witness to the truths we have mentioned.

John Jay to Lindley Murray   BEDFORD, N.Y., JUNE 12, 1805

For a long course of years I had been looking forward with desire to the tranquil retirement in which I now live, and my expectations from it have not been disappointed. I flatter myself that this is the inn at which I am to stop in my journey through life. How long I shall be detained is uncertain, but I rejoice in the prospect of the probability of being permitted to pass my remaining time in a situation so agreeable to me.

John Jay to William Wilberforce   BEDFORD, N.Y., NOVEMBER 8, 1809

To see things as they are, to estimate them aright, and to act accordingly, is to be wise.

James Madison, Conversation with Jared Sparks   APRIL 1830

In speaking of Mr. Jay's suspicions respecting the policy of the French Court at the time of making peace, Mr. Madison observed, that "he had two strong traits of character, suspicion and religious bigotry."

Lindley Murray, Autobiography

He was remarkable for strong reasoning powers, comprehensive views, indefatigable application, and uncommon firmness of mind.

Thomas Jefferson
1743–1826

⊰ BORN AT Shadwell, Albemarle County, Va. Attended College of William and Mary, 1760–62. Studied law under George Wythe, admitted to Virginia bar, 1767. Represented Albemarle County in House of Burgesses, 1769–75, in all Revolutionary conventions (did not attend last two), and in House of Delegates, 1776–79, 1782–83. Delegate to Congress, 1775–76, 1783–84; author and signer, Declaration of Independence, 1776; author, Ordinance for Government of Western Territory, 1784. Governor, 1779–81. Author, Virginia statute of religious freedom, enacted in 1786. Minister plenipotentiary to negotiate treaties in Europe, 1784–85, and to France, 1785–89. U.S. secretary of state, 1790–93. U.S. vice president, 1797–1801. Author, Kentucky Resolutions, 1798. President of the United States, 1801–9. Founder, University of Virginia, 1819, and rector, 1819–26. In 1821 began autobiography but stopped at March 1790; in 1820s collected notes from 1791 to 1806 into what he called the "Anas."

John Adams, Diary OCTOBER 25, 1775

Duane says that Jefferson is the greatest Rubber off of Dust that he has met with, that he has learned French, Italian, Spanish and wants to learn German.

John Adams, Autobiography 1776

Mr. Jefferson had been now about a Year a Member of Congress, but had attended his Duty in the house but a very small part of the time and when there had never spoken in public: and during the whole Time I sat with him in Congress, I never heard him utter three Sentences together. The most of a Speech he ever made in my hearing was a gross insult on Religion, in one or two Sentences, for which I gave him immediately the Reprehension, which he richly merited. It will naturally be inquired, how it happened that he was appointed on a Committee of such importance. There were more reasons than one. Mr. Jefferson had the Reputation of a masterly Pen. He had been chosen a Delegate in Virginia, in consequence of a very handsome public Paper which he had written for the house of Burgesses, which had given him the Character of a fine Writer. Another reason was that Mr. Richard Henry Lee was not beloved by the most of his Colleagues, from Virginia, and Mr. Jefferson was set up to rival and supplant him. This could be done only by the Pen, for Mr. Jefferson could stand no competition with him or any one else in Elocution and public debate. Here I will interrupt the narration for a moment to observe that from all I have read of the History of Greece and Rome, England and France, and all I have observed at home, and abroad, that Eloquence in public Assemblies is not the surest road, to Fame and Preferment, at least unless it be used with great caution, very rarely, and with great Reserve. The Examples of Washington, Franklin and Jefferson are enough to show that Silence and reserve in public are more Efficacious than Argument or Oratory. A public Speaker who inserts himself, or is urged by others into the Conduct of Affairs, by daily Exertions to justify his measures, and answer the Objections of Opponents, makes himself too familiar with the public, and unavoidably makes himself Enemies. Few Persons can bare to be outdone in Reasoning or declamation or Wit, or Sarcasm or Repartee, or Satire, and all these things are very apt to grow out of public debate. In this Way in a Course of Years, a Nation becomes full of a Man's Enemies, or at least of such as have been galled in some Controversy, and take a secret pleasure in assisting to humble and mortify him. The Committee had several meetings, in which were proposed the Articles of which the declaration was to consist, and minutes made of them. The Committee then appointed Mr. Jefferson and me, to draw them up in form, and cloath them in a proper Dress. The Sub Committee met, and considered the Minutes, making such Observations on them as then occurred; when Mr. Jefferson desired me to take them to my Lodgings and make the Draft. This I declined and gave several reasons for declining. 1. That he was a Virginian and I a Massachusettsian. 2. that he was a southern Man and I a northern one. 3. That I had been so obnoxious for my early and constant Zeal in promoting the Measure, that any draft of mine, would undergo a more severe Scrutiny and Criticism in Congress, than one of his composition. 4thly and lastly and that would be reason enough if there were no other, I had a great Opinion of the Elegance of his pen and none at all of my own. I therefore insisted that no hesitation should be made on his part. He accordingly took the Minutes and in a day or two produced to me his Draft. Whether I made or suggested any corrections I remember not. The Report was made to the Committee for five, by them examined, but whether altered or corrected in any thing I cannot recollect. But in substance at least it was reported to Congress where, after a severe Criticism, and striking out several of the most oratorical Paragraphs it was adopted on the fourth of July 1776, and published to the World.*

Jacob Rubsamen to Unknown DECEMBER 1, 1780

The Governor [Jefferson] possesses a Noble Spirit of Building, he is now finishing an elegant building projected according to his own fancy. In his parlor he is creating on the Ceiling a Compass of his own invention by which he can Know the strength as well as Direction of the Winds. I have promised to paint the Compass for it. . . . As all Virginians are fond of Music, he is particularly so. You will find in his House an Elegant Harpsichord Piano forte and some Violins. The latter he performs well upon himself, the former his Lady touches very skillfully and who, is in all Respects a very agreeable Sensible and Accomplished Lady.

Marquis de Chastellux, Travels in North-America, in the Years 1780, 1781, and 1782

Let me describe to you a man, not yet forty, tall, and with a mild and pleasing countenance, but whose mind and understanding are ample substitutes for every exterior grace. An American, who without ever having quitted his own country, is at once a musician, skilled in drawing; a geometrician, an astronomer, a natural

---

*This passage was written in 1802.

philosopher, legislator, and statesman. A senator of America, who sat for two years in that famous Congress which brought about the revolution; and which is never mentioned without respect, though unhappily not without *regret:* a governor of Virginia, who filled this difficult station during the invasions of Arnold, of Philips, and of Cornwallis; a philosopher, in voluntary retirement, from the world, and public business, because he loves them, inasmuch only as he can flatter himself with being useful to mankind; and the minds of his countrymen are not yet in a condition either to bear the light, or to suffer contradiction. A mild and amiable wife, charming children, of whose education he himself takes charge, a house to embellish, great provisions to improve, and the arts and sciences to cultivate; these are what remain to Mr. Jefferson, after having played a principal character on the theater of the new world, and which he preferred to the honorable commission of Minister Plenipotentiary in Europe. The visit which I made him was not unexpected, for he had long since invited me to come and pass a few days with him, in the center of the mountains; notwithstanding which I found his first appearance serious, nay even cold; but before I had been two hours with him we were as intimate as if we had passed our whole lives together; walking, books, but above all, a conversation always varied and interesting, always supported by that sweet satisfaction experienced by two persons, who in communicating their sentiments and opinions, are invariably in unison, and who understand each other at the first hint, made four days pass away like so many minutes.

James Madison to Edmund Pendleton PHILADELPHIA, DECEMBER 25, 1781

It gives me great pleasure to hear of the honorable acquittal of Mr. Jefferson [of malfeasance while governor]. I know his abilities, & think I know his fidelity & zeal for his Country as well, that I am persuaded it was a just one.

James Madison to Edmund Randolph PHILADELPHIA, JUNE 11, 1782

Great as my partiality is to Mr. Jefferson, the mode [i.e., retirement from public life] in which he seems determined to revenge the wrong received from his Country, does not appear to me to be dictated either by philosophy or patriotism. It argues indeed a keen sensibility and a strong consciousness of rectitude.

Edmund Randolph to James Madison RICHMOND, SEPTEMBER 20, 1782

Mrs. Jefferson has at last shaken off her tormenting pains by yielding to them,* and has left our friend inconsolable. I ever thought him to rank domestic happiness in the first class of the chief good; but I scarcely supposed, that his grief would be so violent, as to justify the circulating report, of his swooning away, whenever he sees his children.

James Madison to Edmund Randolph SEPTEMBER 30, 1782

I conceive very readily the affliction & anguish which our friend at Monticello must experience at his irreparable loss. But his philosophical temper renders the circulating rumor which you mention altogether incredible. Perhaps this domestic catastrophe may prove in its operation beneficial to his country by weaning him from those attachments which deprived it of his services. The vacancy occasioned by his refusal of a particular service [as a peace commissioner], you need not be informed, still subsists. As soon as his sensibility will bear a subject of such a nature, will you undertake to obtain his sentiments thereupon, and let me know whether or not his aversion is still insuperable?

Thomas Jefferson to Elizabeth Wayles Eppes OCTOBER 3, 1782

This miserable kind of existence† is really too burthensome to be borne, and were it not for the infidelity of deserting the sacred charge left me [i.e., his three daughters], I could not wish its continuance a moment. For what could it be wished? All my plans of comfort and happiness reversed by a single event and nothing answering in prospect before me but a gloom unbrightened with one cheerful expectation. The care and instruction of our children indeed affords some temporary abstractions from wretchedness and nourishes a soothing reflection that if there be beyond the grave any concern for the things of this world there is one angel at least who views these attentions with pleasure and

---

*Martha Jefferson died on September 6, 1782.

†The distraught Jefferson was speaking of his wife's recent death.

wishes continuance of them while she must pity the miseries to which they confine me.

Thomas Jefferson to James Madison ANNAPOLIS, FEBRUARY 20, 1784

Monroe is buying land almost adjoining me. [William] Short will do the same. What would I not give you could fall into the circle. With such a society I could once more venture home & lay myself up for the residue of life, quitting all its contentions which grow daily more & more insupportable. Think of it. To render it practicable only requires you to think it so. Life is of no value but as it brings us gratifications. Among the most valuable of these is rational society. It informs the mind, sweetens the temper, cheers our spirits, and promotes health.

David Howell to Jonathan Arnold ANNAPOLIS, FEBRUARY 21, 1784

Gov. Jefferson, who is here a Delegate from Virginia, and one of the best members I have ever seen in Congress, has a good Library of French books, & has been so good as to lend me.

Thomas Jefferson to William Short ANNAPOLIS, MARCH 1, 1784

Having to my habitual ill health, had lately added an attack of my periodical headache, I am obliged to avoid reading, writing and almost thinking.

Thomas Jefferson to G. K. van Hogendorp ANNAPOLIS, MAY 4, 1784

Your observation on the situation of my mind is not without foundation: yet I had hoped it was unperceived, as the agreeable conversations into which you led me, often induced a temporary inattention to those events which have produced that gloom you remarked. I have been happy and cheerful. I have had many causes of gratitude to heaven, but I have also experienced its rigors. I have known what it is to lose every species of connection which is dear to the human heart: friends, brethren, parents, children—retired, as I thought myself, to dedicate the residue of life to contemplation and domestic happiness, I have been again thrown by events on the world without an object on which I can

place value. From those which are distant I am excluded by reason and reflection. The sun of life having with me already passed
his meridian.

Elbridge Gerry to John Adams PHILADELPHIA, JUNE 16, 1784

Your Colleague Mr. Jefferson . . . You will find in him an able,
faithful, & impartial Minister. On You & him We place our Reli-
ance, & if You can preserve the Confidence & Friendship of each
other, I am sure your Services will merit the highest approbation
of your Country.

François, Marquis de Barbé-Marbois to Joseph-Matthais Gérard de Rayneval PHILADELPHIA, AUGUST 24, 1784

Mr. Jefferson is an upright, just man, who belongs to no party,
and his representations will have the greatest weight on the general Congress.

Abigail Adams to Cotton Tufts MARCH 8, 1785

Mr. Adams's Colleague Mr. Jefferson is an Excellent Man. Worthy of his station and will do honor to his Country.

John Adams to Richard Cranch AUTEUIL, FRANCE, APRIL 27, 1785

I shall part with Mr. Jefferson, with great Regret, but as he will no
doubt be placed at Versailles, I shall be happy in a Correspondence of Friendship, Confidence and Affection with the Minister
at this Court, which is a very fortunate Circumstance, both for
me, and the public.

John Quincy Adams, Diary MAY 4, 1785

He is a man of great Judgment.

Abigail Adams to Mary Smith Cranch MAY 8, 1785

I shall really regret to leave Mr. Jefferson, he is one of the choice
ones of the Earth.

Abigail Adams to Thomas Jefferson LONDON, JUNE 6, 1785

Mr. Adams has already written you that we arrived in London
upon the 27 of May. We journey'd slowly and sometimes silently.
I think I have somewhere met with the observation that nobody

ever leaves Paris but with a degree of tristness. I own I was loath to leave my garden because I did not expect to find its place supplied. I was still more loath on account of the increasing pleasure, and intimacy which a longer acquaintance with a respected Friend promised, to leave behind me the only person with whom my Companion could associate with perfect freedom, and unreserve: and whose place he had no reason to expect supplied in the Land to which he is destined.

Thomas Jefferson to Abigail Adams PARIS, SEPTEMBER 25, 1785

I do not love difficulties. I am fond of quiet, willing to do my duty, but irritable by slander and apt to be forced by it to abandon my post. These are weaknesses from which reason and your counsels will preserve Mr. Adams.

Abigail Adams to Mary Smith Cranch LONDON, OCTOBER 1, 1785

In Mr. Jefferson he [Adams] has a firm and faithful Friend, with whom he can consult and advise, and as each of them have no object but the good of their Country in view, they have an unlimited confidence in each other, and they have only to lament that the [English] Channel divides their more frequent intercourse.

Marquis de Lafayette to James McHenry PARIS, DECEMBER 3, 1785

No better minister could be sent to France. He is everything that is good, upright, enlightened, and clever, and is respected and beloved by everyone that knows him.

John Adams to Henry Knox DECEMBER 15, 1785

You can Scarcely have heard a Character too high of my Friend and Colleague Mr. Jefferson, either in point of Power or Virtues. My Fellow Laborer in Congress, eight or nine years ago, upon many arduous Trials, particularly in the draft of our Declaration of Independence and in the formation of our Code of Articles of War, and Laws for the Army. I have found him uniformly the same wise and prudent Man and Steady Patriot. I only fear that his unquenchable Thirst for knowledge may injure his Health.

Abigail Adams to Elizabeth Smith Shaw LONDON, JULY 19, 1786

Three of as Learned Men, as ever I had the honor of knowing, are three of the modestest Dr. Priestly, Dr. Price, and Mr. Jefferson, in neither of whom a self importance appears or a wish to force their sentiments and opinions upon Mankind.

Marquis de Lafayette to George Washington PARIS, OCTOBER 26, 1786

Mr. Jefferson is a Most able and Respected Representative, and Such a Man as Makes me Happy to Be His Aid de Camp—Congress Have Made a choice Very favorable to their affairs.

Luigi Castiglioni, Sketches of American Statesmen 1787

Mr. Jefferson is a man of about 50 years of age, lean, of a serious and modest appearance. His uncommon talents are not readily visible at a first encounter, but as one talks with him about the various subjects in which he believes himself to be informed, he very quickly gives evident proof of his judgment and application.

Louis Guillaume Otto to the Comte de Vergennes NEW YORK, FEBRUARY 10, 1787

Mr. Jefferson is for us in Virginia what Franklin has always been in Pennsylvania—that is, the most indefatigable panegyrist of France.

Alexander Donald to Thomas Jefferson RICHMOND, NOVEMBER 12, 1787

Your old school Companion W[arner] Lewis, of Warner Hall was here staying with me when I had the pleasure of receiving your letter. It was so Friendly, and so very Flattering to my Pride, that I could not resist the vanity of showing it to him. He added to my Pride, by declaring (what I was pretty much convinced of before) that of all the Men he ever knew in his Life, he believed you to be the most sincere in your profession of Friendship. I am free to say, that when we used to pass some jovial days together at Hanover Town, I did not then imagine, that at this time you would be in Paris, Ambassador to the Court of Versailles. Some People in your High Character would be very apt to forget their old acquaintance, but you are not, and I must be allowed to do myself the justice to declare, I never entertained an Idea that you would.

Thomas Lee Shippen to William Shippen Jr. FEBRUARY 14–MARCH 26, 1788

[While on the grand tour of Europe, young Thomas Shippen wrote his father.] Mr. Jefferson is in my opinion without exception the wisest and most amiable man I have seen in Europe. He has had the goodness to favor me upon many occasions with his advice. . . . He has supplied to me the want of you better than I thought it could have been supplied, and if any one but yourself were the father, the son should not lose by the substitution.

Marquis de Lafayette to George Washington PARIS, MAY 25, 1788

I am Happy in the Ambassador we Have in this Country, and Nothing Can Excel M. Jefferson's abilities, virtues, pleasing temper, and Every thing in Him that Constitutes the Great Statesman, zealous Citizen, and Amiable Friend.

Edmund Randolph, History of Virginia

As yet Thomas Jefferson had not attained a marked grade in politics. Until about the age of twenty-five years he had pursued general science, with which he mingled the law, as a profession, with an eager industry and unabated thirst. His manners could never be harsh, but they were reserved toward the world at large. To his intimate friends he showed a peculiar sweetness of temper and by them was admired and beloved. In mathematics and experimental philosophy, he was a proficient, assiduously taught by Dr. Small of William and Mary College, whose name was not concealed among the literati of Europe. He panted after the fine arts and discovered a taste in them not easily satisfied with such scanty means as existed in a colony whose chief ambition looked to the general system of education in England as the ultimate point of excellence. But it constituted a part of Mr. Jefferson's pride to run before the times in which he lived. Prudent himself, he did not waste his resources in gratifications to which they were incompetent, but being an admirer of elegance and convenience, and venerated by his contemporaries who were within the scope of his example, he diffused a style of living much more refined than that which had been handed down to them by his and their ancestors. He had been ambitious to collect a library, not merely amassing NUMBERS of books, but distinguishing authors of merit and assembling them in subordination to every art and science; and notwithstanding losses by fire, this library was at this time more happily calculated than any other private one to direct to objects of utility and taste, to present to genius the scaffolding upon which its future eminence might be built, and to reprove the restless appetite, which is too apt to seize the mere gatherer of books.

The theories of human rights he had drawn from Locke, Harrington, Sidney, English history, and Montesquieu he had maturely investigated in all their aspects, and was versed in the republican doctrines and effusions which conducted the first Charles to the scaffold. With this fund of knowledge, he was ripe for stronger measures than the public voice was conceived to demand. But he had not gained a sufficient ascendancy to quicken or retard the progress of the popular current.

Indefatigable and methodical in whatever he undertook, he spoke with ease, perspicuity, and elegance. His style in writing was more impassioned, and although often incorrect, was too glowing not to be acquitted as venial to departures from rigid rules. Without being an overwhelming orator, he was an impressive speaker, who fixed the attention. On two signal arguments before the General Court, in which Mr. Henry and himself were coadjutors, each characterized himself—Mr. Jefferson drew copiously from the depths of the law, Mr. Henry from the recesses of the human heart.

When Mr. Jefferson first attracted notice, Christianity was directly denied in Virginia only by a few. He was adept, however, in the ensnaring subtleties of deism and gave it, among the rising generation, a philosophical patronage, which repudiates as falsehoods things unsusceptible of strict demonstration. It is believed that while such tenets as are in contempt of the Gospel inevitably terminate in espousing the fullest latitude in religious freedom, Mr. Jefferson's love of liberty would itself have produced the same effects. But his opinions against restraints on conscience ingratiated him with the enemies of the establishment, who did not stop to inquire how far those opinions might border on skepticism or infidelity. Parties in religion and politics rarely scan with nicety the peculiar private opinions of their adherents.

When he entered upon the practice of the law, he chose a residence, and traveled to a distance, which enabled him to display his great literary endowments and to establish advantageous connections among those classes of men who were daily rising in weight.

Nathaniel Cutting, Diary COWES, ENGLAND, OCTOBER 12, 1789

I have found Mr. Jefferson a man of infinite information and sound Judgment, becoming gravity, and engaging affability mark his deportment. His general abilities are such as would do honor to any age or Country.

Benjamin Rush, Commonplace Book MARCH 17, 1790

Visited Mr. Jefferson on his way to New York. It was the first time I saw him since his return from France. He was plain in his dress and unchanged in his manners. He still professed himself attached to republican forms of government, and deplored the change of opinion upon this subject in John Adams, of whom he spoke with respect and affection as a great and upright man.

Abigail Adams to Mary Cranch NEW YORK, APRIL 3, 1790

Mr. Jefferson is here, and adds much to the social circle.

James Madison to Edmund Randolph NEW YORK, MAY 6, 1790

Mr. Jefferson has been laid up near a week with his periodical head-Ache which has been very severe.

William Maclay, Diary MAY 24, 1790

Jefferson is a slender Man. Has rather the Air of Stiffness in his Manner. His clothes seem too small for him. He sits in a lounging Manner on One hip, commonly, and with one of his shoulders elevated much above the other. His face has a scrawny aspect. His Whole figure has a loose shackling Air. He had a rambling Vacant look & nothing of that firm collected deportment which I expected would dignify the presence of a Secretary or Minister. I looked for gravity, but a laxity of Manner, seemed shed about him. He spoke almost without ceasing. But even his discourse partook of his personal demeanor. It was lax & rambling and Yet he scattered information wherever he went, and some even brilliant sentiments sparkled from him. The information which he gave Us respecting foreign Ministers &ca. was all high Spiced. He has been long enough abroad to catch the tone of European folly. He gave Us a sentiment which seemed to Savor rather of quaintness. "It is better to take the highest of the lowest, than the lowest of the highest." Translation. It is better to appoint a chargé des affaires with an handsome Salary, than a Minister Plenipotentiary with a small One. He took leave, and the Committee agreed to strike out, the Specific Sum to be given to any foreign appointment, leaving it to the President to account, and appropriated $30,000 generally for the purpose.

Ezra Stiles to Thomas Jefferson YALE COLLEGE, AUGUST 27, 1790

I am rejoiced that the United States are honored with your Counsels and Abilities in the high Department of the Secretary of State. This I say without Adulation, who am a Spectator only and a most cordial Friend to the Liberties and Glory of the American Republic, though without the least Efficiency or Influence in its Councils. There are four Characters which I cannot flatter; their Merit is above it. Such are those of a Franklin, an Adams, an Ellsworth, a Jefferson and a Washington. I glory in them all; I rejoice that my Country is happy in their useful Labors. And for yourself I can only wish, that when that best of Men, the present President, shall be translated to the World of Light, a Jefferson may succeed him in the Presidency of the United States. Forgive me this Effusion of the Sentiments of sincere Respect and Estimation.

James Monroe to Thomas Jefferson RICHMOND, JUNE 17, 1791

Upon political subjects we perfectly agree, & particularly in the reprobation of all measures that may be calculated to elevate the government above the people, or place it in any respect without its natural boundary. To keep it there nothing is necessary but virtue in a part only (for in the whole it cannot be expected) of the high public servants, & a true development of the principles of those acts which have a contrary tendency. The bulk of the people are for democracy, & if they are well informed the risk of such enterprises will infallibly follow.

Oliver Wolcott Jr. to Oliver Wolcott Sr. PHILADELPHIA,
FEBRUARY 14, 1792

Mr. J. appears to have shown rather too much of a disposition to
cultivate vulgar prejudice; accordingly he will become popular in
ale houses, and will do much mischief to his country by exciting
apprehensions that the government will operate unfavorably.

"Catullus" (Alexander Hamilton), No. 3, Gazette of the
United States SEPTEMBER 29, 1792

Mr. Jefferson has hitherto been distinguished as the quiet modest, retiring philosopher—as the plain simple unambitious republican. He shall not now for the first time be regarded as the
intriguing incendiary—the aspiring turbulent competitor.

How long it is since that gentleman's real character may have
divined, or whether this is only the *first time* that the *secret* has
been disclosed, I am not sufficiently acquainted with the history
of his political life to determine; But there is always "a *first time,"*
when characters studious of artful disguises are unveiled; When
the visor of stoicism is plucked from the brow of the Epicurean;
when the plain garb of Quaker simplicity is stripped from the
concealed voluptuary; when Caesar *coyly refusing* the proffered
diadem, is seen to be Caesar *rejecting* the trappings, but tena-
ciously grasping the substance of imperial domination.

Alexander Hamilton to Charles Cotesworth Pinckney
PHILADELPHIA, OCTOBER 10, 1792

[It would be unfortunate if Jefferson defeated Adams as vice
president.] That Gentleman [Jefferson] whom I once very much
esteemed, but who does not permit me to retain that sentiment
for him, is certainly a man of sublimated and paradoxical imagination—entertaining & propagating notions inconsistent with
dignified and orderly Government.

Benjamin Rush, Commonplace Book ANTE AUGUST 22, 1793

The whole of Mr. Jefferson's conversation on all subjects is in-
structing. He is wise without formality, and maintains a consequence without pomp or distance.

John Adams to Abigail Adams PHILADELPHIA, DECEMBER 26, 1793

I am told Mr. Jefferson is to resign [as secretary of state] tomorrow. I have so long been in the habit of thinking well of his Abilities and general good dispositions, that I cannot but feel some regret at this Event: but his want of Candor, his obstinate Prejudices both of Aversion and Attachment his real Partiality in Spite of all his Pretensions and his low notions about many things have so nearly reconciled me to it, that I will not weep. Whether he will be chosen Governor of Virginia, or whether he is to go to France, in Place of Mr. Morris I know not. But this I know that if he is neglected at Monticello he will soon see a Specter like the disgraced Statesman in Gill Blass, and not long afterwards will die, for instead of being the ardent pursuer of Science that some think him, I know he is indolent, and his soul is prisoned with Ambition. Perhaps the Plan is to retire, till his Reputation magnifies enough to force him into the Chair in Case. So be it, if it is thus ordained.

JANUARY 6, 1794

Jefferson went off Yesterday, and a good riddance of bad ware. I hope his Temper will be more cool and his Principles more reasonable in Retirement than they have been in office. I am almost tempted to wish he may be chosen Vice President at the next Election for there if he could do no good, he could do no harm. He has Talents I know, and Integrity I believe, but his mind is now poisoned with Passion Prejudice and Faction.

Abigail Adams to John Adams QUINCY, JANUARY 18, 1794

Mr. Jefferson's designed resignation tho long talked of was not fully credited until it took place. The reason given for it by the French Partisans is that the Nature of his office obliged him to lend his Name to Measures which Militated against his well known principals, and give a sanction to sentiments which his heart disapproved. If this is true he did wisely to withdraw.

They say that he will now appear as the Supporter of Genet and they consider him all their own. But I have always reluctantly believed ill of him and do not credit these reports. Yet I know Mr. Jefferson to be deficient in the only sure and certain security, which binds Man to Man and renders him responsible to his Maker.

James Madison to James Monroe ORANGE, VA., SEPTEMBER 29, 1796

His enemies are as indefatigable as they are malignant.

Alexander Hamilton to Unknown NEW YORK, NOVEMBER 8, 1796

Our excellent President, as you have seen, has declined a reelection. 'Tis all-important to our country that his successor shall be a safe man. But it is far less important who of many men that may be named shall be the person, than that it shall not be Jefferson. We have every thing to fear if this man comes in, and from what I believe to be an accurate view of our political map I conclude that he has too good a chance of success, and that good calculation, prudence, and exertion were never more necessary to the Federal cause than at this very juncture. All personal and partial considerations must be discarded, and every thing must give way to the great object of excluding Jefferson.

Thomas Jefferson to John Adams DECEMBER 28, 1796

I have no ambition to govern men. It is a painful and thankless office.

Alexander Hamilton to Rufus King NEW YORK, FEBRUARY 15, 1797

Mr. Adams is President, Mr. Jefferson Vice President. Our Jacobins say they are well pleased and that the *Lion* & the *Lamb* are to lie down together. Mr. Adams's *personal* friends talk a little in the same way. Mr. *Jefferson* is not half so ill a man as we have been accustomed to think him. There is to be a united and a vigorous administration. Skeptics like me quietly look forward to the event—willing to hope but not prepared to believe. If Mr. Adams has *Vanity* to plan a plot has been laid to take hold of it. We trust his real good sense and integrity will be a sufficient shield.

Abigail Adams to John Adams QUINCY, MARCH 25, 1797

There is one observation in your Letter which struck me as meaning more than is expressed. J. is as he was! Can he still be a devotee to a cause and to a people, run mad, without any wish for Peace, without any desire after a rational system of Government, and whose thirst for power and absolute dominion is become Glutinous? Can it be?

John Nicholas to George Washington CHARLOTTESVILLE, VA., FEBRUARY 22, 1798

I do now know him to be one of the most artful, intriguing, industrious and double-faced politicians in all America.

Thomas Jefferson to Thomas Willing PHILADELPHIA, FEBRUARY 23, 1798

Th: Jefferson presents his respects to Mr. Willing, and other gentlemen managers of the ball of this evening [honoring Washington's birthday]. He hopes his non-attendance will not be misconstrued. He has not been at a ball these twenty years, nor for a long time permitted himself to go to any entertainments of the evening, from motives of attention to health. On these grounds he excused to Genl. Washington when living in the city his not going to his birthnights, to Mrs. Washington not attending her evenings, to Mrs. Adams the same, and to all his friends who have been so good as to invite him to tea- & card parties, the declining to go to them. It is an indulgence which his age and habits will he hopes obtain and continue to him. He has always testified his homage to the occasion by his subscription to it.

Tadeuz Kosciuszko to Thomas Jefferson, [JULY 15–AUGUST 5, 1798]

You may rely upon my partiality towards America that I will do everything in my power to prevent a war so injurious to both republics, and in that respect you will be my Star that will guide my endeavors as you are a True American Patriot, and so disinterested a man who chose only the happiness of your own Country.

Robert Troup to Rufus King NEW YORK, OCTOBER 2, 1798

[Jefferson] on his return home from the last sitting of Congress, was indiscreet enough to accept of the honor of a public entertainment in Virginia on a *Sunday.* This fact has been trumpeted from one end of the continent to the other as an irrefragable proof of his contempt for the Christian religion and his devotion to the new religion of France. It has made an impression much to his prejudice in the Middle and Eastern States.

Charles Carroll of Carrollton to Alexander Hamilton
ANNAPOLIS, APRIL 18, 1800

We have strange reports circulated among us respecting the prevalence of Jacobinical principles in your State; it is asserted with confidence by the antifederal party here, that all your electors will vote for Mr. Jefferson as President; if such an event should really happen, it is probable he will be chosen; of such a choice the consequences to this country may be dreadful. Mr. Jefferson is too theoretical & fanciful a statesman to direct with steadiness & prudence the affairs of this extensive & growing confederacy; he might safely try his experiments, without much inconvenience, in the little Republic of St. Marino, but his fantastic tricks would dissolve this Union. Perhaps the miseries of France & more especially the Government of Buonaparte may have weaned him from his predilection for revolutions. I once saw a letter of his, in which among several others was contained this strange sentiment "that to preserve the liberties of a people, a revolution once in a century was necessary." A man of this way of thinking, surely may be said to be fond of revolutions; yet possibly were he the chief Magistrate he might not wish for a revolution during his presidency.

Alexander Hamilton to John Jay   NEW YORK, MAY 7, 1800

In observing this,* I shall not be supposed to mean that any thing ought to be done which integrity will forbid—but merely that the scruples of delicacy and propriety, as relative to a common course of things, ought to yield to the extraordinary nature of the crisis. They ought not to hinder the taking of a *legal* and *constitutional* step, to prevent an *Atheist in Religion* and a *Fanatic* in politics from getting possession of the helm of the State.

Timothy Pickering to George Cabot   PHILADELPHIA, JUNE 16, 1800

[In a conversation with President Adams, Pickering] remarked that I supposed Mr. Jefferson to be a very learned man, "but

---

*Hamilton was asking Governor John Jay to call a special session of the New York legislature to change the procedure for electing presidential electors that would eliminate the winner take-all method in exchange for a district system. Such a change would have reelected John Adams president.

certainly he is a very visionary man." The President answered,
"Why, yes, he has a certain kind of learning in philosophy, &c.,
but *very little of that which is necessary for a statesman.*"

Arthur Fenner, Report of a Conversation with Alexander Hamilton   NEWPORT, R.I., JUNE 25–26, 1800

[Hamilton said] Mr. Jefferson was a man of no judgment; he
could write a pretty book.

Oliver Wolcott Jr. to Fisher Ames   WASHINGTON, D.C., AUGUST 10, 1800

It is probable that Mr. Jefferson's conduct would be frequently
whimsical and undignified; that he would affect the character of
a philosopher; that he would countenance quacks, impostors,
and projectors; that he would cultivate and increase our national
prejudices, and so relax the principles of government as greatly to
impair its utility as a bond of internal union and bulwark against
foreign influence. He would certainly change all the principal
officers of government, or rather there is no one of the gentlemen now in office who would serve under him. How their places
would be supplied I cannot conjecture, but I know of no individuals of his party in whom are united the indispensable qualifications of character, talents, industry, experience, and integrity.

Chauncey Goodrich to Oliver Wolcott Jr.   HARTFORD, AUGUST 26, 1800

Among all the good people of the state, there is a horrid idea of
Mr. Jefferson. The clergy abominate him on account of his athe-
istical creed.

Fisher Ames to Rufus King   DEDHAM, MASS., SEPTEMBER 24, 1800

His irreligion, wild philosophy and gimmickry in politics are
never mentioned [by John Adams]. On the contrary the great
man has been known to speak of him with much regard, and an
affected indignation at the charge of irreligion, asking what has
that to do with the public and adding that he is a good patriot,
citizen and father.

George Cabot to Alexander Hamilton BROOKLINE, MASS.,
OCTOBER 11, 1800

Dr. [Timothy] Dwight is here stirring us up to oppose the Demon of Jacobinism.

Margaret Bayard Smith, Reminiscences of Washington, D.C.
DECEMBER 1800

"And is this," said I, after my first interview with Mr. Jefferson,
"the violent democrat, the vulgar demagogue, the bold atheist and profligate man I have so often heard denounced by the
federalists? Can this man so meek and mild, yet dignified in his
manners, with a voice so soft and low, with a countenance so benignant and intelligent, can he be that daring leader of a faction,
that disturber of the peace, that enemy of all rank and order?"
Mr. Smith, indeed, (himself a democrat) had given me a very different description of this celebrated individual; but his favorable
opinion I attributed in a great measure to his political feelings,
which led him zealously to support and exalt the party to which
he belonged, especially its popular and almost idolized leader.
Thus the virulence of party-spirit was somewhat neutralized,
nay, I even entertained towards him the most kindly dispositions,
knowing him to be not only politically friendly to my husband;
yet I did believe that he was an ambitious and violent demagogue,
coarse and vulgar in his manners, awkward and rude in his appearance, for such had the public journals and private conversations of the federal party represented him to be.

    In December 1800, a few days after Congress had for the first
time met in our new Metropolis, I was one morning sitting alone
in the parlor, when the servant opened the door and showed in a
gentleman who wished to see my husband. The usual frankness
and care with which I met strangers, were somewhat checked
by the dignified and reserved air of the present visitor; but the
chilled feeling was only momentary, for after taking the chair I
offered him in a free and easy manner, and carelessly throwing his
arm on the table near which he sat, he turned towards me a countenance beaming with an expression of benevolence and with a
manner and voice almost femininely soft and gentle, entered into
conversation on the commonplace topics of the day, from which,
before I was conscious of it, he had drawn me into observations

of a more personal and interesting nature. I know not how it was, but there was something in his manner, his countenance and voice that at once unlocked my heart, and in answer to his casual enquiries concerning our situation in our *new home*, as he called it, I found myself frankly telling him what I liked or disliked in our present circumstances and abode. I knew not who he was, but the interest with which he listened to my artless details, induced the idea he was some intimate acquaintance or friend of Mr. Smith's and put me perfectly at my ease; in truth so kind and conciliating were his looks and manners that I forgot he was not a friend of my own, until on the opening of the door, Mr. Smith entered and introduced the stranger to me as *Mr. Jefferson.*

I felt my cheeks burn and my heart throb, and not a word more could I speak while he remained. Nay, such was my embarrassment I could scarcely listen to the conversation carried on between him and my husband. For several years he had been to me an object of peculiar interest. In fact my destiny, for on his success in the pending presidential election, or rather the success of the democratic party, (their interests were identical) my condition in life, my union with the man I loved, depended. In addition to this personal interest, I had long participated in my husband's political sentiments and anxieties, and looked upon Mr. Jefferson as the corner stone on which the edifice of republican liberty was to rest, the reformer of abuses, the head of the republican party, which must rise or fall with him, and on the triumph of the republican party I devoutly believed the security and welfare of my country depended.

Gouverneur Morris, Diary DECEMBER 11, 1800

It seems to be the general opinion that Colonel Burr will be chosen President by the House of Representatives. Many of them think it highly dangerous that Mr. Jefferson should, in the present crisis, be placed in that office. They consider him as a theoretic man, who would bring the National Government back to something like the old Confederation. Mr. Nicholas comes today, and to him I state it as the opinion, not of light and fanciful but of serious and considerable men, that Burr must be preferred to Jefferson. He is, as I supposed, much wounded at this information.

John Marshall to Alexander Hamilton WASHINGTON, D.C., JANUARY 1, 1801

I received this morning your letter of the 26th of December. It is I believe certain that Jefferson & Burr will come to the house of representatives with equal votes. The returns have been all received & this is the general opinion.

Being no longer in the house of representatives & consequently compelled by no duty to decide between them, my own mind had scarcely determined to which of these gentlemen the preference was due. To Mr. Jefferson whose political character is better known than that of Mr. Burr, I have felt almost insuperable objections. His foreign prejudices seem to me totally to unfit him for the chief magistracy of a nation which cannot indulge those prejudices without sustaining debt & permanent injury. In addition to this solid & immovable objection Mr. Jefferson appears to me to be a man who will embody himself with the house of representatives. By weakening the office of President he will increase his personal power. He will diminish his responsibility, sap the fundamental principles of the government & become the leader of that party which is about to constitute the majority of the legislature. The morals of the Author of the letter to Mazzei* cannot be pure.

William Fitzhugh to Samuel Blachley Webb GENEVA, JANUARY 12, 1801

I will, nevertheless, venture to observe that as the issue of this late electioneering struggle has been the choice of Thomas Jefferson for our President, and as this choice is made by a majority of our countrymen, I am *content,* the more so, as I believe he will make a good President, and grievously disappoint the most violent of his partisans. Mr. Jefferson is a man of too much virtue and good sense to attempt any material change in a system which was adopted by our late beloved Washington, and has been since steadily pursued by Mr. Adams, and which has preserved our

---

*On April 24, 1796, Jefferson wrote a personal letter to his old friend Philip Mazzei in which he alluded to the president (George Washington) and the judiciary drifting toward a favorable policy toward Britain. Mazzei had the letter printed, and it became an embarrassment to Jefferson when he reentered politics.

country in peace and prosperity for 12 years, during which period almost the whole civilized world has been deluged in blood, and this too in defiance of the repeated attempts of France & England by open threats and secret intrigues to draw us into the vortex of their ruinous convulsions.

Alexander Hamilton to James A. Bayard NEW YORK, JANUARY 16, 1801

Perhaps myself the first, at some expense of popularity, to unfold the true character of Jefferson, it is too late for me to become his apologist. Nor can I have any disposition to do it. I admit that his politics are tinctured with fanaticism, that he is too much in earnest in his democracy, that he has been a mischievous enemy to the principle measures of our past administration, that he is crafty & persevering in his objects, that he is not scrupulous about the means of success, nor very mindful of truth, and that he is a contemptible hypocrite. But it is not true as is alleged that he is an enemy to the power of the Executive, or that he is for confounding all the powers in the House of Representatives. It is a fact which I have frequently mentioned that while we were in the administration together he was generally for a large construction of the Executive authority, & not backward to act upon it in cases which coincided with his views. Let it be added, that in his theoretic Ideas he has considered as improper the participation of the Senate in the Executive Authority. I have more than once made the reflection that viewing himself as the reversioner, he was solicitous to come into possession of a Good Estate. Nor is it true that Jefferson is zealot enough to do anything in pursuance of his principles which will contravene his popularity, or his interest. He is as likely as any man I know to temporize—to calculate what will be likely to promote his own reputation and advantage; and the probable result of such a temper is the preservation of systems, though originally opposed, which being once established, could not be overturned without danger to the person who did it. To my mind a true estimate of Mr. J.'s character warrants the expectation of a temporizing rather than a violent system. That Jefferson has manifested a culpable predilection for France is certainly true; but I think it a question whether it did not proceed quite as much from her *popularity* among us, as from sentiment, and in proportion as that popularity is diminished his zeal will cool.

Add to this that there is no fair reason to suppose him capable of being corrupted, which is a security that he will not go beyond certain limits. It is not at all improbable that under the change of circumstances Jefferson's Gallicism has considerably abated.

Gouverneur Morris to Alexander Hamilton WASHINGTON, D.C., JANUARY 26, 1801

They [the Federalist members of the House of Representatives] consider Mr. J. as infected with all the cold blooded Vices and as particularly dangerous from the false Principles of Government which he has imbibed.

Abigail Adams to Mary Cranch WASHINGTON, D.C., FEBRUARY 7, 1801

Have we any claim to the favor or protection of Providence, when we have against warning admonition and advice Chosen as our chief Magistrate a man who makes no pretensions to the belief of an all wise and supreme Governor of the World, ordering or directing or overruling the events which take place in it? I do not mean that he is an Atheist, for I do not think he is—but he believes Religion only useful as it may be made a political Engine, and that the outward forms are only, as I once heard him express himself—mere Mummery. In short, he is not a believer in the Christian system—The other [Aaron Burr] if he is more of a believer, has more to answer for, because he has grossly offended against those doctrines by his practice.

Such are the Men whom we are like to have as our Rulers. Whether they are given us in wrath to punish us for our sins and transgressions, the Events will disclose—But if ever we saw a day of darkness, I fear this is one which will be visible until kindled into flames.

John Marshall to Charles Cotesworth Pinckney WASHINGTON, D.C., MARCH 4, 1801

Today the new political year commences—The new order of things begins. . . . The democrats are divided into speculative theorists & absolute terrorists: With the latter I am not disposed to class Mr. Jefferson. If he arranges himself with them it is not difficult to foresee that much calamity is in store for our country—if he does not they will soon become his enemies & calumniators.

Theodore Sedgwick to Rufus King STOCKBRIDGE, MASS., MAY 24, 1801

Jefferson was believed to be a sincere Democrat—hostile to the principles of our Constitution, and the measures of the administration—desirous of conforming in practice to the imbecile principles of the old confederation, a confederation whose measures would be directed by the arrogance of Virginia aided by those states which looked up to her with servile submission. It was believed that he had given evidence of an entire devotion to France under every form of her government, and that under the dominion of this political passion, aided by a rancorous hatred to Great Britain, he might involve the country in war with the latter, & what is worse form an intimate and subordinate connection with the former.

Robert Troup to Rufus King NEW YORK, MAY 27, 1801

Jefferson's inaugural speech has had a wonderful lullaby effect. I do not apprehend the serious mischiefs from his administration that have been foretold; but my opinion is, that it will be the little contemptible thing that grows of a trimming system and a studied adherence to popular notions. Hamilton is persuaded that neither Jefferson nor his friends have sufficient skill or patriotism to conduct the political vessel in the tempestuous sea of liberty.

Fisher Ames to John Rutledge DEDHAM, MASS., JULY 30, 1801

Mr. Jefferson's removals and appointments afford proof enough of the quo amino* he administers the government. They present a most singular confutation of the puritanism with which his party sought office, and a noiseless efficient instrument of exposing the party to the world. A prevailing party should forbid their chief pen & ink, especially if he is a scribbler by trade and vain of his writing. Tom Payne has said that nobody could write a man down who was up but himself. The two Toms are strong illustrations that the fellow, so often in the wrong, was for once in the right.

Robert Troup to Rufus King NEW YORK, APRIL 9, 1802

Jefferson is the supreme director of measures—he has no levee days—observes no ceremony—often sees company in an undress,

*Intentions with which.

sometimes with his slippers on—always accessible to, and very familiar with, the sovereign people.

Thomas Jefferson to Benjamin Hawkins WASHINGTON, D.C., FEBRUARY 18, 1803

I retain myself very perfect health, having not had twenty hours of fever in forty-two years past. I have sometimes had a troublesome headache, and some slight rheumatic pains; but now sixty years old nearly, I have had as little to complain of in point of health as most people.

William Plumer, Memoranda NOVEMBER 10, 1804

I found the President dressed better than I ever saw him at any time when I called on a morning visit. Though his coat was old & threadbare, his scarlet vest, his corduroy small cloths, & his white cotton hose, were new & clean—but his linen was much soiled, & his slippers old—His hair was cropt & powdered.

MARCH 16, 1806

The more critically & impartially I examine the character & conduct of Mr. Jefferson the more favorably I think of his integrity. I am really inclined to think I have done him injustice in not allowing him more credit for the integrity of heart that he possesses. A city appears very different when viewed from different positions—& so it is with man. Viewed in different situations—different times—place—circumstances—relations & with different dispositions, the man thus examined appears unlike himself. My object is truth—I write for myself—I wish not—I am determined not—to set down ought in malice, or to diminish anything from the fact.

The result of my investigation is that Mr. Jefferson has as much honesty & integrity as men in the higher grades of society usually have—& indeed I think more. He is a man of science. But he is very credulous—he knows little of the nature of man—very little indeed. He has traveled the tour of Europe—he has been Minister at Versailles. He has had great opportunities to know man. He has much knowledge of books—of insects—of shells & of all that charms a virtuoso—but he knows not the human heart. He is a closet politician—but not a practical statesman. He has much *fine sense* but little of that *plain common sense* so requisite to business—& which in fact governs the world.

These observations on his character are founded on facts that have fallen within my own View.

An infidel in religion—but in every thing else credulous to a fault!

Alas man is himself a contradiction! I do not however mean to insinuate that Mr. Jefferson is a model of goodness. He has too much cunning. Still I repeat the errors of his administration proceed more often from the head than the heart. They partake more of credulity than of wickedness. Examine his whole life with a view to this fact & you will meet with proof in almost every official act.

Permit me to mention that no one circumstance tended so much to his elevation as the *great confidence* General Washington reposed in him. Washington did this with a full & perfect knowledge of him. They were both Virginians. His conduct during & after the Revolution was known to Washington. And although Jefferson was publicly opposed to the adoption of the Constitution of the United States yet Genl. Washington when called to administer the government gave to Mr. Jefferson the most important confidential office under him, that of *Secretary of State.* This office Mr. Jefferson held as long as he wished. Mr. Washington did not withdraw his confidence from him while in office. The approbation of Washington, under these circumstances, is honorable.

I do not myself so implicitly yield to the opinion of Mr. Washington as some men do. Still I think his approbation is worthy of great notice. It renders popular, the man on whom it has been conferred, to a certain extent. . . .

Mr. Jefferson is too timid—too irresolute—too fickle—he wants nerve—he wants firmness & resolution. A wavering doubtful hesitating mind joined with credulity is oftentimes as injurious to the nation as a wicked depraved heart.

APRIL 8, 1806

But said Mr. Adair, the President wants nerve—he has not even confidence in himself—For more than a year he has been in the habit of trusting almost implicitly in Mr. Madison. Madison has acquired a complete ascendancy over him. I observed that I considered Mr. M as an honest man—but that he was too cautious—too fearful & timid to direct the affairs of this nation. He replied that is my opinion of the man.

DECEMBER 11, 1806

General [Stephen Roe] Bradley, of the State [Vermont], said to me this day, "That it was time to have some other man president—That Mr. Jefferson's influence in Congress was irresistible—that it was alarming—That if he should recommend to us to repeal the Gospels of the Evangelist, a majority of Congress would do it."

DECEMBER 27, 1806

It appears to me that Mr. Jefferson is growing hard of hearing—that deafness is approaching upon him. I observed him several times to bend his head to listen—& he inquired what I had said. Age has some effect upon him.

He always renders his company easy & agreeable. His table was well furnished—good dinner—rich & various desert—but his wine, except Madeira & Hermitage, not good.

Joseph Story to Samuel P. P. Fay WASHINGTON, D.C., MAY 30, 1807

Jefferson is tall and thin, of a sallow complexion, with a fine, intelligent eye. Dr. M. yesterday introduced me, and we spent a half hour with him, in which time he conversed in a very easy, correct, and pleasant style. His language is peculiarly appropriate, and his manner very unaffected. The negligence of his dress a little surprised me. He received us in his slippers, and wore old-fashioned clothes, which were not in the nicest order, or of the most elegant kind; a blue coat, white worked cassimere waistcoat and corduroy breeches (I beg your pardon, I mean *small clothes*) constituted his dress. You know Virginians have some pride in appearing in simple habiliments, and are willing to rest their claim to attention upon their force of mind and suavity of manners. The President is a little awkward in his first address, but you are immediately at ease in his presence. His manners are inviting and not uncourtly; and his voice flexible and distinct. He bears the marks of intense thought and perseverance in his countenance. . . . I visited him again this morning in company with Mr. Madison, at whose house I breakfasted, and conversed with him upon politics in a perfectly familiar manner. His smile is very engaging and impresses you with cheerful frankness. His familiarity, however, is tempered with great calmness of manner and with becoming propriety. Open to all, he seems willing to stand the test of inquiry, and to be weighed in the balance only by his merit and attainments. You may measure if you please, and cannot easily misjudge. On the whole, I confess he appears to me a clear and intelligent man, ready and discriminating, but more formed by philosophical reflection, than by rapid, enterprising, overbearing genius. If he chooses, he cannot fail to please. If he cannot awe, he will not sink into neglect. The current of his thoughts is gentle and uniform, unbroken by the torrent of eloquence, and unruffled by the fervor of vivid internal flame. Take this passing sketch and color it to your own fancy.

John Adams to Benjamin Rush SEPTEMBER 1807

Jefferson resigned his office as Secretary of State and retired, and his friends said he had struck a great stroke to obtain the presidency. . . . The whole anti-Federal party at that time considered this retirement as a sure and certain step towards the summit of the pyramid and, accordingly, represented him as unambitious, unavaricious, and perfectly disinterested in all parts of all the states in the union. When a man has one of the two greatest parties in a nation interested in representing him to be disinterested, even those who believe it to be a lie will repeat it so often to one another that at last they will seem to believe it to be true. Jefferson has succeeded; and multitudes are made to believe that he is pure benevolence; that he desires no profit; that he wants no patronage; that if you will only let him govern, he will rule only to make the people happy. But you and I know him to be an intriguer.

Margaret Bayard Smith to Susan B. Smith WASHINGTON, D.C., MARCH 1809

[At Madison's presidential inaugural ball.] Mr. Jefferson did not stay above two hours; he seemed in high spirits and his countenance beamed with a benevolent joy. I do believe father never loved son more than he loves Mr. Madison, and I believe too that every demonstration of respect to Mr. M. gave Mr. J. more pleasure than if paid to himself. Oh he is a good man! And the day will come when all party spirit shall expire, that every citizen of the United States will join in saying "He is a good man."

John Adams to Benjamin Rush OCTOBER 25, 1809

There has never been the smallest interruption of the personal friendship between me and Mr. Jefferson that I know of. You should remember that Jefferson was but a boy to me. I was at least ten years older than him in age and more than twenty years older than him in politics. I am bold to say I was his preceptor in politics and taught him everything that has been good and solid in his whole political conduct. I served with him on many committees of Congress, in which we established some of the most important regulations of the army &c., &c., &c.

JUNE 21, 1811

[In speaking of the "masters of the theatrical exhibitions of politics."] We whigs attempted somewhat of the kind. The Declaration of Independence I always considered as a Theatrical Show. Jefferson ran away with all the stage effect of that: i.e. all the Glory of it.

DECEMBER 25, 1811

[In speaking of Jefferson and Benjamin Rush.] I believe you both to mean well to mankind and your country. I might suspect you both to sacrifice a little to the infernal gods, and perhaps unconsciously to suffer your judgments to be a little swayed by a love of popularity and possibly by a little spice of ambition.

Thomas Jefferson to John Adams MONTICELLO, JANUARY 21, 1812

You and I have been wonderfully spared, and myself with remarkable health, and a considerable activity of body and mind. I am on horseback 3 or 4 hours of every day; visit 3 or 4 times a year a possession I have 90 miles distant [Poplar Forest], performing the winter journey on horseback. I walk little however; a single mile being too much for me; and I live in the midst of my grandchildren, one of whom has lately promoted me to be a great grandfather.

Benjamin Rush to John Adams PHILADELPHIA, FEBRUARY 17, 1812

I rejoice in the correspondence which has taken place between you and your old friend Mr. Jefferson. I consider you and him as the North and South Poles of the American Revolution. Some talked, some wrote, and some fought to promote and establish it, but you and Mr. Jefferson *thought* for us all.

Thomas Jefferson to John Adams MONTICELLO, JANUARY 11, 1817

Forty three volumes read in one year, and 12 of them quartos! Dear Sir, how I envy you! Half a dozen 8vos. [octavos] in that space of time are as much as I am allowed. I can read by candle-light only, and stealing long hours from my rest; nor would that time be indulged to me, could I, by that light, see to write. From sunrise to one or two o'clock, and often from dinner to dark, I am drudging at the writing table. And all this to answer letters into which neither interest nor inclination on my part enters; and often for persons whose names I have never before heard. Yet, writing civilly, it is hard to refuse them civil answers. This is the burthen of my life, a very grievous one indeed, and one which I must get rid of.

Thomas Jefferson to Benjamin Waterhouse MONTICELLO, MARCH 3, 1818

I am much debilitated in body, and my memory sensibly on the wane. Still, however, I enjoy good health and spirits, and am as industrious a reader as when a student at college. Not of news-papers. These I have discarded. I relinquish, as I ought to do, all intermeddling with public affairs, committing myself cheer-fully to the watch and care of those for whom, in my turn, I have watched and cared.

John Marshall to Joseph Story RICHMOND, SEPTEMBER 18, 1821

[Jefferson is referred to as] the great Lama of the mountains.

Thomas Jefferson to John Adams MONTICELLO, JUNE 1, 1822

I have ever dreaded a doting old age; and my health has been generally so good, and is now so good, that I dread it still. The rapid decline of my strength during the last winter has made me hope sometimes that I see land. During summer I enjoy its temperature, but I shudder at the approach of winter, and wish I could sleep through it with the Dormouse, and only wake with him in spring, if ever. They say that [General John] Starke could walk about his room. I am told you walk well and firmly. I can only reach my garden, and that with sensible fatigue. I ride however daily. But reading is my delight. I should wish never to put pen to paper; and the more because of the treacherous practice some people have of publishing one's letters without leave.

John Adams to Thomas Jefferson   QUINCY, JULY 12, 1822

I hope one day your letters will be all published in volumes; they will not always appear Orthodox, or liberal in politics; but they will exhibit a Mass of Taste, Sense, Literature and Science, presented in a sweet simplicity and a neat elegance of Style, which will be read with delight in future ages.

Daniel Webster, Notes of Conversation with Thomas Jefferson 1824

Mr. Jefferson is now between eighty-one & eighty-two, above six feet high, of an ample long frame, rather thin & spare. His head, which is not peculiar in its shape, is set rather forward on his shoulders, & his neck being long, there is, when he is walking or conversing, an habitual protrusion of it. It is still well covered with hair, which having been once red, & now turning grey, is of an indistinct sandy color. His eyes are small, very light, & now neither brilliant, nor striking. His chin is rather long, but not pointed, his nose small, regular in its outline, & the nostrils a little elevated. His mouth is well formed, & still filled with teeth; it is generally strongly compressed, bearing an expression of contentment & benevolence. His complexion formerly light, & freckled, now bears the marks of age & cutaneous affection. His limbs are uncommonly long, his hands & feet very large, & his wrists of a most extraordinary size. His walk is not precise & military, but easy & swinging; he stoops a little, not so much from age, as from natural formation. When sitting he appears short, partly from a rather lounging habit of sitting, & partly from the disproportionate length of his limbs. His dress when in the house, is a grey surtout coat, kerseymere buff waistcoat, with an under one faced with some material of a dingy red. His pantaloons are very long, loose, & of the same color as his coat. His stockings are woolen, either white or grey, & his shoes of the kind that bear his name. His whole dress is neglected but not slovenly. He wears a common round hat. He wears when on horseback a grey strait bodiced coat, & a spencer of the same material, both fastened with large pearl buttons. When we first saw him he was riding, & in addition to the above, wore round his throat a knit white woolen tippet, in the place of a cravat, & black velvet gaiters under his pantaloons.

His general appearance indicates an extraordinary degree of health, vivacity, & spirit. His sight is still good, for he needs glasses only in the evening, his hearing is generally good, but a number of voices in animated conversation, confuses it.

Mr. J. rises in the morning, as soon as he can *see* the hands of his clock (which is directly opposite his bed) & examines his thermometer immediately, as he keeps a regular meteorological diary. He employs himself chiefly in writing till breakfast, which is at nine. From that time till dinner, he is in his library, excepting that in fair weather he rides on horseback from seven to fourteen miles. Dines at four, returns to the drawing room at six, when coffee is brought in, & passes the evening, *till nine* in conversation. His habit of retiring at that hour is so strong, that it has become *essential* to his health & comfort. His diet is simple, but he seems restrained only by his tastes. His breakfast is tea & coffee, bread, of which he does not seem afraid, although it is always fresh from the oven, with sometimes a slight accompaniment of cold meat.

He enjoys his dinner well, taking with meat a large proportion of vegetables. He has a strong preference for the wines of the Continent, of which he has many sorts of excellent quality, having been more than commonly successful in his mode of importing, & preserving them. Among others we found the following, which are very rare in this country, & apparently not at all injured by transportation. L'Ednau, Muscat, Samian, & Blanchette de Limoux. Dinner is served in half Virginian, half French style, in good taste & abundance. No wine is put on the table till the cloth is removed.

In conversation, Mr. J. is easy & natural, & apparently not ambitious; it is not loud as challenging general attention, but usually addressed to the person next him. The topics when not selected to suit the character & feelings of his auditor, are those subjects with which his mind seems particularly occupied, & these at present, may be said to be Science & Letters, & especially the University of Virginia, which is coming into existence almost entirely from his exertions, & will rise it is to be hoped, to usefulness & credit under his continued care. When we were with him, his favorite subjects were Greek & Anglo-Saxon, & historical recollections of the times & events of the Revolution & of his residence in France, from 1783–4 to 89.

Daniel Webster to Jeremiah Mason WASHINGTON, D.C., DECEMBER 29, 1824

At Mr. Jefferson's, we remained five days. This was something longer than our intention, but there came rains, which prevented our departure. Mr. Jefferson is a man of whom one may form a very just account, as to person & manners, from description, & pictures. We met him in the road, & I knew him at once, although he was on horseback, & something straighter, & freer from the debility of age, than I had expected. We found him uniformly pleasant, social & interesting. He talked less of present things than might be expected, although in the intercourse with gentlemen under his own roof, he did *not keep back* his opinions, on men or things. But if I were to say what appeared to be the leading topics, with him, & those to which his mind habitually turned itself, I should mention *three*—early anecdotes of Revolutionary times—French society—politics—& literature, such as they were when he was in France—and Genl. Literature, & the Va. University.

On these three general topics he has much to say & he says it all well.

Daniel Webster to Joseph Hopkinson WASHINGTON, D.C., DECEMBER 31, 1824

My visit to Virginia was not unpleasant. Mr. Jefferson is full of conversation, & as it relates, pretty much, to by-gone times, it is replete with information & useful anecdote. All the great men of our Revolutionary epoch necessarily had a circle of which they were, severally, the center. Each, therefore, has something to tell not common to all. Mr. Adams & Mr. Jefferson, for example, though acting together, on a common theater, at Philadelphia, were nevertheless far apart, when in Massachusetts & Virginia, & each was at home, in the midst of men & of events, more or less different from those which surrounded the other. I heard Mr. Jefferson talk over the events of his early life, as your friend [David] Hunter represents the young Indians to listen to the tales of the age-stricken warriors; not without occasionally feeling, like them, an impulse to raise the war song, & grasp the tomahawk. Mr. Jefferson's conversation is little on present things; partly perhaps from the prudence of forbearing to engage in questions which now divide the community, but mostly from a greater love for other topics. Early Revolutionary events, political occurrences, in both Hemispheres, about the time he was in France, & general literature & the *University of Virginia* would seem to be his favorite subjects.

James Madison to Nicholas P. Trist JULY 6, 1826

He lives and will live in the memory and gratitude of the wise and good, as a luminary of science, as a votary of liberty, as a model of patriotism, and as a benefactor of human kind. In these characters, I have known him, and not less in the virtues and charms of social life, for a period of fifty years, during which there was not an interruption or diminution of mutual confidence and cordial friendship, for a single moment in a single instance. What I feel therefore now, need not, I should say, cannot, be expressed.

John Paul Jones
1747–1792

⇥ BORN IN Scotland. Began seafaring career at the age of twelve. Rose from apprentice to merchant captain. Accused twice of murdering his own men. Acquitted of the first charge; he ran off to America rather than face the second. The Continental Congress commissioned him a first lieutenant aboard the *Alfred,* 1775–76. As captain of the *Providence,* 1776–77, he captured sixteen prizes in one cruise. Commanding the *Ranger,* 1777–78, Jones captured British ships and raided British ports in 1778 in the Irish Sea. In September 1779 Jones commanded the *Bonhomme Richard* in its epic naval battle against the British *Serapis.* The *Bonhomme Richard* sank but not before Jones captured the *Serapis,* making him a hero. He commanded the *Alliance,* 1780, the *Ariel,* 1781, and the *America,* 1781–82. After 1783 he was made an agent to solicit payment in Europe for the prizes his ships had taken. He favored the Constitution but did not want the president to command troops in the field. Catherine the Great commissioned him a rear admiral in the Russian navy, 1788–90. He retired to France and was appointed a special envoy to ransom prisoners and negotiate peace with Algiers. He died mysteriously before receiving his commission. In 1905 his body (amazingly well preserved in a lead casket) was exhumed and returned to the U.S. Naval Academy at Annapolis.

John Paul Jones to the Marquis de Lafayette L'ORIENT, MAY 1, 1779

I cannot Insure success but we will endeavor to deserve it.

John Adams, Diary MAY 13, 1779

After Dinner walked out, with C[aptain]s Jones and Landais to see Jones's Marine—dressed in the English Uniform, red and white. A Number of very active and clever Sergeants and Corporals are employed to teach them the Exercise, and Maneuvers and Marches &c.

After which Jones came on Board our ship.

This is the most ambitious and intriguing Officer in the American Navy. Jones has Art, and Secrecy, and aspires very high. You see the Character of the Man in his uniform, and that of his officers and Marines, variant from the Uniforms established by Congress. Golden Button holes, for himself—two Epaulet—Marines in red and white instead of Green.

Eccentricities and Irregularities are to be expected from him—they are in his Character, they are visible in his Eyes. His Voice is soft and still and small, his Eye has keenness, and Wildness and Softness in it.

Benjamin Franklin to Samuel Cooper PASSY, OCTOBER 27, 1779

Few Actions at Sea have demonstrated such steady, cool determined Bravery, as that of Jones in taking the Serapis.

Abigail Adams to Elizabeth Cranch AUTEUIL, FRANCE, DECEMBER 3, 1784

Chevalier Jones you have heard much of. He is a most uncommon Character. I dare Say you would be as much disappointed in him as I was. From the intrepid Character he justly Supported in the American Navy, I expected to have seen a Rough, Stout, warlike Roman. Instead of that, I should sooner think of wrapping him up in cotton wool and putting him into my pocket, than sending him to contend with Cannon Ball.

He is small of stature, well proportioned, soft in his Speech, easy in his address, polite in his manners, vastly civil, understands all the Etiquette of a Lady's Toilite as perfectly as he does the Masts, Sails and rigging of a Ship. Under all this appearance of softness, he is Bold, enterprising, ambitious and active.

He has been here often, and dined with us several times. He is said to be a Man of Gallantry and a favorite amongst the French Ladies whom he is frequently commending for the neatness of their persons, their easy manners and their taste in dress. He knows how often the Ladies use the Baths, what color best suits a Lady's complexion, what Cosmetics are most favorable to the skin. We do not often See the Warrior and the *Abigail** thus united.

Luigi Castiglioni, Sketches of American Soldiers 1787

Paul Jones is about 40 years of age, short, and has none of the ferocious appearance with which some have painted him in affected portraits. He loves the pleasures of life, and readily finds compensation amid the luxuries of Paris for the harsh labors of his excursions on the sea.

Edward Carrington to Thomas Jefferson NEW YORK, NOVEMBER 10, 1787

I find that this brave, and in my mind honest, Man has his enemies.

Thomas Jefferson to Edward Carrington PARIS, MAY 27, 1788

Paul Jones is invited into the Empress's service with the rank of rear admiral, and to have a separate command. I wish it corresponded with the views of Congress to give him that rank from the taking of the Serapis. [I look to] this officer as our great future dependence on the sea, where alone we should think of ever having a force. He is young enough to see the day when we shall be more populous than the whole British dominions and able to fight them ship to ship. We should procure him then every possible opportunity of acquiring experience.

Benjamin Rush, Sketches C. 1800

He united in his military character the *boldness* which is produced by madness, the *bravery* which is the effect of animal spirits, and

---

*Name of a maid in Beaumont and Fletcher's *The Scornful* (1616), thus the term *Abigail* means a lady's maid.

the *courage* which is the result of reflection. He once put into my hands a history of his naval exploits. He exulted in it in having first hoisted the American flag on board the first armed vessel that was commissioned by the United States. I heard him give a minute account of his engagement with the *Serapis* in a small circle of gentlemen at a dinner. It was delivered with great apparent modesty and commanded the most respectful attention. Towards the close of the battle, while his deck was swimming in blood, the captain of the *Serapis* called him to strike. "No, Sir," said he, "I will not, we have had but a small fight as yet." He had been well educated in Scotland (his native country) and discovered style and taste both in writing and conversation. His countenance was strongly marked with thought. I know nothing of his private character.

Nathaniel Fanning, Narrative of the Adventures of an American Naval Officer 1806

I never knew him to drink any kind of ardent spirits. On the contrary, his constant drink was lemonade (lime juice and water, with a little sugar to make it the more palatable). It is true, that every day while at sea, and the weather good, he made it a custom to drink three glasses of wine immediately after the table cloth was removed. . . .

Captain Jones was a man of about five feet six inches high, well shaped below his head and shoulders, rather round shouldered with a visage fierce and warlike, and wore the appearance of great application to study, which he was fond of. He was an excellent seaman, and knew (according to my judgment) naval tactics as well as almost any man of his age; but it must be allowed that his character was somewhat tinctured with bad qualities. . . . His smoothness of tongue, and flattery to seamen when he wanted them was persuasive, and in which he excelled every other man I ever was acquainted with. . . . His pride and vanity, while at Paris and Amsterdam, was not generally approved of after the famous sea battle. This certainly gave great umbrage to many persons who had been his best friends. His conduct however, towards Captain Preston [of the *Serapis*], his antagonist, was highly approved of by many, and was becoming that of a conqueror.

Henry Knox
1750–1806

⚜ Born in Boston. Worked in bookstore and then opened his own. Enlisted in militia, 1768; second in command of Boston grenadiers, 1772. Married daughter of royal secretary, 1774. Volunteer at Bunker Hill, June 1775. Rose in Continental army from colonel in November 1775 to major general in March 1782. Chief of artillery and one of Washington's closest advisers. Commander in chief of Continental army, 1783–84. Organized national Society of the Cincinnati, 1783, and served as its secretary-general, 1783–99; vice president, Massachusetts branch, 1783–85. Confederation secretary at war, 1785–89; U.S. secretary of war, 1789–94.

Benjamin Rush to Richard Henry Lee BORDENTOWN, N.J., JANUARY 6, 1777

I congratulate you upon the addition of Colonel Knox to the list of general officers. He is a brave, sensible, enterprising man. I saw his behavior in the battle of Trenton; he was cool, cheerful, and was present everywhere.

Nathanael Greene to Jacob Greene MIDDLEBROOK, N.J., JUNE 4, 1777

There is a French gentleman sent over by Mr. Dean to have the command of all artillery in America. If his appointment is confirmed, it will rob us of one of the best, or at least, as good an officer as we have in the service—General Knox.

James Lovell to Benjamin Franklin PHILADELPHIA, JULY 4, 1777

The Merit of Br. Genl. Knox is great, and he is beloved by his Corps.

Committee for Foreign Affairs to the Commissioners at Paris YORK, PA., DECEMBER 1, 1777

Genl. Knox, the father of the American Artillery.

Nathanael Greene to Catherine Greene CAMP HOPEWELL NEAR PRINCETON, N.J., JUNE 23, 1778

Mrs. Knox has been in Philadelphia and is now gone to Morristown. She is fatter than ever which is a great mortification to her. The General is equally fat and therefore one cannot laugh at the other. They appear to be extravagantly fond of each other and I think are perfectly happy.

Rev. John Murray to Nathanael Greene GLOUCESTER, MASS., JANUARY 21, 1780

Please to make my Compliments acceptable to General Knox. I hope he has not, or ever will meet, with any thing to prevent his laughing as hearty as ever. I really think he is qualified for a Disciple of who was the Founder of the Sect of laughing Philosophers? Or was there ever so happy a Sect in the world?

Marquis de Chastellux, Travels in North-America, in the Years 1780, 1781, and 1782

Henry Knox . . . is between thirty and forty, very fat, but very active, and of a gay and amiable character. Previous to the war he was a bookseller at Boston, and used to amuse himself in reading some military books in his shop. Such was the origin and the first knowledge he acquired of the art of war, and of the taste he has had ever since for the profession of arms. From the very first campaign, he was entrusted with the command of the artillery, and it has turned out that it could not have been placed in better hands.

John Hancock to Benjamin Franklin BOSTON, OCTOBER 27, 1781

General Knox whose Abilities & Conduct in the Military Line during this Contest has Endeared him to this Country in such a manner as to gain the Universal Esteem of all Whigs & well wishers to their Country.

Alexander Hamilton to George Washington PHILADELPHIA, FEBRUARY 13, 1783

General Knox has the confidence of the army & is a man of sense. I think he may be safely made use of. Situated as I am Your Excellency will feel the confidential nature of these observations.

Francisco de Miranda, Travels in the United States, 1783–1784

General Knox. This man, who from a simple bookseller passed to the militia and from there to the first ranks of the American army, is one of the best informed on the theory and practice of the art of war of the many *caudillos** I have known on this continent, including "The Idol." His manner is very pleasant and his conversation interesting.

Marquis de Lafayette to Henry Knox PARIS, MAY 11, 1785

The patriot and the soldier are nobly united in your person. God grant your advices may be adopted—your pains may fructify.

George Washington to Henry Knox MOUNT VERNON, FEBRUARY 3, 1787

I have the fullest conviction of your friendship for, and attachment to me; know your abilities to judge; and your means of information.

Luigi Castiglioni, Sketches of American Soldiers 1787

Entering the army, he very quickly distinguished himself from the multitude by his range of knowledge and courage. In the course of the war, in which he lost the fingers of his left hand, he commanded the artillery, and was so skillful at directing the artillerymen that by the end of the war the French themselves were amazed at their readiness and activity. His wife always accompanied him in the field and insisted upon sharing the fortunes of war with him. After it was over, it is reported that, upon taking his leave of the other officers, he said laughingly to one of them (who had also been a bookdealer), "Now we can return home and reopen

*Political leaders.

our shops"—so little influence had the well-deserved distinctions had toward rendering him haughty. He is now Secretary of War, lives in New York with his wife, and those who happen to know him are received in their home with complete cordiality.

He is a man of about 50 years of age, of fine stature, but corpulent, with pleasant manners and a face more noble than his humble origins.

Louis Guillaume Otto, Biographies FALL, 1788

Secretary of War. Trustworthy, modest, frank, active, obliging, attached to France. He is of all the servants of Congress the most expeditious and the most serviceable. Born in obscurity* the Revolution put him in his place and atoned the mistake of Fortune. He would be without fault if his imagination was not a little too ardent.

The large holdings of his wife in the province of Maine make him a little uneasy on the dismemberment of this province. He always fears that England will get hold of it, but these apprehensions are hardly founded.

He is from very agreeable Society and he deserves to be among the small number of intimate friends of the foreign minister.

Alexander Hamilton to James Madison NEW YORK, NOVEMBER 23, 1788

As to Knox [for U.S. vice president] I cannot persuade myself that he will incline to the appointment. He must *sacrifice* emolument by it which must *of necessity* be a primary object with him.

---

*He was a bookbinder journeyman in Boston. The daughter of the lieutenant governor passing by chance through the shop to buy some books was taken with his looks and good sense with which he spoke to her. She invited him to come to her house; the young Knox profited by these advances to propose an elopement; they were soon in agreement and were married against the wishes of Mrs. Knox's family. This family was Royalist. It happened through singular circumstances that without this marriage which displeased them so much, all of their property would have been confiscated. The Revolution was at the point of breaking out; Mr. Knox was one of the first to bear arms; he was moreover a captain, and showed his talents to be so extraordinary that in less than two years he was made major general of artillery. He was considered not only by the American but by all the French officers, as the most qualified person to fill this position.

James Madison to Edmund Randolph　NEW YORK, JUNE 17, 1789

High as the existing President stands, I question whether it would be very safe for him even not to reinstate J—y or K—x.

William Maclay, Diary　JUNE 28, 1790

[In comparing Secretary of War Knox to Secretary of the Treasury Hamilton and Secretary of State Jefferson, all of whom attended a dinner hosted by the Pennsylvania delegation to Congress.] Knox is the easiest Man, and the most dignity of Presence. They [the three secretaries] retired at a decent time. One after another. Knox staid longest. As indeed suited his Aspect best, being more of a Bachanalian Figure.

Alexander Hamilton to Edward Carrington　PHILADELPHIA, MAY 26, 1792

Poor *Knox* has come in for a share of their [Madison and Jefferson's] persecution as a man who generally thinks with me & who has a portion of the President's good Will & confidence.

Thomas Jefferson, "Anas"　1793

Knox joined Hamilton in everything.

Thomas Jefferson, Notes on a Cabinet Meeting　PHILADELPHIA, MAY 6, 1793

[On recognizing Citizen Genet and on the viability of the French treaty with the United States.] Knox subscribed at once to H[amilton]'s opinion that we ought to declare the treaty void, acknowledging at the same time, like a fool as he is, that he knew nothing about it. . . . there having been an intimation by E[dmund] R[andolph] that in so great a question he should choose to give a written opinion, & this being approved by the President I gave in mine April 28. H. gave in his. I believe Knox's was never thought worth offering or asking for.

James Madison to Thomas Jefferson　PHILADELPHIA, DECEMBER 21, 1794

Hamilton is to resign, according to his own notification the last of February. His object is not yet unfolded. Knox, as the shadow, follows the substance.

John Adams to Abigail Adams PHILADELPHIA, DECEMBER 30, 1794

Now come great Things. Knox is to go out tomorrow. He insists on beginning the Year 1795 a freeman. He told me Yesterday, he had been 20 Years (next April) in service, that if he should die tomorrow his Wife and Children would not have enough to live on two years. That he had not above ten years to live, that he had the means at the Eastward of making something and that it was his Duty to do it.

This Man is capable of flattering himself with hopes that to others appear Chimerical. He is capable of thinking himself popular enough in Massachusetts to be chosen Governor at the first Vacancy. But I suspect he cherishes another hope, that is being Governor of Maine. These however are hints between you and me and to go no farther.

Oliver Wolcott Jr. to Oliver Wolcott Sr. PHILADELPHIA, JANUARY 6, 1795

General Knox has been unfortunate in some respects, and has not acquired as much reputation as he deserves to have done.

John Adams to Abigail Adams PHILADELPHIA, JANUARY 20, 1795

What is to be the Fortune of General Knox, I know not. I am anxious about him and his Family. He has been raised to an Elevation, for which neither Nature, nor Education ever intended him. Fortune alone has been his Patron. His Family has been worse calculated for his situation than himself. He has been a laborious and I doubt not a faithful servant of the Public, and it would be melancholy to see him unfortunate in his old Age. I wish his Lands may prove a source of Abundance to him and his Family.

Abigail Adams to John Adams NEW YORK, JUNE 22, 1795

Boston Chronical goes on in its accustomed stile of abuse. G[eneral] Knox has got his share, Lord of Maine &c &c.

Timothy Pickering to Alexander Hamilton TRENTON, AUGUST 21, 1798

I know also that not only all your friends, but your political enemies have the highest respect for your abilities: while the latter, the political enemies also of General Knox, estimate his talents by a very moderate scale: and some persons have in my hearing called him a *weak* man. I think him neither *weak* nor *great:* but with pretty good abilities, possessing an imposing manner that impresses an idea of mental faculties beyond what really exist. I am certain that if he had been second to General Washington [in the Provisional Army to be raised to defend against a French invasion] and of course likely to command in chief, great dissatisfaction would have been excited. I much doubt even whether the nomination would have been confirmed by the Senate.

I write this letter in the confidence of friendship, for the public good, which I conceive to be involved in your holding your present superior station. I have always supposed you & General Knox to be cordial friends. I wish you to continue such. I persuade myself he is too good a patriot to suffer the present disappointment to actuate him to any improper conduct; and that he will at least passively acquiesce. I think he will *gain* no honor, by declining to serve under you: I rather believe his refusal will detract from the reputation he now possesses.

Timothy Pickering to George Cabot TRENTON, SEPTEMBER 20, 1798

I knew indeed that Knox was proud and vain and ambitious; but I thought that as for years he had been the daily witness of Hamilton's vast superiority of talents, and had known how highly they stood in the public estimation, and supposing also that he felt an ardent friendship for Hamilton, I was astonished to find him not hesitating, but apparently desirous not to serve under Hamilton. The President's tour to Massachusetts furnished Knox with the lucky opportunity of making and enforcing his claim by the plausibility of his arguments and his adulatory professions of respect, honor, and devotion to the great man. You probably know that Knox is capable of using the deepest flattery; and flattery has often too much effect on the finest minds, and in the present instance would make the stronger impression as operating against a competitor for whom the President had no liking, if he did not feel for him aversion.

George Washington to President John Adams MOUNT VERNON, SEPTEMBER 25, 1798

With respect to General Knox, I can say with truth, there is no man in the United States with whom I have been in habits of greater intimacy; no one whom I have loved more sincerely; nor any for whom I have had a greater friendship.

Oliver Wolcott Jr., to Alexander Hamilton TRENTON, OCTOBER 10, 1798

I sincerely hope that General Knox will decline service. His pecuniary affairs are I believe so embarrassed, that there is no prospect of his preserving his independence & I much fear, that the fortune of modern speculators, some loss of character, awaits him.

Thomas Jefferson to James Madison PHILADELPHIA, JANUARY 3, 1799

Genl. Knox has become bankrupt for $400,000 & has resigned his military commission. He took in Genl. [Benjamin] Lincoln for $150,000 which breaks him. Colo. [Henry] Jackson also sunk with him.

Benjamin Rush, Sketches C. 1800

A brave and intelligent officer, and an open hearted, honest hearted man.

Mercy Otis Warren, History of the American Revolution 1805

Mr. Knox had not the advantages of a literary education; but his natural inquisitive disposition and attention to books, rendered him a well-informed, agreeable man, with ingratiating accomplishments. His love of military parade, and the affability of his manners, brought him forward to the command of a cadet company in Boston, before the commencement of the American war. Naturally of a complacent disposition, his jovial humor and easy deportment rendered him acceptable in all companies, and made him a favorite with the commander in chief, even before his talents as a soldier were called into exercise. With an assemblage of pleasing qualities, it is not strange that he rose rapidly in the military line. He commanded the artillery department for several years before the conclusion of the war; and performed his duty in this line with courage and vigilance, which did honor to his military character.

John Adams to the Printers of the **Boston Patriot** JUNE 1812

[Alexander Hamilton allegedly said that] Knox had no Talents.

John Adams to Richard Rush QUINCY, DECEMBER 12, 1813

You are reading the History of the Revolution, and you do well. But your Father would tell you, there is no History of it extant, and never will be. You have found two or three Genius's. Warren, Montgomery, Green or Arnold, perhaps. Knox, however, contributed, as much as any, to effectual service.

Thomas Jefferson to Martin Van Buren MONTICELLO, JUNE 29, 1824

General Knox, a man of parade.

Marquis de Lafayette
1757–1834

⚓ BORN IN Chavaniac, France. Inherited great wealth and title after the death of parents and grandfather. Moved to Paris, 1768. King's Musketeers, 1771. Marries Adrienne de Noailles, 1774. Joins Noailles regiment and Freemasons, 1775. Sails for the United States, 1777. Commissioned major general in Continental army (without a command), 1777. Wounded at Battle of Brandywine, September 1777. At Valley Forge, 1777–78. Returned to France, January 1779. Returned to the United States with French fleet and army, 1780. In command of all U.S. forces in Virginia, 1781. Commanded capture of Redoubt Ten at Yorktown. Made citizen of Virginia, Maryland, and Connecticut. Returned to France 1782. Visited the United States, 1784. While in France lobbied for the United States. Leader of French Revolution. Sent Washington key to the Bastille, 1789. General of French army. Proscribed by French radicals. While escaping to The Netherlands was captured and imprisoned by Germans-Austrians, 1792–97. Returned to France, 1799. Visited the United States, 1824–25.

John Adams, Autobiography

When I began to attempt a little conversation in French I was very inquisitive concerning this great Family of Noailles and I was told by some of the most intelligent Men in France, ecclesiastics as well as others, that there were no less than six Marshalls of France of this Family, that they held so many Offices under the King that they received Eighteen millions of Livres annually from the Crown. That the Family had been remarkable for Ages, for their harmony with one another and for doing nothing of any consequence without a previous Council and concert. That, when the American Revolution commenced, a family Council had been called to deliberate upon that great Event and determine what part they should take in it, or what Conduct they should hold towards it. After they had sufficiently considered, they all agreed in Opinion that it was a Crisis of the highest importance, in the Affairs of Europe and the World. That it must affect France in so essential a manner, that the King could not and ought not to avoid taking a capital Interest and part of it. That it would therefore be the best policy of the Family, to give their Countenance to it as early as possible. And that it was expedient to send one of their Sons over to America to serve in her Army under General Washington. The Prince de Poix as the Heir apparent, of the Duke of Mouchy, they thought of too much importance to their Views and expectations to be risked in so hazardous a Voyage and so extraordinary a Service, and therefore it was concluded, to offer the Enterprise to the Viscount de Noailles, and if he should decline it, to the Marquis de la Fayette. The Viscount after due consideration, thought it most prudent to remain at home for the present. The Marquis, who was represented as a youth of the finest Accomplishments and most amiable disposition, panting for Glory, ardent to distinguish himself in military Service, and impatient to wipe out a slight imputation which had been thrown, whether by Truth or Calumny upon the Memory of his father who though he had been slain in Battle was suspected to have lost his Life by too much caution to preserve it, most joyfully consented to embark in the Enterprise. All France pronounced it to be the first page in the History of a great Man.

Silas Deane, Agreement with the Marquis de Lafayette PARIS, DECEMBER 7, 1776

The desire which the Marquis de la Fayette shows of serving among the Troops of the United States of North America, and the Interest which he takes in the Justice of their Cause making him wish to distinguish himself in this war and to render himself as useful as he possibly can; but not thinking that he can obtain leave of his Family to pass the seas and serve in a foreign Country till he can go as a General Officer; I have thought I could not better serve my Country and those who have entrusted me than by granting to him in the name of the very honorable Congress the Rank of Major General which I beg the States to confirm to him, to ratify and deliver to him the Commission to hold and take Rank, to count from this Day, with the General Officers of the same degree. His high Birth, his Alliances, the great Dignities which his Family holds at this Court, his considerable Estates in this Realm, his personal merit, his Reputation, his Disinterestedness, and above all his Zeal for the Liberty of our Provinces, have only been able to engage me to promise him the Rank of Major General in the name of the United States.

Silas Deane to President of Congress John Hancock PARIS, C. MARCH 16, 1777

At length, the Marquis de la Fayette, a young Nobleman of the first family and connections at Court, viz. that of Noailles, has equipped a vessel, at his own expense, to transport him and the Baron [de Kalb], with other Officers, to America. As my letters were very particular at the time, and as we shall write express by Capt. Hammond in a few days, will not detain you more than to recommend this young Nobleman to your particular notice and attention. His family are of the first influence here, and have, for ages, been celebrated in the affairs of this Country, as well in peace as war. His fortune puts him above all pecuniary considerations, and he desires none, but wishes to rank with Gentlemen of the first character in the Army.

Marquis de Lafayette to William Carmichael, on board La Victoire APRIL 19, 1777

The only favor that I ask is that they give me every possible opportunity to make use of my fortune, my labors, and all the resources of my imagination, and to shed my blood for my brothers and my friends. The only recompense that I shall request, after success, is to obtain new means of being useful to them.

Henry Laurens to John Lewis Gervais PHILADELPHIA, AUGUST 5, 1777

A Commission of Major General is granted to the Marquis de la Fayette the young nobleman who lately came from Charles Town. He required no pension, no Special Command; the honor of fighting near General Washington & having rank in the Army was all he coveted except opportunities to show his Zeal for the glorious cause of American Freedom either in the Field, or at Court when it shall be judged he can be more Serviceable at Versailles. This illustrious Stranger whose address & manner bespeak his birth will Serve a short Campaign & then probably return to France & Secure to us the powerful Interest of his high & extensive connections.

Richard Henry Lee to Landon Carter PHILADELPHIA, AUGUST 19, 1777

Among other curiosities there, I saw the young Marquis de la Fayette, a Nobleman of the first fortune and family in France, the favorite of Court and Country. He left behind him a most beautiful young wife, and all the soft enjoyments that such a situation, with an immense fortune in a polished Country can furnish to fight in American wilderness for American Liberty! After this can there be a Tory in the World? He has rank of Major General in the Continental Army & fights without pay. He is thirsty for glory but the Commissioners at Paris wish the General may restrain the ardor of youth and not suffer his exposure but on some signal occasion. He is sensible, polite, and good natured. How this example ought to gall the worthless Nobility & Gentry of England, who meanly creep into the Tyrant's service to destroy that liberty which a generous Frenchman quits every delight to defend through every difficulty!

Marquis de Lafayette to Adrienne de Noailles de Lafayette
BETHLEHEM, PA., OCTOBER 1, 1777

Do not be concerned, dear heart, about the care of my wound.* All the physicians in America are paying close attention to me. I have a friend who has spoken to them in such a way that I can be assured of the best care. That friend is General Washington. This estimable man, whom I at first admired for his talents and qualities and whom I have come to venerate as I know him better, has become my intimate friend. His affectionate interest in me soon won my heart. I am a member of his household and we live together like two brothers in mutual intimacy and confidence.

*At the Battle of Brandywine, Lafayette was shot in the left leg.

This close friendship makes me as happy as I could possibly be in this country. When he sent his chief surgeon to care for me, he told him to care for me as though I were his son, for he loved me in the same way.

Henry Laurens to John Lewis Gervais YORK, PA., OCTOBER 8, 1777

[Laurens came to assist a wounded Lafayette.] I . . . returned once more into the City [Philadelphia] . . . to take charge of the Marquis delafayette who lay wounded by a ball through his Leg. . . . I had the honor of conducting the Marquis who is possessed of the most excellent funds of good sense & inexhaustible patience to Bethlehem where the Second day after our arrival I left him in Bed anxious for nothing but to be again in our Army as he always calls it.

George Washington to the President of Congress Henry Laurens WHITE MARSH, PA., NOVEMBER 1, 1777

I would take the liberty to mention, that I feel myself in a delicate situation with respect to the Marquis Le Fayette.* He is extremely solicitous of having a Command equal to his rank, & professes very different Ideas as to the purposes of his appointment from those Congress have mentioned to me. He certainly did not understand them. I do not know in what light they will view the matter, but it appears to me, from a consideration of his illustrious and important connections—the attachment which he has manifested to our cause, and the consequences, which his return in disgust might produce, that it will be adviseable to gratify him in his wishes—and the more so, as several Gentlemen from France, who came over under some assurances, have gone back disappointed in their expectations. His conduct with respect to them stands in a favorable point of view, having interested himself to remove their uneasiness and urged the impropriety of their making any unfavorable representations upon their arrival at home, and in all his letters has placed our affairs in the best situation he could. Besides, he is sensible—discreet in his manners—has made great proficiency in our Language, and from

*Washington repeated the same reservations in his letter to Laurens on November 26, 1777.

the disposition he discovered at the Battle of Brandy Wine, possesses a large share of bravery and Military ardor.

Baron de Kalb to Pierre de Saint-Paul WITH THE AMERICAN ARMY, NOVEMBER 7, 1777

The friendship with which he has honored me since I made his acquaintance, and that which I have vowed to him because of his personal qualities, oblige me to have that deference for him. No one is more deserving than he of the consideration he enjoys here. He is a prodigy for his age; he is the model of valor, intelligence, judgment, good conduct, generosity, and zeal for the cause of liberty for this continent. His wound is healing very well. He has just rejoined the army, so as not to miss any chances for glory and danger.

William Duer to James Wilson YORK, PA., NOVEMBER 30, 1777

On Monday the Marquis de la Fayette with about four or five Hundred Men attacked a Picket of the Enemy in Jersey of about 300, drove them, killed Several, and took twenty or thirty Prisoners. It is said he behaved with great Intrepidity; and I believe with some Experience will make a good officer.

James Lovell to John Adams YORK, PA., DECEMBER 1, 1777

We have nothing of much Importance this morning. Fayette being with Genl. Greene in the Jersies fell upon a Picket of the Enemy, killed 20, took 20 & wounded many without loss. He is delighted with the Militia; and Genl. Greene says the Marquis seems determined to court Danger. I wish more were so determined.

Marquis de Lafayette to Adrienne de Noailles de Lafayette CAMP NEAR VALLEY FORGE, PA., JANUARY 6, 1778

If I depart, many Frenchmen who are useful here will follow my example. General Washington will be truly unhappy if I speak to him of leaving. His confidence in me is greater than my age allows me to admit. In his position, he is surrounded by flatterers and secret enemies. He finds in me a trustworthy friend to whom he can open his heart, and who always tells him the truth. Not a day passes that he does not have long conversations with me or write me long letters, and he likes to consult me about the most important matters. At this very moment there is a particular matter in which my presence is of some use to him; this is not the moment to speak of leaving.

Henry Laurens to Matthew Locke YORK, PA., JANUARY 25, 1778

The Marquis is a most excellent worthy young Noble Man, fighting in our Cause, & using his utmost endeavors to promote our Interest at the Court of France & all without pay or gratuity. He deserves to be considered & respected by every friend to these States.

Gouverneur Morris to Henry Laurens CAMP, JANUARY 26, 1778

I am deeply surprised at the mature Judgment & solid Understanding of this *Young* Man for such he certainly is.

Marquis de Lafayette to Henry Laurens VALLEY FORGE, PA., JANUARY 27, 1778

[In planning an invasion of Canada with Lafayette in command.] If I had that gentleman [Louis Duportail] and the most respectable [Alexander] McDouggall, I should be very happy. I want, my dear Sir, to have men whom I can extract from, as much prudence and as many years (without any sensible injury to their persons) as I believe there is necessary to fill up in my age, which years I think must have a general to be in his point of perfection— and it is my opinion that even when a man is born with those so superior and uncommon talents for the great art of war, the best age for his generalship, after a continued study and experience is between forty and fifty.

Robert Troup to Horatio Gates BETHLEHEM, PA., FEBRUARY 6, 1778

I left the Marquis at Lancaster. He seems to be strongly tinctured with the Fabian Principles* of Head-Quarters.

Henry Laurens to the Marquis de Lafayette YORK, PA., MARCH 6, 1778

[After Lafayette called off an invasion of Canada.] Were I to attempt an intimation of the public opinion of Your Excellency, the

---

*Fabian principles: to fight only when victory is assured.

whole would end in repetition of what is contained in my last. I may nevertheless add by way of anecdote the remark of a sensible candid Man, when he had heard your Letter of the 20th February read. "I," said he, "was averse to this Irruption into Canada not because I thought badly of the scheme but because I feared the Marquis being a Young Man full of Fire would have impetuously rushed our soldiers into too much danger. But his present conduct convinces me he is wise & discreet as well as brave. I now esteem him a worthy valuable Officer." Once more, be assured you have gained great reputation in this Country & that there is not the smallest ground for your apprehensions of the contrary.

Marquis de Lafayette to L'Abbé Fayon CAMP AT VALLEY FORGE, PA., APRIL 13, 1778

Once I set foot in the American camp, I gave up bookish studies. Forgetting belles-lettres, I attempted to educate myself in a cruel and barbarous art. I am so possessed by the demon of war that I have totally abandoned myself to military occupations. Finally, having renounced the gentle company of women, verse, and the Muses, I now find pleasure in the horrible voluptuousness of Bellona.*

Henry Laurens to the Marquis de Lafayette YORK, PA., MAY 29, 1778

[On Lafayette's brilliant escape from Barren Hill, Pa.] I congratulate with your Excellency most heartily on the late honorable Retreat which is spoke of by every body here in the highest terms of applause.

The Marquis delafayette has acquired new Glory by this great Act of Generalship.

Henry Laurens to Cornelius Harnett YORK, PA., MAY 30, 1778

Sir Henry [Clinton] will know every step we take, if he finds we are upon our guard & will not be deceived, he will at least give us Credit for good Generalship, whether he goes or Stays. You have heard, but perhaps crudely, how narrowly Marquis delafayette escaped Burgoyning† last Week. The enclosed narrative will

---

*The Roman goddess of war.

†A reference to the capture of British general John Burgoyne's army at the Battle of Saratoga in October 1777.

inform you circumstantially of almost the whole of his adventure but as it comes from a young man nearly allied to me I request you will not suffer it to be published. The Marquis has gained more applause for his Generalship in the late Retreat than would have been bestowed upon a slight victory.

Marquis de Lafayette to Adrienne de Noailles de Lafayette
VALLEY FORGE CAMP, PA., JUNE 16, 1778

My heart has always been completely convinced that in serving the cause of humanity and that of America, I was fighting for the interests of France.

Marquis de Lafayette to the President of Congress CAMP NEAR
WARREN, R.I., SEPTEMBER 23, 1778

The moment I heard of America, I loved her. The moment I knew she was fighting for freedom, I burnt with the desire of bleeding for her—and the moment I shall be able of serving her in any time or any part of the world, will be among the happiest ones in my life.

President of Congress Henry Laurens to King Louis XVI of France PHILADELPHIA, OCTOBER 21, 1778

The Marquis de la Fayette having obtained our leave to return to his Native Country, we could not suffer him to depart without testifying our deep sense of his Zeal, Courage and attachment.

We have advanced him to the rank of Major General in our Armies, which, as well by his prudent as spirited conduct he hath manifestly merited.

We recommend this young Nobleman to Your Majesty's notice, as one whom we know to be Wise in Council, gallant in the Field and patient under the Hardships of War. His Devotion to his Sovereign hath led him in all things to demean himself as an American, acquiring thereby the confidence of these United States, Your Majesty's good and faithful Friends and Allies, and the Affection of their Citizens.

Marquis de Lafayette, Memoir of 1779
You ask me when I first longed for glory and liberty; I can recall no time in my life when I did not love stories of glorious deeds, or have dreams of traveling the world in search of fame.

Marquis de Lafayette to the Comte de Vergennes LE HAVRE, AUGUST 16, 1779

A diplomatic career would please me very much, Monsieur le Comte, if a strong influence, an inexpressible attraction, did not draw me to the military profession. But if by chance I had the means and abilities to serve my country otherwise than with arms in hand, I should believe myself very fortunate in taking advantage of it.

John Adams to Abigail Adams PARIS, FEBRUARY 28, 1780

If the Marquis should make you a Visit You will treat him with all Distinction that is due to his Merit and Character, as well as his Birth and Rank which are very high.

He has been the invariable and indefatigable Friend of America, in all Times, Places and Occasions, and his Assiduity have done Us much service. He is my particular Friend, and therefore deserves from mine, the greatest Respect, on my private Account as well as on the public.

John Adams to Henry Knox PARIS, FEBRUARY 28, 1780

Your Friend the Marquis, with whom I have sometimes had the Honor to drink your Health after that of General Washington, will deliver you this. His Love of Glory is not diminished, nor his affection for America, as you see by his Return. He has been indefatigable in endeavors to promote the Welfare and Comfort of our Army, as well as to support their Honor and Character, and has had success in both.

John Adams to James Lovell PARIS, FEBRUARY 29, 1780

I cannot let the Marquis go off without a Line to you. He took leave of the King a few days ago, in the Uniform of an American Major General, and attracted the Eyes of the whole Court more than ever. He had on no doubt his American Sword* which is indeed a Beauty, and which he shows with great Pleasure, upon proper Occasions. The workmanship is exquisite, and there are Emblems on it, representing him, in all the most remarkable

---

*Congress resolved on October 21, 1778, that Benjamin Franklin should have an elegant sword made and presented to Lafayette. Lafayette received the sword in August 1779.

Situations he has been in America. He goes out in a Frigate of the King the Hermione from Rochfort, he carries with him Cloaths enough for the Army to make him welcome to them, if they had not known him before.

Samuel A. Otis to Nathanael Greene BOSTON, APRIL 30, 1780

The arrival of the Marquis La Fayette has cheered us in this quarter. If he has any matters particularly in charge, He is as inpenetrable as night; at any rate he has no reason to be dissatisfied with his reception here to the Caresses of a greatful people. And I think him diserving the highest marks of respect. He however either has none or will tell no news.

Alexander Hamilton to James Duane MORRISTOWN, N.J., MAY 14, 1780

The Marquis has a title to all the love of all America; but you know he has a thousand little whims to satisfy—one of these he *will have* me to write to some friend in Congress about. He is desirous of having the Captain of the Frigate in which he came complimented and gives several pretty instances of his punctuality & disinterestedness. He wishes Congress to pass some resolutions of thanks & to recommend him to their Minister in France, to be recommended to the French Court. The first of these is practicable. The last I think might have an officious appearance. The *essential* services the Marquis has rendered America in France give him a claim for all that can be done with propriety; but Congress must not commit themselves.

George Washington to the Comte de Rochambeau JULY 16, 1780

As a General officer I have the greatest confidence in him; as a friend he is perfectly acquainted with my sentiments and opinions; he knows all the circumstances of our army and the country at large; all the information he gives and all the positions he makes, I entreat you will consider as coming from me.

Marquis de Lafayette to Alexander Hamilton LIGHT CAMP, N.J., OCTOBER 21, 1780

Have you yet any thing new, My dear Sir, any thing that May put me in spirits? You know I am not of a desponding, dark temper.

George Washington to Thomas Jefferson NEW WINDSOR, N.Y., DECEMBER 8, 1780

I have the honor of introducing to your Excellency the Marquis de la Fayette, Major General in our army and an officer of Rank in those of France. This Gentleman's character, illustrious birth and fortune, cannot be unknown to you, though you may be unacquainted with his person. I should be wanting in that justice which is due his great merit, to his early attachment to the American Cause, and to his powerful support of it here and at the Court of Versailles; was I to permit him to depart for the Southern Army without this testimony of the sense I entertain of his worth, and recommendations of him to your attention.

Sarah Bache to Benjamin Franklin PHILADELPHIA, JANUARY 14, 1781

The Marquis de Fayette did us the honor of a Visit when in Town. He is expected here again to stay some time. He is greatly admired and beloved wherever he goes.

Marquis de Lafayette to the Prince de Poix NEW WINDSOR, N.Y., JANUARY 30, 1781

My situation with the army and the American people is as pleasant as one can possibly imagine. They overwhelm me with kindness here, and the trust and friendship they are so good as to evince for me makes my service here delightful.

Nathanael Greene to the Marquis de Lafayette CAMP NEAR RUGELEY'S MILL, S.C., MAY 1, 1781

I have only one word of advice to give you, (having entire confidence in your ability, zeal and good conduct), that is not to let the love of fame get the better of your prudence and plunge you into a misfortune, in too eager a pursuit after glory. This is the voice of a friend, and not the caution of a General.

Marquis de Lafayette to Alexander Hamilton RICHMOND, MAY 23, 1781

I request you will write me if you approve of my conduct. The command of the waters, the superiority in cavalry, and the great disproportion of forces, gave the enemy such advantages that I durst not venture out and listen to my fondness for enterprise. To speak the truth I was afraid of myself as much as of the enemy. Independence has rendered me the more cautious, as I know my own warmth; but if the Pennsylvanians come, Lord Cornwallis shall pay some thing for his victory.

Marquis de Lafayette to George Washington MAY 24, 1781

Was I to fight a battle I'd be cut to pieces, the militia dispersed, and the arms lost. Was I to decline fighting the country would think herself given up. I am therefore determined to skirmish, but not to engage too far, and particularly to take care against their immense and excellent body of horse whom the militia fears like they would so many wild beasts.

James McHenry to Nathanael Greene HEAD QUARTERS, 23 MILES FROM RICHMOND, VA., JUNE 20, 1781

Wayne was impetuous, and the Marquis [de Lafayette] loved glory, but then, he was reasonable, and possessed a prudence which the other thinks he can do without.

Nathanael Greene to the Marquis de Lafayette CAMP AT BUSH RIVER IN THE NEIGHBORHOOD OF 96, JUNE 23, 1781

It was my intention to have come to the Northward with the greater part of our Cavalry if the enemy had not received a reinforcement here which enables them to take the field; and they are increasing their Cavalry by every means in their power and have a greater number than we have, though not of equal goodness. We are trying to increase ours. Enlarge your Cavalry or you are inevitably ruined. Don't pay any regard to the murmurs of the people. They will bless you when they find they derive security from them. Let your Army be as light as possible and have your Stores kept at a great distance that you may not be cramped in your movements. Avoid a general action if possible while the enemy have such a superior Cavalry. A defeat to you in that situation may prove your ruin.

Marquis de Lafayette to the Vicomte de Noailles WILLIAMSBURG, JULY 9, 1781

This devil Cornwallis is much wiser than the other generals with whom I have dealt. He inspires me with a sincere fear, and his name has greatly troubled my sleep. This campaign is a good school for me. God grant that the public does not pay for my lessons.

William Carmichael to Benjamin Franklin MADRID, JULY 13, 1781

[The Marquis] was well in the middle of May & greatly respected & beloved by his Troops.

Marquis de Lafayette to Samuel Cooper CAMP NEAR YORKTOWN, VA., OCTOBER 26, 1781

The operations of the siege will be so fully related to you that it is needless for me to enter into details. I shall only observe to my friend that never my feelings have been so delightfully gratified as they were on the 14th in the evening, when the American light infantry in sight of the armies of France, America, and England gallantly stormed a redoubt sword in hand, and proved themselves equal in this business to the grenadiers of the best troops in Europe. I long ago knew what dependence was to be put on them, and was so sure of success, that not a gun had been loaded—but to see this little affair transacted under the eyes of foreign armies, gave me unspeakable satisfaction.

James Madison to Edmund Pendleton PHILADELPHIA, NOVEMBER 13, 1781

Will not the [Virginia] Assembly pay some handsome compliments to the Marquis for his judicious & zealous services whilst the protection of the Country was entrusted to him? His having baffled and finally reduced to the defensive so powerful an army as we now know he had to contend with, and with so disproportionate a force, would have done honor to the most veteran officer and, added to his other merits and services, constitute a claim on their gratitude which I hope will not be unattended to.

Congress, Report on Lafayette's Return to France NOVEMBER 23, 1781

That Major General the Marquis de la Fayette have permission to go to France & that he return at such time as shall be most convenient to him and that he be furnished with the frigate *Alliance* to carry him to France.

That he be informed, that, on a review of his conduct throughout the past campaign, and particularly during the period in which he had the chief command in Virginia, the many new proofs which present themselves of his zealous attachment to the cause he has espoused, & of his judgment, vigilance, gallantry & address in its defense, have greatly added to the high opinion entertained by Congress of his merits & military talents.

That he be requested to make known to the officers & troops whom he commanded during that period, that the brave & enterprising services with which they seconded his zeal and efforts, and which enabled him to defeat the attempts of an enemy far superior in numbers, have been beheld by Congress with particular satisfaction & approbation.

Richard Bache to Benjamin Franklin PHILADELPHIA, NOVEMBER 27, 1781

The Marquis, during his command in Virginia, has shown all the Abilities of a Veteran, he is universally beloved on this side the Atlantic, & we hope to see him again in the Spring, should his Services be wanted in another Campaign—

Comte de Vergennes to the Marquis de Lafayette VERSAILLES, DECEMBER 1, 1781

It is recognized with pleasure that although you did not have the lead in directing this large operation [the Battle of Yorktown], your prudent conduct and your preliminary maneuvers had prepared the way for its success. I followed you step by step, Monsieur le Marquis, throughout your campaign in Virginia. I would often have trembled for you had I not been reassured by your discretion. It takes great skill to stand up, as you did for such a long time despite the extreme disparity of your forces, to Lord Cornwallis, whose military talents are praised. You are the one who led him to that fatal end at which, instead of allowing him to make you a prisoner of war as he might have planned, you forced him to become a prisoner himself. History offers few examples of such a complete success, but it will be a mistake to believe that this success sets the time for an imminent peace.

Marquis de Ségur, French Minister of War, to the Marquis de Lafayette VERSAILLES, C. DECEMBER 5, 1781

You have made a most glorious campaign, Monsieur le Marquis. Our old warriors admire you; the young ones want to take you as a model, without, however, your having excited among them the least impulse of jealousy. You add to perfect conduct a modesty that enhances the value of your virtues.

John Jay to Henry Knox MADRID, DECEMBER 10, 1781

The harmony subsisting between the French troops and ours is an agreeable as well as an important circumstance, and I am glad that the Marquis de Lafayette had an opportunity of cutting some sprigs of laurel on one of the enemy's redoubts [at Yorktown]. He has given strong proofs of attachment to our cause and country, and as military glory seems to be his mistress, he has my best wishes that she may be as constant to him as he has been to us.

Matthew Ridley, Diary 1782

I find the Marquis to be meddling in the Affairs of Peace. He is continually inquisitive as to what is passing wishes to be present at all Mr. Jay's Interviews with those appointed to treat on the part of England wants to know everything passing and as regularly conveys all to Comte de Vergennes and without doubt to the Marquis de Castries as he is his Relation. In short he is a politician who seeks to profit of time and Circumstances in order to advance himself in France. Full of Ambition and not without Intrigue. Feels his consequence and Influence and profits of it to force himself into the knowledge of what relates to us under the character of an American.

William Carmichael to Benjamin Franklin MADRID, FEBRUARY 22, 1782

We think differently of French Gallantry in America, I never can think of it without thinking of the Marquis De la Fayette.

Benjamin Franklin to Secretary for Foreign Affairs Robert R. Livingston PASSY, MARCH 4, 1782

The Marquis de la Fayette was at his Return hither received by all Ranks with all possible Distinction. He daily gains in the General

Esteem and Affection and promises to be a great Man here. He is warmly attached to our Cause; we are on the most friendly and confidential footing with each other, and he is really very serviceable to me in my Applications for additional Assistance.

John Jay to Secretary for Foreign Affairs Robert R. Livingston
PARIS, JUNE 28, 1782

Agreeably to the desire of Congress, as well as my own wishes, I have had the satisfaction of conferring with the Marquis de Lafayette on several interesting subjects. He is as active in serving us in the cabinet as he has been in the field, and (there being great reason to believe that his talents could be more advantageously employed here than an inactive campaign in America would admit of there) Dr. Franklin and myself think it advisable that he should postpone his return for the present. The Marquis inclines to the same opinion, and, though anxious to join the army, will remain here a little longer.

John Adams, Diary NOVEMBER 23, 1782

Unlimited ambition will obstruct his rise. He grasps at all civil, political, and military, and would be the *unum necessarium** in every thing. He has had so much real merit, such family supports, and so much favor at court that he need not recur to artifice. . . . He has gained more applause than human nature at 25 can bear. It has enkindled in him an unbridled ambition . . . this mongrel character of French patriot and American patriot cannot exist long.

John Jay to the Marquis de Lafayette ROUEN, JANUARY 19, 1783

Our warmest acknowledgments are due to you for the zeal you manifest to serve America at all times and in all places.

John Adams to James Warren PARIS, APRIL 16, 1783

The Marquis de la Fayette is an amiable Nobleman and has great Merit. I enjoy his Friendship and wish a Continuance of it; But I will conceal nothing from you. I see in that Youth the seeds of Mischief to our Country if we do not take Care.

---

*The one necessary thing; the essential element.

He was taken early into our Service and placed in an high Command, in which he has behaved well, but he has gained more applause than human nature at twenty-five can bear. It has enkindled in him an unbounded Ambition which it concerns Us much to watch. . . .

The Marquis may live these fifty years. Ten years may bring him by the order of Succession to the Command of your Army. You have given him a great deal too much of Popularity in our own Country. He is connected with a Family of vast Influence in France. He rises fast in the French Army. He may be soon in the Ministry. This Mongrel Character of French Patriot and American Patriot cannot exist long, and if hereafter it should be seriously the Politicks of the French Court to break our Union, Imagination cannot conceive a more Proper Instrument for the Purpose than the Marquis. He is now very active, everlastingly busy, ardent to distinguish himself every Way, especially to increase his Merit towards America, aiming as I believe at some Employment from Congress. Pains are taken to give him the Credit of every Thing. Believe me it is of infinite Importance that you yourselves and your Servants should have the Reputation of their own Measures and of doing your Service.

Marquis de Lafayette to George Washington   NANCY, FRANCE, SEPTEMBER 8, 1783

As to the American trade, it has been represented that my presence here might serve the United States, and to me, that consideration shall ever be a determining one. I hope My Dear General will approve my conduct, which approbation, I confess, in every instance will ever prove necessary to my happiness and self satisfaction. But I grieve to be so long from you, such a distance, such an interval of time cannot agree with the tender feelings of a heart who had taken the happy habit to live in your family, among my American friends, who, in any part of the world, never felt himself so much at home, as when he was at headquarters. Until I return to America, My dear General, until I see you and our fellow supporters of our noble cause, my mind cannot be properly easy, and every mention, every remembrance of America makes me sigh for the moment when I may enjoy the sight of our free and independent shores.

Marquis de Lafayette to William Temple Franklin PARIS, NOVEMBER 19, 1783

The object of my wanting a Declaration of Independence is to have it engraved in golden letters at the most conspicuous part of my cabinet, and when I wish to put myself in spirits, I will look at it, and most voluptuously read it over—So that you will oblige me to procure it for me, printed if you can, in order that a French workman may be less apt to make blunders.*

Samuel Osgood to John Adams ANNAPOLIS, DECEMBER 7, 1783

The Marquis LaFayette has zealously interested himself in all our important Matters. He assumes the Language of a true born American, & is a very popular Character in the Country. But if I Mistake not he is deeply immersed in European Politicks, which are the worst that can possibly exist for America. When he last left this Country he went with an evident Design to assist our Commissioners in negotiating the Peace. It was pretty plainly intimated that he wish'd to be one of the Number. Had he been added to them, it would not have been more extraordinary, than some other Matters that have taken Place. An Instruction however to you, to consult and advise with him, was carried. I do not apprehend you were much the wiser for the Information you might have obtain'd from that Quarter. Few Americans are worthy to be trusted in some of the most important concerns of the United States—& not a single Foreigner.

Marquis de Lafayette to John Adams PARIS, MARCH 8, 1784

As to my democratic principles, let it be remembered that at a time when your situation was to the worst and my disobeying this Court might be ruinous, I went over a Volunteer in the cause from which others could not recede unless they were deserters.

Marquis de Lafayette to George Washington PARIS, MARCH 9, 1784

You will be my compass, My dear General. . . .

I don't Say that I Have Merit—But I Say I Have Consequences

---

*Lafayette eventually placed his engraved copy of the Declaration of Independence on one side of a double frame, leaving the other side empty, as he awaited a parallel declaration of French rights to put beside it.

—viz.—Enemies—My Popularity is Great throughout the Kingdom, and in this City—But Amongst the Great folks I Have a large
party Against me, Because they are jealous of my Reputation.

Marquis de Lafayette to John Adams PARIS, APRIL 9, 1784

As to my going to America, I first went for the Revolution, and
not for the war, and warfaring was truly a secondary incident,
which in support of the rights of mankind had become necessary.
Now I am going for the people, and my motives are, that I love
them, and they love me—that my arrival will please them, and
that I will be pleased with the sight of those whom I have early
joined in our noble and successful cause. I may add, that opinions of honest men, when they have some influence, do more
or less prove serviceable—and how could I refrain from visiting
a nation whose I am an adoptive son, and where, particularly
among your fellow citizens, I have experienced so many marks of
affection and confidence.

Marquis de Lafayette to the Marquise de Lafayette MOUNT VERNON, AUGUST 20, 1784

Though I do not know if my letter will reach you, my dear heart,
I had to write you that I am at Mount Vernon and that I am revel-
ing in the happiness of finding my dear general again; and you
know me too well for me to need to describe to you what I felt.
Crossing the countryside very quickly, I arrived here on the sev-
enteenth, and as the general, though he had been anticipating my
arrival, did not expect me for several more days, I found him in
the routine of his estate, where our meeting was very tender and
our satisfaction completely mutual. I am not just turning a phrase
when I assure you that in retirement General Washington is even
greater than he was during the Revolution. His simplicity is truly
sublime, and he is as completely involved with all the details of
his lands and house as if he had always lived here. To describe to
you the life that we lead here, I shall tell you that after breakfast
the general and I chat together for some time. After having thoroughly discussed the past, the present, and the future, he with-
draws to take care of his affairs and gives me things to read that
have been written during my absence. Then we come down for
dinner and find Mrs. Washington with visitors from the neighborhood. The conversation at table turns to the events of the war

or to anecdotes that we are fond of recalling. After tea we resume our private conversations and pass the rest of the evening with the family.

James Madison to Thomas Jefferson PHILADELPHIA, OCTOBER 17, 1784

The time I have lately passed with the M. has given me a pretty thorough insight into his character. With great natural frankness of temper he unites much address with very considerable talents, a strong thirst of praise and popularity. In his politics he says his three hobby horses are the alliance between France and the United States, the union of the latter and the manumission of the slaves. The two former are the dearer to him as they are connected with his personal glory. The last does him real honor as it is a proof of his humanity. In a word I take him to be as amiable a man as can be imagined and as sincere an American as any Frenchman can be; one whose past services gratitude obliges us to acknowledge, and whose future friendship prudence requires us to cultivate.

Joseph Barrell to Samuel Blachley Webb BOSTON, OCTOBER 21, 1784

The Marquis is with us, & has been treated with a friendship *unknown* by the dishonest, & with a Respect that could not be exceeded if he was a Crown'd head, read Adams & Nourse Paper [Boston *Independent Chronicle*] of this day, & depend the description is not in the least exaggerated.

Resolution of Congress DECEMBER 10, 1784

Resolved, That the Secretary in the War Office do in the name of the United States in Congress Assembled present to Major General the Marquis de Lafayette a standard of those captured at the surrender of . . . Cornwallis . . . as a testimonial of the high sense Congress entertain of the great bravery and prowess evinced on many occasions by the Marquis and particularly during the siege of Yorktown, by carrying, sword in hand with the American column of troops which he commanded in person [against] one of the enemy's redoubts, completely garrisoned, and in an entire state of Military defense.

Marquis de Lafayette, Address to Congress TRENTON,
DECEMBER 13, 1784

Sir: While it please the United States in Congress so kindly, to
receive me, I want words to express the feelings of a heart which
delights in their present situation, and the bestowed marks of
their esteem.

Since I joined the standard of liberty, to this wished for hour of
my personal congratulations, I have seen such glorious deeds performed and virtues displayed by the sons of America, that in the
instant of my first concern for them, I had anticipated but a part of
the love and regard which devote me to this rising empire.

During our revolution, Sir, I obtained an unlimited indulgent
confidence, which I am equally proud and happy to acknowledge; it dates with the time, when, an unexperienced youth, I
could only claim my respected friends' paternal adoption. It has
been most benevolently continued throughout every circumstance of the cabinet and the field; and in personal friendships, I
have often found a support against public difficulties. While on
this solemn occasion I mention my obligations to Congress, the
states, the people at large, permit me also to remember the dear
military companions, to whose services their country is so much
indebted.

Having felt both for the timely aid of my country, and for the
part she, with a beloved king, acted in the cause of mankind, I
enjoy an alliance so well riveted by mutual affection, by interest,
and even local situation. Recollection ensures it. Futurity does
not but enlarge the prospect; and the private intercourse will
every day increase, which independent and advantageous trade
cherishes, in proportion as it is well understood.

In unbounded wishes to America, Sir, I am happy to observe
the prevailing disposition of the people to strengthen the Confederation, preserve public faith, regulate trade, and in a proper
guard over continental magazines and frontier posts, in a general
system of militia, in foreseeing attention to the navy, to ensure
every kind of safety.

May this immense temple of freedom ever stand a lesson to
oppressors, an example to the oppressed, a sanctuary for the
rights of mankind! And may these happy United States attain
that complete splendor and prosperity which will illustrate the

blessings of their government, and for ages to come rejoice the departed souls of its founders.

However unwilling to trespass on your time, I must yet present you with grateful thanks for the late favors of Congress, and never can they oblige me so much as when they put it in my power, in every part of the world, to the latest day of my life, to gratify the attachment which will ever rank me among the most zealous and respectful servants of the United States.

Thomas Jefferson to James Madison PARIS, MARCH 18, 1785

Your character of the M. Fayette is precisely agreeable to the idea I had formed of him. I take him to be of unmeasured ambition but that the means he uses are virtuous. He is returned [to France from America] fraught with affection to America and disposed to render every possible service.

Abigail Adams to Mary Smith Cranch AUTEUIL, FRANCE, MAY 8, 1785

I shall lose part and the greatest part of American intelligence by quitting France, for no person is so well informed from all the states as the Marquis de la Fayette. He has Established a correspondence in all the states and has the News Papers from every quarter.

Abigail Adams to Mercy Otis Warren AUTEUIL, FRANCE, MAY 10, 1785

The Marquis you know. He is dangerously amiable, sensible, polite, affable insinuating pleasing hospitable indefatigable and ambitious. Let our Country Guard let them watch let them fear his virtues and remember that the summit of perfection is the point of declension.

James Madison to Thomas Jefferson ORANGE, VA., AUGUST 20, 1785

Subsequent to the date of mine in which I gave my idea of Fayette I had further opportunities of penetrating his character. Though his foibles did not disappear all the favorable traits presented themselves in a stronger light. On closer inspection he certainly possesses talents which might figure in any line. If he is ambitious it is rather of the praise which virtue dedicates to merit than of the homage which fears renders to power. His disposition is naturally warm and affectionate and his attachment to the United States unquestionable. Unless I am grossly deceived you will find his zeal sincere & useful whenever it can be employed in behalf of the United States without opposition to the essential interests of France.

Virginia Act for the Naturalization of the Marquis de Lafayette OCTOBER 1785

Whereas the Marquis De La Fayette is eminently distinguished by early and signal exertions in defense of American liberty: And whereas this illustrious nobleman continues to afford testimonies of increasing affection to this state, and the general assembly being solicitous to bestow the most decisive mark of regard which a republic can give:

Be it enacted, That the Marquis De La Fayette be henceforth deemed and considered a citizen of this state, and that he shall enjoy all the rights, privileges, and immunities, thereunto belonging.

Marquis de Lafayette to Rabaut de Saint-Etienne PARIS, NOVEMBER 20, 1785

Although less a soldier, thank God, than a citizen, I have a keen taste for that profession, and for all the means of improving myself in it.

Thomas Jefferson to James Madison PARIS, FEBRUARY 8, 1786

I am persuaded that a gift of lands by the state of Virginia to the Marquis de la Fayette would give a good opinion here of our character, and would reflect honor on the Marquis. Nor am I sure that the day will not come when it might be an useful asylum to him. The time of life at which he visited America was too well adapted to receive good & lasting impressions to permit him ever to accommodate himself to the principles of monarchical government; and it will need all his own prudence & that of his friends to make this country a safe residence for him. How glorious, how comfortable in reflection will it be to have prepared a refuge for him in case of a reverse. In the mean time he could settle it with tenants from the freest part of this country, Bretagny. I have never suggested the smallest idea of this kind to him: because the execution of it should convey the first notice. If the state has not a right to give him lands with their own officers, they could buy up at cheap prices the shares of others.

John Jay to the Marquis de Lafayette NEW YORK, JUNE 16, 1786

I can easily conceive that, at the German courts you visited, you have done us service, because I know how able, as well as how willing, you are to do it. I wish all who speak and write of us were equally well-informed and well-disposed. It is a common remark in this country that wherever you go you do us good. For my part, I give you credit, not merely for doing us good, but also for doing it uniformly, constantly, and upon system.

Thomas Jefferson to Edward Carrington PARIS, JANUARY 16, 1787

In my letter to Mr. Jay I have mentioned the meeting of the Notables appointed for the 29th inst. It is now put off to the 7th or 8th of next month. This event, which will hardly excite any attention in America, is deemed here the most important one which has taken place in their civil line during the present century. Some promise their country great things from it, some nothing. Our friend de la Fayette was placed on the list originally. Afterwards his name disappeared: but finally was reinstated. This shows that his character here is not considered as an indifferent one; and that it excites agitation. His education in our school has drawn on him a very jealous eye from a court whose principles are the most absolute despotism. But I hope he has nearly passed his crisis. The king, who is a good man, is favorably disposed towards him: and he is supported by powerful family connections, and by the public good will. He is the youngest man of the Notables, except one whose office placed him on the list.

Thomas Jefferson to James Madison PARIS, JANUARY 30, 1787

The Marquis de Lafayette is a most valuable auxiliary to me. His zeal is unbounded, & his weight with those in power great. His education having been merely military, commerce was an unknown field to him. But his good sense enabling him to comprehend perfectly whatever is explained to him. His agency has been very efficacious. He has a great deal of sounder genius, is well remarked by the king & rising in popularity. He [i.e., the king] has nothing against him but the suspicion [of] republican principles. I think he will one day be of the ministry. His foible is a canine appetite for popularity and fame. But he will get above this.

Thomas Paine, The Rights of Man, Part 1 1791

M. de la Fayette went to America at an early period of the war, and continued a volunteer in her service to the end. His conduct through the whole of that enterprise is one of the most extraordinary that is to be found in the history of a young man, scarcely then twenty years of age. Situated in a country that was like the lap of sensual pleasure, and with the means of enjoying it, how few there are there to be found who would exchange such a scene for the woods and wilderness of America, and pass the flowery years of youth in unprofitable danger and hardship! But such is the fact. When the war ended, and he was on the point of taking his final departure, he presented himself to Congress, and contemplating, in his affectionate farewell, the revolution he had seen, expressed himself in these words: *"May this great monument, raised to Liberty, serve as a lesson to the oppressor, and an example to the oppressed!"* ...

The peculiar situation of the then Marquis de la Fayette is another link in the great chain. He served in America as an American officer under a commission of Congress, and by the universality of his acquaintance, was in close friendship with the civil government of America, as well as with the military line. He spoke the language of the country, entered into the discussions on the principles of government, and was always a welcome friend at any election.

Marquis de Lafayette to Alexander Hamilton WITMOLD-HOLSTEIN, GERMANY, AUGUST 12, 1798

In the passionate love of liberty which brought me to America there were the proper requisites to espouse her democratic system of republicanism. While I was impressed with the dangers of British royalty and aristocracy, and acknowledged the deficiencies in our first experiments, I lately came to think that the science of social representative organization had not been fairly explored and to wish it might have an universal trial—its first principles, however, were to me indubitable. This fundamental doctrine of the rights of men and citizens, reduced to what I thought necessary and sufficient was proclaimed on the 11th July 1789 in an Assembly surrounded with royal troops, and after the National triumph of the 14th, a civil militia was organized as an over match for the standing armies of Europe. . . .

I most heartily thank you for the warm and affectionate manner in which you express the kind dispositions of America in my behalf and your own feelings on the occasion. I am sensible of my obligations to that Beloved Country the welfare of which I would ever be ready to purchase with the last drop of my blood. I am happy and proud of the sentiments which her virtuous and steady inhabitants have uniformly produced to me—and for my more intimate companions, particularly for you, my dear Hamilton, I hope you know that our former friendship has been in my heart unaltered, and that from the early times which have linked our brotherly union to the last Moment of my life I shall Ever be Your Affectionate Friend.

Alexander Hamilton to the Marquis de Lafayette NEW YORK, JANUARY 6, 1799

I have been made happy my dear friend by the receipt of your letter of the 12th of August last. No explanation of your political principles was necessary to satisfy me of the perfect consistency and purity of your conduct. The interpretation may always be left to my attachment for you. Whatever difference of opinion may on any occasion exist between us can never lessen my conviction of the goodness both of your head and heart. . . . Neither have I abandoned the idea that 'tis most advisable for you to remain in Europe 'till the difference is adjusted [between France and America]. It would be very difficult for you here to steer a course which would not place you in a party and remove you from the broad ground which you now occupy in the hearts of all. It is a favorite point with me that you shall find in the universal regard of this country all the consolations which the loss of your own (for so I consider it) may render requisite.

John Quincy Adams to William Vans Murray BERLIN, MARCH 26, 1799

I am glad you have seen La F[ayette], and not surprised that you found him full of the same fanaticism from which he has already suffered so much, a great part of which, however, with him is what it always was, ungovernable ambition in disguise. He is willing to look upon himself as a martyr of liberty, because five years of imprisonment lose almost all their credit and reputation, when they are considered as having been the result of folly or wickedness. There is therefore more address and subtlety in his enthusiasm, than you think. His character, at least as far as judgment combined with honesty is concerned, has long since been irretrievable with thinking men. By recanting he would gain nothing in their opinion, and he would lose most of his personal partisans. I believe he thinks his intentions as good as you allow them to be, but he is a man extremely apt to mistake the operations of his heart as well as those of his head. You will very probably discover before he quits your neighborhood, that he deals largely in a sort of minute intrigue not calculated to inspire confidence.

Marquis de Lafayette to George Washington VIANEN, THE NETHERLANDS, MAY 9, 1799

I have from my youth, head, heart, & hand been devoted to American independence and freedom.

George Washington to Timothy Pickering MOUNT VERNON, NOVEMBER 3, 1799

I have not a doubt of General Lafayette's being *now* on his passage to the United States. I have done every thing in my power to induce him to suspend this determination; by representing the delicate situation in which he would be placed here, and the embarassment it might occasion. Mr. Murray has enforced my observations with all his might; in vain I believe.

He replies, Poor fellow!—with too much truth I fear!—that there is no asylum for him in Europe. That he is determined (without knowing himself, I conceive) to be perfectly neutral. That his wish is to possess a small farm where he can enjoy ease & quiet. Little believing, although he has been told, that he will be assailed by the opposition party in this Country, and that it is hardly possible for him to avoid taking *a side,* without being suspected by *both sides.* That if [he] joins the Government party, he must relinquish all hope, & expectation of countenance from his own Country, under its present form; and if he joins the opposition, he will of course be frowned upon by the Government under whose protection he is settling.

Marquis de Lafayette to Alexander Hamilton LA GRANGE, FRANCE, FEBRUARY 10, 1801

I was on the day of my arrival [back into France after his imprisonment] and am more every day determined for a life of perfect retirement. It has been said I was going to America as an ambassador. My feelings and my habits in the United States I could not well reconcile to the acting a foreign character, however friendly, nor could I with ease to myself, either within or without put off my American regimentals. I may be a happy visitor, and so I shall one day or another, but am not fit to be an ambassador of one country to the other. I feel it better than it can be expressed.

John Adams to Benjamin Rush SEPTEMBER 1807

Mirabeau said of La Fayette, "Il a affiché désintéressement," and he added, "this never fails. You know the sense of the word 'affiché'"? It is as much as to say "he advertised his disinterestedness," that is equivalent to saying that he employed a crier to proclaim through the streets "O Yes! O Yes! O Yes!" All manner of persons may have the benefit of my services, *gratis,* provided always and only that they will yield me their unlimited and unsuspecting confidence and make me commander in chief of five hundred thousand men, and after I shall have gained a few victories, make me a king or an emperor, when I shall take a fancy to be either. This has been the amount and the result of most of the disinterestedness that has been professed in the world. I say most, not all. There are exceptions, and our Washington ought to pass for one. La Fayette imitated his example. So have Jefferson, Hamilton, Governor Strong, Fisher Ames, and many others.

John Adams to Thomas Jefferson QUINCY, JULY 13, 1813

When LaFayette harangued You and me, and John Quincy Adams, through a whole evening in your Hotel in the Cul de Sac, at Paris; and developed the plans then in Operation to reform France: though I was as silent as you was, I then thought I could say something new to him. In plain Truth I was astonished at the Grossness of his Ignorance of Government and History.

NOVEMBER 15, 1824

You and I have been favored with a visit from our old friend General La Fayette. What a wonderful Man at his Age to undergo the fatigues of such long journeys and constant feasts. I was greatly delighted with the sight of him and the little conversation I had with him.

President John Quincy Adams, Speech on the Departure of Lafayette WASHINGTON, D.C., FEBRUARY 23, 1825

We shall look upon you always as belonging to us, during the whole of our life, as belonging to our children after us. You are ours by more than patriotic self-devotion with which you flew to the aid of our fathers at the crisis of our fate; ours by that unshaken gratitude for your services which is a precious portion of our inheritance; ours by that tie of love, stronger than death, which has linked your name for endless ages of time with the name of Washington. . . . Speaking in the name of the whole people of the United States, and at a loss only for language to give utterance to that feeling of attachment with which the heart of the nation beats as the heart of one man, I bid you a reluctant and affectionate farewell.

Marquis de Lafayette, Response to President Adams's Speech WASHINGTON, D.C., FEBRUARY 23, 1825

After a long pause necessary for Lafayette to compose himself, the departing hero responded "God bless you, Sir, and all who surround you. God bless the American people, each of their states and the federal government. Accept this patriotic farewell of a heart that will overflow with gratitude until the moment it ceases to beat."

Richard Henry Lee
1732–1794

⅊ BORN AT Stratford, Westmoreland County, Va. Third of six brothers, including Francis Lightfoot, William, and Arthur Lee; cousin of Henry Lee. Attended Wakefield Academy, Yorkshire, England. Justice of peace, Westmoreland County, 1757. Organized Westmoreland County Nonimportation Association, 1766. Coauthor, intercolonial plan for committees of correspondence, 1773. Represented Westmoreland County in House of Burgesses, 1758–76, in Revolutionary conventions, 1774–76, and in House of Delegates, 1777–78, 1780–81 (speaker, 1781), 1782–85. Delegate to Congress, 1774–79, 1784–85 (president), 1787; made motion for independence and confederation, 1776; signed Declaration of Independence, 1776, and Articles of Confederation, 1778. Declined appointment to Constitutional Convention, 1787. Refused to stand for election to the Virginia ratifying convention, 1788. Opposed ratification of the Constitution. U.S. senator, 1789–92.

John Adams, Diary AUGUST 28, 1774

He [Jonathan Dickinson Sergeant] says the Virginians speak in raptures about Richard Henry Lee and Patrick Henry—one the Cicero and the other the Demosthenes of the Age.

PHILADELPHIA, SEPTEMBER 1, 1774

After Coffee We went to the Tavern, where we were introduced to . . . Richard Henry Lee Esq. . . . Lee is a tall, spare Man.

PHILADELPHIA, SEPTEMBER 3, 1774

Breakfasted at Dr. Shippen's. Dr. Witherspoon was there. Coll. R. H. Lee lodges there. He is a masterly Man.

This Mr. Lee is a Brother of the Sheriff of London [William Lee], and of Dr. Arthur Lee, and of Mrs. Shippen. They are all sensible, and deep thinkers.

Silas Deane to Elizabeth Deane PHILADELPHIA, SEPTEMBER 10, 1774

Col. Lee, is said to be his [Patrick Henry's] Rival in Eloquence, & in Virginia & to the Southward they are styled the *Demosthenes,* & *Cicero* of America. God Grant they may not, Like them, plead in Vain for the Liberties of their Country. These last Gentlemen are Now in full Life, perhaps near Fifty & have made the Constitution, & history of G. Britain, & America their Capital Study ever since the late Troubles between them have arose.

John Adams, Diary PHILADELPHIA, OCTOBER 10, 1774

Lee, Henry, and [William] Hooper are the orators [in Congress].

John Adams, Autobiography FEBRUARY 1776

Jealousies and divisions appeared among the Delegates [to Congress] of no State more remarkably, than among those of Virginia. Mr. [George] Wythe told me, that Thomas Lee the elder Brother of Richard Henry was the delight of the Eyes of Virginia and by far the most popular Man they had. But Richard Henry was not. I asked the reason, for Mr. Lee appeared a Scholar, a gentleman, a Man of uncommon Eloquence, and an agreeable Man. Mr. Wythe said this was all true but Mr. Lee had when he was very young and when he first came into the House of Burgesses moved and urged on an Inquiry into the State of the Treasury which was found deficient in a large Sum, which had been lent by the Treasurer to many of the most influential Families of the Country, who found themselves exposed, and had never forgiven Mr. Lee. This he said had made him so many Enemies, that he never had recovered his Reputation, but was still heartily hated by great Numbers. These feelings among the Virginia Delegates, were a great Injury to Us. Mr. Samuel Adams and myself were very intimate with Mr. Lee, and he agreed perfectly with Us in the great System of our Policy, and by his means We kept a Majority of the Delegates of Virginia with Us, but Harrison, Pendleton and some others, showed their Jealousy of this Intimacy plainly enough, at times.

Richard Henry Lee to Thomas Jefferson PHILADELPHIA, NOVEMBER 3, 1776

I have been informed that very malignant and very scandalous hints and innuendoes concerning me have been uttered in the house [of Delegates]. From the justice of the House I should expect they would not suffer the character of an absent person (and one in their service) to be reviled by any slanderous tongue whatever. When I am present, I shall be perfectly satisfied with the justice I am able to do myself. From your candor Sir, and knowledge of my political movements I hope such misstatings as may happen in your presence will be rectified.

APRIL 29, 1777

If I were to consider punctilio more than the suggestions of friendship, I should expect an answer to some of the letters I have written you, before I dispatched another. But I ever hated ceremonies, and shall not commence ceremony with you.

William Duer to John Jay PHILADELPHIA, MAY 28, 1777

The *Chaste* Colonel Lee will I am credibly informed be left out of the new Delegation for Virginia which is now in Agitation. The mere Contemplation of this Event gives me Pleasure. My mind is full, and I wish to unburden it; but Prudence forbids me.

William Duer to Robert R. Livingston PHILADELPHIA, JULY 9, 1777

I am sorry to inform you that Colonel R. H. Lee is returning to Congress Crowned with Laurels. His Smooth Discourse, and Art of Cabal have blunted the Edge of his Countrymen's Resentment, and they have lauded him Encomiums on his Patriotism and Attention to Business, which he modestly says, he is Anxious of deserving.

Richard Henry Lee to Arthur Lee YORK, PA., MAY 27, 1778

My eyes are so extremely injured by their constant application, that without the aid and support of Spectacles I fear I shall soon lose the use of them. I pray you then to procure me a pair of the best Temple Spectacles that can be had. In fitting these perhaps it may be proper to remember that my age is 46, that my eyes are light colored and have been quick & strong but now weakened by constant use—My head thin between the Temples.

Walter Stewart to Nathanael Greene WILLIAMSBURG, JANUARY 29, 1779

The Affair between Mr. Deane and the Lees have Occasioned much Conversation in this Country. [We] found the People as low down as Fredericksburgh possessed with very Just Ideas of those men and their Colleagues in Congress, but Richard Henry Lee with a few Adherents have been very busy between that place and Williamsburgh. The People heard but one Story, and were from their old Attachment to the Lee Family willing to believe it. However Col. [Burgess] Ball and myself have been equally Industrious in placing things in a proper light, and I flatter myself the day is not far distant when the Junto will receive a Severe Shock by being deprived of one of the most Artful, designing and Wicked men the Country stands Cursed with; I mean Richard Henry Lee. It is amazing to hear of his Artifice in this state in support of a Popular Character, but the People's eyes are now Opened and I doubt whether his Oratory and Weeping will again bring Tears and Lamentations (as Usual) for his sufferings from the Assembly; they have ever been Infatuated when he held forth to them, for whatever he said they were sure to believe.

James Lovell to John Adams PHILADELPHIA, JUNE 13, 1779

The eastern States are charged with wanting what they have no right to, and what is of "no interest to the southern States." Plenty are these local sentiments lately; and R. H. Lee, with H. Laurens, are squinted at as two monsters on the other side of the Susquehanna who pursue points in which the southern States have *no* interest.

Meriwether Smith to Virginia House of Delegates
PHILADELPHIA, FEBRUARY 25, 1781

In Obedience to this Order, Sir, I cannot in any other manner, satisfy the House of Delegates so well as by transmitting to them an Exact Account of my Expenditures from Sept. 1778 to Novr.

1780; during all which Time I have been honored with the pub-lic Confidence in Office [as a delegate to Congress]. They will see, at one View, the whole of my Conduct, and may from thence form a Judgment respecting my Motives & the Advantages I have received; and, I trust, that to every unprejudiced Mind, the Rec-titude of my Intentions in all things relating to the public Inter-est will manifestly appear. At the same Time, I confess that I feel myself but little concerned about the Result of a public Inquiry into my Conduct, having the fullest Confidence in the Justice & Candor of the House of Delegates; and, whatever may be the Event, I am prepared to meet it with that Fortitude & zealous Perseverance in the Service of the Public which have hitherto distinguish[ed] my Conduct, & supported me amidst every Species of Persecution from a Man [R. H. Lee], who, from the *Duplicity of his Conduct,* & the *self-interested Motives by which I discovered him to be actuated,* forfeited the good Opinion I had before entertained of him, and ought to have lost the public Con-fidence. "It is the portion of Humanity to err." I may have erred in this Matter; but ——. nil conscire sibi,* ——.

Robert Hunter Jr., *Travel Diary* OCTOBER 12, 1785

The President [of Congress] was disappointed in fifteen mem-bers of Congress. He is a polite, well-bred man, and quite a gentleman in his manners. His conversation is rather reserved, though he seemed to pay us particular attention as strangers. I am told he is the most elegant speaker in Congress and quite a saint in his disposition. He gave me a very polite invitation to pay him a visit at Alexandria in Virginia. He will be there, he says, about the 15th of November, when His Excellency will be very happy to see me. . . . We came home at seven to drink tea, highly pleased with the President's company. He is one of the richest gentlemen in the state of Virginia.

Edmund Randolph to James Madison RICHMOND, MARCH 22, 1787

Colonel R. H. Lee has been appointed [to the Constitutional Convention]. . . . This seemed proper from the conspicuous-ness of the Character, and the respect, due to past services. The

---

*To be conscious of no wrongdoing.

objection to his unfederal opinions was so urgently pressed, that the council consisting of eight were equally divided. I gave the decision, from a hope that himself and his friends might be attached to the union, on those principles, which can alone support it.

Nathan Dane to Rufus King NEW YORK, JULY 16, 1787

There appears to be a disposition to do business [in Congress], and the arrival of R. H. Lee is of considerable importance. I think his character serves at least in some degree, to check the effects of the feeble habits and lax modes of thinking in some of his Countrymen.

John Armstrong to George Washington CARLISLE, PA., FEBRUARY 20, 1788

Mr. R. Lee's letter too, tho' wrote with decency, contains more of the air, than the Substance of the Statesman; and in which he has fallen below himself.

William Smith of Maryland to Otho H. Williams NEW YORK, JUNE 21, 1789

Colo. R.H.L. was at the head of this scheme, and from his Assiduity & address, he expects, & I have no doubt he will obtain a considerable influence, you are I believe on Such terms with him as to afford an opportunity of corresponding. He is very open to flattery, as is most men.

Thomas Tudor Tucker to St. George Tucker NEW YORK, SEPTEMBER 15, 1789

Mr. L. has been said to be a Man of republican Principles. Whether this be true or not I am entirely ignorant. If it be true in any degree it wou'd be imprudent to drive him over to the aristocratical Party, already too powerful. Were we to make every Man our Enemy who is not *wholly* in Sentiment with us, we shou'd have very little Support left.

Edmund Randolph, History of Virginia

In the quarter of Virginia included in the proprietorship of the Northern Neck, Richard Henry Lee had gained the palm of a species of oratory rare among a people backward in refinement. He had attuned his voice with so much care that one unmusical cadence could scarcely be pardoned by his ear. He was reported to have formed before a mirror his gesture, which was not unsuitable even to a court. His speech was diffusive, without the hackneyed formulas, and he charmed wheresoever he opened his lips. In political reading he was conversant, and on the popular topics dispersed through the debates of Parliament, his recollection was rapid and correct. Malice had hastily involved in censure for a supposed inconsistency of conduct upon the Stamp Act; but the vigor and perseverance of his patriotism extorted from his enemies a confession that he deserved the general confidence which was afterwards conceded to him.

William Maclay, Diary JUNE 12, 1790

R. H. Lee, the Man Who gave independence (in One Sense) to America, a man of a clear head, and great experience in public business. Certainly ambitious, and Vain glorious but his passions seek gratification, in serving the public.

Benjamin Rush, Sketches C. 1800

A frequent, correct and pleasing speaker. He was very useful upon committees and active in expediting business. He made the motion for the Declaration of Independence and was ever afterwards one of its most zealous supporters.

Thomas Jefferson to John Adams MONTICELLO, AUGUST 22, 1813

[On Lee's style of writing.] His was loose, vague, frothy, rhetorical. He was a poorer writer than his brother Arthur.

William Wirt, Sketches of the Life and Character of Patrick Henry 1800

Richard Henry Lee was the Cicero of the house. His face was on the Roman model; his nose Cesarean; the port and carriage of his head, leaning persuasively and gracefully forward; and the whole contour noble and fine. Mr. Lee was, by far, the most elegant scholar in the house. He had studied the classics in the true spirit of criticism. His taste had that delicate touch, which seized with intuitive certainty every beauty of an author, and his genius that native affinity which combined them without an effort. Into every walk of literature and science, he had carried this mind of exquisite selection, and brought it back to the business of life, crowned with every light of learning, and decked with every wreath, that all the muses and all the graces could entwine. Nor did those light decorations constitute the whole value of knowledge, with an activity of observation, and a certainty of judgment, that turned that knowledge to the very best account. He was not a lawyer by profession; but he understood thoroughly the constitution both of the mother-country and her colonies; and the elements also of the civil and municipal law. Thus, while his eloquence was free from those stiff and technical restraints which the habits of forensic speaking are so apt to generate, he had all the legal learning which is necessary to a statesman. He reasoned well, and declaimed freely and splendidly. The note of his voice was deeper and more melodious than that of Mr. Pendleton. It was the canorous voice of Cicero. He had lost the use of one of his hands, which he kept constantly covered with a black-silk bandage, neatly fitted to the palm of his hand, but leaving his thumb free; yet, notwithstanding this disadvantage, his gesture was so graceful and so highly finished, that it was said he had acquired it by practicing before a mirror. Such was his promptitude, that he required no preparation for debate. He was ready for any subject, as soon as it was announced; and his speech was so copious, so rich, so mellifluous, set off with such bewitching cadence of voice, and such captivating grace of action, that, while you listened to him, you desired to hear nothing superior, and indeed thought him perfect. He had a quick sensibility and a fervid imagination, which Mr. Pendleton wanted. Hence his orations were warmer and more delightfully interesting, yet still, to him those keys were not consigned which could unlock the sources either of the strong or tender passions. His defect was, that he was too smooth and too sweet. His style bore a striking resemblance to that of Herodotus, as described by the Roman orator: "He flowed on, like a quiet and placid river, without a ripple."* He flowed, too, through banks covered with all the fresh verdure and variegated bloom of the spring; but his course was too subdued, and too beautifully regular. A cataract, like that of Niagara, crowned with overhanging rocks and mountains, in all the rude and awful grandeur of nature, would have brought him nearer to the standard of Homer and of Henry. . . .

*Orat. 12.39.

On the opposite side of the house sat the graceful [Edmund] Pendleton, and the harmonious Richard Henry Lee, whose aquiline nose, and Roman profile struck me much more forcibly than that of Mr. Henry, his rival in eloquence. . . . I was then between nineteen and twenty, had never heard a speech in public, except from the pulpit—had attached to the idea I had formed of an orator, all the advantages of person which Mr. Pendleton possessed, and even more the advantages of voice which delighted me so much in the speeches of Mr. Lee the fine polish of language, which that gentleman united with harmonious voice, so as to make me sometimes fancy that I was listening to some being inspired with more than mortal powers of embellishment, and all the advantages of gesture which the celebrated Demosthenes considered as the first, second, and third qualification of an orator.

John Adams to Richard Henry Lee   QUINCY, AUGUST 11, 1819

With your grandfather, Richard Henry Lee, I served in Congress from 1774 to 1778, and afterwards in the Senate of the United States in 1789. He was a gentleman of fine talents, of amiable manners, and great worth. As a public speaker, he had a fluency as easy and graceful as it was melodious, which his classical education enabled him to decorate with frequent allusion to some of the finest passages of antiquity. With all his brothers he was always devoted to the cause of his country.

Thomas Jefferson to John Adams   MONTICELLO, DECEMBER 18, 1825

I presume you have received a copy of the life of Richd. H. Lee, from his grandson of the same name, author of the work. You and I know that he merited much during the revolution. Eloquent, bold, and ever watchful at his post, of which his biographer omits no proof. I am not certain whether the friends of George Mason, of Patrick Henry, yourself, and even of Genl. Washington may not reclaim some feathers of the plumage given him, notable as was his proper and original coat.

James Madison, Conversation with Jared Sparks   APRIL 1830

The talents of R. H. Lee were respectable, but not of the highest order.

James Madison
1751–1836

⊰ BORN IN Port Conway, King George County, Va. Attended Donald Robertson's school, King and Queen County, 1762–67, and College of New Jersey (Princeton), 1769–71, receiving an A.B.; pursued graduate studies, 1771–72. Elected to Orange County Committee of Safety, 1774. Represented Orange County in fifth Revolutionary convention, 1776, and in House of Delegates, 1776–77, 1784–87, 1799–1800. Member, Council of State, 1778–79. Delegate to Congress, 1780–83, 1787–88; to Annapolis Convention, 1786; and to Constitutional Convention, 1787 (principal author, Virginia Resolutions). One of three authors of *The Federalist,* 1787–88. Delegate Virginia Convention, voted to ratify the Constitution, 1788. U.S. representative, 1789–97. Married Dolley Payne Todd, 1794. Author, Virginia Resolutions, 1798. Presidential elector, 1800. U.S. secretary of state, 1801–9. President of the United States, 1809–17. Rector, University of Virginia, 1826–34. Member, Virginia constitutional convention, 1829–30.

Thomas Rodney, *"Caractors of Some of the Members of Congress"* POST MARCH 8, 1781

I Take notice of a Mr. Madison of Virginia, Who with some little reading in the Law is Just from the College, and possesses all the Self conceit that is Common To youth and inexperience in like cases—but it is unattended with that gracefulness & ease which Sometimes Makes even the impertinence of youth and inexperience agreeable or at least not offensive.

Martha Dangerfield Bland (Mrs. Theodorick Bland Jr.) to
Frances Bland Tucker (Mrs. St. George Tucker) MARCH 30,
1781

Mr. Madison a gloomy, stiff creature, they say is clever in Congress, but out of it he has nothing engaging or even bearable in his Manners—the most unsociable creature in Existence.

Eliza House Trist to Thomas Jefferson APRIL 13, 1784

He has a Soul replete with gentleness humanity and every social virtue and yet I am certain that some wretch or other will write against him [if he becomes governor of Virginia]. You I am sure wou'd not advise him to it. I have no Idea that men are to live only for the Public. They owe something to themselves. Mr. Madison is too amiable in his disposition to bear up against a torrent of abuse. It will hurt his feelings and injure his health, take my word.

William Short to Thomas Jefferson RICHMOND, MAY 15, 1784

The Assembly have not yet proceeded to active Business. They have formed great Hopes of Mr. Madison, and those who know him best think he will not disappoint their most sanguine Expectations.

Thomas Jefferson to James Madison PARIS, MARCH 18, 1785

Late letters tell us you are nominated for the court of Spain. . . . I need not tell you how much I shall be pleased with such an event. Yet it has its displeasing sides also. I want you in the Virginia Assembly and also in Congress yet we cannot have you everywhere. We must therefore be contended to have you where you choose.

Luigi Castiglioni, Sketches of American Statesmen 1787

He is a man of about 30 years of age, of likable manners and unaffected modesty.

William Pierce, "Character Sketches of Delegates to the Federal
Convention" 1787

Mr. Maddison is a character who has long been in public life; and what is very remarkable every Person seems to acknowledge his greatness. He blends together the profound politician, with the Scholar. In the management of every great question he evidently took the lead in the Convention, and tho' he cannot be called an Orator, he is a most agreeable, eloquent, and convincing Speaker. From a spirit of industry and application which he possesses in a most eminent degree, he always comes forward the best informed Man of any point in debate. The affairs of the United States, he perhaps, has the most correct knowledge of, of any Man in the Union. He has been twice a Member of Congress, and was always thought one of the ablest Members that ever sat in that Council. Mr. Maddison is about 37 years of age, a Gentleman of great modesty,—with a remarkable sweet temper. He is easy and unreserved among his acquaintances, and has a most agreeable style of conversation.

Bushrod Washington to George Washington RICHMOND, JUNE 7, 1788

[In the Virginia ratifying convention.] Mr. Madison followed, and with such force of reasoning, and a display of such irresistible truths, that opposition seemed to have quitted the field. However, I am not so sanguine as to trust appearances, or even to flatter myself that he made many converts. A few I have been confidently informed he did influence, who were decidedly in the opposition.

John Page to James Madison WILLIAMSBURG, AUGUST 6, 1788

Yours of the 27th. Ulto. enclosing the New York Papers, with the joyful News of the Ratification of the Plan of the federal Constitution has just come to Hand. I return you many Thanks for communicating to me so early, an Authentic Account of that important & glorious Event. I heartily congratulate you on the brightening Prospect of our Affairs, & the Success of your Wishes & patriotic Labors—they are crowned with Success, & to your immortal Honor; for it is to you, we are indebted for the Part Virginia took in this great Affair & we see her Influence in the other States. I confess I have always attributed to you the Glory of laying the Foundation of this great Fabric of government; of supporting the Plan of it in Convention & of animating all the States to cooperate in the great Work.

Brissot de Warville, New Travels in the United States of America AUGUST 1788

The name of Madison, famous in America, is also well known in Europe through the amply deserved tributes given him by his fellow countryman and friend, Mr. Jefferson. Although still young, he has rendered important services to Virginia, to the American confederation, and in general to the cause of liberty and humanity. He has contributed much, together with Mr. [Alexander] White, to the reform of the civil and criminal codes of his state, and he distinguished himself particularly at the time that the conventions met to vote on the new Federal Constitution. For a long time Virginia hesitated to join the Union, but by his logic and his eloquence Mr. Madison persuaded the convention to favor acceptance.

This republican seems to be no more than thirty-three years old. When I saw him, he looked tired, perhaps as a result of the immense labors to which he had devoted himself recently. His expression was that of a stern censor; his conversation disclosed a man of learning; and his countenance was that of a person conscious of his talents and of his duties. . . . Mr. Madison [had] the thoughtful look of a wise statesman.

Louis Guillaume Otto, Biographies FALL 1788

Educated, wise, moderate, docile, studious; can be more profound than Mr. Hamilton, but less brilliant; intimate friend of Mr. Jefferson and sincerely attached to France. He has been in Congress since a youth and he seems to be especially dedicated to public affairs. He could one day be governor of his state, if his modesty would allow him to accept this position. In the past he has refused the office of president of Congress. This is a man who must be studied for a long time to form a just opinion of him.

Henry Lee to James Madison ALEXANDRIA, VA., NOVEMBER 19, 1788

You have heard of the election of senators for this state—the friends to the government exerted themselves in your behalf & although you was not chosen, yet you received strong testimonial of the unbounded attachment of one party, & of the excessive jealousy of the other party. Mr. Henry on the floor exclaimed against your political character & pronounced you unworthy of the confidence of the people in the station of Senator. That your election would terminate in producing rivulets of blood throughout the land.

Cyrus Griffin to James Madison NEW YORK, APRIL 14, 1789

We all rejoice greatly at your election [to the U.S. House of Representatives]; indeed, my dear sir, we consider you as the main pillar of the business on the right side.

Fisher Ames to George R. Minot NEW YORK, MAY 3, 1789

Madison is a man of sense, reading, address, and integrity, as 'tis allowed. Very much Frenchified in his politics. He speaks low, his person is little and ordinary. He speaks decently, as to manner, and no more. His language is very pure, perspicuous, and to the point. Pardon me, if I add, that I think him a little too much of a book politician, and too timid in his politics, for prudence and caution are opposites of timidity. He is not a little of a Virginian, and thinks that state the land of promise, but is afraid of their state politics, and of his popularity there, more than I think he should be. . . . He is our first man.

MAY 18, 1789

Madison is cool, and has an air of reflection, which is not very distant from gravity and self-sufficiency. In speaking, he never relaxes into pleasantry, and discovers little of that warmth of heart, which gives efficacy to George Cabot's reasoning, and to [John] Lowell's. His printed speeches are more faithful than any other person's, because he speaks very slow, and his discourse is strongly marked. He states a principle and deduces consequences, with clearness and simplicity. Sometimes declamation is mingled with argument, and he appears very anxious to carry a point by other means than addressing their understandings. He appeals to popular topics, and to the pride of the House, such as that they have voted before, and will be inconsistent. I think him a good man and an able man, but he has rather too much theory, and wants that discretion which men of business commonly have. He is also very timid, and seems evidently to want manly firmness and energy of character.

Abigail Adams to John Adams BRAINTREE, MAY 26, 1789

I read the debates of the House and I have watched a certain character much celebrated and from the whole I have drawn up this conclusion "that he either does not possess so great talents as he has been said to, or he is aiming at popularity, at the expense of his judgment and understanding." Honestus pronounces Mr. Madison the wisest and best man in the house but time will unveil characters. I do not like his politicks nor the narrow jealousy he has discovered.

Fisher Ames to George Richards Minot NEW YORK, MAY 29, 1789

He is probably deficient in that fervor and vigor of character which you will expect in a great man. He is not likely to risk bold measures, like Charles Fox, nor even to persevere in any measures against a firm opposition, like the first Pitt. He derives from nature an excellent understanding, however, but I think he excels in the quality of judgment. He is possessed of a sound judgment, which perceives truth with great clearness, and can trace it through the mazes of debate, without losing it. He is admirable for this inestimable talent. As a reasoner, he is remarkably perspicuous and methodical. He is a studious man, devoted to public business, and a thorough master of almost every public question that can arise, or he will spare no pains to become so, if he happens to be in want of information. What a man understands clearly, and has viewed in every different point of light, he will explain to the admiration of others, who have not thought of it at all, or but little, and who will pay in praise for the pains he saves them. His clear perception of an argument makes him impressive, and persuasive sometimes. It is not his *forte*, however. Upon the whole, he is an useful, respectable, worthy man, in a degree so eminent, that his character will not sink. He will continue to be a very influential man in our country. Let me add, without meaning to detract, that he is too much attached to his theories, for a politician. He is well versed in public life, was bred to it, and has no other profession. Yet, may I say it, it is rather a science, than a business, with him. He adopts his maxims as he finds them in books, and with too little regard to the actual state of things.

JULY 2, 1789

The people of Virginia (whose murmurs, if louder than a whisper, make Mr. Madison's heart quake) . . .

Theodore Sedgwick to Benjamin Lincoln NEW YORK, JULY 19, 1789

Mr. Madison's talents, respectable as they are will for some time be lost to the public, from his timidity. He is constantly haunted with the ghost of Patrick Henry. No man, in my opinion, in this country has more fair and honorable intentions, or more ardently wishes the prosperity of the public, but unfortunately he has not that strength of nerves which will enable him to set at defiance popular and factious clamors.

William Constable to Gouverneur Morris JULY 29, 1789

Many wish you were in the House of Representatives to lead; Madison is too meek to govern.

William L. Smith to Edward Rutledge NEW YORK, AUGUST 9, 1789

Mr. Madison is a great friend to a strong government—his great abilities will always give him much weight with the administration—I believe he now is much in the confidence of the President & he will hereafter stand a chance of being President himself; in the meantime, he will be a leading man in the Cabinet Council. His mildness of character & a certain timidity which accompanies his political conduct render him unfriendly to a republican government.

Robert Morris to Richard Peters NEW YORK, AUGUST 24, 1789

Poor Madison took one wrong step in Virginia by publishing a letter respecting *Amendments* and you, who know every thing, must know what a Cursed thing it is to write *a Book.* He in consequence has been obliged to bring on the proposition for making Amendments; The Waste of precious time is what has vexed me the most, for as to the Nonsense they call Amendments I never expect that any part of it will go through the various Trials which it must pass before it can become a part of the Constitution.

Abigail Adams to Cotton Tufts NEW YORK, SEPTEMBER 1, 1789

Mr. Madison is a very amiable character, a man of virtue & probity.

William Samuel Johnson, Conversation with George Beckwith
NEW YORK, 1789

Mr. Maddison, a Delegate from Virginia took a very active and leading part [in the congressional debates]. He is an Elve of Mr. Jefferson's, who is still our Minister at Paris, and may be esteemed as not exempt from a French bias. . . . and [Madison] being a man of genius and talents, his exertions had a considerable influence.

Theodore Sedgwick to Pamela Sedgwick MARCH 4, 1790

Mr. Madison who is the leader of the opposition is an apostate from all his former principles. Whether he is really a convert to anti-federalism—whether he is actuated by the mean and base motives of acquiring popularity in his own state that he may fill the place of Senator which will probably soon be vacated by the death of Grayson, or whether he means to put himself at the head of the discontented in America time will discover. The last, however, I do not suspect, because I have ever considered him as a very timid man. Deprived of his aid the party would soon be weak and inefficient.

Benjamin Goodhue to Samuel Phillips MARCH 14, 1790

Madison would be an excellent politician if he was not so much warped by local considerations, and popular influences, but with those about him he is a dangerous foe, to those measures which soar above trifling objects, and have national advantages for their basis.

Thomas Hartley to Jasper Yeates NEW YORK, MARCH 14, 1790

He is certainly an extraordinary Man—and when he comes to have a sufficient Knowledge of practical Life—there will be few beyond him.

Benjamin Rush, Commonplace Book MARCH 17, 1790

[Thomas Jefferson on Madison.] He said Mr. Madison "was the greatest man in the world"; that Dr. Witherspoon, his master, had said of him "that he never knew him do or say an improper thing" when at School.

Thomas Lee Shippen to William Shippen APRIL 12, 1790

I am already charmed with Madison. Both before & at dinner yesterday I had a great deal of conversation with him, and I really begin to think that he deserves all his reputation.

John Adams to John Trumbull NEW YORK, APRIL 25, 1790

Mr. Madison is a studious scholar, but his reputation as a man of abilities is a creature of French puffs. Some of the worst measures, some of the most stupid motions stand on record to his infamy. I mean that of compelling American ministers at the peace [negotiations] to tell everything to the French and do nothing without their consent.

Arthur Lee to Thomas Lee Shippen ALEXANDRIA, VA., APRIL 25, 1790

I shall by no means deem you enthusiastic in what you say of Mr. Madison's agreeableness in conversation. I have heard others say the same & as far as I have had experience think with you. It is his political conduct which I condemn. That without being a public knave himself, he has always been the supporter of public knaves, & never, in any one instance has concurred to check, censure, or control them—That he has had such vanity as to suppose himself superior to all other persons, conducting measures without consulting them & intolerant of all advice or contradiction—That in consequence he has been duped by the artful management of the rapacious Morris & the intriguing Marbois. It is possible he may have thought himself right in all this, but in acquitting his intention we hazard the credit of his understanding.

Fisher Ames to John Lowell NEW YORK, MAY 2, 1790

You are acquainted with Mr. Madison, and of course you know that he possesses a most ingenious mind, and extensive learning. He has long been deemed a champion for the Constitution—

Abigail Adams to Cotton Tufts MAY 30, 1790

Madison leads the Virginians like a flock of sheep.

John Trumbull to John Adams JUNE 5, 1790

Maddison's character is certainly not rising in the public estimation. He now acts on a conspicuous stage and does not equal expectation. He becomes more and more a Southern Partisan and loses his assumed candor and moderation. Indeed no man seems to have gained much reputation in the present session of Congress.

Richard Peters to Thomas Jefferson BELMONT, PA., JUNE 20, 1790

I am sorry that Madison, who is a good corrigible Boy a little spoiled by bad Play Mates, should continue to play truant from us [in Congress]. Let me convey my affectionate Regards to him through a Minister of State which he will then receive not for the Value of them but the Channel through which they pass; as if a Man must drink Water, taking it out of a silver Mug at least gives a luxurious Show to the homely Tipple.

George Mason to Thomas Jefferson GUNSTON HALL, JANUARY 10, 1791

I beg the Favor of you to present my best Respects to our Friend Madison. He is one of the few Men, whom from a pretty thorough Acquaintance, I really esteem; though I have been apprehensive some late Difference (and it has only been a late one) on political Questions had caused a Coolness between us.

Alexander Hamilton to Edward Carrington PHILADELPHIA, MAY 26, 1792

Mr. Madison cooperating with Mr. Jefferson . . . have a womanish attachment to France and a womanish resentment against Great Britain.

John Beckley to James Madison PHILADELPHIA, SEPTEMBER 2, 1792

Mr. H[amilton] unequivocally declares, that you are his personal & political enemy.

Catherine Coles to Dolley Payne Todd PHILADELPHIA, JUNE 1, 1794

Now for M—— he told me I might say what I pleas'd to you about him to begin, he thinks so much of you in the day that he has Lost his Tongue, at Night he Dreams of you & Starts in his Sleep a Calling on you to relieve his Flame for he Burns to such an excess that he will be shortly consumed & he hopes that your Heart will be callous to every other swain but himself he has Consented to every thing that I have wrote about him with Sparkling Eyes.

William W. Wilkins to Dolley Payne Todd PHILADELPHIA, AUGUST 22, 1794

Mr. M——n is a Man whom I admire. I knew his Attachment to you and did not therefore content myself with taking his Character from the Breath of popular Applause—but consulted those who knew him intimately in private Life. His personal Character therefore I have every reason to believe is good and amiable. He unites to the great Talents which have secured him public Approbation those engaging Qualities that contribute so highly to domestic Felicity. To such a Man therefore I do most freely consent that my beloved Sister be united and happy.

Edward Livingston to Robert R. Livingston PHILADELPHIA, DECEMBER 24, 1795

His great fault as a politician appears to me a want of decision and a disposition to magnify his adversaries strength. [He has] a habit of considering the objections to his own plans so long and so frequently that they acquire a real weight & influence his conduct. . . . He never determines to act until he is absolutely forced by the pressure of affairs & then regrets that he has neglected some better opportunity. . . . He is a very amiable very well informed, and I believe one of the most honest & upright men this country possesses.

John Adams to Abigail Adams PHILADELPHIA, APRIL 28, 1796

Mr. Madison looks worried to death. Pale, withered, haggard.

JANUARY 14, 1797

Mr. Madison is to retire. It Seems, the Mode of becoming great is to retire. Madison I Suppose after a Retirement of a few Years is to be President or V.P. . . . It is marvelous how political Plants grow in the shade. Continual Day light and sun shine, Show our Faults and record them. Our Persons, Voices, Clothes, Gate, Air, Sentiments, &c. all become familiar to every Eye and Ear and Understanding and they diminish in Proportion, upon the same Principle that no Man is an Hero to his Wife or Valet de Chamber.

Thomas Jefferson to Peregrine Fitzhugh MONTICELLO, APRIL 9, 1797

As no man weighs more maturely than Mr. Madison before he takes a side on any question, I do not expect he has changed either his opinion on that subject, or the expressions of it, and therefore I presume the allegation founded in some misconception or misinformation.

Fisher Ames to Oliver Wolcott Jr. DEDHAM, MASS., JANUARY 2, 1800

The extreme sensibility of the good men in Virginia to silly principles and silly people, has ever been characteristic. Madison crept into the first Congress by some declarations in print, which made some persons say then, there was not room for him to crawl through with his principles, and therefore he was forced to crawl without them.

Charles Pinckney to James Madison CHARLESTON, OCTOBER 26, 1800

I have had your Portrait sent me for my Drawing room—it is a Most exact likeness in the face—But makes you about the Body much fatter than when I saw you. If it is so I suppose you have thriven upon Matrimony & find it a good thing.

Margaret Bayard Smith to Susan B. Smith WASHINGTON, D.C., MAY 26, 1801

I admire the simplicity and mildness of Mr. M's manners, and his smile has so much benevolence in it, that it cannot fail of inspiring good will and esteem.

John Adams to Benjamin Rush AUGUST 23, 1805

When I first took the chair, I was extremely desirous of availing myself of Mr. Madison's abilities, experience, reputation, and amiable qualities. But the violent party spirit of Hamilton's friends, jealous of every man who possessed qualifications to eclipse him, prevented it.

William Plumer, Memoranda MARCH 16, 1806

It seems that Mr. Jefferson & his friends wish that Mr. Madison should succeed to the presidency. John Randolph is against Madison—& the avowed advocate of James Monroe.

Mr. Madison has some talents—but he wants nerve—timid & inefficient—in short he is not a practical man.—And that is a declaration that he is not qualified for the office.

MARCH 19, 1806

Mr. [John] Randolph most explicitly declared that most of the evils which the United States now suffered proceeded from the measures of the Executive—& from the weak feeble and pusillanimous spirit of the keeper of the Cabinet—the Secretary of State.

APRIL 8, 1806

But said [John] Adair, the President wants nerve—he has not even confidence in himself—For more than a year he has been in the habit of trusting almost implicitly in Mr. Madison. Madison has acquired a complete ascendancy over him. I observed that I considered Mr. M. as an honest man—but that he was too cautious—too fearful & timid to direct the affairs of this nation. He replied that is my opinion of the man.

APRIL 11, 1806

Mr. [Nicholas] Gilman told me that he believed the President was an honest man—but he wanted firmness—That Mr. Madison was much more timid—& yet he governed the President—That he consulted the other heads of department but little.

Thomas Jefferson to Henry Guest WASHINGTON, D.C., JANUARY 4, 1809

I have the comfort too of knowing that the person whom the public choice has designated to receive the charge from me, is eminently qualified as a safe depository by the endowments of integrity, understanding, and experience.

John Adams to Benjamin Rush MAY 14, 1812

My confidence in the integrity of Mr. Jefferson and Mr. Madison, in their love of their country and the sincerity of their desires to serve its interests and promote its prosperity, is still entire. Of their genius, talents, learning, industry I am fully convinced, as all the rest of the world is. But either they are shallow statesmen or I am a natural fool. There is no other alternative or dilemma. Mr. Madison has more correct ideas; but as he has been borne up under the wing of Mr. Jefferson, he has been always shackled with Mr. Jefferson's visions and prejudices.

Rufus King to Christopher Gore JAMAICA, N.Y., SEPTEMBER 9, 1812

The imbecility of Madison is daily more manifest, still his friends and party in general adhere to him.

Gouverneur Morris to James Parish MARCH 6, 1813

When I read Mr. Madison's message [his second inaugural address] I supposed him to be out of his senses, and have since been told that he never goes sober to bed. Whether intoxicated by opium or wine was not said, but I learned last winter that pains in his teeth had driven him to use the former too freely.

John Adams to Richard Rush QUINCY, SEPTEMBER 6, 1813

I rejoice that Mr. Madison's Health continues to improve, especially as it confutes an afflicting Report, that he lives by laudanum and could not hold out four months. His Life is of great Importance. The malicious report is contradicted and now understood by the Public, to be false.

DECEMBER 12, 1813
I have read the Message of the President which flew from Washington to Quincy on the Wings of the wind. It is written with his masterly Pen and his deliberate mind. A candid statement, in chaste and elegant style. It is not in that mortal, more than this, to command success, but as far as I can see he has deserved it.

Daniel Webster to Ezekiel Webster WASHINGTON, D.C., NOVEMBER 21, 1814

There is an utter want of confidence in Madison, & his advisers, on all sides.

Thomas Jefferson, Autobiography

Mr. Madison came into the House in 1776. A new member and young; which circumstances, concurring with his extreme modesty, prevented his venturing himself in debate before his removal to the Council of State in Nov. 77. From thence he went to Congress, then consisting of few members. Trained in these successive schools, he acquired a habit of self-possession which placed at ready command the rich resources of his luminous and discriminating mind, & of his extensive information, and rendered him the first of every assembly afterwards of which he became a member. Never wandering from his subject into vain declamation, but pursuing it closely in language pure, classical, and copious, soothing always the feelings of his adversaries by civilities and softness of expression, he rose to the eminent station which he held in the great National convention of 1787, and in that of Virginia which followed, he sustained the new constitution in all its parts, bearing off the palm against the logic of George Mason, and the fervid declamation of Mr. Henry. With these consummate powers were united a pure and spotless virtue which no calumny has ever attempted to sully. Of the powers and polish of his pen, and of the wisdom of his administration in the highest office of the nation, I need say nothing. They have spoken, and will forever speak for themselves.

Thomas Jefferson to James Madison MONTICELLO, FEBRUARY 17, 1826

The friendship which has subsisted between us, now half a century, and the harmony of our political principles and pursuits, have been sources of constant happiness to me through that long period. And if I remove beyond the reach of attentions to the University [of Virginia], or beyond the bourne of life itself, as I soon must, it is a comfort to leave that institution under your care, and an assurance that it will not be wanting. It has also been a great solace to me, to believe that you are engaged in vindicating to posterity the course we have pursued for preserving to them, in all their purity, the blessings of self-government, which we had assisted too in acquiring for them. If ever the earth has beheld a system of administration conducted with a single and steadfast eye to the general interest and happiness of those committed to it, one which, protected by truth, can never know reproach, it is that to which our lives have been devoted. To myself you have been a pillar of support through life. Take care of me when dead, and be assured that I shall leave with you my last affections.

Margaret Bayard Smith to Mrs. Boyd SIDNEY, VA., AUGUST 17, 1828

I could scarcely credit my senses, when dinner was announced and I found it to be four o'clock! So rapidly had the morning passed away. We did not rise from table until six o'clock, when we separated for the night, so rich in sentiments and facts, so enlivened by anecdotes and epigrammatic remarks, so frank and confidential as to opinions on men and measures, that it had an interest and charm, which the conversation of few men now living, could have. He spoke of scenes in which he himself had acted a conspicuous part and of great men, who had been actors in the same theater. No common-places. Every sentence he spoke, was worthy of being written down. The formation and adoption of the Constitution. The Convention and first congress, the characters of their members and the secret debates. Franklin, Washington, Hamilton, John Adams, Jefferson, Jay, Patrick Henry and a host of other great men were spoken of and characteristic anecdotes of all related. It was living History! When I retired for the night, I felt as if my mind was full to over-flowing, as if it could not contain all the new ideas it had received, as if I had feasted to satiety. And this entertaining, interesting and communicative personage, had a single stranger or indifferent person been present, would have been mute, cold and repulsive. After dinner, we all walked in the Portico (or piazza, which is 60 feet long, supported on six lofty pillars) until twilight, then retreated to the drawing room, where we sat in a little group close together and took our coffee while we talked. Some of Mr. M's anecdotes were very droll, and we often laughed very heartily. I wish my letter was large enough to contain a few of them, which I am sure would make you laugh too. He retains all the sportiveness of his character, which he used to reveal now and then to those whom he knew intimately, and Mrs. M says he is as fond of a frolic and of romping with the girls as ever. His little blue eyes sparkled like stars from under his bushy grey eye-brows and amidst the deep wrinkles of his poor thin face. Nor have they lost their look of mischief, that used to lurk in their corners, and which vanished and gave place to an expression ever solemn, when the conversation took a serious turn.

Robert Scott, Diary OCTOBER 26, 1829

[Madison was] in tolerably good health, thin of flesh, rather under the common size, and dressed in his customary black, old-fashioned clothes. His form erect, his step firm but somewhat slow, walks without a staff, his visage pale, and abounding in small wrinkles, his features well-proportioned but not striking, his head bald on the top but excessively powdered showing a point in front. . . . His forehead of common size, his brow grey, heavy, and projecting, his eyes small and faded, his nose of ordinary size and straight, his mouth rather small, ... his ears obscured by whiskers and hair, his sight and hearing both somewhat impaired.

Jared Sparks, Journal APRIL 23, 1830

I have passed five delightful days at Mr. Madison's. The situation of his residence is charming. The blossoms and verdure of the trees are just springing into perfection, and the scenery, embracing a distant view of the Blue Ridge, is commanding and beautiful. But I have had little time for these objects. . . . The intellect and memory of Mr. Madison appear to retain all their pristine vigor. He is peculiarly interesting in conversation, cheerful, gay, and full of anecdote; never a prosing talker, but sprightly, varied, fertile in his topics, and felicitous in his descriptions and illustrations. He seems busy in arranging his papers. While he was in the old Congress he rarely kept copies of his letters, though he wrote many. He has recently succeeded in procuring nearly all the originals from the descendants of the persons to whom he wrote them.

James Madison to Mrs. Margaret Bayard Smith SEPTEMBER 1830

I ought, perhaps, to have another fear, that of being charged with affectation in the microscopic hand in which I write. But the explanation is easy: the fingers, stiffened by age, make smaller strokes, as the feet from the same cause take shorter steps. I hope you will live to verify my sincerity.

Joseph Story to Ezekiel Bacon CAMBRIDGE, MASS., APRIL 30, 1842

I entirely concur with you in your estimate of Mr. Madison—his private virtues, his extraordinary talents, his comprehensive and statesman-like views. To him and Hamilton I think we are mainly indebted for the Constitution of the United States, and in wisdom I have long been accustomed to place him before Jefferson. You and I know something more of each of them in trying times, than the common politicians of our day can possibly arrive at. I wish some one who was perfectly fitted for the task, would write a full accurate biography of Madison. I fear that it can hardly be done now; for the men who best appreciated his excellences have nearly all passed away.

John Marshall
1755–1835

⊰ Born near Germantown, Fauquier County, Va. Officer in militia and Continental army, 1775–81 (inactive after 1779). Briefly attended College of William and Mary (Phi Beta Kappa, 1780). Represented Fauquier County, 1782, 1784–85; Henrico County, 1787–88; Richmond City, 1789–91, 1795–97, in Virginia House of Delegates. Member, Council of State, 1782–84. Henrico County delegate to Virginia Convention, voted to ratify the Constitution, June 1788. U.S. diplomatic commissioner to France, 1797–98. U.S. representative, 1799–1800. U.S. secretary of state under President John Adams, 1800–1801. Chief justice of the United States, 1801–35. Member, Virginia constitutional convention, 1829–30.

Philip Slaughter, *Account of Marshall at Valley Forge*

He was the best-tempered man I ever knew. During his sufferings at Valley Forge nothing discouraged, nothing disturbed him. If he had only bread to eat, it was just as well; if only meat, it made no difference. If any of the officers murmured at their deprivations he would shame them by good-natured raillery, or encourage them by his own exuberance of spirits. He was an excellent companion, and idolized by the soldiers and his brother officers, whose gloomy hours were enlivened by his inexhaustible fund of anecdotes.

John Marshall to Thomas Posey SMITH'S CLOVE, N.Y.,
SEPTEMBER 1, 1779

When the Man who possesses a great, a generous Soul has in-
advertently injured another he will not stop at barely giving him
such satisfaction as will prevent his discovering resentment. He
will repair the injury in the most ample manner imaginable.

Edmund Pendleton to James Madison VIRGINIA, NOVEMBER
25, 1782

Mr. Marshall is elected a Counsellor in the room of Mr. Bannister
who resigned: he is clever, but I think too young for that department, which he should rather have earned as a retirement & reward by 10 or 12 years hard service in the Assembly.

Edmund Randolph to James Madison PETTUS'S, VA.,
NOVEMBER 29, 1782

Capt. Marshall, a promising young gentleman of the law, is
elected into the privy council.

Thomas Jefferson to James Madison PHILADELPHIA, JUNE 29,
1792

I learn that he [Alexander Hamilton] has expressed the strongest desire that Marshall should come into Congress from Richmond, declaring there is no man in Virginia whom he wishes so
much to see there, and I am told that Marshall has expressed half
a mind to come. Hence I conclude that Hamilton has plied him
well with flattery & solicitation, and I think nothing better could
be done than to make him a judge.

George Mason to John Mason GUNSTON HALL, JULY 5, 1792

I beg you will talk with Mr. John Marshall, upon the Subject
of my Suit in the high Court of Chancery against John Hooe,
Banbury & others, & enquire whether it was called & put off at
the last Term. . . . I expected it wou'd have been tried at the last
Term; and am afraid it is neglected by Mr. Marshall; who tho' a
very worthy Man, is an indolent one.

Benjamin Henry Latrobe, Journals MAY 31, 1796

John Marshall (a general of Militia) is inferior to Edmund Randolph in voice and manner. But for talent he substitutes genius,

and instead of talking *about* his subject he talks *upon* it. He possesses neither the energy of expression, nor the sublimity of imagination of [James] Innes, but he is superior to every other orator at the bar of Virginia in closeness of argument, in his most surprising talent of placing his case in that point of view best suited to the purpose he aims at, of throwing a blaze of light upon it, and of keeping the attention of his hearers fixed upon the object to which he originally directed it. He speaks to the man of plain common sense, while he delights and informs the most acute. In a less captivating line of oratory than that which signalizes Innes, he is equally great, and equally successful. The jury obey *Innes* from inclination and *Marshall* from duty.

Abigail Adams to Mary Cranch PHILADELPHIA, JUNE 3, 1797

Mr. Marshall of Virginia is said to be a very fair and Honorable man, and truly American, a Lawyer by profession, against whom no objection is offered, but that he is not Frenchman enough for those who would have sent Jefferson or Madison, [William Branch] Giles or even [Charles] Jarvis.

George Washington to Charles Cotesworth Pinckney MOUNT VERNON, JUNE 24, 1797

This letter will be handed to you by Genl. Marshall, who with Mr. [Elbridge] Gerry joint Envoys with yourself, to try if the difference between France & America can be amicably adjusted. You will find him well worthy of your friendship & confidence. He is a firm friend, upon true principles to his country—sensible & discreet.

George Washington to the Comte de Ségur MOUNT VERNON, JUNE 24, 1797

He is a man of great worth, and of the best disposition.

Abigail Adams to John Quincy Adams PHILADELPHIA, JULY 14, 1797

You will find in Genl. Marshall a sensible upright honest man.

John Adams to Elbridge Gerry PHILADELPHIA, JULY 17, 1797

[Adams found Marshall] a plain Man, very Sensible, cautious, guarded, learned in the Law of Nations. I think you will be pleased with him.

Rufus King to Charles Cotesworth Pinckney LONDON,
OCTOBER 17, 1797

You will be satisfied with General Marshall; his character stands
well on all points. I know little of him, but his head is one of the
best organized of any one that I have known. This I say from general Reputation, and more satisfactorily from an Argument that I
heard him deliver before the federal Court at Philadelphia.

William Vans Murray to John Quincy Adams THE HAGUE,
FEBRUARY 20, 1798

I have not seen much of General P[inckney]'s or G[erry]'s, or
Marshall's writing, but I consider Marshall, whom I have heard
speak on a great subject, as one of the most powerful reasoners I
ever met with in public or in print. Reasoning in such cases will
have a fine effect in America; but to depend upon it in Europe is
really to place Quixote with Genes de Passamente and among
the men of the world whom he reasoned with so sublimely on
their way to the gallies. They answer him, you know, with stones
and blows, though the knight is an *armed,* as well as an eloquent
knight.

Charles Cotesworth Pinckney to Rufus King PARIS, APRIL 4,
1798

General Marshall is a man of extensive ability, of manly candor
and an honest heart.

Julian Ursyn Niemcewicz, Travels through America JUNE
1798

In the evening with the sound of bells, amidst an escort of militia on horseback and on foot and a crowd of people, General
Marshall, one of the commissioners dismissed from Paris, arrived. The more trouble he received in France and the less honor
that he was accorded, the more, on his return, the people with
public show, with honor and respect, have tried to sweeten the
humiliations long undergone. General Marshall is a man of more
than 40 years, quite handsome and one could recognize in his
bearing that he had breathed the air of Paris. In talent, expression and humor he probably surpasses his colleagues Pinckney
and Gerry, and therefore the Directory did not care for him and

dismissed him. I was presented to him. In the evening the town gave him a splendid supper.

The next day, in the morning, when I was getting on the public stage, the very same Mr. Marshall, ambassador extraordinary who, here as everywhere he went, had been greeted with show and pomp was now leaving with bag in hand, and seeing that every seat was occupied, he sat quietly on the seat next to the coachman.

Timothy Pickering to John Adams TRENTON, SEPTEMBER 20, 1798

I shall also this day write to General Marshall to inform him that you have designated him to fill the vacant seat, and urge his acceptance of it: probably no appointment would be more universally approved: but I am sorry to think there is little chance of his gratifying what must be the public wish as well as yours: in a word, there is little hope that an eminent lawyer, in the full tide of practice at the bar, and receiving eight or ten thousand dollars a year, will relinquish it for the meager reward of thirty five hundred dollars, a large part of which must be expended in travelling expenses. The case might be different, if Genl. Marshall was weary of the toils and vexations of business at the bar; or if he possessed a very independent fortune.

John Marshall, To "A Freeholder," Fredericksburg Virginia Herald OCTOBER 2, 1798

I am not an advocate for the alien and sedition bills: had I been in Congress when they passed, I should, unless my judgment could have been changed, certainly have opposed them. Yet, I do not think them fraught with all those mischiefs which many gentlemen ascribe to them. I should have opposed them, because I think them useless; and because they are calculated to create, unnecessarily, discontents and jealousies at a time when our very existence, as a nation, may depend on our union—I believe that these laws, had they been opposed on these principles by a man, not suspected of intending to destroy the government, or of being hostile to it, would never have been enacted. With respect to their repeal, the effort will be made before I can become a member of Congress. If it succeeds, there will be an end of the business—if it fails, I shall, on the question of renewing the effort, should I be chosen to represent the district, obey the voice of my constituents. My own private opinion is, that it will be unwise to renew it for this reason: The laws will expire of themselves, if I recollect rightly the time for which they are enacted, during the term of the ensuing Congress. I shall, indisputably, oppose their revival; and I believe that opposition will be more successful, if men's minds are not too much irritated by the struggle about a repeal of laws which will, at the time, be expiring of themselves.

George Cabot to Timothy Pickering BROOKLINE, MASS., OCTOBER 31, 1798

Mr. Marshall has given great uneasiness here by his answers to the "Freeholder"; and Gerry takes advantage of it to enforce the belief that Marshall's politics will not prove sound according to New England ideas, and he is confident "that Marshall will not in Congress act with New England men, *whom he holds in great contempt.*" I do not yet believe this. Mr. Marshall I know has much to learn on the subject of a practicable system of free government for the United States. I believe, however, he is a man of so much sense that, with honest principles, he cannot fail to discern and pursue a right course, and therefore that he will eventually prove a great acquisition.

Timothy Pickering to George Cabot TRENTON, NOVEMBER 10, 1798

I hope Marshall may get into Congress. His general politics are well known, and his integrity is unblemished. He will assuredly act with the intelligent New England men.

George Cabot to Timothy Pickering BROOKLINE, MASS., NOVEMBER 24, 1798

I concur fully with you in the sentiments that his merit is of the first order, and that he is to be cherished as a most precious acquisition to the cause of order, morality, and good government.

John Marshall to George Washington RICHMOND, JANUARY 8, 1799

I am by no means certain who will be elected for this district. Whatever the issue of the election may be, I shall neither reproach myself nor those at whose instance I have become a candidate, for the step I have taken, I feel with increased force the obligation of duty to make sacrifices and exertions for the preservation of American Union and independence, as I am more convinced of the reality of the danger which threatens them. The exertions made against me by particular characters throughout this State and even from other states have an activity and a malignity which no personal considerations would excite. If I fail I shall regret the failure more on account of the evidence it will afford of the prevalence of a temper hostile to our government and indiscriminately so to all who will not join in that hostility, than of the personal mortification which would be sustained.

George Cabot to Rufus King APRIL 26, 1799

I am ready to join you as well as Ames in reprobating the publication of Marshall's sentiments on the Sedition & Alien Acts, but I still *adhere* to my first opinion that Marshall ought not to be attacked in the Newspapers, nor too severely condemned anywhere, because Marshall has not yet learned his whole lesson but has a mind & disposition which can hardly fail to make him presently an accomplished Scholar & a very useful man. Some allowance too should be made for the influence of the Atmosphere of Virginia which doubtless makes every one who breathes it visionary &, upon the subject of Free Government, incredibly credulous; but it is certain that Marshall at Philadelphia would become a most powerful auxiliary to the cause of order & good Government, & *therefore* we ought not to diminish his fame which would ultimately be a loss to ourselves.

Theodore Sedgwick to Rufus King STOCKBRIDGE, MASS., JULY 26, 1799

General Marshall you know is a member of the House of Representatives. His talents, his character and the situation he has been in, will combine to give him an influence, which will be further aided by the scene which he immediately represents. He may and probably will give a tone to the federal politics South of the Susquehannah. I well know the respect he entertains for you and for your opinions. I have brought this subject to your mind that you may decide on the propriety of a communication of your sentiments to him, which you may do in season to be useful. Should he, which, indeed, I do not expect, conform his public declaration relative to the alien & sedition acts, it would have been better that his insignificant predecessor should have been reelected. There never has been an instance where the commencement of a political career was so important as is that of General Marshall.

Oliver Wolcott Jr. to Fisher Ames PHILADELPHIA, DECEMBER 29, 1799

A number of distinguished men appear from the southward [in Congress], who are not pledged by any act to support the system of the last Congress; these men will pay great respect to the opinions of General Marshall; he is doubtless a man of virtue and distinguished talents, but he will think much of the State of Virginia, and is too much disposed to govern the world according to rules of logic; he will read and expound the constitution as if it were a penal statute, and will sometimes be embarrassed with doubts of which his friends will not perceive the importance.

Theodore Sedgwick to Rufus King PHILADELPHIA, DECEMBER 29, 1799

I have been much in Company with General Marshall since we arrived in this City. He possesses great powers and has much dexterity in the application of them. He is highly & deservedly respected by the friends of the Government from the South. In short we can do nothing without him. I believe his intentions are perfectly honorable, & yet I do believe he would have been a more decided man had his education been on the other side of the Delaware, and he the immediate representative of that country.

George Cabot to Rufus King JANUARY 20, 1800

In Congress, you see Genl. M. is a leader. He is I think a virtuous & certainly an able man; but you see in him the faults of a Virginian. He thinks too much of that State, & he expects the world will be governed according to the Rules of Logic. I have seen such men often become excellent legislators after experience has cured their errors. I hope it will prove so with Genl. M. who seems calculated to act a great part.

George Cabot to Christopher Gore JANUARY 21, 1800

You see General Marshall leads in Congress. He doubtless has great talents and I believe great virtues; but I fear he is not yet a politician, and has much to learn on the subject of *practicable* theories of free government.

Theodore Sedgwick to Rufus King PHILADELPHIA, FEBRUARY 6, 1800

This gentleman is, as you know, a man of fine talents, and I have no doubt, of perfect honor and integrity, but like all the men I have seen from that State, who have talents, too much guided by the refinements of Theory.

MAY 11, 1800

Marshall was looked up to as the man whose great and commanding genius was to enlighten & direct the national councils. This was the general sentiment, while some, and those of no inconsiderable importance, calculating on his foolish declaration, relative to the alien & sedition laws, thought him temporizing, while others deemed him feeble. None had in my opinion justly appreciated his character. As his character has stamped itself on the measures of the present session, I am desirous of letting you know how I view it. He is a man of a very affectionate disposition, of great simplicity of manners and honest & honorable in all his conduct. He is attached to pleasures, with convivial habits strongly fixed. He is indolent, therefore, and indisposed to take part in the common business of the house. He has a strong attachment to popularity but indisposed to sacrifice to it his integrity; hence it is that he is disposed on all popular subjects to feel the public pulse and hence results indecision and *an expression* of doubt. Doubts suggested by him create in more feeble minds those which are irremovable. He is disposed to the erotic refinement, and to express great respect for the sovereign people, and to quote their opinions as an evidence of truth. The latter is of all things the most destructive of personal independence & of that weight of character which a great man ought to possess. This gentleman, when aroused, has strong reasoning powers; they are indeed almost unequalled. But before they are excited; he has frequently, nearly, destroyed any impression from them.

STOCKBRIDGE, MASS., SEPTEMBER 26, 1800

The appointment of Marshall as Secretary of State was a fortunate event—I believe there is not a man in the U.S. of better intentions, and he has the confidence of all good men—no man regrets more than does he the disunion which has taken place, and no one would do more to heal the wounds inflicted by it. In a letter which I received from him a few days since he says, "by union we can securely maintain our ground—without it we must sink & with us all sound, correct American principle." His efforts will, I fear, prove ineffectual.

James McHenry to Oliver Wolcott Jr. BALTIMORE, NOVEMBER 9, 1800

I have been told Mr. Marshall has signified that he does not mean to resign [as secretary of state] in the event of Mr. Jefferson being elected President, but to wait most patiently the development of his politics. Will there, my friend, be so great an antipathy between the politics of the two gentlemen, that one of them must fly off from the other?

Oliver Wolcott Jr. to James McHenry WASHINGTON, D.C., NOVEMBER 26, 1800

The issue of the election in uncertain, but if Mr. Jefferson should be chosen, Mr. Marshall will certainly retire [as secretary of state]. The opposition of sentiment between these men appears to be decided, and I believe is unchangeable; what you have heard is therefore a mistake.

William Paterson to Jonathan Dayton NEW BRUNSWICK, N.J., JANUARY 25, 1801

Your letter of the 17th of this month I had the honor of receiving today. With respect to the office of chief-justice, I have always considered myself as being out of the question. I long ago made up my mind on the subject, and have invariably and repeatedly declared, that if appointed to that office I would not accept. This opinion was the result of due deliberation. After this, if the president had put my name in nomination I should have considered it a complimental thing, a mere feather, which might tickle a vain mind, but which I neither wished nor wanted. Mr. Marshall is a man of genius, of strong reasoning powers, and a sound, correct lawyer. His talents have at once the lustre and solidity of gold. I have no doubt, that he will discharge the duties of the office with ability and honor. But notwithstanding the nomination was unexpected, because the late president laid it down for a rule, which I presumed the present had adopted, not to select two judges from the same state. In casting about, therefore, for a chief-justice, I did not take Virginia into view, but supposed that a gentleman of another state would have been chosen.

William Wirt, The Letters of the British Spy 1804

The Chief Justice of the United States is in his person tall, meager, emaciated; his muscles so relaxed as not only to disqualify him apparently for any vigorous exertion of body, but to destroy everything like harmony in his air and movements. Indeed, in his whole appearance and demeanor, dress, attitude, gesture, sitting, standing, or walking he is as far removed from the idolized graces of Lord Chesterfield as any other gentleman on earth. His head and face are small in proportion to his height; his complexion swarthy; the muscles of his face, being relaxed, make him appear to be fifty years of age, nor can he be much younger. His countenance has a faithful expression of great good humor and hilarity, while his black eyes, that unerring index, possess an irradiating spirit, which proclaims the imperial powers of the mind that sits enthroned within.

Benjamin Rush to John Adams JULY 11, 1806

He is candid and upright.

Joseph Story to Samuel P. P. Fay WASHINGTON, D.C., FEBRUARY 25, 1808

Marshall is of a tall, slender figure, not graceful nor imposing, but erect and steady. His hair is black, his eyes small and twinkling, his forehead rather low, but his features are in general harmonious. His manners are plain, yet dignified; and an unaffected modesty diffuses itself through all his actions. His dress is very simple, yet neat; his language chaste, but hardly elegant; it does not flow rapidly, but it seldom wants precision. In conversation he is quite familiar, but is occasionally embarrassed by a hesitancy and drawling. His thoughts are always clear and ingenious, sometimes striking, and not often inconclusive; he possesses great subtilty of mind, but it is only occasionally exhibited. I love his laugh,—it is too hearty for an intriguer,—and his good temper and unwearied patience are equally agreeable on the bench and in the study. His genius is, in my opinion, vigorous and powerful, less rapid than discriminating, and less vivid than uniform in its light. He examines the intracacies of a subject with calm and persevering circumspection, and unravels the mysteries with irresistible acuteness. He has not the majesty and compactness of thought of Dr. Johnson; but in subtle logic he is no unworthy disciple of David Hume.

Thomas Jefferson to John Adams MONTICELLO, JANUARY 24, 1814

Our cunning Chief Justice would swear to, and find as many sophisms to twist it out of the general terms of our Declarations of rights, and even the stricter text of the Virginia "act for the freedom of religion" as he did to twist Burr's neck out of the halter of treason.

Daniel Webster to Ezekiel Webster WASHINGTON, D.C., MARCH 28, 1814

There is no man in the Court, that strikes one like Marshall. He is a plain man, looking very much like Col. Adams, & about 3 inches taller. I never have seen a man of whose intellect I had a higher opinion.

Thomas Jefferson to William Johnson MONTICELLO, JUNE 12, 1823

This practice of Judge Marshall, of travelling out of his case to prescribe what the law would be in a moot case not before the court, is very irregular and very censurable.

John Adams to John Marshall QUINCEY, AUGUST 17, 1825

There is no part of my Life that I look back upon with more pleasure, than the short time I spent with you. And it is the pride of my life that I have given to this nation a Chief Justice equal to Coke or Hale, Holt or Mansfield.

John Marshall to Mary W. Marshall WASHINGTON, D.C.,
FEBRUARY 12, 1826

I am settled down in my old habits as regularly as if I was still on the right side of seventy. I get up as early as ever, take my walk of three miles by seven, think of you, & then set down to business.

Joseph Story to Charles Sumner WASHINGTON, D.C., FEBRUARY
6, 1833

Chief Justice Marshall is in excellent health, never better, and as firm and robust in mind as in body. He will, I think, justify the remark made of Dr. Franklin, when he was above eighty, that he still remained the ornament of human nature. I deem his life invaluable; for his knowledge of constitutional law, his weight of character, his purity of life, and his devotion to the Union, have gained for him a public confidence, which, in the present crisis of our affairs, cannot be supplied by any other man in the country.

Joseph Story to Samuel P. P. Fay WASHINGTON, D.C., MARCH
2, 1835

Chief Justice Marshall still possesses his intellectual powers in very high vigor. But his physical strength is manifestly on the decline; and it is now obvious, that after a year or two, he will resign, from the pressing infirmities of age. . . . What a gloom will spread over the nation when he is gone! His place will not, nay, it cannot be supplied.

Joseph Story, Eulogy BOSTON, OCTOBER 15, 1835

When can we expect to be permitted to behold again so much moderation united with so much firmness, so much sagacity with so much modesty, so much learning with so much experience, so much solid wisdom with so much purity, so much of every thing, to love and admire, with nothing, absolutely nothing, to regret? What, indeed, strikes us as the most remarkable in his whole character, even more than his splendid talents, is the entire consistency of his public life and principles. There is nothing in either which calls for apology or concealment. Ambition has never seduced him from his principles, nor popular clamor deterred him from the strict performance of duty. Amid the extravagances of party spirit, he has stood with a calm and steady inflexibility; neither bending to the pressure of adversity, nor bounding with the elasticity of success. He has lived, as such a man should live, (and yet, how few deserve the commendation!) by and with his principles. Whatever changes of opinion have occurred, in the course of his long life, have been gradual and slow; the results of genius acting upon larger materials, and of judgment matured by the lessons of experience. If we were tempted to say, in one word, what it was, in which he chiefly excelled other men, we should say, in wisdom; in the union of that virtue, which has ripened under the hardy discipline of principles, with that knowledge, which has constantly sifted and refined its old treasures, and as constantly gathered new. The constitution, since its adoption, owes more to him than to any other single mind, for its true interpretation and vindication. Whether it lives or perishes, his exposition of its principles will be an enduring monument to his fame, as long as solid reasoning, profound analysis, and sober views of government, shall invite the leisure, or command the attention of statesmen and justice.

But, interesting as it is to contemplate such a man in his public character and official functions, there are those, who dwell with far more delight upon his private and domestic qualities. There are few great men, to whom one is brought near, however dazzling may be their talents or actions, who are not thereby painfully diminished in the estimate of those who approach them. The mist of distance sometimes gives a looming size to their character; but more often conceals its defects. To be amiable, as well as great; to be kind, gentle, simple, modest, and social, and at the same time to possess the rarest endowments of mind, and the warmest affections,—is a union of qualities, which the fancy may fondly portray, but the sober realities of life rarely establish. Yet it may be affirmed by those who have had the privilege of intimacy with Mr. Chief Justice Marshall, that he rises, rather than falls, with the nearest survey; and that in the domestic circle he is exactly what a wife, a child, a brother, and a friend would most desire. In that magical circle, admiration of his talents is forgotten, in the indulgence of those affections and sensibilities, which are awakened only to be gratified.

James Monroe
1758–1831

⊀ BORN IN Westmoreland County, Va. Attended College of William and Mary, 1774–76. Militia and Continental army officer, 1775–78. Studied law under Thomas Jefferson, admitted to bar, 1786. Represented King George County, 1782, Spotsylvania County, 1787–89, and Albemarle County, 1810–11, in House of Delegates. Member, Council of State, 1782–83. Delegate to Congress, 1783–86. Delegate Virginia Convention, voted against ratifying the Constitution, 1788. U.S. senator, 1790–94. Minister plenipotentiary to France, 1794–96. Governor of Virginia, 1799–1802, 1811. Special envoy to France, helped negotiate Louisiana Purchase, 1803. U.S. secretary of state, 1811–17; U.S. secretary of war, 1814–15. President of the United States, 1817–25. President, Virginia constitutional convention, 1829–30.

Alexander Hamilton to John Laurens MIDDLEBROOK, N.J., MAY 22, 1779

Monroe is just setting out from Head Quarters and proposes to go in quest of adventures to the Southward. He seems to be as much of a knight errant as your worship; but as he is an honest fellow, I shall be glad he may find some employment, that will enable him to get knocked in the head in an honorable way. He will relish your black scheme* if any thing handsome can be done for

*Laurens was trying to get congressional and state approval to raise black battalions.

him in that line. You know him to be a man of honor a sensible man and a soldier. This makes it unnecessary to me to say any thing to interest your friendship for him. You love your country too and he has zeal and capacity to serve it.

George Washington to Archibald Cary MAY 30, 1779

I very sincerely lament that the situation of our service will not permit us to do justice to the merits of Major Monroe, who will deliver you this, by placing him in the army upon some satisfactory footing. But as he is on the point of leaving us, and expresses an intention of going to the Southward, where a new scene has opened, it is with pleasure I take occasion to express to you the high opinion I have of his worth. The zeal he discovered by entering the service at an early period, the character he supported in his regiment, and the manner in which he distinguished himself at Trenton, when he received a wound, induced me to appoint him to a Captaincy in one of the additional regiments. This regiment failing from the difficulty of recruiting, he entered into Lord Stirling's family, and has served two campaigns as a volunteer aid to his Lordship. He has, in every instance, maintained the reputation of a brave, active, and sensible officer. As we cannot introduce him into the Continental line, it were to be wished that the State could do something for him, to enable him to follow the bent of his military inclination, and render service to his country. If an event of this kind could take place, it would give me particular pleasure; as the esteem I have for him, and a regard to his merit, conspire to make me earnestly wish to see him provided for in some handsome way.

Charles Lee to James Monroe JULY 18, 1780

The good figure you make flatters my vanity, as I have always asserted that you would appear one of the first characters of this country, if your shyness did not prevent the display of the knowledge and talents you possess. Mr. White tells me you have got rid of this *mauvaise honte,** and only retain a certain degree of recommendatory modesty. I rejoice in it with all my soul, as I really love and esteem you most sincerely and affectionately.

*Diffidence, bashfulness.

James Monroe to Thomas Jefferson RICHMOND, SEPTEMBER 9, 1780

A variety of disappointments with respect to the prospects of my private fortune previous to my acquaintance with your Excellency, upon which I had built as on ground which could not deceive me, & which failed in a manner which could not have been expected, perplexed my plan of life & exposed me to inconveniences which had nearly destroyed me. In this situation had I not formed a connection with you I should most certainly have retired from society with a resolution never to have entered on the stage again. I could never have prevailed on myself to have taken an introduction to the Country, or to have derived any advantages or even to have remained in connection with one by whom I felt myself injured, but whose near relationship & situation in life put it in his power to serve me. In this situation you became acquainted with me & undertook the direction of my studies & believe me I feel that whatever I am at present in the opinion of others or whatever I may be in future has greatly arisen from your friendship.

Thomas Jefferson to James Madison ANNAPOLIS, MAY 8, 1784

I think Colonel Monroe will be of the Committee of the states. He wishes a correspondence with you; and I suppose his situation will render him an useful one to you. The scrupulousness of his honor will make you safe in the most confidential communications. A better man there cannot be.

Sarah Vaughan to Catherine W. Livingston OCTOBER 10, 1784

Poor Col. Monroe! The man is in despair he has written a letter to Gen. Gates telling him that he has lost his heart on board the Albany sloop, and fills the sheet with a panegyric upon his fair one. I fear his love did not meet with a return, but we were blind and not acquainted with one half his perfections of person or mind, they were summed up to me this day and amounted to eight which includes every perfection that a female can wish or a man envy. He is a member of Congress, rich, young, sensible, well read, *lively,* and *handsome.* I forget the other accomplishment, and will not subscribe to the last unless you prove the dimple on his chin to be what constitutes beauty, and I have a doubt about the sixth unless it is agreed that affording subject for gaiety and liveliness to the company you are in, is the same thing as being gay and lively yourself. If you are the goddess at whose shrine he worships inform me of it that I may think higher of his perfection. His being *your* choice will have great influence upon me, and stop me when I might be saucily inclined, for at present he is more the object of my diversion than admiration.

Marquis de Lafayette to James Madison NEW YORK, DECEMBER 15, 1784

Our friend Munro is very much Beloved and Respected in Congress.

William Temple Franklin to Thomas Jefferson NEW YORK, JANUARY 18, 1786

In the Opportunity I have had of being with him, I have found him very sensible and agreeable, and possessing those pleasing Manners, which take off from the formality of a new Acquaintance and smooth the Way to Friendship.

Thomas Jefferson to William Temple Franklin PARIS, MAY 7, 1786

You have formed a just opinion of Monroe. He is a man whose soul might be turned wrong side outwards without discovering a blemish to the world.

James Monroe to Thomas Jefferson FREDERICKSBURG, VA., JULY 27, 1787

The Governor [Edmund Randolph], I have every reason to believe is unfriendly to me & hath shown (If I am well informed) a disposition to thwart me; Madison, upon whose friendship I have calculated, whose views I have favored, and with whom I have held the most confidential correspondence since you left the continent, is in strict league with him & hath I have reason to believe concurred in arrangements unfavorable to me; a suspicion supported by some strong circumstances that this is the case, hath given me great uneasiness—however in this I may be disappointed & I wish it may be so.

French Strother to James Higginbotham 1788

[On Monroe running for the U.S. House of Representatives.] I hope you will consider the necessity of uniting in favor of a Gentleman who has been uniformly in favor of Amendments [to the Constitution]. I mean James Monroe Esq., a man who possesses great abilities, integrity and a most amiable Character who has been many years a member of Congress, of the House of Delegates and of the Privy Council and whom I have prevailed on to offer in our District: Considering him as being able to render his Country Great Services on this important occasion.

Reverend James Madison to James Madison WILLIAMSBURG, NOVEMBER 12, 1794

Our Friend Monro's Speech [as U.S. minister to France] shows a good republican Heart, but I wish it had been a little more luminous.

John Quincy Adams to John Adams THE HAGUE, MAY 11, 1797

It is with extreme reluctance that I have given you, though in the most intimate confidence, my sentiments upon Mr. Monroe's conduct during his mission to France. A most unfortunate mission it has been for his country, and where its consequences will lead, I am more able to conjecture than willing to foretell. I hope he was not aware of them himself, because I had rather consider him as prejudiced and improvident, but honest, than something worse.

John Quincy Adams to William Vans Murray HAMBURG, OCTOBER 26, 1797

Mr. Monroe has called upon the Secretary of State for the reasons of his recall; he seems to think that the tenure of the President's pleasure, expressed in his commission meant the pleasure of Mr. Monroe. He is trying to make a noise, and add one more puff to the bellows of faction, but his breath happens to be weak. He talks about liberty, and enlightened principles, and despotism, and coalition, as much as Molière's Tartuffe talks of piety, devotion, the love of God and sin. Mr. Pickering has answered him by plainly referring to the constitutional principles, which made an assignment of the reasons demanded improper; but at the same time gives him to understand what the reasons were, and offers in his individual character to tell him the reasons why *he* advised to it. This, however, Mr. Monroe chooses to decline, and the offer appears to have vexed him. He is going to publish a pamphlet; for you know with us everything ends in a pamphlet, as in France all ends in a song.

BERLIN, JANUARY 27, 1798

Have you seen Hamilton's vindication of himself against a charge of speculation? This affair must injure him with the rigid moralists, and makes him liable to a sort of censure, which he acknowledges and which I cannot but consider as just. But in the conduct of those who compelled him to uncover his nakedness to the public, there is something much worse than his offense. There is a skulking, cowardly, malignant wish to stigmatize him with corruption, without daring to assert it. Monroe especially has shown himself at this time, what he was when he set Tom Paine to howl at his benefactor Washington, silencing him in word, while he instigated him in deed. There is no distinction of weapons in the modern philosophy; poison is just as freely used as the sword.

DECEMBER 8, 1798

Monroe's greatest enemy is himself, and his own book. The most malignant foe could not pronounce so complete a sentence of damnation both upon his head and heart as that work. It is so unanswerably bad that you see even faction is ashamed of it.

Thomas Jefferson to John Taylor PHILADELPHIA, JANUARY 24, 1799

Many points in Monro's character would render him the most valuable acquisition the republican interest in this legislature [Congress] could make.

Mercy Otis Warren, History of the American Revolution 1805

Mr. Munroe, a gentleman of unimpeachable integrity, much knowledge and information, united with distinguished abilities, great strength of mind, and a strong attachment to the republican system, was appointed and sent forward [as minister to France] by President Washington.

William Plumer, Memorandum MARCH 16, 1806

Mr. Monroe, is I believe honest—a man of plain common sense—practical—but not scientific. His conduct in France in the time of their revolution partook of the delirium of the times. It was censurable.

He was an aid in our revolutionary army to Baron Steuben, or Lord Stirling. He was well known to Genl. Washington—& was by him honored with the important office of Minister plenipotentiary to the Court of France in a critical time.

Thomas Jefferson to William Duane MONTICELLO, OCTOBER 1, 1812

I clearly think with you on the competence of Monroe to embrace great views of action. The decision of his character, his enterprise, firmness, industry, and unceasing vigilance, would, I believe, secure, as I am sure they would merit, the public confidence, and give us all the success which our means can accomplish.

Aaron Burr to Joseph Alston NOVEMBER 15, 1815

A Congressional Caucus will, in the Course of the ensuing month, nominate James Monroe for President of the U.S. and will call on all good republicans to support the nomination—

Whether we consider the Measure itself—the Character & Talents of the Man or the State whence he comes, this Nomination is equally exceptionable & odious— ...

Independently of the Manner of the Nomination & of the location of the Candidate, the Man himself is one of the Most improper & incompetent that could have been selected—Naturally dull & stupid—extremely illiterate—indecisive to a degree that would be incredible to one who did not know him—pusillanimous & of course hypocritical—has no opinion on any subject & will be always under the Government of the worst Men—pretends as I am told, to some Knowledge of Military Matters, but never commanded a platoon nor was ever fit to command one—"He served in the revolutionary War"—that is, he acted a short time as aide de camp to Lord Stirling who was regularly drunk from Morning to Morning—Monroe's whole duty was to fill his Lordship's Tankard and hear with indications of admiration his Lordship's long stories about himself—Such is Monroe's

Military experience. I was with my regiment in the same division at the time—As a Lawyer, Monroe was far below Mediocrity— He never rose to the Honor of trying a Cause of the Value of an hundred pounds. This is a character exactly suited to the Views of the Virginia Junto—

John Adams to Thomas Jefferson QUINCY, OCTOBER 10, 1817

Mr. Monroe has got the universal Character among all our Common People of "A very smart Man." And verily I am of the same Mind.

Joseph Story to Ezekiel Bacon WASHINGTON, D.C., MARCH 12, 1818

The old notions of republican simplicity are fast wearing away, and the public taste becomes more and more gratified with public amusements and parade. Mr. Monroe, however, still retains his plain and gentlemanly manners, and is in every respect a very estimable man.

James Madison to Tench Ringgold JULY 12, 1831

I need not say to you who so well know, how highly I rated the comprehensiveness and character of his mind; the purity and nobleness of his principles; the importance of his patriotic services; and the many private virtues of which his whole life was a model, nor how deeply therefore I must sympathize, on his loss, with those who feel it most. A close friendship, continued thro' so long a period and such diversified scenes, had grown into an affection very imperfectly expressed by that term; and I value accordingly the manifestation in his last hours that the reciprocity never abated.

Gouverneur Morris
1752–1816

⫷ BORN AT Morrisania, the Bronx, New York; graduated from King's College (Columbia), 1768. Member New York Provincial Congress, 1775; delegate state convention, helped write New York constitution, 1776–77. Member Continental Congress, 1778–79. Became citizen of Pennsylvania, 1779; allied with Republican Party; admitted to Pennsylvania bar, 1781. Assistant in Confederation Office of Finance, 1781–85. Delegate Constitutional Convention, delivered more speeches than any other delegate. As member of Committee of Style, 1787, wrote final version of Constitution including Preamble. Returned to New York and then went to France as Robert Morris's business agent, 1788; U.S. special envoy to Britain, 1791; U.S. minister to France, 1792–94. Returned to America, 1798; U.S. senator, 1800–1803; opposed War of 1812; supported Hartford Convention, 1814.

Edward Rutledge to Robert R. Livingston PHILADELPHIA, OCTOBER 19, 1776

I am Amazed at Gouverneur! Good God what will mankind come to! Is it not possible to awake him to a sense of his Duty? Has he no one Virtue left that can plead in favor of an oppressed & bleeding Country? Has he no Friendship for those who are standing so opposed as you & Jay are to the attacks of open and secret Enemies? One would think he would find a solid Satisfaction in acting and even suffering with such Men in such a Cause. Does he desire to live forever in Obscurity, or would he prefer being "damned of ever Lasting Fame," to a Life devoted to his Country? Tis a hard case indeed my dear Robert that the Burden should be cast upon the Shoulders of a few—but the Honor will bear a just proportion to the Trouble, & the Reflection of having deserved well of the Community will elevate you I trust beyond the reach of Affliction.

William Duer to Robert R. Livingston PHILADELPHIA, JULY 9, 1777

At present there are no very great Matters in which our State is particularly interested before Congress; and indeed if they were, Mr. [Gouverneur] Morris can supply my place with great Advantage to the Reputation of the State, as well as his own. His Coolness of Temper, and happy Vein of Irony are Qualifications, which would render him a very powerful Antagonist to Mr. R. H. Lee.

William Duer to Francis Lightfoot Lee READING, PA., FEBRUARY 14, 1778

I must confess that I do not think there are many Men in America, who can be considered as Financiers, our contracted dependent System of Government not affording Scope for Abilities of this Species. Yet some undoubtedly might be found whose Genius fits them in a peculiar Manner for such a Line of Business. Two occur to me at present Mr. R. Morris of this State, and my Colleague Govr. Morris. With respect to the former, you know him so well, that it is unnecessary to enlarge upon his Character—the latter, tho' Young, has turned his thoughts and Course of reading much to the Subject of Money as a Science, and from his Genius would I am convinced make an Useful, and Shining Member in such a Department.

Gouverneur Morris to His Mother, Sarah Morris YORK, PA., APRIL 16, 1778

I would that it were in my Power to solace and comfort your declining Age. The Duty I owe to a tender Parent demands this of me but a higher Duty hath bound me to the Service of my Fellow Creatures. The natural Indolence of my Disposition hath unfitted me for the Paths of Ambition and the early Possession of Power taught me how little it deserves to be prized. Whenever the present Storm subsides I shall rush with Eagerness into the Bosom of private Life but while it continues and while my Country calls for the Exertion of that little Share of Abilities which it hath pleased God to bestow on me I hold it my indispensable Duty to give myself to her. I know that for such Sentiments I am called a Rebel and that such Sentiments are not fashionable among the Folks you see. Let me however entreat that you be not concerned on my Account. I shall again see you. Perhaps the Time is not far off.

Gouverneur Morris to John Jay YORK, PA., APRIL 29, 1778

I am a busy Man tho as heretofore a pleasurable one.

Gouverneur Morris to Robert R. Livingston YORK, PA., MAY 3, 1778

I believe all is right but you know I am quite a Candid.

PHILADELPHIA, AUGUST 17, 1778

You tell me that I must be with you at the opening of the Session [of the New York legislature] but you do not let me know when the Session is. Let me paint my Situation [in Congress]. I am on a Committee to arrange the Treasury & Finances. I am of the medical Committee and have to prepare the Arrangements of that Department. I have the same Thing to go thro with Relation to the Commissary's, Quarter Master's & Clothier General's Departments. I am to prepare a Manifesto on the Cruelties of the British. I have drawn and expect to draw almost if not all the Publications of Congress of any Importance. These are leading Things but the every Day Minutia are infinite. From Sunday Morning to Saturday Night I have no Exercise unless to walk from where I now sit about fifty Yards to Congress and to return. My Constitution sinks under this and the Heat of this pestiferous Climate. Duer talks daily of going hence. We have nobody else here so that if I quit the State will be unrepresented. Can I come to you? If there be a Practicability of it with any Kind of Consistency I will take half a dozen Shirts and ride Post to meet you. Oh that a Heart so disposed as mine is to social Delights should be worn and torn to Pieces with public Anxieties.

Gouverneur Morris to Robert Morris PHILADELPHIA, OCTOBER 20, 1778

As to Personalities I am fully of Opinion with you that I speak too often and too long of which the Bearer of this Letter will give you I doubt not many Instances. To my Sorrow I add that I am by no Means improved in my public Speaking. I have no Doubt that the Instance you allude to is exceptionable and the Party by his own Wrong deprived of the Benefit of that Protection which altho given by the Law that is the Consent of Nations does by no Means suspend the Laws of civil Society so far as to excuse a Breach of those Laws. But I am a Civilian. That I am not a punctual Correspondent must be attributed to Distractions arising from an Attention to Business of so many different Kinds that your poor Friend hath but little in him of the gay Lothario. But you must believe, at least I entreat it, that my Heart holds you dear nor shall any Objects exclude you from the Place in it which you have acquired a double Title to by Right and by long Possession. The American* is mine or I am the American which you please. Both it and the Writer have Faults, Alas a great Many.

John Adams, Diary JUNE 22, 1779

In the Evening I fell into Chat with the Chevalier [de La Luzerne]. He asked me, about Governeur Morris. I said it was his Christian Name—that he was not Governor. The Chevalier said He had heard of him as an able Man. I said he was a young Man, chosen into Congress since I left it. That I had sat some Years with his Elder Brother in Congress. That Governeur was a Man of Wit, and made pretty Verses—but of a Character trés legere.† That the Cause of America had not been sustained by such Characters as that of Governeur Morris or his Colleague Mr. Jay.

John Jay to Governor George Clinton PHILADELPHIA, AUGUST 27, 1779

Several circumstances which have come to my knowledge, lead me to suspect that pains have been taken to injure Morris in the opinion of his constituents. Justice to him as well as regard to

---

*Gouverneur Morris wrote four essays signed "An American" to the British peace commission led by Lord Carlisle.

†A very light character.

truth obliges me to say that he deserves well of New York and America in general. It has been the uniform policy of some from the beginning of the contest, to depreciate every man of worth and abilities who refused to draw in their harness.

SEPTEMBER 29, 1779

Morris will be serviceable [in Congress]—His Abilities enable him to promote every Cause he may advocate, but if I may be permitted to advise he should restrain himself from taking any Part or pushing any Measure respecting your Disputes [with Vermont and New England], without previous Concert with Livingston and Hobart.

John Jay to Robert R. Livingston and Gouverneur Morris
PHILADELPHIA, SEPTEMBER 29, 1779

I exceedingly regret his [Morris's] not being sent to Europe where his abilities would have done Honor as well as Service to his Country—but it seems that Period is not yet arrived. & Congress must for some time longer remain his Field. . . . if Morris governs his Imagination will conciliate Friends.

Lewis Morris Jr., to Nathanael Greene ESOPUS, N.Y.,
OCTOBER 1, 1779

This morning the legislature proceeded to the choice of delegates [to Congress]; Mr. Jay, Mr. Scott, Mr. Duane, Mr. Floyd and a Mr. LeHommodieu are the persons chosen. The last is a refugee from Long Island, a man of sense but not out of the common track. Mr. [Gouverneur] Morris was dropt from a vulgar prejudice which prevailed in the assembly that he ridiculed the Christian religion and was a man of very bad morals. Thus from this idle notion they have lost the services of the ablest politician in the state.

John Laurens to Alexander Hamilton PHILADELPHIA,
DECEMBER 18, 1779

The world in general allows greater credit for his abilities than his integrity.

William Bingham to John Jay PHILADELPHIA, JULY 1, 1780

An unlucky accident lately happened to Gouvernuer Morris.

In attempting to drive a pair of wild horse in a phaeton, he was thrown out and in the fall his left leg caught in the wheel and was greatly shattered. He was under the necessity of having it amputated below the knee and is now in a fair way of recovery.

John Jay to Robert Morris ST. ILDEFONSO, SPAIN, SEPTEMBER 16, 1780

Gouverneur's Leg has been a Tax on my Heart. I am almost tempted to wish he had lost something else.

Robert Morris to Gouverneur Morris OFFICE OF FINANCE, JULY 6, 1781

The cheerful manner in which you agreed to render me the assistance I solicited, soon after my appointment to the Superintendency of the Finances of the United States, gave me great pleasure on my own Account, and a still more solid satisfaction on Account of my Country; depending solely on my self, I trembled at the Arduous task I had reluctantly undertaken; aided by your Talents and Abilities I feel better Courage and dare to indulge the fond hope, that Uniting our utmost exertions in the Service of our Country, we may be able to extricate it from the present embarrassments, and dispel those only Clouds, that seem to hang destruction over it. The Honorable Congress by their act of this date have fixed a Salary for the Assistant I may appoint agreeable to the Powers annexed to my office by a former Act of Congress. My entire Conviction of the great and essential Services your Genius, Talents and Capacity enable you to render to your Country, and of that aid, ease and Confidence you can and will Administer to my own exertions and Feelings, never left me one moment to hesitate about the choice I shou'd make. I only lament that the provision allowed by Congress is not more adequate to your deserts, but as I know you are incapable of Mercenary Views and considerations, this circumstance shall be overlooked for the present in expectation that the Utility of our measures may draw a proper attention from those that employ us and at any rate we will have the Consolation to pursue the interests of the United States to the best of our Judgment and abilities whether we meet with suitable rewards or not. Therefore it is with the utmost satisfaction that I do hereby appoint you, an Assistant to the Superintendent of the Finances of the

United States of North America, and I do assure you nothing will make me more happy than to acquire and divide with you the thanks of our Country and applause of the World.

Mary Morris to Sally Jay   PHILADELPHIA, JULY 12, 1781

Mr. Gov. Morris's friends here and, indeed, all who know him, were exceedingly shocked at his irreparable misfortune—the loss of his leg. . . . I never knew an individual more sympathized with.

Robert Morris to John Jay   PHILADELPHIA, OCTOBER 19, 1781

Gouverneur is with me and a most useful and able adjunct he is. I hope our joint labors will in the end have the desired effect. We have mended the appearance of things very much, and are regaining public credit and confidence by degrees.

John Jay to George Clinton   MADRID, NOVEMBER 16, 1781

It gave me much pleasure to hear that G. Morris would probably be in your delegation [to Congress] this fall. Independent of my regard for him, it appears to me of great importance to the State that every valuable man in it should be preserved, and that it is particularly our interest to cultivate, cherish, and support all such of our citizens, especially young and rising ones, as are, or promise to be, able and honest servants of the public.

Nathanael Greene to Charles Pettit   DECEMBER 21, 1782

[On the rumor that Superintendent of Finance Robert Morris had been killed in a duel, it was thought that Gouverneur Morris might fill the superintendent's vacancy.] Gouverneur Morris is in the order of promotion; but the confidence of the people is wanting. His abilities are great; but I fear he has more of genius than judgment.

Robert Morris to John Jay   PHILADELPHIA, JANUARY 3, 1783

Your friend Gouverneur writes you political letters, but as he tells you nothing of himself, it is just that I tell you how industrious, how useful he is; his talents and abilities, you know; they are all faithfully and disinterestedly applied to the service of his country. I could do nothing without him, and our quiet labors do but just keep the wheels in motion.

Charles Thomson to Hannah Thomson PRINCETON, N.J., JUNE 30, 1783

At Trenton I shaved, washed & breakfasted & waited till eight in hopes of seeing Govr. Morris. . . . Govr. was gone a fishing and though I sent him a note to inform him of my arrival, I suppose he thought it too great a sacrifice to forego the pleasure of fishing.

John Jay to Robert Morris PASSY, JULY 20, 1783

Gouverneur is happy in your esteem; it adds to mine for him. I have long been attached to him, and sincerely wish that our friendship, instead of being diminished, may continue to gain strength with time.

Robert Morris to John Jay PHILADELPHIA, NOVEMBER 4, 1783

I do not know whether Gouverneur writes to you by this opportunity; you must cherish his friendship, it is worth possessing. He has more virtue than he shows, and more consistency than anybody believes. He values you exceedingly, and hereafter you will be very useful to each other.

Samuel Osgood to Elbridge Gerry PHILADELPHIA, APRIL 3, 1784

I have had an Opportunity of conversing freely with the D——M——r [Dutch minister Pieter Johan van Berckel]. He has observed a very good Line of Conduct in my Opinion since he has been here—& I apprehend he will fall in, fully with the independent Americans. He is much opposed to intriguing. He has a good Opinion of R—— M—— but says he has very bad Councillors about him. I found he meant G—— M——. He has the same Sentiments of him that I have.

Arthur Lee to John Adams ANNAPOLIS, MAY 11, 1784

Our Treasury is as low & the prospect of raising it by taxes, as unpromising as possible. Either the present Superintendent must continue on with powers calculated solely to convert every thing to the emolument of himself & his Creatures; or if a reform is made, he & his immoral Assistant have malignity enough to ruin where they can no longer plunder. However there is now a plan before Congress for reforming the department, by putting it into Commission & prohibiting the Commissioners from being engaged in trade or commerce; which I hope will take place.

Francisco de Miranda, Travels in the United States, 1783-1784

Mr. Gouverneur Morris, the lively intellect of the town, and it seems to me he has more ostentation, audacity, and tinsel than real value.

Luigi Castiglioni, Sketches of American Statesmen 1787

All those who have the good fortune to know him marvel at his talents and can only profit from his conversation and his pleasant company. As courteous and refined as a European, free as an American, he combines the talents of French bon ton* and republican frankness, and is welcomed with pleasure in Philadelphia society.

William Pierce, "Character Sketches of Delegates to the Federal Convention" 1787

Mr. Gouverneur Morris is one of those Geniuses in whom every species of talents combine to render him conspicuous and flourishing in public debate;—He winds through all the mazes of rhetoric, and throws around him such a glare that he charms, captivates, and leads away the senses of all who hear him. With an infinite stretch of fancy he brings to view things when he is engaged in deep argumentation, that render all the labor of reasoning easy and pleasing. But with all these powers he is fickle and inconstant,—never pursuing one train of thinking,—nor ever regular. He has gone through a very extensive course of reading, and is acquainted with all the sciences. No Man has more wit,— nor can any one engage the attention more than Mr. Morris. He was bred to the Law, but I am told he disliked the profession, and turned merchant. He is engaged in some great mercantile matters with his namesake Mr. Robt. Morris. This Gentleman is about 38 years old, he has been unfortunate in losing one of his Legs, and getting all the flesh taken off his right arm by scald, when a youth.

---

*Fashionable society.

Louis Guillaume Otto, Biographies FALL 1788

Citizen of the state of New York, but always connected with Robert Morris and having represented Pennsylvania several times. Celebrated lawyer, one of the best organized minds on the continent, but without manners, and, if one believes his enemies, without principles; extremely interesting in conversation having studied finances with special care. He works constantly with Robert Morris. He is feared more than admired, but few regard him with esteem.

George Washington to Thomas Jefferson MOUNT VERNON, NOVEMBER 27, 1788

You will find [him] full of affability, good nature, vivacity and talents. As you will also find in him a deportment calculated to do credit to the national character, I cannot hesitate to believe that you will be desirous of having opportunities of being useful to him.

George Washington, Diary OCTOBER 8, 1789

Mr. Madison . . . thought with Colonel Hamilton, and as Mr. Jay also does, that Mr. Morris is a man of superior talents—but with the latter that his imagination sometimes runs ahead of his judgment—that his Manners before he is known—and where known are oftentimes disgusting—and from that, and immoral & loose expressions had created opinions of himself that were not favorable to him and which he did not merit.

George Washington to Gouverneur Morris PHILADELPHIA, JANUARY 28, 1792

[On the opposition to Morris's appointment as minister plenipotentiary to France.] Whilst your abilities, knowledge in the affairs of this Country, & disposition to serve it were adduced, and asserted on one hand, you were charged on the other hand, with levity, and imprudence of conversation and conduct. It was urged, that your habit of expression, indicated a hauteur disgusting to those who happen to differ from you in sentiment; and among a people who study civility and politeness more than any other nation, it must be displeasing. That in France you were considered as a favourer of Aristocracy, & unfriendly to its Revolution—

(I suppose they meant Constitution). That under this impression you could not be an acceptable public character—of consequence, would not be able, however willing, to promote the interests of this Country in an essential degree. That in England you indiscretely communicated the purport of your mission, in the first instance, to the Minister of France, at that Court; who, availing himself in the same moment of the occasion, gave it the appearance of a movement through his Court. This, and other circumstances of a cimilar nature, joined to a closer intercourse with the opposition members, occasioned distrust, & gave displeasure to the Ministry; which was the cause, it is said, of that reserve which you experienced in negotiating the business which had been entrusted to you.

But not to go further into detail—I will place the ideas of your political adversaries in the light which their arguments have presented them to my view—viz.—That the promptitude with wch your brilliant, & lively imagination is displayed, allows too little time for deliberation, and correction; and is the primary cause of those sallies which too often offend, and of that ridicule of characters which begets enmity not easy to be forgotten, but which might easily be avoided if it was under the control of more caution and prudence. In a word, that it is indispensably necessary that more circumspection should be observed by our Representatives abroad than they conceive you are disposed to adopt.

In this statement you have the pros & the cons; by reciting them, I give you a proof of my friendship, if I give none of my policy or judgment. I do it on the presumption, that a mind conscious of its own rectitude, fears not what is said of it; but will bid defiance to and dispise shafts that are not barbed with accusations against honor or integrity; and because I have the fullest confidence (supposing the alligations to be founded in whole or part) that you would find no difficulty, being apprised of the exceptionable light in which they are received, and considering yourself as the representative of this Country, to effect a change; and thereby silence, in the most unequivocal and satisfactory manner, your political opponents. Of my good opinion, & of my friendship & regard, you may be assured.

George Mason to James Monroe GUNSTON HALL, JANUARY 30, 1792

I see by a late Paper, that Gr. Morris is appointed our Minister, to the Court of France; so that, I suppose, the Opposition in the Senate has been outvoted.

I don't think a more injudicious Appointment cou'd have been made. In the present Situation of France, to appoint a Man of his known monarchical Principles has rather the Appearance of Insult, than of Compliment, or Congratulation. And altho' Mr. Morris's Political Creed may not be known generally in France, it must be well known to Mr. de la Fayette, the most influential Character in the Nation. What a Man seems to value himself upon, and glory in, can't long remain a Secret, in a public Character. "Coercion by G—d" is his favorite Maxim in government. And in his place, as a Member of the federal Convention in Philadelphia, I heard him express the following sentiment. "We must have a Monarch sooner or later" (tho' I think his word was a *Despot*) "and the sooner we take him, while we are able to make a Bargain with him, the better."

Gouverneur Morris to George Washington LONDON, APRIL 6, 1792

I now promise you that Circumspection of Conduct which has hitherto I acknowledge formed no Part of my Character. And I make the *Promise* that my Sense of Integrity may enforce what my Sense of Propriety dictates.

Thomas Jefferson, "Anas" 1792

The fact is, that Gouverneur Morris, a high flying monarchy-man, shutting his eyes & his faith to every fact against his wishes, & believing everything he desires to be true, has kept the President's [Washington's] mind constantly poisoned with his forebodings [respecting the French Revolution].

Alexander Hamilton to Rufus King NEW YORK, OCTOBER 2, 1798

Why does not Gouverneur Morris come home? His talents are wanted. Men like him do not superabound.

Robert Troup to Rufus King NEW YORK, APRIL 19, 1799

Mr. Gouverneur Morris is at Morrisania. . . . He is in excellent health and is very happy to see his friends, to whom he is all hospitality. His wines are of superior quality and given with great liberality. His attachments to his own country and government have increased by what he has seen in Europe. . . . He seems determined to remain a farmer, and not again to embark in public life.

Manasseh Cutler, Journal JANUARY 8, 1802

Mr. Gouverneur Morris delivered in the Senate a truly Ciceronian philippic on the repeal of the Judiciary [Act of 1801].

Manasseh Cutler to Joseph Torrey WASHINGTON, D.C., FEBRUARY 1, 1802

You will find there has been much able speaking on both sides [of] the question [in Congress]. Mr. G. Morris has shown with distinguished luster. His eloquence has never been surpassed, it is said, in either House of Congress.

Gouverneur Morris to John Dickinson APRIL 13, 1803

In adopting a republican form of government, I not only took it as a man does his wife, for better, for worse, but, what few men do with their wives, I took it knowing all its bad qualities.

Mercy Otis Warren, **History of the American Revolution** 1805

A character eccentric from youth to declining age; a man of pleasure, pride, and extravagance, fond of the trappings of monarchy, and implicated by a considerable portion of the citizens of America, as deficient in principle, was not a suitable person for a resident minister in France at so important a crisis. . . . These circumstances required a man of character, rather than a dexterous agent of political mischief, whose abilities and address were well adapted either for private or court intrigue.

Gouverneur Morris to Jared Sparks C. DECEMBER 1809

I have no notes or memorandums of what passed during the war. I led then the most laborious life, which can be imagined. This you will readily suppose to have been the case, when I was engaged with my departed friend, Robert Morris, in the office of finance. But what you will not so readily suppose is, that I was still more harassed while a member of Congress. Not to mention the attendance from eleven to four in the House, which was common to all, and the appointment to special committees, of which I had a full share, I was at the same time chairman, and of course did the business, of three standing committees, viz. on the commissary's, quartermaster's, and medical departments. You must not imagine, that the members of these committees took any charge or burden of the affairs. Necessity, preserving the democratical forms, assumed the monarchical substance of business. The chairman received and answered all letters and other applications, took every step which he deemed essential, prepared reports, gave orders, and the like, and merely took the members of a committee into a chamber, and for the form's sake made the needful communications, and received their approbation, which was given of course. I was moreover obliged to labor occasionally in my profession, as my wages were insufficient for my support. I would not trouble you with this abstract of my situation, if it did not appear necessary to show you why I kept no notes of my services, and why I am perhaps the most ignorant man alive of what concerns them.

Gouverneur Morris to Timothy Pickering NOVEMBER 1, 1814

Propositions to counterbalance the issue of paper money, and the consequent violations of contracts, must have met with all the opposition I could make. But, my dear sir, what can a history of the Constitution avail towards interpreting its provisions? This must be done by comparing the plain import of the words with the general tenor and object of the instrument. That instrument was written by the fingers which write this letter. Having rejected redundant and equivocal terms, I believed it to be as clear as our language would permit; excepting, nevertheless, a part of what relates to the judiciary. On that subject, conflicting opinions had been maintained with so much professional astuteness that it became necessary to select phrases which, expressing my own notions, would not alarm others nor shock their self-love; and, to the best of my recollection, this was the only part which passed without cavil.

James Madison to Jared Sparks MONTPELIER, APRIL 8, 1831

[Sparks had asked Madison whether it was true that Gouverneur Morris had written the final form of the Constitution in the Constitutional Convention of 1787.] The *finish* given to the style and arrangement of the Constitution fairly belongs to the pen of Mr. Morris; the task having, probably, been handed over to him by the chairman of the Committee [of Style, William Samuel Johnson], himself a highly respectable member, and with the ready concurrence of the others. A better choice could not have been made, as the performance of the task proved. It is true, that the state of the materials, consisting of a reported draft in detail, and subsequent resolutions accurately penned, and falling easily into their proper places, was a good preparation for the symmetry and phraseology of the instrument, but there was sufficient room for the talents and taste stamped by the author on the face of it. The alterations made by the Committee are not recollected. They were not such, as to impair the merit of the composition. Those, verbal and others made in the Convention, may be gathered from the Journal, and will be found also to leave that merit altogether unimpaired. . . .

It is but due to Mr. Morris to remark that, to the brilliancy of his genius, he added what is too rare, a candid surrender of his opinion when the lights of discussion satisfied him that they had been too hastily formed, and a readiness to aid in making the best of measures in which he had been overruled.

James Kent to Mrs. Elizabeth Hamilton NEW YORK, DECEMBER 10, 1832

The appearance of Mr. Morris was very commanding. His noble head, his majestic mien, the dignity of his deportment were all impressive.

Robert Morris

1734–1806

⊰ BORN IN Liverpool, England; arrived in Maryland, 1747; apprenticed to Philadelphia merchant Charles Willing; formed mercantile partnership with Thomas Willing. Member Continental Congress, 1775–76; voted against independence but signed Declaration of Independence; contracted with Congress for war supplies, 1775 onward. Founder, Bank of North America, 1781. Confederation superintendent of finance, 1781–84, formulated long-range plans to strengthen central government. Political plans, business methods, and charges of corruption forced resignation in 1784. Elected Philadelphia assemblyman, 1776, 1778, 1780, 1785, 1786; delegate Constitutional Convention, 1787. U.S. senator, 1789–95. Land speculation and overextension in commerce led to bankruptcy; in debtors' prison, 1798–1801.

John Adams to Horatio Gates PHILADELPHIA, APRIL 27, 1776

You ask me what you are to think of Robt. Morris? I will tell you what I think of him. I think he has a masterly Understanding, an open Temper and an honest Heart: and if he does not always vote for What you and I should think proper, it is because he thinks that a large Body of People remains, who are not yet of his Mind. He has vast designs in the mercantile Way. And no doubt pursues mercantile Ends, which are always gain; but he is an excellent Member of our Body [Congress].

Robert Morris to Horatio Gates   PHILADELPHIA, OCTOBER 27, 1776

I am not one of those Testy Politicians that run resty when my own plans are not adopted, for I think it the duty of a good Citizen to follow when he cannot lead, & happy would it be for America if all her Inhabitants would adopt this Maxim, and make it an invariable Rule during this great Contest for the Minority on every question to Submit to & cooperate with the Majority; but alas this cannot be. It is not to be expected from Human Nature. We must take Men as we find them, and do the best we can.

John Jay to Gouverneur Morris   WHITE PLAINS, N.Y., AUGUST 29, 1778

Few men have more of my esteem.

Robert Morris to James Duane   PHILADELPHIA, SEPTEMBER 8, 1778

Ambition had no share in bringing me forward into Public life nor has it any Charms to keep me there. The time I have spent in it has been the severest Tax of my life and really I think those who have had so much, should now be relieved & let some fresh hands take the Helm. These notions prompt me to get out of Congress at the next appointment of Delegates, but my Namesake [Gouverneur Morris] swears I shall not depart.

John Swanick to Robert Morris   PHILADELPHIA, C. FEBRUARY 20, 1781

I declare to you sir most solemnly—Pardon the Expression—that I do not believe there is in America any Man fit for this office of Financier but you. And if I prove this assertion, the Result must be, that either you will accept and discharge this high office with your Usual Zeal, or else that you will by Refusing, perhaps Contribute Indirectly to the Ruin of yourself and this Country. For this is my Opinion: That the Fate of this Country is so nearly tied to yours that as she Rises or Falls so is your Fate determined; and that unless her Finances be regularly Ordered by an Able and diligent officer, she must forsake her Trophies and under an Ignoble Shade await the first bold Invader who shall seize her.

In the Character of a General director of the Finances of a
Country I think these things are wanting. *Fortune* that he be not
subservient to Temptation of wealth or the offers of a job. *Abilities* that he do not Injury to the Country by Neglect or Ignorance.
Credit so Whigs and even disaffected People may Repose Confidence in what he shall say as coming from a Man of tried Honor
who Scorned ever to take advantages. By this Means the Miller at
Brandywine and thousands others would do for him what not even
Gold Could tempt them to do for others. *Intelligence of and in the
Country* so that he may know how to take his Measures and how
to Conciliate and if need be enforce them, for if he be known to the
Principal Characters in the Country and respected by all he will
be able to gain knowledge from even such as would not be fond of
Imparting it to others and Men in office will execute his pleasure
Readily whom from early Life they have Esteemed and are Used
to repose Confidence in. *A Man of Weight Abroad,* and to be this
he must be known there by very extensive dealings Conducted
with Probity and Fame. The two principal Financiers of Europe
Mr. Neckar and Lord North are Certainly Men of Surprising Genius. We have to hope that the former would be agreeably surprised to hear that the affairs of the Treasury of the Allies were no
longer in their Wretched needy State, that they were no longer a
draw back on him and doubtless his Esteem for America would
be greatly enhanced by the Reflection that their Resources were
in the hands of a Man whose Name must ensure Economy and
Integrity those two Corner Stones of Public Fortune; and as to the
latter, with what Ingenuity will he tell Parliament that the Affairs of
America are deserted to amass Private Fortunes, when he can be
told that a Merchant of great Eminence forsaking this Narrow System consents to live or die with his Country? A Man a Financier
ought to be Accustomed to Rank and Honors not a Man indebted
for them to this single appointment, for then he will not be Lord-
ing it in his new Jurisdiction, but observing that happy Medium
between the State of Office and the Manner of a Gentleman which
will secure him Love and Respect. He ought to be a Man of true *Industry and Application* and where shall that be sought more properly than in the Life of a Man who from early Youth accustomed to
business has made it at once his Pleasure and his Study. And now
sir, where is the Man Uniting these Qualities? I will not answer.
This Country knows him and has declared him in her Choice.

Alexander Hamilton to Robert Morris DE PEYSTER'S POINT, N.Y., APRIL 30, 1781

I hope Sir you will not consider it as a compliment when I assure you that I heard with the greatest satisfaction of your nomination to the department of finance. In a letter of mine last summer to Mr. Duane, urging among other things the plan of an executive ministry, I mentioned you as the person, who ought to fill that department. I know of no other in America who unites so many advantages, and of course, every impediment to your acceptance is to me a subject of chagrin. I flatter myself Congress will not preclude the public from your services by an obstinate refusal of reasonable conditions; and as one deeply interested in the event I am happy in believing you will not easily be discouraged from undertaking an office, by which you may render America and the world no less a service than the establishment of American independence! Tis by introducing order into our finances—by restoring public credit—not by gaining battles, that we are finally to gain our object. Tis by putting ourselves in a condition to continue the war not by temporary, violent and unnatural efforts to bring it to a decisive issue, that we shall in reality bring it to a speedy and successful one. In the frankness of truth I believe, Sir, you are the Man best capable of performing this great work.

Robert Morris to John Jay PHILADELPHIA, JUNE 5, 1781

Our friend Gouverneur has acquainted you with my appointment to the superintendent of finance; the motives of my acceptance are purely patriotic, and I would this moment give much of my property to be excused; but pressed by my friends, acquaintances, fellow-citizens, and almost by all Americans, I could not resist. I will therefore most assiduously try to be useful, and if in this I do but succeed, my recompense will be ample. Gouverneur and others have promised me the assistance of their abilities. Congress promise support; if the Legislatures and individuals will do the same, we will soon change the face of our affairs, and show our enemies that their hopes of our ruin, through the channel of finance, is as vain as their hope of conquest.

Gouverneur Morris to Robert Morris PHILADELPHIA, JULY 7, 1781

Your Industry, your Abilities, and above all your Integrity will extricate America from her Distresses; and consequently, Malice will blacken and Envy traduce you. I will freely share in this bitter Portion of Eminence.

If, contrary to the common Course of human Affairs, you meet with the just tribute of Applause; you will have this additional Title to it, that your Conduct has been actuated by a Love of your Country, and not by the Thirst of popular Acclamation.

Benjamin Franklin to Robert Morris PASSY, JULY 26, 1781

I have just received your very friendly Letter of the 6th of June past, announcing your Appointment to the Superintendence of our Finances. This gave me great Pleasure, as from your Intelligence, Integrity and Abilities, there is reason to hope every Advantage that the Public can possibly receive from such an Office. You are wise in estimating beforehand, as the principal Advantage you can expect, the Consciousness of having done Service to your Country. For the Business you have undertaken is of so complex a Nature, and must engross so much of your Time, and Attention, as necessarily to hurt your private Interests; and the Public often niggardly even of its Thanks, while you are sure of being censured by malevolent Critics and Bug Writers, who will abuse you while you are serving them, and wound your Character in nameless Pamphlets, thereby resembling those little dirty stinking Insects, that attack us only in the dark, disturb our Repose, molesting and wounding us while our Sweat and Blood is contributing to their Subsistence.

John Jay to Benjamin Franklin ST. ILDEFONSO, SPAIN, SEPTEMBER 10, 1781

The sanguine expectations entertained by our country from the appointment of Mr. Morris, his known abilities, integrity, and industry, the useful reformations he has begun, and the judicious measures he is pursuing abroad, as well as at home, afford reason to hope that, under his direction, American credit will be re-established, and the evils which have long threatened us on that head avoided.

Nathanael Greene to Gouverneur Morris SOUTH CAROLINA, NOVEMBER 21, 1781

I have the highest opinion of Mr. Morris the Minister of finance and had I the least inclination to enter the department you propose [as secretary of war] a connection with him would be a strong motive. My acquaintance with him is small, but from what I know of him I venerate his character and the more for his engaging in his present employment under such unfavorable appearances. Was I the fiftieth part as independent as he is in his private fortune I should have fewer objections to the place of secretary of war, then a failure could only affect my reputation and not my living. Not that the appointment I hold [commander of the Southern Army] is more lucrative but less expensive [*crossed out:* and perhaps upon the whole less hazardous].

Joseph Reed to Nathanael Greene PHILADELPHIA, C. DECEMBER 1781

If you retain any Resentment against Congress you will now give it up. The Humiliation is sufficient to disgust their greatest Enemies. For in fact they now [must?] register Mr. Morris Edicts which they do with an obsequiousness as any Parliament in the Dominion of the Grand Monarque. He has engrossed all the Affairs of the Continent at the Head of the Treasury & Admiralty. All Estimates of every kind in the Department & civil subject to his Control & if not, a Penny of Money attainable but with much Difficulty & profound Submission. In the mean time he is largely concerned in Trade being Principal for capital Houses: Had the Paper Money in his Hands which he raises or falls occasionally so that it is computed his Profits by this alone last year amounted to £30, or 40,000. In short he bids fair to show no Trinculos* Government in the Play. You shall be King and I will be King over you.

Samuel Osgood to John Lowell PHILADELPHIA, FEBRUARY 2, 1782

I think Mr. Morris is very well calculated for his Office, perhaps no Man in the united States is better qualified.

*Trinculos is the jester in Shakespeare's *The Tempest.*

James Madison to Edmund Randolph PHILADELPHIA, JUNE 4, 1782

My charity I own cannot invent an excuse for the prepense malice with which the character and service of this gentleman are murdered. I am persuaded that he accepted his office from motives which were honorable and patriotic. I have seen no proof of malfeasance. I have heard of many charges which were palpably erroneous. I have known others somewhat suspicious vanish on examination. Every member in Congress must be sensible of the benefit which has accrued to the public from his administration. No intelligent man out of Congress can be altogether insensible of it. The Court of France has testified its satisfaction at his appointment which I really believe lessened its repugnance to lend us money. These considerations will make me cautious in lending an ear to the suggestions even of the impartial; to those of known and vindictive enemies very incredulous. The same fidelity to the public interest which obliges those who are its appointed guardians, to pursue with every rigor a perfidious or dishonest servant of the public requires them to confront the imputations of malice against the good and faithful one. I have in the conduct of my colleague here [Theodorick Bland] a sure index of the sentiments and objects of one of my colleagues who is absent [Arthur Lee] relative to the department of finance.

Marquis de Chastellux, Travels in North-America, in the Years 1780, 1781, and 1782

Mr. Morris . . . is a very rich merchant, and consequently a man of every country, for commerce bears every where the same character. . . . It is scarcely to be credited, that amidst the disasters of America, Mr. Morris, the inhabitant of a town [Philadelphia] just emancipated from the hands of the English, should possess a fortune of eight millions (between 3 and 400,000 £ sterling). It is, however, in the most critical times that great fortunes are acquired. The fortunate return of several ships, the still more successful cruises of his privateers, have increased his riches beyond his expectations, if not beyond his wishes. . . .

Mr. Morris is a large man, very simple in his manners; but his mind is subtle and acute, his head perfectly well organized, and he is as well versed in public affairs as in his own. He was a member of Congress in 1776, and ought to be reckoned among those personages who have had the greatest influence in the revolution of America. He is the friend of Dr. Franklin, and the decided enemy of Mr. Read [Joseph Reed]. His house is handsome, resembling perfectly the houses in London; he lives there without ostentation, but not without expense, for he spares nothing which can contribute to his happiness, and that of Mrs. Morris, to whom he is much attached. A zealous republican, and an Epicurean philosopher, he has always played a distinguished part at table and in business.

John Jay to Gouverneur Morris PARIS, OCTOBER 13, 1782

I find you are industrious and, of consequence, useful; so much the better for yourself, for the public, and for our friend Morris, whom I consider as the pillar of American credit.

Arthur Lee to James Warren IN CONGRESS, DECEMBER 12, 1782

Mr. Morris, Mr. [William] Bingham, Mr. [George] Ross, and others, who have made large fortunes during this war, employ their wealth in a manner not very consistent with that unostentatious virtue which ought to animate our Infant republic. Extravagance, ostentation and dissipation distinguish what are called the Ladies of the first rank. There are however exceptions, there being prudent, amiable and worthy persons of both Sexes. But the generality seem to be intoxicated with a sudden change of manners and unexpected elevation.

Robert Morris to Congress JANUARY 24, 1783

I should be unworthy of the Confidence reposed in me by my fellow Citizens, if I did not explicitly declare that I will never be the Minister of Injustice.

James Madison to Edmund Randolph PHILADELPHIA, MARCH 11, 1783

The peremptory style & publication of Mr. M's letters have given offense to many without & to some within Congress. His enemies of both descriptions are industrious in displaying their impropriety. I wish they had less handle for the purpose.

Joseph Reed to Nathanael Greene PHILADELPHIA, MARCH 14, 1783

Mr. Morris has been for a long Time the Dominus Factotum,* whose Dictates none dare oppose, & from whose Decisions lay no Appeal: he has in Fact exercised the Power really of the three great Departments, & Congress have only had to give their Fiat to his Mandates.

Edmund Randolph to James Madison PETTUS'S, VA., MARCH 15, 1783

There is a report, that Mr. Morris has actually resigned his superintendency: and the speculations are various on the subject. Some impute the step to weariness and fatigue; others to an excess of private business; while others, whose disposition is not cordial towards him, ascribe it to a more disagreeable motive. For my part, I conjecture, that he must have been led to this measure by disgust, & want of due support. But even my respect for him will not suffer me to acquit him for resigning at this hour, when fresh vigor may be added to the arms of the enemy, by an assurance, that he abandoned the office through despair of our finances; and the affections of France herself, or rather her inclination to succor us with seasonable loans, may be diminished, from the apprehension of her aid, being misapplied, if thrown into other hands than his.

RICHMOND, MARCH 22, 1783

Lucius† has expressed the destructiveness of Mr. Morris's resignation in colors not very tender, nor yet very extravagant on the score of cruelty. At such a season to quit his office, even if it were steeped to the lips in poverty and difficulty! Personal embarrassments from personal engagements he might have avoided. He ought to have avoided an obedience to that impulse of petulance, which caused him to proclaim the bankruptcy of America.

Alexander Hamilton to George Washington PHILADELPHIA, APRIL 8, 1783

As to Mr. Morris, I will give Your Excellency a true explanation of his conduct. He had been for some time pressing Congress

*The leader of every aspect of government.
†See "Lucius," Philadelphia *Freeman's Journal,* March 15, 1783.

to endeavor to obtain funds, and had found a great backwardness in the business. He found the taxes unproductive in the different states—he found the loans in Europe making a very slow progress—he found himself pressed on all hands for supplies; he found himself in short reduced to this alternative either of making engagements which he could not fulfill or declaring his resignation in case funds were not established by a given time. Had he followed the first course the bubble must soon have burst—he must have sacrificed his credit & his character, and public credit already in a ruinous condition would have lost its last support. He wisely judged it better to resign; this might increase the embarrassments of the moment, but the necessity of the case it was to be hoped would produce the proper measures; and he might then resume the direction of the machine with advantage and success. He also had some hope that his resignation would prove a stimulus to Congress.

He was however ill-advised in the publication of his letters of resignation. This was an imprudent step and has given a handle to his personal enemies, who by playing upon the passions of others have drawn some well meaning men into the cry against him. But Mr. Morris certainly deserves a great deal from his country. I believe no man in this country but himself could have kept the money-machine a going during the period he has been in office. From every thing that appears his administration has been upright as well as able.

Stephen Higginson to Samuel Adams   PHILADELPHIA, MAY 20, 1783

It is the avowed intention of some to create a Congressional influence by the disposal of places of honor & profit, but the effect of this plan if adopted will be a very great increase of particular individual influence & not Congressional. Congress may appear to appoint but it will be, of such persons only as may be nominated by others. Some late instances will show you what extensive influence some Gentlemen have—& many I dare say wonder that after what has passed Mr. Morris should remain in Office. It is however not an easy matter to set him aside. His Friends in Congress are many & powerful. His continuance in Office is by others deemed absolutely necessary at present. It is supposed, & perhaps justly, that if any other person was to be appointed to his Office, or if the business was attempted by a Board, he would be able to so obstruct & oppose their measures that no success could be expected. I confess that I am much of that opinion myself, I should wish however to run the risk, persuaded that the difficulty will not lessen but increase. He will always have it in his power to embarrass if displaced & the disposition is not to be doubted. Disappointed Views in ambitious minds will certainly produce resentment.

Stephen Higginson to Unknown PHILADELPHIA, MAY 1783

I have mentioned to You the large Peace Establishment, the formation of a Navy, and other favorite projects of the *Financier* and his Followers and Adherents. But these Propositions ought to be rejected by Congress, and I think they will, tho' they will be back'd by that Influence which I have already described as being far too great. A thorough Understanding betwixt *Morris,* [*Robert R.*] *Livingston,* the French Minister, the Spanish Agent, and some of the wealthier Citizens of this place, forms a Phalanx that attacks with great force, and when their whole Efforts are brought to a point, and their numerous Dependents are brought forth to action, they are almost irresistible. It is their practice to *hunt* down every man that can't be brought over to their Views, and so many Engines are set at work to depress every individual Opposer, that a man must have more than a common Share of good fortune to escape them, so that an Independent Spirit here is in a constant State of Warfare. I find it difficult to be well with these people, and at the same time act honestly; but as I am not easily discomposed I am determined they shall finally respect me in spite of themselves.

John Jay to Catherine W. Livingston PASSY, JULY 20, 1783

Mr. Morris it seems has postponed his resignation, and I rejoice at it. That resolution is fortunate for the public, and in my opinion conducive to his reputation. He has his enemies it is true, and so all men so circumstanced ever have had and ever will have.

John Jay to Robert Morris PASSY, JULY 20, 1783

Your intended resignation alarmed me, and would have been followed with ill consequences to our affairs. I rejoice that you continue in office, and by no means regret that it will be less in your power than inclination to retire soon. I am well aware of the difficulties you will continue to experience. Every man so circumstanced must expect them. Your office is neither an easy nor a pleasant one to execute, but it is elevated and important, and therefore envy, with her inseparable companion injustice, will not cease to plague you. Remember, however, that triumphs do not precede victory, and that victory is seldom found in the smooth paths of peace and tranquility. Your enemies would be happy to drive you to resign, and in my opinion both your interest and that of your country oppose your gratifying them. You have health, fortune, talents, and fortitude, and you have children too. Each of these circumstances recommends perseverance.

Arthur Lee to St. George Tucker PHILADELPHIA, JULY 21, 1783

Congress are yet at Princeton. The Citizens here are signing an Address intended to effect their return to this City. As Mr. Robert Morris's undue & wicked influence depends so much upon the residence here, it is presumed that he will use his utmost authority for that purpose. But his influence has manifestly diminished since the removal from Philadelphia, & the fixing of Congress in any other place will I hope restrain it within due bounds. It is much suspected that he & his friends have been the prime movers of all the disturbances in the Army, for the purpose of enforcing the 5 per Cent [Impost] in the shape most parental of a corrupt influence in Congress of which he with reason expected to be the prime Minister.

Charles Thomson to Hannah Thomson PRINCETON, N.J., OCTOBER 24, 1783

Mr. Morris had entered into his Office at a time when there was an end of all public credit, when our army was on the point of disbanding for want not of pay but of provisions, when those who were enemies to our cause were pluming themselves with hopes of our speedy ruin, the timid & wavering seemed ready to provide for their safety by going over to the enemy & the most stout hearted had the most serious apprehensions of distress & danger. Without a farthing in the public treasury, without any well grounded hopes of a speedy supply, Mr. M stept into office & by his personal credit & wise measures retrieved & established credit, & fed & kept the army together, until our enemy was compelled to acknowledge our independence and agree to a cessation of hostilities.

James Warren to Elbridge Gerry MILTON, MASS., NOVEMBER 16, 1783

The People see the Cloven foot and have no Confidence in those or rather in him who is Invested with such Indefinite powers.

Samuel Osgood to John Adams ANNAPOLIS, DECEMBER 7, 1783

The Financier & Secretary for foreign Affairs [Robert R. Livingston] were admirably well adapted to support, and not only so, but to become the principal Engines of Intrigue. The first mentioned Officer, is a Man of inflexible Perseverance. He Judges well in almost all Money Matters; and mercantile Transactions. He well knows what is necessary to support public Credit. But never thinks it necessary to secure the Confidence of the People, by making Measures palatable to them. A Man destitute of every Kind of theoretic Knowledge; but from extensive mercantile Negotiations, he is a good practical Merchant; more than this cannot be said with Justice. He Judges generally for himself; and acts with great Decision. He has many excellent Qualities for a Financier, which however do not comport so well with Republicanism, as Monarchy. Ambitious of becoming the first Man in the united States, he was not so delicate in the Choice of Means, and Men for his Purpose, as is indispensably necessary in a free Government. The good Ally of the united States could assist him in Money, & he was heartily dispos'd to make her very grateful Returns. The United States abound with Men absolutely devoted. With such a Financier and with such Materials, it is easy to conceive what an amazing Power he would soon acquire. He stood in need of foreign Support, & they stood in need of him; thus far the political Machinery was in Unison, and republicanism grated harsh Discords.

David Howell to Jabez Bowen ANNAPOLIS, MAY 31, 1784

I hope & trust that the time is near at hand when the sanguine pursuit of new-fangled and (to use the modern phrase) balloon Schemes of financiering will be abandoned.

François, Marquis de Barbé-Marbois to Joseph-Matthais Gérard de Rayneval PHILADELPHIA, AUGUST 24, 1784

From the superintendent we ought not to expect anything but that which he will not be able to prevent himself from doing. . . . I do not think Mr. Morris susceptible of affection or aversion for any power; but I have reason to believe that his avidity can make him capable of very reprehensible irregularities; and that, unless he is bound by the instructions of Congress, he will take very little pains to fulfill the obligations of the United States towards his Majesty.

Francisco de Miranda, Travels in the United States, 1783–1784

Robert Morris, superintendent of finance, etc., seems to me, without doubt, the official of greatest capacity and performance in his line that the United States has had during the past strife, in any department! It is nevertheless said that the extraordinary assistance of Gouverneur Morris has contributed principally to this.

David Jackson to George Bryan NEW YORK, JULY 13, 1785

The business of appointing commissioners to investigate the accounts of the late superintendent of finance, has been for sometime at a stand, because suitable characters seem difficult to be found. I confess myself at a loss on the subject—the influence of the great man is so extensive in Philadelphia, that few probably of the citizens there properly qualified could be found perfectly free from bias—Can you point out any persons either in Pennsylvania or elsewhere which you would suppose fully qualified?

Abigail Adams to Cotton Tufts LONDON, SEPTEMBER 16, 1785

The Board of Commissioners [Treasury] consists of able Men and I hope they will bring order out of confusion, tho I fear they will find the public money making voyages to China. I have been informed that the late Financier lived at an expense of 5000 sterling a year.

Benjamin Rush to Richard Price PHILADELPHIA, OCTOBER 27, 1786

An important revolution took place on the 10th day of this instant in favor of the wisdom, virtue, and property of Pennsylvania. Mr.

Robt. Morris, the late financier of the United States, is at the head of the party that will rule our state for the ensuing year. This gentleman's abilities, eloquence, and integrity place him upon a footing with the first legislators and patriots of ancient and modern times.

Luigi Castiglioni, *Sketches of American Statesmen* 1787

Mr. Morris is now the wealthiest merchant in America, but he shares his fortune with friends who are welcomed to his table and into his home without ceremony, but with complete cordiality. He devotes his mornings to business and evenings to joviality and conversation. He has given a good education to his children, two of whom are now traveling in Europe; and he will leave his wealth to whoever is capable of making good use of it. Many persons have not failed to speak badly of him, asserting that he made his fortune by illicit means. Among others, M. Chastellux, ill-informed, fell into this error. It is certain, however, that he is esteemed by all his correspondents as most exact, punctual, and clear in his dealings—qualities forming the active and honest businessman. He has of late gotten much involved in politics, and being very influential both because of his money and a natural, unstudied, eloquence, he was made head of the Republican party, or of the city inhabitants—a party that exerted a great influence in legislation in the year 1787; and he succeeded in obtaining from the State the legal foundation of the Bank of North America in Philadelphia.

He is a man of more than 50 years of age, with a rustic and pleasant-like face, fond of the table and the bottle, which he gladly shares with his friends.

William Pierce, *"Character Sketches of Delegates to the Federal Convention"* 1787

Robert Morris is a merchant of great eminence and wealth; an able Financier, and a worthy Patriot. He has an understanding equal to any public object, and possesses an energy of mind that few Men can boast of. Although he is not learned, yet he is as great as those who are. I am told that when he speaks in the Assembly of Pennsylvania, that he bears down all before him. What could have been his reason for not Speaking in the Convention I know not,—but he never once spoke on any point. This Gentleman is about 50 years old.

Louis Guillaume Otto, Biographies FALL 1788

Superintendent of Finances during the war, the most powerful merchant in his state. A good head above all, and experienced, but not well-educated. He has somewhat cooled toward France since M. de Marbois has taken the side of Mr. Holker* with so much eagerness and that one has disapproved his contract with the firm [the Farmers General]. It will be easy, however, to win him over with proper handling. This is a man of the greatest consequence whose friendship is not a matter of indifference to us.

George Thatcher to Sarah Thatcher NEW YORK, OCTOBER 1, 1788

Robert Morris & William Maclay were chosen federal Senators for that State. The former lives in the City of Philadelphia—and is the greatest Merchant, perhaps, in all America. He was for several years Financier-General of the United States, in which Office, he acquired immense Riches—whether honestly or dishonestly—is not for you or me to determine, nor is it of any consequence to us now. And it may be enough to regulate his future Conduct for him to know, which I believe he does, that the people in general think pretty independently upon this subject; and three to one don't hesitate to say, in speaking of his wealth, that ill-gotten Riches are of short duration.

Andrew Craigie to Daniel Parker NEW YORK, OCTOBER 2, 1788

Morris is not so popular as he once was and I doubt if his influence will ever again cause much jealousy.

James Campbell to Tench Coxe YORK, PA., OCTOBER 7, 1788

The city Senator is at once the genius of commerce, the patron of manufactures and an extensive landholder.

Benjamin Rush to Jeremy Belknap PHILADELPHIA, OCTOBER 7, 1788

Our senators are both highly federal. Mr. Morris' character for abilities and integrity is well known.

---

*John Holker, a native of France, had been mercantile partners with Robert Morris until 1784 when they had a bitter falling out.

James Madison to Thomas Jefferson   PHILADELPHIA,
DECEMBER 8, 1788

The affairs of R. Morris . . . are still much deranged.

Tench Coxe to James Madison   NEW YORK, JANUARY 27, 1789

In this particular instance it is fortunate that our Senator is a
man of extensive political information, and landed property and,
though a practical Merchant, a friend to a pretty System of Trade.
I do not think the most captious agriculturist in the Senate will
find Mr. Morris tenacious of any principle that will be injurious
to the landed interest.

Samuel A. Otis to Nathan Dane   NEW YORK, MARCH 28, 1789

Here is Bobbe in all his glory nor do I see anybody disposed to
eclipse it.

Paine Wingate to Timothy Pickering   NEW YORK, SEPTEMBER
14, 1789

It is suspected that Mr. Morris has the ear of the President as
much or more than any man. How it is or where the influence lies
I can not say, nor do I care if that influence is not abused.

Fisher Ames to Alexander Hamilton   BOSTON, JULY 31, 1791

Mr. Morris, whom they [the eastern stockholders of the Bank of
the United States] fear as a man of talents & intrigue, with his
connections, will make a property of this man [Thomas Willing
as possible president of the Bank of the United States] & govern
him at their pleasure.

John Adams to Abigail Adams   PHILADELPHIA, JUNE 23, 1795

I went out to Lansdowne [Morris's country estate] on Sunday
about half a mile on this Side Judge Peter's where you once
dined. The Place is very retired, but very beautiful a Splendid
House, gravel Walks, Shrubberies and Clumps of Trees in the
English Style—on the Bank of the Skuykill.

Robert Morris to Alexander Hamilton PHILADELPHIA, JUNE 2, 1797

I am to be sure disagreeably situated, but my affairs are retrievable if I could get the Common aid of Common times and I will struggle hard. Keep All this to Yourself.

John Marshall to Mary W. Marshall PHILADELPHIA, JULY 14, 1797

I like no body so well as the family of Mr. Morris. There is among them throughout a warmth & cordiality which is extremely pleasing.

Julian Ursyn Niemcewic, Travels through America JANUARY 1798

The house of Robert Morris, recently sold, is a monument to the folly of this man who, in spite of all his genius for commerce, has finished by becoming bankrupt. He undertook it in a spirit of rivalry with Bingham. He took as his architect another fool, Major Enfant. He built for him a real confection which was to be all covered with white marble. The undertaking was abandoned in that state most suitable to show all its extravagances.

Robert Morris to Alexander Hamilton HILLES, NEAR PHILADELPHIA, JANUARY 17, 1798

I am Sensible that I have lost the Confidence of the World as to my pecuniary ability, but I believe not as to my honor or integrity and I shall certainly deem myself unhappy if yours is diminished in any respect.

Abigail Adams to Mary Cranch PHILADELPHIA, FEBRUARY 21, 1798

Mr. Morris delivered himself to his bail and went to Jail last week.

Benjamin Rush, Sketches C. 1800

A bold, sensible, and agreeable speaker. His perceptions were quick and his judgment sound upon all subjects. He was opposed to the *time* (not to the *act*) of the Declaration of Independence, but he yielded to no man in his exertions to support it, and a year after it took place he publicly acknowledged on the floor of Congress that he had been mistaken in his former opinion as to its time, and said that it would have been better for our country had it been declared sooner. He was candid and liberal in a debate so as always to be respected by his opponents, and sometimes to offend the members of the party with whom he generally voted. By his extensive commercial knowledge and connections he rendered great services to his country in the beginning, and by the able manner in which he discharged the duties of Financier he revived and established her credit in the close of the Revolution. In private life he was friendly, sincere, generous and charitable, but his peculiar manners deprived him of much of that popularity which usually follows great exploits of public and private virtue. He was proud and passionate, and hence he always had virulent enemies, as well as affectionate friends.

Gouverneur Morris to James Parish JANUARY 14, 1803

I would trust the matter to your decision if you could spend this summer with me as your old acquaintance Robert Morris did the last. He came to me lean, low-spirited, and as poor as a commission of bankruptcy can make a man whose effects will, it is said, not pay a shilling in the pound. Indeed, the assignees will not take the trouble of looking after them. I sent him home fat, sleek, in good spirits and possessed of the means of living comfortably the rest of his days.

John Adams to F. A. Vanderkemp QUINCY, FEBRUARY 16, 1809

Robert Morris (since you ask me my opinion of him) was a frank, generous, and manly mortal. He rose from nothing but a naked boy, by his industry, ingenuity, and fidelity, to great business and credit as a merchant. At the beginning of our revolution, his commerce was stagnated, and as he had over-traded, he was much embarrassed. He took advantage of the times, united with the w[h]igs, came into Congress, and united his credit, supported by my loans in Holland, and resources of the United States. By this means he supported his credit for many years; but at last grew extravagant, as all conquerors and extraordinary characters do, and died as he had lived, as I believe, all his days, worth very little solid capital.

Mathew Carey, Memoirs JUNE 1829

This celebrated man lived too long for his honour.

Thomas Paine
1737–1809

⊰ BORN IN Thetford, Norfolk, England. Radical writer. Five years of formal education in grammar school. Apprenticed to father as staymaker. Excise tax collector. Arrived in Philadelphia with letter of introduction from Benjamin Franklin, November 1774. Edited *Pennsylvania Magazine*, published *Common Sense*, January 1776. Army, 1776, aide to General Nathanael Greene. Wrote sixteen numbers of "The American Crisis," 1776–83. Secretary to Committee for Foreign Affairs (forced to resign), 1777–79. Clerk, Pennsylvania Assembly, 1779–80. Traveled to France with John Laurens to raise funds from French government, 1781. Wrote for Congress and army, 1782. Elected to American Philosophical Society, 1785. Published *Dissertation on Government*, 1786. Defended Bank of North America, 1786. Sailed for Europe with design for iron bridge, April 1787. Published *Rights of Man* (2 pts.), 1791, 1792. Elected to French National Convention, 1792. Opposed execution of Louis XVI. Imprisoned, 1793–94. Published *Age of Reason* (2 pts.), 1794, 1795. Published letter attacking Washington, 1797. Published *Agrarian Justice*, 1797. Returned to the United States, 1802. Unofficial adviser to President Thomas Jefferson.

Thomas Paine and the Pennsylvania Magazine, *1775, from* Isaiah Thomas, History of Printing in America 1810

[Robert] Aitken contracted with Paine to furnish, monthly, for this work [the *Pennsylvania Magazine*] a certain quantity of original matter; but he often found it difficult to prevail on Paine to comply with his engagement. On one of the occasions, when Paine had neglected to supply the materials for the Magazine, within a short time of the day of publication, Aitken went to his lodgings, and complained of his neglecting to fulfill his contract. Paine heard him patiently, and coolly answered, "You shall have them in time." Aitken expressed some doubts on the subject, and insisted on Paine's accompanying him and proceeding immediately to business, as the workmen were waiting for copy. He accordingly went home with Aitken, and was soon seated at the table with the necessary apparatus, which always included a glass, and a decanter of brandy. Aitken remarked, "he would never write without *that.*" The first glass put him in a train of thinking; Aitken feared the second would disqualify him, or render him untractable; but it only illuminated his intellectual system; and when he had swallowed the third glass, he wrote with great rapidity, intelligence, and precision; and his ideas appeared to flow faster than he could commit them to paper. What he penned from the inspiration of the brandy, was perfectly fit for the press without any alteration, or correction.*

John Adams, Autobiography 1776

Paine soon after the Appearance of my Pamphlet [*Thoughts on Government*] hurried away to my Lodgings and spent an Evening with me. His Business was to reprehend me for publishing my Pamphlet. Said he was afraid it would do hurt, and that it was repugnant to the plan he had proposed in his Common Sense. I told him it was true it was repugnant and for that reason, I had written it and consented to the publication of it: for I was as much afraid of his Work as he was of mine. His plan was so democratical, without any restraint or even an Attempt at any Equilibrium or Counterpoise, that it must produce confusion and every Evil Work. I told him further, that his Reasoning from the Old Testament was ridiculous, and I could hardly think him sincere. At this he laughed, and said he had taken his Ideas in that part from Milton; and then expressed a Contempt of the Old Testament and indeed of the Bible at large, which surprised me. He saw that

---

* Isaiah Thomas: Aitken was a man of truth, and of an irreproachable character. This anecdote came from him some years before his death.

I did not relish this, and soon checked himself, with these Words "However I have some thoughts of publishing my Thoughts on Religion, but I believe it will be best to postpone it, to the latter part of Life." This Conversation passed in good humor, without any harshness on either Side: but I perceived in him a conceit of himself, and a daring Impudence, which have been developed more and more to this day.

The third part of Common Sense which relates wholly to the Question of Independence, was clearly written and contained a tolerable Summary of the Arguments which I had been repeating again and again in Congress for nine months. But I am bold to say there is not a Fact nor a Reason stated in it, which had not been frequently urged in Congress. The Temper and Wishes of the People, supplied every thing at that time: and the Phrases, suitable for an Emigrant from New Gate, or one who had chiefly associated with such Company, such as "The Royal Brute of England," "The Blood upon his Soul," and a few others of equal delicacy, had as much Weight with the People as his Arguments. It has been a general Opinion, that this Pamphlet was of great Importance in the Revolution. I doubted it at the time and have doubted it to this day. It probably converted some to the Doctrine of Independence, and gave others an Excuse for declaring in favor of it. But these would all have followed Congress, with Zeal: and on the other hand it excited many writers against it, particularly Plain Truth, who contributed very largely to fortify and inflame the Party against Independence, and finally lost us the Allens, Penns, and many other Persons of Weight in the Community.

Notwithstanding these doubts I felt myself obliged to Paine for the Pains he had taken and for his good Intentions to serve Us which I then had no doubt of. I saw he had a capacity and a ready Pen, and understanding he was poor and destitute, I thought We might put him into some Employment, where he might be useful and earn a Living. Congress appointed a Committee of foreign affairs not long after and they wanted a Clerk. I nominated Thomas Paine, supposing him a ready Writer and an industrious Man. Dr. Witherspoon the President of New Jersey College and then a Delegate from that State rose and objected to it, with an Earnestness that surprised me. The Dr. said he would give his reasons; he knew the Man and his Communications:

When he first came over, he was on the other Side and had written pieces against the American Cause: that he had afterwards been employed by his Friend Robert Aitken, and finding the Tide of Popularity run rapidly, he had turned about: that he was very intemperate and could not write until he had quickened his Thoughts with large drafts of Rum and Water: that he was in short a bad Character and not fit to be placed in such a Situation.—General Roberdeau spoke in his favor: no one confirmed Witherspoon's Account, though the truth of it has since been sufficiently established. Congress appointed him: but he was soon obnoxious by his Manners, and dismissed. . . .

At this day it would be ridiculous to ask any questions about Tom Paine's Veracity, Integrity or any other Virtue.*

John Adams to Abigail Adams PHILADELPHIA, APRIL 28, 1776

The Writer of Common Sense, and the Forrester,† is the same Person. His Name is Payne, a Gentleman, about two Years ago from England, a Man who General [Charles] Lee says has Genius in his Eyes.

Thomas Paine to Henry Laurens 1778

I am neither farmer, manufacturer, mechanic, merchant nor shopkeeper. I believe, however, I am of the first class. I am a Farmer of thoughts.

Gouverneur Morris, Speech in Congress JANUARY 9, 1779

[Paine was] a mere Adventurer from England, without Fortune, without Family or Connections, ignorant even of Grammar.

Marquis de Chastellux, Travels in North-America, in the Years 1780, 1781, and 1782

I know not how it happened, that since my arrival in Philadelphia, I had not seen Mr. Payne, that author so celebrated in America, and throughout Europe, by his excellent work, entitled, *Common Sense,* and several other political pamphlets. M. de la Fayette and I had asked the permission of an interview for the 14th in the

---

*This passage was written in 1802.

†Paine used this pseudonym in writing four letters published in the spring of 1776.

morning, and we waited on him accordingly with Colonel Laurens. I discovered, at his apartments, all the attributes of a man of letters; a room pretty much in disorder, dusty furniture, and a large table covered with books lying open, and manuscripts begun. His person was in a correspondent dress, nor did his physiognomy belie the spirit that reigns throughout his works. Our conversation was agreeable and animated, and such as to form a connection between us, for he has written to me since my departure, and seems desirous of maintaining a constant correspondence. His existence at Philadelphia is similar to that of those political writers in England, who have obtained nothing, and have neither credit enough in the state, nor sufficient political weight to obtain a part in the affairs of government. Their works are read with more curiosity than confidence, their projects being regarded rather as the play of imagination, than as well concerted plans, and sufficient in credit ever to produce any real effect: theirs is always considered as the work of an individual, and not that of a party; information may be drawn from them, but not consequences; accordingly we observe, that the influence of these authors is more felt in the satirical, than in the dogmatical style, as it is easier for them to decry other men's opinions than to establish their own. This is more the case with Mr. Payne than any body; for having formerly held a post in government, he has now no connection with it; and as his patriotism and his talents are unquestionable, it is natural to conclude that the vivacity of his imagination, and the independence of his character, render him more calculated for reasoning on affairs, than for conducting them.

Sarah Bache to Benjamin Franklin PHILADELPHIA, JANUARY 14, 1781

I hear Mr. Payne is gone to France with Mr. Lawrence [John Laurens]. He did not call on us. I had a little dispute with him more than a year ago about Mr. [Silas] Deane, since which time he has never even moved his hat to me. He has lately wrote a Pamphlet called Public Good, which you will receive. Tis called sensible, but he appears throughout to be much afraid of his old employers the Lees, who are interested Virginians. There never was a man less beloved in a place than Payne is in this, having at different times disputed with everybody. The most rational thing he could have done would have been to have died the instant he had finished his Common Sense, for he never again will have it in his power to leave the World with so much credit.

Elkanah Watson, Memoirs 1781

About this period, the notorious Tom Paine arrived at Nantes, in the *Alliance* frigate, as Secretary of Colonel [John] Laurens, Minister Extraordinary from Congress, and took up his quarters at my boarding-place. He was coarse and uncouth in his manners, loathsome in his appearance, and a disgusting egotist; rejoicing most in talking of himself, and reading the effusions of his own mind. Yet I could not repress the deepest emotions of gratitude towards him, as the instrument of Providence in accelerating the declaration of our Independence. He certainly was a prominent agent, in preparing the public sentiment of America for that glorious event. The idea of Independence had not occupied the popular mind, and when guardedly approached on the topic, it shrunk from the conception, as fraught with doubt, with peril, and with suffering.

In 1776 I was present, at Providence, Rhode Island, in a social assembly of most of the prominent leaders of the State. I recollect that the subject of independence was cautiously introduced by an ardent Whig, and the thought seemed to excite the abhorrence of the whole circle.

A few weeks after, Paine's *Common Sense* appeared, and passed through the continent like an electric spark. It everywhere flashed conviction, and aroused a determined spirit, which resulted in the Declaration of Independence, upon the 4th of July ensuing. The name of Paine was precious to every Whig heart, and had resounded throughout Europe.

On his arrival being announced, the Mayor, and some of the most distinguished citizens of Nantes, called upon him to render their homage of respect. I often officiated as interpreter, although humbled and mortified at his filthy appearance, and awkward and unseemly address. Besides, as he had been roasted alive on his arrival at L'Orient, for the —— and well basted with brimstone, he was absolutely offensive, and perfumed the whole apartment. He was soon rid of his respectable visitors, who left the room with marks of astonishment and disgust. I took the liberty, on his asking for the loan of a clean shirt, of speaking to him frankly of his dirty appearance and brimstone odor, and prevailed upon him to stew for an hour, in a hot bath. This, however, was not done without much entreaty, and I did not succeed, until receiving a file of English newspapers, I promised, after he was in the bath, he should have the reading of them, and not before. He at once consented, and accompanied me to the bath, where I instructed the keeper in French (which Paine did not understand) to gradually increase the heat of the water, until "le Monsieur etait bien bouilli."* He became so much absorbed in his reading that he was nearly par-boiled before leaving the bath, much to his improvement and my satisfaction.

Joseph Reed to Nathanael Greene PHILADELPHIA, C. DECEMBER 1781

Your old Friend Mr. Paine has proved himself the Mercenary his Enemies formerly called him having deserted his old Friends & Connections. He is now in the actual Pay of the Men & a supporter of the measures a few Years ago he labored so much to demolish. I am told he pleads Necessity. Many a poor Dog has gone to the Gallows with the same Plea.

Thomas Paine, Philadelphia Freeman's Journal MAY 1, 1782

I have ever kept a clear head and an upright heart, and am not afraid of being replied to. I never took up a matter without fully believing it to be right, and never yet failed in proving it so.

Thomas Paine, The Crisis 1783

It was the cause of America that made me an author.

Gouverneur Morris, Diary JANUARY 26, 1790

Although he has an excellent Pen to write he has but an indifferent Head to think.

Benjamin Rush to Jeremy Belknap PHILADELPHIA, JUNE 6, 1791

Have you read Paine's† and [Joseph] Priestley's answers to [Edmund] Burke's pamphlet? They are both masterly performances,

---

*He should be boiled through and through.

†Paine's first part of *Rights of Man* (1791).

although they possess different species of merit. Paine destroys error by successive flashes of lightning. Priestley wears it away by successive strokes of electricity.

Gouverneur Morris, Diary JULY 4, 1791

Paine is here, inflated to the Eyes and big with a Litter of Revolutions.

Etienne Dumont, Recollections of Mirabeau and of the First Two Legislative Assemblies of France 1791

I could easily excuse, in an American, his prejudice against England but his egregious conceit and presumptuous self-sufficiency quite disgusted me. He was drunk with vanity. If you believed him, it was he who had done everything in America. He was an absolute caricature of the vainest of Frenchmen. He fancied that his book upon the Rights of Man ought to be substituted for every other book in the world; and he told us roundly that, if it were in his power to annihilate every library in existence, he would do so without hesitation in order to eradicate the errors they contained and commence with the Rights of Man, a new era of ideas and principles. He knew all his own writings by heart, but he knew nothing else. . . . Yet Paine was a man of talent, full of imagination, gifted with popular eloquence, and wielded, not without skill, the weapon of irony.

Thomas Paine, Rights of Man, Part 2 1792

Independence is my happiness, and I view things as they are, without regard to place or person; my country is the world, and my religion is to do good.

Gouverneur Morris, Diary FEBRUARY 23, 1792

[Paine] seems to become every Hour more drunk with Self Conceit.

John Adams to Abigail Adams PHILADELPHIA, JANUARY 14, 1793

I expect e'er long to hear that Pain is Split and pliced for an Aristocrat: perhaps roasted or broiled or fried. He is too lean to make a good Pye, but he is now in company with a Number, who are admirably qualified and disposed to feed upon each other.

MARCH 2, 1793

[William Stephens] Smith says that my Books are upon the Table of every Member of the Committee for framing a Constitution of Government for France except Tom Paine, and he is so conceited as to distain to have any Thing to do with Books.

DECEMBER 22, 1793

It is reported this Luminary is coming to America. I had rather two more Genets* should arrive.

Thomas Paine, Age of Reason, *Part 1* 1794

I believe in one God, and no more; and I hope for happiness beyond this life.

Gouverneur Morris to William Short PARIS, JUNE 16, 1794

In the best of times, he had a larger share of every other sense than of common sense, and lately the intemperate use of ardent spirits has, I am told, considerably impaired the small stock, which he originally possessed.

John Adams to Abigail Adams PHILADELPHIA, DECEMBER 28, 1794

The Clergy of New England have trumpeted Paine and Robespierre till they begin to tremble for the Consequences of their own Imprudence.

JANUARY 2, 1796

This sounds like the Bombast of Mad Tom.

Abigail Adams to John Adams QUINCY, JANUARY 15, 1796

[On the rumor of Paine's death.] So poor Tom Paine is gone to see whether there is any State besides the present. Heaven be praised that he is gone there, instead of coming to America. "If plagues and Earthquakes break not heaven's design Why then a Paine or Jacobine?" He was an instrument of much mischief.

---

*Edmond Genet was the young obnoxious French minister to the United States who appealed directly to the American people to support the French war effort, violating the Washington administration's policy of neutrality.

John Adams to Abigail Adams PHILADELPHIA, DECEMBER 8, 1796

They kept back Paine's Letter* Several Weeks, presuming no doubt that it would not promote their Election. It appeared for the first, this morning. I think, of all Paine's Productions it is the weakest and at the same time the most malicious. The Man appears to me to be mad—not drunk. He has the Vanity of the Lunatic who believed himself to be Jupiter the Father of Gods and Men.

Eli Whitney to Josiah Stebbins WASHINGTON, D.C., NOVEMBER 1802

You have doubtless heard of the arrival of the notorious Tom Paine in this country—Being informed, previous to my arrival here, that he was in this neighborhood I had some curiosity to see him—I stopped at the public house where I am now writing to spend one day (it being in a central situation & convenient to the Public Offices where I do business)—I walked out for an hour & returned to dinner—on entering the room—to my great surprise I found that T. Paine was there & a lodger in the house & in less than five minutes we were seated opposite each other at the table—

I was not disappointed in my expectation of his appearance— I found him the same filthy old sot that he has ever been represented. . . . I should judge from his appearance that he is nearly 70 years of age. . . . He is about five feet 10 inches high—his hair three-fourth white—black eyes—a large bulbous nose—a large mouth drawn down at the corners with flabby lips—with more than half decayed, horrid looking teeth—his complexion of a brick color—his face & nose covered with carbuncles & spots of a darker hue than the general color of his skin—his dress rather mean & his whole appearance very slovenly—his hands so convulsed that while his expansive lips almost encompassed a wine glass, he could hardly get the contents of it into his head without spilling it. . . . In short he is a mere loathsome carcass, which has withstood the ravages & rackings of brutal intemperance for an uncommon length of time & from which (were it exposed on

*Paine's published letter to George Washington severely attacked the president for not pursuing efforts to free Paine from his eleven-month incarceration in a French prison.

the barren heath of Africa) the Hyena & Jackals would turn away with disgust.

He observed that he had dined with Mr. Jefferson yesterday & the Day before—& I make no doubt he is a "bosom friend" of the President. . . . Though some of the democrats will swallow common carrion with a good relish, I think most of them will loath the putrid rattle snake which has died from the venom of his own bite.

William Dickson to Andrew Jackson WASHINGTON, D.C., DECEMBER 10, 1802

The Author of Rights of Man—Common Sense &c is here. But that energy of mind and forcible language of which he was formerly possessed is gone. He is now in the sixty-sixth year of his age, but the hardships sustained in the French Prisons have made him much older—he receives due attention from the Republicans.

Manasseh Cutler to Joseph Torrey WASHINGTON, D.C., JANUARY 3, 1803

In answer to your inquiries respecting Paine, I hear very little said about him here. You see by his fourth letter that his "useful labors" are to be suspended during the session. I have not heard of his being at the President's since the commencement of the session, and it is believed that Mr. Jefferson sensibly feels the severe, though just, remarks which have been made on his inviting him to this country. You see by the Message, that courting popularity is his darling object, but we have convincing proof that his caressing of Paine has excited his fears. . . . Paine's venom against the character of the great Washington was occasioned by his not interfering on his behalf when he was confined in France, and any affront from Mr. Jefferson would induce the same kind of treatment. I cannot believe it will be in the power of this degraded wretch to do much mischief. It is certain the more sensible Democrats here view him with contempt, and there are very few so abandoned as openly to associate with him. He lives at Lovell's hotel, who has many lodgers. The members who are there are not willing to acknowledge they have any society with him. He dines at the public table, and, as a show, is as profitable to Lovell as an *Ourang Outang,* for many strangers who come to the city feel a curiosity to see the creature. They go to Lovell's and call for the show—even some members of Congress have done it. I have not yet seen him, nor shall I go out of my way for the sight. He has not, I believe, been in the Hall.

John Adams to Benjamin Waterhouse OCTOBER 29, 1805

I am willing you should call this the Age of Frivolity ... and would not object if you had named it the Age of Folly, Vice, Frenzy, Brutality, Daemons, Buonaparte, Tom Paine, or the Burning Brand from the Bottomless Pit, or anything but the Age of Reason. I know not whether any man in the world has had more influence on its inhabitants or affairs for the last thirty years than Tom Paine. There can be no severer Satyr on the Age. For such a Mongrel between Pigg and Puppy, begotten by a wild Boar on a Bitch Wolf, never before in any Age of the World was suffered by the Poltroonery of Mankind, to run through such a Career of Mischief. Call it then the Age of Paine.

Benjamin Rush, Commonplace Book JUNE 8, 1809

Died at New York Thomas Paine, author of "Common Sense," "Rights of Man," "Age of Reason," and many other political and deistical publications. I knew him well soon after his arrival in America in 1773, at which time he was unfriendly to the claims of America. He wrote "Common Sense" at my request. I gave it its name. He possessed a wonderful talent of writing to the tempers and feelings of the public. His compositions, though full of splendid and original imagery, were always adapted to the common capacities. He was intemperate and otherwise debauched in private life. His vanity appeared in everything he did or said. He once said he was at a loss to know whether he was made for the times or the times made for him. His "Age of Reason" probably perverted more persons from the Christian faith than any book that ever was written for the same purpose. Its extensive mischief was owing to the popular, perspicuous, and witty style in which it was written, and to its constant appeals to the feelings and tempers of his readers.

Thomas Jefferson to Francis Eppes   MONTICELLO, JANUARY 19, 1821

You ask my opinion of Lord Bolingbroke and Thomas Paine. They were alike in making bitter enemies of the priests and pharisees of their day. Both were honest men; both advocates for human liberty. Paine wrote for a country which permitted him to push his reasoning to whatever length it would go. . . . These two persons differed remarkably in the style of their writing, each leaving a model of what is most perfect in both extremes of the simple and the sublime. No writer has exceeded Paine in ease and familiarity of style, in perspicuity of expression, happiness of elucidation, and in simple and unassuming language. In this he may be compared with Dr. Franklin; and indeed his Common Sense was, for awhile, believed to have been written by Dr. Franklin, and published under the borrowed name of Paine, who had come over with him from England.

Thomas Jefferson to John Cartwright   MONTICELLO, JUNE 5, 1824

Paine . . . thought more than he read.

Benjamin Rush

1745–1813

❧ BORN NEAR Philadelphia; educated at College of New Jersey (Princeton); received medical degree, University of Edinburgh, Scotland. Began medical practice in Philadelphia, 1769. Member Continental Congress, 1776–77; signed Declaration of Independence. Appointed surgeon general, Middle Department, 1777; member Republican Society, 1779; helped found Dickinson College at Carlisle, 1782. Delegate Pennsylvania Convention, voted to ratify U.S. Constitution, 1787; wrote many newspaper essays supporting ratification of Constitution; campaigned for revision of Pennsylvania constitution. Member Pennsylvania Democratic Society, 1794. Treasurer of U.S. Mint, 1797–1813. Supported movement for prison reform, educational reform, female education, temperance, and abolition of slavery. Coordinated rapprochement between Thomas Jefferson and John Adams, 1812.

John Adams, Diary SEPTEMBER 24, 1775

Dr. Rush came in. He is an elegant, ingenious Body. Sprightly, pretty fellow. He is a republican. He has been much in London. ...But Rush I think, is too much of a Talker to be a deep Thinker. Elegant not great.

John Adams to Benjamin Rush PARIS, NOVEMBER 7, 1782

You have been a little too busy in your profession of late and are getting Money too fast for my Comfort.

Benjamin Rush to John King   PHILADELPHIA, APRIL 2, 1783

In some of their letters and conversations I am considered as a fool and a madman. In others I am considered as a sly, persevering, and dangerous kind of fellow. Almost every epithet of ridicule and resentment in our language has been exhausted upon me in public newspapers and in private cabals since the humble part I have acted in endeavoring to found a college at Carlisle [Dickinson College].

Benjamin Rush to John Montgomery   PHILADELPHIA, JANUARY 4, 1785

Mr. Hall will send you some newspapers and a new pamphlet written by that turbulent spirit Dr. Rush, who I hope will never be quiet while there is ignorance, slavery, or misery in Pennsylvania.

Louis Guillaume Otto, Biographies   FALL 1788

Doctor and politician. Knowledgeable, eloquent, active but vain and bombastic in debates. He affects too much enthusiasm for France to be believed sincere.

John Adams to Abigail Adams   PHILADELPHIA, JANUARY 26, 1794

I drank Tea last Evening with Dr. Rush. He seems worn and weakened by his great Exertions and fatigues and sickness altogether: but is still agreeable and cheerful. He enquired after your health and sends his respects &c. He had an Awful summer of last.

Benjamin Rush, Commonplace Book 1794

I have been accused of poligamy in my studies. But unlike a plurality of wives, my studies all agree, and are handmaids to each other.

Benjamin Rush to Horatio Gates   PHILADELPHIA, DECEMBER 26, 1795

The word *Republican* is still music in my ears. I still abhor the substance and shadows of monarchy. I still love the common people with all their weaknesses and vices, both of which in our country I ascribe in part to the errors and corruptions of our government. . . . In one thing more I am unchanged. I still love and esteem my old friend General Gates. He was always dear to me. Do come and pass a few weeks in our city. Bring Mrs. Gates along with you. Let us feast once more, before we are parted by the grave, upon the republican principles and maxims with which our bosoms glowed in the years 1774, 1775, and 1776. We will fancy Richard Henry Lee and Samuel Adams are part of our company.

Oliver Wolcott Jr. to John Adams ⸢GRAY'S NEAR PHILADELPHIA, SEPTEMBER 26, 1797

Doctor Rush's pretensions [to be director of the U.S. Mint], founded on public service and celebrity of character, are certainly superior to any of the candidates who have been named. I do not know that he has any other fault, than being somewhat addicted to the modern philosophy. Being, however, of a disposition naturally benevolent, and not apt to be long tenacious of any particular system, his error, if it be one, will probably yield to topical remedies. But to be serious, my opinion is, that though Doctor Rush's mind is not exactly of the right cast, no better selection can be made among the candidates.

William Stephens Smith to Oliver Wolcott Jr. LISBON, FEBRUARY 25, 1798

I see the old dispute revived with great violence for bleeding for fever and ague, and that Dr. Rush is charged with bleeding many hundreds to death. I was not very much surprised of this charge, but I confess I was surprised to see him appointed treasurer of the mint. I hope he won't bleed that to death also. . . . I always considered the Doctor a wrong-headed politician. I know for a fact he was, at the election of President [Adams], very much in favor of the Vice President [Thomas Jefferson].

Abigail Adams to Mary Cranch PHILADELPHIA, MARCH 5, 1798

Upon making inquiries of my intelligencer, Dr. Rush, who knows everybody and their connections . . .

Benjamin Rush, Sketches C. 1800

He aimed well.

John Adams to Benjamin Rush MARCH 26, 1806

You, my friend, I see, are a greater proficient in this philosophy Than I am. You are grown as wise as a serpent and as harmless as a dove.

Benjamin Rush to John Adams SEPTEMBER 8, 1810

I have sometimes amused myself by enumerating the different kinds of hatred that operate in the world. They are the "odium theologicum," the "odium politicum," the "odium philologium," and the "odium medicum." It has been my lot—I will not call it my misfortune—to be exposed to them all. The divines hate me for holding tenets that they say lead to materialism and that are opposed to the rigid doctrines of Calvin. The politicians hate me for being neither a democrat nor a monarchist, neither a Frenchman nor an Englishman. The philologists hate me for writing against the dead languages; and the physicians for teaching a system of medicine that has robbed them by its simplicity of cargoes of technical lumber by which they imposed upon the credulity of the world.

John Adams to Benjamin Rush AUGUST 14, 1811

I know your prudence, your reserve, your caution, your wisdom.

DECEMBER 25, 1811

[In speaking of Jefferson and Benjamin Rush.] I believe you both to mean well to mankind and your country. I might suspect you both to sacrifice a little to the infernal gods, and perhaps unconsciously to suffer your judgments to be a little swayed by a love of popularity and possibly by a little spice of ambition.

BRAINTREE, JANUARY 8, 1812

[Adams had heard it reported that Washington had said:] He had been a good deal in the world and seen many bad Men, but Dr. Rush was the most black hearted scoundrel he had ever known. . . .

   In my opinion there is not in Philadelphia a single citizen more universally esteemed and beloved by his fellow citizens than Dr. Benjamin Rush. There is not a man in Pennsylvania more esteemed by the whole state. I know not a man in America more esteemed by the nation. There is not a citizen of this Union more esteemed throughout the literary, scientifical, and moral world in Europe, Asia, and Africa.

John Adams to Elbridge Gerry QUINCY, APRIL 26, 1813

As a man of Science, Letters, Taste, Sense, Philosophy, Patriotism, Religion, Morality, Merit, Usefulness, taken all-together Rush has not left his equal in America, nor that I know in the World. In him is taken away, and in a manner most sudden and totally unexpected a main Prop of my Life.

John Adams to Richard Rush QUINCY, MAY 5, 1813

In what terms can I address you? There are none that can express my Sympathy with you and your Family, or my own personal Feelings on the loss of your excellent father. There is not another Person, out of my own Family, who can die, in whom my personal Happiness can be so deeply affected. The World would pronounce me extravagant and no Man would apologize for me if I should say that in the Estimation of unprejudiced Philosophy, he has done more good in this World than Franklin or Washington.

Thomas Jefferson to John Adams MONTICELLO, MAY 27, 1813

Another of our friends of 76 is gone, my dear Sir, another of the Co-signers of the independence of our country. And a better man, than Rush, could not have left us, more benevolent, more learned, of finer genius, or more honest.

Thomas Jefferson to Richard Rush MONTICELLO, MAY 31, 1813

No one has taken a more sincere part than myself in the affliction which has lately befallen your family, by the loss of your inestimable and ever to be lamented father. His virtues rendered him dear to all who knew him, and his benevolence led him to do all men every good in his power. Much he was able to do, and much therefore will be missed. My acquaintance with him began in 1776. It soon became intimate, and from that time a warm friendship has been maintained by a correspondence of unreserved confidence. [Jefferson asks for the return of several letters he wrote to Benjamin Rush that contained personal information, such as Jefferson's thoughts on religion.]

John Adams to Thomas Jefferson QUINCY, JUNE 11, 1813

I received yesterday your favor of May 27th. I lament with you the loss of Rush. I know of no Character living or dead, who has done more real good in America.

Roger Sherman

1721–1793

⊰ BORN IN Newton, Mass.; cordwainer, shopkeeper, lawyer. Moved to New Milford, Conn., 1743. Surveyor for New Haven County, 1745–52. New Milford town offices (grand juryman, list taker, leather sealer, fence viewer, selectman, town agent), 1749–53. Surveyor for Litchfield County, 1752–58. Admitted to bar, 1754. New Milford delegate to house, 1755–56, 1758–61. Litchfield County justice of peace, 1755–61 (justice of quorum, 1759–61). New Haven County justice of quorum, 1766–67. Member of council, 1766–85. Judge of Superior Court, 1766–89. Delegate to Congress, 1774–81, 1783–84 (member of committee on Declaration of Rights, signed declaration, 1774; signed Articles of Association, 1774; signed Olive Branch petition, 1775; member of committee to draft Declaration of Independence, signed Declaration, 1776; member of committee to draft Articles of Confederation, 1776, signed Articles, 1778; signed ratification of Treaty of Paris, 1784). Delegate to Springfield Convention, 1777, to New Haven Convention, 1778, to Philadelphia Convention, 1780. Member council of safety, 1777–80, 1782. Mayor of New Haven, 1784–93. Delegate to Constitutional Convention, signed U.S. Constitution, 1787. Author of "A Countryman" and "A Citizen of New Haven" essays, 1787–88. Delegate to Connecticut Convention, voted to ratify U.S. Constitution, 1788. New Haven County justice of peace, 1789–90. Member U.S. House of Representatives, 1789–91. U.S. senator, 1791–93.

John Adams, Diary SEPTEMBER 15, 1775

Sherman's Air is the Reverse of Grace. There cannot be a more striking Contrast to beautiful Action, than the Motions of his Hands. Generally, he stands upright with his Hands before him. The fingers of his left Hand clenched into a Fist, and the Wrist of it, grasped with his right. But he has a clear Head and sound Judgment. But when he moves a Hand, in any thing like Action, Hogarth's Genius could not have invented a Motion more opposite to grace. It is Stiffness, and Awkwardness itself. Rigid as Starched Linen or Buckram. Awkward as a junior Bachelor, or a Sophomore. . . .

OCTOBER 10, 1775

Dyer and Sherman speak often and long, but very heavily and clumsily.

Silas Deane to Elizabeth Deane PHILADELPHIA, JANUARY 21, 1776

I have not sat in Congress since last Tuesday when with pleasure, I gave place to my Successor of whom as Our Neighbor says, *I say Nothing.* But of my Old Colleague, Sh——n suffice it to say, that if the order of Jesuits is extinct, their practices are not out of fashion, even among *modern New Light Saints,* or some of them, for I will never particularize any Sect.

William Williams to Jabez Huntington PHILADELPHIA, SEPTEMBER 30, 1776

If our Assembly rechose their Delegates, I hope They will be guided by Wisdom & Prudence. I must say that Mr. Sherman from his early acquaintance, his good sense, Judgment, Steadiness & inflexible Integrity, has acquired much Respect & is an exceeding valuable Member, & so is Mr. [Samuel] Huntington & truly judicious, upright & worthy the Trust in Spite of that awful Contempt of Religion & Goodness too visible &c. Integrity & Virtue does & will Command Respect.

John Adams to Abigail Adams PHILADELPHIA, MARCH 16, 1777

Mr. [Samuel] Adams has removed to Mrs. Cheeseman's [boardinghouse], in fourth Street near the Corner of Market Street, where he has a curious Group of Company consisting of Characters as opposite, as North and South. [Jared] Ingersol[l], the Stamp man and Judge of Admiralty, Sherman, an old Puritan, as honest as an Angel and as staunch as a blood Hound firm as a Rock in the Cause of American Independence, as Mount Atlas, and Coll. [Matthew] Thornton, as droll and funny as Tristram Shandy. Between the Fun of Thornton, the Gravity of Sherman, and the formal Toryism of Ingersol, Adams will have a curious Life of it.

Nathanael Greene to Samuel Blachley Webb CAMP, PRECKNESS NEAR PARAMUS, N.J. JULY 4, 1780

The Congress are dreaming as usual; your very good friend Sir Roger is playing his old game of little tricks, and pursuing his former scale of penny happenny politics; and unfortunately for America, he finds enough of his kidney to join him, to form a majority in the House.

Nathanael Greene to Jeremiah Wadsworth CAMP TAPPAN, N.Y. AUGUST 14, 1780

Roger Sherman is doing all the mischief he can in Congress, he is at the head of this affair. It appears to be his intention to get our public affairs in as bad a train as possible at the time he leaves Congress; that the confusion and disorder that will follow, may appear to be owing to his having left the house. I am of opinion that he is one of the most wicked and ignorant politicians that ever disgraced an Assembly or that had such an extensive influence.

Joseph Webb to Nathanael Greene WETHERSFIELD, CONN., SEPTEMBER 16, 1780

[Members of Congress led by Sherman who advocated reduced salaries for officers in the Quartermaster Department:] Messrs. Penny Halfpenny Shermanites.

William Ellery to Benjamin Huntington ANNAPOLIS, APRIL 3, 1784

Your description of the attendants upon the Lady Mayoress, the day Old Roger was chosen Lord Mayor of the City of New Haven, and the design of their visits diverted me hugely. I believe the election was not disagreeable to our old friend. He sucked his tooth, threw his thighs across each other when he heard the news, looked foolish, and was persuaded to sprinkle his commission with wine. The company, consisting of delegates from N. Hampshire, R. Island, Connecticut and N. Jersey, who all board together, indulged a merry vein on the occasion. When a person gives a treat with us, upon his being elected to a new office, we call it cutting or docking the colt's tail. This was mentioned, and naturally and punnicly bro't up a *mare's* tail, and a *Mayor's* tail, and that produced this anecdote from friend Roger. When his little son was told that his father was made a *mayor*, what says the boy and are they agoing to *ride* him? We made Yankey Hall roar with laughter, for so we call our dining room.

Jeremiah Wadsworth to Rufus King HARTFORD, JUNE 3, 1787

I am satisfied with the appointments [to the Constitutional Convention]—except Sherman, who, I am told, is disposed to patch up the old scheme of Government. This was not my opinion of him, when we chose him: he is as cunning as the Devil, and if you attack him, you ought to know him well; he is not easily managed, but if he suspects you are trying to take him in, you may as well catch an Eel by the tail.

William Pierce, "Character Sketches of Delegates to the Federal Convention" 1787

Mr. Sherman exhibits the oddest shaped character I ever remember to have met with. He is awkward, un-meaning, and unaccountably strange in his manner. But in his train of thinking there is something regular, deep and comprehensive; yet the oddity of his address, the vulgarisms that accompany his public speaking, and that strange New England cant which runs through his public as well as his private speaking make everything that is connected with him grotesque and laughable,—and yet he deserves infinite praise,—no Man has a better Heart or a clearer Head. If he cannot embellish he can furnish thoughts that are wise and useful. He is an able politician, and extremely artful in accomplishing any particular object,—it is remarked that he seldom fails. I am told he sits on the Bench in Connecticut, and is very correct in the discharge of his Judicial functions. In the early part of his life he was a Shoe-maker,—but despising the lowness of his condition, he turned Almanack maker, and so progressed upwards to a

Judge. He has been several years a Member of Congress, and discharged the duties of his Office with honor and credit to himself, and advantage to the State he represented. He is about 60.

Benjamin Rush, Sketches   c. 1800

A plain man of slender education. He taught himself mathematicks, and afterwards acquired some property and a good deal of reputation by making almanacks. He was so regular in business, and so democratic in his principles that he was called by one of his friends "a republican machine." Patrick Henry asked him in 1774 why the people of Connecticut were more zealous in the cause of liberty than the people of other States; he answered "because we have more to lose than any of them." "What is that," said Mr. Henry. "Our beloved charter" replied Mr. Sherman. He was not less distinguished for his piety than his patriotism. He once objected to a motion for Congress sitting on a Sunday upon an occasion which he thought did not require it, and gave as a reason for his objection, a regard of the commands of his Maker. Upon hearing of the defeat of the American army on Long Island, where they were entrenched and fortified by a chain of hills, he said to me in coming out of Congress "Truly in vain is salvation hoped for from the hills, and from the multitude of mountains" (Jeremiah 12:23).

George Washington
1732–1799

⁌ BORN IN Westmoreland County, Va. Culpeper Co. surveyor, 1749. District adjutant, 1752–53. Appointed lieutenant colonel, 1754. Commander in chief of Virginia forces, 1755–58. Represented Frederick County, 1758–65, and Fairfax County, 1766–76, in House of Burgesses. Delegate to Congress, 1774–75. General and commander in chief, Continental army, 1775–83. President-general, Society of the Cincinnati, 1783–99. President, Constitutional Convention, 1787. Chancellor, College of William and Mary, 1788–99. President of the United States, 1789–97. Lieutenant general and commander in chief, U.S. Provisional Army, 1798–99.

Charles Willson Peale RECOLLECTION OF DECEMBER 28, 1773

One afternoon several young gentlemen, visitors at Mount Vernon, and myself were engaged in pitching the bar, one of the athletic sports common in those days, when suddenly the colonel appeared among us. He requested to be shown the pegs that marked the bounds of our efforts; then, smiling, and without putting off his coat, held out his hand for the missile. No sooner . . . did the heavy iron bar feel the grasp of his mighty hand than it lost the power of gravitation, and whizzed through the air, striking the ground far, very far, beyond our utmost limits. We were indeed amazed, as we stood around, all stripped to the buff, with shirt sleeves rolled up, and having thought ourselves very clever fellows, while the colonel, on retiring, pleasantly observed, "When you beat my pitch, young gentlemen, I'll try again."

Silas Deane to Elizabeth Deane PHILADELPHIA, SEPTEMBER 10, 1774

Col. Washington is nearly as Tall a Man as Col. Fitch and almost as hard a Countenance, yet with a very young Look, & an easy Soldierlike Air, & gesture. He does not appear above Forty-five, yet was in the first Action in 1753 & 1754 on the Ohio, & in 1755 was with Braddock, & was the means of saving the remains of that unfortunate Army. It is said That in the House of Burgesses in Virginia, on hearing of the Boston port Bill, he offered to raise & Arm & lead One Thousand Men himself at his Own Expense for the defense of the Country were there Need of it. His Fortune is said to be equal to such an Undertaking. . . . [Richard Bland is a tolerable speaker] as is Col. Washington who speaks very Modestly, & in cool but determined Style & Accent.

Eliphalet Dyer to Joseph Trumbull PHILADELPHIA, JUNE 17, 1775

You will hear that Coll. Washington is Appointed General or Commander in Chief over the Continental Army by I don't know but the Universal Voice of the Congress. I believe he will be Very Agreeable to our officers & Soldiery. He is a Gentleman highly Esteemed by those acquainted with him, though I don't believe as to his Military, & for real service he knows more than some of ours, but so it removes all jealousies, more firmly Cements the Southern to the Northern, and takes away the fear of the former lest an Enterprising eastern New England General providing Successful, might with his Victorious Army give law to the Southern & Western Gentry. This made it absolutely Necessary in point of prudence, but he is Clever, & if any thing too modest. He seems discrete & Virtuous, no harum Scarum ranting Swearing fellow, but Sober, steady, & Calm. His modesty will Induce him I dare say to take & order every step with the best advice possible to be obtained in the Army.

John Adams to Elbridge Gerry PHILADELPHIA, JUNE 18, 1775

There is something charming to me in the conduct of Washington. A gentleman of one of the first fortunes upon the continent, leaving his delicious retirement, his family and friends, sacrificing his ease, and hazarding all in the cause of his country! His views are noble and disinterested. He declared, when he accepted the mighty trust, that he would lay before us an exact account of his expenses, and not accept a shilling for pay.

George Washington to Martha Washington PHILADELPHIA, JUNE 18, 1775

My Dearest, I am now set down to write to you on a subject which fills me with inexpressable concern—and this concern is greatly aggravated and Increased when I reflect on the uneasiness I know it will give you—It has been determined in Congress, that the whole Army raised for the defense of the American Cause shall be put under my care, and that it is necessary for me to proceed immediately to Boston to take upon me the Command of it. You may beleive me my dear Patcy, when I assure you, in the most solemn manner, that, so far from seeking this appointment, I have used every endeavour in my power to avoid it, not only from my unwillingness to part with you and the Family, but from a consciousness of its being a trust too great for my Capacity and that I should enjoy more real happiness and felicity in one month with you, at home, than I have the most distant prospect of reaping abroad, if my stay was to be Seven times Seven years. But, as it has been a kind of destiny that has thrown me upon this Service, I shall hope that my undertaking of it, is designed to answer some good purpose—You might, and I suppose did perceive, from the Tenor of my letters, that I was apprehensive I could not avoid this appointment, as I did not even pretend to intimate when I should return—that was the case—it was utterly out of my power to refuse this appointment without exposing my Character to such censures as would have reflected dishonour upon myself, and given pain to my friends—this, I am sure could not, and ought not to be pleasing to you, & must have lessend me considerably in my own esteem. I shall rely therefore, confidently, on that Providence which has heretofore preservd, & been bountiful to me, not doubting but that I shall return safe to you in the fall—I shall feel no pain from the Toil, or the danger of the Campaign—My happiness will flow, from the uneasiness I know you will feel from being left alone—I therefore beg of you to summon your whole fortitude & Resolution, and pass your time as agreeably as possible—nothing will give me so much sincere satisfaction as to hear this, and to hear it from your own Pen.

John Adams to William Tudor PHILADELPHIA, JUNE 20, 1775

You will be pleased with him. He is brave, wise, generous and humane.

Thomas Cushing to James Bowdoin Sr. PHILADELPHIA, JUNE 21, 1775

You will doubtless have been informed that the Congress have unanimously appointed George Washington, Esqr., General & Commander in Chief of the American forces. I beg leave to recommend him to your respectful notice. He is a complete gentleman. He is sensible, amiable, virtuous, modest, & brave. I promise myself that your acquaintance with him will afford you great pleasure, and I doubt not his agreeable behavior & good conduct will give great satisfaction to our people of all denominations.

Charles Carroll of Annapolis to Charles Carroll of Carrollton JUNE 24, 1775

I am pleased with Washington's appointment to be Generalissimo, there may be as brave & as good Officers to the Northward, but we know Him to be a Cool, prudent Man.

Abigail Adams to John Adams BRAINTREE, JULY 16, 1775

I was struck with General Washington. You had prepared me to entertain a favorable opinion of him, but I thought the one half was not told me. Dignity with ease, and complacency, the Gentleman and Soldier look agreeably blended in him. Modesty marks every line and feature of his face.

Elkanah Watson, Memoirs 1775

I delivered my letter to Gen Washington in person, and was deeply impressed with an awe I cannot describe in contemplating that great man, his august person, his majestic mien, his dignified and commanding deportment, more conspicuous perhaps at that moment from the fact that he was in the act of admonishing a militia colonel with some animation.

Benjamin Rush to Thomas Ruston PHILADELPHIA, OCTOBER 29, 1775

General Washington has astonished his most intimate friends with a display of the most wonderful talents for the government of an army. His zeal, his disinterestedness, his activity, his politeness, and his manly behavior to General Gage in their late correspondence have captivated the hearts of the public and his friends. He seems to be one of those illustrious heroes whom providence raises up once in three or four hundred years to save a nation from ruin. If you do not know his person, perhaps you will be pleased to hear that he has so much martial dignity in his deportment that you would distinguish him to be a general and a soldier from among ten thousand people. There is not a king in Europe that would not look like a valet de chamber by his side.

Thomas Paine, "The American Crisis," No. 1 DECEMBER 19, 1776

Voltaire has remarked, that King William never appeared to full advantage but in difficulties and in action; the same remark may be made on General Washington, for the character fits him. There is a natural firmness in some minds which cannot be unlocked by trifles, but which, when unlocked, discovers a cabinet of fortitude; and I reckon it among those kind of public blessings, which we do not immediately see, that GOD hath blest him with uninterrupted health, and given him a mind that can even flourish upon care.

Samuel Shaw to Francis Shaw MORRISTOWN, N.J., JANUARY 7, 1777

Our army love our General very much, but yet they have *one thing against him,* which is the little care he takes of himself in any action. His personal bravery, and the desire he has of animating his troops by example, make him fearless of any danger. This, while it makes him appear great, occasions us much uneasiness. But Heaven, who has hitherto been his shield, I hope will still continue to guard so valuable a life.

William Hooper to Robert Morris BALTIMORE, FEBRUARY 1, 1777

I congratulate you upon the new face which our affairs have assumed in the Jersies* under every difficulty that a military genius could possibly have to struggle with. General Washington

*A reference to Washington's victories at Trenton and Princeton.

sometimes almost without an army, at best with one composed of raw undisciplined troops, impatient of Command & vastly inferior in numbers to the Enemy, has been able to check a victorious army, with every thing that could afford a probability of Success, thundering at the very gates of the Capital of America, to change their Course, & is now pursuing them in turn to the only spot which they have possession of in America. Will Posterity believe the Tale? When it shall be consistent with policy to give the history of that man from his first introduction into our service, how often America has been rescued from ruin by the mere strength of his genius, conduct & courage encountering every obstacle that want of money, men, arms, Ammunition could throw in his way, an impartial World will say with you that he is the Greatest Man on Earth. Misfortunes are the Element in which he shines. They are the Groundwork on which his picture appears to the greatest advantage. He rises superior to them all, they serve as foils to his fortitude, and as stimulants to bring into view those great qualities which in the serenity of life his great modesty keeps concealed. I could fill the side in his praise, but anything I can say cannot equal his Merits or raise your Idea of them.

Robert Morris to George Washington PHILADELPHIA, FEBRUARY 27, 1777

I do not like to be too sanguine & yet it is very necessary in a Contest like this we are engaged in to view the best side of the picture frequently, remember good Sir, that few men ever Keep their feelings to themselves, & that it is necessary for example sake, that all leaders should feel & think old in order to inspirit those that look up to them. Heaven (no doubt for the Noblest purposes) has blessed you with a Firmness of Mind, Steadiness of Countenance and patience in Sufferings that give You infinite advantages over other Men. This being the case You are not to depend on other People's exertions being equal to your own. One Mind feels & thrives on misfortunes by finding resources to get the better of them, another sinks under their weight, thinking it impossible to resist and as the latter description probably includes the Majority of Mankind we must be cautious of alarming them.

John Adams to Abigail Adams YORK, PA., OCTOBER 26, 1777

[After word of the victory over Burgoyne at Saratoga.] Congress will appoint a Thanksgiving, and one Cause of it ought to be that the Glory of turning the Tide of Arms, is not immediately due to the Commander in Chief, nor to southern Troops. If it had been, Idolatry, and Adulation would have been unbounded, so excessive as to endanger our Liberties for what I know.

Now We can allow a certain Citizen to be wise, virtuous, and good, without thinking him a Deity or a savior.

Jonathan Dickinson Sergeant to James Lovell LANCASTER, PA., NOVEMBER 20, 1777

Things look gloomy enough below. We want a General; thousands of Lives & Millions of Property are yearly sacrificed to the Insufficiency of our Commander in Chief. Two Battles he has lost for us by two such Blunders as might have disgraced a Soldier of three Months Standing; and yet we are so attached to this Man that I fear we shall rather sink with him than throw him off our Shoulders. And sink we must under his Management. Such Feebleness & Want of Authority, such Confusion & Want of Discipline, such Waste, such Destruction will exhaust the Wealth of both the Indies & annihilate the Armies of all Europe & Asia. Twenty Thousand Recruits annually would be absolutely necessary to maintain an Army of forty thousand. I believe this is the most moderate Calculation. In the mean Time People are so disaffected to the Service that no more Recruits can be got. In short, I am quite a Convert to Abraham Clarke's Opinion; that we may talk of the Enemy's Cruelty as we will, but we have no greater Cruelty to complain of than the Management of our Army.

John Adams, Autobiography DECEMBER 1777

The News of my Appointment was whispered about, and General Knox came up to dine with me, at Braintree. The design of his Visit was as I soon perceived to sound me in relation to General Washington. He asked me what my Opinion of him was. I answered with the utmost Frankness, that I thought him a perfectly honest Man, with an amiable and excellent heart, and the most important Character at that time among Us, for he was the center of our Union. He asked the question, he said, because, as

I was going to Europe it was of importance that the General's Character should be supported in other Countries. I replied that he might be perfectly at his ease on the Subject for he might depend upon it, that both from principle and Affection, public and private I should do my Utmost to support his Character at all times and in all places.

Marquis de Lafayette to the Duc d'Ayen IN CAMP AT GULPH, PA., DECEMBER 16, 1777

Our general is a man truly made for this revolution, which could not succeed without him. I am closer to him than anyone else, and I find him worthy of his country's veneration. His warm friendship and his complete confidence in me regarding all military and political matters, great and small, put me in a position to know all that he has to do, to reconcile, and to overcome. I admire him more each day for the beauty of his character and his spirit. Certain foreigners piqued because they did not receive commissions (although such things were not within his authority), others whose ambitious projects he did not wish to serve, and still other jealous intriguers would like (perhaps) to tarnish his reputation, but his name will be revered down through the centuries by all those who love liberty and humanity.

Henry Laurens to Isaac Motte YORK, PA., JANUARY 26, 1778

We have been from time to time for above a Month past alarmed by accounts from the Commander in Chief of the near & almost inevitable dispersion of the Army from a want of provision. Nakedness is cheerfully submitted. The General has made the most affecting complaints of neglect in the principal departments, has proceeded even to say, that "never was Officer so impeded as he has been," yet I intimate it with deep feeling & much regret, too little regard has been paid to his sensible, spirited, Manly Representations. This great & virtuous Man has not acted the *half patriot,* by a hasty resignation. His Complaints are well founded, nevertheless he will not take a Step which may greatly injure thirteen United States because of the inconsiderate conduct, design, ignorance or negligence of a Majority of *twenty-one,* too often only of *fifteen* Men. No internal Enemy can hurt him without his own consent.

Benjamin Harrison to Robert Morris FEBRUARY 19, 1778

The general is fully inform'd of all those Cabals, they prey on his Constitution, sink his Spirits, and will in the end I fear prove fatal to him, if this should be the case excuse me for once more repeating it, America, will lose perhaps her only prop. He well knows bad consequences would follow his resignation, or he would not leave it in the power of the wicked and designing, thus to insult him.

Marquis de Lafayette to the Baron von Steuben ALBANY, MARCH 12, 1778

Allow me, sir, to congratulate you on being so near General Washington. This great man has no enemies but those of his own country, and yet every noble and sensitive soul must love the excellent qualities of his heart. I think I know him as well as anyone, and that is precisely the idea I have of him. His honesty, his candor, his sensitivity, his virtue in the full sense of the word are above all praise. It is not for me to judge his military abilities, but as far as my feeble judgment can discern, his opinion in the council always seemed to me to be the best, though his modesty sometimes kept him from sustaining it, and his predictions have always been fulfilled. In all sincerity, it has been a pleasure for me to give you some idea of the character of my friend, because some people would have tried perhaps to deceive you in this matter.

Samuel Shaw to the Rev. Mr. Eliot of Boston ARTILLERY PARK, ABOUT 24 MILES WEST OF PHILADELPHIA, APRIL 12, 1778

It would be paying very little attention to that warm attachment which you so justly have to our illustrious Commander-in-chief, were I to omit acquainting you, that he enjoys a perfect state of health, and is the same steady, amiable character he ever has been. His fortitude, patience, and equanimity of soul, under the discouragements he has been obliged to encounter, ought to endear him to his country,—it has done it exceedingly to the army. When I contemplate the virtues of the man, uniting in the citizen and soldier, I cannot too heartily coincide with the orator for the Fifth of March last, who so delicately describes him, as a person that appears to be raised by Heaven to show how high humanity can soar.* It will afford you no small pleasure to be told, that the faction which was breeding last winter in order to traduce the first character on the Continent is at an end.

Thomas Burke to the North Carolina Assembly YORK, PA., APRIL 29, 1778

[After a debate in Congress over a draft letter responding to General Washington's criticism of the inconsistent policy of Congress toward prisoners.] I have penetrated the personal character of General Washington. In my Judgment he is a good officer and most excellent Citizen, moved only by the most amiable and disinterested Patriotism, he perseveres in encountering extreme difficulties, dangers and fatigues under which he seems Sensible of no uneasiness but from the misfortunes of his Country, and of no pleasure but from her success. His few Defects are only the Excess of his amiable Qualities, and though I am not of opinion that any Individual is absolutely Essential to the success of our Cause, yet I am persuaded his loss would be very severely felt, and would not be easily supplied. With this Idea of him, I could not but deem it very impolitic to hazard giving him disgust when no good cause required it. Nor could I avoid deeming it unjust, and ungenerous to give unnecessary offense and Insult to so worthy a man who had so well deserved of his Country.

Alexander Hamilton to Elias Boudinot NEW BRUNSWICK, N.J., JULY 5, 1778

[On Washington at the Battle of Monmouth.] As we approached the supposed place of action we heard some flying rumors of what had happened in consequence of which the General rode forward and found the troops retiring in the greatest disorder and the enemy pressing upon their rear. I never saw the general to so much advantage. His coolness and firmness were admirable. He instantly took measures for checking the enemy's form and make a proper disposition. He then rode back and had

---

*In the Boston Massacre commemorative speech delivered on March 5, 1778, Jonathan Williams Austin said "our EXALTED GENERAL . . . seems to have been raised up by Heaven, to show to what an height Humanity may soar; who generously sacrificing affluence and domestic ease, wishes to share with you in every danger and distress."

the troops formed on a very advantageous piece of ground; in which and in other transactions of the day General Greene & Lord Stirling rendered very essential service, and did themselves great honor. The sequel is, we beat the enemy and killed and wounded at least a thousand of their best troops. America owes a great deal to General Washington for this day's work; a general rout, dismay and disgrace would have attended the whole army in any other hands but his. By his own good sense and fortitude he turned the fate of the day. Other officers have great merit in performing their parts well; but he directed the whole with the skill of a Master workman. He did not hug himself at a distance and leave an Arnold to win laurels for him;* but by his own presence, he brought order out of confusion, animated his troops and led them to success.

Henry Laurens to George Washington PHILADELPHIA, JULY 7, 1778

I arrived here on Thursday last, but hitherto have not collected a sufficient number of States to form a Congress, consequently I have received no Commands. Your Excellency will therefore be pleased to accept this as the address of an Individual intended to assure you Sir of my hearty congratulations with my Country Men on the success of the American Arms under Your Excellency's immediate Command in the late Battle of Monmouth & more particularly of my own happiness in the additional Glory achieved by Your Excellency in retrieving the honor of these States in the Moment of an alarming dilemma.

It is not my design to attempt encomiums upon Your Excellency. I am as unequal to the task as the Act is unnecessary, Love & respect for Your Excellency is impressed on the Heart of every grateful American, & your Name will be revered by posterity. Our acknowledgements are especially due to Heaven for the preservation of Your Excellency's person necessarily exposed for the Salvation of America to the most imminent danger in the late Action; that the same hand may at all times guide & Shield Your

---

*A reference to the Battle of Saratoga (October 1777) in which General Benedict Arnold heroically led the troops, while his commanding officer, General Horatio Gates, did not actively participate in the combat.

Excellency is the fervent wish of, Dear sir, Your much obliged & faithful humble servant.

Elias Boudinot to Alexander Hamilton PHILADELPHIA, JULY 8, 1778

With the utmost sincerity I congratulate you & my Country on the kind Interposition of Heaven in our favor on the 28 Ultimo. It seems as if on every Occasion we are to be convinced that our political Salvation is to be as through the fire. . . . The General I always revered & loved ever since I knew him, but in this Instance he has rose superior to himself. Every Lip dwells on his Praise for even his pretended Friends (for none dare to acknowledge themselves his Enemies) are obliged to croak it forth. The share that his family (for whom I retain a real friendship) has in the Honors of the day has afforded me real Pleasure, and among the rest none more than that of your Lordship.

John Jay to George Washington PHILADELPHIA, APRIL 21, 1779

I have perused the several papers with which you favoured me. The delicacy, candor, and temper diffused through your letters form a strong contrast to the evasions and design observable in some others.

Marquis de Lafayette to George Washington ST. JEAN D'ANGELY, NEAR ROCHEFORT HARBOR, FRANCE, JUNE 12, 1779

Forgive me for what I am going to say. But I can't help reminding you that a commander in chief should never too much expose himself, that in case General Washington was killed, Nay was seriously wounded, there is no officer in the army who might fill that place. The Battle or action whatsoever should most certainly be lost, and the American army, the American cause itself would perhaps be entirely Ruined.

Moses Hazen to Nathanael Greene PREAKNESS, N.J., JULY 24, 1780

[George Washington] is the very Idol of His Country, and who I love, regard, and Esteem, as one of the best men since the Creation of Adam.

Nathanael Greene to Alexander Hamilton CAMP ON PEDEE RIVER, S.C., JANUARY 10, 1781

It is my opinion that General Washington's influence will do more than all the Assemblies upon the Continent. I always thought him exceeding popular; but in many places he is little less than adored; and universally admired. His influence in this Country might possibly effect something great. However I found myself exceedingly well received; but more from being the friend of the General's than from my own merit.

Alexander Hamilton to Philip Schuyler NEW WINDSOR, N.Y., FEBRUARY 18, 1781

I always disliked the office of an Aide de Camp as having in it a kind of personal dependence. I refused to serve in this capacity with two Major Generals at an early period of the war. Infected however with the enthusiasm of the times, an idea of the General's character which experience soon taught me to be unfounded, overcame my scruples and induced me to accept his invitation to enter into his family. I believe you know the place I held in the General's confidence and councils of which will make it the more extraordinary to you to learn that for three years past I have felt no friendship for him and have professed none. The truth is our own dispositions are the opposites of each other & the pride of my temper would not suffer me to profess what I did not feel. Indeed when advances of this kind have been made to me on his part they were received in a manner that showed at least I had no inclination to court them, and that I wished to stand rather upon a footing of military confidence than of private attachment. You are too good a judge of human nature not to be sensible how this conduct in me must have operated on a man to whom all the world is offering incense. . . .

The General is a very honest man. His competitors have slender abilities and less integrity. His popularity has often been essential to the safety of America, and is still of great importance to it. These considerations have influenced my past conduct respecting him, and will influence my future. I think it is necessary he should be supported.

Marquis de Lafayette to the Prince de Poix CAMP NEAR YORKTOWN, VA., OCTOBER 20, 1781

As for the commander in chief, his genius, his greatness, and the nobility of his manners attach to him the hearts and veneration of both [American and French] armies.

John Jay to Henry Knox MADRID, DECEMBER 10, 1781

General Washington has favored me with copies of the articles of capitulation and returns of the prisoners, etc. It gives me very sensible pleasure to find that he commanded in person on this glorious occasion, and had the satisfaction of bringing deliverance to his native, and, consequently, favorite part of America. If Providence shall be pleased to lead him, with safety and success, through all the duties of his station, and carry him home with the blessings of all America on his head, I think he will exhibit to the world the most singular instance of virtue, greatness, and good-fortune united which the history of mankind has hitherto recorded.

Stephen Higginson to John Lowell PHILADELPHIA, MARCH 4, 1783

I arrived here the 26th ult. . . . Three days We spent at head Quarters with Genl. Washington, with whose steadiness & great prudence I was much pleased, he surely was made expressly for these times & no other than such a Character could have answered Our purpose.

Chevalier de La Luzerne to the Comte de Vergennes MARCH 29, 1783

General Washington conducts himself with his usual wisdom. It conciliates to him more and more the respect and affection of the people. After a war of eight years, during which he has scarcely ever left his army, and has never taken any repose, he has received the news of the peace with the greatest joy. It made him shed tears, and he said it was the happiest hour of his life. It will be in vain for him to wish to conceal himself and to live as a private man. He will always be the first citizen of the United States; and, although military men are not agreed as to his military talents, all the world is agreed touching his republican virtues, and agreed that there is no character more eminent among those who have taken part in this grand revolution.

Samuel Shaw to the Rev. Mr. Eliot APRIL 1783

[At a meeting of the officers of the Continental army at Newburgh, N.Y., to force Congress to live up to its promises to compensate the officers.] The meeting of the officers was in itself exceedingly respectable, the matters they were called to deliberate upon were of the most serious nature, and the unexpected attendance of the Commander-in-chief heightened the solemnity of the scene. Every eye was fixed upon the illustrious man, and attention to their beloved General held the assembly mute. He opened the meeting by apologizing for his appearance there, which was by no means his intention when he published the order which directed them to assemble. But the diligence used in circulating the anonymous pieces rendered it necessary that he should give his sentiments to the army on the nature and tendency of them, and determined him to avail himself of the present opportunity; and, in order to do it with greater perspicuity, he had committed his thoughts to writing, which, with the indulgence of his brother officers, he would take the liberty of reading to them. It is needless for me to say any thing of this production; *it speaks for itself.* After he had concluded his address, he said, that, as a corroborating testimony of the good disposition in Congress towards the army, he would communicate to them a letter received from a worthy member of that body, and one who on all occasions had ever approved himself their fast friend. This was an exceedingly sensible letter; and, while it pointed out the difficulties and embarrassments of Congress, it held up very forcibly the idea that the army should, at all events, be generously dealt with. One circumstance in reading this letter must not be omitted. His Excellency, after reading the first paragraph, made a short pause, took out his spectacles, and begged the indulgence of his audience while he put them on, observing at the same time, that he had grown gray in their service, and now found himself growing blind. There was something so natural, so unaffected, in this appeal, as rendered it superior to the most studied oratory; it forced its way to the heart, and you might see sensibility moisten every eye. The General, having finished, took leave of the assembly. . . .

I cannot dismiss this subject without observing, that it is happy for America that she has a *patriot army,* and equally so that a *Washington* is its leader. I rejoice in the opportunities I have had of seeing this great man in a variety of situations;—calm and intrepid where the battle raged, patient and persevering under the pressure of misfortune, moderate and possessing himself in the full career of victory. Great as these qualifications deservedly render him, he never appeared to me more truly so, than at the assembly we have been speaking of. On other occasions he has been supported by the exertions of an army and the countenance of his friends; but in this he stood single and alone. There was no saying where the passions of an army, which were not a little inflamed, might lead; but it was generally allowed that longer forbearance was dangerous, and moderation had ceased to be a virtue. Under these circumstances he appeared, not at the head of his troops, but as it were in opposition to them; and for a dreadful moment the interests of the army and its General seemed to be in competition! He spoke,—every doubt was dispelled, and the tide of patriotism rolled again in its wonted course. Illustrious man! What he says of the army may with equal justice be applied to his own character. "Had this day been wanting, the world had never seen the last stage of perfection to which human nature is capable of attaining."

John Jay to George Washington PASSY, JUNE 13, 1783

I have, within these few days past, read and admired your address to the army, and their proceedings in consequence of it. Such instances of patriotism are rare, and America must find it difficult to express, in adequate terms, the gratitude she owes to both. Such a degree of glory, so virtuously acquired, and so decently sustained, is as new as our political constellation, and will for ever give luster to it. May every blessing be yours.

John Adams to Robert R. Livingston PARIS, JUNE 16, 1783

The happy turn given to the discontents of the army by the General is consistent with his character, which, as you observe, is above all praise, as every character is whose rule and object are duty, not interest nor glory, which I think has been strictly true with the General from the beginning, and I trust will continue to the end. May he long live and enjoy his reflections and the confidence and affections of a free, grateful, and virtuous people.

Marquis de Lafayette to George Washington CHAVANIAC IN
THE PROVINCE OF AUVERGNE, FRANCE JULY 22, 1783

I must again tell you how happy you made your friend by your
letters enclosing the proceedings of the army. In every instance,
My dear General, I have the satisfaction to love and to admire
you. The conduct you had on that occasion was highly praised
throughout all Europe, and your returning to a private station is
called the finishing stroke to an unparalleled character. Never did
a man exist who so honorably stood in the opinions of mankind,
and your name, if possible, will become still greater in posterity. Everything that is Great, and everything that is Good were
not hitherto united in one man. Never did one man live whom
the soldier, statesman, patriot, and philosopher could equally admire, and never was a Revolution brought about, that in its motives, its conduct, and its consequences could so well immortalize
its Glorious Chief. I am proud of you, My dear General, your
Glory makes me feel as if it was my own—and while the world is
gaping at you, I am pleased to think, and to tell, the qualities of
your heart do render you still more valuable than anything you
have done.

David Howell to William Greene PRINCETON, N.J., SEPTEMBER
9, 1783

In consequence of a polite card from his Excellency the General to his Excellency the President [of Congress]—The latter,
with all the present members, Chaplains & great officers of Con-
gress had the Honor of dining at the General's Table last Friday.
The Tables were spread under a Marquis, or tent taken from the
British. The repast was elegant—but the General's Company
crowned the whole. As I had the fortune to be seated facing the
General; I had the pleasure of hearing all his Conversation. The
President of Congress was seated on his right & the minister of
France on his left.

I observed with much pleasure that the General's front was
uncommonly open & pleasant—the contracted, pensive Air beto-
kening deep thought & much care, which I noticed on Prospect
Hill in 1775 is done away; & a pleasant smile sparkling vivacity
of wit & humor succeeds. It will please you to hear the following
which occur out of many. On the president observing that in the

present Situation of our affairs he believed that *Mr. Morris had his HANDS full.* The General replied at the same Instant—*"He wished he had his POCKETS full too."* . . .

Congress have ordered an Equestrian Statue of General Washington to be erected at the place where they may establish their permanent residence. No honor short of those, which the Deity vindicates to himself, can be too great for Gen. Washington.

John Price to John Jay GREAT BOURTON, NEAR BANBURY, OXFORDSHIRE, ENGLAND, OCTOBER 29, 1783

Immortal Washington . . . has outshined and Eclipsed all Asiatic, African, and European Generals, and Commanders from the Creation of the World, to this Day.

Thomas Jefferson to Benjamin Harrison PHILADELPHIA, NOVEMBER 11, 1783

I had the happiness of seeing Genl. Washington the other day after an interval of 7 years. He has more health in his countenance than I ever saw in it before.

James McHenry to His Fiancée Margaret Caldwell ANNAPOLIS, DECEMBER 23, 1783

Today my love the General at a public audience made a deposit of his commission and in a very pathetic [i.e., emotional] manner took leave of Congress. It was a Solemn and affecting spectacle; such an one as history does not present. The spectators all wept, and there was hardly a member of Congress who did not drop tears. The General's hand which held the address shook as he read it. When he spoke of the officers who had composed his family, and recommended those who had continued in it to the present moment to the favorable notice of Congress he was obliged to support the paper with both hands. But when he commended the interests of his dearest country to almighty God, and those who had the superintendence of them to his holy keeping, his voice faltered and sunk, and the whole house felt his agitations. After the pause which was necessary for him to recover himself, he proceeded to say in the most penetrating manner, "Having now finished the work assigned me I retire from the great theater of action, and bidding an affectionate farewell to this august body under whose orders I have so long acted I here offer my commission and take my leave of all the employments of public life." So saying he drew out from his bosom his commission and delivered it up to the president of Congress. He then returned to his station, when the president read the reply that had been prepared—but I thought without any show of feeling, though with much dignity.

This is only a sketch of the scene. But, were I to write you a long letter I could not convey to you the whole. So many circumstances crowded into view and gave rise to so many affecting emotions. The events of the revolution just accomplished—the new situation into which it had thrown the affairs of the world—the great man who had borne so conspicuous a figure in it, in the act of relinquishing all public employments to return to private life—the past—the present—the future—the manner—the occasion—all conspired to render it a spectacle inexpressingly solemn and affecting.

James Tilton to Gunning Bedford Jr. ANNAPOLIS, DECEMBER 25, 1783

The General came to town last Friday, and announced his arrival, by a letter to Congress, requesting to know in what manner they choosed he should resign his authority; whether by private letter or public audience? The latter was preferred without hesitation. Some etiquette being settled on Saturday, a public dinner was ordered on Monday and the audience to be on Tuesday. The feast on Monday was the most extraordinary I ever attended. Between 2 and 3 hundred Gentlemen dined together in the *ball-room.* The number of cheerful voices, with the clangor of knives and forks made a din of a very extraordinary nature and most delightful influence. Every man seemed to be in heaven or so absorbed in the pleasures of imagination, as to neglect the more sordid appetites, for not a soul got drunk, though there was wine in plenty and the usual number of 13 toasts drank, besides one given afterwards by the General which you ought to be acquainted with: it is as follows. "Competent powers to Congress for general purposes."

In the evening of the same day, the Governor gave a ball at the State House. To light the rooms every window was illuminated. Here the company was equally numerous and more brilliant, consisting of ladies and Gentlemen. Such was my villainous awkwardness, that I could not venture to dance on this occasion, you must therefore annex to it a cleverer Idea, than is to be expected from such a mortified whelp as I am. The General danced every set, that all the ladies might have the pleasure of dancing with him, or as it has since been handsomely expressed, *get a touch of him.*

Tuesday morning, Congress, met, and took their seats in order, all covered [i.e., wearing their hats]. At twelve o'clock the General was introduced by the Secretary, and seated opposite to the president, until the throng, that filled all the avenues, were so disposed of as to behold the solemnity. The ladies occupied the gallery, as full as it would hold, the Gentlemen crowded below stairs. Silence ordered, by the Secretary, the General rose & bowed to Congress, who uncovered but did not bow. He then delivered his speech, and at the close of it, drew his commission from his bosom & handed it to the president. the president replied in a set speech, the General bowed again to Congress, they uncovered & the General retired. After a little pause, the company withdrew, Congress adjourned. The General then stepped into the room again, bid every member farewell and rode off from the door intent upon eating his Christmas dinner at home. Many of the spectators particularly the fair ones shed tears, on this solemn & affecting occasion.

John Marshall to James Monroe RICHMOND, JANUARY 3, 1784

At length then the military career of the greatest Man on earth is closed. May happiness attend him wherever he goes. May he long enjoy those blessings he has secured to his Country. When I speak or think of that superior Man my full heart overflows with gratitude. May he ever experience from his Countrymen those attentions which such sentiments of themselves produce.

Marquis de Lafayette to George Washington PARIS, JANUARY 10, 1784

My dear general Now is at Mount Vernon where He Enjoys those titles Every Heart Gives Him, As the Savior of His Country, the Benefactor of Mankind, the Protecting Angel of liberty, the pride of America, and the Admiration of the two Hemispheres—and Among all those Enjoyments I know He Will Most tenderly feel the pleasure of Embracing His Best His Bosom friend, His Adopted Son, who Early in the Spring Will Be Blessed With a direct Course to the Beloved landing that leads to the House at Mount Vernon.

George Washington to the Marquis de Lafayette MOUNT VERNON, FEBRUARY 1, 1784

At length my Dear Marquis I am become a private citizen on the banks of the Potomac, & under the shadow of my own Vine & my own Fig tree, free from the bustle of a camp & the busy scenes of public life, I am solacing myself with those tranquil enjoyments, of which the Soldier who is ever in pursuit of fame— the Statesman whose watchful days & sleepless Nights are spent in devising schemes to promote the welfare of his own—perhaps the ruin of other countries, as if this Globe was insufficient for us all—& the Courtier who is always watching the countenance of his Prince, in hopes of catching a gracious smile, can have very little conception. I am not only retired from all public employments, but I am retireing within myself; & shall be able to view the solitary walk, & tread the paths of private life with heartfelt satisfaction—Envious of none, I am determined to be pleased with all, & this my dear friend, being the order for my march, I will move gently down the stream of life, until I sleep with my Fathers.

And to tell you that . . . at Annapolis, where Congress were then, and are now sitting, I did, on the 23d of December present them my Commission, & made them my last bow—& on the Eve of Christmas entered these doors an older man by near nine years, than when I left them, is very uninteresting to any but myself.

George Washington to James Craik MOUNT VERNON, MARCH 25, 1784

I do not think vanity is a trait of my character.

Thomas Jefferson to George Washington ANNAPOLIS, APRIL 16, 1784

The objections of those opposed to the institution* shall be briefly sketched . . . that the moderation & virtue of a single character has probably prevented this revolution from being closed

*The Society of the Cincinnati was a fraternal order of former Continental military officers, whose male heirs could obtain membership.

as most others have been by a subversion of that liberty it was intended to establish: that he is not immortal, & his successor or some one of his successors at the head of this institution may adopt a more mistaken road to glory.

George Washington to the Marquis de Lafayette MOUNT VERNON, DECEMBER 8, 1784

In the moment of our separation upon the road as I traveled, & every hour since—I felt all that love, respect & attachment for you, with which length of years, close connexion & your merits, have inspired me. I often asked myself, as our Carriages distended, whether that was the last sight, I ever should have of you? And tho' I wished to say no—my fears answered yes. I called to mind the days of my youth, & found they had long since fled to return no more; that I was now descending the hill, I had been 52 years climbing—& that tho' I was blessed with a good constitution, I was of a short lived family—and might soon expect to be entombed in the dreary mansions of my father's—These things darkened the shades & gave a gloom to the picture, consequently to my prospects of seeing you again: but I will not repine—I have had my day.

Elkanah Watson, Memoirs JANUARY 23–25, 1785

I had feasted my imagination for several days in the near prospect of a visit to Mount Vernon, the seat of Washington. No pilgrim ever approached Mecca with deeper enthusiasm. I arrived there in the afternoon of January 23d, '85. I was the bearer of the letter [of introduction] from Gen. Greene with another from Col. [John] Fitzgerald, one of the former aids of Washington, and also the books from Granville Sharp. Although assured that these credentials would secure me a respectful reception, I trembled with awe as I came into the presence of this great man. I found him at table with Mrs. Washington and his private family, and was received in the native dignity and with that urbanity so peculiarly combined in the character of a soldier and eminent private gentleman. He soon put me at ease, by unbending, in a free and affable conversation.

The cautious reserve, which wisdom and policy dictated, whilst engaged in rearing the glorious fabric of our independence, was evidently the result of consummate prudence, and not characteristic of his nature. Although I had frequently seen him in the progress of the Revolution, and had corresponded with him from France in '81 and '82, this was the first occasion on which I had contemplated him in his private relations. I observed a peculiarity in his smile, which seemed to illuminate his eye; his whole countenance beamed with intelligence, while it commanded confidence and respect. The gentleman who had accompanied me from Alexandria, left in the evening, and I remained alone in the enjoyment of the society of Washington, for two of the richest days of my life. I saw him reaping the reward of his illustrious deeds, in the quiet shade of his beloved retirement. He was at the matured age of fifty-three. Alexander and Caesar both died before they reached that period of life, and both had immortalized their names. How much stronger and nobler the claims of Washington to immortality! In the impulses of mad and selfish ambition, they acquired fame by wading to the conquest of the world through seas of blood. Washington, on the contrary, was parsimonious of the blood of his countrymen, and stood forth, the pure and virtuous champion of their rights, and formed for them (not himself), a mighty Empire.

To have communed with such a man in the bosom of his family, I shall always regard as one of the highest privileges, and most cherished incidents of my life. I found him kind and benignant in the domestic circle, revered and beloved by all around him; agreeably social, without ostentation; delighting in anecdote and adventures, without assumption; his domestic arrangements harmonious and systematic. His servants seemed to watch his eye, and to anticipate his every wish; hence a look was equivalent to a command. His servant Billy [William Lee], the faithful companion of his military career, was always at his side. Smiling content animated and beamed on every countenance in his presence.

The first evening I spent under the wing of his hospitality, we sat a full hour at table by ourselves, without the least interruption, after the family had retired. I was extremely oppressed by a severe cold and excessive coughing, contracted by the exposure of a harsh winter journey. He pressed me to use some remedies, but I declined doing so. As usual after retiring, my coughing increased. When some time had elapsed, the door of my room was gently opened, and on drawing my bed-curtains, to my utter astonishment, I beheld Washington himself, standing at my bedside, with a bowl of hot tea in his hand. I was mortified and distressed beyond expression. This little incident, occurring in common life with an ordinary man, would not have been noticed; but as a trait of the benevolence and private virtue of Washington, deserves to be recorded.

George Washington to Francis Hopkinson MOUNT VERNON, MAY 16, 1785

[In response to Hopkinson's request that Washington sit for his portrait by Robert Edge Pine.] In for a penny, in for a pound, is an old adage. I am so hackneyed to the touches of the Painters pencil, that I am *now* altogether at their beck, and sit like patience on a Monument whilst they are delineating the lines of my face.

It is a proof among many others, of what habit & custom can effect. At first I was as impatient at the request, and as restive under the operation, as a Colt is of the Saddle—The next time, I submitted very reluctantly, but with less flouncing. Now, no dray moves more readily to the Thill, than I do to the Painters Chair. It may easily be conceived therefore that I yielded a ready obedience to your request, and to the views of Mr. Pine.

Robert Hunter Jr., Travel Diary NOVEMBER 16, 1785

At half past eleven we left Alexandria with Mr. [Richard Henry] Lee, the president of Congress, his son, and the servants.* You have a fine view of the Potomac, till you enter a wood. A small rivulet here divides the General's estate from the neighboring farmer's. His seat breaks out beautifully upon you when you little expect, being situated upon a most elegant rising ground on the banks of the Potomac, ten miles from Alexandria. We arrived at Mount Vernon by one o'clock—so called by the General's eldest brother, who lived there before him, after the admiral of that name.

When Colonel Fitzgerald introduced me to the General, I was struck with his noble and venerable appearance. It immediately brought to my mind the great part he had acted in the late war. The General is about six foot high, perfectly straight and well made, rather inclined to be lusty. His eyes are full and blue and seem to express an air of gravity. His nose inclines to the aquiline; his mouth small; his teeth are yet good; and his cheeks indicate

---

*The twenty-year-old Hunter was sent to America to collect pre-Revolutionary War debts by his father, a Scottish factor living in London.

perfect health. His forehead is a noble one, and he wears his hair turned back, without curls (quite in the officer's style) and tied in a long queue behind. Altogether, he makes a most noble, respectable appearance, and I really think him the first man in the world. After having had the management and care of the whole Continental Army, he has now retired without receiving any pay for his trouble. And though solicited by the King of France and some of the first characters in the world to visit Europe he has denied them all and knows how to prefer solid happiness in his retirement to all the luxuries and flattering speeches of European courts.

The General was born and educated near Fredericksburg on the Rappahannock. He must be a man of great abilities and a strong natural genius, as his master never taught him anything but writing and arithmetic. People come to see him here from all parts of the world; hardly a day passes without. But the General seldom makes his appearance before dinner, employing the morning to write his letters and superintend his farms, and allotting the afternoon to company. But even then he generally retires for two hours, between tea and supper, to his study to write.

He is one of the most regular men in the world. When no particular company is at his home, he goes to bed always at nine, and gets up with the sun. It's astonishing the packets of letters that daily come for him, from all parts of the world, which employ him most of the morning to answer, and his secretary Mr. [William] Shaw (an acquaintance of mine) to copy and arrange. The General has all the accounts of the war yet to settle. Shaw tells me he keeps as regular books as any merchant whatever—and a daily journal of all his transactions. It's amazing the number of letters he wrote during the war. There are thirty large folio volumes of them upstairs, as big as common ledgers, all neatly copied. The General is remarked for writing a most elegant letter. Like the famous Addison, his writing excels his speaking.

But to finish this long digression—when I was first introduced to him, he was neatly dressed in a plain blue coat, white cashmere waistcoat, and black breeches and boots, as he came from his farms. After having sit with us some time, he retired and sent in his lady, a most agreeable woman about fifty, and Major [George Augustine] Washington, his nephew, married about three weeks ago to a Miss Besser [Frances Bassett]. She is Mrs. Washington's niece, and a most charming young woman; she is about nineteen. After chatting with them for half an hour, the General came in again, with his hair neatly powdered, a clean shirt on, a new plain, drab coat, white waistcoat, and white silk stockings.

At three dinner was on the table, and we were shown by the General into another room, where everything was set off with a peculiar taste and at the same time very neat and plain. The General sent the bottle about pretty freely after dinner, and gave success to the navigation of the Potomac for his toast, which he has very much at heart, and when finished will, I suppose, be the first river in the world. He never undertakes anything without having first well considered of it and consulted different people. But when once he has begun anything, no obstacle or difficulty can come in his way but what he is determined to surmount. The General's character seems to be a prudent but a very persevering one. He is quite pleased at the idea of the Baltimore merchants laughing at him and saying it was a ridiculous plan and would never succeed. They begin now, says the General, to look a little serious about the matter, as they know it must hurt their commerce amazingly.

The Colonel and I had our horses ready after dinner to return to Alexandria, and, notwithstanding all we could do, the General absolutely insisted upon our staying, on account of the bad afternoon. We therefore complied . . . as I could not refuse the pressing and kind invitation of so great a general. Though our greatest enemy, I admire him as superior even to the Roman heroes themselves.

After tea the General retired to his study and left us with the President, his lady, and the rest of the company. If he had not been anxious to hear the news of Congress from Mr. Lee, most probably he would not have returned to supper but gone to bed at his usual hour, nine o'clock—for he seldom makes any ceremony. We had a very elegant supper about that time.

The General with a few glasses of champagne got quite merry, and being with his intimate friends laughed and talked a good deal. Before strangers, he is generally very reserved and seldom says a word. I was fortunate in being in his company with his particular acquaintances. I'm told during the war he was never seen to smile. The care indeed of such an army was almost enough to make anybody thoughtful and grave. No man but the General could have kept the army together without victuals or clothes.

They placed a confidence in him that they would have had in no other person. His being a man of great fortune and having no children showed them it was quite a disinterested part that he was acting with regard to money-making, and that he only had the good of his country at heart. The soldiers, though starving at times, in a manner adored him.

We had a great deal of conversation about the slippery ground, as the General said, that Franklin was on; and also about Congress, the Potomac, improving their roads, etc.

At twelve I had the honor of being lighted up to my bedroom by the General himself.

Henry Knox to George Washington NEW YORK, MARCH 19, 1787

As you have thought proper my dear Sir, to request my opinion respecting your attendance at the convention, I shall give it with the utmost sincerity and frankness.

I imagine that your own satisfaction or chagrin and that of your friends will depend entirely on the result of the convention—For I take it for granted that however reluctantly you may acquiesce, that you will be constrained to accept of the president's chair. Hence the proceedings of the convention will more immediately be appropriated to you than to any other person.

Were the convention to propose only amendments, and patch work to the present defective confederation, your reputation would in a degree suffer—But were an energetic, and judicious system to be proposed with Your signature, it would be a circumstance highly honorable to your fame, in the judgment of the present and future ages; and doubly entitle you to the glorious republican epithet—THE FATHER OF YOUR COUNTRY.

William Pierce, "Character Sketches of Delegates to the Federal Convention" 1787

Genl. Washington is well known as the Commander in chief of the late American Army. Having conducted these states to independence and peace, he now appears to assist in framing a Government to make the People happy. Like Gustavus Vasa, he may be said to be the deliverer of his Country;—like Peter the great he appears as the politician and the States-man; and like Cincinnatus he returned to his farm perfectly contented with being only a plain Citizen, after enjoying the highest honor of the Confederacy,—and now only seeks for the approbation of his Country-men by being virtuous and useful. The General was conducted to the Chair as President of the Convention by the unanimous voice of its Members. He is in the 52d. year of his age.

Gouverneur Morris to George Washington PHILADELPHIA, OCTOBER 30, 1787

I have observed that your Name to the new Constitution has been of infinite Service. Indeed I am convinced that if you had not attended the Convention, and the same Paper had been handed out to the World, it would have met with a colder Reception, with fewer and weaker Advocates, and with more and more strenuous Opponents. As it is, should the Idea prevail that you would not accept of the Presidency it would prove fatal in many Parts. Truth is, that your great and decided Superiority leads Men willingly to put you in a Place which will not add to your personal Dignity, nor raise you higher than you already stand: but they would not willingly put any other Person in the same Situation because they feel the Elevation of others as operating (by Comparison) the Degradation of themselves. And however absurd this Idea. You will agree with me that Men must be treated as Men and not as Machines, much less as Philosophers, & least of all Things as reasonable Creatures; seeing that in Effect they reason not to direct but to excuse their Conduct.

Thus much for the public Opinion on these Subjects, which must not be neglected in a Country where Opinion is every Thing. I will add my Conviction that of all Men you are best fitted to fill that Office. Your steady Temper is *indispensably necessary* to give a firm and manly Tone to the new Government. To constitute a well poised political Machine is the Task of no common Workman; but to set it in Motion requires still greater Qualities. When once a-going, it will proceed a long Time from the original Impulse. Time gives to primary Institutions the mighty Power of Habit, and Custom, the Law both of Wise Men and Fools, serves as the great Commentator of human Establishments, and like other Commentators as frequently obscures as it explains the Text. No Constitution is the same on Paper and in Life. The Exercise of Authority depends on personal Character; and the Whip and Reins by which an able Charioteer governs unruly Steeds will only hurl the unskillful Presumer with more speedy

& headlong Violence to the Earth. The Horses once trained may be managed by a Woman or a Child; not so when they first feel the Bit. And indeed among these thirteen Horses now about to be coupled together there are some of every Race and Character. They will listen to your Voice, and submit to your Control; you therefore must I say *must* mount the Seat. That the Result may be as pleasing to you as it will be useful to them I wish but do not expect. You will however on this, as on other Occasions, feel that interior Satisfaction & Self Approbation which the World cannot give; and you will have in every possible Event the Applause of those who know you enough to respect you properly.

Thomas Jefferson to Edward Carrington PARIS, MAY 27, 1788

Our jealousy is only put to sleep by the unlimited confidence we all repose in the person to whom we all look as our president. After him, inferior characters may perhaps succeed and awaken us to the danger which his merit has led us into.

Brissot de Warville, New Travels in the United States of America 1788

You have heard me criticize M. Chastellux for having put so much art in his character sketch of the general. To paint a pretentious portrait of an unpretentious man is nonsense. The general's kindness of heart shines in his eyes, which, although they no longer have the piercing gleam his officers knew when he was at the head of the army, still grow animated in conversation. His face has no distinctive features, which is why it has always been difficult to paint a good likeness of him, and why few of his portraits resemble him. His answers to queries are full of common sense. He is very cautious and hesitant about committing himself, but once he has made a decision he is firm and unshakable. His modesty is astonishing, particularly to a Frenchman. He speaks of the American War as if he had not been its leader, and of his victories with a greater indifference than even a foreigner would. I saw him lose his characteristic composure and become heated only when he talked about the present state of affairs in America. The schisms within his country torture his soul, and he feels the necessity of rallying all lovers of liberty around one central issue, the need to strengthen the government. He is still ready to sacrifice his peaceful life, which gives him such happiness. "Happiness like

this," he told me, "is not to be found in great honors or in the tu-
mult of life." This philosopher believed in this truth so strongly
that from the moment of his retirement he severed every political
connection and renounced all offices. And yet, despite his spirit
of abnegation, his disinterestedness, and his modesty, this astonishing man has enemies! He has been viciously attacked in the
newspapers and has been accused of being ambitious and con-
niving, when all his life, when indeed all America, can testify to
his selflessness and integrity. Virginia is perhaps the only state
where he does have enemies, for everywhere else I have heard his
name pronounced with nothing but respect mingled with affection and gratitude. Americans speak of him as they would of a
father. Perhaps Washington is not to be compared to the most
famous military leaders, but he has all the qualities and all the
virtues of the perfect republican. . . .

After spending about three days in the home of this famous
man, who showered me with kindness and gave me a great deal
of information both on the recent war and on present conditions
in America, I reluctantly returned to Alexandria.

Benjamin Franklin, Codicil to His Will 1789

My fine crab-tree walking-stick, with a gold head curiously
wrought in the form of the cap of liberty, I give to my friend, and
the friend of mankind, *General Washington.* If it were a Scepter,
he has merited it, and would become it.

Samuel Phillips Jr. to Benjamin Goodhue IPSWICH, MASS., APRIL 8, 1789

I well remember the plain neat appearance of Genl. Washington
when he first came to Cambridge in 1775 had a surprising effect
on the whole army: on his parting with his earlocks the Officers
at once followed his example, & the time & expense saved in so
small an article, was not inconsiderable.

Ebenezer Hazard to Jeremy Belknap NEW YORK, APRIL 25, 1789

Both the President & Vice President have arrived; both were
duly attended to, but the Evidences of universal Attachment to
the former cannot be described; every Countenance discovered
gladness of heart, & Curiosity, excited by Love, crowded every

Street through which "the Man of the People" was to pass: it was indeed a Day of Joy.

John Langdon to Governor John Pickering NEW YORK, MAY 2, 1789

You have no doubt seen by the papers, the Manner in which we Received our President—I had the honor to be Chairman of a Committee or Delegation, from Both houses of Congress to Receive and Conduct him from the Jersey Shore to his Residence in this City—His Installation, was Truly Solemn and Magnificent—he Delivered his Speech to Both Houses, with a Majesty, Dignity and propriety, that almost exceeded himself. All his movements are Truly Natural, and he Appears in the Cabinet, as in the Field A Washington.

Fisher Ames to George Richards Minot NEW YORK, MAY 3, 1789

I was present [at the inauguration of Washington] in the pew with the President, and must assure you that, after making all deductions for the delusion of one's fancy in regard to characters, I still think of him with more veneration than for any other person. Time has made havoc upon his face. That, and many other circumstances not to be reasoned about, conspire to keep up the awe which I brought with me. He addressed the two Houses in the Senate chamber; it was a very touching scene, and quite of the solemn kind. His aspect grave, almost to sadness; his modesty, actually shaking; his voice deep, a little tremulous, and so low as to call for close attention; added to the series of objects presented to the mind, and overwhelming it, produced emotions of the most affecting kind upon the members. I, Pilgaric, sat entranced. It seemed to me an allegory in which virtue was personified, and addressing those whom she would make her votaries. Her power over the heart was never greater, and the illustration of her doctrine by her own example was never more perfect.

Fisher Ames to Nathaniel Bishop NEW YORK, C. MAY 17, 1789

I saw and listened to Washington with as much emotion as you have supposed. It seemed to be a deception—a kind of allegorical vision, which over-whelmed the senses with vast objects, and the mind with vast reflections. The crowd was great—but not a stupid one—each expressing as much admiration and joy as a painter would have on his canvas. The modesty, benevolence and dignity of the President cannot be described. Your own feeling heart must finish the picture.

John Adams to Richard Peters NEW YORK, JUNE 5, 1789

Your confidence in the thoughtful Temper and prudent Foresight of the President is perfectly well founded, and these qualities will be greatly assisted by proper Ministers.

Daniel George to George Thatcher PORTLAND, MAINE, JUNE 5, 1789

The difference in opinion, between the senate and the house, on the subject of *titles,* has excited the wonder of many wise heads. The opinion of the house, I humbly conceive, was truly republican, and philosophical; and I pray to God that it may prevail. There is more majesty in "GEORGE WASHINGTON, PRESIDENT OF THE UNITED STATES OF AMERICA," than there is in all the pompous titles of Europe and the East! Nobody used to say Mr. Cesar; and nobody ought to add titles to GEORGE WASHINGTON. The name cannot be magnified. Besides, the title proposed by the senate is a servile imitation: for it is almost the very title that Oliver Cromwell wore—but I have said too much.

William Smith of South Carolina to Edward Rutledge NEW YORK, JUNE 21, 1789

While we were struggling & contending about the President's prerogatives,* he was lying extremely ill in bed—it was not known at the time, but we have been since told, that he was in some danger—I had a long conversation yesterday with his Doctor [Samuel Bard], who informed me that the President had been troubled with a Bile on his Seat, which had been so inflamed by his riding on horseback as to grow into an Imposthume as large as my two fists—this occasioned a fever of a threatening nature—it was apprehended that it would turn to a malignant one & the Doctor sat up with him one night—the fever however abated & the Imposthume has been opened—he is now considerably

*The bill requiring the Senate's approval of dismissals of department heads was defeated in the Senate by the casting vote of Vice President John Adams.

better & out of all danger, but will be prevented for some time
from sitting up. . . .

What a blessing to this Country is a Man in this high Station
who is so generally beloved that those things which would alarm
& give uneasiness if committed by any one else are overlooked
when done by him. I am in hopes that before his death, a number
of questions will be settled, the discussion of which under his
Successor would give rise to parties & factions: there is danger
however to be apprehended on the other hand that some points
may be conceded to him from a Sense of his virtues & a confidence that he will never make an improper use of his power,
which ought not to be yielded from a dread of his Successor being less virtuous & moderate.

Samuel Nasson to George Thatcher SANFORD, MAINE, JULY 9, 1789

Suffer me to tell you in few words what is now Spreading in
this Country—you know that I am in friendship with almost all
the Revd. Clergy in this Country [i.e., Maine] or at least they
pretend friendship for me although it may be for Nothing more
than they can turn it to advantage that when they travel they may
know where to Call for a Dinner or lodging thus much for the
Prologue.

Now for the Play that is acting they praise your President to
me for all his Virtues but none more than for his attendance to
Public Worship for this they almost Adore him and I Join with
them and Could almost fill a Volume with his Virtues but why
Should I attempt to paint the Sun.

Abigail Adams to Mary Cranch RICHMOND HILL, NEW YORK, JULY 12, 1789

Our August President is a singular example of modesty and diffidence. He has a dignity which forbids Familiarity mixed with
an easy affability which creates Love and Reverence.

Archibald Stuart to James Madison STAUNTON, VA., JULY 31, 1789

I never knew the Minds of men so much disposed to acquiesce
in public Measures as at present. Their Language is all is well.
While G. Washington lives he will crush both men & Measures

that would abridge either our happiness or Liberty. In short we are all in the same State of Security with Passengers on board a Vessel navigated by an Able captain & skillful Mariners.

Abigail Adams to Mary Cranch RICHMOND HILL, NEW YORK, AUGUST 9, 1789

The House was New furnished for the President & cost ten thousand dollars as the Board of Treasury say. The use & improvement of this they have granted him, which is but just & right. He never rides out without six Horses to his Carriage, four servants, & two Gentlemen before him. This is no more state than is perfectly consistent with his Station, but then I do not Love to see the News writers fib so. He is Perfectly averse to all marks of distinction, say they, yet on the 4th of July when the Cincinnati committee waited upon him he received them in a Regimental uniform with the Eagle most richly set with diamonds at his Button. Yet the News writers will fib, to answer particular purposes. I think he ought to have still more state, & time will convince our Country of the necessity, of it.

John Adams to Silvanus Bourn NEW YORK, AUGUST 30, 1789

I must caution you, my dear Sir, against having any dependence on my influence or that of any other person. No man, I believe, has influence with the President. He seeks information from all quarters, and judges more independently than any man I ever knew. It is of so much importance to the public that he should preserve this superiority, that I hope I shall never see the time that any man will have influence with him beyond the powers of reason and argument.

James Kent, Memoirs

I visited the President at one of his public levees. They are every Tuesday from three to four o'clock P.M. You enter, make a bow; the President and company all stand with their hats in their hands, and after exchanging a few words retire *sans cérémonie.** . . . The President was dressed in a suit of plain cloth of a snuff color, with silk stockings, and a sword by his side. His manners were easy, but distant and reserved. His eye was expressive of

*Without ceremony.

mildness and reflection. His person was tall and full of dignity. No person can approach him without being penetrated with respect and reverence. Without the brilliancy of Caesar's talents, or the daring exertions of Frederick, such has been his steadiness, discretion, good sense, and integrity that no man ever attained a greater ascendancy over free minds or ever reigned so long and so completely in the hearts of a sober and intelligent people.

Abigail Adams to Mary Cranch NEW YORK, JANUARY 5, 1790

[Washington] has so happy a faculty of appearing to accommodate & yet carrying his point, that if he was not really one of the best intentioned men in the world he might be a very dangerous one. He is polite with dignity, affable without familiarity, distant without Haughtiness, Grave without Austerity, Modest, Wise & Good. These are traits in his Character which peculiarly fit him for the exalted station he holds, and God Grant that he may Hold it with the same applause & universal satisfaction for many many years, as it is my firm opinion that no other man could rule over this great people & consolidate them into one mighty Empire but He who is set over us.

Abraham Baldwin to Joel Barlow NEW YORK, MAY 8, 1790

Our great and good man has been unwell again this spring. I never saw him more emaciated, he has been out for a ride on Long Island for ten days, and since his return appears manifestly better. If his health should not get confirmed soon, we must send him out to Mount Vernon to farm it a-while, and let the Vice manage here; his habits require so much exercise, and he is so fond of his plantation, that I have no doubt it would soon restore him. It is so important to us to keep him alive as long as he can live, that we must let him cruise as he pleases, if he will only live and let us know it. His name is always of vast importance but any body can do the greater part of the work that is to be done at present, he has got us well launched in the new ship.

Samuel Osgood to Henry Knox MAY 22, 1790

All upset at President's illness. As Sancho said to the Don,* He

---

*Sancho Panza, the simple squire to Cervantes' Don Quixote. Sancho's commonsense attitude contrasts well against the visionary idealism of his master.

must not, he shall not die, at least not for 10 years. God knows where our troubles would end. . . . He alone has the confidence of the People. In Him they believe and through him they remain United.

Abigail Adams to Mary Cranch   NEW YORK, MAY 30, 1790

He has been in a most dangerous state, and for two or three days I assure you I was most unhappy. I dreaded his death from a cause that few persons, and only those who know me best, would believe. It appears to me that the union of the states, and consequently the permanency of the Government depend under Providence upon his Life. At this early day when neither our Finances are arranged nor our Government sufficiently cemented to promise duration, His death would I fear have had most disastrous consequences. I feared a thousand things which I pray I never may be called to experience. Most assuredly I do not wish for the highest Post.

Marquis de Lafayette to George Washington   PARIS, AUGUST 28, 1790

For God's sake, my dear General, take care of your health! Do not devote yourself so much to the Cabinet, while your habit of life has, from your young years, accustomed you to constant exercise. Your conservation is the life of your friends, the salvation of your country. It is for you a religious duty, not to neglect what may concern your health.

Thomas Jefferson to William Short   PHILADELPHIA, MARCH 16, 1791

[In response to Short's several requests to obtain President Washington's nomination of Short as U.S. minister to France.] To overdo a thing with him is to undo it.

Connecticut Courant   JUNE 20, 1791

Many a private man might make a great President; but will there ever be a President who will make so great a man as WASHINGTON?

George Washington to John Sinclair PHILADELPHIA, MARCH 15, 1793

I keep more Sheep than is usual in this Country (from Six hundred to a thousand head) and whilst I resided thereon and could attend to the management of them myself their fleeces averaged full 5 lbs.; & the Mutton from 18 to 22 lbs. a quarter.

John Adams to Abigail Adams PHILADELPHIA, DECEMBER 30, 1794

But the Man the most to be pitied is the President. With his Exertions, anxieties, Responsibilities for twenty years without fee or reward or Children to enjoy his Renown, to be the Butt of the Insolence of Genets and Clubs is a Trial too great for human Nature to be exposed to. Like The Starling he can't get out of his Cage but Knox says and I believe it, he is sick very sick in it. I could tell you a great deal more but this must be reserved for a Tete a Tete.

DECEMBER 13, 1795
The President is serene, healthy, in good Spirits and so is his Lady.

Thomas Jefferson to William Branch Giles MONTICELLO, DECEMBER 31, 1795

[The president] errs as other men do, but errs with integrity.

John Adams to Abigail Adams PHILADELPHIA, FEBRUARY 15, 1796

I could name you however as good Federalists and as good Men as any, who think and say that he will retire and that they would, if they were he. And who would not? I declare upon my honor I would. After 20 Years of such Service, with such Success, and with no Obligation to any one, I would retire before my Constitution failed, before my Memory failed, before my Judgment failed, before I should grow peevish and fretful, irresolute or improvident. I would no longer put at hazard a Character so dearly earned at present so uncontaminated, but liable by the Weakness of Age to be impaired in a Moment.

APRIL 9, 1796
The Old Hero looks very grave of late.

George Washington to James McHenry MOUNT VERNON, MAY 29, 1797

[In retirement] I begin my diurnal course with the Sun; that if my hirelings are not in their places at that time I send them messages expressive of my sorrow for their indisposition—then having put these wheels in motion, I examine the state of things farther; and the more they are probed, the deeper I find the wounds are, which my buildings have sustained by an absence, and neglect of eight years. By the time I have accomplished these matters, breakfast (a little after seven o'clock, about the time I presume you are taking leave of Mrs. McHenry) is ready. This over, I mount my horse and ride round my farms, which employs me until it is time to dress for dinner; at which I rarely miss seeing strange faces— come, as they say, out of respect to me. Pray, would not the word curiosity answer as well? and how different this, from having a few social friends at a cheerful board? The usual time of sitting at Table—a walk—and Tea—brings me within the dawn of Candlelight; previous to which, if not prevented by company, I resolve, that as soon as the glimmering taper, supplies the place of the great luminary, I will retire to my writing Table and acknowledge the letters I have received; but when the lights are brought, I feel tired, and disinclined to engage in this work, conceiving that the next night will do as well; the next comes, and with it the same causes for postponement, & effect; and so on.

This will account for *your* letters remaining so long unacknowledged—and having given you the history of a day, it will serve for a year; and I am persuaded you will not require a second edition of it: but it may strike you, that in this detail no mention is made of any portion of time allotted for reading; the remark would be just, for I have not looked into a book since I came home, nor shall be able to do it until I have discharged my workmen; probably not before the nights grow longer; when, possibly, I may be looking in doomsday book.

James Madison to Thomas Jefferson FEBRUARY 18, 1798

There never was perhaps a greater contrast between two characters, than between those of the present President [John Adams]

& of his predecessor, although it is the boast & prop of the latter, that he treads in the steps of the former: The one cold considerate & cautious, the other headlong & kindled into flame by every spark that lights on his passions: the one ever scrutinizing into the public opinion, and ready to follow where he could not lead it: the other insulting it by the most adverse sentiments & pursuits: W. a hero in the field, yet over-weighing every danger in the Cabinet—A. without a single pretension to the character of Soldier, a perfect Quixote as a Statesman: the former chief Magistrate pursuing peace every where with sincerity, though mistaking the means; the latter taking as much pains to get into war, as the former took to keep out of it. The contrast might be pursued into a variety of other particulars—the policy of the one in shunning connections with the arrangements of Europe, of the other in holding out the U.S. as a makeweight in its Balances of power: the avowed exultation of W. in the progress of liberty every where, & his eulogy on the Revolution & people of France posterior even to the bloody reign & fate of Robespierre—the open denunciations by Adams of the smallest disturbance of the ancient discipline, order & tranquility of Despotism, &c. &c. &c.

Julian Ursyn Niemcewicz, Travels through America MAY 21, 1798

We arrived there [at Thomas Peters's house near Georgetown] between six and seven o'clock. (I saw him [Washington] through the window and I recognized him immediately.) One can guess how my heart was beating; I was going to see the man for whom, since my youth, I had had such a great respect, such a man as my unhappy fatherland lacked for its own salvation. There were about ten people coming out toward us. I saw only him. I was presented to him by Mr. Law. He held out his hand to me and shook mine. We went into the parlor; I sat down beside him; I was moved, speechless. I had not eyes enough to look on him. He is a majestic figure in which dignity and gentleness are united. The portraits that we have of him in Europe do not resemble him much. He is nearly six feet tall, square set, and very strongly built; aquiline nose, blue eyes, the mouth and especially the lower jaw sunken, a good head of hair. In a word *"Iam senior, sed cruda Deo viridisque Senectus."** He

---

*"Now aged, but a god's old age is hardy and green." Virgil, *Aeneid* 6.304.

wore a coat of deep nut brown, black stockings, a waistcoat and breeches of satin of the same color. He began by questioning me about General Kosciuszko. . . . He continued then—*"How long are you in this country?"*—*"Eight Months"*—*"How do you like it?"* *"I am happy, Sir, to see in America those blessings which I was so ardently wishing for in my own country. To you, Sir, are the Americans indebted for them—"* He bowed his head with a modest air and said to me, *"I wished always to your country well and that with all my heart."* He uttered these last words with feeling.

JUNE 5, 1798

Since his retirement he has led a quiet and regular life. He gets up at 5 o'clock in the morning, reads or writes until seven. He breakfasts on tea and cakes made from maize; because of his teeth he makes slices spread with butter and honey. He then immediately goes on horseback to see the work in the fields; sometimes in the middle of a field he holds council of war with Mr. Addison [the overseer]. He returns at two o'clock, dresses, goes to dinner. If there are guests, he loves to chat after dinner with a glass of Madeira in his hand. After dinner he diligently reads the newspapers, of which he receives about ten of different kinds. He answers letters, etc. Tea at 7 o'clock; he chats until nine, and then he goes to bed.

Abigail Adams to Mary Cranch PHILADELPHIA, JUNE 8, 1798

It was General W.'s wish to make Friends of foes, and he aimed at converting over those who were lukewarm.

John Marshall, Speech in U.S. House of Representatives PHILADELPHIA, DECEMBER 19, 1799

The melancholy event which was yesterday announced with doubt, has been but too certain. Our Washington is no more! The hero, the sage, and the patriot of America—the man on whom in times of danger every eye was turned and all hopes were placed, lives now, only in his own great actions, and in the hearts of an affectionate and afflicted people.

If, sir, it had even not been unusual openly to testify respect for the memory of those whom Heaven had selected as its instruments for dispensing good to men, yet such has been the uncommon worth, and such the extraordinary incidents which have marked the life of him whose loss we all deplore, that the whole American nation, impelled by the same feelings, would call with one voice for public manifestations of that sorrow which is so deep and so universal.

More than any other individual, and as much as to one individual was possible, has he contributed to found this our wide spreading empire, and to give to the western world its independence and its freedom.

Having effected the great object for which he was placed at the head of our armies, we have seen him converting the sword into the plough-share, and voluntarily linking the soldier in the citizen.

When the debility of our federal system had become manifest, and the bonds which connected the parts of this vast continent were dissolving, we have seen him the chief of those patrons who formed for us a constitution, which, by preserving the union, will, I trust, substantiate and perpetuate those blessings our revolution had promised to bestow.

In obedience to the general voice of his country, calling on him to preside over a great people, we have seen him once more quit the retirement he loved, and in a season more stormy and tempestuous than war itself, with calm and wise determination, pursue the true interests of the nation, and contribute more than any other could contribute, to the establishment of that system of policy, which will, I trust, yet preserve our peace, our honor and our independence.

Having been twice unanimously chosen the Chief Magistrate of a free people, we see him, at a time when his re-election with the universal suffrage, could not have been doubted, affording to the world a rare instance of moderation, by withdrawing from his high station to the peaceful walks of private life.

However the public confidence may change, and the public affections fluctuate with respect to others, yet with respect to him they have, in war and in peace, in public and in private life, been as steady as his own firm mind, and as constant as his own exalted virtues.

Let us then, Mr. Speaker, pay the last tribute of respect and affection to our departed friend—Let the grand council of the nation display those sentiments which the nation feels. . . .

Resolved, That a committee, in conjunction with one from the Senate, be appointed to consider on the most suitable manner of paying honor to the memory of the man, first in war, first in peace, and first in the hearts of his countrymen.

Alexander Hamilton, General Orders PHILADELPHIA, DECEMBER 21, 1799

'Tis only for me to mingle my tears with those of my fellow soldiers, cherishing with them the precious recollection, that while others are paying a merited tribute to *"The man of the age,"* we in particular allied as we were to him by a close tie, are called to mourn the irreparable loss of a kind and venerated Patron and father!

Abigail Adams to Mary Cranch PHILADELPHIA, DECEMBER 22, 1799

I wrote to you the day after we received the account of the death of General Washington. This Event so important to our Country at this period, will be universally deplored. No Man ever lived, more deservedly beloved and Respected. The praise and I may say adulation which followed his administration for several years, never made him forget that he was a Man, subject to the weakness and frailty attached to human Nature. He never grew giddy, but ever maintained a modest diffidence of his own talents, and if that was an error, it was of the amiable and engaging kind, tho it might lead sometimes to a want of decisions in some great Emergencies. Possessed of power, possessed of an extensive influence, he never used it but for the benefit of his Country. Witness his retirement to private Life when Peace closed the scenes of War; When called by the unanimous suffrages of the People to the chief Magistracy of the Nation, he acquitted himself to the satisfaction and applause of all Good Men. When assailed by faction, when reviled by Party, he suffered with dignity, and Retired from his exalted station with a Character which malice could not wound, nor envy tarnish. If we look through the whole tenor of his Life, History will not produce to us a Parallel. Heaven has seen fit to take him from us. Our Mourning is sincere, in the midst of which, we ought not to lose sight of the Blessings we have enjoyed and still partake of, that he was spared to us, until he saw a successor filling his place, pursuing the same system which he had adopted, and that in times which have been equally dangerous and Critical. It becomes not me to say more upon this Head.

Alexander Hamilton to Tobias Lear NEW YORK, JANUARY 2, 1800

Your letter of the 15 of December last was delayed in getting to hand by the circumstance of its having gone to New York while I was at Philadelphia and of its having arrived at Philadelphia after I had set out on my return to New York.

The very painful event which it announces had, previously to the receipt of it, filled my heart with bitterness. Perhaps no man in this community has equal cause with myself to deplore the loss. I have been much indebted to the kindness of the General, and he was an Aegis very essential to me. But regrets are unavailing. For great misfortunes it is the business of reason to seek consolation. The friends of General Washington have very noble ones. If virtue can secure happiness in another world he is happy. In this the Seal is now put upon his Glory. It is no longer in jeopardy from the fickleness of fortune.

P.S. In whose hands are his papers gone? Our very confidential situation will not permit this to be a point of indifference to me.

Alexander Hamilton to Rufus King NEW YORK, JANUARY 5, 1800

The irreparable loss of an inestimable man removes a control [over factiousness] which was felt and was very salutary.

Daniel Webster to James Hervey Bingham SALISBURY, MASS., FEBRUARY 5, 1800

Washington, the great political cement dead.

Timothy Dwight, Discourse on the Character of Washington FEBRUARY 22, 1800

Wherever he appeared, an instinctive awe and veneration attended him on the part of all men. Every man, however great in his own opinion, or in reality, shrunk in his presence, and became conscious of an inferiority, which he never felt before. Whilst he encouraged every man, particularly every stranger, and peculiarly every diffident man, and raised him to self possession, no sober person, however secure he might think himself of his esteem, ever presumed to draw too near him. . . .

To his conduct, both military and political, may, with exact propriety, be applied the observation, which has been often made concerning his courage; that in the most hazardous situations no man ever saw his countenance change.

Letter from Alexander Hamilton concerning the Public Conduct and Character of John Adams NEW YORK, OCTOBER 24, 1800

Very different from the practice of Mr. Adams was that of the modest and sage Washington. He consulted much, pondered much, resolved slowly, resolved surely.

Thomas Jefferson to the Earl of Buchan WASHINGTON, D.C., JULY 10, 1803

I feel a pride in the justice which your Lordship's sentiments render to the character of my illustrious countryman, Washington. The moderation of his desires, and the strength of his judgment, enabled him to calculate correctly, that the road to that glory which never dies is to use power for the support of the laws and liberties of our country, not for their destruction; and his will accordingly survives the wreck of everything now living.

Gouverneur Morris to John Marshall JUNE 26, 1807

In approving highly your character of Washington [in Marshall's biography of the president], permit me to add that few men of such steady, persevering industry ever existed, and perhaps no one who so completely commanded himself. Thousands have learned to restrain their passions, though few among them had to contend with passions so violent. But the self-command to which I allude was of higher grade. He could, at the dictate of reason, control his will and command himself to act. Others may have acquired a portion of the same authority; but who could, like Washington, at any moment command the energies of his mind to a cheerful exertion?

John Adams to Benjamin Rush SEPTEMBER 1807

Washington had great advantages for obtaining credence. He possessed a great fortune, immense lands, many slaves, an excellent consort, no children. What could he desire more for felicity here below? His professions therefore of attachment to private life, fondness for agricultural employments, and rural amusements were easily believed; and we all agreed to believe him and make the world believe him. Yet we see he constantly betrayed apprehensions that he should not be seriously believed by the world. He was nevertheless believed, and there is not an example in history of a more universal acknowledgment of disinterestedness in any patriot or hero than there is and will be to the latest posterity in him. . . .

I have sometimes amused myself with inquiring where Washington got his system. Was it the natural growth of his own genius? Had there been any examples of it in Virginia? Instances enough might have been found in history of excellent hypocrites, whose concealments, dissimulations, and simulations had deceived the world for a time; and some great examples of real disinterestedness, which produced the noblest efforts and have always been acknowledged. But you know that our beloved Washington was but very superficially read in history of any age, nation, or country. When then did he obtain his instruction? I will tell you what I conjecture.

Rollin's *Ancient History,* you know, is very generally diffused through this country because it has been and is in England. The reading of most of our men of letters extends little further than this work and Prideaux's *Connections of the Old and New Testament.* From Rollin I suspect Washington drew his wisdom, in a great measure. In the third chapter of the third book . . . there are in the character of Dejoces several strokes which are very curious as they resemble the politics of so many of our countrymen, though the whole character taken together is far inferior in purity and magnanimity to that of Washington.

"He retired from public business, pretending to be over fatigued with the multitudes of people that resorted to him." "His own domestic affairs would not allow him to attend those of other people" &c.

Benjamin Rush to John Adams OCTOBER 31, 1807

It is indeed a rare virtue. . . . I do not think the gentleman you alluded to in your letter upon this subject formed himself or his conduct upon the model of the character described in Rollin. He was self-taught in all the arts which gave him his immense elevation above all his fellow citizens. An intimate friend of Colonel Hamilton's informed me that he once told him that he had never read a single military book except Sime's *Guide.* ...

Our great man wrote a great deal, thought constantly, but read (it is said) very little, and hence the disrespect with which his talents and character have been treated by his aide-de-camp.

John Adams to Benjamin Rush NOVEMBER 11, 1807

Self-taught or book-learned in the arts, our hero was much indebted to his talents for "his immense elevation above his fellows." Talents! You will say, what talents? I answer. 1. An handsome face. That this is a talent, I can prove by the authority of a thousand instances in all ages: and among the rest Madame Du Barry, who said "Le vèritable royaut, est la beaut."* 2. A tall statue, like the Hebrew sovereign chosen because he was taller by the head than the other Jews. 3. An elegant form. 4. Graceful attitudes and movements. 5. A large, imposing fortune consisting of a great landed estate left him by his father and brother, besides a large jointure with his lady, and the guardianship of the heirs of the great Custis estate, and in addition to all this, immense tracts of land of his own acquisition. There is nothing, except bloody battles and splendid victories, to which mankind bow down with more reverence than to great fortune. ...

Mankind in general are so far from the opinion of the lawyer that there are no disinterested actions, that they give their esteem to none but those which they believe to be such. They are oftener deceived and abused in their judgments of disinterested men and actions than in any other, it is true. But such is their love of the marvelous, and such their admiration of uncommon generosity, that they will believe extraordinary pretensions to it, and the Pope says, "Si bonus populus vult decipi, decipiatur."†

Washington, however, did not deceive them. I know not that they gave him more credit for disinterestedness than he deserved, though they have not given many others so much. 6. Washington

---

*The true royalty is beauty.

†Pope Paul IV: "If the good people wish to be deceived, let them be deceived."

was a Virginian. This is equivalent to five talents. Virginian geese are all Swans. Not a bairn in Scotland is more national, not a lad upon the Highlands is more clannish, than every Virginian I have ever known. . . . The Philadelphians and New Yorkers, who are local and partial enough to themselves, are meek and modest in comparison with Virginian Old Dominionism. Washington, of course, was extolled without bounds. 7. Washington was preceded by favorable anecdotes. The English had used him ill in the expedition of Braddock. They had not done justice to his bravery and good counsel. They had exaggerated and misrepresented his defeat and capitulation, which interested the pride as well as compassion of Americans in his favor. President Davies* had drawn his horoscope by calling him "that heroic youth, Col. Washington." Mr. [Thomas] Lynch of South Carolina told me before we met in Congress in 1774 that "Colonel Washington had made the most eloquent speech that ever had been spoken upon the controversy with England, viz. that if the English should attack the people of Boston, he would raise a thousand men at his own expense and march at their head to New England to their aid." . . . 8. He possessed the gift of silence. This I esteem as one of the most precious talents. 9. He had great self-command. It cost him a great exertion sometimes, and a constant constraint, but to preserve so much equanimity as he did required a great capacity. 10. Whenever he lost his temper as he did sometimes, either love or fear in those about him induced them to conceal his weakness from the world. Here you see I have made out ten talents without saying a word about reading, thinking, or writing, upon all which subjects you have said all that need be said. You see I use the word talents in a larger sense than usual, comprehending every advantage. Genius, experience, learning, fortune, birth, health are all talents, though I know not how the word has been lately confined to the faculties of the mind.

Benjamin Rush to John Adams DECEMBER 15, 1807

I admire the correctness of your history of the *ten* talents committed to the subject of your letter. Upon the talent of his taciturnity,

---

*Samuel Davies, president of the College of New Jersey, had praised Washington in his 1775 pamphlet *Religion and Patriotism: The Constituents of a Good Soldier.*

Mr. Liston* gave me the following anecdote: "That he was the only person he had ever known (and he had conversed with several crowned heads and many of the first nobility in Europe) who made *no reply* of any kind to a question that he did not choose to answer."

John Jay to Richard Peters BEDFORD, N.Y., MARCH 29, 1811

His administration raised the nation out of confusion into order, out of degradation and distress into reputation and prosperity. It found us withering—it left us flourishing.

John Adams to Benjamin Rush JUNE 21, 1811

[In speaking of the "masters of the theatrical exhibitions of politics."] Washington understood this art very well, and we may say of him, if he was not the greatest President, he was the best actor of presidency we have ever had. His address to the states when he left the army, his solemn leave taken of Congress when he resigned his commission, his Farewell Address to the people when he resigned his presidency: these were all in a strain of Shakespearian and Garrickal excellence in dramatical exhibitions.

Benjamin Rush to John Adams FEBRUARY 12, 1812

In the summer of 1775 or thereabouts I dined in company with General, then Colonel, [Adam] Stephen on his way from Virginia to the camp. I sat next to him. In a low tone of voice he asked me who constituted General Washington's military family. I told him Colonel J[oseph]. Reed and Major Thomas Mifflin. "Are they men of talent?" said he. "Yes," said I. "I am glad to hear it," said the General, "for General Washington will require such men about him. He is a *weak man.* I know him well. I served with him during the last French war."

FEBRUARY 12, 1812

I do not even wish it to be known that General W. was deficient in that mark of true greatness which so preeminently characterized Julius Caesar, Henry the 4th of France, and Frederick the 2nd of Prussia—the talent to forgive.

---

*Robert Liston was the British minister to the United States.

PHILADELPHIA, JUNE 4, 1812

General Washington I have heard felt public abuse in the most sensible manner. Mr. Jefferson told me he once saw him throw the *Aurora* hastily upon the floor with a "damn" of the author, who had charged him with the crime of being a slaveholder. It is even said that paper induced him to retire from the President's chair of the United States.

John Adams to Benjamin Rush JUNE 12, 1812

I have heard much of Washington's impatience under the lash of scribblers, some of it from his own mouth. Mr. Lear related to me one morning the General's ripping and rascalling Philip Freneau for sending him his papers full of abuse.

Benjamin Rush to John Adams JULY 8, 1812

Among the national sins of our country that have provoked the wrath of Heaven to afflict us with a war, I ought to have mentioned in my last letter the idolatrous worship paid to the name of General Washington by all classes and *nearly* all parties of our citizens, manifested in the impious application of names and epithets to him which are ascribed in Scripture only to God and to Jesus Christ. The following is a part of them: "our Savior," "our Redeemer," "our cloud by day and our pillar of fire by night," "our star in the east," "to us a Son is borne," and "our advocate in Heaven."

Thomas Jefferson to John Melish MONTICELLO, JANUARY 13, 1813

General Washington did not harbor one principle of federalism. He was neither an Angloman, a monarchist, nor a separatist. He sincerely wished the people to have as much self-government as they were competent to exercise themselves. The only point on which he and I ever differed in opinion, was, that I had more confidence than he had in the natural integrity and discretion of the people, and in the safety and extent to which they might trust themselves with a control over their government. He has asseverated to me a thousand times his determination that the existing government should have a fair trial, and that in support of it he would spend the last drop of his blood. He did this the more repeatedly, because he knew General Hamilton's political bias, and my apprehensions from it.

Thomas Jefferson to Walter Jones MONTICELLO, JANUARY 2, 1814

I think I knew General Washington intimately and thoroughly; and were I called on to delineate his character, it should be in terms like these.

His mind was great and powerful, without being of the very first order; his penetration strong, though not so acute as that of a Newton, Bacon, or Locke; and as far as he saw, no judgment was ever sounder. It was slow in operation, being little aided by invention or imagination, but sure in conclusion. . . . He was incapable of fear, meeting personal dangers with the calmest unconcern. Perhaps the strongest feature in his character was prudence, never acting until every circumstance, every consideration, was maturely weighed; refraining if he saw a doubt, but, when once decided, going through with his purpose, whatever obstacles opposed. His integrity was most pure, his justice the most inflexible I have ever known, no motives of interest or consanguinity, of friendship or hatred, being able to bias his decision. He was, indeed, in every sense of the words, a wise, a good, and a great man. His temper was naturally high toned; but reflection and resolution had obtained a firm and habitual ascendancy over it. If ever, however, it broke its bonds, he was most tremendous in his wrath. In his expenses he was honorable, but exact; liberal in contributions to whatever promised utility; but frowning and unyielding on all visionary projects and all unworthy calls on his charity. His heart was not warm in its affections; but he exactly calculated every man's value, and gave him a solid esteem proportioned to it. His person, you know, was fine, his stature exactly what one would wish, his deportment easy, erect and noble; the best horseman of his age, and the most graceful figure that could be seen on horseback. Although in the circle of his friends, where he might be unreserved with safety, he took a free share in conversation, his colloquial talents were not above mediocrity, possessing neither copiousness of ideas, nor fluency of words. In public, when called on for a sudden opinion, he was unready, short and embarrassed. Yet he wrote readily, rather diffusely, in an easy and correct style. This he had acquired by conversation with the world, for his education was merely reading, writing and common arithmetic, to which he added surveying at a later day. His time was employed in action chiefly, reading little, and that only in agriculture and English history. His correspondence became necessarily extensive, and with journalizing his agricultural proceedings, occupied most of his leisure hours within doors. On the whole, his character was, in its mass, perfect, in nothing bad, in few points indifferent; and it may truly be said, that never did nature and fortune combine more perfectly to make a man great, and to place him in the same constellation with whatever worthies have merited from man an everlasting remembrance. For his was the singular destiny and merit, of leading the armies of his country successfully through an arduous war, for the establishment of its independence; of conducting its councils through the birth of a government, new in its forms and principles, until it had settled down into a quiet and orderly train; and of scrupulously obeying the laws through the whole of his career, civil and military, of which the history of the world furnishes no other example.

. . . He was no monarchist from preference of his judgment. The soundness of that gave him correct views of the rights of man, and his severe justice devoted him to them. He has often declared to me that he considered our new constitution as an experiment on the practicability of republican government, and with what dose of liberty man could be trusted for his own good; that he was determined the experiment should have a fair trial, and would lose the last drop of his blood in support of it.

. . . I felt on his death, with my countrymen, that "verily a great man hath fallen this day in Israel."

Martha Washington

1731–1802

⇥ BORN IN New Kent County, Va., she was the eldest of eight children in a middle-gentry family. Her education consisted of reading, writing, arithmetic, music, dance, domestic arts, and household management. She was an accomplished equestrienne. In May 1750 she married Daniel Parke Custis, a wealthy Virginia planter. He died in July 1757, leaving an estate of over £23,000 (more than 17,500 acres and 300 slaves). Martha had four children, two of whom survived. She married George Washington on January 6, 1759. She was five feet tall; he six feet three inches. Martha ran the household staff at Mount Vernon, which consisted of eleven slaves: two cooks, two waiters, two laundresses, one seamstress, and a personal servant for each family member. She had control over the mansion house, the kitchen, the smokehouse, the spinning house, and the washhouse. Her daughter, Patsy Custis, died at the age of seventeen in 1773 and her son, John Parke Custis, somewhat indolent and lacking ambition, died in 1781. Two of his children were raised at Mount Vernon by Martha and George. Unlike Abigail Adams, Martha Washington avoided politics, but she always served as the perfect hostess for the frequent visitors to Mount Vernon and to the President's Mansion in New York City and then in Philadelphia. When Washington died, Martha destroyed their correspondence. In Washington's will he provided for the emancipation of all of his slaves when Martha died and she freed hers. She freed the slaves in 1801.

George Washington to Richard Washington MOUNT VERNON, SEPTEMBER 20, 1759

I am now I beleive fixed at this Seat with an agreable Consort for Life and hope to find more happiness in retirement than I ever experienced amidst a wide and bustling World.

From Edmund Pendleton SEPTEMBER 1774

I was much pleased with Mrs. Washington and her spirit. She seemed ready to make any sacrifice and was cheerful though I knew she felt anxious. She talked like a Spartan mother to her son on going to battle. "I hope you will stand firm—I know George will," she said. The dear little woman was busy from morning until night with domestic duties, but she gave us much time in conversation and affording us entertainment. When we set off in the morning, she stood in the door and cheered us with the good words, "God be with you gentlemen."

John Adams to Mercy Otis Warren PHILADELPHIA, NOVEMBER 25, 1775

The General is amiable and Accomplished and judicious and cool; You will soon know the Person and Character of his Lady. I hope She has as much Ambition for her Husband's Glory, as Portia [Abigail Adams] & Marcia [Mercy Otis Warren] have, and then the Lord have Mercy on the Souls of [Generals William] Howe and [John] Burgoyne & all the [British] Troops in Boston.

Mercy Otis Warren to Abigail Adams WATERTOWN, APRIL 17, 1776

I Arrived at my Lodgings before Dinner the day I Left you: found an obliging Family, Convenient Room and in the Main an agreeable set of Lodgers. Next Morning I took a Ride to Cambridge and waited on Mrs. Washington at 11 o'clock, where I was Received with that politeness and Respect shown in a first interview among the well bred and with the Ease and Cordiality of Friendship of a much Earlier date. If you wish to hear more of this Lady's Character I will tell you I think the Complacency of her Manners speaks at once the Benevolence of her Heart, and her affability, Candor and Gentleness Qualify her to soften the hours of private Life or to sweeten the Cares of the Hero and smooth the Rugged scenes of War.

Elizabeth Drinker, Diary APRIL 6, 1778

Requested an audience with the General—set with his Wife (a sociable pretty kind of Woman) until he came in.

Pierre Etienne du Ponceau, Remembrance of a Visit at Mount Vernon NOVEMBER 1780

She reminded me of the Roman matrons of whom I had read so much, and I thought that she well deserved to be the companion and friend of the greatest man of the age.

Catharine Macaulay Graham to George Washington NEW YORK, JULY 13, 1785

The benevolence of Mrs. Washington's temper with that polite and captivating attention with which she exercises the virtues of hospitality to all the numerous visitors which resort to Mount Vernon are the favorite topics of conversation on which we have dwelt ever since we have had the honor of being entertained under your roof.

George Washington to Jonathan Trumbull Jr. MOUNT VERNON, OCTOBER 1, 1785

My principal pursuits are of a rural nature, in which I have great delight, especially as I am blessed with the enjoyment of good health—Mrs. Washington on the contrary is scarcely ever well, but thankful for your kind remembrance of her.

George Washington to Robert Morris MOUNT VERNON, MAY 5, 1787

Mrs. Washington is become too Domestick, and too attentive to two little Grand Children to leave home.

Martha Washington to Fanny Bassett Washington MOUNT VERNON, FEBRUARY 25, 1788

We have not a single article of news but politic which I do not concern myself about.

Brissot de Warville, New Travels in the United States of America 1788

Everything was simple in the general's home. He provides a good table but not a sumptuous one, and his household is run with regularity and order. Mrs. Washington keeps an eye on everything. She combines with the qualities of an excellent countrywoman the simple dignity which befits a wife whose husband has played the greatest role in his country's history. She is gracious as well, and she shows strangers that courtesy which is the flower of hospitality.

Abigail Adams to Mary Cranch RICHMOND HILL, NEW YORK CITY, JUNE 28, 1789

I took the earliest opportunity (the morning after my arrival [in New York City]) to go & pay my respects to Mrs. Washington. Mrs [Abigail Adams] Smith accompanied me. She received me with great ease & politeness. She is plain in her dress, but that plainness is the best of every article. She is in mourning. Her Hair is white, her Teeth beautiful, her person rather short than otherways, hardly so large as my Ladyship, and if I was to speak sincerely, I think she is a much better figure. Her manners are modest and unassuming, dignified and feminine, not the Tincture of hauteur about her.

JULY 12, 1789

Mrs. Washington is one of those unassuming characters which creates Love & Esteem. A most becoming pleasantness sits upon her countenance & an unaffected deportment which renders her the object of veneration and Respect. With all these feelings and Sensations I found myself much more deeply impressed than I ever did before their Majesties of Britain.

AUGUST 9, 1789

I propose to fix a Levee day soon. I have waited for Mrs. Washington to begin and she has fixed on every Friday 8 o'clock. I attended upon the last, Mrs. [Abigail Adams] Smith & Charles [Adams]. I found it quite a crowded Room. The form of Reception is this, the servants announce & Col. [David] Humphries or Mr. Lear, receives every Lady at the door, & Hands her up to Mrs. Washington to whom she makes a most Respectful courtsey and then is seated without noticing any of the rest of the company.

The President then comes up and speaks to the Lady, which he does with a grace dignity & ease, that leaves Royal George far behind him. The company are entertained with Ice creames & Lemonade, and retire at their pleasure performing the same ceremony when they quit the Room.

OCTOBER 11, 1789

Whilst the Gentlemen are absent we propose seeing one another on terms of much sociability. Mrs. Washington is a most friendly, good Lady, always pleasant and easy, dotingly fond of her Grandchildren, to whom she is quite the Grandmamma.

Martha Washington to Fanny Bassett Washington NEW YORK, OCTOBER 23, 1789

I live a very dull life here and know nothing that passes in the town—I never go to the public place—indeed I think I am more like a state prisoner than anything else, there is certain bounds set for me which I must not depart from—and as I can not do as I like I am obstinate and stay at home a great deal.

Abigail Adams to Mary Cranch NEW YORK, AUGUST 28, 1790

Mrs. Washington . . . sets out tomorrow for Mount Vernon. I am [going] into Town . . . and shall part with her, tho I hope only for a short time, with much Regret. No Lady can be more deservedly beloved & esteemed than she is, and we have lived in habits of intimacy and Friendship. In short the Removal of the principal connections I have here serves to render the place, delightful as it is, much less pleasant than it has been.

Abigail Adams to John Adams QUINCY, JANUARY 12, 1794

My best Respects to Mrs. Washington with many thanks for the honor done me by her repeated kind inquiries. I honor her for a prudence, which I know I do not possess. I could not keep silence as She does.

Benjamin Henry Latrobe, Journals JULY 19, 1796

Upon my return to the house [Mount Vernon], I found Mrs. Washington and her granddaughter Miss Custis in the hall. I introduced myself to Mrs. Washington as a friend of her Nephew, and she immediately entered into conversation upon the prospect from the Lawn and presently gave me an account of her family in a good humored free manner that was extremely pleasant and flattering. She retains strong remains of considerable beauty, seems to enjoy very good health and to have as good humor. She has no affectation of superiority in the slightest degree, but acts completely in the character of the Mistress of the house of a respectable and opulent country gentleman.

Abigail Adams to John Adams QUINCY, JANUARY 29, 1797

I shall think myself the most fortunate among women if I can glide on for four Years with as spotless a Reputation, beloved and esteemed by all as that Good and amiable Lady has done. My endeavors shall not be wanting.

Martha Washington to Lucy Knox POST MAY 1797

I cannot tell you, My dear friend, how much I enjoy home after having been deprived of one so long, for our dwelling in New York and Philadelphia was not home, only a sojourning. The General and I feel like children just released from school or from a hard taskmaster, and we believe that nothing can tempt us to leave the sacred roof-tree again, except on private business or pleasure. We are so penurious with our enjoyment that we are loath to share it with anyone but dear friends, yet almost every day some stranger claims a portion of it, and we cannot refuse. . . .

Our furniture and other things sent to us from Philadelphia arrived safely; our plate we brought with us in the carriage. How many dear friends I have left behind. They fill my memory with sweet thoughts. Shall I ever see them again? Not likely, unless they shall come to me here, for the twilight is gathering around our lives. I am again fairly settled down to the pleasant duties of an old fashioned Virginia house-keeper, steady as a clock, busy as a bee, and as cheerful as a cricket.

Martha Washington to Elizabeth Powel MOUNT VERNON, DECEMBER 18, 1797

It was indeed with sympathetic concern we heard of the late calamitous situation of Philadelphia; and of the death and indisposition of some of your friends. These occurrences, however, are inflicted by an invisible hand as trials of our Philosophy, resignation, and patience, all of which it becomes us to exercise.

Paul Ferdinand Fevot to George Washington BALTIMORE,
APRIL 4, 1798

I am distressed for proper words to express my gratitude for the
reception Your very respectable Lady had favoured me with;
Her gracious civility, the anxiousness The Lady had for my being obliged to wait for Your Excellency; Her condescendency to
keep up a conversation, in short those manners of the Lady of the
highest birth, & the most refined education, has raised in me the
most precious & most thankful remembrance.

Julian Ursyn Niemcewicz, Travels through America MAY 21,
1798

I then went up to Mrs. Washington. She is the same age as the
General (both were born in 1732), small, with lively eyes, a gay
air and extremely kind. She had on a gown, with an even hem,
of stiff white cotton, fitting very tightly, or rather attached from
all sides with pins. A bonnet of white gauze, ribbons of the same
color, encircling her head tightly, leaving the forehead completely
uncovered and hiding only half of her white hair which in back
was done up in a little pigtail. She was at one time one of the most
beautiful women in America and today there remains something
extremely agreeable and attractive about her. She has never had
any children by General Washington. She had four by her first
husband, Mr. Custis.

JUNE 5, 1798

Mrs. Washington is one of the most estimable persons that one
could know, good, sweet, and extremely polite. She loves to talk
and talks very well about times past.

Oliver Wolcott Jr. to Elizabeth Wolcott WASHINGTON, D.C.,
JULY 17, 1800

In May last, I mentioned my intentions of visiting Alexandria and
Mount Vernon, which I have since done. . . . Mrs. Washington
received me with great cordiality, and inquired after you and the
children with lively affection. She appeared to be grieved that you
were not of the party. Her mind is generally serene, but the decay
of strength, the increasing marks of age, and occasional suffusion
of countenance, plainly show that the zest of life has departed.

Manasseh Cutler, Journal JANUARY 2, 1802

When our coaches entered the yard [at Mount Vernon], a number of servants immediately attended, and when we had all stepped out of our carriages a servant conducted us to Madam Washington's room, where we were introduced by Mr. Hillhouse, and received in a very cordial and obliging manner. Mrs. Washington was sitting in rather a small room, with three ladies (granddaughters), one of whom is married to a Mr. [Lawrence] Lewis, and has two fine children; the other two are single. Mrs. Washington appears much older than when I saw her last at Philadelphia, but her countenance very little wrinkled and remarkably fair for a person of her years. She conversed with great ease and familiarity, and appeared as much rejoiced at receiving our visit as if we had been of her nearest connections. She regretted that we had not breakfast sooner, for she always breakfasted at seven, but our breakfast would be ready in a few minutes. In a short time she rose, and desired us to walk into another room, where a table was elegantly spread with ham, cold corn beef, cold fowl, red-herring, and cold mutton, the dishes ornamented with sprigs of parsley and other vegetables from the garden. At the head of the table was the tea and coffee equipage, where she seated herself, and sent the tea and coffee to the company. We were all Federalists, which evidently gave her particular pleasure. Her remarks were frequently pointed, and sometimes very sarcastic, on the new order of things and the present administration. She spoke of the election of Mr. Jefferson, whom she considered as one of the most detestable of mankind, as the greatest misfortune our country had ever experienced. Her unfriendly feelings toward him were naturally to be expected, from the abuse he has offered to General Washington, while living, and to his memory since his decease. She frequently spoke of the General with great affection, viewing herself as alone, and her life protracted, until she had become a stranger to the world. She repeatedly remarked the distinguished mercies heaven still bestowed upon her, for which she had daily cause of gratitude, but she longed for the time to follow her departed friend.

James Wilson
1742–1798

⊰ BORN IN Scotland; educated at St. Andrews, Glasgow, and Edinburgh universities; came to Pennsylvania, 1765; studied law with John Dickinson; admitted to Pennsylvania bar, 1767. Moved to Reading and then to Carlisle. Elected to Continental Congress, May 1775; opposed independence but voted for it on July 2, 1776. Moved to Philadelphia, 1778. Opponent of democratic state constitution (1776); a member Republican Society, 1779. Reelected to Congress, 1776, 1777, 1782, 1785; advocated measures to strengthen central government; defended Bank of North America. Delegate Constitutional Convention, member Committee of Detail, 1787. Speech at Pennsylvania State House Yard, October 6, 1787, provided standard argument for supporters of Constitution. Delegate Pennsylvania Convention, voted to ratify the Constitution, 1787. Presidential elector, 1789; delegate state constitutional convention and principal author of new Pennsylvania constitution, 1789–90. Associate justice, U.S. Supreme Court, 1789–98. Failure of land speculations led to flight to New Jersey in 1797 and then to North Carolina to escape imprisonment for debt in Pennsylvania. Died in North Carolina.

John Adams to Abigail Adams JULY 23, 1775
There is a young Gentleman from Pennsylvania whose Name is Wilson, whose Fortitude, Rectitude, and Abilities too, greatly outshine his Masters.

Robert Whitehill to Various Friends PHILADELPHIA, JUNE 10, 1776

Dickinson, Wilson, and the others, have Rendered themselves obnoxious to Every Whig in town, and Every Day of their Existence are losing the Confidence of the people.

William Hooper to Robert Morris BALTIMORE, FEBRUARY 1, 1777

I have the next delegation of your State much at heart & should be very sorry that any change should take place to the exclusion of Wilson. He is a Character some what particular, but after a long and pretty intimate acquaintance with him I am extremely deceived, if pure Integrity & love to America, a just and generous Attachment to the State which he represents, a strong natural Capacity improved by extensive reading & retentive memory where cool Judgment has matured & digested what he has read are not the genuine Characteristics of my friend Wilson. His removal from Congress in my opinion would work an essential political Evil.

William Churchill Houston to Robert Morris PHILADELPHIA, OCTOBER 4, 1779

Be sure to press Mr. Wilson to return to the Assembly. He is a worthy and capable Man, and fully justifies the Character you gave of him to me the first Time I saw him. I well recollect it.

"Common Sense" (Thomas Paine), Pennsylvania Packet OCTOBER 16, 1779

That Mr. Wilson is not a favorite in the State, is a matter which I presume, he is fully sensible of.

William Pierce, "Character Sketches of Delegates to the Federal Convention" 1787

Mr. Wilson ranks among the foremost in legal and political knowledge. He has joined to a fine genius all that can set him off and show him to advantage. He is well acquainted with Man, and understands all the passions that influence him. Government seems to have been his peculiar Study, all the political institutions of the World he knows in detail, and can trace the causes and effects of every revolution from the earliest stages of the Grecian common-wealth down to the present time. No man is more clear, copious, and comprehensive than Mr. Wilson, yet he is no great Orator. He draws the attention not by the charm of his eloquence, but by the force of his reasoning. He is about 45 years old.

Francis Hopkinson to Thomas Jefferson PHILADELPHIA, DECEMBER 14, 1787

[In the Pennsylvania ratifying convention] Mr. Wilson exerted himself to the astonishment of all Hearers. The Powers of Demosthenes and Cicero seemed to be united in this able Orator.

Benjamin Rush to Tench Coxe PHILADELPHIA, FEBRUARY 26, 1789

J——n [James Wilson] is indefatigable—& confident—But more unpopular than ever. His appointment [as chief justice] would be very disagreeable to some of the best men in the State of Pennsylvania.

Philadelphia Federal Gazette MARCH 9, 1789

It is with singular pleasure we hear that James Wilson, esq. of this state, is destined by the voice of many thousand federalists, to fill the state of CHIEF JUSTICE of the UNITED STATES. This worthy citizen devoted himself to the cause of American freedom in 1774, and has shared in every toil and danger of the revolution. His hand, his heart, his tongue and his pen, have ever been at the command of his country. To his laborious investigations into the principles and forms of every species of government that has ever existed in the world—and to his powerful reasonings in the late federal convention, the United States are indebted for many of the perfections of the new constitution.

The office allotted for that distinguished patriot and legislator by his grateful countrymen, will require an uncommon share of *legal* and *political* abilities and information. A new system of federal jurisprudence must be formed; a new region in the administration of justice must be explored, in which genius alone can supply the defect of precedent; and who so equal to those great and original undertakings as that favorite son of Pennsylvania, James Wilson, esq.

Frederick A. Muhlenberg to Benjamin Rush NEW YORK, MARCH 21, 1789

Nor is there a Man in the U. States who entertains a more favorable Opinion of Mr. Wilson than myself. In Point of abilities I do not know his equal nor any one so well calculated for the Duties of that important Station [chief justice of the United States]. From my personal Regard for him I would sooner forego any Advantage* than be in any Manner the Means of injuring him or his Views.

Benjamin Rush to John Adams PHILADELPHIA, APRIL 22, 1789

Your influence in the Senate over which you have been called to preside, will give you great weight (without a vote) in determining upon the most suitable Characters to fill the first offices in government. Pennsylvania looks up with anxious Solicitude for the commission of Chief Justice for Mr. Wilson. It was from an expectation of this honor being conferred upon him, that he was left out of the Senate, and House of Representatives. His Abilities & knowledge in framing the Constitution, & his zeal in promoting its establishment, have exposed him to a most virulent persecution from the Antifederalists in this state. With these our president general Mifflin has joined. . . . Should Mr. Wilson be left to sink under this opposition, I shall for ever deplore the ingratitude of republics.

John Adams to Benjamin Rush NEW YORK, MAY 17, 1789

Mr. Wilson, I have long known esteemed and respected: but, if I had a Vote, I could not promise to give it for him to be Chief Justice. All Things considered, that have ever come to my Knowledge I feel myself inclined to wish, because I am fully convinced that Services, Hazards, Abilities and Popularity, all properly weighed, the Balance, is in favor of Mr. Jay. One of the judges, I wish Mr. Wilson to be: and the difference is not great between the first and the other Judges.

Boston Federal Gazette JUNE 10, 1793

Friday last the Circuit Court of the United States opened in this town.

---

*Muhlenberg was expected to be, and was, elected Speaker of the House of Representatives.

It is said that a Charge has been delivered "replete with the happiness of *equal* government." This idea comes with an ill grace from a man, who parades our streets with a coach and four horses, when it is known his exorbitant salary enables him to make this *flashy parade,* and the money is taken from the pockets of the industrious part of the community.—Query. Where is the "*equality*" when an officer of government is enabled by his excessive salary, to live in a style vastly superior to any member in the society that supports him?

John Quincy Adams to Thomas Boylston Adams BOSTON, JUNE 23, 1793

The most extraordinary intelligence, which I have to convey is that the wise and learned Judge & Professor Wilson, has fallen most lamentably in love with a young Lady in this town, under twenty, by the name of Gray. He came, he saw, and was overcome. The gentle Caledon, was smitten at meeting with a first sight love—unable to contain his amorous pain, he breathed his sighs about the Streets; and even when seated on the bench of Justice, he seemed as if teeming with some woeful ballad to his mistress eye brow—He obtained an introduction to the Lady, and at the second interview proposed his lovely person and his agreeable family to her acceptance; a circumstance very favorable to the success of his pretensions, is that he came in a very handsome chariot and four. In short his attractions were so powerful that the Lady actually has the subject under consideration, and unless the Judge should prove as fickle as he is amorous and repent his precipitate impetuosity so far as to withdraw his proposal, you will no doubt soon behold in the persons of those well assorted lovers a new edition of January and May.—Methinks I see you stare at the perusal of this intelligence, and conclude that I am attempting to amuse you, with a *bore;** no such thing. It is the plain and simple truth that I tell—and if you are in the habit of seeing the Miss Breck's as frequently as your wishes must direct you to see them, you may inform them, that their friend and mine, *Miss Hannah Gray,* has made so profound an impression upon the Heart of judge Wilson, and received in return an impression so

*A trick.

profound upon her own, that in all probability they will soon see her at Philadelphia, the happy consort of the happy judge.

Cupid himself must laugh at his own absurdity, in producing such an Union; but he must sigh to reflect that without the soft persuasion of a deity who has supplanted him in the breast of modern beauty, he could not have succeeded to render the man ridiculous & the woman contemptible.

Henry Jackson to Henry Knox BOSTON, JUNE 23, 1793

Judge Wilson is violently in love with Miss Gray—the second daughter of Mr. Ellis Gray, she is about 18 or 19—& he it's said is 55—he saw her for the first time at Doctor Thatcher's meeting, and Cupid with his dart *instantly* struck him in the heart—he has accordingly addressed her on the subject of Love—which she has under consideration until his return from the Circuit Court—it is conjectured from all circumstances that this Passion will not prove tragical, and that the wound will be healed by the Lady's giving him her fair hand—it will be highly flattering to see one of our Boston Girls in her *Coach & four* rolling the streets of Philadelphia—

William Richardson Davie to James Iredell HALIFAX, N.C., DECEMBER 15, 1794

Judge Wilson's affability and politeness gave great satisfaction to both the bar and the people; a circumstance I mention with pleasure because I have observed its conciliatory effect with respect to the Government.

John Adams to Abigail Adams PHILADELPHIA, MARCH 5, 1796

Mr. Wilson's ardent Speculations had given offense to some, and his too frequent affectation of Popularity to others.

Benjamin Rush, Commonplace Book DECEMBER 1796

Judge Wilson deeply distressed [after suffering bankruptcy]; his resource was reading novels constantly.

James Iredell to Hannah Iredell PHILADELPHIA, AUGUST 11, 1797

All the Judges here but Wilson who unfortunately is in a manner absconding from his creditors—his Wife with him—the rest of the Family here! What a situation! It is supposed his object is to wait until he can make a more favorable adjustment of his affairs than he could in a state of arrest.

Jacob Rush to Benjamin Rush READING, PA., SEPTEMBER 8, 1798

The Death of Judge Wilson was to me an unwelcome & unexpected Event—I fear he hastened it by some unjustifiable Means. His Constitution was too good to have sunk in so short a Time, under the Weight of mere Intemperance. What a miserable Termination to such distinguished Abilities, and what a dark Cloud overcast the last Days of a Life that had once been marked with uncommon Lustre—

Robert Troup to Rufus King NEW YORK, OCTOBER 2, 1798

Poor [Robert] Morris remains in gaol. Judge Wilson lately died in North Carolina in the hands of the Sheriff—a victim to misfortune and liquor!

Benjamin Rush, Sketches c. 1800

An eminent lawyer and a great and enlightened statesman. He had been educated for a clergyman in Scotland, and was a profound and accurate scholar. He spoke often in Congress, and his eloquence was of the most commanding kind. He reasoned, declaimed, and persuaded according to circumstances with equal effect. His mind, while he spoke, was one blaze of light. Not a word ever fell from his lips out of time, or out of place, nor could a word be taken from or added to his speeches without injuring them. He rendered great and essential services to his country in every stage of the Revolution.

For Further Reading

GENERAL

Bowling, Kenneth R., and Helen E. Veit, eds. *The Diary of William Maclay and Other Notes on Senate Debates, March 4, 1789–March 3, 1791.* Vol. 9 of *The Documentary History of the First Federal Congress.* Ed. Linda Grant De Pauw et al. Baltimore, 1988.

Brissot de Warville, J. P. *New Travels in the United States of America, 1788.* Ed. Durand Echeverria. Cambridge, Mass., 1964.

Chastellux, Marquis de. *Travels in North-America, in the Years 1780, 1781, and 1782.* 1st English trans., London, 1787; rept. New York, 1968. Rev. trans. and ed. Howard C. Rice Jr., 2 vols., Chapel Hill, N.C., 1963.

Otto, Louis Guillaume. List of the Members and Officers of Congress, 1788. French Archives: Ministère des Affaires Etrangères. Archives. Etats-Unis. Correspondance Politique. Supplement vol. 26, pp. 1–72. My translations. Cited as Louis Guillaume Otto, Biographies.

Pierce, William. "Character Sketches of Delegates to the Federal Convention." *The Records of the Federal Convention of 1787.* Ed. Max Farrand. 3 vols. New Haven, 1911. A new edition of Pierce's Sketches taken from Pierce's original journal edited by Richard Leffler and John P. Kaminski will be published in 2008.

Smith, Paul H., et al., eds. *Letters of Delegates to Congress, 1774–1789.* 26 vols. Washington, D.C., 1976–2000.

ABIGAIL ADAMS

Akers, Charles W. *Abigail Adams: An American Woman.* Boston, 1980.

Butterfield, L. H., Marc Friedlaender, and Mary-Jo Kline, eds. *The Book of Abigail and John: Selected Letters of the Adams Family, 1762–1784.* Cambridge, Mass., 1975.

Gelles, Edith B. *Portia: The World of Abigail Adams.* Bloomington, Ind., 1992.

Hogan, Margaret A., and C. James Taylor, eds. *My Dearest Friend: Letters of Abigail and John Adams.* Cambridge, Mass., 2007.

Kaminski, John P. *Abigail Adams: An American Heroine.* Madison, Wis., 2007.

Levin, Phyllis Lee. *Abigail Adams: A Biography.* 1987. Rept. New York, 2001.

Stewart, Mitchell, ed. *New Letters of Abigail Adams, 1788–1801.* Boston, 1947.

Withey, Lynne. *Dearest Friend: A Life of Abigail Adams.* New York, 1981.

JOHN ADAMS

Butterfield, L. H., et al., eds. *Adams Family Correspondence.* Cambridge, Mass., 1963–.

———. *Diary and Autobiography of John Adams.* 4 vols. Cambridge, Mass., 1961.

Ellis, Joseph J. *Passionate Sage: The Character and Legacy of John Adams.* New York, 1994.

Ferling, John. *John Adams: A Life.* New York, 1992.

Kurtz, Stephen G. *The Presidency of John Adams: The Collapse of Federalism, 1795–1800.* Philadelphia, 1957.

McCullough, David. *John Adams.* New York, 2001.

Shaw, Peter. *The Character of John Adams.* Chapel Hill, N.C., 1976.

Smith, Page. *John Adams.* 2 vols. New York, 1962.

Taylor, Robert J., et al., eds. *Papers of John Adams.* Cambridge, Mass., 1977–.

Thompson, C. Bradley. *John Adams and the Spirit of Liberty.* Lawrence, Kans., 1998.

SAMUEL ADAMS

Alexander, John K. *Samuel Adams: America's Revolutionary Politician.* Lanham, Md., 2002.

Fowler, William M., Jr., *Samuel Adams: Radical Puritan*. New York, 1997.

Harlow, Ralph Volney. *Samuel Adams, Promoter of the American Revolution: A Study in Psychology and Politics*. New York, 1975.

Miller, John C. *Sam Adams: Pioneer in Propaganda*. Boston, 1936.

Aaron Burr

Isenberg, Nancy. *Fallen Founder: The Life of Aaron Burr*. New York, 2007.

Kline, Mary-Jo, et al., eds. *Political Correspondence and Public Papers of Aaron Burr*. 2 vols. Princeton, N.J., 1983.

Lomask, Milton. *Aaron Burr*. 2 vols. New York, 1979–82.

Samuel Chase

Hawe, James, et al. *Stormy Patriot: The Life of Samuel Chase*. Baltimore, 1980.

George Clinton

Kaminski, John P. *George Clinton: Yeoman Politician of the New Republic*. Madison, Wis., 1993.

Spaulding, E. Wilder. *His Excellency George Clinton: Critic of the Constitution*. New York, 1938.

John Dickinson

Flower, Milton E. *John Dickinson: Conservative Revolutionary*. Charlottesville, Va., 1983.

Jacobson, Davie L. *John Dickinson and the Revolution in Pennsylvania, 1764–1776*. Berkeley, Calif., 1965.

Oliver Ellsworth

Brown, William Garrott. *The Life of Oliver Ellsworth*. New York, 1905.

Casto, William R. *The Supreme Court in the Early Republic: The Chief Justiceships of John Jay and Oliver Ellsworth*. Columbia, S.C., 1995.

Littieri, Ronald J. "Connecticut's 'Publius': Oliver Ellsworth, the 'Landholder' Series, and the Fabric of Connecticut Republicanism." *Connecticut History* 23 (April 1982): 24–25.

———. *Connecticut's Young Man of the Revolution: Oliver Ellsworth*. Cambridge, Mass., 1978.

Benjamin Franklin

Brands, H. W. *The First American: The Life and Times of Benjamin Franklin*. New York, 2000.

Isaacson, Walter. *Benjamin Franklin: An American Life*. New York, 2003.

Labaree, Leonard W., et al., eds. *The Papers of Benjamin Franklin*. New Haven, Conn., 1959–.

Morgan, Edmund S. *Benjamin Franklin*. New Haven, Conn., 2002.

Van Doren, Carl. *Benjamin Franklin*. New York, 1938.

Wright, Esmond. *Benjamin Franklin: His Life As He Wrote It*. Cambridge, Mass., 1989.

Elbridge Gerry

Billias, George A. *Elbridge Gerry: Founding Father and Republican Statesman*. New York, 1976.

Alexander Hamilton

Brookhiser, Richard. *Alexander Hamilton: American*. New York, 1999.

Chernow, Ron. *Alexander Hamilton*. New York, 2004.

Cooke, Jacob E. *Alexander Hamilton*. New York, 1982.

Hickey, Donald R., and Connie D. Clark, eds. *Citizen Hamilton: The Wit and Wisdom of an American Founder*. Lanham, Md., 2006.

McDonald, Forrest. *Alexander Hamilton: A Biography*. New York, 1979.

Miller, John C. *Alexander Hamilton and The Growth of the New Nation*. New York, 1959.

Mitchell, Broadus. *Alexander Hamilton*. 2 vols. New York, 1957–62.

Morris, Richard B. *Alexander Hamilton and the Founding of the Nation*. New York, 1957.

Schachner, Nathan. *Alexander Hamilton*. New York, 1946.

Stourzh, Gerald. *Alexander Hamilton and the Idea of Republican Government*. Stanford, Calif., 1970.

Syrett, Harold C., et al., eds., *The Papers of Alexander Hamilton*. 27 vols. New York, 1961–87.

John Hancock

Allan, Herbert S. *John Hancock: Patriot in Purple*. New York, 1948.

Fowler, William M., Jr. *The Baron of Beacon Hill: A Biography of John Hancock.* Boston, 1980.

Unger, Harlow Giles. *John Hancock: Merchant King and American Patriot.* New York, 2000.

Patrick Henry

Beeman, Richard R. *Patrick Henry: A Biography.* New York, 1975.

Mayer, Henry. *Son of Thunder: Patrick Henry and the American Revolution.* New York, 1986.

Meade, Robert Douthat. *Patrick Henry: Practical Revolutionary.* Philadelphia, 1969.

Wirt, William. *Patrick Henry: Life, Correspondence, and Speeches.* 3 vols. New York, 1891.

———. *Sketches of the Life and Character of Patrick Henry.* Philadelphia, 1817.

John Jay

Johnston, Henry P., ed. *The Correspondence and Public Papers of John Jay.* 4 vols. New York, 1890–93.

Monaghan, Frank. *John Jay: Defender of Liberty.* New York, 1935.

Morris, Richard B. *The Peacemakers.* New York, 1965.

Stahr, Walter. *John Jay: Founding Father.* New York, 2005.

Thomas Jefferson

Boyd, Julian P., et al., eds. *The Papers of Thomas Jefferson.* Princeton, N.J., 1950–.

Burstein, Andrew. *The Inner Jefferson: Portrait of a Grieving Optimist.* Charlottesville, Va., 1995.

Cunningham, Noble, Jr. *In Pursuit of Reason: The Life of Thomas Jefferson.* Baton Rouge, La., 1987.

Ellis, Richard E. *The Jeffersonian Crisis: Courts and Politics in the Young Republic.* New York, 1971.

Kaminski, John P. *The Quotable Jefferson.* Princeton, N.J., 2006.

———. *Thomas Jefferson: Philosopher and Politician.* Madison, Wis., 2005.

Kukla, Jon. *Mr. Jefferson's Women.* New York, 2007.

Looney, J. Jefferson, et al., eds. *The Papers of Thomas Jefferson: Retirement Series.* Princeton, N.J., 2004–.

Malone, Dumas. *Jefferson and His Time.* 6 vols. Boston, 1948–81.

Mayer, David N. *The Constitutional Thought of Thomas Jefferson.* Charlottesville, Va., 1994.
Risjord, Norman K. *Thomas Jefferson.* Madison, Wis., 1994.

JOHN PAUL JONES

Morison, Samuel Eliot. *John Paul Jones: A Sailor's Biography.* Boston, 1959.

HENRY KNOX

Callahan, North. *Henry Knox: General Washington's General.* New York, 1958.
Drake, Francis S. *Life and Correspondence of Henry Knox.* Boston, 1873.

MARQUIS DE LAFAYETTE

Gottschalk, Louis R. *Lafayette Comes to America.* 4 vols. Chicago, 1935–50.
Idzerda, Stanley I., et al., eds. *Lafayette in the Age of the American Revolution: Selected Letters and Papers, 1776–1790.* 5 vols. Ithaca, N.Y., 1977–83.
Kaminski, John P. *Lafayette: The Boy General.* Madison, Wis., 2006.
Unger, Harlow Giles. *Lafayette.* Hoboken, N.J., 2002.

RICHARD HENRY LEE

Ballagh, James C., ed. *The Letters of Richard Henry Lee.* 2 vols. New York, 1911.
Chitwood, Oliver Perry. *Richard Henry Lee: Statesman of the Revolution.* Morgantown, W.Va., 1967.
McGaughy, J. Kent. *Richard Henry Lee of Virginia: A Portrait of a Revolutionary.* Lanham, Md., 2004.

JAMES MADISON

Banning, Lance. *The Sacred Fire of Liberty: James Madison and the Founding of the Federal Republic.* Ithaca, N.Y., 1995.
Brant, Irving. *James Madison.* 6 vols. Indianapolis, 1941–61.
Hutchinson, William T., et al., eds., *The Papers of James Madison.* Chicago and Charlottesville, Va., 1962–.
Kaminski, John P. *James Madison: Champion of Liberty and Justice.* Madison, Wis., 2006.

Ketcham, Ralph. *James Madison: A Biography.* New York, 1971.

Koch, Adrienne. *Jefferson and Madison: The Great Collaboration.* New York, 1950.

Madison, James. "Detatched Memorandum." Ed. Elizabeth Fleet. *William and Mary Quarterly,* 3d ser., 3 (Oct. 1946): 534–68.

McCoy, Drew R. *The Last of The Fathers: James Madison and the Republican Legacy.* Cambridge, Mass., 1989.

Matthews, Richard K. *If Men Were Angels: James Madison and the Heartless Empire of Reason.* Lawrence, Kans., 1995.

Rakove, Jack N. *James Madison and the Creation of the American Republic.* New York, 2002.

Rutland, Robert A. *James Madison: The Founding Father.* New York, 1987.

———, ed. *James Madison and the American Nation, 1751–1836: An Encyclopedia.* New York, 1994.

John Marshall

Baker, Leonard. *John Marshall: A Life in Law.* New York, 1974.

Hobson, Charles F. *The Great Chief Justice: John Marshall and the Rule of Law.* Lawrence, Kans., 1996.

Johnson, Herbert Alan. *The Chief Justiceship of John Marshall, 1801–1835.* Columbia, S.C., 1997.

Johnson, Herbert A., et al., eds. *The Papers of John Marshall.* 12 vols. Chapel Hill, N.C., 1974–2006.

Nelson, William E. *Marbury v. Madison: The Origins and Legacy of Judicial Review.* Lawrence, Kans., 2000.

Newmeyer, R. Kent. *John Marshall and the Heroic Age of the Supreme Court.* Baton Rouge, La., 2001.

Simon, James F. *What Kind of Nation: Thomas Jefferson, John Marshall, and the Epic Struggle to Create a United States.* New York, 2002.

Smith, Jean Edward. *John Marshall: Definer of a Nation.* New York, 1996.

James Monroe

Ammon, Harry. *James Monroe: The Quest for National Identity.* Charlottesville, Va., 1971.

Cunningham, Noble, Jr. *The Presidency of James Monroe.* Lawrence, Kans., 1996.

Gouverneur Morris

Brookhiser, Richard. *Gentleman Revolutionary: Gouverneur Morris, The Rake Who Wrote the Constitution.* New York, 2003.

Kirschke, James J. *Gouverneur Morris: Author, Statesman, and Man of the World.* New York, 2005.

Kline, Mary-Jo. *Gouverneur Morris and the New Nation, 1775–1788.* New York, 1978.

Miller, Melanie Randolph. *Envoy to Terror: Gouverneur Morris and the French Revolution.* Dulles, Va., 2005.

Morris, Anne Cary, ed. *The Diary and Letters of Gouverneur Morris.* 2 vols. 1888. Rept. New York, 1970.

Muntz, Max M. *Gouverneur Morris and the American Revolution.* Norman, Okla., 1970.

Sparks, Jared. *The Life of Gouverneur Morris with Selections from His Correspondence and Miscellaneous Papers.* Boston, 1832.

Robert Morris

Ferguson, E. James. *The Power of the Purse: A History of American Public Finance, 1776–1790.* Chapel Hill, N.C., 1961.

Ferguson, E. James, et al., eds. *The Papers of Robert Morris.* 9 vols. Pittsburgh, 1973–99.

Oberholtzer, Ellis Paxson, *Robert Morris: Patriot and Financer.* New York, 1903.

Ver Steeg, Clarence L. *Robert Morris: Revolutionary Financier.* New York, 1976.

Thomas Paine

Foner, Eric. *Tom Paine and Revolutionary America.* London, 1976.

Foner, Philip S., ed. *The Complete Writings of Thomas Paine.* New York, 1945.

Fruchtman, Jack, Jr. *Thomas Paine: Apostle of Freedom.* New York, 1994.

Hawke, David Freeman. *Paine.* New York, 1974.

Kaminski, John P. *Citizen Paine: Thomas Paine's Thoughts on Man, Government, Society, and Religion.* Lanham, Md., 2002.

Keane, John. *Tom Paine.* Boston, 1995

Williamson, A. *Thomas Paine: His Life, Work and Times.* London, 1973.

Benjamin Rush

Butterfield, L. H., ed. *Letters of Benjamin Rush.* 2 vols. Princeton, N.J., 1951.

Corner, George W., ed. *The Autobiography of Benjamin Rush: His "Travels through Life" together with his Commonplace Book for 1789–1813.* Princeton, N.J., 1948.

Hawke, David Freeman. *Benjamin Rush: Revolutionary Gadfly.* Indianapolis, 1971.

Schutz, John A., and Douglas Adair, eds. *The Spur of Fame: Dialogues of John Adams and Benjamin Rush, 1805–1813.* San Marino, Calif., 1966.

Roger Sherman

Boutell, Lewis Henry. *The Life of Roger Sherman.* Chicago, 1896.

Collier, Christopher. *Roger Sherman's Connecticut: Yankee Politics and the American Revolution.* Middletown, Conn., 1971.

George Washington

Abbot, W. W., et al., eds. *The Papers of George Washington.* Charlottesville, Va., 1983–.

Cunliffe, Marcus. *George Washington: Man and Monument.* Boston, 1958.

Ellis, Joseph J. *His Excellency George Washington.* New York, 2004.

Flexner, James Thomas. *Washington: The Indispensable Man.* New York, 1969.

Freeman, Douglas S. *George Washington: A Biography.* 7 vols. New York, 1948–57.

Grizzard, Frank E., Jr. *George Washington: A Biographical Companion.* Santa Barbara, Calif., 2002.

Higginbotham, Don. *George Washington and the American Military Tradition.* Athens, Ga., 1985.

Jackson, Donald, et al., eds. *The Diaries of George Washington.* 6 vols. Charlottesville, Va., 1976–79.

Kaminski, John P. *George Washington: "The Man of the Age."* Madison, Wis., 2004.

Lucas, Stephen E., comp. and ed. *The Quotable George Washington: The Wisdom of an American Patriot.* Madison, Wis., 1999.

Smith, Richard Norton. *Patriarch: George Washington and the New American Nation.* Boston, 1993.

MARTHA WASHINGTON

Brady, Patricia. *Martha Washington: An American Life.* New York, 2005.

Bryan, Helen. *Martha Washington: First Lady of Liberty.* New York, 2002.

Clark, Ellen McCallister. *Martha Washington: A Brief Biography.* Mount Vernon, Va., 2002.

Fields, Joseph E., comp. *"Worthy Partner": The Papers of Martha Washington.* Westport, Conn., 1994.

JAMES WILSON

Conrad, Stephen A. "Metaphor and Imagination in James Wilson's Theory of Federal Union," *Law and Social Inquiry* 13 (1988): 1–70.

Hall, Kermit L., ed. *Collected Works of James Wilson.* 2 vols. Indianapolis, 2007.

Hall, Mark David. *The Political and Legal Philosophy of James Wilson, 1742–1798.* Columbia, Mo., 1997.

McCloskey, Robert Green, ed. *The Works of James Wilson.* 2 vols. Cambridge, Mass., 1967.

Seed, Geoffrey. *James Wilson.* Milford, N.Y., 1978.

Smith, Charles Page. *James Wilson: Founding Father, 1742–1798.* Chapel Hill, N.C., 1956.

Index